The U.S. Savings Challenge

Published in cooperation with
American Council for Capital Formation
Center for Policy Research

The U.S. Savings Challenge

Policy Options for Productivity and Growth

EDITED BY

Charls E. Walker, Mark A. Bloomfield, and Margo Thorning

Routledge
Taylor & Francis Group
LONDON AND NEW YORK

First published 1990 by Westview Press

Published 2019 by Routledge
52 Vanderbilt Avenue, New York, NY 10017
2 Park Square, Milton Park, Abingdon, Oxon OX14 4RN

Routledge is an imprint of the Taylor & Francis Group, an informa business

Library of Congress Cataloging-in-Publication Data
The U.S. savings challenge : policy options for productivity and growth / edited by Charls E. Walker, Mark A. Bloomfield, and Margo Thorning.
p. cm.
"Published in cooperation with American Council for Capital Formation Center for Policy Research"—
Includes bibliographical references and index.
ISBN 0-8133-7921-0
1. Saving and investment—United States. 2. Taxation—United States. I. Walker, Charls E. (Charls Edward), 1923– . II. Bloomfield, Mark A. III. Thorning, Margo. IV. Title: US savings challenge.
HC110.S3U8 1990
339.4'3'0973—dc20 90-38801
CIP

ISBN 13: 978-0-367-29682-7 (hbk)
ISBN 13: 978-0-367-31228-2 (pbk)

Contents

Tables

Figures

Preface

Concern about the low U.S. saving rate and its negative impact on capital formation and economic growth prompted the American Council for Capital Formation (ACCF) Center for Policy Research to launch a multifaceted, three-year project to explore this issue in 1988. This volume is one element of that project. This book contains slightly updated versions of the papers presented at a two-and-one-half-day conference entitled Saving: The Challenge for the U.S. Economy, held in Washington, D.C., in October 1989.

The conference assembled prominent academicians, administration and congressional policymakers, fiscal policy experts, business leaders, and members of the financial and economic media for an in-depth discussion of the reasons for low U.S. national saving, the consequences for our economy, and public policy alternatives to reverse the situation. More than two hundred fifty policymakers, corporate representatives, economists, and members of the press attended the conference sessions.

The conference was generously underwritten by the following corporations, foundations, and individuals: American Business Conference; R. C. Baker Foundation; BankAmerica Foundation; The Boeing Company; Deloitte Haskins & Sells; The Equitable Life Assurance Society of the United States; Exxon Company USA; Fidelity Investments Foundation; *Fortune;* General Electric Foundation; The Henley League; IBM Corporation; Intel Corporation; Investment Company Institute; Manufacturers' Alliance for Productivity and Innovation; Merrill Lynch & Co., Inc.; National Association of Home Builders; National Venture Capital Association; New York Stock Exchange; Oryx Energy Company; Pennzoil Company; T. Rowe Price Associates; The Principal Financial Group; John and Lolita Renshaw; Shell Oil Company; Harold Simmons Foundation; Texaco Philanthropic Foundation, Inc.; Thermo Electron Corporation; USF&G Corporation; United States League of Savings Institutions; and Weyerhaeuser Company.

The combined efforts of many individuals made the conference and this book possible. Along with the groups and individuals already named, we thank our other contributors for their ongoing support and

Westview Press for its expert guidance and assistance. We would like to express special thanks to Donna Brodsky, the center's communications director, for her editorial judgment and tireless efforts, which contributed significantly to the quality of this book. Our thanks also go to the other ACCF Center for Policy Research staff members whose hard work contributed to the success of the saving conference: Mari Lee Dunn, vice president; Ernestine Johnson, assistant conference director; Vicky Agnew, Margaret Burrell, and Doreen Kreger, support staff; and David Tumblin, research associate. Finally, we express our gratitude to Danette Lewis, who enthusiastically assumed most of the monumental burden of typing the 800-page manuscript.

Charls E. Walker
Mark A. Bloomfield
Margo Thorning
Washington, D.C.

Introduction

Charls E. Walker, Mark A. Bloomfield, and Margo Thorning

Because economic growth depends on the availability of an adequate pool of saving to finance new investment in both physical and human capital, the low U.S. saving rate is an increasing concern for many economists and policymakers. Recent changes in the U.S. tax code have weakened incentives to save for individuals and businesses. This, along with our multibillion-dollar federal budget deficit, has contributed to a national saving rate less than one-half that of the 1960s and 1970s. We now save at about one-half the rate of West Germans and about one-third the rate of the Japanese, which means that our primary competitors in the world economy can invest a far larger share of their gross national product in physical and human capital and in research and development.

A low rate of saving puts the U.S. economy at risk in a number of ways. First, our low saving rate leads to increased capital costs, which in turn contribute to a low rate of investment. For productivity to increase, we must maintain a high and sustained level of investment in modern, state-of-the-art machinery and equipment. As research presented by John Shoven in Chapter 13 shows, capital costs of short-lived equipment are as much as 150 percent higher in the United States than in Japan, for example.

Second, the major cause of growing U.S. international indebtedness and our large current account deficits is the substantial decline in our national saving rate. Lower U.S. saving rates, reflected in both large federal deficits and lower private saving rates, mean that a net inflow of saving from abroad is required to finance even our reduced levels of domestic investment.

On balance, this foreign capital has been beneficial: It has helped keep U.S. investment from falling. Foreigners are willing to invest here largely because of the fundamental attractiveness of the U.S. economy with its record-breaking economic expansion, skilled work force, political stability, and large, free markets. As Michael Boskin notes in Chapter 2, the solution to the U.S. trade deficit is *not* to close off our markets for either goods or capital. This would seriously disrupt our economy and our prospects for growth and might even set off a destructive trade war. Instead, we must boost national saving in order to finance the domestic investment necessary to provide the rising living standards for future generations on the scale enjoyed by previous generations.

Third, low national saving translates into a low rate of investment and slow productivity growth. The extent of our problem is indicated by the fact that from 1973 to 1988, productivity in U.S. manufacturing grew by only 2.5 percent annually; this contrasts with 3.3 percent in the United Kingdom and West Germany and 5.7 percent in Japan. This overall poor performance prevailed even with a spurt in U.S. manufacturing productivity in the early 1980s. Although investment can be financed for a time through foreign borrowing, the U.S. economy eventually must pay its own way, which means that in the long run our ability to invest is constrained by our willingness to save.

This investment squeeze can be postponed for a time to the extent that the United States can continue to attract inflows of foreign capital. But these inflows carry their own costs: An increasing share of U.S. assets ends up being foreign owned, which implies that in the future a growing share of U.S. output will be claimed by foreigners. This will require real transfers of resources abroad; the result will be slower growth in living standards for our children and grandchildren. Also, as Fred Bergsten notes in Chapter 6, the United States—the world's wealthiest nation—becomes a competitor for capital with the poorest nations in the world.

What can be done to bolster U.S. saving? Contributors to this book have suggested a number of promising answers. The quickest and surest route to a higher domestic saving rate is to reduce the deficit in the federal budget. During most of the 1980s, federal dissaving (the deficit) offset more than one-half of the saving attributed to individuals, businesses, and state and local governments. Unfortunately, the outlook is for continuing large federal dissaving in the years ahead. This is especially true if the emerging surpluses connected with the Social Security and other federal trust funds are excluded from budget computations or if Social Security revenues are reduced. Personal saving can be encouraged through a continuation of the reduced income tax rates of the Tax Reform Act of 1986 as well as through capital gains tax reductions and expanded individual retirement accounts and pension law reforms. Business saving, which like personal saving trended down as a share of net national product in the 1980s, can be encouraged most efficiently through direct incentives such as the investment tax credit and other capital cost recovery provisions.

Finally, the United States must shift its focus toward the long term in its public and private decisions. Raising the U.S. saving and investment rate is the key to increasing productivity and maximizing economic growth, which will result in rising incomes and employment opportunities for Americans.

This book provides policymakers with a comprehensive discussion of the concept of saving, the deleterious impact of our low national saving rate on the U.S. economy, and policy options to raise our saving rate and thereby ensure our economic future. We hope that it will serve as a catalyst in putting the challenge of our national saving rate at the top of the U.S. economic policy agenda.

The U.S. Savings Challenge

PART ONE

The U.S. Saving Challenge: Policymaker Perspectives

1

U.S. Economic Growth and the National Saving Rate

Nicholas F. Brady

I believe that we are at the beginning of a new era of thinking about the relationship of government and politics to the economy. Attitudes about economic growth and economic equity in society are changing. Many who used to see achieving "fairness" as the goal of government economic policy now recognize that stimulating economic growth is inextricably linked to this goal.

To see this, one need only look at the House of Representatives, where in late 1989 sixty-four Democrats joined Republicans in voting to support a cut in the capital gains tax. They did so because they recognized that a lower capital gains tax will encourage saving and investment and that saving and investment are the foundations on which growth is built. They recognized that growth is essential to an economically strong and just society. By voting to cut the capital gains tax, they acknowledged that the debate about capital gains should be about the benefits of growth for all Americans, not about the politics of division and economic confrontation. I will return to the subject of capital gains later, but I wanted to stress here what a significant change in perspective the 1989 congressional debate represented.

As we look at saving and investment as an essential foundation and engine for growth in our economy, we can do so with the knowledge that there is a burgeoning understanding in the policy realm: Just as there is a direct relationship between investment and growth, there is an equally direct correlation between growth and economic well-being throughout our country. Our recent impressive economic performance provides a positive launching pad for an analysis of the issue of saving. Since 1982 the United States has experienced eight consecutive years of economic growth. Americans enjoy a high standard of living and relatively low rates of inflation and unemployment. But we must not let our pride in these accomplishments distract us from focusing on the question of whether the United States is adequately preparing to compete over the long term in an integrated world economy.

In my view, we are *not* adequately preparing for the future. By any measure, our national saving rate has been declining since the late 1970s. This decline inevitably raises questions about our ability to fund investment and therefore to sustain economic growth in the face of ever-increasing competition from abroad.

Historically, investment capital in the United States has come from foreign capital as well as from domestic saving, a combination that has served us well. However, our ability to attract foreign capital must not lead us to neglect the fostering of domestic sources of capital. It would be extremely unwise for us to lose sight of the difference between benefiting from foreign investment capital and being dependent on it.

Because we are not saving at a sufficient rate, our cost of capital in the United States is consistently higher than that of our major trading partners. In some cases, U.S. companies face capital costs fully twice as high as our foreign competitors pay. The consequence is clear: If one of the essential inputs of production is so much more expensive in the United States, we are at a disadvantage in world trade. We simply cannot pay more than our competitors for a basic component of production and still hope to come out ahead. Ultimately, the higher cost of capital endangers the competitive position of U.S. companies. And if our capital costs are consistently higher than those of our competitors over a long period of time, our leadership in the international economy, and even our standard of living, will be placed in jeopardy. This is the problem we face.

The solutions lie in changing the practices and attitudes of government, of business, and of individual Americans. These categories are not independent of one another, nor are the solutions. It is a fundamental fact that the most important step the government can take to increase national saving is to decrease the greatest source of national dissaving: the federal budget deficit. Until we have eliminated the budget deficit, it will necessarily shape our thinking and dominate our actions across the spectrum of policy issues.

Several of the proposals to increase saving that I will discuss here would be constrained by the demands of reducing the deficit. For that reason, some might say we should not discuss these proposals at all because we cannot move forward immediately. I agree that there is an inevitable tension between prescriptions for increasing saving and investment and the need to maintain the current revenue base. It's a fact of life. But I do not believe that just because we are grappling with one large problem, we have the luxury of dismissing other great challenges as unsolvable. We cannot afford to stop planning and working toward worthwhile long-term goals solely because we have to address the budget deficit first. At Treasury, the goal is to deal with the current problems and at the same time plan for the country's future.

We have made progress on the deficit. We reduced its size as a percentage of gross national product (GNP) from 6.3 percent in 1983 to 2.9 percent of GNP in fiscal 1989. Because the fiscal 1990 Gramm-Rudman-Hollings target of a $100 billion deficit was met, that percentage declined to 1.8 percent. If we meet the fiscal 1991 Gramm-Rudman-Hollings target of $64 billion, the deficit will be 1.1 percent of GNP. We have achieved this decrease primarily by reducing the rate of increase of federal spending from double-digit levels to single-digit levels, while increasing federal revenues through economic growth.

It was not easy to reach the $100 billion mark for fiscal 1990, even with a bipartisan commitment to do so. The fiscal year 1991 target will be even tougher to achieve, but the Bush administration remains committed to meet the deficit-reduction targets set forth by law.

As I mentioned earlier, as part of the debate over the fiscal year 1990 budget, Congress and the Bush administration were involved in a great debate over another means of lowering capital costs and promoting capital formation: the reduction of the capital gains tax. For sixty-five years, from 1922 to 1986, the United States taxed long-term capital gains at a preferential rate. The logic was simple and compelling: A permanently lower taxation rate for capital gains promotes long-term investment and economic growth.

President Bush proposed the restoration of a permanent reduction in the capital gains rate in his budget presentation to Congress in February 1989. The House of Representatives took a step in the right direction by approving a temporary reduction later in the year. The Senate, however, failed to pass a capital gains measure in 1989, largely due to procedural roadblocks. We should build upon the efforts of the House of Representatives, and we encourage the Senate to finish the job by putting in place a permanent reduction in the capital gains tax rate.

The debate in Congress and the support of many Democrats for a reduction in the capital gains rate have made clear in Washington, D.C., what the majority of Americans already know: The benefits of a lower capital gains rate reach across society. At one time or another capital gains are received by individuals of all income brackets. For example, in 1987, 70 percent of the taxpayers reporting long-term capital gains had income other than capital gains of less than $50,000. So it can no longer be argued that capital gains are only for the wealthy.

But it definitely can be argued that by not lowering the capital gains tax, we are reducing our international competitiveness. We have higher taxes on capital gains than most of our trading partners. Belgium, Italy, and the Netherlands have no tax at all on capital gains. Hong Kong, Singapore, and South Korea also do not tax capital gains. In West Germany the gain on assets held more than six months is exempt from taxation. And France and Japan provide a preferential rate for long-term capital gains that is considerably below that of the United States.

We cannot expect to remain competitive when our tax structure provides so little incentive for new investment.

Our trading partners also have the advantage when it comes to the tax treatment of corporate earnings. All of our partners to some extent integrate individual and corporate taxes to prevent fully taxing the same income twice. In the United States, corporate earnings are taxed twice: once when the company pays taxes on its profits and again when the shareholders pay tax on their dividends.

Elimination of the double taxation of dividends obviously would involve a loss of revenue to the Treasury, so our options in this area will be limited by the reality of the budget deficit. But whenever it could be accomplished, such a change would lower the cost of capital and help corporations of every size. A lower cost of capital means a corporation can invest in projects with lower returns or longer term payoffs and still provide the same or better return to its shareholders. Every corporation would benefit, even those that pay no dividends or raise no new equity. Without this extra layer of tax, which reduces returns to shareholders, the stock prices of every corporation would be higher.

Such a change in the policy of double taxation would provide an incentive for long-term growth by lowering the overall cost of capital. And this change would do more. It would end the bias of the tax system toward debt financing and thereby return Americans to active participation in our equity markets. This change would also substantially reduce the incentives for leveraged buyouts.

A great deal of concern has been expressed recently about the leveraging of the United States. Congress has correctly traced most of this increased leverage to the unequal tax treatment of debt and equity. The answer put forth by some in Congress is to limit the deductibility of interest on corporate debt. But this would in effect just further increase the cost of capital to U.S. business, which clearly is not in our national interest. Removing the double taxation of dividends would eliminate the bias toward debt without raising the cost of capital.

Just as there is an important role for the government to play in assisting business, there is also a role for government in encouraging individual Americans to increase their private saving. We at Treasury, along with others in the administration, are examining ways to improve Americans' private saving rate. Among the ideas we are examining is the possibility of expanding individual retirement accounts (IRAs).

There are some options that merit more careful analysis. These include an increase in the liquidity of IRAs by permitting early withdrawals without penalty for certain specific purposes, such as catastrophic illness, education, or a first-time home; and a delay in the budget impact of IRAs by permitting no tax deduction for contributions but still allowing the accumulation of interest and the final withdrawal of funds to be tax free.

While we pursue these proposals, we must recognize that there will always be limits to what can be accomplished by government action alone, especially in the realm of individual saving. Thus, I believe that government also has a valuable role to play in educating the American public about the importance of saving and capital formation to our long-term economic well-being. But, of course, the government cannot do this alone. It must be a truly collaborative effort. A consensus must be created across the country that saving and investment are the foundations on which economic growth rests and that economic growth holds the key to a prosperous future for us all. I believe we can meet this challenge to the U.S. economy.

2

Policy Prescriptions for Raising U.S. Saving

Michael J. Boskin

I would like to address four questions. First, why are saving and investment important? Second, what constitutes saving and investment, and how do U.S. saving patterns differ from those of other nations? Third, why should the federal government be involved in policies to raise national saving and capital formation? Fourth, what policies has the administration proposed in order to raise national saving and to raise the level and efficiency of investment in physical and human capital? In each of these areas, I will attempt to highlight the importance of a comprehensive view of national saving as the sum of personal, business, and government saving.

THE IMPORTANCE OF SAVING AND INVESTMENT

Higher rates of national saving are a critical element of long-run successful economic performance. Higher rates of saving lead to a lower cost of capital and to greater investment, although these effects may be partially offset by the movement of some capital across international borders. Higher rates of saving lead to greater national wealth and higher standards of living for the future. For these reasons, it is important that national policies not discriminate against capital formation. Instead, our goal should be to provide an economic environment that treats saving and investment in as neutral a way as possible and permits capital markets to work as efficiently as possible.

Indeed, it is the history not only of the United States but of all success stories of sustained economic growth in the modern era that high rates of saving and investment have been a primary element in those successful growth episodes. As examples, I would cite the United States in the late nineteenth century and first half of the twentieth century, Japan in the postwar era, and the newly industrializing economies today.

National saving performs the critical role of providing funds to finance the investment needed for economic growth. Although at least in the short run and perhaps over a sustained length of time, one can finance investment by importing capital, over the long run investment in the economy will be closely tied to the domestic supply of capital available for investment finance.

People have become more and more concerned about foreign investment in the United States. My own view is that the inflow of foreign capital has been good for our economy. It has kept our investment from falling and interest rates from rising further than they otherwise would have. Foreigners have been lured to invest here largely by the fundamental attractiveness of the U.S. economy. We have a record-breaking economic expansion, we have a skilled labor force, we are politically stable, and we have enormous free markets. The answer to our various concerns, including our trade deficit, is not to close off our markets for either goods or capital. This would seriously disrupt our own economy and our prospects for growth. Instead, part of the answer is to raise our own national saving rate.

MEASURING U.S. SAVING

The first step in analyzing any issue is to define the problem clearly. Most economists adopt the notion of saving as the change in net worth. Alternatively, they define saving as what remains of income after consumption is subtracted. If all measurement problems could be solved, we could go about measuring and analyzing saving in either of these two complementary ways. The national income and product accounts (NIPAs) measure saving as a residual by subtracting consumption from income, and that causes some problems. For example, if there is income in the underground economy that is not properly captured in the NIPAs, but some of the consumption resulting from that income is captured, we will understate the saving rate. Also, capital gains and losses are not recorded in the NIPAs. The list goes on. The alternative way to look at saving—use of the Federal Reserve's flow of funds or other measures of net worth—has similar measurement problems.

Despite the differences in the measures, both practically and conceptually, these two complementary approaches to the measurement of saving tell essentially the same story concerning the current U.S. saving rate: The rate of U.S. saving was lower in the 1980s than in the previous few decades. Part of that decline was due to a decline in the private, including the personal, saving rate, and part was due to a rise in the federal budget deficit.

Another important aspect of measuring saving involves the question, Who is saving? It is conventional to divide saving into government saving and private saving. In addition, many go further and divide private saving into personal saving and business, primarily corporate, saving. Which measure is most important and why? Which should be the focus of economic policy?

The answers to these questions go beyond the issue of measurement. These answers depend on how the economy actually operates. One extreme view—not supported by the data—is that tax and debt finance of government spending are equivalent. Some believe that should the government choose debt finance, reducing government saving thereby, individuals and businesses will increase their saving pari passu, leaving national saving unchanged. I reject this so-called Ricardian equivalence notion, which suggests that we can analyze government and private saving in toto and that we need not separate them out. I think we have to look at both.

A similar issue occurs with private saving. If credit markets operated perfectly, it would not matter if changes in private saving derived from individuals or from corporate behavior. But much recent research into the operation of credit markets suggests that imperfect information can cause at least some firms to treat a dollar of internal finance as less costly than a dollar of external finance. If so, the cash flow of firms will directly affect their investment. Thus to understand the link between saving and investment, we must analyze separately both saving by firms and saving by households—not simply their total.

In both examples, national saving becomes more than a measurement issue. To understand why national saving changes, why it has fallen, and how we can improve our saving performance, we must keep track of who is doing the saving and what is affecting incentives and patterns of saving. We need a coordinated, comprehensive approach to national saving, not one that deals with improving one element of national saving at the expense of worsening another.

U.S. SAVING TRENDS

A quick look at U.S. history reveals a substantial fall in net national saving in the United States. I mentioned that part of this is due to an increase in the federal budget deficit and part of it is due to a decline in personal saving. Also, if one looks at net saving as opposed to gross saving, one will see there has been a substantial increase in the measured capital consumption allowance. Whether one should be looking at gross saving or net saving, gross investment or net investment, or net investment inclusive or exclusive of replacement investment really depends on a variety of factors. Among these is one's view of how technology works its way through the economy—that is, whether technology is disproportionately embodied in new capital. In my view, one must keep track of all these measures. To look at net national saving only is not sufficient; one must be concerned about gross saving and about the components of saving.

We should not be blind to the fact that the decline of saving in the United States has not occurred in a worldwide vacuum. Many other countries have witnessed substantial declines in their national saving. Indeed, we should draw a distinction between the fact that the United States ranks low on the list of our major trading partners and competitors in terms of our saving rate and the fact that for many of them, saving has fallen even more than in the United States. Although Japan, for example, has a much higher saving rate than the United States has, over the last ten or fifteen years that rate has fallen substantially more than the U.S. rate has.

What do we know about saving, and what can be done about it? First, government saving or, to be more accurate, dissaving, is the most directly controllable of all the components of saving. The simplest and most effective way to raise national saving is to continue reducing the federal budget deficit. Supplementarily and importantly, the decline in personal saving has exacerbated the impact of government deficits, thereby making it desirable to increase private saving to the extent possible through the removal of the barriers, obstacles, and distortions to private saving put up by our tax system and other sources.

Some progress has been made in the last couple of years on both fronts. Despite all the flaws and the angst that the Gramm-Rudman-Hollings process produces, it has helped reduce federal deficits. The federal budget deficit was 5.4 percent of gross national product (GNP) in fiscal 1985; in fiscal 1989, it was 2.9 percent. If the 1990 target is met, the deficit will drop to 1.8 percent of GNP, back to the levels of the 1970s. The Gramm-Rudman-Hollings balanced budget law remains indispensable to the improvement of our national saving performance and acts as an anchor in the reduction of the federal budget deficit.

There is also evidence of a modest rebound in personal saving, which reached an appallingly low ebb of 3.2 percent in 1987. In the first half of 1989, the personal saving rate averaged about 5.5 percent of disposable income, much closer to its historical average.

The budget deficit has directly lowered our national saving and has drained away resources available for investment. In assessing the impact of the federal deficit on national saving, one must realize that the unified budget deficit is important because it measures the federal government's net drain of private saving from capital markets.

Although we have made some progress in recent years, we need to go further. Our highest priority must be to reduce the unified budget deficit and move it into balance along the lines of the Gramm-Rudman-Hollings targets.

WHY SHOULD GOVERNMENT INTERVENE?

The federal government currently discourages private saving and investment. U.S. tax policies favor consumption and tilt against saving, particularly saving in the form of equity finance. Taxes raise the cost of capital more than is necessary, which reduces the international competitiveness of U.S. firms. The double taxation of corporate dividends not only raises the cost of capital but biases investment and saving away from equity and toward debt.

A working group established by the Bush administration, led by Treasury, the Council of Economic Advisers, and the Office of Management and Budget, is analyzing and addressing some of these issues. The group will propose no policies that merely try to raise private saving—whether business saving or personal saving—at the expense of a larger budget deficit. That would only cosmetically transfer our low national saving rate from one part of our books to another part and would replace a too low rate of private saving with a still larger budget deficit.

Reducing or eliminating barriers to saving and investment is a priority of the Bush administration. But such policies must be developed with care. Although there is merit to the general concept of individual retirement accounts (IRAs), for example, any specific proposal must be carefully evaluated to make sure it does not cost the Treasury substantial revenue. We must make sure that we do not wind up increasing the deficit through our efforts to encourage private saving. It is my reading of the evidence that the IRAs introduced in 1981 did raise personal saving somewhat, but they also cost the Treasury revenues. A more promising approach is back-end-loaded IRAs and/or IRAs with increased liquidity that permit penalty-free withdrawals for specific purposes. We must also reexamine, as resources permit, the double taxation of dividends and the bias against equity in our system of corporate taxation.

In addition to raising the level of saving and investment, the United States must increase the efficiency of saving and investment. The Bush administration believes strongly that private capital markets do the best job of allocating saving and investment to their most efficient use. The federal government should not attempt to steer investment into favored industries or technologies. History shows that such efforts are misguided and lead to waste because winners and losers are picked on the strength of their public relations and lobbying efforts, rather than on the basic economic value of the investments.

In the same way, we need to get a larger return from our public investment, for example, in the education system. We spend more per pupil than most of the other major industrialized economies, yet our students rank near the bottom in test scores. We spend a very large amount of our national income on education, and we need to allocate those resources in a way that provides us with much greater output for this substantial human and physical capital input.

ADMINISTRATION PROPOSALS TO RAISE SAVING

Among the most important policies the Bush administration is trying to follow in order to raise national saving and investment—or at least to prevent them from falling—is the promotion of continued economic growth coupled with the control of inflation. The administration believes the U.S. economy is capable of sustaining economic growth and low unemployment while controlling and reducing inflation. The administration favors a credible monetary policy that supports sustained growth while predictably controlling inflation.

The administration's regulatory, trade, budget, and tax policies are designed with the same goals in mind. The administration believes that the notion that the only way to keep inflation in check is to run a slack economy with relatively high unemployment and excess capacity is not only wrong but irresponsible. A recession will result in a permanent loss of output, higher unemployment, and a sharp reduction in investment. The Bush administration sees no reason a recession is likely to occur, just as it sees no reason the United States cannot make continued progress toward the goals of reducing inflation and maintaining high employment while sustaining economic growth.

The reduction of the federal budget deficit is equally important. It is the surest and safest way to raise national saving, so long as it is accomplished in a manner that does not decrease private saving. The president has made a number of other specific proposals to increase U.S. investment and productivity. Prominent among these is the proposal to encourage long-term investment through restoration of the capital gains tax differential.

The Tax Reform Act of 1986 was a historic achievement in many ways. The Bush administration supports the basic principles of tax reform—a broadened base and lower rates. One of the disappointments accompanying the 1986 reform, however, was the removal of the capital gains differential. The United States is burdened with a higher capital gains tax than are all of our trading partners, particularly Japan. Several do not tax capital gains at all; most have a differential that creates lower capital gains rates than we have in the United States.

It has been the history of the United States, recent and otherwise, that a disproportionate share of jobs and employment growth is created by small and medium-sized firms. The high cost of capital is a particularly onerous problem for new ventures and small businesses, which have only limited access to traditional sources of finance. Lower capital gains tax rates will increase entrepreneurial activity, risk-taking, and investment and ultimately benefit all of us in the form of rising incomes and employment.

Some see IRAs as a substitute for a capital gains tax reduction. It is the Bush administration view and my own view that reducing capital gains tax rates is a far more promising proposal in terms of increasing investment, increasing employment, and stimulating the economy than expanding IRAs is. The two approaches should not be regarded as even approximate substitutes. An IRA is designed to increase saving, whereas a capital gains tax rate cut is designed to raise saving as well as spur investment, encourage entrepreneurial activity, and accelerate economic growth.

In addition to the capital gains tax proposal, the Bush administration has a variety of other proposals. The president has called for several steps to improve the U.S. position in science and technology. These include increasing investment in basic research and making the research and experimentation tax credit permanent. He also favors expansion of our knowledge base through efforts to improve the quality of our economic statistics, a particular concern of mine. The president has also offered initiatives to improve the quality and productivity of our investment in our most precious resource: our human capital, particularly our children.

In September 1989, I joined the president and the state governors in a historic occasion: the president's education summit with governors. (This was only the third time in the history of our country that a president thought an issue so important as to call a summit with the governors of the states. Teddy Roosevelt called the first such summit—on the environment—in the early part of the century. Franklin Roosevelt did so to talk about the economy, but he called the summit during a bank holiday period, and therefore all the governors did not attend.) This summit was very successful. The president and the governors came to a historic agreement that for the first time will lead us to set national performance standards and goals for our schools. The administration and the governors are working together to develop long-term structural reforms in the U.S. education system by stressing choice, improved incentives, greater flexibility, and increased accountability.

The administration has also put forward proposals to expand our investment in efforts to eliminate the scourge of drugs and to increase low-income parents' access to quality child care with choice. The president is also determined to avoid an excessive increase in the minimum wage and to institute a training wage.

In conclusion, we must shift our orientation toward the long term in public and private decisions. Raising our national saving and investment rate is the key to raising productivity and maximizing economic growth to provide rising incomes and employment opportunities for U.S. families.

The first and foremost priority must be to reduce the unified budget deficit. Despite the various problems that people lay at its door, the Gramm-Rudman-Hollings balanced budget law and its target of a balanced, unified budget by fiscal year 1993 are the best anchor we have to achieve that goal. We must reduce the federal deficit in order to reduce the drain on our scarce private saving pool and thereby make greater resources available for investment. (From an ethical perspective, we must reduce the deficit in order to decrease the liabilities we leave to our children and grandchildren.)

Various people have called for a change in the accounting treatment in our budget for Social Security. Whatever the ultimate long-run merit of these proposals, they should not be allowed to divert attention from the primary goal, which for the foreseeable future must be to balance the unified budget.

The administration believes that the private capital markets are the best vehicle to allocate saving and investment. Historically, government policy that picks winners and losers has been a dismal failure. We must, however, make sure that impediments to saving and investment are removed; the administration will try to do that as it moves forward with various reforms of the type I mentioned earlier, whether those be tax or nontax reforms.

Although it is important for us to address our tangible capital, we must also be concerned about our human capital—not only the level of saving and investment but also the productivity or efficiency of such investment. We must spend more efficiently, rather than just spend more, in a variety of areas, and education is the prime example.

3

U.S. Fiscal Policy and Saving

Manuel H. Johnson

The topic of saving has always been important, but today it is more important for the U.S. economy, which must increasingly compete in a rapidly changing, integrated world. The determinants of saving are many, and the issue of the effects of government policy on saving is both controversial and enormously complex.

Although I cannot hope to clarify all of the complex issues, there are points of agreement. Most economists agree that saving is important because it constitutes the supply of capital that, combined with labor, forms the primary inputs to production. Capital growth works to increase productivity; the more capital there is per worker, the higher is the output per worker. With more capital per worker, returns to labor are higher and workers' real incomes are higher. The productivity-enhancing character of capital growth works to improve overall economic growth as well as the living standards of workers. In short, economic growth cannot occur without capital formation which, in turn, is dependent on saving. Stated simply, saving can determine which nations are rich and which are poor and whether living standards are high or low.

Another principle on which there is widespread agreement among many economists relates to the operation of the market system. Economic theory argues that an unencumbered world with a competitive private capital market produces an optimal rate of saving. In such circumstances, the return to saving accurately reflects real investment opportunities. Savers determine the volume of saving according to their desire for future consumption relative to current consumption. In more technical parlance, individuals save until their subjective time discount rate matches the return to capital or the equilibrium real interest rate. In short, a well-functioning price system efficiently allocates resources intertemporally. The optimal saving rate is a derivative of free choice and accurately reflects the intertemporal saving desires of the population.

Today, there is widespread agreement that the current U.S. saving rate is relatively low and also less than the optimal rate. There is a good deal of disagreement, however, concerning the level of U.S. saving. Some, referring to the personal saving rate measured by the national income and product accounts, argue that the saving rate is so low that a crisis exists. Others contend that although we do not have a crisis, we nonetheless face an important problem and a difficult policy challenge.

Of course, many measurement and definitional issues are important and lie at the root of these disagreements. Recently, several important and thorough studies addressing these measurement problems have been published. The 1989 National Bureau of Economic Research volume, *The Measurement of Saving, Investment and Wealth,* by Robert E. Lipsey and Helen Stone Tice, serves as an excellent example. Suffice it to say that all the relevant measurement and definitional issues have not been fully resolved. But overall it is fair to say that the U.S. saving rate is low relative to both its earlier history and the saving rate of most industrialized nations today.

Economists agree that even though saving is determined by a host of factors, government policies can have an important impact on saving. Most importantly, fiscal policies, both taxation and spending, can significantly influence saving and therefore affect prospects for long-term economic growth. Of course, disagreement exists as to both the proper policies to influence saving and the degree of influence that a particular policy may have. Nonetheless, fiscal policy is viewed as having a potentially important impact on saving. And economists generally agree that the current low saving rate is at least partly the result of government policies. It is widely recognized that there are numerous types of government tax and spending policies that distort behavior by increasing the cost of and lowering the reward for saving and thereby lower saving.

In recent years, important progress has been made in reforming the tax code. Tax rates are lower, and some distortions that plagued the tax system have been removed or lessened, particularly with regard to the interaction between the tax structure and inflation. But we are very far from an ideal tax system. The U.S. tax system is still quite biased against saving in a number of ways. The current income tax, for example, encourages consumption over saving. Income that is saved is taxed twice: once when it is earned and once again when it generates additional income. Thus, there is a higher rate of tax on income that is saved and invested than on income that is consumed immediately.

The income tax is not the only important form of tax distortion that adversely affects saving. Other forms of federal, state, and local taxes also exact funds from income produced by saving and capital formation. By reducing the future income that can be obtained by the foregoing of current consumption, these tax systems add to the cost of saving.

For individuals who save by purchasing shares in a taxable corporation, the income produced by the corporation is first subject to the corporate income tax. If the corporation distributes its earnings as dividends, the shareholders must pay tax on the dividends they receive, which effectively results in a double taxation of dividends. (The United States is the only country in the G-7 that taxes dividends twice.) If rather than distribute dividends, the corporation retains earnings, and if share prices advance, shareholders must pay capital gains taxes when they sell the stock, even if share values only keep up with inflation.

In cases such as these, the interaction of corporate income taxes, personal taxes on dividends, and capital gains taxes works to substantially increase the cost of saving. Similarly, inadequate depreciation allowances on capital investment work to overstate corporate profits, thereby raising the effective corporate tax rate. Property taxes and estate, gift, inheritance, and other wealth taxes imposed at the federal, state, or local level also amount to taxes on saving.

Tax policy is not the only way in which fiscal policy adversely affects saving. Various government spending programs—especially those oriented toward consumption—can also have important distorting effects. The growth of government consumption spending in excess of revenue growth works to adversely impact saving. This occurs because the government borrowing used to finance such spending absorbs private saving that would otherwise be used to finance more productive private investment activity. Because such government consumption spending in effect works to divert private saving to less productive public-sector activity, this spending lowers the overall return to saving and thereby discourages saving.

Furthermore, various government welfare programs supposedly designed to provide security or insurance to workers and citizens may also adversely affect motives for saving in a more direct way. Social Security, medical disability, and health and unemployment insurance, for example, all provide workers with a substitute for what historically would have been a strong motive for saving. Because these programs supposedly provide income for the retired worker, medical expenses, and unemployment benefits, workers may not save as much as they otherwise would have. Ironically, some of these programs have imposed tax burdens that have reduced both the ability of and incentive for people to save while at the same time promising benefits that may have further reduced the motivation to save.

Similarly, other forms of governmental intervention may adversely affect saving in less obvious ways. Well-intended governmental regulations imposed on business often adversely affect returns of capital, and therefore saving, regardless of whether these regulations achieve their stated objectives. Credit allocation schemes (direct loans, loan guarantees, and credit market rules and regulations) in effect constitute implicit forms of taxation of private capital that also work to lower returns to saving.

Finally, government policies may unintentionally influence many demographic factors known to be important determinants of saving. Although little research has addressed these issues, government policies working to change retirement ages, divorce rates, college attendance, fertility rates, and family formation may also have important effects on or implications for saving.

To summarize, there appears to be a consensus among economists and others on many issues pertaining to saving. They generally agree (1) that saving is important, (2) that an unencumbered market will allow saving to seek its optimal rate, (3) that the current U.S. saving rate is less than the optimal rate, (4) that fiscal policies can influence saving, and (5) that at least part of the reason for the low U.S. saving rate is a whole host of government-policy-induced distortions that have an adverse impact on saving.

Before discussing specific policy proposals to improve our saving performance, I wish to emphasize some very important policy objectives. An understanding of these objectives is essential to set the stage for any lasting, successful strategy to solve our saving problem. First, even if no specific action is undertaken to improve our saving performance, we must support policies that continue to maintain or foster both a healthy investment climate and open trading arrangements. Restrictions to capital flows should be minimized. Even though U.S. saving is less than optimum, saving in the rest of the world may not be. If the United States maintains an environment that fosters relatively healthy returns to investment, the country may supplement its domestic saving with foreign saving to finance productive investment without necessarily endangering its future. If the U.S. economy offers higher relative returns to productive investment and attracts foreign saving, we are likely to be better off than if foreign saving had not migrated here. In particular, our workers will likely be more productive, earn higher wages, and enjoy higher living standards than if such foreign saving were prevented from entering. Of course, it is important to acknowledge that such an approach has exchange rate consequences. Despite an overall macroeconomic benefit, export- and import-competing industries will likely suffer as a result.

Nonetheless, just as it is important to improve our domestic saving performance, it also is important to maintain an environment conducive to both domestic and foreign investment and to maintain and promote open trading arrangements. Offering attractive opportunities for foreign investment and saving is not only good policy; it also is a sign of strength rather than weakness. We can achieve gains from free and open trade and commerce just as we can achieve gains from removing distortions to domestic saving. Restrictions on foreign capital flows or the erection of trade barriers is not a solution to our saving problem. The best approach, of course, is to adopt policies that improve our domestic saving performance, continue to promote a healthy environment for investment, and dismantle barriers to trade and capital flows.

Second, it is important for policymakers to adopt an appropriate framework for analyzing the long-term effects of fiscal policy. The evidence about our saving behavior indicates that in recent decades, a variety of fiscal policy initiatives on both the tax and the spending side introduced distortions (perhaps inadvertently) that adversely impacted our saving performance. These well-intentioned initiatives were probably introduced without a recognition of the adverse effects they might have on saving.

A common thread connecting the fiscal-policy initiatives of recent decades is that they were devised and promoted within a framework that implicitly emphasized the short-term rather than the long-term effects of policy. The framework used for fiscal policy was based on a theory whereby taxation and spending were intended to stabilize the business cycle, manage aggregate demand, or redistribute income—but not foster long-run growth. The framework underlying this theory used data that did not measure wealth and used government budget accounting that did not acknowledge capital investment.

This theory was based on an income-expenditure framework emanating from the 1930s, when the stimulation of spending was critical and saving was actually discouraged. Indeed, it is useful to remember that Keynesians promulgated the so-called paradox of thrift—the idea that saving is bad and consumption is good for the macroeconomy. This view may have been appropriate for the peculiar circumstances of the 1930s, when aggregate demand collapsed and excess supply and capacity prevailed, but it is not an appropriate framework for long-term growth.

I believe that ideas do have consequences. If we are to change fiscal policies to improve our saving performance, we need to extricate ourselves from a theory premised on the notion that saving is bad for the economy, and we need to adopt a longer term, growth-oriented perspective. We need a framework in which the beneficial effects of saving, investment, and long-term growth receive prominent attention and in which incentives to save and invest are recognized as important. In short, a progrowth paradigm is needed within which to frame fiscal policies intended to improve our saving performance. Until this is done, it may be difficult to properly analyze or assess our persistently poor saving performance.

Third, a saving-promoting public policy should have the overall objective of removing the many distortions to saving mentioned previously so that saving can increase and approach its optimal level. In short, government policy should have the goal of fostering a system in which the unencumbered saving preferences of the populace work to determine the actual overall saving rate. Such effects are likely to occur in an environment in which the signals of the market system are allowed to function so as to bring about this desired result. A proper policy approach should seek to minimize the many government spending, tax-related distortions and impediments that work to adversely affect saving behavior.

A long list of distortions is working to adversely affect saving in the United States. Correcting any one or a number of these distortions is likely to improve our saving performance. Overall, emphasis should be placed on minimizing the taxation of saving and reducing the cost of capital. The recommendations in Chapter 1 are consistent with such an approach and overall appear quite good. These proposals certainly move us in the right direction.

My policy preference is generally consistent with recent Treasury proposals that involve some movement toward consumption-based taxation or, for institutional reasons, toward a consumed-income tax. This proposal, of course, is not novel. It has been recommended by many distinguished public finance experts and is the essence of the well-known 1977 Treasury proposal entitled *Blueprints for Basic Tax Reform*, by David Bradford.

The reasons for advocating consumption-based taxation are also well known. An income tax raises the cost of saving relative to consumption, which discourages saving, investment, and capital formation, whereas a consumption tax does not. A consumption tax is neutral with respect to intertemporal consumption decisions. Nevertheless, like all other taxes, consumption taxes do continue to distort the labor-leisure choice. But on balance a consumption tax is more efficient than an income tax given that they both produce a labor-leisure distortion. Although there are many good arguments to support a value-added tax or a national sales tax, I do not believe they are practical or appropriate. Taxes should be clearly discernible, not disguised. Moreover, institutionally, we have an entrenched income-tax structure. The income tax is the mainstay of the federal tax system, and it is unlikely to change in the near future. Given this fact, the last thing we need to do is to create an additional revenue structure or bureaucracy by imposing more layers of taxation. Unlike old soldiers, we know that bureaucracies—whether old or new—neither die nor fade away; instead, they seem to grow forever.

An appropriate alternative is to move in the direction of a consumed-income tax. If an income tax is to be adjusted so as to be neutral with respect to the saving-consumption choice, it must either allow deductions for current saving while taxing all the returns to saving, or it must fully exempt all income from saving while taxing current saving. Accordingly, movement to a consumed-income tax would require exempting either saving or returns to saving. Thus, a practical, revenue-neutral approach is to expand the deductibility of saving or the returns to saving as well as the tax base on consumption. In fact, the United States has already made some progress in lowering tax rates and broadening the tax base. To improve our saving performance and minimize the antisaving bias of the tax code, however, the tax base should be broadened on consumed income rather than on saved income. Of course, such an approach argues for exempting individual retirement accounts (IRAs) as well as reforming certain types of taxation, such as on capital gains and corporate income.

Another distortion adversely affecting our overall saving performance is government dissaving. As indicated earlier, the growth of government spending—especially government consumption spending—in excess of revenue growth negatively affects our saving performance because the government borrowing used to finance such spending absorbs private saving that would otherwise be used to finance more productive private-investment activity. Such government consumption spending in effect works to divert private saving to less productive public-sector activity, thereby both lowering the overall return to saving and discouraging additional saving.

Increasing government saving is best achieved by reducing the growth of government consumption spending. This reduces the likelihood that government borrowing will absorb private saving as well as the likelihood of saving-distorting taxation. Attempts to reduce government dissaving through increases in taxes are potentially counterproductive. Tax increases can lead to additional government consumption spending and can also adversely affect private saving behavior.

What role should monetary policy play in affecting saving behavior? A credible goal of price stability would contribute not only to lower long-term interest rates because of the minimization of both inflation and risk premiums; price stability would also result in less volatile interest rates. In short, the achievement of price stability would enable the price system to work better and allow the saving preferences of the public to be accurately registered in the markets—and thereby impact actual saving.

One manifestation of such a smoothly functioning price system is that saving is neither destroyed by inflation nor diverted into unproductive inflation hedges. A smoothly operating price system contributes to a smoothly operating intermediation process—the uninterrupted channeling of saving into productive investment. Thus, monetary policy is the policy tool for price stabilization and consequently for economic stabilization. A stable, predictable monetary policy will promote a more stable environment, which should allow fiscal policy to focus more attention on capital formation and long-term growth.

Economists agree on a number of important issues relating to our suboptimal saving performance. They generally agree that fiscal policy can distort behavior so as to adversely affect the economy's saving rate. Adopting an appropriate longer run growth framework for fiscal policy, promoting open trading arrangements, and removing distortions to saving are all important components of an overall prosaving macroeconomic policy.

Many politicians and pundits continue to rail about our low saving rate and budget deficits and their implications for trade deficits and long-term capital formation. Yet these same individuals normally do not address the continued distortions that are adversely affecting saving, and these individuals often promote policies that exacerbate these very distortions. Their policy prescriptions include both tax increases and the continued promotion of the growth of government consumption spending within an income-expenditure framework. If adopted, such policies will probably worsen rather than improve our saving performance. As long as such inappropriate policy proposals continue to be made, we should welcome rather than discourage the inflow of foreign capital.

4

Lagging U.S. Saving: Threat to U.S. World Leadership

Paul A. Volcker

Several years ago, I began to sound the alarm about all the U.S. deficits—budget deficit, foreign trade deficit, and current account deficit—and the low level of saving in this country. While I was at the Federal Reserve, I used to remark that we were running the risk of a very serious economic problem, perhaps even a crisis. Yet the crisis has not materialized. Was I all that misguided, or is there something new going on? Is the business cycle obsolete? Do we not have to save anymore? Does investment not make any difference? Or is the problem simply deferred?

In assessing all those possibilities, we must note that ever since 1982 we have had expansion and lower unemployment than we have seen in fifteen or twenty years, with inflation somewhat contained and certainly lower than at the start of the expansion period. I think there is a very good chance that with reasonable management and some good luck, we will move through this current period of sluggish growth without a recession. There is no necessary reason to look for a recession as far ahead as I can see; indeed, I think a period of slower growth was necessary at some point because we were growing faster than we had capacity in terms of employment or plant equipment.

The 1980s witnessed quite a performance, one that was not limited to the United States. In fact, the buoyancy of the Japanese economy and of the economies throughout Asia and the strength of Europe, particularly West Germany, provide a large part of the base for my optimism about the relatively near-term outlook. I think it is fair to say that the U.S. economy carried the world economy in the 1980s. Now that situation has been somewhat reversed.

What was not fully predictable was the extent to which we could bridge the basic deficit between our willingness to save and our desire to invest and to run government deficits. We have been able to bridge that shortfall of saving by a continuing, very large inflow of saving from abroad. We have not had a collision, and we have not had a crunch in domestic credit markets because we have been able to draw so heavily and so freely on foreign saving. That is particularly interesting and surprising in view of the fact that during 1985, 1986, and a good part of 1987 the dollar was declining—rather rapidly by most standards. But this decline did not give rise to a panicky run by foreign investors.

In 1987 and 1988, when domestic saving was at its low point, the current account deficit was bigger and we were borrowing even more from abroad; there were quarters when we were borrowing more from abroad than we were generating in total personal saving at home. I think that is an interesting comparison that suggests the magnitude of the problem. We have had a recovery in personal saving since then, and we have had a reduction in the foreign deficit, although the deficit is still large.

Foreign saving is flowing very freely into this country, even though our external liabilities have mounted quite rapidly over this period. The foreign saving is coming in so freely that the dollar goes up, which worries some people. But the fact is that we are totally dependent upon that saving, whether it is flowing in freely or not. We are dependent in the most immediate sense because we have to pay for the trade deficit and the current account deficit. That is very clear.

But what we sometimes forget is that we need that saving to balance our government deficit. If we did something dramatic to eliminate the trade imbalance and the external current account imbalance, and if the deficit disappeared, we would not need to borrow any money to cover that particular deficit. But if we did not borrow any money from abroad, we would be left with an internal deficit and with enormous pressures on the capital market and on the economy. We would end up balancing the internal markets with an unacceptable kind of recession. For all our concern about the external balance, we do not have the manufacturing capacity or the financial capacity to see that deficit eliminated.

Is our low saving rate really fundamental to our future? I believe it is. Even during this long and glorious period of economic advance with relative price stability, we have had some very close calls. The most obvious year in point is 1987, when, temporarily at least, saving from abroad was not flowing so freely from private lenders. We by necessity were borrowing from abroad very heavily, but it was largely through lending by foreign governments and central banks for very short-term periods—hardly the most stable, desirable, continuing form of financing. There was increasing concern about confidence in our financial markets, particularly as the spring and summer wore on, and fear that our dependence on foreign official lending rather than on spontaneous private flows would cause the dollar to go down. Nervousness in the bond markets caused the government bond yields to reach 10.5 percent when there was still quite a lot of unemployment and more excess capacity than there is today. All those events had something to do with the culmination of the stock market boom. The culmination actually began in August 1987, when interest rates peaked. Then there was the subsequent collapse in October. We got through that without much impact on the economy. But it was a close call in those few days in October as to whether there would be damage to the financial and economic outlook.

That all seems distant now. There is nothing like two years of rising stock prices and a continually rising economy to shorten memories. But maintenance of confidence is extremely important. If we had a sense of lack of progress on both the domestic deficit and external deficit, we would be in trouble. We have not had very much progress, but we have had some. The trend has been in the right direction, and inflation is being contained. If that were not the case, I would worry about confidence among our foreign as well as our domestic lenders. The news generally has been modestly reassuring on these scores, and with reasonable management and luck we can look ahead to continuing economic advances and even continuing progress on the inflation front. Nonetheless, we are running a high-consumption, low-saving economy. In the long run, that is debilitating.

All the reassuring remarks I have made about the economy do not obscure some other rather fundamental factors. We have a high cost of capital relative to other countries. Now that I am in investment banking, the high cost of capital in the United States has been driven home to me more forcibly. Like other investment bankers, our firm has educated young people peering over computers projecting cash flows of various corporations. Then these young people take that cash flow and discount it by 15 percent, which is a magic number these days. And they say if the company cannot show a projected cash flow adequate to return 15 percent the investment is not a good one. In the history of humankind, however, there are not that many investments that return 15 percent a year for any length of time, even allowing for inflation around current levels. The really good ones do, but the great bulk of investments do not.

Look at the people in this country making that calculation in today's market, and then look at foreigners whose cost of capital is much lower—particularly the Japanese. It is not a great surprise that the money tends to flow from Japan to the United States because the Japanese are not insisting on a 15 percent return on capital. They are looking for a strategic investment, for a piece of technology, to ensure a market position. They are hoping to enlarge their worldwide market share, and they hope to get a decent return over ten or twenty years.

The capital is flowing from them to us, and we are in the position where we need that capital. We dislike this situation in a political sense, but this cannot be entirely a political question. That technology is flowing from the United States to Japan and Europe is cause for concern. Others are making strategic investments for the future and increasing their market share by rounding out product lines. U.S. companies do that also, but to a lesser extent. It seems to me that this investment pattern is a reflection of relative economic weakness in the United States, which will be revealed over a period of time in a slower rate of economic growth for our citizens and a diminished role in the world economy.

Even in these past years of good economic conditions, U.S. productivity growth has been low by world standards. The U.S. investment rate by our own past standards relative to gross national product (GNP) net investment is also relatively low, particularly considering that since 1982 business has been expanding. By international standards, the rate is very low, and the investing we are doing is, at the margin, increasingly owned by foreigners. We are doing very poorly in terms of private saving and in terms of the public deficit. We are spending more than ever before. We are indeed, by any objective measure, richer than ever before. But somehow we feel poor.

We are not spending any more on defense as a proportion of GNP than we did earlier in the postwar period, but somehow the burdens of troops in Europe or Korea or of bases in the Philippines begin to seem insurmountable. I am not arguing for big military expenditures. I am arguing that our defense spending ought to be set in a reasonable range by our security needs—not by some sense that we are feeling poor when the economy is generating more income than it ever has in its history—and there should be more left over for both private and other public needs.

Symbolic of the decline in the U.S. international role are our December 1989 negotiations with the World Bank on the International Development Association (IDA) replenishment, which is highly subsidized aid to the poorest countries, including those in Africa and Asia. When the IDA program started in 1960 the United States provided 42 percent of the money. Our share has gone down steadily since then, as perhaps it should, to 25 percent. If we maintain the real purchasing power of our contribution for the World Bank's 1988, 1989, and 1990 fiscal years, which would require an increase of about $100 million a year (and even this is very much in jeopardy), our relative share will fall to 22 percent. The Japanese share will rise to between 20 and 21 percent. I am not at all sure that is a reasonable measure of the relative wealth of the United States and Japan and of our relative influence in the world. But that is the direction in which the situation is going.

Take the World Bank capital itself. A country's capital contributions to the World Bank determine its voting rights in that body. Our contribution is steadily going down. We arranged a few years ago that our proportionate share could be reduced to as little as 15 percent and we could still maintain our veto right over charter amendments. (We are the only country that has a veto.) Our share is still greater than

15 percent. But if Congress does not provide the appropriation of $60 or $70 million for the capital installment due in 1990, our contribution to the World Bank could drop to less than 15 percent and we could lose our veto. Is this really a desirable or appropriate measure of the kind of influence we should bear in the world economy? Should we not play a greater role?

This question of voting rights at the World Bank may seem a pretty esoteric issue. Nevertheless I was struck when President Bush came back from his July 1989 trip to Poland and spoke so enthusiastically about the communist system breaking up, about reliance on private enterprise and private markets, and about political systems changing. But in spite of all that bright promise, he said that the United States could not afford more than $119 million of aid. It struck me as troubling that in the midst of this promising situation heralding the end of the cold war, we could not afford more than the equivalent of one-tenth of one cent on the gas tax. What this implicitly said about U.S. leadership in the world disturbed me. Further, we are not providing any bilateral official money to the heavily indebted nations of Latin America; we instead ask Japan to provide loans.

My point is that we can smooth over all those problems because we can borrow so readily from abroad for a variety of reasons, mainly because our cost of capital is relatively high. The cost is not high because capital investment is booming. It is not high because we are having an enormous burst of productivity; productivity is rather modest. Our cost of capital is high because our saving is low.

We are not on the edge of catastrophe. But it is a risky strategy to finance our spending and investment by borrowing and relying so much on foreign capital. This seems to me a tough balancing act, and over time it is inherently debilitating. This strategy does to some degree undermine our economic future, and it is undercutting our leadership.

Let me offer just one warning on particular measures to raise the U.S. saving rate. Capital gains are fun to debate. There are all kinds of technical issues; we can argue about individual retirement accounts, and the evidence is a bit ambiguous as to whether they help saving or only increase the deficit. These seem to me to be side issues; neither of these measures is going to attack in any very substantial way the basic dilemma that I am describing. We need to get to work on this basic imbalance that we are still grappling with after so many years. We must take some constructive action—whether to reduce government spending or change the tax structure. And we must build some support for addressing this underlying dilemma and imbalance in national policy.

PART TWO

U.S. Saving and Investment Rate: Cause for Concern?

5

What Is National Saving? Alternative Measures in Historical and International Context

David F. Bradford

INTRODUCTION

Among policymakers and commentators there is a virtual consensus today that the United States saves too little, and there is only scattered disagreement about whether something can and should be done about it. But journalistic analysis, if not professional opinion, is actually based on a rather unreflective reliance on one, or perhaps two, statistical measures of national saving behavior. It would assist intelligent discussion of these issues to have in view the multiple meanings of the term *saving.* My object here is to lay out some of the main alternative conceptions of saving and their interpretation and to present data comparing recent U.S. saving behavior with its own past and with the saving behavior of other nations.

NATIONAL INCOME, CONSUMPTION, AND SAVING

A good place to start is with the identity Y = C + S, income equals the sum of consumption and saving. The simplicity of this identity is apparent but is not real. All it accomplishes is to establish a relationship among three measures of economic performance and thereby to imply that when an empirical or accounting content is given to any two of the concepts, the empirical or accounting content of the third is implied. National income accounting generally starts with definitions of income and consumption (by households and governments) from which saving is defined by subtraction. All beginning students of economics learn that saving is a residual.

Analysis of U.S. national saving is quite likely to start with the income data and definitions of the U.S. Department of Commerce's national income and product accounts (NIPAs).[1] To make life confusing, the term *income* in the NIPAs is attached to factor payments and distinguishes between taxes that fall on factor payments and taxes that do not (indirect business taxes). It is doubtful that there is an economically meaningful distinction between taxes that bear on factor payments and those that do not. When speaking of the nation, I here use the terms *income* and *product* interchangeably to mean "product" (gross or net) as measured in the NIPAs. Instead of income, consumption, and saving, the three related notions in the NIPA context are product, consumption, and saving. Which two of the three are fundamental (in determining the third as a residual) in the case of the NIPAs is not immediately obvious.

National income and product accounts are primarily focused on measuring output, of which there are two major conceptions: gross and net. The beginning student's deceptively simple truism applies to the concepts of gross national income (or product) and gross national saving. Gross national product (GNP)—"the market value of the goods and services produced by labor and property supplied by residents of the United States"[2]—and consumption—personal and government—can reasonably be described as fundamental ideas. Together (by subtraction) they define gross saving.

Gross national product may perhaps be of behavioral interest because of its relationship to the aggregate employment of labor. But it has always been recognized, and more advanced students understand, that a gross measure of output is defective as a measure of performance because it ignores the using up of national capital and that gross saving is purely an accounting residual concept with no normative or behavioral interpretation. As measures of economic performance, more advanced students look to net national product (NNP) (or income) and net national saving. To reach net product, net investment, and net saving, it is necessary to subtract an allowance for the using up of the reproducible capital stock. Here, the defining ideas are consumption and net investment (or saving), the latter understood as the increase in the nation's capital stock. We will have it about right if we think of net product (income) as definitionally equal to the sum of consumption (personal and governmental) and saving (the change in the reproducible capital stock owned by U.S. residents).

It is thus true that net national saving is equal to the difference between net national product (income) and national consumption, but it is misleading to describe net saving as a residual because net saving has a normative and behavioral interpretation as the change in the nation's capital stock. The interpretation is normative because we regard more capital as desirable, and it is behavioral because we think people and businesses seek to optimize the level of capital. Indeed, it is reasonable to describe net national product (income) as the piece of the identity that is defined residually (as the sum of consumption and net saving), even if this is disguised by the way the statisticians describe the derivation of net national product as gross national product less the depreciation of the capital stock (capital consumption allowances).

Whereas gross saving does not have normative content, net saving does. It measures the increment to the nation's capital stock. When we speak of saving as an indicator of economic performance, we have in mind this quality: that it measures a change in a stock of wealth or productive potential. The difference among alternative measures of saving from a policy perspective consists of differences among the stocks of wealth or capital to which the saving is an increment.

WEALTH AND CAPITAL

The Flow of Funds Division of the Board of Governors of the Federal Reserve System compiles balance sheets for the various private sectors of the U.S. economy. Table 5.1 gives a summary of the figures on the national net worth for year end 1988. Note that the figures do not include the assets of governments, whereas the financial liabilities of governments are in effect treated as national liabilities. Another, less obvious, feature of the data is the treatment of asset location. "Domestic net worth" consists of reproducible assets plus land located in the United States. The reproducible assets other than consumer durables constitute the stock that is augmented each year by "net private domestic investment" in the NIPAs. To obtain a figure representative of the aggregate of the capital owned by U.S. residents, it is necessary, first, to add assets located abroad but owned by U.S. residents ("direct foreign investment" plus financial claims on foreigners, including portfolio equity); second, to subtract the corresponding foreign claims against U.S. assets; and third, to add the U.S. stock of gold and special drawing rights (SDRs). Note, too, that except for land and net international portfolio investment in corporate equities, the assets are carried on the national balance sheet on a "financial accounting basis," by which I mean to draw the analogy with the financial accounting for a business firm and to contrast with estimated market value.[3] "Financial accounting" for assets is often the only method available, and I do not mean to imply by the term a crude historical cost record. The Federal Reserve data on reproducible assets are the U.S. Department of Commerce "current" (that is, replacement) cost estimates.[4] For this reason, the "total consolidated national net assets" figure in Table 5.1 is not identical to the aggregate wealth represented by those assets. I will say more on this point.

Some of the components of total consolidated net assets can be considered more closely. According to the Federal Reserve Board, as of the end of 1988, the "net claims on foreign" item was negative. This is roughly the same as saying that U.S. residents owed more to foreigners than vice versa, but it is important to keep in mind that the direct investment stocks are valued at replacement, rather than at market,

TABLE 5.1
National Net Worth of the United States,
Year End 1988

	Millions of Dollars	Percent Distributions		
Domestic Net Worth	14,964,435	104	100	
Reproducible Assets	11,410,041		76	100
Residential Structures	4,235,330			37
Nonresidential Plant and Equipment	4,364,789			38
Inventories	1,003,997			9
Consumer Durables	1,805,925			16
Land at Market	3,554,394		24	
Net Claims on Foreign	-558,463	-4		
Foreign Assets, U.S. owned	738,367			
U.S. Assets, Foreign owned	-1,296,830			
U.S. Gold and SDRs	20,789	0		
Total Consolidated National Net Assets	14,426,761	100		

Source: Board of Governors, Federal Reserve System, *Balance Sheets for the U.S. Economy,* Flow of Funds publication C.9 (October 1989).

TABLE 5.2
Wealth of U.S. Households at Market Value, Year End 1988

	Millions of Dollars	Percent Distributions	
Household-Owned Tangible Assets	6,560,104	48	100
Owner-Occupied Structures and Land	4,388,381		67
Other Structures and Nonprofit Tangible	3,185,804		49
Consumer Durables	1,805,925		28
Net Financial Assets	7,205,731	52	
Net Household Financial Assets	9,334,094		
Total Private Financial Assets	12,600,638		100
Deposits and Credit Market Instruments	4,543,226		36
Corporate Equities	2,242,924		18
Life Insurance and Pension Fund Reserves	2,906,337		23
Equity in Noncorporate Business[a]	2,654,300		21
Miscellaneous Other	253,851		2
Total Private Liabilities	3,266,544		
Public Sector Financial Assets Less Liabilities	-2,128,363		
National Wealth at Market Value	13,765,835	100	
Memo: Net Household-Owned Assets	15,894,198		

Source: Board of Governors, Federal Reserve System, *Balance Sheets for the U.S. Economy,* Flow of Funds publication C.9 (October 1989).

[a]Household equity in noncorporate business includes equity in noncorporate private financial institutions, omitted in the Federal Reserve's household sector balance sheet.

value. Land value is estimated to have accounted for almost one-quarter of the tangible assets located in the United States. Of the reproducible assets, housing and industrial plant and equipment are of almost equal importance, together accounting for 75 percent. Inventories account for almost 10 percent, and consumer durables, at 16 percent, make up the rest.

Table 5.2 presents data on the aggregate wealth of U.S. households (including nonprofit institutions). The household totals include all the assets indirectly owned by households via life insurance and pension reserves. The totals therefore include government financial obligations, directly or indirectly owned, and they make no allowance for the implicit liability of U.S. taxpayers to foreign holders of U.S. government financial obligations. A better measure of national wealth is therefore obtained by netting out these financial liabilities, yielding the figure for "national wealth at market value" shown in Table 5.2.

Where possible, the market values of assets have been used in Table 5.2, in particular, for land and corporate equity. For this reason, as well as slightly different coverage, the national wealth in Table 5.2, at $13.8 trillion, differs from the consolidated national net asset total of $14.4 trillion shown in Table 5.1.

I noted earlier that the Federal Reserve Board's national balance sheets do not include the assets of governments. We should remember that the figures also exclude a form of wealth that swamps both private and public tangible capital in importance: human capital.[5]

U.S. SAVING IN INTERNATIONAL CONTEXT: NATIONAL ACCOUNTS MEASURES

I turn now to some data on the behavior of national saving over time in the United States and in selected foreign countries as reflected in national accounts. Table 5.3 presents decade averages of the ratio of national saving (net national product less government and personal consumption) to GNP for the 1950–1988 period, taken from the NIPAs. The table makes clear that there was a sharp drop in the NIPA net national saving rate in the 1980s. Figure 5.1 displays the annual data from the NIPAs, together with its downward trend line.

National accounting within the Organisation for Economic Co-operation and Development (OECD) follows rules laid down in the system of national accounts (SNA) developed by the United Nations, which differs in various ways from the conventions of the U.S. NIPAs.[6] The treatment of government expenditure is probably the most important of these differences. In the case of the NIPAs, all government expenditure on goods and services is regarded as consumption; the SNA, by contrast, divides government expenditure into consumption and investment components and keeps track of the associated capital stocks, depreciation, and so on. In fact, although the U.S. federal government

TABLE 5.3
U.S. National Saving: NIPA Definition
(decade average percent of GNP)

Period	Percent of GNP
1950–1959	7.4
1960–1969	7.9
1970–1979	7.1
1980–1988	3.0

Sources: U.S. Department of Commerce, *National Income and Product Accounts of the United States, 1929–82; Survey of Current Business* (July 1987–1989).

TABLE 5.4
U.S. National Saving: Two Definitions
(decade average percent of NDP)

	System of National Accounts	NIPA-Type Measure
1960–1969	10.9	9.2
1970–1979	9.3	8.6
1980–1987	4.3	4.0

Source: Organisation for Economic Co-operation and Development, *National Accounts.*

FIGURE 5.1
U.S. NIPA National Saving
(percent of GNP)

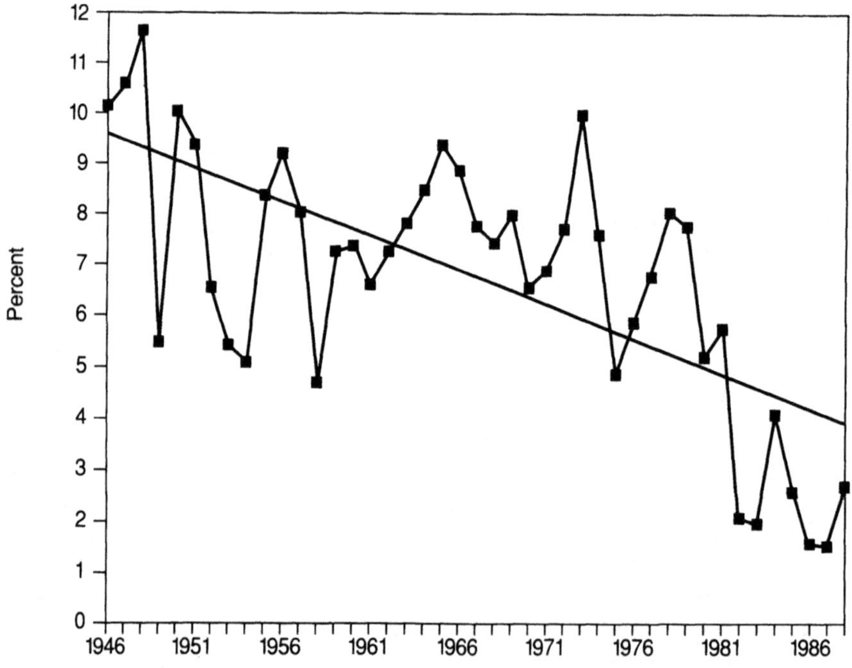

Source: U.S. Department of Commerce, Bureau of Economic Analysis, *National Income and Product Accounts.*

does not distinguish current and capital expenditures in its budget, the U.S. Department of Commerce nonetheless compiles and publishes the figures. These are incorporated in the multination compilations of the OECD.

A second difference between U.S. accounting practice and that of all the other OECD countries is in the denominator typically chosen for measuring economic magnitudes. The U.S. practice is to express aggregates such as consumption as fractions of GNP, or perhaps NNP. In the other OECD countries, the typical denominator is gross or net domestic product (GDP or NDP). For purposes of exploring long-term saving trends, the difference is not important. Table 5.4 suggests the difference implied by the differing treatments of government expenditure in the two accounting systems. The first column shows the U.S. national saving rate (as a ratio to net domestic product) according to the SNA definitions; the other column subtracts government net investment from the SNA definition. Because net government capital formation has been positive over the time period covered, the SNA saving rates are larger than the "NIPA" saving rates. We can infer from the table that the rate of net capital formation by the U.S. government dropped from about 1.7 percent of NDP in the 1960s to about 0.3 percent of NDP in the 1980s. (Barry Bosworth has suggested to me that major influences on the decline have been the completion of the interstate highway system and the slowdown in construction of new schools attributable to the shifting U.S. demographic structure.) Figure 5.2 displays the annual time series with trend lines. Again, a sharp decline of the saving rate is evident in both measures.

A common system of national accounts preparation permits international comparisons free of one possibly significant source of differences. Table 5.5 compares national saving rates for six countries: the United States, the United Kingdom, Japan, Sweden, West Germany, and Canada. Large differences are noticeable, particularly the high saving propensity of Japan. National saving rates in most countries have declined in recent years. Figure 5.3 displays annual national savings rates, based on the same OECD data, for four of the countries for which I have also assembled data on wealth at market value.

One should not be too quick to draw conclusions from these international differences. Derek Blades and Peter Sturm have warned that depreciation conventions have not been unified under the SNA,[7] and Barry Bosworth has expressed to me the view that the Japanese national accounts understate depreciation, which would tend to increase the numerator relative to the denominator of the Japanese national saving rate. Fumio Hayashi has suggested that the relatively large place of land value in Japanese wealth also gives a somewhat misleading quality to a simple comparison of national account saving rates.[8]

FIGURE 5.2
U.S. National Saving: Comparison of Measures with Trends

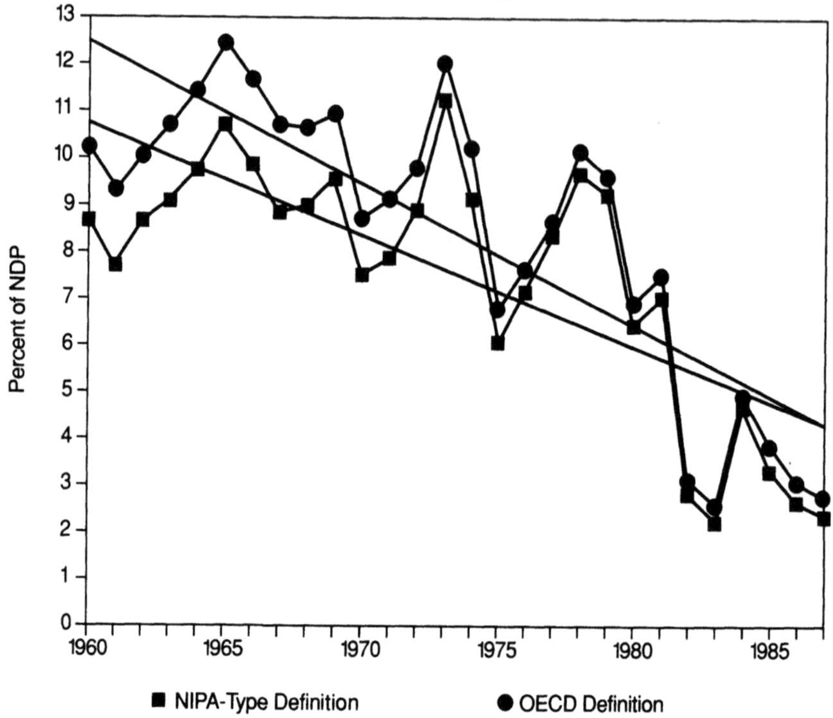

Source: Organisation for Economic Co-operation and Development, *National Accounts.*

TABLE 5.5
Comparison of National Accounts Saving Rates
(national saving as a percent of NDP)

	United States	United Kingdom	Japan	Sweden	West Germany	Canada
1963–1967	11.5	11.1	23.5	17.1	19.0	12.3
1968–1972	9.9	12.2	28.9	15.8	19.0	12.0
1973–1977	9.0	7.2	24.8	13.0	13.9	13.7
1978–1982	7.4	7.3	21.2	5.9	11.0	11.7
1983–1987	3.4	6.4	20.3	6.7	11.5	8.4

Source: Organisation for Economic Co-operation and Development, *National Accounts.*

FIGURE 5.3
International Comparison of National Accounts Saving

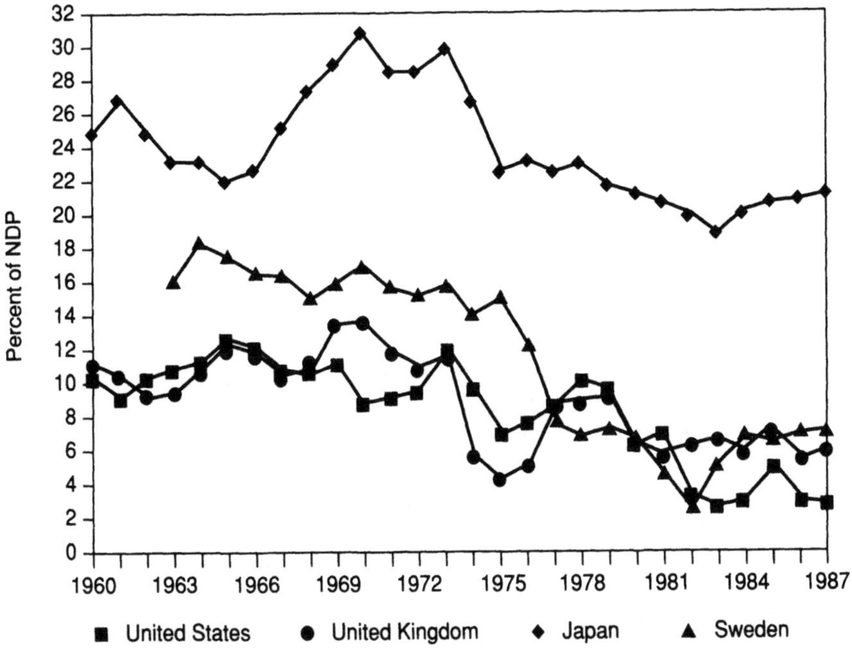

Source: Organisation for Economic Co-operation and Development, *National Accounts.* For details, see Appendix 5.A.

PERSONAL SAVING AND THE FLOW OF FUNDS

The discussion thus far has concentrated on *national* saving, for which all accumulation by U.S. residents, whether directly on their own account or indirectly via the retained earnings of corporations, is aggregated. The NIPAs also distinguish the income and expenditure of various sectors of the economic system, in particular, of the household or personal sector (which includes nonprofit institutions as well as households in the ordinary sense of the term).[9] The underlying idea of personal income is the payment to households for supplying productive services (plus net transfers), but the idea's implementation emphasizes cash flow to households as reflected in such transactions as receipt of wages and dividends. In the context of defining income for purposes of taxation, economists customarily argue that accruing gain is equivalent to, say, interest payments as a reward to the capitalist who supplies capital services. But accruing gains and losses on assets held by households are not included in NIPA personal income. Accrual accounting (in the usual financial accounting sense) is applied to directly owned businesses (and thus income of proprietors is net of depreciation on capital used in the business, for example).

As mentioned, economics casts doubt on the validity of cash-flow income as a good measure of the compensation for services rendered by or of the economic opportunities of a household. Most obviously, a family that owns a readily marketable asset that increases in value during the year is in much the same position as one that owns a bank account to which the same amount of interest is credited during the year. (That is the argument for including *real* capital gains in income subject to tax.) Similarly, a worker whose employer deposits a certain amount in a defined-contribution pension plan is arguably in the same position as one who receives the payment in cash and makes a deposit in an individual retirement account. Whether personal income is a useful concept, either behaviorally or normatively, is thus very questionable.

Be that as it may, the NIPAs provide a measure of a statistically well-defined quantity: personal income. The NIPA personal income measure includes most transfer payments from the government (Social Security benefits and the like). The worker's share of payroll tax "contributions" for social insurance is deducted from amounts reported as received as wage and salary disbursements by employers. (The employer's share is not regarded as received by the employee in the first place.)

Of course, employee contributions to social insurance are not the only compulsory outlays by households. So the NIPAs define "disposable personal income" as what is left from personal income after income taxes (along with other similar taxes) have been paid. (The line item in the accounts "personal tax and nontax payments" always amuses students.) Personal saving is disposable personal income less "personal outlays" (personal consumption expenditures, constituting the vast bulk, plus consumer interest plus personal transfer payments to foreigners).

The Flow of Funds Section of the Board of Governors of the Federal Reserve System also provides a measure of personal saving that is alternative to that presented in the NIPAs.[10] This measure differs conceptually from NIPA personal saving in two respects. First, the flow of funds account (FFA) saving measure treats net acquisition of consumer durables as a form of saving, whereas the NIPAs regard outlays on consumer durables simply as a component of personal consumption expenditures. Second, the FFAs adopt a slightly different definition of personal income and count in certain credits from government insurance programs and capital gains distributions from mutual funds, items excluded from the NIPA definition of personal income.

There is, however, a further difference between the NIPA and FFA personal saving measures that is in some ways more important. This difference is the nature of the data. In the NIPAs, personal saving is a residual between a measure of personal income and a measure of consumption.[11] By contrast, FFA personal saving is a direct measure of the net acquisitions of assets by households. It should be emphasized, however, that apart from the two specific differences already mentioned, the NIPAs and FFAs purport to measure the same thing. That is, both use the same basic concepts of income, consumption, and saving.

The differences in statistical approaches sometimes have resulted in fairly large differences in saving rates. Table 5.6 presents data on NIPA personal saving side by side with FFA personal saving, both as defined in the FFAs and as the NIPA personal saving rate would be if derived from the FFAs. Columns 1–3 of the table show how FFA personal saving is built up from data on net capital expenditures (from the NIPAs, including purchases of consumer durables less the depreciation on the stock of consumer durables) and acquisitions of financial assets less increases in financial liabilities. The net of these three forms of saving is FFA personal saving (column 3). From 1979 to 1988 the FFA personal saving rate thus defined was 8.3 percent, the same level as in the 1960s. This rate was considerably less than the levels of 9.1 percent during the 1970s and 8.7 percent during the 1950s.

The FFAs provide data from which we can construct an estimate of personal saving according to the NIPA definitions of income. The required adjustments are also shown in Table 5.6 (columns 4 and 5). The NIPA personal saving rates are substantially less than the FFA personal saving rates. The main reasons for the difference are the inclusion of acquisitions of consumer durables and extra receipts (credits from government insurance and mutual fund capital gains distributions) in income and saving according to the FFAs. Of these, the investment in consumer durables is the larger piece (although both adjustments are significant). Like the FFA personal saving rate, the NIPA personal saving rate estimated from the FFAs was down in the 1980s from its high level in the 1970s.

The FFA estimate of the NIPA saving rate differs from the actual NIPA saving rate because of the different statistical sources used. The NIPA figures are also shown in Table 5.6 (column 6). The difference between the two (column 7), known as the "household discrepancy," has always been volatile but generally positive (that is, direct estimates of household net acquisitions of assets exceed the amount implied in the national income data). As Figure 5.4 shows, the household discrepancy had appeared to be declining as a fraction of the saving being measured until the 1980s, when its volatility and apparent magnitude increased. As discussed in detail by John Wilson and colleagues, there is no single explanation for the discrepancy, which must be regarded as one measure of our uncertainty about household saving behavior.[12]

The ratio of personal saving to disposable personal income, often referred to as *the* "personal saving rate," is used as a measure of the saving choices of households. The line labeled "NIPA" in Figure 5.5 shows the annual personal saving rate for the United States from 1949 to 1988. The well-known downward trend in the NIPA personal saving rate since the mid-1970s is dramatically clear. The other two lines in

TABLE 5.6
U.S. Personal Saving
(FFA and NIPA)

	(1) Net Capital Expenditure	(2) Acquisition of Financial Assets (net)	(3) FFA Net Personal Saving	(4) Income Adjustments[a]	(5) FFA Personal Saving—NIPA Basis	(6) NIPA Personal Saving	(7) Household Discrepancy	(8) Household Discrepancy/NIPA Saving
1949–1958	6.5	2.2	8.7	3.3	5.4	4.5	0.9	20.7
1959–1968	4.8	3.6	8.3	2.8	5.5	4.6	0.9	20.7
1969–1978	4.7	4.4	9.1	3.3	5.8	5.4	0.4	8.0
1979–1988	4.6	3.7	8.3	3.8	4.5	3.8	0.7	20.2

Sources: Board of Governors, Federal Reserve System, and U.S. Department of Commerce.

Note: FAA denotes flow of funds accounts; NIPA denotes national income and product accounts. Figures are the average percentage of GNP for each decade.

[a]Includes consumer durables.

FIGURE 5.4
U.S. Household Discrepancy
(Ratio to NIPA Saving)

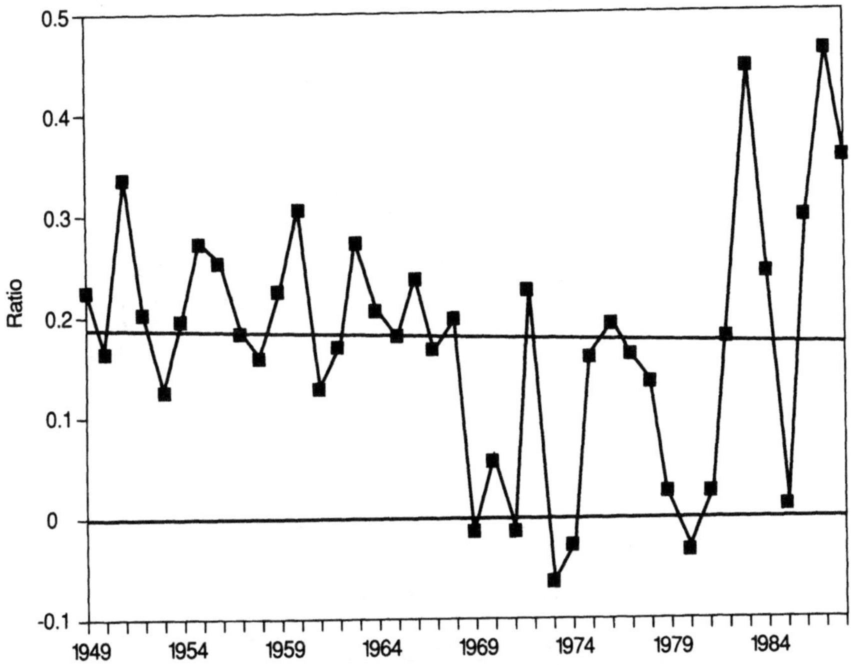

Sources: U.S. Department of Commerce, Bureau of Economic Analysis, *National Income and Product Accounts*; and Board of Governors, Federal Reserve System, Flow of Funds Section, *Flow of Funds Accounts.*

Figure 5.5 show the estimate of the NIPA concept of the personal saving rate from the FFAs, together with the FFA personal saving rate expressed as a percentage of disposable personal income. Figure 5.5 suggests what Table 5.6 may also have led us to expect: that for purposes of assessing the broad trend, it matters little whether we use the personal saving rate from the NIPAs or the estimate of the same quantity from the FFAs. It does apparently matter somewhat more whether we look at the NIPA concept or the FFA concept as there is no down trend in the latter (the top line in Figure 5.5).

My own inclination is to prefer (slightly) the FFA personal saving concept, including its extra income elements and inclusion of consumer durables in saving. But both measures are lacking insofar as they depend on a somewhat arbitrary definition of what constitutes disposable personal income. As I have suggested, we may reasonably doubt that disposable income is a good measure of the opportunities of households, dependent as it is on the degree to which households see through various transactions to underlying economic reality (such as accruing gains and losses or the change in pension claims). A better measure of the resources out of which households in the aggregate may be thought

FIGURE 5.5
U.S. Personal Saving: Three Measures
(percent of disposable personal income)

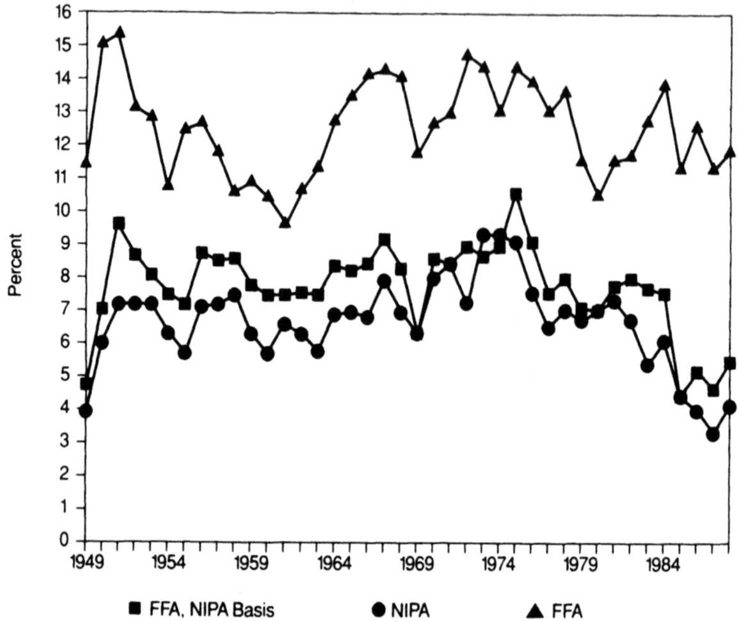

Sources: U.S. Department of Commerce, Bureau of Economic Analysis, *National Income and Product Accounts*, and Board of Governors, Federal Reserve System, Flow of Funds Section, *Flow of Funds Accounts*.

Notes: FFA denotes flow of funds accounts; NIPA denotes national income and product accounts.

TABLE 5.7
U.S. Net National Saving Rates
(corrected measures)

Period	(1) (Y-G-C)/Y	(2) (Y-G-C)/(Y-G)	(3) G/Y
1940–1949	0.086	0.101	0.271
1950–1959	0.133	0.167	0.203
1960–1969	0.130	0.166	0.215
1970–1979	0.118	0.152	0.223
1980–1985	0.072	0.093	0.230

Source: Laurence J. Kotlikoff, testimony before the U.S. House of Representatives, Committee on Ways and Means, April 20, 1989.

Notes: Y is national income and product account (NIPA) net national product plus imputed rent on consumer durables and government tangible assets (excluding military equipment) less depreciation on the stock of consumer durables and government tangible assets (excluding military equipment).

G is NIPA government expenditures less government expenditures on tangible assets (excluding military equipment) plus imputed rent on the government's stock of tangible assets (excluding military equipment).

C is NIPA personal consumption less consumer expenditures on durables plus imputed rent on the stock of consumer durables.

Imputed rent on an asset is calculated as annual depreciation plus 3 percent times the stock of the asset. Annual depreciation of consumer durables and government tangible assets as well as the stocks of consumer durables and government tangible assets are reported in U.S. Department of Commerce, *Fixed Reproducible Tangible Wealth in the United States, 1925–1985* (Washington, D.C.: U.S. Government Printing Office, June 1987).

to draw their consumption is the amount of national output that is left over after the government's exhaustive uses.

Laurence Kotlikoff has provided the figures in Table 5.7 to measure the behavior of households in relation to their real economic opportunities. Table 5.7 shows the behavior over time of two measures of national saving. The first is a version of the usual national saving rate constructed by the addition to national output estimates of the flows of services from government tangible capital (excluding military capital) and from consumer durables; similar modifications are made to the NIPA figures for personal and government consumption. The national saving rate in column 1 of Table 5.7 thus differs from the usual national saving rate in that it uses these modified income and consumption concepts and has net rather than gross product in the denominator. This national saving rate is larger than the usual NIPA measure, but it also displays a sharp downturn in the 1980s. Column 2 presents a modified "personal" saving rate, one that in effect assumes no substitutability between government and personal consumption and therefore conceives of households as making their choices from what remains from national output after government consumption has been subtracted. This modified personal consumption rate shows an even more marked decline in the 1980s, suggesting that households are "to blame" for the decline in saving—not the government, whose claims have only modestly increased.

NATIONAL ACCOUNTS AND MARKET VALUE SAVING

The national accounts of the United States and other countries generally seek to produce a measure of "current production" of goods and services. Because the measure of production is value, not physical units, there are many definitional problems, particularly those associated with what may be generically described as accruing changes in value. For example, the value of an inventory of wine held from the beginning of the year to the end typically increases. This increase in value, if it occurs in the context of a wine-producing business, is presumably economically equivalent to the increase in value of the grapes that are grown in the field, harvested, and sold to the wine producer. This increase is probably not, however, captured in either business or national income accounts. Much the same can be said of most other accruing changes in value of assets (both up and down).

Accruing changes in value in fact are significant elements of the performance of the U.S. economy. Figure 5.6 displays, for example, the ratio of the market value of the net assets of U.S. nonfinancial corporations to their replacement value for the period 1945–1988. Two aspects are notable. First, the market value of corporate equity is typically considerably less than the replacement cost of the underlying physical

FIGURE 5.6
Market Value of U.S. Corporate Equity Relative to Corporate Net Worth
(percent)

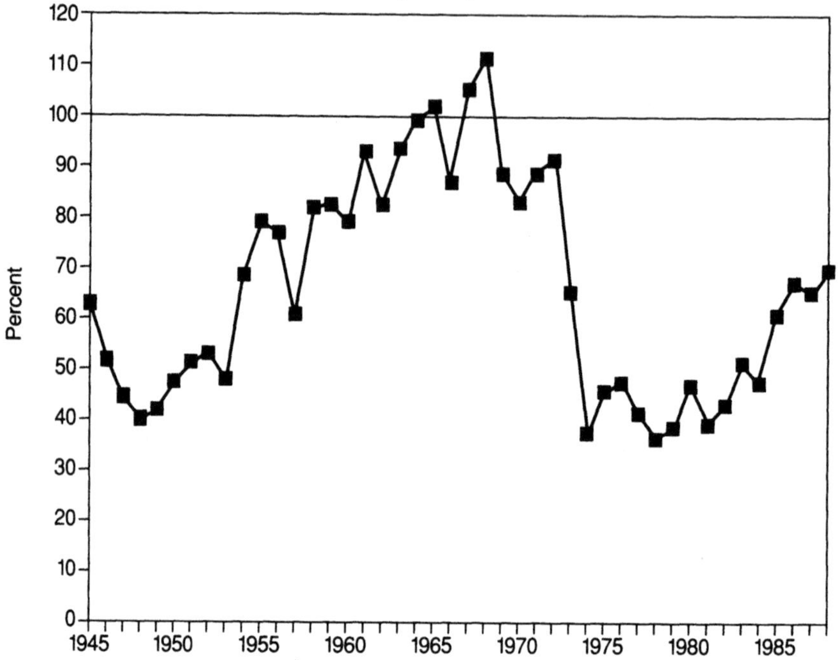

Source: U.S. Federal Reserve.

TABLE 5.8
U.S. National Saving: Comparison of Measures
(percentage of GNP decade averages)

	Market Value		
	Government Assets		National Income and Product Accounts
	Excluded	Included	
1950–1959	14.8	16.6	7.4
1960–1969	10.0	12.0	7.9
1970–1979	6.9	9.2	7.1
1980–1988	7.0	7.1	3.0

Note: NIPA saving is net national saving (see Table 5.3); market value saving is the year-to-year change in national wealth at market value based on the Federal Reserve national balance sheets (see Table 5.2), deflated to 1982 price levels using the GNP deflator and augmented by Department of Commerce estimates of the replacement value of government capital.

assets, including land. Second, the ratio of the market value to the accounting value is far from constant, having varied over a range between 37 and 110 percent during the forty-three-year period.

In the economic theory of household consumption, it is the market value of wealth, not its accounting value, that plays an economic role.[13] Saving by a household consists of the accumulation of wealth as valued in asset markets and is measured by the change in the value of wealth between the beginning and end of the accounting period. The Flow of Funds Division's national balance sheets provide data from which a measure of the aggregate of household wealth can be constructed. Table 5.8 presents decade averages of the ratio of national saving to GNP when national saving is defined as the annual change of the aggregate wealth of U.S. households (including the claims they hold indirectly through pension funds and the like). The first column of the table shows saving rates when wealth is defined as in Table 5.2, exclusive of government assets and with government debt netted out of household wealth. The second column shows the rates when national wealth is extended to incorporate the net worth of governments, using the Department of Commerce estimates of government capital stocks. These rates usually differ from the national saving rates according to the NIPAs (shown in the third column of the table). As with the NIPA saving rates, a downward trend is suggested by the decade averages.

Figure 5.7 displays the annual data on national market value saving, together with NIPA saving, where national market value saving is defined to include the value of government assets. Because the value of assets is highly volatile (the main driving element in the data is the stock market), the market value saving rate generates a jagged picture. Its sawtooth record contrasts with the smooth path of the NIPA saving rate, but like the NIPA record, the market value saving rate also drifts downward. The trend in the market value saving rate is far from sharp, however; the regression on time is negative, but statistically insignificant, even when 1946 is excluded.

Students of taxation generally accept what has come to be known as the Schanz-Haig-Simons (SHS) definition of income for purposes of income taxation.[14] Rather than treat saving as a residual, the SHS definition defines income as the sum of the taxpayer's consumption and change in wealth during the year, where wealth is measured at market value. Having a time series of national wealth at market value puts us in a position to produce a measure of aggregate SHS income: the sum of the year-to-year change in wealth and the aggregate consumption, where wealth and consumption are defined consistently. Consistent definition of consumption requires an imputation for the flow of consumption services for forms of wealth not used for production for market. To construct a series for aggregate SHS income using private wealth (that is, excluding government assets), we have imputed consumption out of consumer durables in the amount of the sum of the

FIGURE 5.7
U.S. Market Value and NIPA Saving
(percent of GNP)

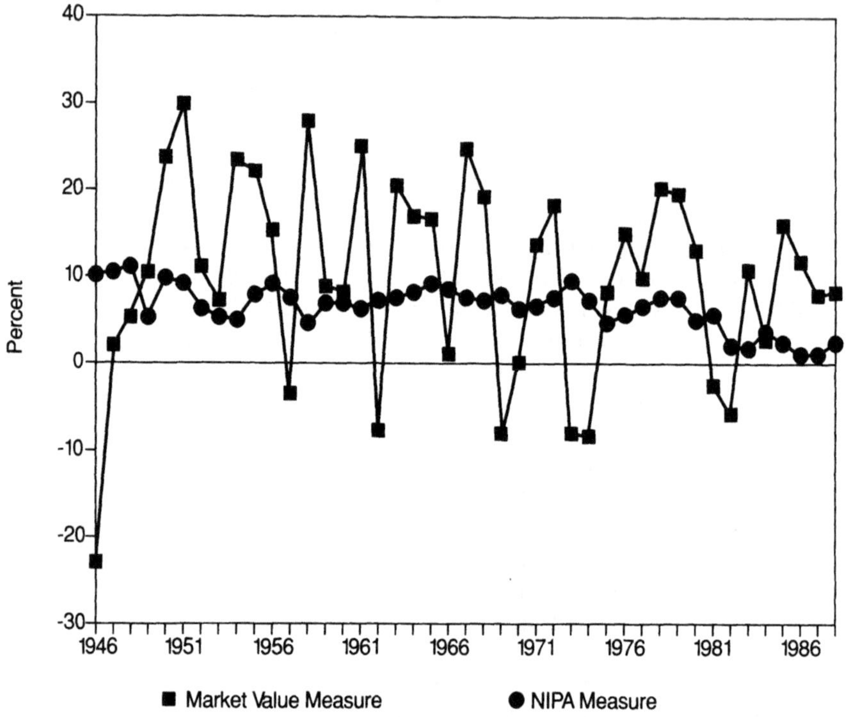

Sources: U.S. Federal Reserve; U.S. Department of Commerce.

depreciation of the stock of durables during the year and the assumed yield on the stock. The latter is calculated as 5.2 percent of the average of the beginning and end-of-year stocks. (The 5.2 percent real rate of return is the average real rate of return on owner-occupied housing implicit in the Department of Commerce's imputation of the rental value in the NIPAs.) Depreciation is the difference between the "gross investment" (outlays on consumer durables) and the year-to-year increase in real stock. Figure 5.8 displays the graph of the resulting national SHS income series, together with the net national product from the NIPAs. Because the two measures have so much in common, it should not be surprising that they follow roughly similar paths, but the SHS measure is considerably more volatile.

SAVING, CAPITAL FORMATION, AND ECONOMIC PERFORMANCE

The object of saving is the accumulation of wealth, which in turn supports consumption. Conversely, high rates of consumption may

FIGURE 5.8
U.S. National Income: Comparison of Two Measures

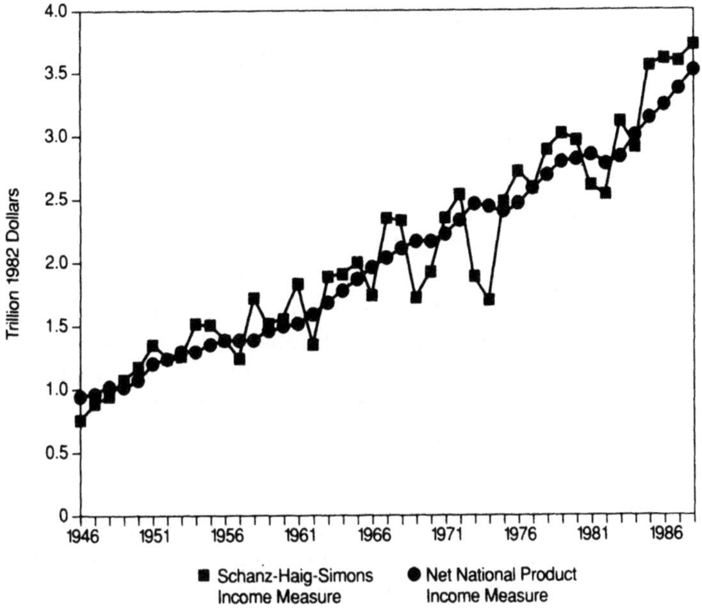

Sources: U.S. Federal Reserve; U.S. Department of Commerce.

FIGURE 5.9
U.S. Real Wealth Per Capita

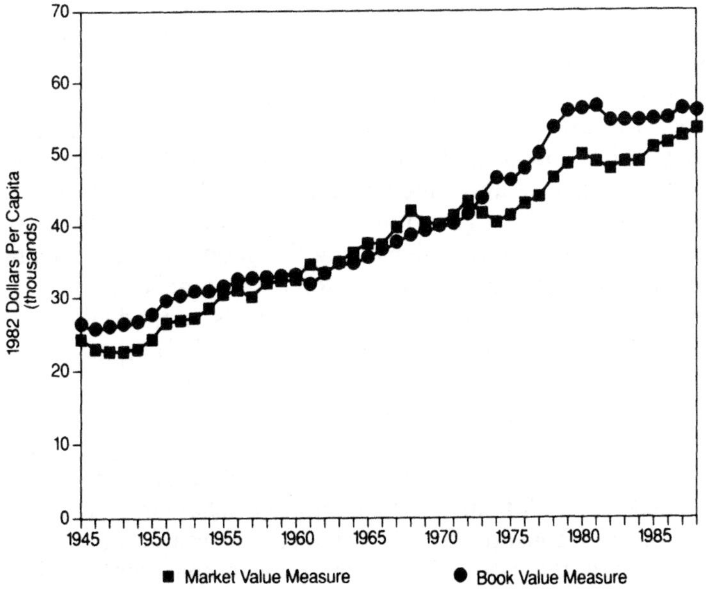

Sources: U.S. Federal Reserve; U.S. Department of Commerce; *Economic Report of the President*, 1989.
Note: Includes government tangible assets.

imply "too low" rates of saving. In this section I present data on the effects of U.S. saving behavior as reflected in the accumulation of wealth and measures of consumption. Figure 5.9 makes clear what is not readily inferred from the study of saving rates: that over a forty-three-year period U.S. residents achieved a substantial increase in wealth per capita. The data graphed include government tangible assets in the measure of wealth, which in the case of tangible assets is converted from current-value to constant-dollar units by deflating at an estimate of the end-of-year GNP deflator. The path labeled "book value" describes the history of the accounting value of per capita capital, whereas the path labeled "market value" uses the market value for corporate equity. The "accounting value" here is the "total consolidated national net assets" figure of Table 5.1, deflated, augmented by the Department of Commerce estimate of the value of the government tangible capital stock. Land is included at market value in both wealth concepts. Figure 5.9 reveals that in the aggregate (as well as in the case of equity claims to U.S. nonfinancial corporations), "book" value (the quotation marks are to remind us that the data are adjusted for inflation) has often been above market, substantially so between 1975 and 1985. The data also show a significant contrast between a slight down trend in "book" wealth per capita since the late 1970s and something more like a continuation of the historical uptrend in market value wealth.

The object of production is consumption, but too much consumption implies too little accumulation. Figure 5.10 shows what happened to per capita consumption, both private and government, over the period 1946–1988. The data in the figure follow the NIPA convention of treating all government purchases of goods and services as consumption. But purchases of consumer durables are treated two alternative ways: either as simple consumption (again, as in the NIPAs) or as an imputed rent on a stock (by use of the imputation method described previously). It is rather striking how little difference it makes which approach is taken to the measurement of aggregate consumption. The pronounced upward trend in private and in government consumption per capita is both evidence that the economy is delivering the goods to U.S. residents and a signal that their saving may be in some sense deficient.

The theory of consumption behavior models individuals as seeking to smooth their consumption, typically over their lifetimes or at least over an extended future run of years. This model does not readily generate a particular relationship between consumption and income, but with certain simplifying assumptions it does suggest a constant ratio between consumption and wealth, including human wealth. One place to look for a shift in the consumption behavior of U.S. residents is in the ratio of consumption to the piece of wealth we can observe. Figure 5.11 plots the ratio of aggregate private consumption (including the imputed rent on consumer durables) to three different versions of national wealth. The first and smallest measure of wealth is national

FIGURE 5.10
U.S. Consumption Per Capita

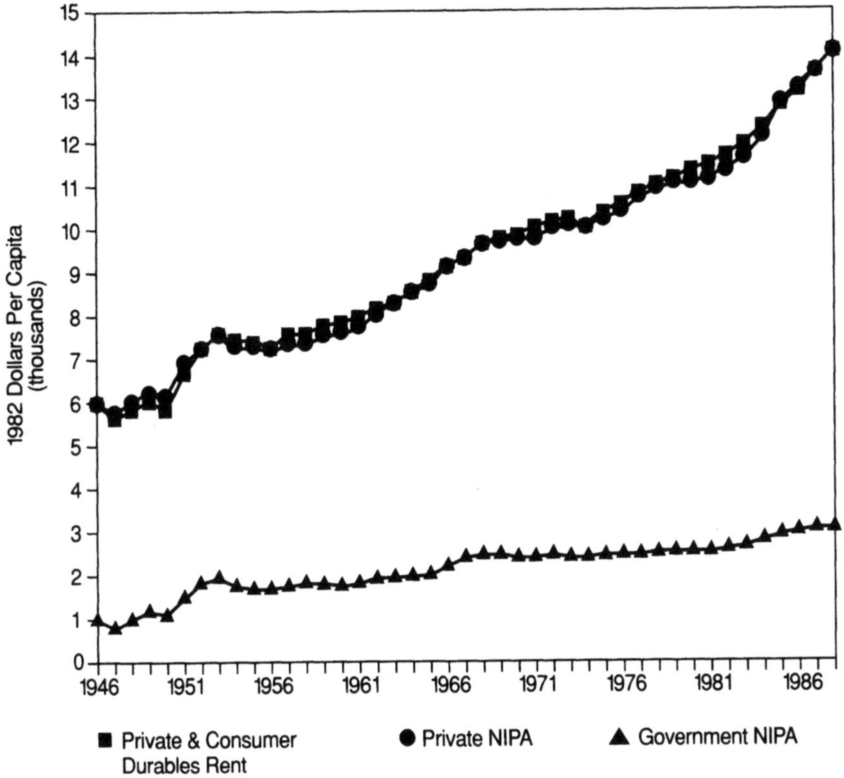

Source: U.S. Department of Commerce, Bureau of Economic Analysis, *National Income and Product Accounts.*

wealth excluding both government assets and debt. Use of this measure yields the highest ratio of consumption to national wealth, as shown in Figure 5.11. This measure is the wealth that would govern the behavior of households that see through the government debt in their aggregate portfolio to the future taxes they must pay to service and retire that debt but do not see through the veil of government to the assets their taxes and lending to government may be financing. (Alternatively, they see through to the assets and do not believe they will have a positive yield.)

The next largest measure of wealth since the early 1950s has been aggregate wealth including the value of government debt but excluding government assets. This is the wealth most people seem to regard as operative in household calculations. In other words, government issue of bonds has the effect of increasing the perceived stock of wealth to be held by someone. It is the wealth of a world of fiscal illusion (in which, perhaps, we live). Third, and largest, is the stock of wealth

FIGURE 5.11
U.S. Private Consumption
(ratio to national wealth)

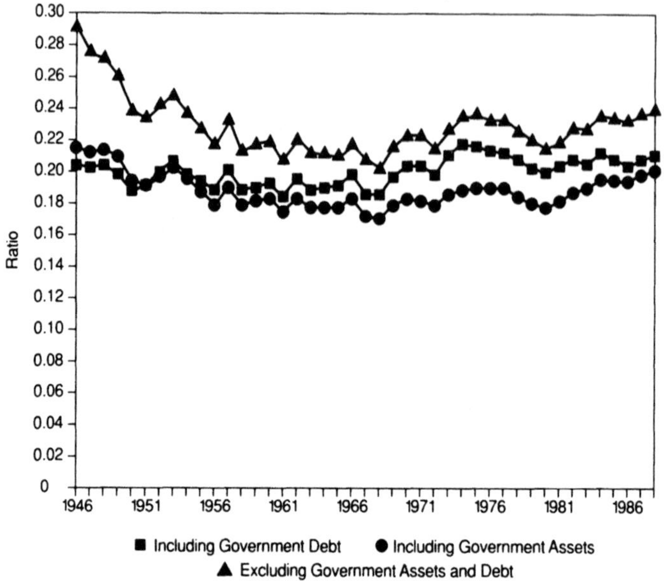

Sources: U.S. Federal Reserve; U.S. Department of Commerce.

FIGURE 5.12
U.S. Private Consumption, 1980-1988
(ratio to national wealth)

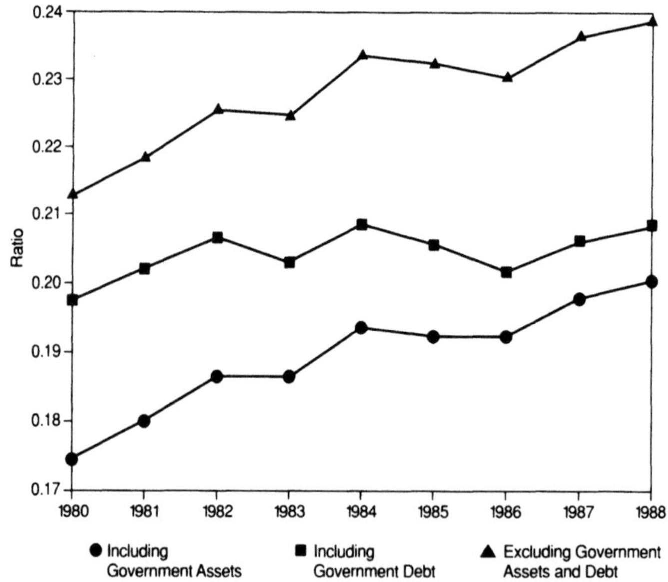

Sources: U.S. Department of Commerce, Bureau of Economic Analysis, *National Income and Product Accounts*; and Board of Governors, Federal Reserve System, Flow of Funds Section, *Flow of Funds Accounts*.

including government assets. If government assets are really productive (at least of reduced future taxes), this is the wealth that should operate in the world of super-rational households that see through the government veil.

If we work from an assumption of no trend in the relationship between human and nonhuman wealth, inspection of Figure 5.11 suggests that there has been no very sharp break in recent years with behavior in the past, as reflected in the chosen ratio of consumption to wealth. I can see in the differences in the curves, however, some support for the fiscal illusion view that consumption is regulated to maintain a constant ratio to the stock of wealth including government. A growing stock of debt will cause the level of consumption to rise relative to one or the other "rational" perceptions of wealth (to include government). In recent years certainly, the ratio of consumption to wealth including government debt has risen relative to its ratio to either of the other two wealth measures. Figure 5.12 offers a magnified view of the portion of Figure 5.11 that covers the period 1980–1988.

I noted previously that aggregate wealth at book value has been declining or constant for the past few years. Figure 5.13 presents another facet of the same fact, showing the tangible capital stock (including inventories, housing, consumer durables, and government reproducible assets) per U.S. worker (represented by the civilian labor force) annually from 1948 to 1987. The divergence from trend of this very broadly conceived capital-labor ratio, while not conclusive evidence of suboptimal performance, is quite noticeable. The failure of book value to track market value is important to this record, and one should not be too quick to accept the view that it is "real" capital, as measured in the current-value accounts kept by the Department of Commerce, that contributes to the productivity of workers. Certainly, the entrepreneur expects to get the same extra productivity from the last $1 million spent on any form of capital, be it in the form of machines, patents, or land.

U.S. SAVING IN INTERNATIONAL CONTEXT: MARKET VALUE WEALTH AND SAVING

The previous section considered the recent saving behavior of the United States in comparison with its own past, with reference particularly to the accumulation of wealth measured at market value and to consumption in relation to the value of wealth. In this section U.S. behavior is compared with that of other countries. Although comparable national accounting data are available for a large group of countries, estimates of national wealth are available for few. We have been able to assemble such data for three countries in addition to the United States: the United Kingdom, Japan, and Sweden.

There are three figures for each of the four countries, in each case for as long a time series as we have been able to construct. For each

FIGURE 5.13
U.S. Capital Stock
(ratio to labor force)

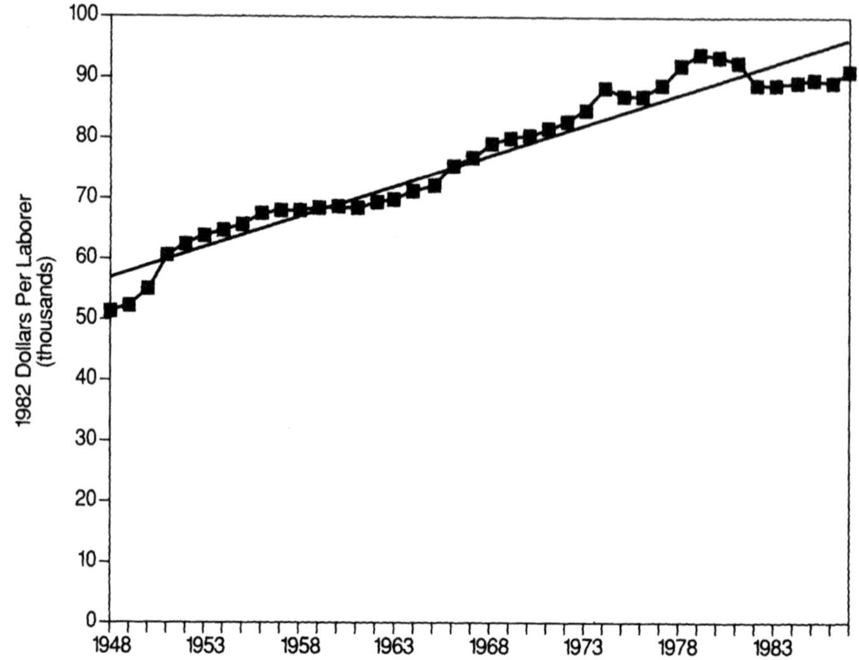

Sources: U.S. Federal Reserve; U.S. Department of Commerce; *Economic Report of the President,* 1989.

country, the first figure presents wealth per capita, where wealth is defined as the market value of privately owned assets excluding government debt. The second displays national saving rates (national saving to GNP or GDP), for saving defined as the change in market value wealth and on a national accounts basis. The third figure in each case shows the ratio of market value wealth to GNP or GDP, as suggestive both of possible differences in economic structure across the four countries and of possible shifts in the character of production within each.

The data reveal a good deal of diversity. In the case of the United States, the good news is that the real wealth per capita is about on its forty-three-year upward trend line (Figure 5.14). U.S. residents managed to accumulate about $800 (1988) per person per year over that period. The saving behavior described in Figure 5.15 is a repeat of an earlier display. The wealth-output ratio in the United States has wavered around 2.8 over the whole period and shows no obvious trend (Figure 5.16).

The British story, for which we have a much shorter record, reveals a drop in wealth per capita in the early 1970s, just as in the United States, but a rather longer and stronger upward trend since then (Figure 5.17). (A more careful international comparison will follow.) The path

FIGURE 5.14
Real Wealth Per Capita: United States

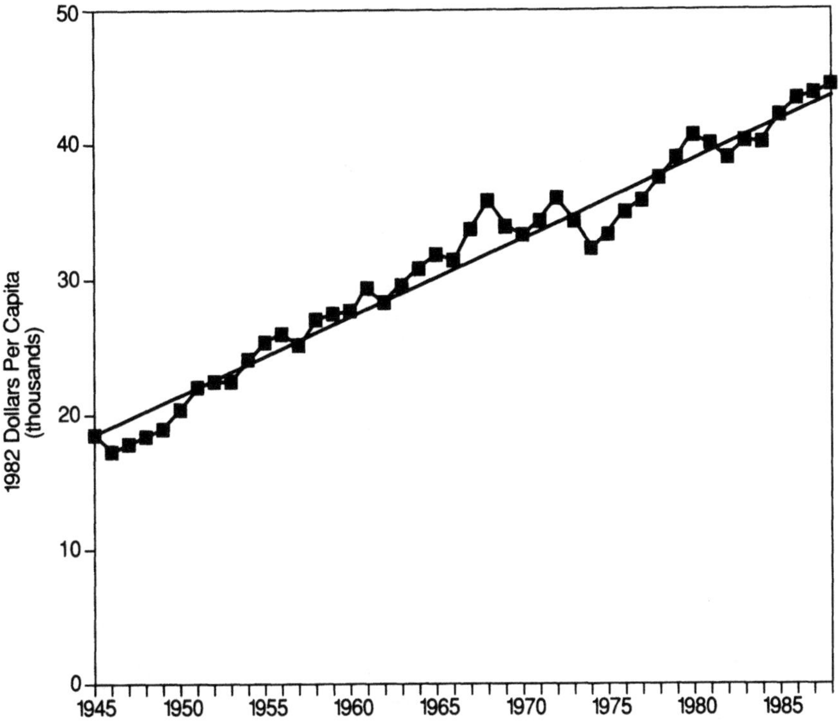

Sources: U.S. Federal Reserve; U.S. Department of Commerce; *Economic Report of the President,* 1989.
Note: Excludes government tangible assets.

of the market value saving rate has even wider swings than that of the U.S. rate along a similarly downward-drifting national accounts measure (Figure 5.18). At a fairly steady 3, the wealth-output ratio is close to that of the United States (Figure 5.19).

In Japan, wealth per capita has increased steadily and rapidly (Figure 5.20). The comparative behavior of market value and national accounts measures of national saving rates is qualitatively similar to that in the United States and the United Kingdom (Figure 5.21). The different feature in the Japanese record is the strong upward drift in the wealth-output ratio, from about 3 at the end of the 1960s to more than 5 in 1987 (Figure 5.22)—possibly a sign that assets are "overvalued."

Sweden presents the most surprising picture. After twenty years of steady increase, from the mid-1950s to the mid-1970s, per capita wealth turned sharply down, falling by 1985 to about its 1965 level (Figure 5.23). Naturally, the saving rates were consistent with this path, with large negative saving in the late 1970s to the mid-1980s (Figure 5.24). For Sweden, even the national accounts saving rate was negative in 1986 (when the market value saving rate was significantly positive). As

FIGURE 5.15
U.S. Saving Rate: Comparison of Measures

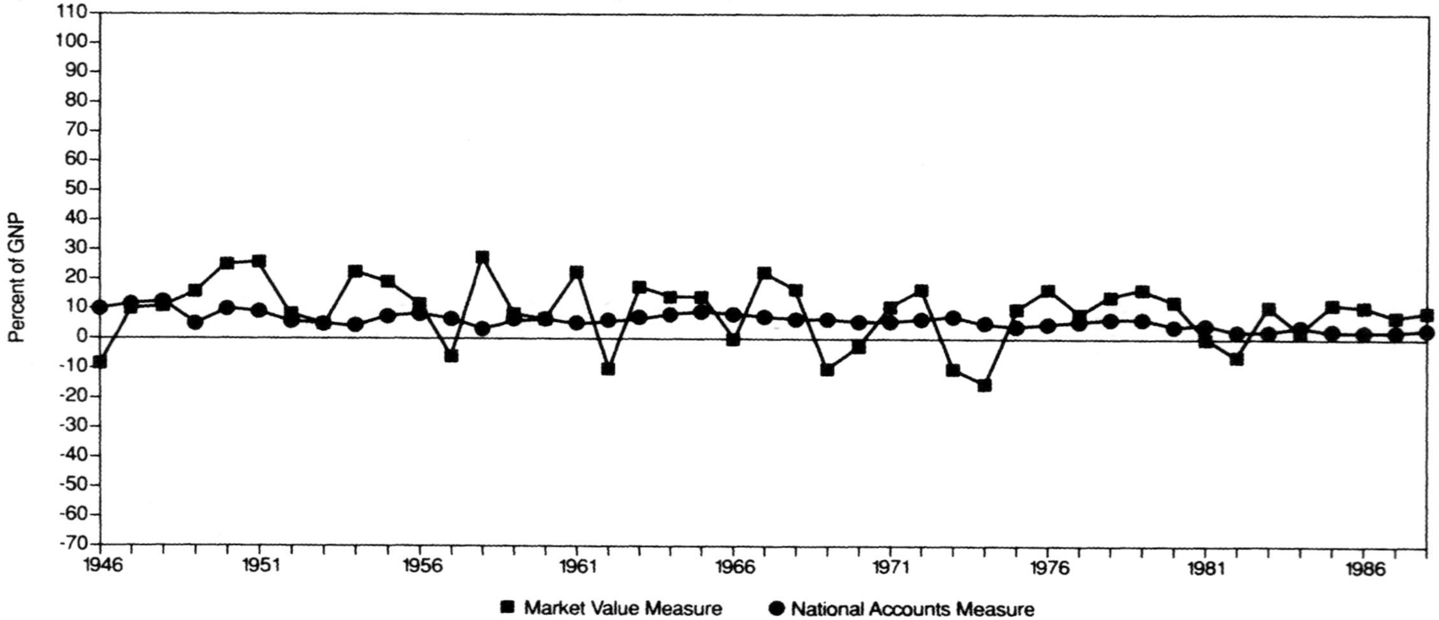

Sources: U.S. Federal Reserve; U.S. Department of Commerce; *Economic Report of the President*, 1989.

FIGURE 5.16
Wealth-GNP Ratio: United States

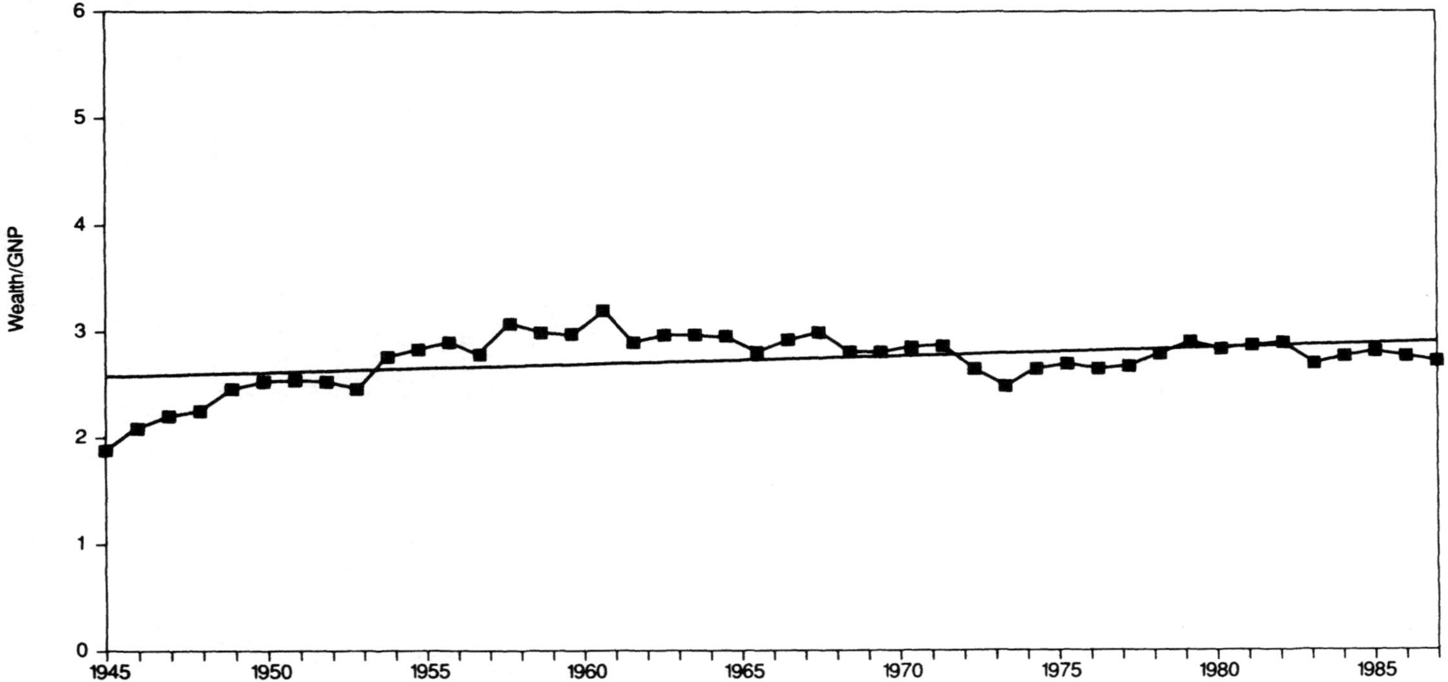

Sources: U.S. Federal Reserve; U.S. Department of Commerce; *Economic Report of the President*, 1989.

FIGURE 5.17
Real Wealth Per Capita: United Kingdom

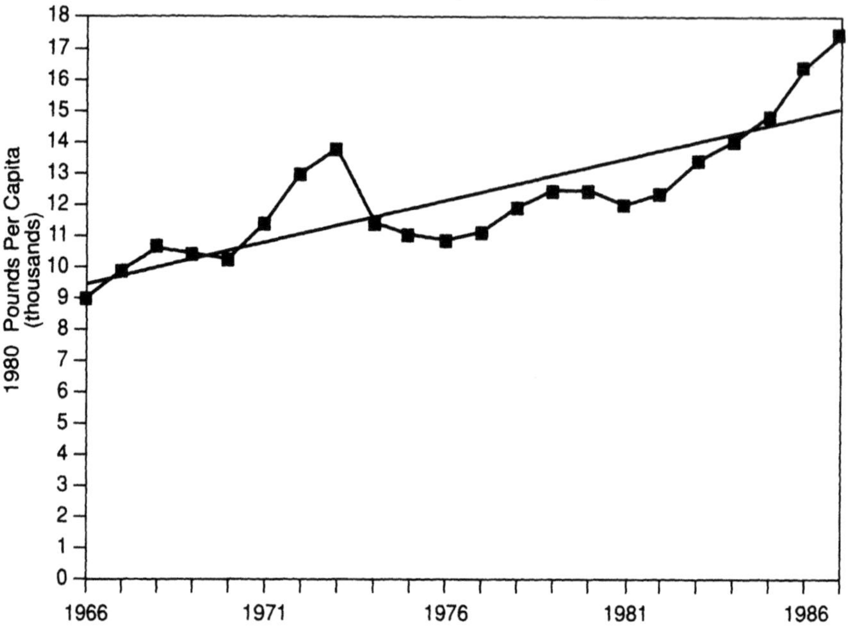

Sources: See Appendix 5.A.

there has been no sharp contraction in Swedish national output, it follows that the wealth-output ratio also fell sharply in the 1977–1984 years (Figure 5.25). As in the case of Japan, one wonders if the market is "improperly" valuing Swedish assets, in this case undervaluing them. It is also of interest that even in the period when it was fairly steady, the wealth-output ratio in Sweden was, at about 1.8, substantially less than that observed in the other countries—perhaps a signal of undiscovered differences in coverage of the data.

It is of interest to compare the four countries' wealth accumulation. The comparison is facilitated here by the fact that the wealth-per-capita amounts were presented in constant real units of the respective currencies. Figures 5.26 and 5.27 make the attempt. Figure 5.26 plots on a single graph the relative paths of per capita wealth, indexed to 1970, the earliest year in the data for Japan. The remarkable rate of accumulation in Japan, compared with the three other countries, jumps out of the figure, as do the strong recent growth in wealth in Britain and the slump in wealth per capita in Sweden.

Figure 5.27 uses GDP purchasing power parity exchange rates compiled by the OECD to convert all four wealth-per-capita series to 1982 U.S. dollars of purchasing power. Naturally, we have to take with a grain of salt the idea of selling a house in Japan to acquire U.S. consumer goods. Nevertheless, the rapid growth in Japanese per capita

FIGURE 5.18
British Saving Rate: Comparison of Measures

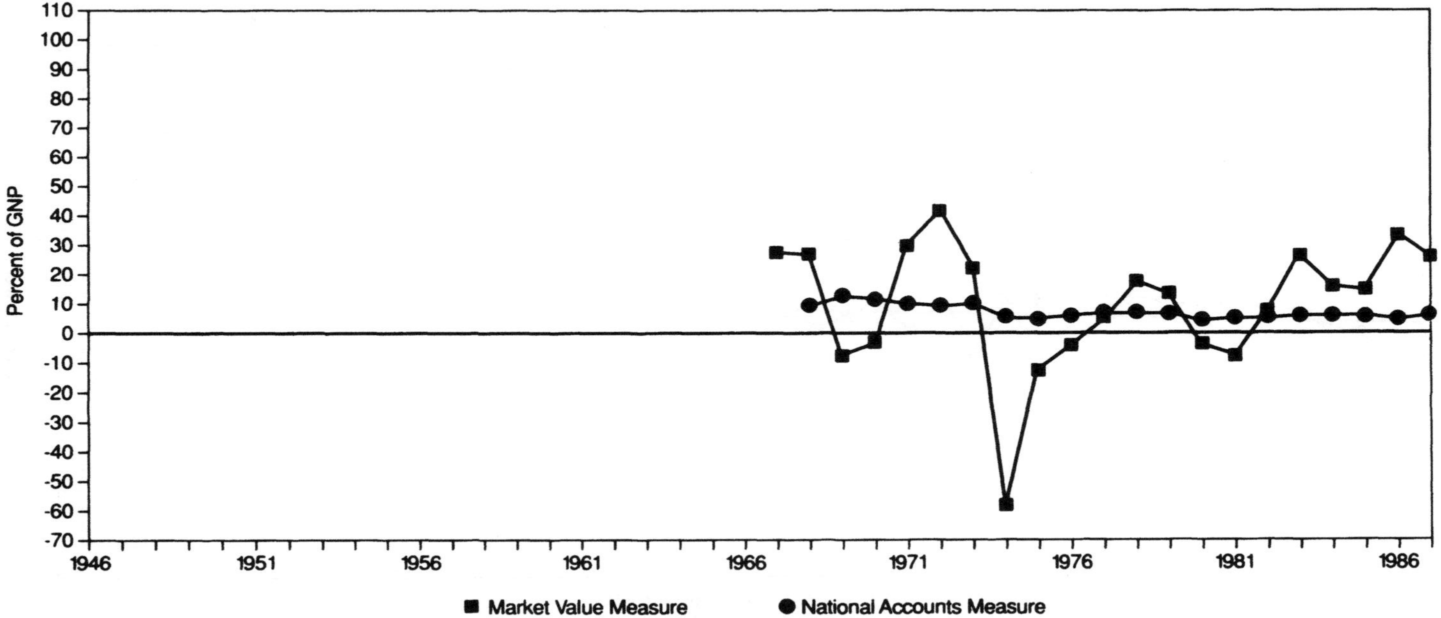

Sources: See Appendix 5.A

FIGURE 5.19
Wealth-GNP Ratio: United Kingdom

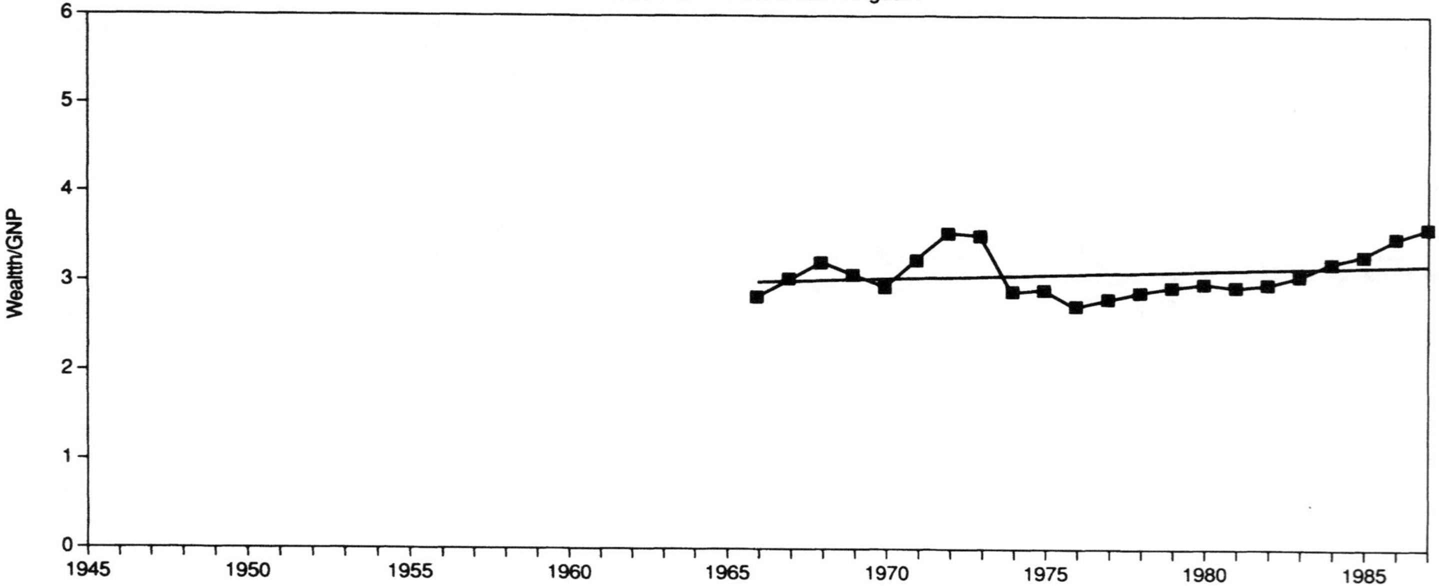

Sources: See Appendix 5.A

FIGURE 5.20
Real Wealth Per Capita: Japan

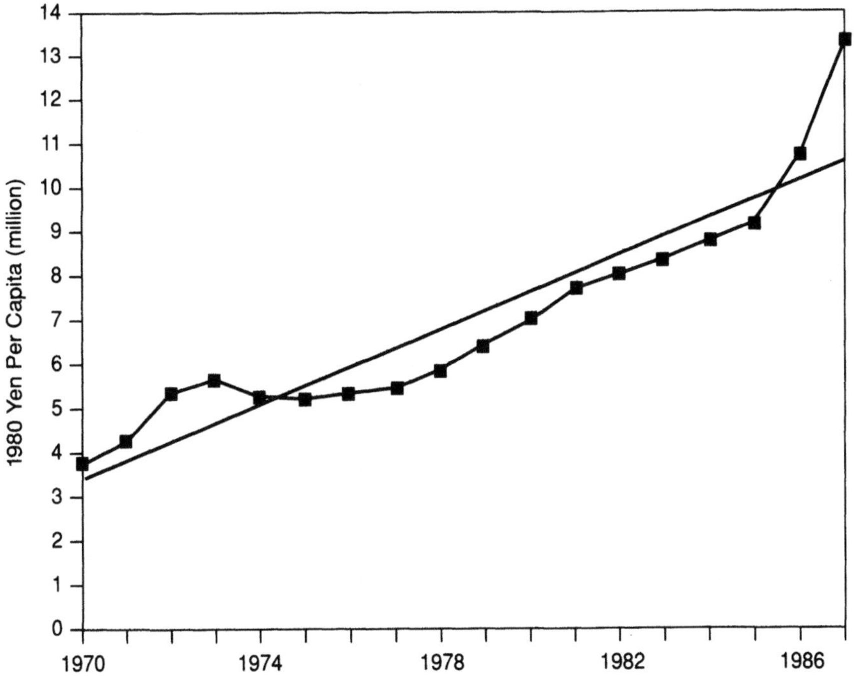

Sources: See Appendix 5.A.

wealth (from almost the bottom to the top of the group) is striking, as are the recent tendency toward convergence of the British and U.S. levels and the low level of Swedish wealth. Given the evident high living standard in Sweden, we must again wonder whether there is an undiscovered difference in coverage of the data.

In view of the exceptional character of Japan's economic performance and the high degree of current U.S. interest in Japan, two additional figures comparing the two countries are provided. Figure 5.28 displays annual data on the fraction of national private wealth consisting of land value. It is widely known that real estate prices in Japan are very high, but it may not be generally appreciated that land value accounted for nearly 90 percent of the country's wealth as early as 1970 and did not account for less than 70 percent during the period 1970–1987. The comparable fraction for the United States drifted upward from about 20 percent in 1970 to about 25 percent in 1987.

It might be argued that high wealth owing to high land prices should be interpreted as bad, rather than good, a signal of crowding and agricultural protection. Figure 5.29 presents wealth per capita in the United States and in Japan, converted to 1982 U.S. dollars of purchasing

FIGURE 5.21
Japanese Saving Rate: Comparison of Measures

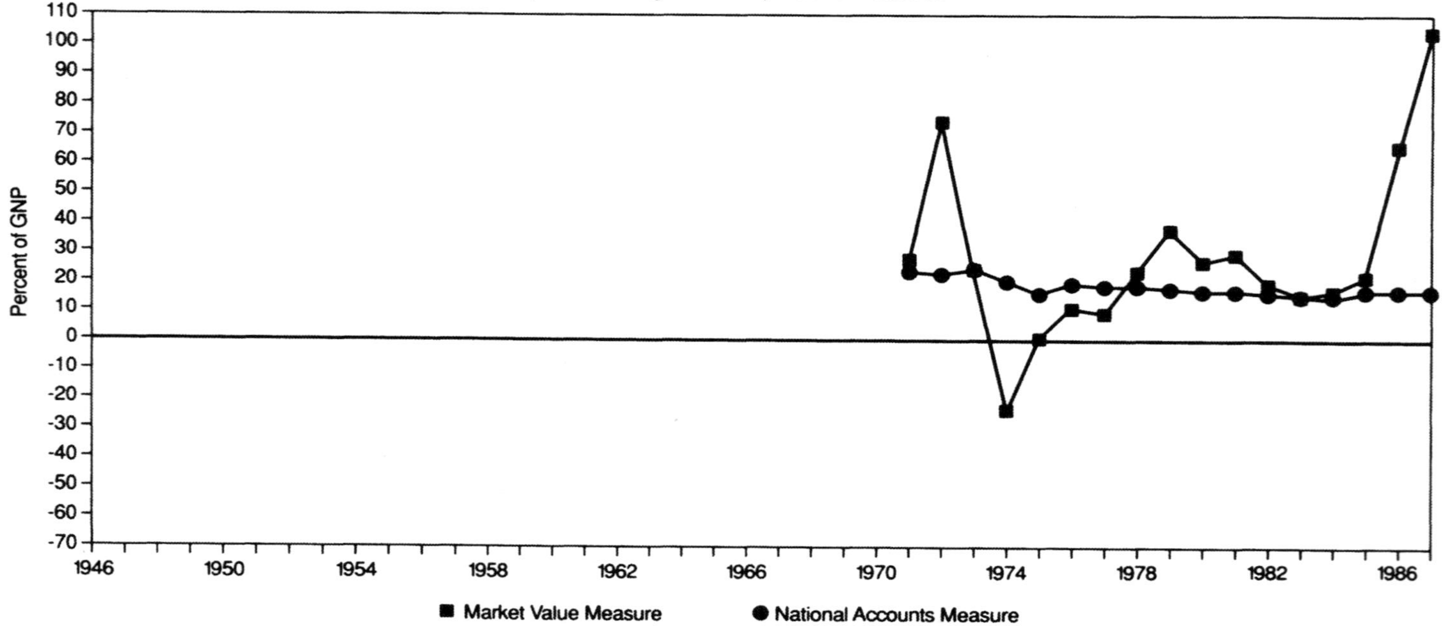

Sources: See Appendix 5.A.

FIGURE 5.22
Wealth-GNP Ratio: Japan

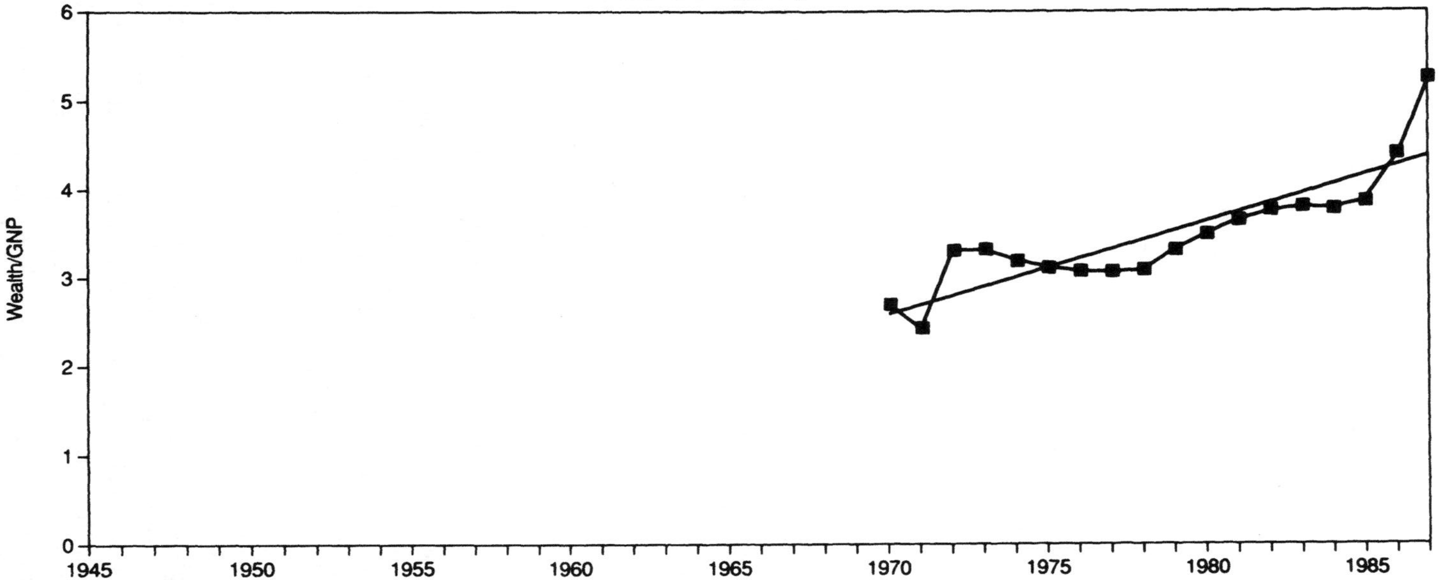

Sources: See Appendix 5.A

FIGURE 5.23
Real Wealth Per Capita: Sweden

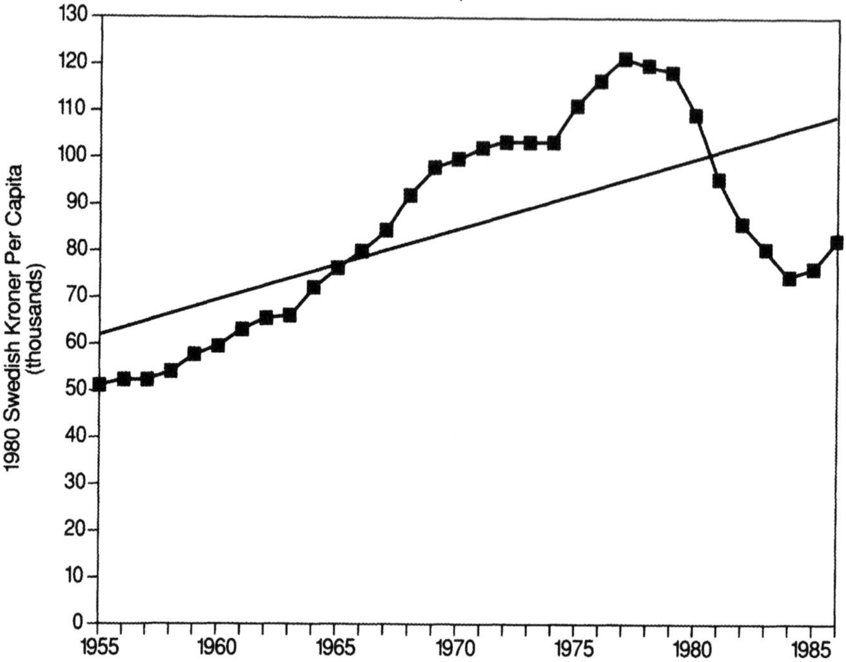

Sources: See Appendix 5.A.

power using the OECD purchasing power parity exchange rates. In wealth-less-land per capita, Japan has substantially less than the United States.

CONCLUDING REMARKS

In devoting so much attention to matters of measurement, I have perforce had to slight the development of policy assessment and policy analysis. I therefore offer some only loosely supported reflections.

The major question addressed in this book is why the United States is saving so little. I would rephrase that question and ask, Why is the United States consuming so much? On my reading of the record of the behavior of wealth in the sense that most people mean the term, the recent consumption (and therefore saving) behavior of the U.S. public is not glaringly out of line with its past behavior. A reasonable standard of consistency with past behavior would be for consumption to maintain its past ratio to wealth. Figure 5.30 presents a further excerpt from Figure 5.11, in this case showing the trend in the consumption-wealth ratio from 1946–1979 and its projection through 1988, where wealth is interpreted to include the public's holding of government debt and to exclude government assets. The figure shows that the consumption-

FIGURE 5.24
Swedish Saving Rate: Comparison of Measures

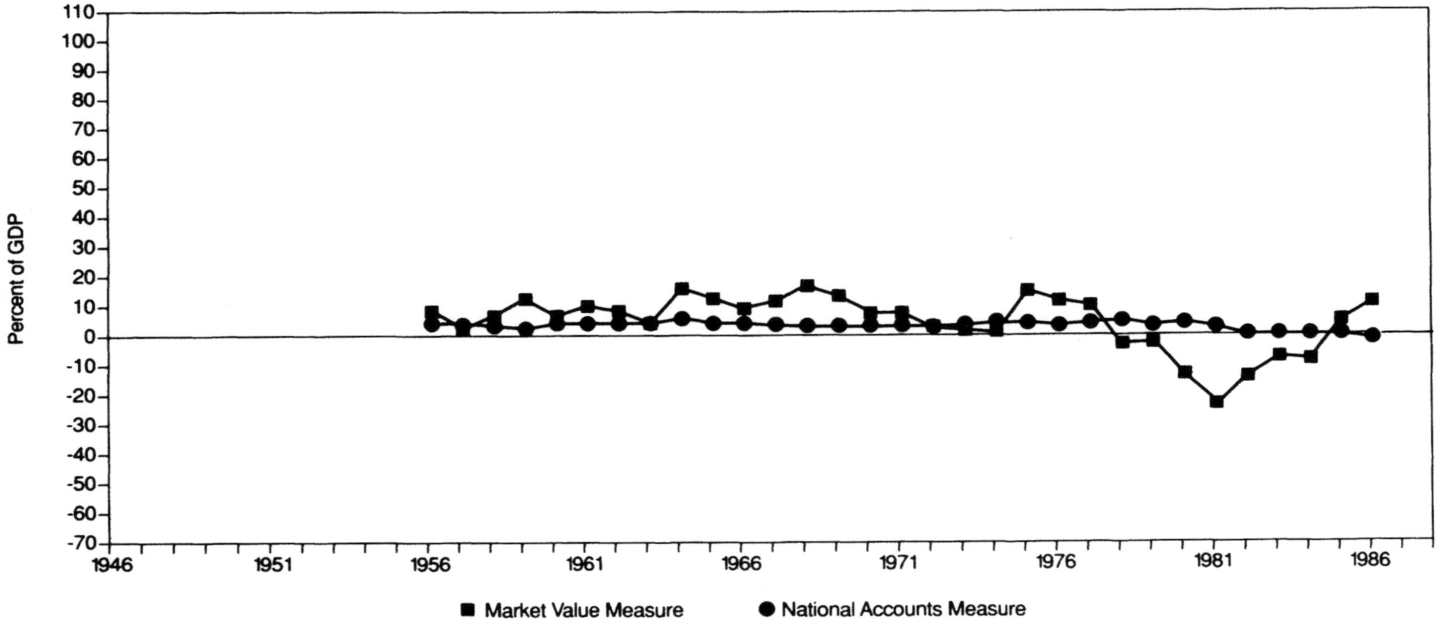

Sources: See Appendix 5.A.

FIGURE 5.25
Wealth-GDP Ratio: Sweden

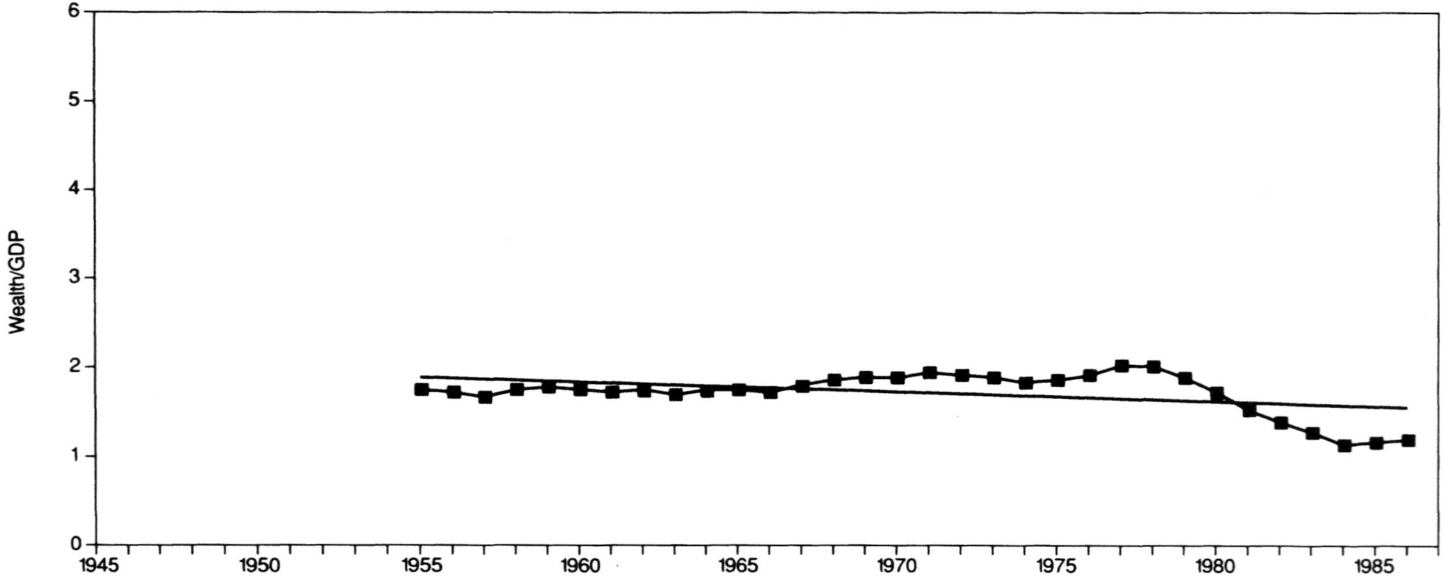

Sources: See Appendix 5.A.

FIGURE 5.26
International Comparison of
Real Wealth Per Capita Index

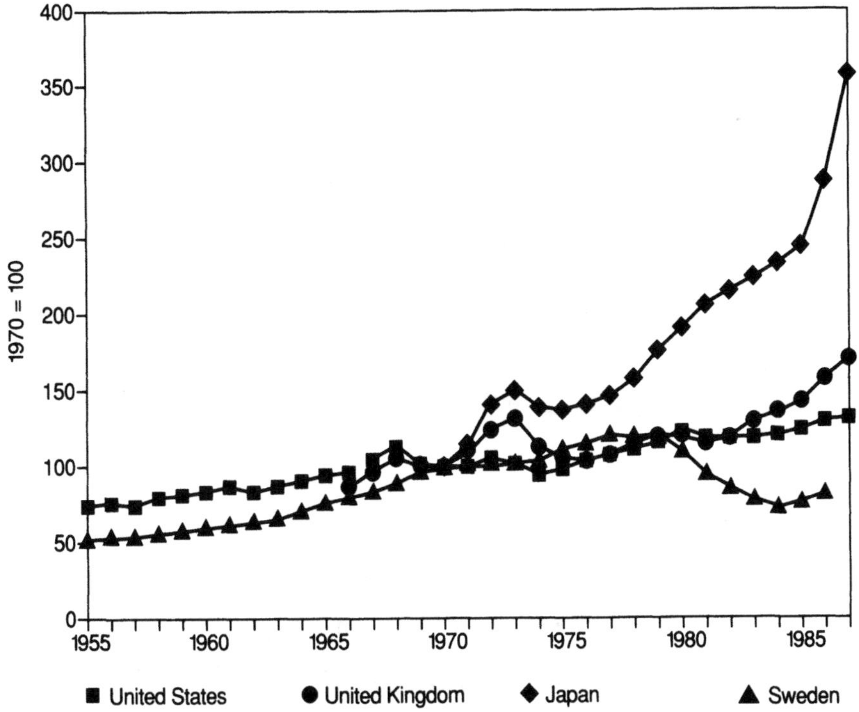

Sources: Figures 5.14, 5.17, 5.20, and 5.23.

wealth ratio in the 1980s was very close to its historic trend value. (Obviously, a plot of one or two variables against time is not an analytical model. I indicated previously that these reflections would be loosely supported. In any case, most argumentation on this subject is at this level.)

From a policy perspective, of course, the regularity of consumption suggested in Figure 5.30 is not welcome insofar as it reflects private prudence but not public prudence, which might rather imply a steady ratio between consumption and wealth exclusive of government debt and perhaps inclusive of government assets. It is thus possible to find U.S. consumption behavior explicable in terms of what people *perceive* as their circumstances but too low by reference to their *actual* circumstances.

By "actual circumstances" I mean the market assessment of the aggregate wealth of the country. There is a further question whether we should rely on the market assessment in thinking about policy and whether U.S. consumers have historically "believed" the financial market results in the way that the projection in Figure 5.30 implies they

FIGURE 5.27
International Comparison of
Real Wealth Per Capita

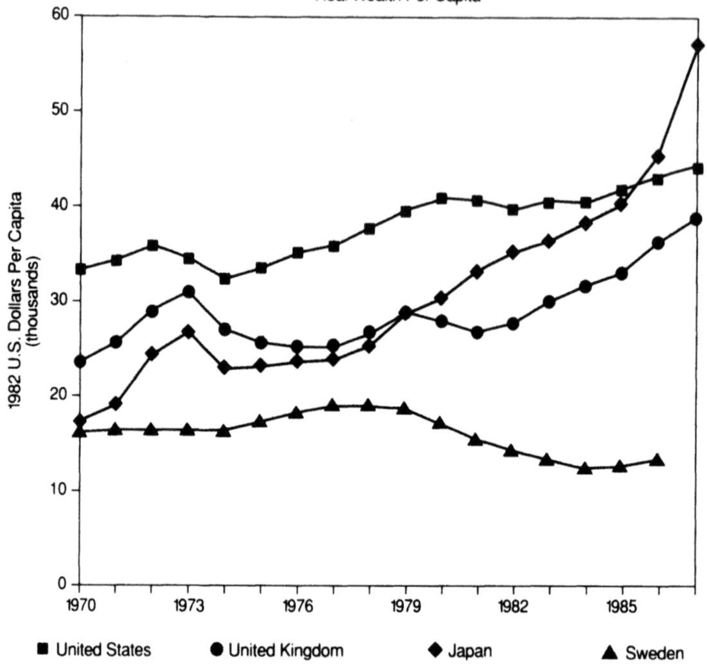

Source: Conversion based on GDP purchasing power parity exchange rates from Organisation for Economic Co-operation and Development. *Annual National Accounts*, 1987.

FIGURE 5.28
U.S. and Japanese
Land-Wealth Ratios

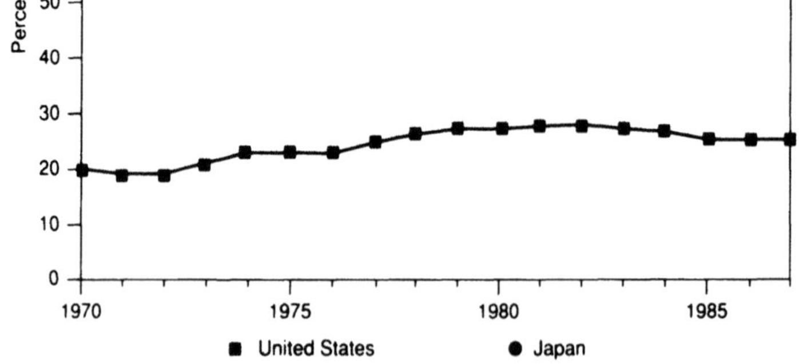

Sources: U.S. data are from the U.S. Federal Reserve and U.S. Department of Commerce. See Appendix 5.A for Japanese data sources.

FIGURE 5.29
U.S. and Japanese Wealth Per Capita

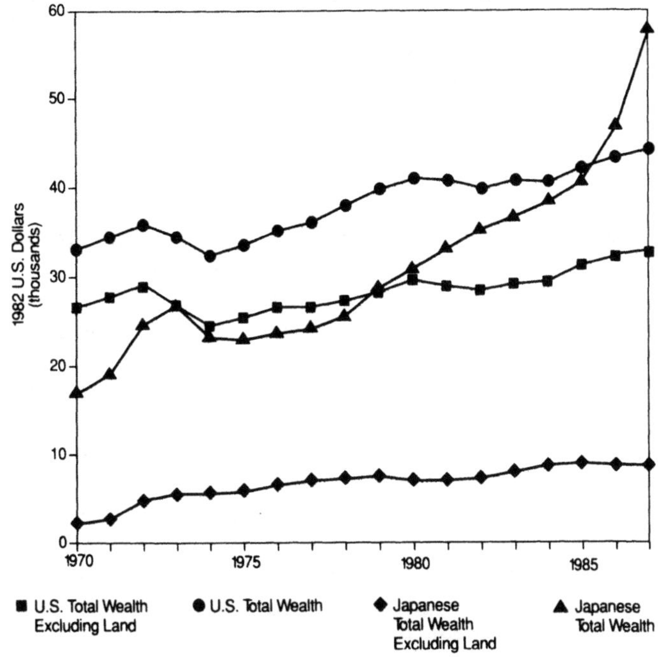

Sources: U.S. data are from the U.S. Federal Reserve and U.S. Department of Commerce. See Appendix 5.A for Japanese data sources.

FIGURE 5.30
U.S. Private Consumption: Comparison of Actual and Extrapolated Trend
(ratio to national wealth)

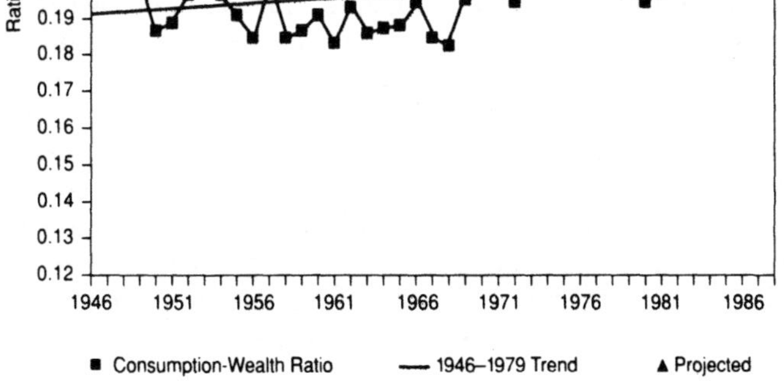

Sources: U.S. Federal Reserve; U.S. Department of Commerce.

Note: Includes government debt; government assets not included.

might. It is notoriously hard to outguess the market. But Patric Hendershott suggests in his commentary that follows that the measured consumption-wealth ratio has tended to do that, being lower in stock market booms than in busts. If we presume we are presently in a boom, consumption is unexpectedly high, relative to wealth, in comparison with past behavior, and the basis for policy concern is all the greater. The hypothesis seems to me well worth further exploration.

We should recognize that even if the U.S. public has shifted its behavior toward a higher consumption, lower accumulation path, it is not self-evident that that fact alone provides a basis for a policy to reverse that choice. Nor is it immediately clear that it should be a matter of policy concern that Americans choose to accumulate less rapidly than the Japanese do.

We might argue that most people are insufficiently reflective about their saving behavior. Most people apparently never accumulate anything beyond a bare minimum of financial assets (although it is not clear that they rationally should, given Social Security and other retirement resources). But some of the studies of individual retirement accounts, for example, indicate that people are not much motivated by a calculus of rate of return and are much motivated by advertising. Although philosophically not very attractive, a dose of paternalism sometimes seems rather sensible.

I do think, however, that there are reasons quite consistent with respect for the rationality of our fellow citizens to advocate significant changes in policy toward accumulation. By and large, existing policy discriminates against accumulation. (I was interested to see the survey evidence gathered by John Immerwahr that indicated that the U.S. public regards accumulation as socially bad.[15]) It would be easy to compile a long list of discriminatory policies, from the income tax to asset tests for receipt of health insurance benefits or scholarships. In many such cases, the antiaccumulation feature may be a necessary screen to focus some sort of help on the truly needy, but I wonder how carefully the matter has been considered. To be sure, there are exceptions, such as the heavy government investment in schooling and the income-tax-free imputed return on investment in consumer durables and owner-occupied housing. But even some of the apparent exceptions, such as tax-sheltered retirement saving, are often organized with features (for example, the contribution ceiling) that negate their effects at the critical margin.

Steps to ameliorate some of the many penalties on accumulation might reasonably be justified on grounds of a presumption in favor of neutrality toward saving. But we could argue that policies should not merely be neutral but should promote saving because it has positive externalities. To the extent that each of us places a positive value on the *current* standard of living of others, it is in our interest to encourage each other to save.

APPENDIX 5.A: NOTES ON THE INTERNATIONAL DATA

General Considerations

Except where specifically indicated to the contrary, the figures reflect the following conventions, adopted in part because data needed to improve upon them are lacking or unreliable:

1. National government tangible assets are ignored.
2. All government spending is classified as consumption.
3. Local government assets and liabilities are ignored; local governments are treated as having zero net worth.
4. Consumer durables are counted as part of national wealth.

United Kingdom

All publications referred to in this section are by the Central Statistical Office in London. Data are reproduced by permission of the Controller of Her Majesty's Stationery Office.

GNP Deflator

The deflator used for an end-of-year stock is the average of the fourth and following first quarter figures.

1979–1987 *Monthly Digest of Statistics* (March 1989), p. 6.
1957–1978 *Economic Trends Annual Supplement* (1987), pp. 5–6.

Real GNP

Nominal GNP has been taken from the same sources as the GDP deflator. Nominal GNP is converted to real terms using GDP deflators.

National Accounts Saving

United Kingdom National Accounts (1988), pp. 36–37.

Population

Monthly Digest of Statistics (October 1989), p. 19; and *Annual Abstract of Statistics* (1987), p. 6. Midyear estimates for the current and following years are averaged to approximate the year-end figures.

Personal Sector Net Worth

1976–1987 *United Kingdom National Accounts* (1988), p. 87. The stock of consumer durables, detailed in the same source, are added in.

1975 C.G.E. Bryant, "National and Sector Balance Sheets," *Economic Trends* (May 1987) (pp. 92–119), p. 102.

1966–1974 Central Statistical Office, "Personal Sector Balance Sheets," *Economic Trends* (January 1978) (pp. 97–107), p. 102; C. W. Pettigrew, "National and Sector Balance Sheets for the United Kingdom," *Economic Trends* (November 1980) (pp. 82–100), p. 92. The former source is annual but does not include nonprofit organizations, whereas the latter has balance sheets at three-year intervals. The figures used in the chapter are from Pettigrew, with the gaps filled using the Central Statistical Office report to indicate approximate year-to-year changes.

Public Net Worth

Public net worth is public corporation net worth plus national government financial assets minus national government liabilities.

1976–1987 *United Kingdom National Accounts* (1988).

1975 C.G.E. Bryant, "National and Sector Balance Sheets," *Economic Trends* (May 1987), pp. 92–119.

1966–1974 C. W. Pettigrew, "National and Sector Balance Sheets for the United Kingdom," *Economic Trends* (November 1980), pp. 82–100. Because these balance sheets are at three-year intervals, interpolation has been used. The public debt series in *Financial Statistics* (1978–1982), Table s11, have been used to estimate year-to-year changes.

Japan

Private Net Worth

Kokumin Keizai Keisan Nempo (*Annual Report on National Accounts;* hereafter *KKKN*) (Tokyo: 1989), Economic Planning Agency, pp. 346–353, line 6. Consumer durables have been added using *KKKN* (1989), p. 413; (1988), p. 445; (1986), p. 387; (1983), pp. 628–629. A change in definition of the consumer durable measure between 1983 and 1986 forced a modification of some of the figures for consistency. The difference is insignificant in comparison to total wealth.

Government Net Worth

KKKN (1989), pp. 364–365; (1988), pp. 384–385; (1983), pp. 522–526. The figure is the net financial assets of the central government and social security fund.

GNP Deflator

KKKN (1989), pp. 130–133; (1988), pp. 504–505. For 1980–1987, the given figure is the average of the fourth and following first quarter figures. Before 1980, the given figures are the average of the annual figures for the current and following years.

Real GNP

Keizai Tokei Nempo (Economic Statistics Annual) (Tokyo: Bank of Japan, 1976–1988). The pages for 1988 are 337–338. Nominal GNP is deflated using the GNP Deflator.

National Accounts Saving

KKKN (1989), pp. 82–83; (1988), pp. 82–83; (1983), pp. 10–11.

Population

Japanese Statistical Yearbook (Tokyo: Statistics Bureau, Management and Coordination Agency, 1987), p. 24; *Keizai Tokei Nempo (Economic Statistics Annual)* (Tokyo: Bank of Japan, 1988), p. 300. Populations are as of October 31.

Sweden

Private Net Worth; Price Index; National Accounts Savings

Estimates provided by Lennart Berg.

National Debt

Statistisk Arsbok for Sverige (Stockholm: Statistiska Centralbyrån, 1958–1988). In 1988, Table 284, p. 249.

Population

Statistisk Arsbok for Sverige (Stockholm: Statistiska Centralbyrån, 1963, 1981, 1988). In 1988, Table 241, p. 231.

International Comparisions

Purchasing Power Parity

For purposes of international comparison, wealth per capita is converted to U.S. dollar units using the purchasing power parity ratios published in the *National Accounts Main Aggregates Volume 1, 1960–1987* (Paris: OECD, Department of Economics and Statistics, 1989), pp. 150–151. The U.S. dollar figures are converted to constant 1982 dollars using the GNP deflator.

NOTES

For helpful discussions and leads on data, I particularly thank Albert Ando, Barry Bosworth, Angus Deaton, R. Glenn Donaldson, Elizabeth Fogler, Charles Horioka, Laurence J. Kotlikoff, Robert E. Lipsey, James Poterba, Jan Södersten, and Frederick O. Yohn. Michael Williams of Princeton University provided quick and ingenious research assistance.

1. For a clear exposition of saving concepts in the U.S. national income and product accounts, see Thomas M. Holloway, "Present NIPA Saving Measures: Their Characteristics and Limitations," in Robert E. Lipsey and Helen Stone Tice, eds., *The Measurement of Saving, Investment and Wealth* (Chicago: University of Chicago Press, 1989), pp. 21–100.

2. U.S. Department of Commerce, Bureau of Economic Analysis, *National Income and Product Accounts of the United States, 1929–82* (Washington, D.C.: U.S. Government Printing Office, 1986).

3. For an extensive discussion of the issues, see David F. Bradford, "Market Value vs. Financial Accounting Measures of National Saving," *NBER Working Paper No. 2906* (Cambridge, Mass.: National Bureau of Economic Research, March 1989). For a good introduction to financial accounting concepts, see George Foster, *Financial Statement Analysis,* 2nd ed. (Englewood Cliffs, N.J.: Prentice-Hall, 1986).

4. U.S. Department of Commerce, Bureau of Economic Analysis, *Fixed Reproducible Tangible Wealth in the United States, 1925–85* (Washington, D.C.:

U.S. Government Printing Office, June 1987). See also John C. Musgrave, "Fixed Reproducible Wealth in the United States, 1979–82," *Survey of Current Business* 63, no. 8 (August 1983), pp. 62–67; John C. Musgrave, "Fixed Reproducible Tangible Wealth in the United States, 1972–82, Revised Estimates," *Survey of Current Business* 66, no. 1 (January 1986), pp. 51–75; and John C. Musgrave, "Fixed Reproducible Tangible Wealth in the United States, 1982–85," *Survey of Current Business* 66, no. 8 (August 1986), pp. 36–39.

5. For recent studies of the magnitude of these two forms of investment, in addition to Chapter 7 in this book, see Dale W. Jorgenson and Barbara M. Fraumeni, "The Accumulation of Human and Nonhuman Capital, 1948–84," in Lipsey and Tice, eds., *The Measurement of Saving, Investment and Wealth,* pp. 227–282; and Michael J. Boskin, Marc S. Robinson, and Alan M. Huber, "Government Saving, Capital Formation and Wealth in the United States, 1947–85," in Lipsey and Tice, eds., *The Measurement of Saving, Investment and Wealth,* pp. 287–353.

6. See Derek W. Blades and Peter Sturm, "The Concept and Measurement of Savings: The United States and Other Industrialized Countries," in Federal Reserve Bank of Boston, *Saving and Government Policy* (Boston: Federal Reserve Bank of Boston, 1982), pp. 1–30.

7. Ibid.

8. See Fumio Hayashi, "Is Japan's Saving Rate High?" *Quarterly Review of the Federal Reserve Bank of Minneapolis* (Spring 1989), pp. 3–9.

9. The data for personal income and outlays are presented in the Table 2 series in *Survey of Current Business.*

10. For a clear discussion, see John F. Wilson, James L. Freund, Frederick O. Yohn, Jr., and Walther Lederer, "Household Saving Measurement: Recent Experience from the Flow of Funds Perspective," in Lipsey and Tice, eds., *The Measurement of Saving, Investment and Wealth,* pp. 101–152.

11. For a clear display of the NIPA concepts in this respect, see Table 2.1 in *Survey of Current Business.*

12. John F. Wilson et al., "Household Saving Measurement: Recent Experience from the Flow of Funds Perspective."

13. A number of authors have emphasized this point, developed at length in Bradford, "Market Value vs. Financial Accounting Measures of National Saving."

14. David F. Bradford, *Untangling the Income Tax* (Cambridge, Mass.: Harvard University Press, 1986).

15. John Immerwahr, *"Saving: Good or Bad?"* (New York: Public Agenda Foundation, 1989).

ADDITIONAL REFERENCES

Federal Reserve System, Board of Governors. *Balance Sheets for the U.S. Economy 1949–88.* Washington, D.C.: Board of Governors of the Federal Reserve System, 1989.

______. *Flow of Funds Accounts.* Washington, D.C.: Board of Governors of the Federal Reserve System, various dates.

Japan Economic Planning Agency. *Annual Report on National Accounts, 1989.* Tokyo: Economic Planning Agency, 1989.

______. *Report on National Accounts from 1955 to 1969.* Tokyo: Economic Planning Agency, 1989.

Lipsey, Robert E., and Irving B. Kravis. "Is the U.S. a Spendthrift Nation?" *NBER Working Paper No. 2274*. Cambridge, Mass.: National Bureau of Economic Research, June 1987.
Lipsey, Robert E., and Helen Stone Tice, eds., *The Measurement of Saving, Investment and Wealth*. Chicago: University of Chicago Press, 1989.
Organisation of Economic Co-operation and Development. *Annual National Accounts*. Paris. OECD, various issues.

Discussion

Patric H. Hendershott

The title of this chapter is far too modest. David Bradford does not simply ask how saving should be measured and then discuss a U.S. national saving series. Rather, he examines numerous alternative measures of national saving and consumption in a number of countries: the United States, the United Kingdom, Japan, and Sweden. In addition, he reports a variety of other interesting statistics, most relating to real wealth accumulation in these countries but also including the capital-labor ratio in the United States and the land-wealth ratios in the United States and Japan. (I was particularly struck by the fact that even though Japanese wealth per capita now exceeds that of the United States, U.S. nonland wealth per capita is still more than three times that of Japan.) This mother lode of data will no doubt stir debates regarding wealth accumulation in each of the countries analyzed.

I divide my comments into two broad parts. I begin with the evidence on U.S. saving and discuss the causes and consequences of the saving rate decline in the 1980s. I then report data on the composition of real U.S. capital gains since 1950 and compare the "quality" of real capital gains in the 1970s and 1980s. Like Dr. Bradford, I confine myself to the accumulation of nonhuman capital.

U.S. NATIONAL SAVING

Bradford's Evidence

The traditional NIPA and FFA saving measures indicate a significant decline in U.S. national saving in the 1980s, although the decline is less pronounced when net consumer durables purchases are correctly interpreted as saving, not consumption (Table 5.6). The change-in-real-wealth saving measure indicates an earlier and even sharper decline in U.S. saving (Table 5.8). Alan Auerbach did not find the 1970s decline in his change-in-real-wealth variable, apparently because he used the Department of Commerce's valuation of corporate assets, not the stock market's, and the stock market declined so precipitously in 1973–1974.[1]

In spite of the declines in all of his saving measures, Dr. Bradford concludes that recent consumption (and thus saving) is not glaringly out of line with the past, referring specifically to the consumption-wealth ratio in Figure 5.11. Although interpretation of what is or is not glaring can certainly vary from individual to individual, I would contend that recent consumption and saving, using Dr. Bradford's own data, *are* glaringly out of line. As noted, the various saving measures are down, and a close look at Figure 5.11 suggests that private consumption is up. Moreover, not only did the ratio of consumption to wealth rise in the 1980s; past experience would have led us to expect a decline.

Movements during the 1960s and 1970s in the consumption-wealth ratio were driven by the corporate stock market. Every jump in the ratio in Figure 5.11 corresponded to a market decline (1962, 1966, 1969–1970, and 1973–1974), and all declines in the consumption-wealth ratio were reflections of two-year stock market booms (1967–1968, 1971–1972, 1975–1976, and 1979–1980) in which the market rose by 42 percent on average. Two additional booms occurred in the 1980s: a 27 percent gain in 1982–1983 and a 44 percent gain in 1985–1986. In spite of these stock market gains, the consumption-wealth ratio has risen, not fallen. A careful empirical investigation that takes into account the effect of equity capital gains on the ratio, will, I am convinced, find that consumption in 1987 was at least 10 percent higher than previous experience would have suggested.

The same argument holds for the U.S. wealth-GNP ratio in Figure 5.16. Historically, this ratio has been driven by the stock market, and given the enormous stock market gains since 1981, one would have expected the ratio to have been near an all-time high in 1987. In fact, however, the ratio was below trend. In summary, I am less sanguine about recent aggregate wealth accumulation in the United States than Dr. Bradford is.

Causes, Consequences, and Cures

Drawing on work of Kotlikoff, Dr. Bradford concludes that households, not the government, "are 'to blame' for the decline in saving." To blame the slowdown in real wealth accumulation on households when the federal government is running large deficits at full employment, and spending the buildup in the Social Security fund to boot, is astonishing—unless one is simply blaming households for the high reelection rate of their congressional representatives.

Households did not reduce their saving in the 1980s; they simply shifted its composition from the accumulation of assets officially counted as saving (financial assets, real estate, and private pensions) to the accumulation of those not counted (consumer durables and government pensions, including Social Security). Let me dwell for a moment on the misclassification of contributions to government retirement plans and durable outlays. The national income and product accounts treat household investment in retirement accounts and real assets in an inconsistent manner.[2] When a household contributes dollars to a private retirement plan set up either by itself (for example, individual retirement accounts) or its private-sector employer, these dollars are counted as household, not business, saving. But when the dollars are contributed to a government retirement plan, including Social Security, the dollars are counted as government saving. Consistency requires similar treatment of these contributions, and logic requires the counting of all of them as household saving.

When a household purchases a house, rather than renting one, the purchase is classified as saving (and investment). When an automobile is purchased, however, the acquisition is treated entirely as consumption (if a business purchases automobiles to rent to households, the acquisition is labeled investment). Similarly, if appliances, bookcases, carpeting, and so on are part of the house purchased, they are saving, but if these goods are bought separately, they are consumption. Consistency requires that these purchases be treated similarly, and logic dictates that purchases net of depreciation be counted as saving.

Data on sectoral net saving and investment (as a percent of net national product) are listed in Table 5.9 for the decade 1979–1988. (Earlier years in the 1970s were like 1979.) The data in the top of the table indicate that household net durables purchases and net contributions to government retirement plans in 1985–1988 totally offset the 1980s plunge in personal saving. In contrast, moving net contributions to government retirement plans from government saving to household saving lowered the government saving rate by 1.5 percentage points in 1988 versus 1980–1981. As a result, total household saving was flat between 1979 (the last year in which the U.S. economy was operating at full employment) and 1988, while total government saving—and total domestic saving—was down a full 5 percentage points.

The problem of a low U.S. national saving rate is shown in the lower part of Table 5.9: the 3-percentage-point decline between 1979 and 1988 in net investment, which took the form of reduced business, not household, capital formation. The direct cause of the problem was the huge negative government dissaving (and to a lesser extent the biases in the tax code against business investment and in favor of household investment).

Nonetheless, one should realize that reduction of government dissaving will not automatically increase net business investment. For example, a $100 billion tax increase on businesses and higher income households, two-thirds of which is used for deficit reduction and one-third of which is used to expand federal benefits of various sorts, would lower the deficit by $67 billion but might not increase total saving at all and could actually decrease business net investment. It is low capital formation, especially business capital formation, that should concern us, not whether a specific sector is saving a lot or a little.

TABLE 5.9
Net Saving and Investment
(percent of NNP[a])

	1979	1980	1981	1982	1983	1984	1985	1986	1987	1988
Household Saving										
Personal	5.8	6.1	6.4	6.0	4.7	5.3	3.8	3.6	2.7	3.6
Durables	2.7	1.4	1.5	1.4	2.3	3.2	3.5	3.6	3.1	3.2
Government Retirement[b]	1.2	1.4	1.6	1.7	1.9	2.2	2.5	2.4	2.6	3.1
Total Household	9.7	8.9	9.5	9.2	8.9	10.7	9.8	9.6	8.4	9.9
Business Saving[c]	3.0	1.7	1.7	0.8	2.3	3.0	3.1	2.4	2.0	2.0
Government Saving[d]	–0.6	–3.0	–2.8	–6.0	–6.5	–5.6	–6.5	–6.5	–5.5	–5.5
Total Domestic Saving	12.1	7.6	8.4	3.9	4.7	8.1	6.4	5.5	4.9	6.4
Foreign	–0.1	–0.5	–0.4	0.0	1.2	2.9	3.4	3.9	4.0	2.9
TOTAL SAVING	12.0	7.1	8.0	3.9	5.9	11.0	9.8	9.4	8.9	9.3
Net Business Investment[e]	5.4	3.3	4.6	1.2	1.2	5.1	3.4	2.6	2.3	2.4
Net Household Investment										
Owner Housing	3.9	2.7	2.1	1.3	2.6	2.9	2.8	3.1	3.4	3.5
Durables	2.7	1.4	1.5	1.4	2.3	3.2	3.5	3.6	3.1	3.2
TOTAL INVESTMENT[f]	12.0	7.4	8.2	3.9	6.1	11.2	9.7	9.3	8.8	9.1

Sources: U.S. Department of Commerce, Bureau of Economic Analysis, *National Income and Product Accounts; Survey of Current Business*, various issues.

[a] Net national product (NNP) equals gross product less capital consumption, including that on consumer durables.

[b] Net contributions to government insurance programs, including Social Security.

[c] Retained earnings plus capital consumption allowances and inventory valuation adjustment.

[d] Federal and state and local "surpluses" less net household contributions to government retirement and insurance programs.

[e] Net private domestic investment excluding owner housing (and consumer durables).

[f] Total investment and saving differ by the statistical discrepancy.

SHOULD REAL CAPITAL GAINS BE INCLUDED IN SAVING?

Adding real capital gains to, and subtracting real capital losses from, saving has become popular in recent years. But not all real gains and losses should be viewed as saving or dissaving. Only real capital gains that reflect a more productive capital stock and thus greater future consumption possibilities should be added to saving, and only real losses that reflect reduced future consumption possibilities should be subtracted. It is not obvious that routinely adding these real gains to traditional saving numbers improves our measure of saving.

Joe Peek and I divided real gains/losses into four broad categories: losses on net fixed-valued assets due to inflation; losses on consumer durables due to a steady or even accelerating decline in the real price of durables since 1965; real gains on housing, land, and noncorporate equity; and gains or losses on corporate equity.[3] (We aggregated noncorporate equity with land because more than one-half of real noncorporate-equity gains in the 1950–1982 period were attributable to increases in real land prices.) The key question is, Which categories of real gains or losses likely reflect an increase or decrease in the productivity of the asset?

Inflation-induced losses on net fixed-valued assets are likely small for the United States as a whole because fixed-valued assets and liabilities roughly cancel out. Thus, this is not a major issue for measuring national saving, although correcting for inflation is important in measuring private saving and public dissaving. In principle, losses on net fixed-valued assets should be subtracted from saving because inflation erodes the income stream from the assets.

In contrast, the real losses on consumer durables consistently recorded in the United States since the early 1960s probably should not be subtracted from saving. The one-third decline in the real price of consumer durables between 1965 and 1988 likely reflected the introduction of superior close substitutes at attractive prices, owing to sharp technological advances in the durables-producing industry. Although this introduction drove down the prices of existing durables, it did not reduce their productivity; for example, the introduction of color television did not reduce the quality of black-and-white TV reception. Thus, the real losses on consumer durables should not be construed as dissaving. (To the extent that the consumer durables stock is a larger component of wealth in the United States than in other countries, a measure that does not subtract these losses would improve the relative U.S. saving performance vis-à-vis a saving measure that does subtract the losses.)

How the other two categories of real gains should be treated is less clear, but before addressing this issue I report the magnitude of these real gains. Table 5.10 reproduces the cumulated real gains on these assets between 1950 and 1982, along with cumulated NIPA personal

TABLE 5.10
Real Household Wealth Accumulation
(billions of 1972 dollars)

	Real Cumulated Capital Gains				
	Housing, Land, and Noncorporate Equity	Corporate Equity	Housing, Land, and Total Equity	Cumulated Saving	Ratio of Gains to Saving
1950–1968	248	825	1,066	638	1.67
1969–1982	643	-376	267	875	0.31
1983–1988	-32	516	484	343	1.41

Sources: Data for 1950–1982 and the method of calculations are given in Patric H. Hendershott and Joe Peek, "Real Household Capital Gains and Wealth Accumulation," in Patric H. Hendershott, ed., *The Level and Composition of Household Saving,* copyright ©1985 by Ballinger Publishing Company. Used by permission of Harper Business, a division of Harper & Row, Publishers, Inc., New York, N.Y. The 1983-1988 update is based on Board of Governors, Federal Reserve System, *Balance Sheets of the U.S. Economy, 1949–1988* (Washington, D.C.: Board of Governors of the Federal Reserve System, 1989).

Note: The real gains (losses) on corporate equities held indirectly by households via their insurance and pension fund reserves are included in the corporate equity data.

TABLE 5.11
Adjusted Real Household Wealth Accumulation
(billions of 1972 dollars)

	Real Cumulated Capital Gains			
	Housing, Land, and Noncorporate Equity	Adjusted Corporate Equity	Housing, Land, and Total Adjusted Equity	Cumulated Adjusted Saving
1950–1968	241	426	667	1,037
1969–1982	643	-724	-81	1,223
1983–1988	-32	296	264	343

Sources: Data for 1950–1982 and the method of calculations are given in Patric H. Hendershott and Joe Peek, "Real Household Capital Gains and Wealth Accumulation," in Patric H. Hendershott, ed., *The Level and Composition of Household Saving,* copyright ©1985 by Ballinger Publishing Company. Used by permission of Harper Business, a division of Harper & Row, Publishers, Inc., New York, N.Y. The 1983-1988 update is based on Board of Governors, Federal Reserve System, *Balance Sheets of the U.S. Economy, 1949–1988* (Washington, D.C.: Board of Governors of the Federal Reserve System, 1989).

Note: In the adjustment, cumulated real retained earnings are subtracted from the change in real corporate equity holdings and added to cumulated saving.

saving, in billions of 1972 dollars, and reports comparably computed data for the 1983–1988 period. Table 5.11 reports the same data but with cumulated real retained earnings shifted from corporate equity gains to cumulated saving (now personal and corporate).

The overwhelming impression given in Tables 5.9, 5.10, and 5.11 is that the 1983–1988 period was far more like the 1950s and 1960s than like the 1970s. In both the early and late periods, cumulated total real gains were about one and one-half times cumulated personal saving, versus only one-third in the 1970s. Also, corporate equities were the dominant source (the total source in 1983–1988) of real gains in the beginning and ending periods, whereas real equity losses were recorded in the 1970s. The value of real corporate equities grew at an annual rate of 8.5 percent in both the beginning and ending periods and fell at a 3 percent annual rate in the 1969–1982 span. In contrast, the real value of housing, land, and noncorporate equity grew at 1 percent in the 1950–1968 period, 2.5 percent in the 1969–1982 span, and not at all in 1983–1988.

How should we view real gains in these two categories of assets? My own view is that the 1 percent growth in real land and so on values in the 1950s and 1960s might reasonably be attributed to productivity gains and thus could be added to saving. In contrast, deviations from this growth in later years have been largely a reflection of changes in real after-tax discount rates. The decline in real after-tax discount rates in the 1970s increased real values, and the rise in discount rates to more normal levels in the 1980s tended to lower real values.[4] As such, these gains/losses relative to the normal 1 percent do not reflect changes in the productivity of assets and thus should not be added to/subtracted from saving.

Real corporate equity gains are probably a more controversial issue. Over the longer haul, I would say that these gains reflect changes in the productivity of capital, although this is obviously not true from year to year. These gains certainly do not move inversely with real after-tax interest rates.[5] If equity real gains reflect changes in the productivity of capital, then these should be added to saving.

CONCLUSION

My look at the historical record reveals both good news and bad news. The bad news is that real wealth accumulation slowed in the United States in the 1980s owing to the federal government's dissaving. The good news is that the quality of wealth accumulation improved in the 1980s relative to the 1970s because the quality of real capital gains improved. On net, the record on capital accumulation for the 1980s is unclear. What is clear, however, is that counting on high-quality real capital gains to offset government dissaving is risky business.

The consequence of low government saving is low business capital formation. The cure for this low formation undoubtedly entails reducing government dissaving. But the way in which the dissaving is reduced is crucial. Increased government saving that is matched by decreased private saving is no solution at all.

NOTES

1. See Table 2-2 in Alan Auerbach, "Saving in the U.S.: Some Conceptual Issues," in Patric H. Hendershott, ed., *The Level and Composition of Household Saving* (Cambridge, Mass.: Ballinger, 1985), pp. 15–38.

2. Patric H. Hendershott and Joe Peek, "Aggregate U.S. Private Saving: Conceptual Measures and Empirical Tests," in Robert E. Lipsey and Helen Stone Tice, eds., *The Measurement of Saving, Investment and Wealth* (Chicago: University of Chicago Press, 1989), pp. 185–226.

3. Patric H. Hendershott and Joe Peek, "Real Household Capital Gains and Wealth Accumulation," in Hendershott, ed., *The Level and Composition of Household Saving,* pp. 41–62.

4. A regression for the 1952–1982 period that supports this conjecture is reported in Patric H. Hendershott and Joe Peek, "Household Saving: An Econometric Investigation," in Hendershott, ed., *The Level and Composition of Household Saving,* pp. 63–100.

5. Franco Modigliani and Richard Cohn have argued that real equity gains and losses reflect changes in nominal pretax rates, although why households can be fooled by the wrong discount rate in their stock investments but not in their housing investments is unclear. See Franco Modigliani and Richard A. Cohn, "Inflation, Rational Valuation and the Market," *Financial Analysts Journal* (March-April 1979), pp. 24–44.

Discussion

Charles L. Schultze

David Bradford brings together—partly from other sources and partly from his own research—a whole series of alternative measures of national saving. The measures differ along three major dimensions:

- First, the measures differ with respect to what they include or exclude from the definition of productive assets—for example, the stock of consumer durables, the "stock" of research and development (R&D), and the stock of educational investment.
- Second, the measures differ according to the source of the statistical estimates. The NIPAs rely on income and consumption measure. The FFAs rely on data relating to the net issuance of financial assets by business and other sectors.
- Third, and most importantly, the alternative measures differ according to whether they use the reproduction cost of additions to productive assets or the change in the market value of the stock of assets as the measure of saving.

After arraying and discussing a number of alternative measures of national saving, Dr. Bradford concludes that on the evidence presented, especially the market value measures of the change in private wealth, national saving is "not glaringly out of line with past experience." He also argues that even if the national saving rate were significantly lower than in the past, that fact *alone* may not necessarily provide a basis for a policy to reverse that choice. At the very end of his discussion, however, he notes that many of the nation's tax and other policies are biased against saving and that a removal of those penalties to saving might well be warranted.

Bringing together and comparing the time path of these alternative saving series as Dr. Bradford has done represent a most important and welcome contribution to the discussion about the current status of the U.S. saving rate. But I disagree strongly with many of the implications he draws from the data. Contrary to Dr. Bradford, I believe that when properly interpreted, all the relevant data do in fact provide strong evidence that the U.S. saving rate has fallen sharply and is well out of line both with U.S. history and with other countries and that this should be a major source of national concern.

In the first place *every* measure of national saving in which saving is defined to be equal to the net increase in productive capital valued at reproduction cost shows a steep drop in the national saving rate since 1980 from a relatively stable average in the thirty years prior to that time. This drop in saving shows up, of course, in the most familiar measure of national saving derived from the official NIPAs of the U.S. government. As measured there, the national saving rate falls from 8 percent of national income in the early period to a 1989 level of a little more than 3 percent.

The U.S. saving rate decline also shows up in the OECD measures of national saving rates that use a standardized definition for all countries. The OECD measures include in saving and investment net investment in nondefense tangible assets by governments. But because net government investment in the United States as a share of national income has fallen, the decline in the net national saving rate is larger when government assets are included in the measure of saving. Of the twenty-one countries whose national saving rates are measured by the OECD, the United States stood lowest in 1986 and 1987. The U.S. saving rate has increased a little since then but not by enough to change any of these conclusions.

On the basis of data on gross investment in R&D as a share of national income in the United States, one can easily infer that the inclusion in saving of the net change in the stock of R&D would not alter in any significant way the conclusion that the U.S. saving rate has fallen sharply. Barry Bosworth has constructed an NIPA saving series that includes net investment in the stock of consumer durables as part of saving and also adjusts private saving for the effect of inflation on private holdings of government debt. This measure also shows a substantial drop in national saving between the years prior to 1980 and 1986–1987.

The FFA measures of *household* saving show a more favorable picture than do the NIPA measures of household saving (see Figure 5.5, top line). But once we go to the more inclusive *national* saving concept—which in addition to household saving includes business and government saving or dissaving—most of the favorable discrepancy disappears, and national saving as measured by the FFA declines almost as much as it does by the NIPA measure. One reason the FFA measure of household saving declines less than does the NIPA measure is that the latter includes in household saving the accumulation of pension funds for state and local employees, which the NIPAs include in the government sector. But this is only a statistical reassignment of saving from one sector to another, and so although FFA household saving performs better than does NIPA saving, the government dissaving is worse to an exactly offsetting degree.

A large, positive statistical discrepancy has recently emerged between the two series; household saving in the FFA, even when adjusted to NIPA conceptual definitions, has risen relative to the NIPA measure. But again this is mainly an allocational phenomenon that is largely matched by an offsetting movement in the sum of the statistical discrepancies of the other sectors. Again, the discrepancy does not represent a substantially more favorable picture for total national saving.

Analysis of the two series—NIPA and FFA—yields the conclusion that the only important systematic difference between their measures of *national* saving is that the FFA includes and the NIPA excludes increases in the stock of consumer durables as saving. Compared to its pre-1980 average, such accumulation has risen as a share of national income by about 0.5 percentage point. And so instead of falling by roughly 4.5 percentage points since its pre-1980 level, national saving by this measure has fallen by about 4 percentage points.

Dr. Bradford then turns from measures of national saving based on the annual flow of capital accumulation valued at reproduction cost to measures based on the change in the real market value of the stock of private assets held by U.S. residents. Conceptually, saving as measured in this way is equal to the annual accumulation of new assets plus any revaluation in the (real) value of existing assets. Dr. Bradford gives *two* related sets of market value measures: the flow of national saving and the stock of national wealth.

As I will explain shortly, I strongly disagree that changes in the market value of existing assets are relevant in judging national saving performance. But let us nonetheless accept for the moment the relevance of such a concept and look at the two measures Dr. Bradford presents. First, even if we use his market value measure of saving, we see that the national saving rate fell sharply—even more so than in the NIPA or OECD measures—from an average of 12.4 percent of GNP in the 1950s and 1960s to 7.0 percent in the 1970s and 1980s (see Table 5.8). The decline also started earlier in the market value measure than it did in the NIPA.

Dr. Bradford places particular reliance on an alternative set of data shown in Figure 5.16, which indicates that the *wealth-GNP* ratio has cycled around a constant value and has not shown any substantial decline. He also notes that the uptrend in wealth per capita has been constant over the postwar years. The growth in wealth per capita, however, has been constant only in arithmetic terms; the percentage rate of growth, which is the relevant measurement for assessing the saving rate, has fallen substantially.

That the wealth-GNP ratio has been constant is somewhat misleading in terms of its implications for the U.S. saving rate. The rate of growth of GNP fell sharply after 1973, from its 1948–1973 average of 3.7 percent a year to a 1973–1988 average of 2.6 percent. But the combination of falling income growth and a constant wealth-income ratio necessarily implies a decline in the annual saving rate, defined as the increment to market value of wealth.[1] Indeed, the numbers underlying the constant wealth-income ratio in Figure 5.16 imply a fall in the saving rate from approximately 10 percent in the 1948–1973 era to approximately 7 percent today—a 3-percentage-point decline compared to the 4.5-percentage-point decline shown in the national income accounts.

One might still argue that a saving rate that maintains a constant wealth-income ratio, even though it represents a lower saving rate than in the past, represents satisfactory performance. But as I will demonstrate, changes in the market value of *existing* private wealth should not be included in a measure of national saving; that the wealth-income ratio, thus defined, has remained constant in no way warrants a conclusion that we should be unconcerned about the drop in national saving implied by such constancy.

For purposes of explaining the consumption and saving behavior of individuals, we must indeed consider the changes in the market value of individuals' existing wealth to be quite relevant. People base their saving decisions in part on the size of their wealth relative to their income. Nevertheless, the aggregate change in the market value of individuals' wealth is not an appropriate measure by which to assess national saving *performance*. For that purpose, we should be interested in the volume of national saving, and the investment in productive assets that it makes possible, because additions to those assets contribute to future national income and production. Future national income can also change, however, for a host of reasons that have nothing to do with the volume of saving and capital input. For example, the future pace of scientific and technological advance may speed up or slow down, or the overseas price of oil may surge or collapse. To the extent that such developments generate changes in income streams that are appropriable by private firms, correct expectations about those developments will increase or decrease the current market value of real estate and of existing corporate assets and so affect the measure of national saving as defined by Dr. Bradford. But however much these developments affect future national income, they have nothing to do with the contribution of *current saving and investment* to that future national income. Therefore, the capital gains or losses on existing assets that these developments generate do not belong in a measure used to evaluate the nation's saving and investment performance.

To say it another way, we want a measure of national saving that generates the capital inputs into a national production function. There are many other elements in addition to capital inputs that affect future production, some (but not all) of which may be anticipated, may be appropriable by private firms, and may therefore change the value of existing assets. But the anticipation of these developments does not represent a capital input into the production function, and I know of no body of research that incorporates them into production function analyses of national growth.

Not only is the sum of change in the private market value of real estate and business enterprises not the right measure by which to judge national saving and capital input; this sum may often bear little relationship to changes in *national* productive wealth. An increase in wealth to an individual or firm is often not an increase in wealth for the nation as a whole, as several examples may help make clear. Legal limits on the supply of taxicabs in New York City, through restrictions on the number of cab medallions, have increased the financial value of those medallions tremendously and thus the wealth of the individuals or businesses that own them. If entry into the taxi business were made free, the financial value of the medallions would collapse, but national wealth would not fall; indeed, future national income would rise. Or, if there were a sudden and well-forecasted halt to all new innovations in the United States, the future obsolescence of the existing stock of tangible capital assets would fall to zero, and the stock prices of firms owning those assets would rise. But future national production would decline.

To take another case, imagine a sudden, large increase in population. Urban land values would skyrocket, even as the disamenities of urban living increased sharply. This change in market value would surely not mean that the nation had added to its saving, its investment, and its productive wealth. To drive this point home, consider Japan. As Dr. Bradford points out, 80 percent of the market value of its wealth is represented by the value of real estate. Once the value of land is included, Japan—with one-half the U.S. population—is much wealthier than the United States. But does anyone really believe that in any important sense the Japanese nation in recent years has gained real wealth as the price of land has soared? Of course not. The increase in land values does not represent an increase in national wealth but simply a redistribution of wealth between those who own land and those who do not.

In sum, the annual increment to the market value of private wealth may be a very important piece of data in explaining the saving behavior of households. But changes in the market value of existing assets have no place in a measure of *national* saving, which ought to tell us how much of its current output the nation is setting aside to be available as a capital input into the production of future wealth. Here the national income accounts measure of national saving, perhaps supplemented by data on changes in the stock of government capital and the stock of R&D, is the appropriate one. By any of these measures—whether those of the United States or the OECD—the U.S. saving rate has declined very sharply since 1980.

Indeed, the current national saving rate so measured would not be sufficient to provide enough capital to maintain the nation's already slow growth of output per worker were it not for the fact that U.S. saving is being supplemented by the inflow of saving from abroad. In a recent article, I calculated that the financing of the capital inputs that would be necessary simply to maintain the current low rate of growth, in the absence of that overseas borrowing, would require an increase of several percentage points in the current (1988, first half 1989) national saving rate.[2]

Moreover, in view of the demographic situation facing the United States early in the next century, when the number of retirees will rise sharply relative to the number of workers, we ought to be saving and adding to our national wealth more, not less, than enough to maintain the status quo with respect to the growth of worker productivity. The magnitudes of the needed extra saving are very roughly given by the size of the annual surplus in the Social Security trust funds. To the extent that we were to achieve that objective, our national saving rate would have to be not 2, but more like 4 percentage points higher than it now is. In short, on any *relevant* set of data, U.S. saving has fallen and is undesirably low by any reasonable set of criteria. Government policy should be addressed to increasing it, principally by moving the federal budget from deficit to surplus.

NOTES

1. Let $\dot{w}$, $\dot{y}$ = rates of growth of wealth and income respectively; s = the saving rate; R_w = the ratio of wealth to income. If R_w remains constant, then $\dot{w} = \dot{y}$ and $s = \dot{y} \times R_w$. If the rate of growth of income falls, then s must also have fallen.

2. Charles L. Schultze, "Setting Long-Run Deficit Reduction Targets: The Economics and Politics of Budget Design," in Henry J. Aaron, ed., *Social Security and the Budget, Proceedings of the First Conference of the National Academy of Social Insurance* (Washington, D.C.: NASI and University Press of America, 1990), pp. 15–42.

6

Domestic and International Consequences of Low U.S. Saving

C. Fred Bergsten

THE CENTRAL ISSUE

Conventional wisdom holds that the main consequence of the low U.S. saving rate will be slow growth in the future standard of living in the United States. Low saving means low investment; low investment means low productivity growth. One result will be a lower standard of living than if domestic saving and the two intermediate variables—investment and productivity—were higher. Another result will be a relative decline in the international position of the United States, perhaps in the political as well as in the economic sphere.

The U.S. saving rate has been "low" by contemporary international standards throughout the postwar period (see Table 6.1).[1] Nevertheless, the living standards and international competitive position of the United States remained largely satisfactory at least into the early 1970s. Most present concerns focus on the *decline* in U.S. saving, which may have begun in the 1970s and which accelerated sharply in the 1980s.

U.S. investment held up reasonably well in the 1980s despite the sharp fall in domestic saving. To be sure, net domestic investment fell by 1.5 to 2.0 percentage points of net national product (NNP) from the average of the previous three decades (see Table 6.2). Net domestic saving, however, declined by 5 to 6 percentage points; this decline was divided about equally between reductions in private and in government saving.

Domestic investment was sustained to such a surprising degree by the large net inflow of foreign capital to the United States. *Two-thirds of the decline in our domestic saving rate has been offset to date by the importation of foreign saving.* This influx of capital even permitted a *rise* in U.S. living standards in the short run by enabling the United States to raise domestic expenditure above the level of domestic output—through consuming and investing more than our domestic re-

TABLE 6.1
Historical Gross Saving Rates, Ten Countries

Country	Percentage of GNP				Ratio to Pre-WW II	
	Pre-World War II		1950–1959	1960–1984	1950–1959	1960–1984
United States	18.7	(1869–1938)	18.4	18.0	0.99	0.96
Australia	12.4	(1861–1938)	26.2	22.7	2.12	1.84
Canada	14.0	(1870–1930)	22.4	21.2	1.61	1.52
Japan	11.7	(1887–1936)	30.2	32.5	2.59	2.79
Denmark	10.1	(1870–1930)	18.9	19.6	1.87	1.94
West Germany	20.0	(1851–1928)	26.8	23.7	1.34	1.19
Italy	12.0	(1861–1930)	19.8	21.0	1.65	1.75
Norway	11.5	(1865–1934)	27.5	27.1	2.40	2.36
Sweden	12.2	(1861–1940)	21.4	21.4	1.75	1.75
United Kingdom	12.3	(1860–1929)	16.2	18.1	1.32	1.47

Sources: Robert E. Lipsey and Irving B. Kravis, "Is the U.S. a Spendthrift Nation?" *NBER Working Paper 2274*, 1987, Table 1; Simon Kuznets, "Long Term Changes in the National Income of the United States of America Since 1870," in Simon Kuznets, ed., *Income and Wealth of the United States: Trends and Structure, Income and Wealth Series II*, International Association for Research in Income and Wealth (Cambridge: Bowes and Bowes, 1952), Table 5.3; OECD, *Historical Statistics*, 1960–1984.

Note: Average of the figures for the periods weighted by lengths of periods.

Reprinted by permission from Bela Balassa and Marcus Noland, *Japan in the World Economy* (Washington, D.C.: Institute for International Economics, August 1988), p. 83.

TABLE 6.2
U.S. Net Saving and Investment[a]
(percent of net national product)

	1951–1960	1961–1970	1971–1980	1981–1985	1986	1987	1988 (1st Half)
Net Saving							
Private Saving[b]	8.7	9.4	9.7	8.2	7.4	6.1	6.7
Government Saving	-0.7	-1.0	-2.0	-4.6	-5.3	-4.1	-3.6
Total National Saving-Investment	8.0	8.4	7.7	3.6	2.1	2.0	3.0
Net Foreign Investment	0.3	0.7	0.3	-1.3	-3.8	-4.0	-3.3
Net Domestic Investment	7.7	7.7	7.5	5.0	5.6	5.8	6.1

Source: U.S. Department of Commerce, Bureau of Economic Analysis, *National Income and Product Accounts*.

Note: Full-year data for 1988 show a slightly greater increase in total saving and investment, due to a small further pickup in net private saving and a corresponding further fall in net foreign investment.

[a]Net saving and investment equal the gross flow minus capital consumption allowances (the depreciation of existing capital). Net national product equals gross national product minus capital consumption allowances. The sum of the investment components does not add to the total because of statistical discrepancy.

[b]Business and household saving. Employee pension funds of state and local governments are allocated to household saving to match the treatment of private pension funds.

Reprinted with permission of publisher, M.E. Sharpe, Inc., Armonk, New York, from Barry P. Bosworth, "The Saving Shortfall," *Challenge* (July-August 1989), p. 28.

sources would support. *Any comprehensive analysis of the consequences of the low and falling U.S. saving rate in the 1980s must therefore emphasize the impact of these foreign capital inflows on both our domestic economy and the world as a whole.*

At the outset, it is important to note the ambiguity as to whether the foreign funding has financed higher consumption or higher investment in the United States—an issue of great importance when I discuss later the sustainability of the large foreign debt that the United States is accumulating as a result. As indicated, U.S. net investment fell from its level of the previous three decades. The shares of (especially) private consumption and government spending in the economy rose concomitantly. A straightforward comparison over time thus suggests that the incoming foreign investment has primarily financed higher U.S. consumption.

Nevertheless, the sharp decline in domestic saving would presumably have led to a much sharper fall in investment in the absence of the capital inflow. We cannot know whether domestic private saving would have behaved precisely as it did in the absence of that inflow. But the sharp rise in the federal budget deficit in the 1980s by itself would have produced a substantial cutback in private investment in the absence of foreign capital, mainly by driving domestic interest rates considerably higher,[2] unless private saving had somehow risen by 3 percentage points rather than declining by 3 percentage points. At the margin, the capital inflow from abroad thus financed U.S. private investment to a significant degree. This phenomenon has already lasted since about 1983. Expansion has continued over the same period, with unemployment falling to its lowest level since the Vietnam War.

It is also important to distinguish between *sustainability* and *desirability* as criteria for assessing the shifts in the U.S. international economic position during the 1980s. The foreign capital inflow has continued for considerably longer than many observers, myself included, had thought possible. Some conclude that it therefore can continue indefinitely, or at least for a good while longer, and that no corrective action needs to be taken.

This conclusion could turn out to be correct for some time to come. But we should not forget that the private capital inflow largely dried up in 1987 and triggered sharp falls both in the bond market in the spring and in the stock market in the fall ("Black Monday") before foreign central banks came to the rescue with $120 billion of dollar support. In addition, the continuance of the capital inflows to date could just as easily be bringing us close to the world's saturation point for dollar assets as it could be demonstrating that "automatic" external funding will continue indefinitely. Even more important, an economic outcome is not necessarily desirable simply because it is sustainable in the marketplace, even over a considerable period of time. Much of this analysis in fact is devoted to assessing the desirability of the new U.S.

reliance on foreign funds to maintain domestic investment and the U.S. standard of living.

The "real" counterpart of the net capital inflow of the 1980s is the deficit in the U.S. current account balance with the rest of the world. From a small surplus in 1980–1981, the external balance rose steadily and rapidly to a peak deficit (to date) of more than $150 billion—about 3.4 percent of GNP—in 1987. The deficit was still at $105 billion in 1989, and *it seems likely on the basis of present policies and exchange rates that the deficit will start rising again in 1990 and will exceed $200 billion by 1992.*[3]

The stock counterpart of these capital inflows has been the shift of the United States from being the world's largest creditor nation, as recently as 1983, to the world's largest debtor nation. Net capital inflows to the United States exceeded $800 billion during 1982–1989. At the end of 1988, the U.S. net international investment position had become negative by $533 billion. *This "net debt" is virtually certain to rise to at least $1 trillion in the early to middle 1990s.*[4] An increasing share of the debt buildup has taken the form of selling off U.S. assets, such as companies and real estate, as well as borrowing in the financial markets.

In assessing the net effect of the saving shortfall on the U.S. economy, we must set the costs of these external deficits and debts against the returns on the continuing domestic investment made possible by the capital inflows. My analysis makes the critical assumption that the recovery from the recession of 1982 and the subsequent expansion could have been achieved with an alternative policy mix—lower budget deficits, lower interest rates, and avoidance of most of the dollar appreciation of 1981–1985—that would have avoided the buildup of external difficulties.

DOMESTIC CONSEQUENCES

There are six major domestic costs of the precipitate reversal in the international economic position of the United States in the 1980s:[5]

- Major adjustment costs as the effects of dollar overvaluation and the trade deficits fell primarily on manufacturing, including a potentially permanent loss in the U.S. position in world markets because U.S. firms were discouraged by the high dollar from competing internationally and foreign firms were able to establish strong footholds here.
- A permanent drain of real resources from the United States to service the debt to foreigners generated by the deficits. These debt-service costs will probably amount to at least $100 billion annually, in contrast to the sizable investment *income* received as recently as 1980–1981, and will require a much larger decline in the ex-

change rate of the dollar to restore equilibrium in the current account. This decline will have adverse effects on the U.S. living standard.

- The perennial risk of a drying up of the capital inflow, which (especially with the economy near full employment and full capacity utilization) could trigger a sharp rise in inflation and in interest rates, financial disruption, and perhaps a sharp and prolonged recession.
- Even absent such a "hard landing," increased constraints on the independent conduct of U.S. economic policy and foreign policy and increased vulnerability to decisions made abroad. One particularly important risk is consistently higher interest rates (than called for by domestic considerations) to avoid capital flight.
- A steady increase in protectionism and the consequent erosion of the world trading system as dollar overvaluation alters the balance of domestic trade politics.
- Feedback to the U.S. economy of the increased instability of the global economic system stemming from the weakened position of the world's key currency country and foremost champion of free trade as well as from the U.S. response to the debt (and other economic) problems of other countries.

Adjustment Costs

The decline in the trade balance in manufactured goods from 1981 to 1987 ($153 billion) was considerably greater than the decline in the overall trade balance ($132 billion). (The reduction in the agricultural surplus was more than offset by the fall in oil imports.) It is clear that most of the correction of the trade imbalance will require a sharp recovery of manufactured trade. In addition, the trade balance as a whole will have to improve considerably more than it previously declined to offset the rise in debt-service costs resulting from the shift to debtor status.[6]

The United States will therefore have undergone a substantial shift of resources out of and then back into the same sector, on the order of 3 to 4 percent of GNP in nominal terms (perhaps 5 to 6 percent in real terms).[7] One million jobs were displaced, and many will have to be recreated.[8] Similarly disruptive variations will have occurred in domestic consumption, which rose above the long-term sustainable level and was oriented toward nontradeables as the deficits rose, and now must fall below that level with a shift toward tradeables in the correction phase. Popular dissatisfaction arising from this alternation of splurge and austerity is predictable and represents both a welfare cost of the imbalance[9] and a political impediment to achievement of the correction. Needless adjustment costs will clearly ensue.

Moreover, it now is widely recognized that the adjustment process is asymmetrical. Firms that gain or lose international market share because of a large and prolonged currency appreciation, such as that experienced by the dollar in the first half of the 1980s, may not be able to recoup their positions from a subsequent depreciation of like magnitude. Startup or renewal costs can be quite high. The firms may require price changes (via additional dollar depreciation) that exceed—perhaps by a considerable margin—those that triggered their original difficulties.[10]

Debt Service

Closely related to these adjustment costs is the inevitable cost of servicing the foreign debt accumulated to finance the current account deficits. In 1980–1981, the United States was able to balance the current account while running merchandise deficits of $25 billion to $30 billion. To achieve balance in the mid-1990s, merchandise trade and nonfactor services will have to be in surplus—thereby transferring real resources to the rest of the world—by $50 billion to $75 billion. *The annual impact on national income of the swing in the U.S. international investment position could therefore be upwards of about $100 billion*—about 2 percent of current GNP and still about 1 percent of projected GNP in the year 2000.[11]

"Extra" dollar depreciation of 10 to 15 percent will be needed to accomplish this additional adjustment.[12] Each additional decline of 10 percent adds 1.5 to 2.0 percentage points to our price level and erodes the real value of our wealth and income. *The large and prolonged deficits of the 1980s mean that a restoration of equilibrium in the U.S. international economic position could levy considerable long-term costs on the economy as a whole.* The alternative to such adjustment is for the United States to continue borrowing abroad to service the previously accumulated debt. The debt would continue to rise, but the cost of transferring real resources would be deferred. This is what most of the Third World debtors did prior to 1982.

A critical variable at this point is whether the capital inflows have been used to finance productive, self-financing investment—as in the United States in the nineteenth century and in Korea in contemporary times. As noted, the inflow has kept investment from falling to lower levels, but its net impact has been to maintain (or even increase) domestic consumption rather than investment. This raises substantial doubts about the prospect for continued borrowing to finance debt service and suggests that the United States will at some point have to begin transferring real resources abroad to finance at least a substantial part of the servicing costs of the external debt accumulated in the 1980s and early 1990s.

The Risk of a Hard Landing

An abrupt cessation or shrinkage of the foreign capital inflow could trigger a hard landing for the dollar and the U.S. economy. If the private capital inflow were to dry up (as in 1987) and if (unlike 1987) foreign central banks failed to come to the rescue, the U.S. monthly borrowing requirement of more than $10 billion would go unmet in an ex ante sense, and the dollar would plunge.

If this occurred when the economy was near full employment and full capacity utilization, as is now the case, inflation and interest rates would rise sharply. Given the fragility of parts of the financial system, considerable financial disruption would result. A sharp recession could ensue—possibly a prolonged one because of the inability of either fiscal or monetary policy to respond. The trade balance would improve considerably, but only after a year or two. The traditional impact of low saving would come crashing home as the reliance on foreign borrowing as an offset became unsustainable.[13]

We cannot know when, or even if, such a catastrophe will occur. We do know, however, that imbalances of the current magnitude have always proved to be unsustainable in the past. There is no reason to believe that the United States, even borrowing in its own currency, can indefinitely attract capital at a rate that raises its foreign debt relative to its GNP—especially when that borrowing is primarily funding consumption rather than increased investment.

It is easy to construct scenarios in which the dollar would fall sharply: a renewed upturn of the external (and perhaps the budget) deficit, as is now widely forecast; lower interest rates in the United States resulting from a slowdown in the economy; continued rapid growth and higher interest rates in Japan and Europe; a restoration of political stability in those areas; or a decision by foreign monetary authorities—with their economies growing strongly from increased domestic demand and facing inflationary pressures—to cease supporting the seemingly endless U.S. deficits and thereby to force adjustment on us. The playing out of any such scenario would levy substantial costs on the United States.

Constraints and Vulnerability

A continuing buildup of foreign debt will increasingly constrain the ability of the United States to conduct its economic policy and foreign policy independent of external considerations and will perhaps produce a significant degree of vulnerability to external events, even in the absence of a cataclysmic hard landing. Such constraints and vulnerability were *not* caused by our swing to debtor status. Major runs on the dollar occurred in the early 1970s and again in the late 1970s when the United States was still the world's largest creditor country. Our vulnerability derives inevitably from global economic and especially financial interdependence. This vulnerability is particularly acute for a key currency country whose external liabilities are inherently large and whose external assets (especially foreign direct investment but most others held privately as well) are of little or no use in defending the country against currency runs.

Moreover, currency runs are unlikely to be triggered by debtor status per se. Both theory and history suggest that a restoration of flow equilibrium—that is, equilibrium in the current account and underlying economic performance and policies—will sustain stability for the currency under most conditions. It is not only foreign dollar holdings that could cause trouble; domestic investors would be likely to join, or even lead, any market retreat from the dollar.

The *extent* of U.S. vulnerability, however, is increased considerably by the onset of large debtor status. The magnitude of external liabilities is obviously much higher, and the psychological impact of debtor status could be considerable. When the flow position slides into disequilibrium, as inevitably happens even for the best-managed economies, sales from the "dollar overhang" could substantially exacerbate the situation—as occurred for the United States in the two periods cited, for the United Kingdom throughout the lengthy period of the sterling's decline, and even for West Germany when part of the newly created "deutsche mark Überhang" collapsed when that country moved into large flow deficit after the second oil shock.

As a result, the consequent U.S. adjustment would have to be much larger. The costs for the economy would be much larger as well. In particular, as revealed by the British case and that of contemporary debtor countries such as Canada, interest rates would have to be maintained at higher levels to avoid withdrawals of foreign funds and, if the deficits continue (even just to finance interest on existing debt), to keep the net inflow coming. Continued high interest rates would in turn depress investment and U.S. living standards—the traditional result of low saving; this effect would occur with a lag and indeed partly via the delayed impact of the foreign borrowing that obviated that effect in the short run.

Protectionism

The postwar history of U.S. trade policy reveals that dollar overvaluation is the most accurate leading indicator of an upsurge of protectionism. Overvaluation prices many normally competitive U.S. industries out of world markets, thereby swelling the ranks of those seeking import controls and weakening the countervailing force of export interests. The result is a sharp swing in the balance of trade politics.[14]

Such cycles have produced protectionist outbreaks in the late 1960s and early 1970s, in the mid-1970s (to a lesser degree), and most notably in the 1980s. President Reagan, despite his devotion to open markets and free trade, "granted more import relief to U.S. industry than any of his predecessors in more than half a century."[15] The impact of the Reagan administration's domestic policy mix simply swamped its predilections; the economic effects of overvaluation, working through domestic politics, forced the administration to adopt an array of new trade controls (for autos, steel, textiles and apparel, machine tools, and so forth).

Some of the protectionist measures adopted during the period when the U.S. saving shortfall savaged the country's trade position may turn out to be temporary. For example, the Bush administration has announced that it intends in 1992 to terminate the voluntary restraint agreements now in effect for the steel industry; these were adopted at the height of the dollar overvaluation in 1984. Nevertheless, protection tended to ratchet upward during the 1970s and the 1980s primarily because of the three cycles of dollar overvaluation in the United States. Therefore, the steady erosion of the trading system is another cost of low U.S. saving.

A new form of protectionism may develop as a result of the reliance on foreign saving: resistance to foreign direct investment (FDI) in the United States. It is doubtful that the influx of FDI is causally related to the large U.S. external deficits to any great extent, having started much earlier and probably deriving largely from firm-specific microeconomic factors.[16] Deficits and FDI are closely linked in public perception, however, and action to curb FDI could result if the inflow of foreign saving continues to take this form to a significant extent—as is likely for at least some time to come.

Renewed growth in the U.S. trade deficit over the next year or two, resulting from the failure to raise domestic saving adequately (as reflected in the incomplete correction of the dollar in 1985–1987 and its renewed appreciation since early 1988), could accelerate the protectionist trend. The traditional shift in the balance of trade politics would recur. In addition, such a development would imply failure of the Baker/G-7/Plaza strategy of correcting the trade imbalances through currency changes and macroeconomic policy cooperation. Although the adjustment failure would be due primarily to U.S. unwillingness to correct its saving shortfall, the political message could be that the agreed strategy had been tried for five years and had been found wanting. One likely result would be a renewed surge of protectionism and increasing calls for managed trade.

Erosion of the Global System

Closely related to the protectionist threat is the likely adverse impact on the United States itself of the erosion of the world economic system that seems inevitable as the lead country, the United States, faces a steadily weakened international position because of its deficits and debt. The United States has derived considerable national benefits from the key currency role of the dollar, an open trading system, and the U.S. ability to provide constructive leadership on issues such as Third World debt. That leadership is increasingly difficult to sustain, however, because of the domestic constraints stemming from low saving and the resulting deficits and because of a reduced willingness of other countries to follow the lead of the world's largest debtor. As noted, *the United States is likely to face growing constraints on its international actions—political and even military—until it corrects its external imbalances.* This country could even find itself doing the bidding of its creditors to maintain the inflow of capital and to avoid withdrawals of existing balances.

To be sure, a large debtor accrues power over its creditors as well. The situation may be likened to one of mutual strategic deterrence: Large creditors (such as Japan) and large debtors (such as the United States) can do enough damage to each other that neither would rationally trigger a conflict. This mutual deterrence reduces the risk of concerted pressure on the United States by one or more creditors.

Unlike in the military sphere, however, the dominant role of private actors greatly increases the risk of accidental conflict via the markets and thus of hard landings or other financial disruptions. In any event, *global superpower status is hardly compatible with being the world's largest debtor and with running massive external deficits.* The United States will have to choose between these roles sometime in the foreseeable future.

INTERNATIONAL CONSEQUENCES

The Global Economic System

As just noted, the leadership position of the United States is eroding more rapidly as a result of its deficits and foreign debt. That erosion will continue to accelerate until the saving shortfall is corrected. The resulting global problem is that international economic stability seems to require a "hegemonic power" with both the ability and the willingness to provide such leadership.[17] The only stable periods in the modern era have been those led by the United Kingdom in the latter part of the nineteenth century and by the United States in the first postwar generation. The years just before World War I, between the two wars, and during the 1980s reveal the difficulties that arise when such leadership is absent.

It is possible to envisage effective joint management of the world economy in the early twenty-first century by a newly competitive United States, a newly internationalized Japan, and a truly United States of Europe. At best, however, it will take some time to reach such a steady state. Moreover, historic transition periods are always fraught with risk and uncertainty.

It is conceivable that the weakness of the United States—rooted in the sharp fall in the U.S. saving rate—will galvanize a more rapid assumption of international responsibility by Europe and Japan. But it is equally likely that *premature abdication by the United States could plunge the world economy into a period of considerable turmoil,* as did the decline of the United Kingdom in the interwar period, when the United States was not yet willing to provide a replacement. The results could include endemic financial instability, growing protectionism and a resort to managed trade, and the evolution of economic blocs that would divide the world politically as well as economically.

Third World Debt

One immediate international consequence of low U.S. saving, and the resulting importation of huge amounts of foreign capital, is the competition thereby provided for the debtor countries (and others) in the Third World. The debtors of Latin America hardly face a "level playing field" when they must compete for capital with the U.S. Treasury.

To be sure, the taste of the United States for foreign capital has certain international advantages. As a "borrower of last resort," the United States offers an attractive outlet for investors from other countries, notably Japan, but also for a large number of Europeans *and* Latin Americans (whose foreign investments we call "capital flight"). But the U.S. readiness to borrow also obviates the pressure on surplus countries to contribute to adjustment of the imbalances and thereby supports the desire of these countries to continue running large trade surpluses. Unbridled U.S. borrowing thus perpetuates the costs of the imbalances and their risks both for the United States itself and for the world economy as a whole. Indeed, there will be no real pressure on the United States to adjust—to raise its saving rate through budget deficit reduction or other measures—as long as other countries continue to finance (or even overfinance, as they have of late) this country's external imbalances.

It is no coincidence that the United States started running its large external deficit just as Latin America had to cease running a large external deficit. To be sure, Latin America's problems are mainly homegrown, and the debt problem of the continent would have emerged even if the United States had remained a capital exporter. But in the 1980s U.S. capital that had been moving south suddenly stayed home, and Japanese and European capital that had ventured into Latin America was redirected north. The U.S. trade deficit notched further upward as Latin America had to cut its buying sharply, and the "negative resource transfer" from the Third World commenced.

It is highly unlikely that this negative resource transfer of $40 billion to $50 billion annually can be eliminated or substantially reduced, let alone reversed to the logical and normal state of net capital inflow to developing countries, until the United States ceases draining the bulk of the world's internationally mobile funds. *Low saving in the United States thus probably means continued low growth and instability in large parts of the developing world, notably the United States' "back yard."*

Adjustment in the Surplus Countries

Just as the United States must shift resources back into the tradeables sector and cut domestic expenditure sharply during the adjustment period, so must the major surplus countries (notably Japan, Europe, and the Asian newly industrializing countries) adjust in the opposite direction. They will almost certainly turn out to have allocated excessive resources to exporting and import-competing industries, and they (especially Japan and Korea) have already experienced sharp adjustment shocks as their currencies soared. Needless adjustments will arise on the surplus as well as the deficit side of the international imbalances.

CONCLUSIONS

I have attempted in this analysis to trace the domestic and international consequences of the recent fall in the already low U.S. saving rate. These consequences derive largely from the massive deterioration that has resulted in our international trade and financial positions. I have deliberately made no effort to add up these costs because some are difficult to quantify, some overlap to a degree, and some are highly conjectural.

Nevertheless, these consequences taken together seem to produce an overwhelming case for the adoption of remedial measures. *The current external position of the United States is neither sustainable nor desirable. We should set a national goal of eliminating the current account deficit, and thus halting the buildup of foreign debt, by the mid-1990s.*[18] This in turn will require a sharp rise in our domestic saving—thus getting at the root of the problem.

Measures that offer promise of raising private saving in the United States have proven extremely elusive to date. I therefore reiterate the importance of our reducing and preferably eliminating the federal budget deficit according to the current Gramm-Rudman-Hollings schedule, without gimmicks.[19] In combination with continued rapid growth of domestic demand abroad and a further fall of the dollar against the currencies of the major surplus countries (which must then be maintained through the adoption of target zones or some equivalent international monetary reform), such action should eliminate the current account deficit and halt the further buildup of the U.S. foreign debt by the middle of the 1990s. Failure to take such steps will continue to jeopardize the economic future of the United States as well as that of the world as a whole.

NOTES

1. As indicated in Table 6.1, this comparison stands in sharp contrast to the prewar period, when the United States had one of the world's highest saving rates. Research is needed to verify these data and to determine why

saving in most other countries appears to have jumped so sharply after World War II but remained relatively constant in the United States.

2. Stephen N. Marris, *Deficits and the Dollar: The World Economy at Risk,* rev. ed. (Washington, D.C.: Institute for International Economics, August 1987), p. 44, estimated that the foreign capital inflow held U.S. real interest rates down by "at least 5 percentage points" during the early recovery period in 1983–1984.

3. William R. Cline, "Impact of the Strong Dollar on U.S. Trade" (Washington, D.C.: Institute for International Economics, June 1989, mimeograph). The International Monetary Fund foresaw a rise to about $140 billion in 1990 in its *World Economic Outlook*, October 1989.

4. This issue is analyzed in detail in C. Fred Bergsten and Shafiqul Islam, *The United States As a Debtor Country* (Washington, D.C.: Institute for International Economics, forthcoming). As noted in Chapter 2 of that study, there are substantial data problems on both sides of the U.S. international balance sheet. On the asset side, foreign direct investment by U.S. firms is substantially underestimated because it is based on book value (and is considerably older than is inward foreign direct investment, which is recorded in the same manner). On the liability side, the data exclude the net inflow of "errors and omissions," most of which is probably capital inflow, which totaled almost $200 billion during 1978–1987. The recorded balance is thus probably not too far off; in any event, its deteriorating trend is unambiguously clear.

5. For somewhat different categorizations of the "costs of misalignments," see John Williamson, *The Exchange Rate System,* rev. ed. (Washington, D.C.: Institute for International Economics, June 1985), pp. 38–45; and Paul Krugman, "Long-Run Effects of the Strong Dollar," in Richard C. Marston, ed., *Misalignment of Exchange Rates: Effects on Trade and Industry* (Chicago: University of Chicago Press, 1988), pp. 277–298.

6. Robert Z. Lawrence, "The International Dimension," in Robert E. Litan, Robert Z. Lawrence, and Charles L. Schultze, eds., *American Living Standards: Threats and Challenges* (Washington, D.C.: Brookings Institution, 1988), estimated that the share of manufacturing in GNP would have to rise by at least 1 percentage point to restore balance in the U.S. current account in the future.

7. The arithmetic is in C. Fred Bergsten, *America in the World Economy: A Strategy for the 1990s* (Washington, D.C.: Institute for International Economics, November 1988), Chapter 4.

8. William H. Branson and James P. Love, "U.S. Manufacturing and the Real Exchange Rate," in Marston, ed., *Misalignment of Exchange Rates*, pp. 259–269.

9. Harry Johnson called these "The Welfare Costs of Exchange Rate Stabilization," *Journal of Political Economy* 74, no. 5 (1966), pp. 512–518.

10. Richard E. Baldwin, "Hysteresis in Import Prices: The Beachhead Effect," *American Economic Review* 4 (1978), pp. 773–785.

11. The *change* in the merchandise trade balance required to achieve equilibrium in light of future debt-service costs, compared with the U.S. "creditor country equilibrium" of the early 1980s, would be the same at whatever *level* turns out to represent equilibrium for the United States in the future.

12. This is suggested by the need for such further depreciation to restore the U.S. current account position to the rough balance of 1980–1981 despite the fact that the real value of the dollar has already returned to the level of those years. See William R. Cline, *United States External Adjustment and the*

World Economy (Washington, D.C.: Institute for International Economics, March 1989); and Cline, "Impact of the Strong Dollar on U.S. Trade."

13. The full story is in Marris, *Deficits and the Dollar.* For an update, see C. Fred Bergsten, "The Hard Landing Scenario," in Martin Feldstein, ed., *Reducing the Risk of Economic Crisis* (Chicago: University of Chicago Press, forthcoming).

14. C. Fred Bergsten and John Williamson, "Exchange Rates and Trade Policy," in William R. Cline, ed., *Trade Policy in the 1980s* (Washington, D.C.: Institute for International Economics, 1983), pp. 99–120; and I. M. Destler, *American Trade Politics: System Under Stress* (Washington, D.C.: Institute for International Economics, and New York: Twentieth Century Fund, 1986).

15. Remarks of Secretary of the Treasury James A. Baker III at the Institute for International Economics, Washington, D.C., September 14, 1987.

16. Edward M. Graham and Paul R. Krugman, *Foreign Direct Investment in the United States* (Washington, D.C.: Institute for International Economics, December 1989).

17. Charles P. Kindleberger, *The World in Depression, 1929–1939* (London: Penguin, 1973).

18. A comprehensive strategy is offered in Bergsten, *America in the World Economy.*

19. The personal saving rate would have to rise from 5.4 percent in the second quarter of 1989, already up sharply from 1987–1988, to 7.3 percent by the second quarter of 1993 to eliminate the need for foreign borrowing, with the budget deficit remaining at $150 billion even if business saving recovered to its late-1988 level.

Discussion

Clive Crook

I congratulate Fred Bergsten on his very clear and persuasive analysis. I agree with much, but not quite all, of it.

The Institute for International Economics has been stressing the risk of a hard landing for a long time, and it has not happened yet. Many commentators, as Dr. Bergsten notes, are inclined to dismiss the idea. I commend the example of Britain to the skeptics. There are differences between the British case and the U.S. case, but the similarities are revealing. Britain is heading for a hard landing of the sort that Dr. Bergsten fears for the United States. In Britain, we have had a collapse of private saving; we have an enormous current account deficit, and the government is being forced to raise interest rates to prevent a run on the pound. Interest rates may already be high enough to bring about a hard landing.

So these things can happen—and when the economic situation starts to deteriorate, it can do so with surprising speed. In 1988 the outlook was a moderate deterioration of the current account, not the very sharp deterioration we have seen. In 1989, sentiment shifted abruptly, and a hard landing became not merely plausible but likely.

There are clearly great differences between the situations of the two countries. In particular, Britain's external deficit does not reflect a public-sector budget deficit. The British government's budget is actually in large surplus. Despite that important difference, Britain does show how quickly a hard landing can materialize, which is why I think that Dr. Bergsten is right to stress the risks in the outlook for the U.S. economy.

But some of the cures he suggests may be worse than the disease. He argues, for example, that the dollar has to fall. The question is, How? Other things equal, a lower dollar will require lower U.S. interest rates. This is what the Bush administration seems to want. But lower interest rates would be risky with the U.S. economy at, or close to, full capacity. In other words, getting the dollar down as a matter of policy runs a severe risk of causing higher inflation.

This leads to a broader point. Is the core of the problem really the current account deficit, as Dr. Bergsten argues, or is it the exchange rate regime? Dr. Bergsten puts the current account deficit at the center of his calculation—describing the costs of adjusting to the current account deficit and organizing policy implicitly around a target for the current account deficit. But many of the adjustment costs he talks about—the costs of shifting economic activity from one sector to another—are related to dollar instability. The appreciation of the dollar in the early 1980s accelerated the decline in the U.S. current account position and put U.S. manufacturers under tremendous pressure. Then the process went into reverse as the dollar fell. It is not obvious that the dollar was an innocent bystander—still less a helpful shock absorber. So it seems odd to argue that the way to reduce those adjustment costs is to lean on the dollar as a variable instrument of government policy. That may only be adding to the problem.

Dr. Bergsten's argument about the costs and risks can be recast, I think more persuasively, as an argument for pursuing exchange rate stability as a goal of policy rather than as an argument for pursuing a specific target for the current account deficit. Moreover, if policymakers listen to his prescription and try to achieve what he calls a modest decline in the dollar, they may end up with a highly immodest decline instead. If the Federal Reserve did announce such an intention, it might serve nicely as the proximate cause of the hard landing Dr. Bergsten fears. I think currency stability is the core to this dilemma and is a much more important problem in its own right than the current account deficit is.

I quarrel with Dr. Bergsten's implication that any current account deficit is bad. Indeed, he describes the requirement on the trade side for achieving balance in the current account. He wants the United States to run a trade surplus in order to achieve "equilibrium" in the current account. To this end, he wants to organize policy around a target for the current account. This is a sort of neomercantilism: the idea that countries grow rich and powerful by accumulating claims on foreigners. This, of course, is absolutely false. Countries grow rich and powerful by building up their productive capacity. Often, as South Korea found, a current account deficit can be an extremely useful way of doing so.

Equally, steps to reduce the current account deficit as an end in itself can easily become obstacles to this process of enrichment. Dr. Bergsten himself would be the last person to propose protectionist solutions to the current account deficit. But his approach, in putting the current account deficit at the center of the problem, does lend support to the U.S. protectionist battalion. If the current account deficit is so vital, if it is essential to reduce it very quickly, perhaps protectionism (which, in principle, we all know to be bad) is a price we should be willing to pay. If the U.S. accumulation of foreign debt is such a worrying development, perhaps there is also a case for laws to discourage foreign direct investment. Again, we know this is bad in itself, and in an ideal world nobody would propose it. But we have the current account deficit to think about.

Focusing micropolicy on the external deficit can be extremely harmful; focusing macropolicy on it can be almost as bad. An approach that ties monetary policy to short-term objectives for the current account is likely to be profoundly hostile to growth. The Federal Reserve's aim should be to pursue a credible anti-inflationary monetary policy. The Federal Reserve cannot do this if it must set interest rates partly with a view to hitting short-term targets for the current account.

So far I have said nothing about saving. A question I would like to see answered is, How much saving is enough? We usually take for granted that the United States needs to save more. Most of the arguments used to support this view, including Dr. Bergsten's, apply just as well to Japan. If we think that more saving must always be "good," and that is how we talk, a country can never have too much. But this is an absurd position. It is plausible to argue that Japan, in fact, saves "too much"; that is what the comparison between its living standards and its productive capacity suggests. In any case, it is obvious that we cannot all be net savers. So I would question the presumption that more saving is automatically better and the policy prescriptions that flow from it.

Britain's present discomfiture shows that it is not enough to say, "Balance the public-sector budget, and then leave saving and investment decisions to the private sector." Even so, I am more comfortable with this than with the unquestioned assumption that the United States has too little saving and that the government should therefore do something about it. Certainly, there is plenty that the U.S. government could do to reduce the disincentives it has created for savers and to reduce its own demands on the financial markets. The U.S. tax system greatly favors borrowing and discourages saving. I am interested in policy prescriptions that aim toward neutrality in the way the tax system treats saving. I am not convinced that the debate on the capital gains tax reduction is actually going to move the tax system in that direction. That is a complicated question. I agree that bringing the federal budget deficit down is first and foremost. I am very disappointed that Treasury Secretary Brady says in Chapter 1 that he wants the capital gains tax reduction regardless of what happens to the budget deficit. I think it is inexcusable that the administration and Congress cannot reduce the budget deficit. This is, by far, the biggest element in the current U.S. saving shortage.

On the tax side, I agree with Mervyn King's proposal that Britain and the United States move to a system of expenditure taxes rather than income taxes. The income tax system has the inherent defect of taxing saving twice. An individual saves out of taxed income to begin with and then has to pay tax on the income the saving generates. I think that is a powerful disincentive to saving. So I would like to see in the long run a deep change in the British and U.S. taxation systems that moves toward taxing consumption rather than income.

I am much more skeptical about putting distortions back in order to make saving more attractive than it would be under a neutral tax system, especially if the implicit target for saving is entirely arbitrary. I am happier to leave these decisions to the private sector, at least in the longer run. In the short run, as in Britain, financial deregulation and mistakes in macroeconomic policy can cause difficulties. But this has nothing to do with the question of the optimal long-term saving rate. In other words, if it turned out, as it probably would, that Americans chose in an undistorted world to save less than the Japanese did, I would say, "So be it. And let the United States have the current account deficit that goes with this decision."

These antisaving distortions should be put right, and the budget deficit should undoubtedly be cut. But when all of that has been done, the United States may still have a current account deficit. If so, I think I would be willing to say—the British case notwithstanding—that it was no cause for concern.

Discussion

Lee H. Hamilton

Fred Bergsten has, as usual, provided a cogent analysis of the international consequences of a low U.S. saving rate. He focuses his attention on the costs to the United States and to the world of our substituting foreign borrowing for our own domestic saving in financing

U.S. domestic investment. Bergsten concludes that "the current external position of the United States is neither sustainable nor desirable." He also concludes that reduction of the federal budget deficit is critically important if we are to raise national saving and reduce our dependence on foreign borrowing.

I agree with Dr. Bergsten that large budget and trade deficits do not represent a healthy state of affairs for the United States or for the world economy. Capital is being attracted to the United States that is probably better invested elsewhere from the standpoint of efficient global development. The United States is eroding its future standard of living by consuming too much now and selling assets and accumulating debt to pay for that consumption. The U.S. ability to be an effective world economic and political leader is severely constrained by our seeming inability to put our domestic affairs in order. These long-term, yet cumulatively corrosive, effects on growth and economic development are the real risks associated with low saving and continuing imbalances—although concerns about financial instability and dollar flight sometimes get more attention.

Thus, I agree fully with Dr. Bergsten that the consequences of our low saving are undesirable, but I take issue with him about whether this position is unsustainable. Dr. Bergsten and others at his institute have become associated with the view that the world economy is headed for a hard landing if prompt action is not taken to reduce the budget deficit. In fact, our experience following the 1987 stock market panic gives reason to be cautiously optimistic about the risk of financial panic that throws the real economy into a recession. True, concern that the United States is not making sufficient progress to reduce its budget and trade deficits could cause a flight from the dollar, but once the dollar has fallen sufficiently, dollar-denominated assets are cheap and international investors seem willing to come back in. Moreover, U.S. output and employment growth were largely unaffected by the turbulence in the foreign exchange and bond markets leading to the stock market crash in 1987, and the market itself has recovered steadily. I wonder whether it helps the debate to paint too apocalyptic a picture of what will happen if we continue to try to muddle through as we have so far.

If I am correct, we will not be prodded into action by an external crisis. But we do need to take action, and, as Dr. Bergsten observes at the conclusion of his discussion, one key action is to reduce the federal budget deficit. There is no iron link between budget deficits and trade deficits, but in the United States in the 1980s the drain on national saving caused by the budget deficit was not offset by an increase in private saving, despite the enactment of numerous saving incentives. As Dr. Bergsten points out, the situation might have been worse for domestic investment if we had not been able to attract foreign saving to offset the loss in domestic saving that resulted from the budget deficit, but we lose many of the benefits of investment when it is financed by foreign borrowing rather than by our own saving.

I am unpersuaded by arguments that the budget and trade deficits are benign artifacts of good policy. The U.S. saving rate is too low, and it is important that we raise national saving by reducing the budget deficit. The argument that the trade deficit reflects a boom in investment relative to saving would carry more force if U.S. saving were high by historical standards and if U.S. investment were even higher. Neither is the case. Expressed as a share of national income, U.S. saving is well below historical levels, and investment is about equal to or somewhat below historical levels depending on which exact measure is used.

Unfortunately, the president and Congress have been playing too many games with the deficit in recent years, and we have not pursued a serious policy of deficit reduction. The actual budget deficit has grown over the past few years ($150 billion in fiscal year [FY] 1987, $155 billion in FY 1988, and between $150 billion and $160 billion in FY 1989) rather than declining toward balance in 1993 as required under Gramm-Rudman, yet we have always found enough gimmicks to meet the requirement that we *project* a declining deficit. We need a prudent and realistic budget, and that may require reform of the budget process. For example, we need a way to cut down on the use of overly optimistic economic assumptions and to eliminate the use of budget gimmicks that produce onetime savings but make future deficit reduction even more difficult.

We also need a realistic deficit reduction plan. In my view, such a plan must be a package deal with broadly based spending reductions as well as moderate tax increases. We continue to be seduced by rhetoric about the incentive effects of various tax cuts when our experience over the past several years has been that the direct negative effects of budget deficits on national saving have swamped any indirect positive effects from the numerous saving incentives that were enacted. Thus, I feel about current plans to cut the capital gains tax the way Samuel Johnson felt about second marriages—they represent the triumph of hope over experience.

There is a further danger in pursuing additional tax loopholes that violate the spirit of tax neutrality underlying the 1986 tax reform effort: Tax rates will eventually have to go up to restore the revenues lost by the opening of loopholes. No one likes tax increases, but prudent changes can make an important contribution to saving and growth by reducing the budget deficit without seriously affecting incentives.

Finally, I want to reemphasize Dr. Bergsten's observation that our inability to deal with our budget and trade deficits hurts us as a world leader. As the *Wall Street Journal* concluded in an interesting series of articles a while back, the United States remains the foremost political and economic power in the world today. No other country possesses a comparable combination of industrial, financial, military, and political strengths. Nevertheless, the 1980s demonstrated the limitations of an emphasis on military strength and a failure of political resolve and leadership. As Secretary of the Treasury Nicholas Brady acknowledged at a Joint Economic Committee hearing immediately after the Paris summit, the United States reacted "on the cheap" in response to the major initiatives on Poland/Hungary, the environment, and Third World debt. In each case, the United States has vital interests in the development of prompt and effective programs. Similarly, we have yet to identify where we will find the resources to meet important domestic priorities such as fighting drugs, providing national defense, protecting the environment, educating our citizens, and rebuilding our infrastructure.

Only a lack of will—not a lack of resources—explains the current U.S. tendency to respond so cheaply to these kinds of issues. Although they are large, neither the budget deficit nor the trade deficit justifies the United States in making small financial contributions *and* being assigned an inferior seat in the resolution of the major problems and opportunities facing the world economy. We lived beyond our means—spending more than our productive income could support—in the 1980s. To finance this excess spending, we reduced our net asset position by $700 billion. But in terms of the physical and human resources that we continue to control and expand, we remain the world's most wealthy country.

If we can make the tough decisions to bring down future deficits, we will reap several benefits. First, at international meetings U.S. negotiators can propose adequate resources for the problem at hand, rather than blaming Congress for having to participate "on the cheap." Second, because we will finally set an example of making tough decisions at home, we will have more credibility in asking other countries to make sacrifices to address important international problems such as those raised at the summit. Third, the international financial markets will respond favorably to evidence of U.S. resolve and thereby substantially reduce the risks of financial panic and the hard landing about which Dr. Bergsten has warned us. Finally, we will begin to lay the groundwork for an investment-based economic recovery rather than one driven by consumption and debt.

Discussion

Mervyn A. King

One of the most striking developments in economic thinking in the last decade has been the rediscovery of the importance of international factors for domestic economic developments. In many areas of our subject—macroeconomics and tax policy, to name but two—it is no

TABLE 6.3
Comparison of Net National Saving Rates
(percent of net national product)

	1960–1970	1971–1980	1981–1987	1987
United States	10.6	8.9	3.9	2.7
OECD (average)	14.6	13.5	8.7	8.5
Japan	25.6	24.6	20.2	21.3
United Kingdom	11.2	8.2	6.2	6.1

Source: Organisation for Economic Co-operation and Development, *National Accounts.*

longer possible to pretend that the United States, or any other country, is a closed economy. Few institutions have done more to awaken the profession to the importance of international economic issues than the Institute for International Economics, of which Fred Bergsten is the director. It is therefore a pleasure to comment on his analysis.

In an economy that is either closed or characterized by little international capital mobility, saving and investment must be equal. Tax incentives to affect one will also affect the other. But in an open economy with free movement of capital, domestic saving and domestic investment can differ. This has important consequences that have been widely acknowledged in recent discussions of the U.S. saving rate and the trade deficit. The accounting identity that holds that the current account balance of payments is, in the absence of capital transfers, equal to the difference between saving and investment has played a central role in recent discussions of the twin U.S. deficits. The low U.S. saving rate is held primarily responsible for the trade, or more broadly, the balance-of-payments current account deficit. It is indeed most important that the balance of payments is discussed within the context of national saving and investment rates. But it is also necessary to recognize that at different stages of economic development, countries may vary in their structural saving and investment rates with the implication that balance-of-payments deficits and surpluses are phenomena that may persist over many years—and indeed did so in the nineteenth century. Therefore, such occurrences should no longer be seen, as they were in the 1960s, as symptoms of policy failure.

The debate in the United States on this issue has lacked an important dimension by focusing exclusively on developments in saving and trade within the United States; this focus fails to take into account that the world economy is a closed economy. Despite the efforts of international statisticians, it is not possible for the world to have a balance-of-payments deficit with itself. It is instructive to examine the behavior of saving rates in the developed world. Table 6.3 shows national net saving rates for the 1960s, 1970s, and 1980s in the United States, Japan, the United Kingdom, and the OECD countries as a whole. It is striking that in the United States as well as in the OECD there was a marked fall in saving rates in the 1980s. It is possible that part of the fall in saving rates in the OECD can be attributed to a reduction in capital outflows to the Third World. But it is difficult to argue that such a dramatic change in national saving rates—a fall of about 6 percentage points during the 1980s—can be attributed to, or can be said to have caused, a corresponding increase in the trade deficit of the OECD as a whole. There has been no change on this scale. Given that national saving rates have fallen by roughly the same amount in the United States and its major trading partners, the U.S. trade deficit cannot be blamed on lower U.S. saving.

It is therefore worth asking whether the fall in the U.S. saving rate has resulted from factors that are common to the OECD as a whole. It is then worth asking a supplementary question: Given that falls in saving rates in many OECD countries did not lead to trade deficits, why did this happen in the United States? I do not pretend to have simple answers to these questions, but they must be tackled. It was during the French Revolution that the Abbé Augustin wrote that "to all the enemies of God and his Christ, I add another sect known under the name of economists. These men, disciples of Turgot, for thirty years tormented France, claiming to reform its Government and restore its finances by schemes which ruined its monarchy and wasted its treasure. All the science of these sophists was contained in what they called the 'clear consequences.'"[1] Perhaps economists should be more cautious in describing the consequences of a fall in the national saving rate.

Fred Bergsten's view is that the major cost of the low U.S. saving rate is a dramatic change in U.S. international indebtedness and the wider role of the United States in the world economy. Whereas the latter has indeed followed from the prolonged and substantial trade deficits experienced in recent years, it is, as I have argued, by no means obvious that we should lay the blame entirely at the door of a lower national saving rate. One hypothesis that deserves more attention is that in many countries the 1980s saw the adoption of more "realistic" economic policies and the stabilization of public finances (although not in the United States). The unhealthy symptoms of the 1970s—high inflation rates and excessively low, often negative real interest rates—are a distant memory. There is greater confidence that governments will take steps both to stabilize public finances and keep down rates of inflation. Supply-side measures in tax policy and in efforts to increase the effectiveness of the market mechanism have come to the fore. It would not be surprising if an increase in confidence of this kind had led to expectations of increased future incomes. These will show up to some extent in higher values of current net worth. For given levels of current income, an increase in net worth will lead under almost any view of how consumption is determined to an increase in consumption relative to current income or, in other words, to a fall in the saving

FIGURE 6.1
U.S. and Japanese Household Saving Rates, 1960–1987

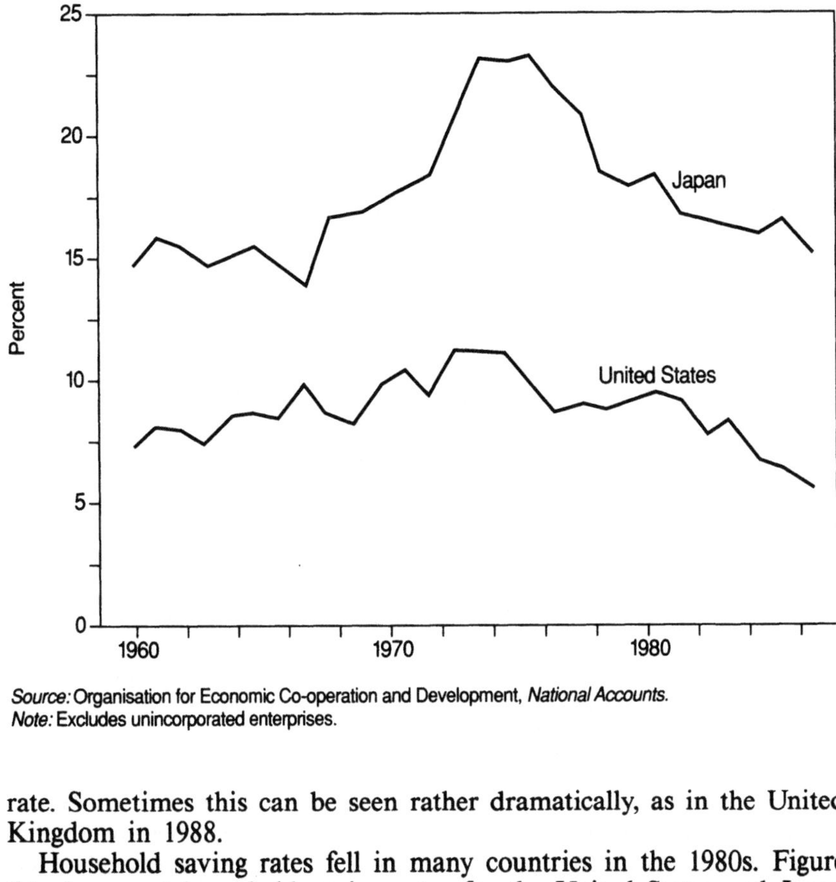

Source: Organisation for Economic Co-operation and Development, *National Accounts.*
Note: Excludes unincorporated enterprises.

rate. Sometimes this can be seen rather dramatically, as in the United Kingdom in 1988.

Household saving rates fell in many countries in the 1980s. Figure 6.1 shows net household saving rates for the United States and Japan over the period 1960–1987. In *both* countries there was a substantial fall in the household saving rate. In both countries there were significant increases in the wealth-income ratios during the 1980s. The same was also true for the United Kingdom. This line of thought suggests that consumers in the developed world have been raising consumption levels in anticipation of higher future levels of output. If these expectations turn out to have been excessively rosy, there will be a period of stagnation in the growth of consumption. This would not be a happy period over which to preside, and it is not surprising that in recent years governments have encouraged consumers in their optimism that structural changes to the economy mean that growth prospects have improved. But it would be a period in which saving rates would return to their previous levels.

Although Dr. Bergsten is absolutely right to point out that a reduction in the future trade deficit will require—for unchanged levels of investment—a higher U.S. saving rate, the proximate cause of the current deficit is the buoyancy of the U.S. investment rate relative to rates elsewhere. For much of the 1980s the United States acted as the locomotive of the world economy. Saving rates fell in most major countries, as did investment rates. But growth in the United States led to a relatively good investment performance and a resulting trade deficit. Equally, the rapid deterioration of the U.K. trade deficit in 1988–1989—to a level of 4 percent of GNP—was the result of a boom in consumption *and* investment. With a rise in the investment rate and a fall in the saving rate, a current account deficit was inevitable. The resumption of growth in Japan and West Germany may alter their saving and investment rates in a way conducive to the reduction of deficits in the United States and the United Kingdom.

I conclude from this that we should be cautious in advocating widespread changes in tax and other policies in order to encourage an increase in the saving rate. Rather, we should target policy changes at areas where there is some reason to suppose that an increase in saving can be achieved at low budgetary cost. Two policies come to mind. The first is of particular relevance to the United States, where the federal budget deficit remains. There is one type of new tax that might be popular and that could be defended by those whose "lips have been read": "green taxes" to protect the environment. Such taxes could be explained as a charge on the users of our environment, and if international agreement could be secured among at least a small number of developed countries, the United States would need not feel that its government had unilaterally reversed policy when raising additional revenue by legislating for such taxes. Indeed, many governments would welcome the chance to introduce popular taxes in order to reduce unpopular and distortionary taxes elsewhere in the economy. Green taxes that are worth considering include a carbon tax, a tax on other forms of emissions, and other charges on pollutants. Governments have a clear incentive to agree on the desirability of introducing such charges: Some governments could lower other taxes, and the United States could reduce its budget deficit. Thus, national saving would rise as a result of a reduction in public dissaving.

The second type of policy that I advocate is the introduction of tax incentives to saving that are specifically focused on reaching that part of the market that other incentives cannot reach. Most tax incentives for saving—including many for retirement saving—are highly complicated and require the assistance of accountants to exploit. Tax incentives that harness the marketing power of successful financial institutions that already enjoy the confidence of low-income households may have a major role to play in increasing household saving. These incentives have the additional benefit that there might be great social good in their encouraging low-income households, which have negligible financial assets, to accumulate at least some minimum amount of financial reserves. The argument for the introduction of an expenditure or cash-flow tax system should be made primarily in terms of the difficulty the operation of a true income tax poses and the need for fiscal neutrality. I am less confident that such a tax system will raise the level of national saving. But in the context of our present concerns, measures to increase taxes of a new rather different form and tax incentives to saving targeted to low-income and low-wealth households have an important role to play and can be defended in their own right irrespective of their ultimate impact on national saving.

NOTES

1. Augustin Barruel, *Histoire de clergé pendant la révolution française* (London: J. P. Coglan, 1893), p. 6.

7

Investment in Education and U.S. Economic Growth

Dale W. Jorgenson and Barbara M. Fraumeni

INTRODUCTION

This analysis describes the impact of investment in education on U.S. economic growth. Beginning with the seminal contributions of Theodore Schultz in 1961, Gary Becker in 1964, and Jacob Mincer in 1974, economists have found it useful to characterize the benefits of education by means of the notion of investment in human capital.[1] This idea captures the fact that an investment in human beings, like an investment in tangible forms of capital such as buildings and industrial equipment, generates a stream of future benefits. Education is regarded as an investment in human capital because benefits accrue to an educated individual over a lifetime of activities.

One of the most important benefits of education is higher income from participation in the labor market. This increase in income is the key to an understanding of the link between investment in education and economic growth. People differ enormously in their effectiveness on the job. Substituting more effective for less effective workers increases output per worker. More highly educated or better trained people are more productive than are less educated or poorly trained people. Nevertheless, because education and training are costly, substitution of people with more education and training requires an investment in human capital.

Although the relationship between educational investment and productivity growth is well understood at a conceptual level, not all data on productivity reflect this relationship. For example, the official statistics on multifactor productivity for the U.S. economy, produced by the Bureau of Labor Statistics and published annually in the *Economic Report of the President,* do not differentiate among the hours worked by individuals with different levels of educational attainment. As a consequence, the contribution of changes in the educational composition of the labor force to increased output is confounded with a host of other omitted factors that affect productivity.

The most common approach to compiling data on educational investment is to measure the inputs, rather than the output, of the educational system.[2] Data on the expenditures of educational institutions for teachers and other personnel, buildings and equipment, and materials can be compiled from accounting records. This information can be supplemented by estimates of the value of time spent by students (and their parents) as part of the educational process. Costs of schooling and the value of the time spent by students can be used to measure the flow of resources into schools and universities.

Athough the costs of education are highly significant in economic terms, the cost-based approach to the measurement of educational investment ignores a fundamental feature of the process of education. This is the lengthy gestation period between the application of educational inputs—mainly the services of teachers and the time of their students—and the emergence of human capital embodied in the graduates of educational institutions. Furthermore, some of the benefits of investment in education, such as greater earning power, are recorded in transactions in the labor market, whereas others, such as better parenting skills or more rewarding enjoyment of leisure, remain unrecorded.[3]

This analysis presents new data on investment in education that make it possible to analyze the impact of educational investment on U.S. economic growth. In the measurement of investment in education, the first step is to compile data on the economic value of labor market activities. Section two of this analysis ("Market and Nonmarket Labor Incomes") shows that the current dollar value of time spent working has expanded very rapidly in the postwar United States. The growth of this value has been greater for women than for men at all levels of educational attainment, which reflects the rapid increase in labor force participation by women relative to men. The proportional increase in the value of market labor time has been greatest for college-educated men and women. This corresponds to the substantial growth in levels of educational attainment.

The second step in measuring investment in education is to estimate the value of nonmarket labor activities, which include time spent in investment in education as well as time spent in the consumption of leisure. Rates of compensation for nonmarket activities are inferred from market wage rates. When measured in this way, the value of nonmarket activities exceeds the value of market activities, primarily because nonmarket time exceeds time in the labor market. Nevertheless, the value of nonmarket labor activities has grown more slowly. The expansion of the value of nonmarket time has been more rapid for men than for women.

In section three ("Investment in Education") lifetime labor incomes for all individuals in the U.S. population are estimated. These incomes include the value of both market and nonmarket labor time. The impact of increases in educational attainment on the lifetime incomes of all individuals enrolled in school is estimated. When measured in this way, investment in education exceeds the value of working time for all individuals participating in the labor force. Furthermore, the growth of investment in education has exceeded the growth of market labor activities during the postwar period. Investment in education has increased much more rapidly for women than for men, especially at the college level.

In section four ("Sources of Growth") new estimates of the sources of U.S. economic growth are presented that incorporate the effects of changes in the educational composition of the labor force. These estimates include a measure of changes in the quality of hours worked based on the impact of substitution among workers with different characteristics—including age, sex, and education—on output per worker. We identify the growth of labor quality with an increase in the proportion of more highly trained and better educated workers. An important part of this increase in labor quality is a consequence of investment in education.

The conclusions of the study are presented in section five ("Conclusion"). The most important finding is that investment in human and nonhuman capital accounts for the largest part of U.S. economic growth during the postwar period. Since 1973 the growth rate of the U.S. economy has slowed by 1 full percentage point relative to the postwar average. A revival of U.S. economic growth will require the mobilization of vastly increased capital and labor resources. Educational investment will continue to predominate in the investment requirements for more rapid economic growth.

MARKET AND NONMARKET LABOR INCOMES

In order to measure investment in human capital as an output of the educational system, we constructed a new data base for measuring lifetime labor incomes for all individuals in the U.S. population. This data base includes demographic accounts for the population in each year, cross-classified by sex, individual year of age, and individual year of highest educational attainment. The demographic accounts include data on the number of individuals enrolled in formal schooling and the number employed. These demographic accounts are based on annual population data from the U.S. Bureau of the Census.[4]

Table 7.1 presents our estimates of the numbers of students between five and thirty-four years of age enrolled in school, cross-classified by sex and level of education.[5] Enrollments in grades 1–8 and high school peaked during the 1970s and gradually drifted downward through 1984, the last year for which data are available. College enrollments flattened in the 1980s for both men and women. Enrollments in primary schools

TABLE 7.1
U.S. School Enrollment by Sex and Level, 1948–1984
(thousands)

		Male			Female		
Year	Total	Grades 1–8	High School	College	Grades 1–8	High School	College
1948	28876	10120	3570	1694	9387	3341	764
1949	29581	10485	3555	1719	9731	3324	767
1950	30318	10840	3562	1741	10069	3333	773
1951	30980	11120	3623	1702	10352	3403	780
1952	31721	11407	3712	1669	10639	3503	791
1953	33011	11954	3810	1648	11177	3611	811
1954	34433	12545	3922	1644	11751	3731	840
1955	35791	13072	4055	1655	12259	3873	877
1956	37166	13551	4232	1685	12718	4055	925
1957	38577	13954	4493	1730	13097	4324	979
1958	40028	14368	4756	1788	13497	4579	1040
1959	41492	14819	4969	1870	13950	4771	1113
1960	43198	15382	5157	1999	14497	4943	1220
1961	44643	15683	5442	2164	14767	5238	1349
1962	46121	15929	5797	2335	15002	5588	1470
1963	47645	16203	6154	2498	15283	5927	1580
1964	49140	16496	6475	2668	15580	6229	1692
1965	50432	16759	6636	2950	15838	6347	1902
1966	51665	16991	6756	3271	16072	6458	2117
1967	52894	17206	6901	3582	16276	6607	2322
1968	54068	17358	7080	3899	16417	6788	2526
1969	55102	17421	7268	4218	16511	6966	2718
1970	55907	17392	7434	4567	16450	7130	2934
1971	56447	17282	7616	4764	16352	7300	3133
1972	56717	17048	7783	4957	16129	7451	3349
1973	56736	16739	7908	5129	15833	7562	3565
1974	56554	16389	7989	5273	15503	7638	3762
1975	56301	16037	8037	5401	15171	7679	3976
1976	55996	15723	8048	5499	14878	7677	4171
1977	55680	15476	8017	5562	14647	7635	4343
1978	55200	15202	7968	5577	14381	7565	4507
1979	54437	14863	7843	5563	14062	7427	4679
1980	53552	14560	7644	5511	13775	7214	4848
1981	52775	14362	7406	5565	13577	6982	4883
1982	51989	14207	7157	5577	13422	6743	4883
1983	51323	14075	6967	5565	13286	6568	4862
1984	50831	13947	6896	5519	13151	6512	4806

increased over the period 1948–1984 as a whole, while secondary school enrollments nearly doubled. Enrollments in higher education have increased very dramatically, especially for women.

To measure lifetime labor incomes for all individuals in the U.S. population, we began with a data base on market activities constructed by Frank Gollop.[6] Estimates of hours worked and labor compensation were derived for each sex by 61 age groups and 18 education groups, for a total of 2,196 groups for each year. Table 7.2 presents our estimates of the value of time spent working, cross-classified by sex and educational attainment, for all individuals in the U.S. economy from 1948 to 1984. In this and subsequent tables, estimates of the value of labor time are given in current prices in order to ensure comparability within each year for the values of market labor activities presented in Table 7.2 and for the values of nonmarket labor activities and investment in education given in the following discussion. It is important to bear in mind that comparisons across years involve differences in rates of labor compensation as well as differences in the amounts of labor time.

The current dollar value of market labor activities has increased fourteenfold over the postwar period. The proportional increases have been greatest for college-educated workers—more than thirty times for men and fifty times for women. The proportional increase for women exceeds that for men for all levels of educational attainment. For the population as a whole, the growth of labor compensation is due to a rise in employment and to very substantial increases in rates of labor compensation per hour worked. The contrasting trends for men and women are due to a modest rise in employment for men and a much greater increase in employment for women. Hours worked per employed person have declined for both sexes.

We turn next to the task of evaluating labor time spent in nonmarket activities, considering activities, such as formal schooling, that enter into investment in human capital and activities that result in consumption. The importance of evaluating time spent in nonmarket activities is widely recognized.[7] For example, William Nordhaus and James Tobin have incorporated measures of the value of these activities into their measure of economic welfare.[8] John Kendrick and Robert Eisner have also imputed values for time spent outside the labor market.[9] Five types of nonmarket activities are commonly distinguished in studies of time allocation: household work, human capital investment, travel, leisure, and maintenance (the satisfaction of physical needs such as eating and sleeping).[10]

The total time available for all individuals in the population was allocated among maintenance, work, school, and household production and leisure. Studies of time allocation show that maintenance time per capita has changed very little during the postwar period. We estimated that time spent in maintenance is ten hours per day per person and excluded this time from our measure of the value of nonmarket activ-

TABLE 7.2
Value of Market Activities by Sex and Educational Attainment, 1948–1984
(billions of current dollars)

		Male			Female		
Year	Total	Grades 1–8	High School	College	Grades 1–8	High School	College
1948	151.4	45.3	52.9	25.5	7.3	14.5	6.0
1949	155.2	45.5	54.1	26.6	7.5	15.0	6.4
1950	168.9	49.0	57.7	29.8	8.0	16.4	7.8
1951	191.7	54.7	66.9	34.4	9.1	18.5	8.0
1952	205.4	55.5	72.2	39.1	9.3	20.3	8.9
1953	220.0	56.8	78.1	44.0	9.7	21.8	9.5
1954	224.7	55.6	80.3	46.3	9.6	22.8	10.2
1955	233.9	54.3	84.5	49.3	10.1	24.6	11.1
1956	249.2	56.1	90.4	53.1	10.7	26.9	12.0
1957	266.2	57.5	96.9	58.7	11.0	28.9	13.2
1958	276.5	57.4	100.7	62.8	11.1	30.2	14.3
1959	289.1	55.6	106.4	67.9	11.6	32.2	15.4
1960	302.7	58.8	112.1	74.7	10.8	29.5	16.7
1961	315.3	55.2	115.3	79.8	11.5	34.6	18.9
1962	333.8	53.6	123.9	87.0	11.1	37.3	21.0
1963	346.7	54.2	129.6	90.3	11.5	40.0	21.1
1964	373.3	53.5	141.4	99.4	11.6	44.2	23.2
1965	398.1	55.5	152.1	105.1	11.8	48.5	25.1
1966	440.1	59.1	168.8	116.4	12.4	54.8	28.5
1967	470.5	59.9	177.0	130.6	12.6	59.0	31.4
1968	514.9	60.9	193.9	144.9	13.1	66.0	36.1
1969	561.4	63.5	210.7	158.7	13.7	74.8	40.0
1970	613.4	69.7	229.9	177.9	14.3	76.4	45.4
1971	664.5	65.6	245.8	200.4	13.9	86.5	52.4
1972	719.9	67.1	266.6	218.6	13.7	96.3	57.6
1973	820.1	72.7	303.0	252.7	14.6	109.6	67.6
1974	893.1	72.6	322.2	285.8	14.4	118.6	79.6
1975	959.7	64.4	334.1	327.2	14.1	128.4	91.4
1976	1057.6	68.6	365.6	361.6	15.0	142.4	104.4
1977	1162.6	70.6	395.4	402.7	15.1	160.1	118.8
1978	1312.8	81.4	448.0	457.1	16.5	175.3	134.5
1979	1466.5	81.5	483.3	520.2	17.6	197.6	166.4
1980	1593.9	73.8	495.1	563.2	19.0	230.5	212.3
1981	1733.5	74.2	531.9	616.5	19.1	252.2	239.6
1982	1812.4	69.1	543.1	653.8	18.7	260.9	266.8
1983	1937.9	67.8	565.7	713.2	18.2	273.2	299.9
1984	2126.3	72.0	624.7	777.5	21.9	298.4	331.8

ities. We estimated the time spent in formal education for all individuals enrolled in school and allocated this time to investment. Finally, we allocated the time not spent on maintenance, work, or school to consumption. We imputed rates of labor compensation for nonmarket activities from wage rates for employed individuals with the same age, sex, and educational attainment. Market wage rates were reduced by taxes on labor incomes estimated by Kun-Young Yun.[11]

Table 7.3 gives the value of nonmarket activities, cross-classified by sex and educational attainment, for all individuals in the U.S. population for the period 1948–1984. The value of nonmarket activities exceeds the value of market activities by a factor of two. This is due to the fact that nonmarket time, as we measure it, is greater than time spent at work. For the population as a whole, the growth of the value of nonmarket time is roughly comparable to the growth of the value of work time; but the distribution of this growth is considerably different. Because each individual has a fixed time budget of fourteen hours per day to be allocated between market and nonmarket activities, the general pattern for nonmarket time is a mirror image of that for work time. For both men and women, the value of nonmarket time has grown considerably more slowly than the value of time spent working.

With increased rates of labor force participation for women, the value of work time has grown more rapidly for women than for men. Given fixed time budgets for both men and women, the value of nonmarket time has increased faster for men. For example, the value of nonmarket time for college-educated men has increased by thirty-four times, while the value for college-educated women has grown by a factor of only twenty-five. The relative increase in the value of nonmarket time is greater for individuals of both sexes with higher education than for individuals with only secondary education. This increase is greater for individuals with secondary education than for those with only primary education. These trends reflect increases in the levels of educational attainment for both men and women.

The final step in measuring lifetime labor incomes for all individuals in the U.S. population was to project incomes for future years and discount these incomes back to the present, weighting income for each individual by the probability of survival.[12] We obtained these probabilities by sex from life tables published by the National Center for Health Statistics.[13] We combined estimates of lifetime labor incomes by sex, age, and educational attainment with demographic accounts for the numbers of individuals to obtain estimates of human capital, investment in this capital, and the flow of human capital services. The value of the services of human capital is, of course, equal to the sum of the values of market and nonmarket time presented in Tables 7.2 and 7.3.

TABLE 7.3
Value of Nonmarket Activities by Sex and Educational Attainment, 1948–1984
(billions of current dollars)

		Male			Female		
Year	Total	Grades 1–8	High School	College	Grades 1–8	High School	College
1948	339.9	75.8	69.8	33.8	59.0	74.6	26.8
1949	369.9	81.1	79.0	38.1	60.9	81.2	29.6
1950	390.4	80.3	84.7	41.7	63.7	87.5	32.5
1951	404.9	84.7	89.7	46.1	62.3	88.1	33.9
1952	420.3	85.3	93.8	50.1	63.4	91.8	36.0
1953	462.6	91.1	105.1	58.2	67.1	101.0	40.1
1954	499.3	96.6	114.6	64.3	69.7	109.4	44.6
1955	505.6	92.9	117.7	68.8	67.5	112.2	46.5
1956	532.5	97.1	125.5	73.8	68.4	118.0	49.6
1957	579.3	105.9	138.2	83.1	71.4	126.9	53.9
1958	633.3	117.9	153.8	92.2	74.6	136.1	58.7
1959	640.0	110.3	157.0	96.5	72.9	141.8	61.5
1960	665.3	111.8	164.7	98.6	73.9	151.7	64.6
1961	716.8	121.7	180.9	108.0	77.7	159.9	68.5
1962	746.5	122.8	189.1	115.7	78.5	167.6	72.9
1963	766.6	120.4	195.1	122.3	77.2	173.5	78.2
1964	841.5	125.5	215.7	138.9	81.7	191.9	87.8
1965	909.0	131.5	233.9	151.9	85.9	209.6	96.1
1966	985.7	137.1	255.6	168.3	89.7	227.5	107.4
1967	1055.7	141.2	276.3	182.9	91.4	245.9	117.9
1968	1119.1	140.1	297.1	198.8	93.2	263.2	126.7
1969	1194.7	144.0	320.0	214.7	95.9	281.7	138.4
1970	1346.5	151.7	359.6	246.2	101.2	324.8	162.9
1971	1521.9	169.6	406.8	290.4	109.9	358.3	186.9
1972	1621.9	177.7	431.9	315.9	112.8	378.6	204.9
1973	1791.2	200.5	476.3	350.3	122.7	413.5	228.0
1974	1968.1	201.5	522.3	407.5	126.6	454.7	255.4
1975	2182.2	205.5	576.5	474.9	131.2	501.3	292.8
1976	2364.5	221.6	627.3	517.4	137.6	538.8	321.7
1977	2520.3	221.0	665.4	569.6	139.7	571.6	353.0
1978	2812.2	256.1	753.4	647.4	147.6	624.5	383.1
1979	3184.8	268.2	837.2	758.9	166.8	697.8	455.9
1980	3289.7	236.6	855.0	821.1	164.9	717.9	494.2
1981	3561.0	256.4	928.4	891.7	177.8	773.9	532.8
1982	3944.5	283.4	1036.4	985.4	196.4	859.4	583.6
1983	4274.7	311.1	1128.6	1063.2	214.4	932.7	624.7
1984	4590.9	337.6	1204.7	1149.2	230.9	999.3	669.2

INVESTMENT IN EDUCATION

To estimate investment in education, we used data on lifetime labor incomes, cross-classified by sex, age, and single grade of highest educational attainment. We used the increments in lifetime labor incomes and the estimates of the number of individuals enrolled in school presented in Table 7.1 to measure the value of investment in education.[14] This is the point at which our approach to measuring investment in education incorporates the crucial time dimension of the educational process. Lifetime incomes reflect the impact of educational attainment on the values of future market and nonmarket labor activities over the entire lifetime of an educated individual. These values were discounted back to the present in order to reflect the time value of money, because future incomes are obviously worth less in the present than are current incomes.

The gestation periods between educational outlays and the final emergence of human capital embodied in the graduates of educational institutions are very lengthy: eight years for individuals completing primary education, twelve years for secondary education graduates, and sixteen or more years for graduates of higher education. These long gestation periods imply that educational investment must reflect the increase in the value of previous investments in education because of the time value of money as well as the current outlays of educational institutions. In measuring investment in education, we focus on increments in lifetime labor incomes due to increases in educational attainment. These increments incorporate the time value of money for investments in education in earlier time periods. Of course, increments in lifetime labor incomes, as we define them, incorporate the effects of enhanced earning power on the values of both work time and nonmarket time.

Table 7.4 presents our estimates of the value of educational investment. The most remarkable finding is that these values are comparable in magnitude to the values of time spent at work presented in Table 7.2. The value of investment in education, as we measured it, accrues in the form of increments to the lifetime incomes of individuals enrolled in school. This value is similar in amount to the value of the time spent at work by the whole labor force. The growth in the value of educational investment, however, is almost eighteen times the initial level, whereas the increase in the value of work is only fourteen times the initial level. This reflects the rising educational investment associated with increases in levels of educational attainment.

The growth of investment in education is greater in relative terms for women than for men. While the value of market activities for college-educated women has increased by a factor of fifty-five, the value of investment in higher education for women has grown by more than twice as much. The corresponding growth in the value of market activities for college-educated men is thirty times the initial level, while

TABLE 7.4
Investment in Formal Education by Sex and Level of Enrollment, 1948–1984
(billions of current dollars)

		Male			Female		
Year	Total	Grades 1–8	High School	College	Grades 1–8	High School	College
1948	184.5	52.7	49.1	29.5	16.9	29.4	6.8
1949	195.7	56.6	51.0	30.5	18.4	31.6	7.6
1950	209.0	61.7	52.8	35.4	17.5	32.1	9.5
1951	218.9	63.3	55.8	38.6	18.0	32.7	10.4
1952	239.3	68.6	62.2	43.3	18.5	35.0	11.7
1953	275.0	79.7	72.5	48.5	21.8	39.3	13.3
1954	295.5	84.4	75.4	51.7	24.2	43.4	16.4
1955	325.5	93.9	82.7	56.0	27.4	47.2	18.4
1956	339.7	95.1	86.5	58.6	27.9	50.5	21.2
1957	371.0	99.0	96.8	67.6	27.6	55.5	24.6
1958	391.2	97.0	104.8	73.7	25.5	61.1	29.1
1959	440.1	111.1	117.5	81.2	29.6	67.6	33.0
1960	455.0	110.5	118.6	87.4	29.6	70.9	37.9
1961	487.0	115.5	133.0	95.1	29.1	73.0	41.4
1962	531.8	121.5	148.0	106.0	31.1	78.5	46.8
1963	564.6	122.9	156.1	113.7	32.3	87.1	52.4
1964	650.6	137.5	181.4	132.7	36.2	101.9	60.8
1965	679.3	139.3	185.8	144.0	36.6	107.3	66.3
1966	742.8	149.0	199.3	163.4	38.5	113.4	79.2
1967	807.3	145.3	205.4	200.1	40.3	122.2	94.1
1968	914.8	165.5	230.8	230.5	45.5	133.3	109.2
1969	980.1	167.2	241.8	257.5	47.6	142.7	123.2
1970	1106.5	173.4	252.3	316.5	50.5	159.4	154.4
1971	1270.9	191.5	296.3	363.8	59.9	183.2	176.2
1972	1325.1	193.5	304.8	375.7	63.0	194.9	193.0
1973	1359.0	178.0	321.6	388.9	55.5	201.8	213.2
1974	1587.3	213.0	365.2	467.2	71.4	233.4	237.1
1975	1894.5	258.4	424.1	576.0	89.4	271.0	275.6
1976	1897.8	242.0	432.9	569.9	81.0	272.9	299.1
1977	2052.1	266.1	459.6	613.3	90.5	295.3	327.2
1978	1928.9	245.5	425.3	600.0	82.7	262.3	313.0
1979	2210.1	259.4	463.3	698.0	84.0	281.7	423.7
1980	2611.3	328.5	541.1	776.3	94.0	305.6	565.6
1981	2815.4	342.9	578.6	850.2	97.5	325.7	620.4
1982	2970.2	357.2	609.7	910.7	100.6	317.2	674.9
1983	3148.8	376.8	629.4	981.9	105.7	327.0	728.0
1984	3318.9	390.1	664.6	1042.7	107.5	334.8	779.1

investment in higher education for men has increased by a factor of thirty-five. The massive rise in investment in education for women is associated with the costs of substantially higher levels of educational attainment, which have preceded the entry of more highly educated women into the labor force.

Table 7.5 presents investment in education per student enrolled, which makes it possible to separate trends in the number of students from trends in per capita levels of educational investment. The value of educational investment per student is far greater than per capita income from market activities. This difference reflects the fact that the value of investment in education includes the impact of formal schooling on the value of nonmarket as well as market activities. At all levels of education, the value of investment in education for men exceeds that for women, which reflects differences in labor compensation between the two sexes. The value of investment per student in higher education considerably exceeds that for secondary education, which in turn exceeds the value of investment per student in primary education.

To bring out the importance of nonmarket activities in our estimates of lifetime labor incomes, we reestimated the value of investment in education by eliminating the value of these activities. For this purpose, we redefined lifetime labor incomes to include only the value of time spent at work (presented in Table 7.2), thereby excluding the value of nonmarket time (given in Table 7.3). We then reestimated the value of increments to lifetime labor incomes from higher levels of educational attainment by excluding the value of nonmarket time. We expressed this more limited concept of the benefits of education as a percentage of the full measure of educational investment given in Table 7.5.

In Table 7.6 we give the ratio of investment in education based only on time spent at work to the estimates of investment in education presented in Table 7.5 in percentage form. As shown in Table 7.6, the value of work time accounted for substantially less than one-half of the value of investment in education at the beginning of the period 1948–1984, but a rising trend over the period lifted this proportion to more than one-half. This reflects the growing importance of time spent at work over this period, as indicated in Tables 7.2 and 7.3. The exclusion of nonmarket time leads to a very substantial downward bias in estimates of the value of investment in education for women relative to that for men at the beginning of the period 1948–1984.[15]

Human wealth is the sum of lifetime labor incomes for all individuals in the U.S. population. Table 7.7 presents estimates of human wealth by sex and level of educational attainment. We obtained these estimates by multiplying lifetime labor incomes by numbers of individuals in the population, both cross-classified by sex, age, and education. We obtained the totals by sex and education by summing over age groups. The value of human wealth reflects the value of market and nonmarket activities given in Table 7.2 and 7.3. Nevertheless, the estimates of human wealth

TABLE 7.5
Investment Per Student by Sex and Level of Enrollment, 1948–1984
(thousands of current dollars)

		Male			Female		
Year	Total	Grades 1–8	High School	College	Grades 1–8	High School	College
1948	6.4	5.2	13.8	17.4	1.8	8.8	8.9
1949	6.6	5.4	14.3	17.7	1.9	9.5	9.9
1950	6.9	5.7	14.8	20.3	1.7	9.6	12.3
1951	7.1	5.7	15.4	22.7	1.7	9.6	13.3
1952	7.5	6.0	16.8	25.9	1.7	10.0	14.8
1953	8.3	6.7	19.0	29.4	2.0	10.9	16.4
1954	8.6	6.7	19.2	31.4	2.1	11.6	19.5
1955	9.1	7.2	20.4	33.8	2.2	12.2	21.0
1956	9.1	7.0	20.4	34.8	2.2	12.5	22.9
1957	9.6	7.1	21.5	39.1	2.1	12.8	25.1
1958	9.8	6.8	22.0	41.2	1.9	13.3	28.0
1959	10.6	7.5	23.6	43.4	2.1	14.2	29.6
1960	10.5	7.2	23.0	43.7	2.0	14.3	31.1
1961	10.9	7.4	24.4	43.9	2.0	13.9	30.7
1962	11.5	7.6	25.5	45.4	2.1	14.0	31.8
1963	11.9	7.6	25.4	45.5	2.1	14.7	33.2
1964	13.2	8.3	28.0	49.7	2.3	16.4	35.9
1965	13.5	8.3	28.0	48.8	2.3	16.9	34.9
1966	14.4	8.8	29.5	50.0	2.4	17.6	37.4
1967	15.3	8.4	29.8	55.9	2.5	18.5	40.5
1968	16.9	9.5	32.6	59.1	2.8	19.6	43.2
1969	17.8	9.6	33.3	61.0	2.9	20.5	45.3
1970	19.8	10.0	33.9	69.3	3.1	22.4	52.6
1971	22.5	11.1	38.9	76.4	3.7	25.1	56.2
1972	23.4	11.4	39.2	75.8	3.9	26.2	57.6
1973	24.0	10.6	40.7	75.8	3.5	26.7	59.8
1974	28.1	13.0	45.7	88.6	4.6	30.6	63.0
1975	33.6	16.1	52.8	106.7	5.9	35.3	69.3
1976	33.9	15.4	53.8	103.6	5.4	35.5	71.7
1977	36.9	17.2	57.3	110.3	6.2	38.7	75.3
1978	34.9	16.1	53.4	107.6	5.8	34.7	69.4
1979	40.6	17.5	59.1	125.5	6.0	37.9	90.6
1980	48.8	22.6	70.8	140.9	6.8	42.4	116.7
1981	53.3	23.9	78.1	152.8	7.2	46.7	127.1
1982	57.1	25.1	85.2	163.3	7.5	47.0	138.2
1983	61.4	26.8	90.3	176.4	8.0	49.8	149.7
1984	65.3	28.0	96.4	188.9	8.2	51.4	162.1

TABLE 7.6
Percentage of Investment Based on Market Activities to
Total Educational Investment, 1948–1984

		Male			Female		
Year	Total	Grades 1–8	High School	College	Grades 1–8	High School	College
1948	40.6	48.1	53.6	38.5	22.2	28.4	23.6
1949	37.9	42.6	50.3	37.9	15.8	25.3	25.3
1950	37.7	38.6	43.2	44.3	23.5	26.0	30.9
1951	39.4	42.1	48.7	41.4	17.6	28.1	23.3
1952	41.3	43.3	50.6	42.9	23.5	31.0	23.6
1953	39.8	43.3	47.9	42.5	20.0	30.3	22.0
1954	39.5	41.8	50.0	41.1	19.0	30.2	21.5
1955	38.5	41.7	49.5	39.3	18.2	30.3	21.9
1956	39.6	44.3	51.0	39.1	22.7	32.0	21.4
1957	40.6	43.7	52.1	38.6	23.8	33.6	22.3
1958	40.8	42.6	54.1	38.6	21.1	32.3	23.2
1959	40.6	42.7	53.8	39.2	19.0	32.4	23.6
1960	40.0	47.2	48.3	43.9	25.0	23.1	29.3
1961	42.2	44.6	54.5	43.7	25.0	30.2	29.6
1962	45.2	46.1	59.6	42.1	28.6	33.6	31.4
1963	44.5	48.7	59.8	41.3	28.6	32.0	27.7
1964	45.5	49.4	62.5	39.4	26.1	34.1	27.3
1965	45.2	48.2	64.3	36.7	30.4	36.7	25.8
1966	45.1	51.1	63.4	36.2	37.5	38.1	23.8
1967	45.1	48.8	62.4	40.6	32.0	37.3	25.2
1968	45.6	48.4	61.7	42.0	32.1	39.3	28.0
1969	45.5	43.7	61.6	42.5	37.9	43.4	26.5
1970	42.4	52.0	49.6	45.0	38.7	30.8	28.3
1971	43.6	39.6	65.3	39.7	29.7	40.2	26.2
1972	44.9	43.9	66.8	39.3	38.5	43.9	25.0
1973	48.3	48.1	74.2	40.1	48.6	47.6	25.6
1974	46.3	43.1	70.7	38.7	39.1	46.7	29.0
1975	46.7	43.5	72.2	39.3	33.9	45.9	29.6
1976	48.1	46.8	72.9	41.3	42.6	45.9	30.0
1977	49.3	52.9	71.0	42.1	50.0	48.8	29.6
1978	51.9	55.3	76.6	42.8	50.0	51.9	32.7
1979	49.3	45.1	73.3	41.7	53.3	54.1	33.8
1980	48.0	42.0	64.4	42.4	54.4	57.5	37.5
1981	50.1	43.9	66.7	44.1	55.6	61.5	39.3
1982	50.8	40.6	68.1	45.5	52.0	61.3	42.5
1983	52.8	42.5	70.0	47.1	55.0	64.9	45.4
1984	52.5	42.9	71.9	45.8	51.2	61.7	46.2

TABLE 7.7
Human Wealth by Sex and Educational Attainment, 1948–1984
(billions of current dollars)

		Male			Female		
Year	Total	Grades 1–8	High School	College	Grades 1–8	High School	College
1948	14542	4104	3520	1564	2366	2243	743
1949	15536	4355	3773	1699	2485	2409	812
1950	16512	4502	3983	1855	2689	2578	903
1951	17687	4978	4352	2096	2727	2607	926
1952	18618	5110	4612	2325	2839	2739	989
1953	20372	5441	5102	2665	3056	3012	1093
1954	21574	5742	5347	2849	3233	3203	1197
1955	21904	5650	5474	3013	3236	3283	1245
1956	23209	6084	5763	3189	3417	3435	1318
1957	25417	6692	6301	3602	3685	3698	1437
1958	27737	7408	6869	3947	3963	3980	1566
1959	28174	7136	7082	4142	4000	4170	1641
1960	29603	7582	7422	4377	4143	4346	1731
1961	31551	8019	7873	4712	4475	4608	1862
1962	32971	8153	8268	5089	4584	4861	2014
1963	34056	8304	8554	5339	4659	5057	2140
1964	37187	8739	9410	5990	5025	5614	2407
1965	40171	9429	10114	6446	5425	6111	2642
1966	43886	10129	11120	7194	5783	6671	2987
1967	47137	10717	11833	8031	6046	7183	3325
1968	50331	10924	12832	8900	6241	7765	3367
1969	54184	11578	13846	9754	6563	8390	4051
1970	60722	12662	15471	11195	7117	9491	4782
1971	67478	13589	17241	12993	7598	10522	5533
1972	71999	14404	18471	13970	7877	11212	6063
1973	80686	16263	20721	15753	8692	12382	6872
1974	87523	16463	22580	18173	8888	13596	7819
1975	95046	16280	24517	21188	9064	14946	9049
1976	103214	17769	26613	22983	9725	16091	10031
1977	110041	18043	28350	25349	9920	17227	11149
1978	121597	20951	31494	28062	10902	18326	11861
1979	134457	21894	34136	32128	11815	20245	14236
1980	139442	20043	34744	34686	12068	21484	16415
1981	151185	21309	37516	38163	12866	23262	18067
1982	163916	22644	40254	41527	14052	25383	20054
1983	176481	24103	43007	45180	15058	27250	21880
1984	190755	25940	46207	49197	16263	29317	23828

incorporate not only investment in education but all forms of investment in human capital. These include, for example, investments by the family in childrearing and the value of new individuals added to the population before any rearing or educational investment has taken place.

Table 7.8 provides the average value of human wealth per person for individuals cross-classified by sex and educational attainment. As the table shows, these values have grown steadily throughout the postwar period, and the relative values for men and women have remained fairly constant. The greatest proportional increases for both men and women have been for those with college education. The increase is slightly greater for women than for men. Growth in human wealth for the population as a whole is due to the increase in the population, the rise in average levels of educational attainment, and the growth in rates of labor compensation. Growth in rates of compensation is by far the most important of these components of the increase in human wealth.

These estimates of the value of human wealth are based on measures of lifetime labor incomes that include both market and nonmarket activities. In order to bring out the significance of nonmarket time, it is useful to consider estimates based on market time alone. This required, as before, that we reestimate lifetime incomes for all individuals in the U.S. population. For this purpose we included the value of work time given in Table 7.2 but excluded the value of nonmarket time presented in Table 7.3. In Table 7.9 we present measures of human wealth that do not include the value of nonmarket time as a ratio of the full measures of human wealth given in Table 7.7 in percentage form.

For the population as a whole, the percentage of human wealth based on market labor activities alone is remarkably stable, varying from 29.4 percent in 1950 to 30.6 percent in 1959 and 1960. But this percentage has fallen for men—rapidly for men with only primary education, substantially for men with secondary education, and only modestly for college-educated men. By contrast, the percentage has grown slowly for women with elementary education, more rapidly for women with secondary education, and very rapidly for college-educated women. As with the estimates of investment in education presented in Table 7.6, the omission of nonmarket activities produces a downward bias for women that greatly exceeds the downward bias for men.

SOURCES OF GROWTH

In Table 7.10 we present an analysis of the sources of U.S. economic growth. The output of the U.S. economy at the aggregate level is defined in terms of value added for the domestic economy. The growth of output is decomposed into the contributions of capital and labor inputs and growth in productivity. Our estimate of the contribution of labor input to U.S. economic growth incorporates the information on labor

TABLE 7.8
Human Wealth Per Person by Sex and Educational Attainment, 1948–1984
(thousands of current dollars)

		Male			Female		
Year	Total	Grades 1–8	High School	College	Grades 1–8	High School	College
1948	95.9	87.2	162.8	212.5	54.1	88.9	112.4
1949	100.7	91.8	170.6	222.0	56.2	93.1	118.4
1950	105.4	94.1	175.9	233.3	60.2	97.3	127.0
1951	111.1	103.1	188.4	254.1	60.4	96.2	126.6
1952	115.0	104.7	195.7	272.2	62.1	98.8	131.7
1953	123.8	110.4	212.2	302.2	66.0	106.2	141.9
1954	128.9	115.3	217.7	312.7	69.0	110.3	151.4
1955	128.7	112.2	218.0	320.4	68.2	110.4	153.6
1956	134.0	119.5	224.2	328.5	71.1	112.7	158.5
1957	144.2	130.2	239.2	359.7	75.8	118.1	168.4
1958	154.8	143.1	253.9	382.7	80.8	123.6	179.0
1959	154.8	137.0	254.5	389.8	81.0	125.9	182.9
1960	159.4	144.2	258.4	397.9	83.0	127.0	187.0
1961	167.1	151.7	267.8	409.3	89.0	131.6	192.3
1962	172.0	154.3	273.3	421.9	91.0	134.9	198.7
1963	175.2	157.8	274.4	423.1	92.7	136.2	202.0
1964	188.7	166.8	293.1	454.6	100.3	146.9	217.7
1965	201.3	181.3	306.0	468.9	108.8	155.4	229.2
1966	217.4	196.7	327.7	498.5	116.9	165.3	246.8
1967	231.0	210.6	340.0	529.4	123.4	173.3	261.4
1968	244.3	217.9	359.3	559.5	129.1	182.3	275.1
1969	260.4	234.6	377.5	586.2	137.5	191.7	290.6
1970	288.9	260.8	410.5	643.2	151.4	211.0	327.9
1971	317.7	283.1	449.5	710.3	163.2	229.8	359.4
1972	336.1	305.0	473.1	727.0	171.7	240.3	373.4
1973	373.9	351.3	521.6	781.2	193.0	260.8	401.9
1974	402.7	363.3	558.9	859.0	201.4	281.4	434.4
1975	434.0	366.8	597.1	954.9	209.4	304.2	477.8
1976	467.8	409.3	638.3	988.0	229.4	322.3	503.4
1977	494.8	424.5	670.2	1039.8	238.7	339.8	532.7
1978	542.3	503.2	734.5	1099.3	267.4	356.2	539.7
1979	594.6	536.3	786.4	1203.2	295.3	388.3	617.8
1980	611.3	499.5	792.3	1243.3	306.5	407.5	680.2
1981	656.1	529.1	847.4	1340.3	325.4	436.7	734.7
1982	704.1	558.8	901.8	1431.3	352.8	472.2	800.8
1983	750.8	590.7	956.8	1529.8	375.2	502.9	859.4
1984	803.9	631.4	1020.6	1638.6	402.4	536.6	922.3

TABLE 7.9
Percentage of Human Wealth Based on Market Activities to Total Human Wealth by Sex and Educational Attainment, 1948–1984

		Male			Female		
Year	Total	Grades 1–8	High School	College	Grades 1–8	High School	College
1948	29.9	35.8	43.0	42.7	10.6	14.4	16.7
1949	29.5	35.2	41.7	41.7	10.6	14.3	16.6
1950	29.4	36.0	41.1	41.5	10.7	14.3	17.2
1951	29.7	36.7	41.5	41.8	11.2	14.7	17.3
1952	29.9	37.1	41.9	42.2	11.6	15.2	17.7
1953	30.2	37.2	42.0	42.3	11.8	15.4	17.7
1954	30.3	36.9	41.9	42.2	11.8	15.5	17.7
1955	30.4	36.9	41.9	42.0	12.0	15.8	17.9
1956	30.5	36.8	41.9	42.0	12.2	16.1	18.0
1957	30.5	36.5	41.8	41.8	12.4	16.3	18.1
1958	30.5	36.0	41.5	41.5	12.4	16.4	18.2
1959	30.6	35.8	41.3	41.3	12.6	16.6	18.4
1960	30.6	35.7	41.2	41.4	12.6	16.6	18.5
1961	30.5	35.3	41.0	41.5	12.6	16.7	18.8
1962	30.5	34.8	40.9	41.5	12.6	16.8	19.1
1963	30.5	34.5	40.8	41.5	12.7	17.0	19.3
1964	30.5	34.1	40.7	41.5	12.7	17.1	19.4
1965	30.4	33.7	40.6	41.4	12.7	17.2	19.5
1966	30.4	33.4	40.5	41.3	12.6	17.4	19.6
1967	30.4	33.2	40.4	41.3	12.6	17.5	19.7
1968	30.3	33.1	40.4	41.4	12.7	17.6	19.8
1969	30.3	33.1	40.4	41.6	12.7	17.9	20.0
1970	30.3	33.1	40.4	41.6	12.8	18.0	20.1
1971	30.3	32.9	40.2	41.5	12.7	18.0	20.2
1972	30.3	32.7	40.1	41.4	12.6	18.2	20.2
1973	30.3	32.5	40.0	41.3	12.6	18.3	20.3
1974	30.3	32.3	39.8	41.2	12.5	18.5	20.4
1975	30.3	31.9	39.6	40.9	12.4	18.6	20.5
1976	30.3	31.5	39.4	40.8	12.3	18.7	20.7
1977	30.2	31.1	39.2	40.7	12.2	18.9	20.9
1978	30.2	30.9	39.1	40.6	12.2	19.0	21.1
1979	30.2	30.7	38.9	40.4	12.2	19.2	21.4
1980	30.2	30.5	38.7	40.3	12.2	19.5	22.1
1981	30.2	30.3	38.5	40.3	12.2	19.8	22.8
1982	30.2	29.9	38.2	40.2	12.1	20.1	23.5
1983	30.2	29.4	37.8	40.1	11.9	20.2	24.2
1984	30.1	28.8	37.5	40.0	11.8	20.4	24.9

TABLE 7.10
Aggregate Output, Inputs, and Productivity: Rates of Growth, 1947–1985

Variable	1947–1985	1947–1953	1953–1957	1957–1960	1960–1966	1966–1969	1969–1973	1973–1979	1979–1985
Value-Added	0.0328	0.0529	0.0214	0.0238	0.0472	0.0360	0.0306	0.0212	0.0222
Capital Input	0.0388	0.0554	0.0401	0.0229	0.0367	0.0437	0.0421	0.0392	0.0262
Labor Input	0.0181	0.0251	0.0037	0.0124	0.0248	0.0226	0.0128	0.0219	0.0146
Contribution of Capital Input	0.0145	0.0215	0.0149	0.0083	0.0142	0.0167	0.0149	0.0140	0.0098
Contribution of Labor Input	0.0112	0.0153	0.0022	0.0077	0.0151	0.0140	0.0082	0.0139	0.0089
Rate of Productivity Growth	0.0071	0.0160	0.0043	0.0078	0.0179	0.0053	0.0074	-.0067	0.0034
Contribution of Capital Quality	0.0058	0.0126	0.0069	0.0016	0.0053	0.0058	0.0054	0.0045	0.0022
Contribution of Capital Stock	0.0088	0.0090	0.0080	0.0067	0.0089	0.0108	0.0095	0.0095	0.0077
Contribution of Labor Quality	0.0039	0.0060	0.0038	0.0084	0.0041	0.0030	0.0018	0.0024	0.0026
Contribution of Hours Worked	0.0073	0.0093	-.0016	-.0007	0.0110	0.0110	0.0065	0.0114	0.0063

market activities presented in section two. Growth rates for the period 1947–1985 are given for output and the two inputs in the first column of Table 7.10. Value added grows at the rate of 3.28 percent per year, while capital grows at 3.88 percent, and labor input grows at 1.81 percent.[16]

We obtained the contributions of capital and labor inputs to the growth of output by weighting the growth rates of these inputs by their shares in value added. This calculation produced the familiar allocation of growth to its sources. Capital input is the most important source of U.S. economic growth by a substantial margin, accounting for 44.2 percent of growth during the period; labor input accounts for 34.1 percent of growth; and productivity growth accounts for only 21.6 percent of U.S. economic growth during the period.

The findings summarized in Table 7.10 are not limited to the period as a whole. In the first three rows of the table, the growth of output is compared with the contributions of capital and labor inputs and productivity growth for eight subperiods: 1947–1953, 1953–1957, 1957–1960, 1960–1966, 1966–1969, 1969–1973, 1973–1979, and 1979–1985. The end points of the periods identified in the table, except for the last period, are years in which a cyclical peak occurred. The growth rate presented for each subperiod is the average annual growth rate between cyclical peaks. The contributions of capital and labor inputs are the predominant sources of U.S. economic growth for the period as a whole and for all eight subperiods.

The contribution of capital input is the most significant source of output growth for the period 1947–1985 as a whole. It is also the most important source of growth for seven of the eight subperiods; productivity growth is the most important source for the subperiod 1960–1966. The contribution of capital input exceeds the contribution of productivity growth for seven of the eight subperiods; the contribution of labor input exceeds that of productivity growth in the last four of the eight subperiods.

In 1985 the output of the U.S. economy stood at more than three times the level of output in 1947. Our overall conclusion is that the driving force behind the expansion of the U.S. economy between 1947 and 1985 was the growth in capital and labor inputs. Growth in capital input is the most important source of growth in output, growth in labor input is the next most important source, and productivity growth is least important. This perspective focuses attention on the mobilization of capital and labor resources rather than on advances in productivity.

These findings are consistent with a substantial body of research. For example, these findings coincide with early findings by Laurits Christensen for the United States for the period 1929–1969;[17] and Angus Maddison gave similar results for six industrialized countries, including the United States, for the period 1913–1984.[18] But these findings contrast sharply with those in individual studies by Moses Abramovitz, John Kendrick, and Robert Solow, all three of which emphasized productivity as the predominant growth source.[19] At this point it is useful to describe the steps required to go from these earlier findings to the results summarized in Table 7.10.

The first step is to decompose the contributions of capital and labor inputs into the separate contributions of capital and labor quality and the contributions of capital stock and hours worked. Capital stock and hours worked are a natural focus for input measurement because capital input would be proportional to capital stock if capital inputs were homogeneous, whereas labor input would be proportional to hours worked if labor inputs were homogeneous. In fact, capital and labor inputs are enormously heterogeneous, so that measurement of these inputs requires detailed data on the components of each input. The growth rate of each input is a weighted average of the growth rates of its components. Weights are given by the shares of the components in the value of the input.

The development of measures of labor input reflecting heterogeneity is one of the many pathbreaking contributions by Edward Denison to the analysis of sources of economic growth.[20] Table 7.10 is based on the results we obtained in a previous study with Frank Gollop in which we disaggregated labor input among 1,600 categories at the aggregate level, cross-classified by age, sex, education, class of employment, and occupation.[21] These data on labor input incorporated all the annual detail on employment, weeks, hours worked, and labor compensation published in the decennial *Census of Population* and the *Current Population Survey.*

Our measures of capital input involve weighting of components of capital input by rental prices. Assets are cross-classified by age of the asset, class of asset, and legal form of organization. Different ages are weighted in accord with profiles of relative efficiency constructed by Charles Hulten and Frank Wykoff.[22] An average of 3,535 components of capital input are distinguished at the aggregate level.[23] Similarly, the data on capital input have incorporated all the available detail on investment in capital goods by class of asset and on property compensation by legal form of organization from the U.S. national income and product accounts (NIPAs).[24]

The growth rates of capital and labor quality are defined as the differences between growth rates of input measures that take account of heterogeneity and measures that ignore heterogeneity. Increases in capital quality reflect the substitution of more highly productive capital goods for those that are less productive. This substitution process requires investment in tangible assets or nonhuman capital. Similarly, growth in labor quality results from the substitution of more effective for less effective workers. This process of substitution requires the massive investments in human capital documented in section three.

In the Abramovitz-Kendrick-Solow approach, the contributions of growth in capital and labor quality are ignored because inputs are treated as homogeneous. The omission of growth in labor quality destroys the link between investment in human capital and economic growth; the omission of growth in capital quality leads to the drastic underestimation of the impact of investment in nonhuman capital on economic growth. The results presented in Table 7.10 reveal that the assumption of homogeneous capital and labor inputs is highly misleading.

We find that growth in the quality of capital stock accounts for two-fifths of the growth of capital input during the period 1947–1985. This quantitative relationship also characterizes the eight subperiods. For the period as a whole, we find that the growth of hours worked exceeds the growth of labor quality. But the growth in hours worked is actually less than the growth in the quality of hours worked for the period 1953–1960. For the period 1960–1985, the contribution of hours worked accounts for almost two-thirds of the contribution of labor input. The relative proportions of growth in hours worked and labor quality are far from uniform.

CONCLUSION

Our new estimates of investment in education will help to bring the role of human capital formation in the process of economic growth into proper perspective.[25] Economic growth is measured through increments in the national product, as recorded in the U.S. NIPAs compiled by the Bureau of Economic Analysis of the U.S. Department of Commerce.[26] The accumulation of human and nonhuman capital accounts for the predominant share of economic growth.[27] The revival of U.S. economic growth will require huge investments in both human and nonhuman capital.

Although human and nonhuman capital formation are both important sources of economic growth, the information required to measure investment in human capital is not available in standard sources of economic data such as the U.S. NIPAs. For example, the Bureau of Economic Analysis publishes a great deal of valuable information on investment in physical or nonhuman capital.[28] By contrast the NIPAs provide no data on investment in human capital,[29] primarily because the accounts are limited to economic activities recorded through market transactions. Even though there have been numerous attempts at augmenting the NIPAs to incorporate human capital formation, none measures investment in education as an output of the educational system.[30]

Investment in education, which is a major portion of investment in human capital, is produced almost entirely outside the business sector of the economy.[31] Fortunately, participation in schooling is recorded in enrollment statistics. Furthermore, levels of educational attainment for individuals are routinely collected as part of the census of the population. Transmission of education from schools and universities to their students involves increases in educational attainment that are not evaluated in the marketplace, at least not initially. Nevertheless, the economic value of these increases can be traced through their impact on the lifetime incomes of individuals enrolled in school.

We have emphasized the critical importance of including both market and nonmarket activities in the value of labor incomes for purposes of estimating the value of investment in education. In section A of Table 7.11, we compare our estimates of the value of nonmarket activities and the well-known estimates of Nordhaus and Tobin[32] for three years in which comparable data are available. Their estimates are derived on the basis of rates of labor compensation before taxes, whereas ours employ after-tax wage rates. The use of before-tax wage rates imparts a substantial upward bias to the estimates of Nordhaus and Tobin; nevertheless, the trend in these estimates is nearly identical to that in the estimates presented in greater detail in Table 7.3.

We have pointed out that existing estimates of the value of human wealth are based on the costs of education. Estimates of this type have been constructed by Kendrick for an augmented system of U.S. national accounts.[33] We present a comparison of our estimates with those of Kendrick for the period 1948–1969 in section B of Table 7.11. The ratio of our estimates to Kendrick's varies from 16.66 to 14.64, with a gradually declining trend from 1948 to 1969. We conclude that his cost-based estimates differ from our lifetime labor income-based esti-

TABLE 7.11
Comparison with Other Results

A. Value of Nonmarket Activities for Selected Years
(billions of current dollars)

	Current		
Year	Jorgenson-Fraumeni	Nordhaus-Tobin	Ratio
1954	499.3	637.0	0.784
1958	633.3	794.6	0.797
1965	909.0	1096.9	0.829

B. Private National Human Wealth, 1948–1969
(billions of current dollars)

	Current		
Year	Jorgenson-Fraumeni	Kendrick	Ratio
1948	14542.3	908.8	16.00
1949	15536.7	938.9	16.55
1950	16512.9	991.3	16.66
1951	17687.9	1097.7	16.11
1952	18618.4	1172.6	15.88
1953	20372.5	1236.8	16.47
1954	21574.4	1294.4	16.67
1955	21904.1	1364.2	16.06
1956	23209.8	1462.7	15.87
1957	25417.2	1576.8	16.12
1958	27737.3	1682.6	16.48
1959	28174.9	1786.9	15.77
1960	29603.6	1901.4	15.57
1961	31551.9	2012.8	15.68
1962	32971.7	2137.4	15.43
1963	34056.3	2273.0	14.98
1964	37187.6	2423.9	15.34
1965	40171.4	2594.4	15.48
1966	43886.3	2818.7	15.57
1967	47137.4	3049.7	15.46
1968	50331.7	3344.4	15.05
1969	54184.1	3699.9	14.64

Sources: William D. Nordhaus and James Tobin, *Economic Growth* (New York: National Bureau of Economic Research, 1972); and John W. Kendrick, *The Formation of Stocks of Total Capital* (New York: published for the National Bureau of Economic Research by Columbia University Press, 1976). Reprinted with permission.

mates by more than an order of magnitude.[34] The trends in the two sets of estimates are broadly similar but far from identical.

It is important to note that Kendrick's cost-based estimates of human capital include the accumulated costs of rearing within the family as well as the costs of formal schooling. Our lifetime income-based estimates include all sources of lifetime labor income, including investment in education, the value of rearing—which is partly offset by depreciation of human capital with aging—and the lifetime incomes of individuals added to the population prior to any investment in education or rearing. Nonetheless, the disparities between the two sets of estimates of human capital are very striking. These disparities provide a graphic demonstration of the conceptual differences between the cost-based approach and the income-based approach to the measurement of investment in human capital.

Although cost-based estimates of investment in education reflect the current flow of resources into educational institutions, they do not capture the crucial time dimension of educational investment. There is a lengthy gestation period between the current outlays of educational institutions and the emergence of human capital embodied in their graduates. A very substantial proportion of educational investment is attributable to the time value of money applied to previous investments in the education of individuals who are still enrolled in school. This feature of investment in education is entirely disregarded in estimates limited to current educational outlays.

We conclude that the time scale for measuring human capital formation is given by the life span of an educated individual. The appropriate value of investment in education is given by its impact on the individual's lifetime income. The relevant concept of income must not be limited to market activities alone because many of the benefits of education accrue in the form of enhanced value to nonmarket activities. Our estimates of investment in education incorporate the impact of higher educational attainment on the value of nonmarket activities such as parenting or enjoyment of leisure as well as the effect of increased education on earning power in the labor market.

Our estimates of investment in education are based on very detailed information on the value of working time. We have based our estimates of the value of nonmarket labor time on market wage rates, however. The valuation of nonmarket activities could be refined considerably, especially for individuals not in the labor force. An alternative approach is to infer the value of nonmarket time from labor supply behavior. We have estimated the value of increments in lifetime incomes resulting from increases in educational attainment by comparing the incomes of individuals of the same age and sex with different levels of education. An important further refinement would base estimates of differences on lifetime incomes on the determinants of educational attainment for a given individual. These limitations of our existing estimates suggest opportunities for significant new research on the benefits of education.

Another important source of new research opportunities is the extension of our methods to encompass other forms of investment in human capital. We have already mentioned three extensions of this type. First, fertility behavior is influenced by the lifetime incomes of children added to the population and by the effects of childbearing on the lifetime incomes of parents. Second, investment in childrearing is an important component of investment in human capital and can be measured on the basis of its impact on the lifetime incomes of children. Third, the value of on-the-job training can be appraised by employers and workers in terms of its impact on lifetime labor incomes.[35]

NOTES

1. Rates of return to investment in human capital are discussed in G. S. Becker, *Human Capital,* 2nd ed. (New York: Columbia University Press, 1975); and J. Mincer, *Schooling, Experience, and Earnings* (New York: Columbia University Press, 1974). F. Welch presented estimates of relative rates of return for different age cohorts of the U.S. population in his article "Effect of Cohort Size on Earnings: The Baby Boom Babies' Financial Bust," *Journal of Political Economy* 87 (1979), pp. S65–S98. Estimates of rates of return for higher education are provided in K: Murphy and F. Welch, "Wage Premiums for College Graduates: Recent Growth and Possible Explanations," *Educational Researcher* 18 (1989), pp. 27–34. For surveys of different aspects of the literature, see Z. Griliches, "Estimating the Returns to Schooling: Some Econometric Problems," *Econometrica* 45 (1977), pp. 1–22; and S. Rosen, "Human Capital: A Survey of Empirical Research," in R. G. Ehrenberg, ed., *Research in Labor Economics, Vol. 1* (Greenwich, Conn.: JAI Press, 1977), pp. 3–39. Schultz's early contribution is found in T. W. Schultz, "Investment in Human Capital," *American Economic Review* 51 (1961), pp. 1–17.

2. In this context we use the notion of "output" as the economic value produced within the educational sector. "Outputs" of the educational system can also be defined in terms of measures of educational achievement, such as performance on standardized tests. This definition is the basis for the literature on educational production functions reviewed in E. A. Hanushek, "The Economics of Schooling," *Journal of Economic Literature* 24 (1986), pp. 1141–1178; and E. A. Hanushek, "The Impact of Differential Expenditures on School Performance," *Educational Researcher* 18 (1989), pp. 45–51.

3. Nonmarket benefits of education are discussed in R. H. Haveman and B. L. Wolfe, "Schooling and Economic Well-Being: The Role of Nonmarket Effects," *Journal of Human Resources* 19 (1984), pp. 377–407; and R. T. Michael, "Measuring Non-monetary Benefits of Education: A Survey," in W. W. McMahon and T. G. Geske, eds., *Financing Education: Overcoming Inefficiency and Inequity* (Urbana: University of Illinois Press, 1982), pp. 119–149.

4. See, for example, U.S. Department of Commerce, Bureau of the Census, *Census of Population, 1980* (Washington, D.C.: U.S. Government Printing Office, 1980). We employ a system of demographic accounts for the United States constructed by K. C. Land and M. M. McMillen, "Demographic Accounts and the Study of Social Change, with Applications to Post–World War II United States," in F. T. Juster and K. C. Land, eds., *Social Accounting Systems* (New York: Academic Press, 1981), pp. 242–306. Demographic accounting is also

discussed in R. Stone, "The Relationship of Demographic Accounts to National Income and Product Accounts," in Juster and Land, eds., *Social Accounting Systems,* pp. 307–376.

5. See, for example, U.S. Department of Education, National Center for Education Statistics, *Digest of Education Statistics* (Washington, D.C.: U.S. Department of Education, National Center for Education Statistics, 1988). A compendium of educational statistics is given in D. M. O'Neill and P. Sepielli, *Education in the United States: 1940–1983* (Washington, D.C.: U.S. Government Printing Office, 1985).

6. See F. M. Gollop and D. W. Jorgenson, "U.S. Productivity Growth by Industry, 1947–73," in J. W. Kendrick and B. N. Vaccara, eds., *New Developments in Productivity Measurement and Analysis* (Chicago: University of Chicago Press, 1980), pp. 17–136; and F. M. Gollop and D. W. Jorgenson, "Sectoral Measures of Labor Cost for the United States, 1948–1979," in J. E. Triplett, ed., *The Measurement of Labor Cost* (Chicago: University of Chicago Press, 1983), pp. 185–235.

7. An economic theory of time allocation is presented in Becker, *Human Capital.* Detailed references to the literature are given in M. Murphy, *The Measurement and Valuation of Household Nonmarket Time* (Washington, D.C.: U.S. Department of Commerce, Bureau of Economic Analysis, 1980). Time use accounts for the United States for 1975–1976, based on data collected by the Survey Research Center of the University of Michigan, are presented in J. A. Gates and M. Murphy, "The Use of Time: A Classification Scheme and Estimates for 1975–76," in J. Peskin, ed., *Measuring Nonmarket Economic Activity* (Washington, D.C.: U.S. Government Printing Office, 1982), pp. 3–22.

8. See W. D. Nordhaus and J. Tobin, *Economic Growth* (New York: National Bureau of Economic Research, 1972).

9. See J. W. Kendrick, *The Formation and Stocks of Total Capital* (New York: Columbia University Press, 1976); and R. W. Eisner, "Extended Accounts for National Income and Product," *Journal of Economic Literature* 24 (1988), pp. 1611–1684.

10. See, for example, Gates and Murphy, "The Use of Time"; and F. T. Juster, P. N. Courant, and G. K. Dow, "The Theory and Measurement of Well-Being: A Suggested Framework for Accounting and Analysis," in Juster and Land, eds., *Social Accounting Systems,* pp. 23–94.

11. D. W. Jorgenson and K.-Y. Yun, "Tax Policy and Capital Allocation," *Scandinavian Journal of Economics* 88 (1986), pp. 355–377.

12. Estimates of lifetime labor incomes for men based on market labor activities are presented in B. A. Weisbrod, "The Valuation of Human Capital," *Journal of Political Economy* 69 (1961), pp. 425–436; H. P. Miller, "Lifetime Income and Economic Growth," *American Economic Review* 55 (1965), pp. 834–844; and J. W. Graham and R. H. Webb, "Stocks and Depreciation of Human Capital: New Evidence from a Present-Value Perspective," *Review of Income and Wealth* 25 (1979), pp. 209–224.

13. See U.S. Department of Health, Education, and Welfare, National Center for Health Statistics, *Vital Statistics of the United States* (Washington, D.C.: Public Health Service, U.S. Department of Health and Human Services, various years).

14. For details, see D. W. Jorgenson and B. M. Fraumeni, *Productivity and U.S. Economic Growth, 1979–1985* (Cambridge, Mass.: Harvard Institute for Economic Research, 1988).

15. Estimates of investment in education based on lifetime labor incomes from market activities for men and women are given in E. Kroch and K. Sjoblom, "Education and the National Wealth of the United States," *Review of Income and Wealth* 32 (1986), pp. 87–106.

16. These estimates are based on D. W. Jorgenson, F. M. Gollop, and B. M. Fraumeni, *Productivity and U.S. Economic Growth* (Cambridge, Mass.: Harvard University Press, 1987), revised and updated by Jorgenson and Fraumeni, *Productivity and U.S. Economic Growth, 1979–1985*. An excellent overview of research on sources of economic growth, including alternative data sources and methodologies, is provided by National Research Council, *Measurement and Interpretation of Productivity* (Washington, D.C.: National Academy of Sciences, 1979).

17. L. R. Christensen and D. W. Jorgenson, "Measuring the Performance of the Private Sector of the U.S. Economy, 1929–1969," in M. Moss, ed., *Measuring Economic and Social Performance* (New York: National Bureau of Economic Research, 1973), pp. 233–338.

18. A. Maddison, "Growth and Slowdown in Advanced Capitalist Economies: Techniques of Quantitative Assessment," *Journal of Economic Literature* 25 (1987), pp. 649–698.

19. See M. Abramovitz, "Resources and Output Trends in the United States Since 1870," *American Economic Review* 46 (1956), pp. 5–23; J. W. Kendrick, "Productivity Trends: Capital and Labor," *Review of Economics and Statistics* 38 (1956), pp. 248–257; and R. M. Solow, "Technical Change and the Aggregate Production Function," *Review of Economics and Statistics* 39 (1957), pp. 312–320.

20. E. F. Denison, "Measurement of Labor Input: Some Questions of Definition and the Adequacy of Data," in Conference on Research in Income and Wealth, *Output, Input, and Productivity Measurement* (Princeton, N.J.: Princeton University Press, 1961), pp. 347–372.

21. The application of the theory of index numbers to the measurement of labor input requires a weighting of the components of labor input by wage rates. This was carried out at the aggregate level by Denison and implemented for all industrial sectors of the U.S. economy by Gollop and Jorgenson. See E. F. Denison, *Sources of Economic Growth in the United States and the Alternatives Before Us* (New York: Committee for Economic Development, 1962); and Gollop and Jorgenson, "U.S. Productivity Growth by Industry, 1947–73," pp. 17–136.

22. C. Hulten and F. Wykoff, "The Estimation of Economic Depreciation Using Vintage Asset Prices: An Application of the Box-Cox Power Transformation," *Journal of Econometrics* 15 (1981), pp. 367–396.

23. The measurement of capital as a factor of production involves a weighting of components of capital input by rental rates. This was carried out at the aggregate level by Jorgenson and Griliches and by Christensen and Jorgenson and at the sectoral level by Fraumeni and Jorgenson and by Gollop and Jorgenson. See D. W. Jorgenson and Z. Griliches, "The Explanation of Productivity Change," *Review of Economic Studies* 34, no. 3 (1967), pp. 249–283; Christensen and Jorgenson, "The Measurement of U.S. Real Capital Input, 1929–1967"; B. M. Fraumeni and D. W. Jorgenson, "The Role of Capital in U.S. Economic Growth, 1948–1976," in G. von Furstenberg, ed., *Capital Efficiency and Growth* (Cambridge, Mass.: Ballinger, 1980), pp. 9–250; B. M. Fraumeni and D. W. Jorgenson, "The Role of Capital in U.S. Economic Growth, 1948–1979," in A. Dogramaci, ed., *Measurement Issues and Behavior of Pro-*

ductivity Variables (Boston: Martinus Nijhoff, 1986), pp. 161–244; and Gollop and Jorgenson, "U.S. Productivity Growth by Industry, 1947–73."

24. Denison continues to adhere to capital stock as a measure of capital input. See E. F. Denison, "Some Major Issues in Productivity Analysis: An Examination of Estimates by Jorgenson and Griliches," *Survey of Current Business* 49 (1969), pp. 1–27. This approach ignores the heterogeneity of capital inputs reflected in Table 7.10.

25. For estimates of the contribution of education to U.S. economic growth, see Jorgenson, Gollop, and Fraumeni, *Productivity and U.S. Economic Growth,* especially Chapter 8. A complete set of national accounts, incorporating the estimates of market and nonmarket labor time, investment in education, and human wealth given above, is given in D. W. Jorgenson and B. M. Fraumeni, "The Accumulation of Human and Nonhuman Capital, 1948–1984," in R. E. Lipsey and H. S. Tice, eds., *The Measurement of Saving, Investment, and Wealth* (Chicago: University of Chicago Press, 1989), pp. 227–282. For surveys of the contribution of education to economic growth, see E. Dean, ed., *Education and Economic Productivity* (Cambridge, Mass.: Ballinger, 1984); J. Mincer, "Human Capital and Economic Growth," *Economics of Education Review* 3 (1984), pp. 195–205; and R. Murnane, "Education and the Productivity of the Work Force: Looking Ahead," in R. E. Litan, R. Z. Lawrence, and C. L. Schultze, eds., *American Living Standards: Threats and Challenges* (Washington, D.C.: Brookings Institution, 1988), pp. 215–245.

26. See Jorgenson, Gollop, and Fraumeni, ibid., especially Chapters 1 and 9.

27. See, for example, U.S. Department of Commerce, Bureau of Economic Analysis, *The National Income and Product Accounts of the United States, 1929–1974, Statistical Tables, A Supplement to the Survey of Current Business* (Washington, D.C.: U.S. Government Printing Office, 1976).

28. Investment and capital stocks for sixty-one industries broken down by seventy-two categories of physical assets are provided in U.S. Department of Commerce, Bureau of Economic Analysis, *Fixed Reproducible Tangible Wealth in the United States, 1925–85* (Washington, D.C.: U.S. Government Printing Office, 1987).

29. Time series estimates of education and training costs for 1976–1979 are provided in J. A. Gates, "Education and Training Costs: A Measurement Framework and Estimates for 1965–79," in Peskin, ed., *Measuring Nonmarket Economic Activity,* pp. 107–135. This compendium also includes other studies of nonmarket activities conducted at the Bureau of Economic Analysis. Unfortunately, the bureau has discontinued this line of investigation.

30. The cost-based approach to measuring investment in human capital was originated by Machlup and Schultz. See F. Machlup, *The Production and Distribution of Knowledge in the United States* (Princeton, N.J.: Princeton University Press, 1962); and Schultz, "Investment in Human Capital." Campbell and Peskin as well as Eisner surveyed augmented accounting systems, including those containing cost-based estimates of investment in human capital. See B. Campbell and J. Peskin, *Expanding Economic Accounts and Measuring Economic Welfare: A Review of Proposals* (Washington, D.C.: U.S. Department of Commerce, Bureau of Economic Analysis, 1979); and Eisner, "Extended Accounts for National Income and Product." Kendrick's accounting system was also discussed by Engerman and Rosen. See Kendrick, *The Formation and Stocks of Total Capital;* and S. Engerman and S. Rosen, "New Books on the

Measurement of Capital," in D. Usher, ed., *The Measurement of Capital* (Chicago: University of Chicago Press, 1980), pp. 153–170.

31. The educational sector is discussed from the economic point of view in J. T. Froomkin, D. T. Jamison, and R. Radner, eds., *Education as an Industry* (Cambridge, Mass.: Ballinger, 1976).

32. Nordhaus and Tobin, *Economic Growth.*

33. Kendrick, *The Formation and Stocks of Total Capital.*

34. A comparison of Kendrick's estimate of human wealth for 1969 with estimates based on lifetime labor incomes for males, excluding the value of nonmarket activities, is found in Graham and Webb, "Stocks and Depreciation of Human Capital." Kroch and Sjoblom compared their estimates of human capital accumulated through education, based on lifetime labor incomes from market activities for men and women, with Kendrick's estimates, based on costs of education and training. See Kroch and Sjoblom, "Education and the National Wealth of the United States."

35. A survey of recent research on the prevalence and impact of on-the-job training is presented in J. Mincer, "Human Capital and the Labor Market," *Educational Researcher* 18 (1989), pp. 27–34. Estimates of the annual costs of training in the United States for 1958, 1976, and 1987 are provided in J. Mincer, *Job Training: Costs, Returns, and Wage Profiles* (New York: Columbia University, Department of Economics, 1989). For 1976, these costs amount to one-half of the costs of formal schooling.

ADDITIONAL REFERENCES

Juster, F. T., and K. C. Land, eds. *Social Accounting Systems.* New York: Academic Press, 1981.

Peskin, J., ed. *Measuring Nonmarket Economic Activity,* Washington D.C.: U.S. Government Printing Office, 1982.

U.S. Council of Economic Advisers. *Economic Report of the President.* Washington, D.C.: U.S. Government Printing Office, 1989.

U.S. Department of Labor, Bureau of Labor Statistics. *Trends in Multifactor Productivity, 1948–81.* Washington, D.C.: U.S. Department of Labor, Bureau of Labor Statistics, 1983.

Discussion

Roberts T. Jones

I agree with the basic thesis that the "black hole" in the availability of statistics on the value of investment in human capital—particularly regarding education's impact on future earning power—needs to be addressed. Simply increasing the hours of work no longer plays a major role in increasing productivity rates. Capital investment in new technology is difficult to confine within our borders and thus has a decreasing effect on this country's comparative advantage in productivity. These considerations, along with demographic trends and the increased skill levels demanded in new jobs, have brought us to the conclusion that investment in education, in the human factor, may be the most important contribution we can make during the next few years to an increase in U.S. productivity and economic growth.

The actual numbers for investment in education are a bit troubling. Dr. Jorgenson and Dr. Fraumeni suggest that one set of numbers represents a basically stable investment in education. The trend may not be quite as stable as they suggest, however. From 1959 to 1971, investment in education was about 4.7 percent of gross national product (GNP), which for those years was equal to or slightly greater than capital investment as a percentage of GNP. But from 1971 to 1985, investment was about 2.7 percent of GNP, considerably less than the percentage for capital investment. So it is almost contradictory that at a time when this factor clearly should contribute more and more to economic growth and productivity, our overall investment in education, in real dollars, is going down or, at best, is stabilizing.

There are three dimensions of this discussion that have particular relevance for U.S. public policy, as contrasted with that of most industrialized countries in Europe and in the Pacific Rim. The first dimension involves the low end of the population and of the work force. We have a critical issue here because the data include about a 30 percent failure rate of individuals who leave our school systems either because they drop out or because they have skills deficiencies. They represent potential labor market failures. These are individuals who cannot read, cannot compute, and lack a whole range of work readiness skills. They enter the labor market at a time when the skill demands are, on average, about one year to two years of post–high school work. Unless significant changes are made, these people are not going to be part of the productivity equation. Investment in this significant portion of our population has to take place if we are, in fact, to substantially increase U.S. productivity. This situation, frankly, is an opportunity. Given the statistics presented by Dr. Jorgenson and Dr. Fraumeni, probably the greatest impact can be made by a substantial investment in just that sector of the population.

The second issue is one that the September 1989 education summit focused on: the skill levels achieved by high school graduates in relation to the demands of the workplace. In the next two or three years, this subject will stimulate major discussions, I suspect, on national norms, national achievement standards, and whether major investments should be made to develop meaningful policies in this area.

I believe that this issue is relevant in two ways. The first of these points, emphasized by Dr. Jorgenson and Dr. Fraumeni, is how significant each year of education is to the future economic earnings of people across the board. I suspect that a 9 or 10 percent increase in lifetime earnings for each year of education achieved is not too far off the mark. That message is not clearly articulated to young people in our educational system, whether they are college-bound or non-college-bound students. They see no relationship among their educational experience, their prospects in the job market, and this type of earning structure. The second point is that there is no structure within our system that articulates the level and type of investment needed in our students in order for them to achieve success in the labor market.

We made a mistake a few years ago: We stopped testing, and we graduated everybody. In fact, what will probably have to take place is a reemergence of testing but as part of an overall national strategy to invest in remediation. If the reported data are correct, investment in testing is probably the most important investment we can make, and it must take place early enough to allow for remediation during high school. We cannot solve the problem in second-chance or postsecondary systems.

Finally, I want to examine Dr. Jorgenson's and Dr. Fraumeni's suggestion that the majority of investment in education and the value it produces are almost entirely outside the business sector of the economy. I am not sure that is the case. Most of the current data seem to suggest that expenditures for training and education in the institutional setting and for both formal and informal training and education in the private sector are roughly equal. The data also suggest that for the next few years more training and education will go on in the workplace than in institutional settings. This circumstance drives us to look at a whole set of public policies related to how we enhance the investment by business in education and training. That debate, I assume, will involve policies ranging from training tax credits to a variety of other incentives to increase workers' investment in their lifetime learning. Many issues are going to be raised concerning how to enhance that process of lifetime education and training and achieve a continuing investment in that process by both business and individuals.

Discussion

Jacob Mincer

One purpose of Dale Jorgenson's and Barbara Fraumeni's long-term research in growth accounting is, in their words, "to describe the impact of investment in education on U.S. economic growth." This description is contained in the section of their analysis entitled "Sources of Growth." The bulk of the analysis which precedes that section but is conceptually related to it, really stands on its own and is more directly related to the topic of saving. Clearly, magnitudes of investments in education must imply corresponding volumes of saving, which are not recorded in national income accounts.

Although Dr. Jorgenson and Dr. Fraumeni sometimes use the terms *education, human capital,* and *labor quality* interchangeably, we should note that they are not synonymous. Thus, education is a component of human capital investments, as are job training, labor mobility, and investment in health—all of which enhance skills and capacities. Labor quality as quantified by Dr. Jorgenson and Dr. Fraumeni summarizes labor heterogeneity, which may in large part reflect differences in human capital but does not completely correspond to these differences.

A major contribution of Dr. Jorgenson's continuing empirical study of U.S. economic growth is the development and inclusion of "quality" measures of capital and labor along with the conventional measures of the two inputs for growth accounting purposes. Looking at Table 7.10, we see that without the quality components barely one-half of U.S. growth is explainable by conventional measures of physical capital and labor hours. This wide gap between the growth of inputs and output—known as the residual or as multifactor productivity growth—has stimulated a whole industry of growth accounting since the mid-1950s. Dr. Jorgenson's work has by now filled out more than one-half of the residual by the quality components of capital and labor. As Table 7.10 shows, close to 80 percent of the growth of output (value added) over the period 1947–1985 is accounted for by the quantity and quality components. The residual, a measure of our ignorance, has been reduced by more than one-half—no mean accomplishment!

Growth accounting by itself does not inquire into the relation between the factors of growth. Yet human capital formation is not only a cause but also a consequence of economic growth. In particular, recent empirical research reveals that technological change and new vintages of capital increase demands for human capital, thus reinforcing the process of growth as well as keeping investment in education profitable, despite the huge, long-run increases in educational attainment.

Table 7.10 also contains some information on a more recent puzzle: the drastic decline in economic growth since the early 1970s. This decline amounted to more than 1 full percentage point from the average of more than 3 percent in the 1947–1985 period. That table makes clear that changes in conventional capital and labor are not responsible for the decline. The growth of capital did not slacken, and the growth of labor hours actually accelerated. But the reduction in growth is evident in both quality measures and accounts for one-third of the decline in the growth of output, whereas the residual (unexplained or "disembodied" productivity growth) accounts for two-thirds of the decline.

In the bulk of their discussion, to which I now turn, Dr. Jorgenson and Dr. Fraumeni present a new approach to the quantification of the benefits from education and derive new annual estimates of investment in education over the 1947–1985 period. One innovation in this approach is the use of values of educational outputs, or benefits, rather than the value of inputs, or costs, to measure educational investments. The other is the inclusion in the benefits of education of the value of activities outside the labor market, such as parenting or enjoyment of leisure time.

These innovations are part of a larger scheme whereby Dr. Jorgenson and Dr. Fraumeni propose to revise national income accounts to include not merely economic activities reported in market transactions but all activities that have economic outcomes or value. Such a scheme, the details of which are necessarily controversial, is useful in showing the incompleteness of the standard picture of economic activity when it leaves out human capital from the capital accounts and consumption goods and services supplied by nonmarket activities from the income accounts.

According to Dr. Jorgenson and Dr. Fraumeni, there are two ways to measure investments in education. In a cost-based approach, the sum of direct expenditures on schools and universities is added to the opportunity costs of students attending school to measure the flow of resources into education. In the income-based approach, investment is defined as an increment in the value of human assets that is in the present value of lifetime income because of the increment in education. All of this is summed over the total labor force and includes imputed income from nonmarket activities. Dr. Jorgenson and Dr. Fraumeni prefer the income-based approach because it makes the methodology of calculating human and nonhuman capital investments fully comparable in their scheme of revised national income and wealth accounts.

Not surprisingly, the resulting estimates of investment are far larger than we have ever seen. This is mainly due to the inclusion of nonmarket time in lifetime income, all of which is valued at market wage rates per hour when hours of market work take up an average of less than one-third of the available time—even after ten hours a day are put aside for maintenance, including sleep. It can be shown, of course, that if labor incomes are restricted to market transactions and the rate at which they are discounted is equal to the internal rate of return, the two approaches should yield the same results. The discount rate used by Dr. Jorgenson and Dr. Fraumeni is 4 percent, about one-half of the internal rate, on average. Consequently their income-based approach to the estimation of educational investments yields numbers that are six times as large as the cost-based approach; the latter are tripled by the inclusion of nonmarket time valued at the market wage rate and doubled again by the discount rate chosen.

We should note that the income-based accounting as presented does not distinguish between returns to investment that are due to increases in units of investment (say, years of schooling) and to increases (or decreases) in the profitability or efficiency of the investment. The cost-based approach—of which I am one of the practitioners—sharply distinguishes between costs and returns *in order to* make possible the profitability or rate of return calculations, which in turn provide insights into incentives to invest in human capital. To list a few recent developments, the decline in rates of return to education in the 1970s resulted from the influx of more-educated baby boomers, the subsequent retardation in college enrollment rates, and the present rise in the rates of return to college as the baby boom waned and education-using technology grew on the demand side are examples of the insights the cost-based approach is capable of providing.

The large magnitude of educational investments that Dr. Jorgenson and Dr. Fraumeni estimate implies correspondingly huge figures for saving. Indeed, in a previous study these numbers amount to close to one-half of the revised private national income.[1] Actually, even if we stay with the cost-based estimate and exclude nonmarket imputations of income, my estimates of the current costs of schooling including opportunity costs yield a figure of 14 percent of gross national product (GNP). When the costs of job training are added, the figure rises to more than 20 percent of GNP.

Do these numbers suggest that the worry about meager U.S. saving is spurious because it is not meager? It is certainly true that saving provides resources for investment and thus for economic growth. Therefore, the large numbers we get raise the question, If things are so good, why are they so bad? First, although the larger numbers are impressive, they do show a decline in the 1980s. More importantly, they suggest that the availability of resources for investment does not guarantee that the resources will be used efficiently. Efficient use of resources is more likely to occur in nonhuman private capital investments, where market competition usually prevails. This is not the case with educational investments, where the competitive process is usually severely restricted. As we are told repeatedly, despite the largest investments per student, standardized international tests show our students below the college level to be close to the bottom of the ranks across industrialized countries—even including some of the lesser developed countries. There are even indications that "the rising tide of mediocrity" is beginning to reach the college level.

I suspect the response to the question might be that although inefficiency may be a problem in human capital investments, inadequate saving is a problem in "nonhuman" capital investments. Thus, instead of one problem we have two. Indeed, the two problems are related because of complementarity between human capital and physical capital. This means that the efficiency of investments in physical capital suffers as well if the quality of workers is inadequate. Within the human capital sector a similar problem arises because of the complementarity between school education and job training. The worse the quality of their school education, the more difficult it is to train workers. Although learning on the job is to some extent substitutable for learning at school, a solid foundation of school learning is necessary for efficient training.

Are the problems insurmountable in the United States, given that they do not even arise in some of our trade partners? I find this difficult to believe.

NOTES

1. Dale W. Jorgenson and Barbara M. Fraumeni, *Productivity and U.S. Economic Growth, 1979–1985* (Cambridge, Mass.: Harvard Institute for Economic Research, 1988).

Discussion

Paul S. Sarbanes

It is very clear that during the 1990s, the United States will not be able to count on rapid labor force growth to contribute in a significant way to economic growth. The Bureau of Labor Statistics estimates that during the 1990s, the labor force will grow by only about 1.0 or 1.25 million people per year, compared to 2.4 million per year during the 1970s and a little less than 2.0 million per year during the 1980s. The bureau projects that the 1990s will have the slowest rate of labor force growth since the Depression. Therefore, although any vast increase in labor resources is a contribution to economic growth, in the 1990s the contribution must come from an improvement in the *quality* of labor, unless we are either going to start people working sooner or have them work longer.

To start people working sooner would require very significant changes in how we educate our young people. We would have to shift our whole educational system downward, much as in some European countries where people enter the work force at an earlier age prepared for at least certain aspects and then through an on-the-job or continuing education process are able to develop their skills.

A longer work life is an interesting concept. It is embodied somewhat in the revisions to the Social Security law that will slowly move back the retirement age for receipt of full benefits. This concept is also reflected in the growing practice of retiring from a prime or major career and then continuing to work, but in a new area. The experience of William Macomber, a very distinguished U.S. ambassador and later head of the Metropolitan Museum of Art in New York, is a case in point. Macomber retired from the museum some years ago and is now a high school teacher in New England. He says he works harder than he has ever worked in his life, and he seems to be doing a very good job of it.

But in any event, we must improve the quality of labor. Some of the projected trends will help improve the quality; others will reduce it. It is estimated that the average age of the work force will rise from thirty-five to thirty-nine by the end of the century. By the year 2000, 75 percent of the work force will be in the twenty-five to fifty-four age bracket, when workers are typically most productive; in 1980, the comparable figure for that age group was 63 percent of the work force. But 45 percent of the new entrants into the work force in the 1990s will be from ethnic groups—blacks and Hispanics—whose educational attainment is lower and for whom the dropout rate is much higher than for the rest of the population. Twenty-five percent of new entrants will be immigrants. This situation brings us right back to the question of the quality of education.

It is my view that improving labor force quality will require a significant commitment of resources—public and private—to both education and job training. At the federal level, this means a major turnaround in 1980s educational policies.

During the 1980s, one of the major goals of the Reagan administration was to reduce federal government involvement in spending for education and job training. At the very beginning of the Reagan administration, there were some even within the Department of Education whose objective was to move the federal government entirely out of education. This did not happen. But that administration, in each of its eight years, sought to cut appropriations for the Department of Education by an average of about 20 percent. Such cuts did occur in all of the eight years except for election years (1984 and 1988). This gives some insight into the importance of education to the U.S. electorate.

Congress, of course, funded education programs at higher levels than the administration requested, but real federal spending on education nevertheless was lower in every year from fiscal 1981 through 1989 than it had been during fiscal 1980. For job training, the decline was even more severe. Federal government outlays for training and employment fell from $10.3 billion in fiscal year 1980 to $5.0 billion in fiscal 1989. Department of Labor outlays fell from 5 percent of federal spending to 2 percent. So there was a very marked drop in the commitment to both education and job training.

At the time a theory was advanced about the withdrawal of the federal government, and I want to put this forward as a matter of political dynamics. If the federal government recedes, according to the theory, the state and local governments will have room to move in, so there will be a compensating movement in the other direction. Generally speaking, such political dynamics do not work that way. What instead happens is that the state and local governments draw the same lesson, or their constituents impose on them the same lesson, that is being drawn at the federal level. So if the federal government recedes, the state and local governments tend to do the same. The pressure of circumstance was such, and the direct responsibility in education was so much more clearly defined, that some states did, in fact, move in the other direction. But I think it was contrary to the general public sentiment.

In July 1989 the Joint Economic Committee conducted a hearing on government investment in human and physical infrastructure that focused on the contribution of publicly provided capital to the growth of the economy and to the productivity of the private sector. The committee heard Jim Tobin, a Nobel Prize winner; Don Strassheim from Merrill Lynch; and Jack Meyer from the Ford Foundation. The major thrust of the testimony was the importance of government investment in human and physical infrastructures—that is, in economic growth and productivity.

An open letter from more than three hundred economists to Congress and the president expressed concern that underinvestment in human and physical infrastructure will impair our economic growth, and thereby reduce our competitiveness. That letter began, "In addition to our trade and fiscal deficits, America faces a third deficit, the deficiency of public investment in our people and our economic infrastructure. The deficit will have a crippling effect on America's future competitiveness." The letter continued, "Just as business must continually reinvest in order to prosper, so must the nation. Higher productivity, the key to higher living standards, is a function of both public and private investment. If America is to succeed in an increasingly competitive world, we must expand efforts to equip our children with better education and our workers with more advanced skills."

We should begin to think about certain public expenditures not as expenditures but as investments in the future strength of the country; these would include education, health, research and development, and the nation's physical infrastructure. The failure to make wise, prudent, and adequate investments in each of those categories will only undercut the future strength of the economy.

We must marshal our efforts to ensure the necessary investment, both in human capital and in physical capital, and draw on the complementary relationship between public investment and private activity. We must be prepared to make the investments in the development of these resources that are absolutely essential to the future strength and viability of our economy.

PART THREE

Strategies for Increasing U.S. Saving

8

Tax Policies for Increasing Personal Saving

A. Stimulating U.S. Personal Saving

Lawrence H. Summers

It is widely recognized that low national saving is the most serious problem facing the U.S. economy. Low saving accounted for the trade deficit and the slow growth in standards of living that continued throughout the 1980s. Part of the reason for low national saving is the excessive federal budget deficits. But the low U.S. saving rate is increasingly the result of insufficient personal saving by U.S. households. During the period 1985–1989, U.S. households saved an average of only 4 percent of their incomes, down from an average of nearly 8 percent during the 1970s.

In this analysis, I review trends in national saving, highlighting the reasons why they pose such a serious problem, and examine the behavior of private and personal saving. I consider the reasons for the collapse in personal saving during the 1980s as well as policy levers that the government can use to increase personal saving. I argue strongly that the traditional view that holds that public policy can have only a small impact on private saving behavior is supported neither by logic nor by evidence. The restoration and expansion of individual retirement account (IRA) benefits, reforms in employee-benefit rules, and more neutral taxation of corporate restructuring activities all can have an important impact on personal saving behavior.

The first section of this analysis ("The U.S. National Saving Problem") considers the dimensions of the U.S. national saving problem and its consequences. Section two ("Why Is U.S. National Saving So Low?") considers a number of possible explanations for declining national saving and highlights the fact that most U.S. families essentially do no direct financial saving. Section three ("Can Public Policy Stimulate Personal Saving?") considers policy levers with the potential to increase personal saving. It argues that measures that change attitudes toward saving are likely to be the most effective stimulants to personal saving. Section four ("Conclusion") offers some concluding observations.

THE U.S. NATIONAL SAVING PROBLEM

In 1990, the U.S. economy entered its eighth year of the longest cyclical expansion in its history. Unemployment and inflation are at levels that were thought to be unachievable just a few years ago, the market is at an all-time high, and the economy continues to grow. These are real achievements, but the indicators contained in Figures 8.1, 8.2, and 8.3 suggest that they rest on a shaky foundation:

- During the current recovery, the United States has drawn down its foreign asset position by nearly $1 trillion and is now the world's largest debtor nation. The trade deficit, which extends even to high technology, continues to damage the economy and is expected to increase in the near term.
- Stock markets reflect sentiments about the future. In 1980 the U.S. stock market accounted for 50 percent of the world total; today it accounts for less than 30 percent. The value of the land in Tokyo today exceeds the combined value of all the corporations and all the land in the United States by nearly $1 trillion.
- Growth in U.S. standards of living has stagnated. The real wages of full-time workers today are no greater than they were in 1973. Even as Japanese firms have gained market share in world markets, Japanese wages, measured in a common currency, have increased almost 5 percent a year faster than U.S. wages have.

These problems all have a single root cause: the low level of national saving in the United States.[1] As Figures 8.4 and 8.5 illustrate, as a nation we have consumed publicly and privately more than ninety-seven cents of every one dollar of income that we earned over the last several years. Our current national saving rate is about one-third of the rate we enjoyed during the 1970s, when supply-side concerns about inadequate saving began to emerge. Official figures suggest that the U.S. national saving rate is less than one-half of the average saving rate of the major industrialized countries and about one-fifth of the saving rate of Japan.

Before considering the implications of low U.S. national saving, I want to consider the recent widely publicized research by Fumio Hayashi, which suggested that official figures might have presented a misleading picture of the difference between U.S. and Japanese saving.[2] Hayashi argued that differences in the treatment of depreciation and of public investment caused Japanese saving to be significantly overstated

FIGURE 8.1
U.S. Trade Deficit, 1970–1988

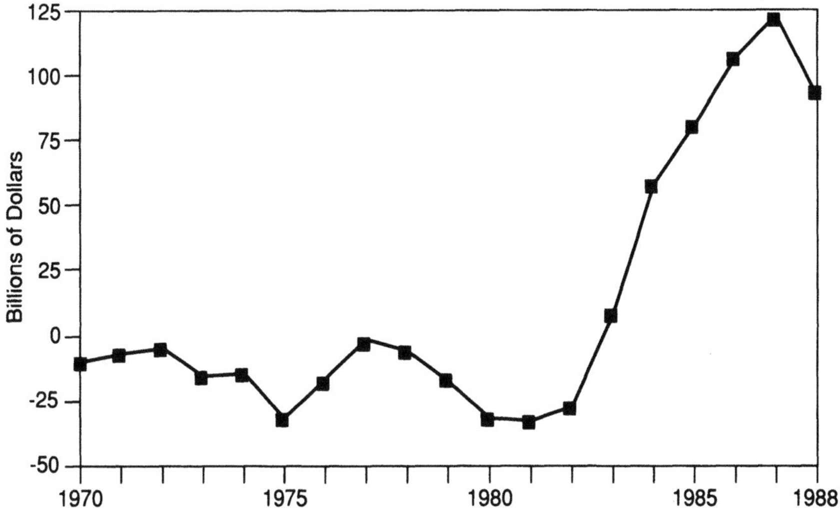

Source: Economic Report of the President, 1989.

FIGURE 8.2
U.S. Share of World Stock Market Value,
1974–1988

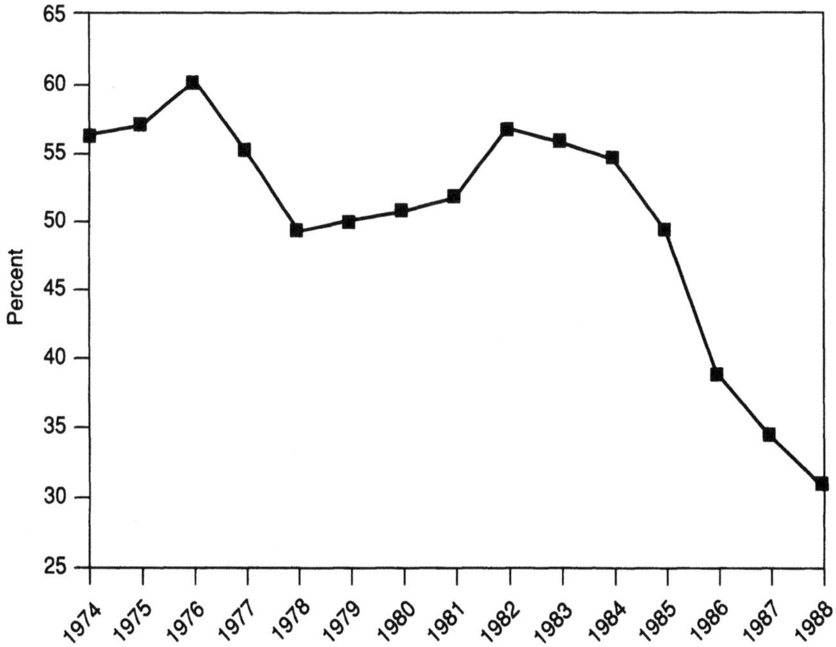

Source: Data from *Morgan Stanley Capital International Perspective* (New York: Morgan Stanley & Co., Inc., 1989), various issues; reprinted with permission.

FIGURE 8.3
Real Hourly Compensation in Manufacturing

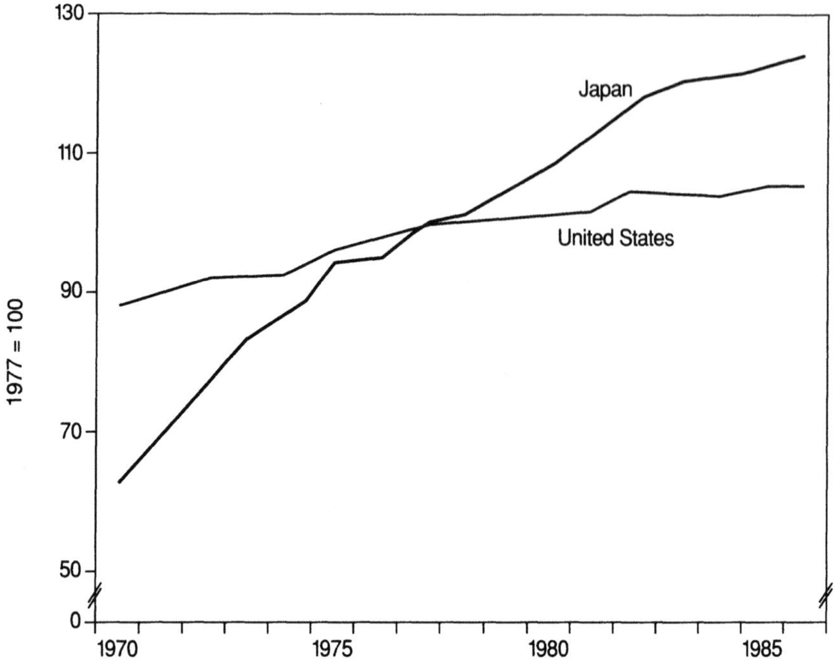

Source: U.S. Department of Labor, Bureau of Labor Statistics, unpublished data.

FIGURE 8.4
U.S. National Saving Rate, 1970–1988
(percent of GNP)

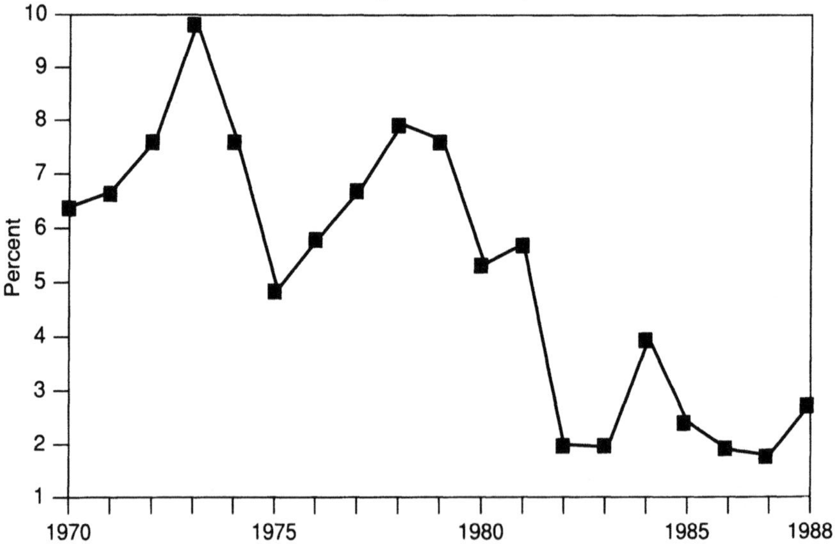

Source: Economic Report of the President, 1989.

FIGURE 8.5
Net National Saving, 1980–1986

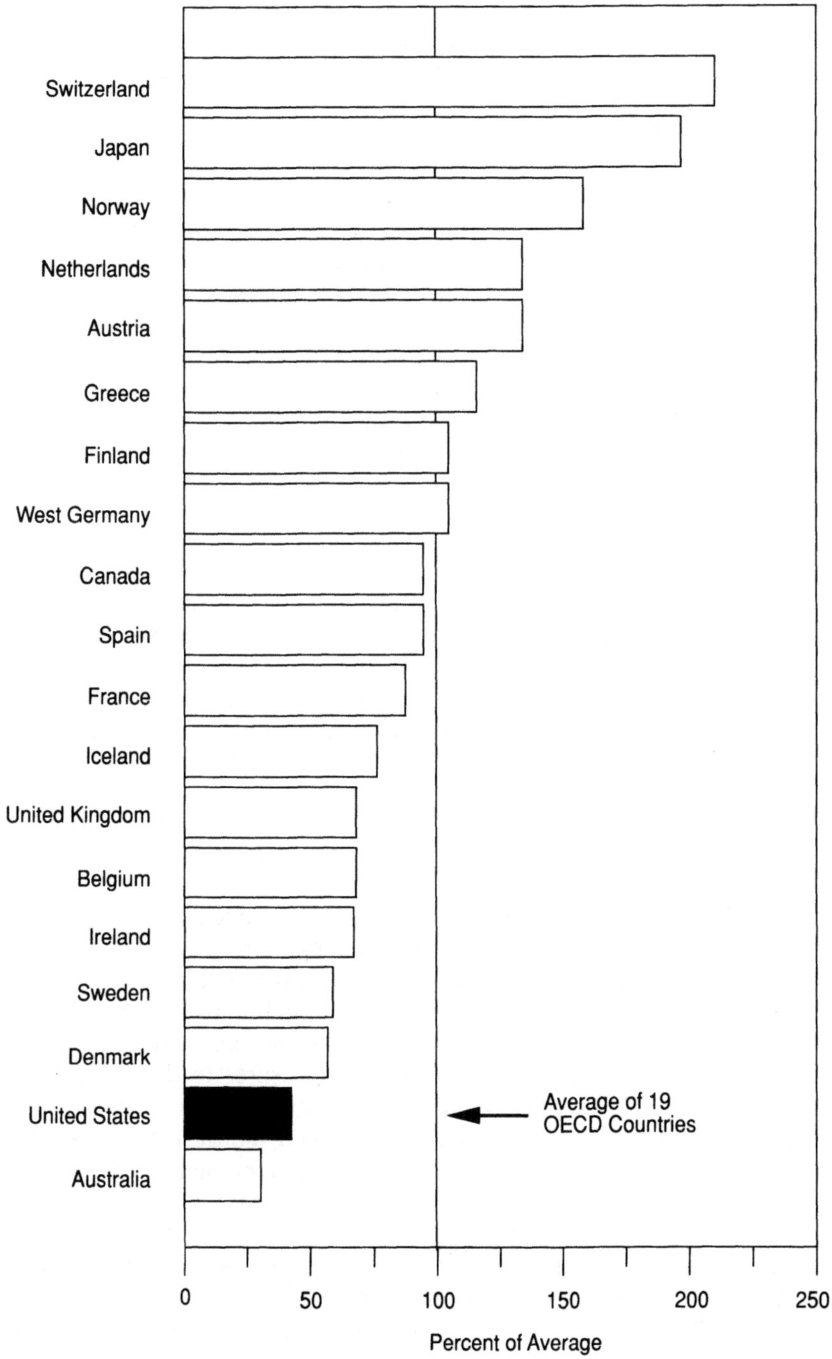

Source: Congressional Budget Office calculations based on data of the Organisation for Economic Co-operation and Development.

relative to U.S. saving. After making a complex set of calculations designed to put the two countries' saving rates on a comparable basis, he concluded that Japan saves at a rate only slightly higher than the United States does.

This conclusion is dubious. Hayashi subtracted all Japanese public investment from Japanese saving on the grounds that the U.S. accounts treat all government spending as consumption. But much of Japanese public investment represents spending by public corporations on goods that would represent private investment in the United States. Furthermore, Hayashi's depreciation estimates rather implausibly suggested that capital consumption represents nearly one-fourth of Japanese gross national product (GNP). Statistics on gross saving of the Organisation for Economic Co-operation and Development (OECD), which are free from the problems that concerned Hayashi, indicate a spread of nearly 15 percentage points between U.S. and Japanese saving rates during the 1980s.

Domestic Consequences of Low Saving

The U.S. investment rate is woefully low, as evidenced by the fact that the United States, with twice as large a work force as Japan, invested less than Japan did in plant and equipment in 1988. As low as our investment rate is, it is only possible through borrowing from abroad. The only way foreign funds can enter the United States is for us to import more than we export. For example, the U.S. current account deficit of 3.5 percent of GNP in 1987 occurred because the United States saved only *2 percent* of GNP while it invested *5.5 percent* of GNP. Japan, whose saving exceeds its investment, has enjoyed consistent trade surpluses.

Any desirable program to reduce the U.S. current account deficit must have an increase in U.S. national saving as its central element. If the U.S. current account deficit were to decline without increases in national saving, the result would be a major decline in U.S. investment. *Without foreign borrowing, U.S. net investment would fall to approximately one-half its current level.* Although measures to drive the value of the dollar down or restrict foreign investment in the United States could influence the current account, they would reduce U.S. investment by as much as they reduced the current account deficit unless they were coupled with steps that increased national saving.

Even supplemented by foreign borrowing, low national saving has reduced investment in recent years. The United States invested less in plant and equipment (as a percentage of GNP) during the 1980s than in any of the three preceding decades. As a consequence, capital-labor ratios have grown less rapidly in the United States than in any of our major competitor nations, resulting in disastrous consequences for living standards. International evidence confirms that there is a close relationship between rates of capital formation and rates of productivity growth.

The channel through which low national saving leads to reduced investment is through increases in the *cost of capital*. When low saving leads to a reduced supply of capital, the cost of capital rises. Differential saving rates are an important reason the price-earnings ratios in Japan are so much greater than U.S. price-earnings ratios. High costs of capital lead investors to set high hurdle rates of return that cheat the future. Economic fundamentals alone can account for much of the myopia often thought to afflict U.S. businesspeople; there is no need to blame cultural factors. Consider this comparison: A U.S. investor, given his or her costs of capital, would be willing to invest only thirty-seven cents in return for receiving one dollar six years from now, compared with sixty-six cents for his or her Japanese counterpart. It is hardly surprising that Japanese managers often appear to take a longer view than their U.S. counterparts do.

The combined effect of reduced investment and the foreign financing of a large fraction of the investment that does take place is a gradual reduction in U.S. living standards. Although this reduction does not occur overnight, as Figure 8.6 illustrates, there is a clear relationship between national saving rates and rates of growth. As a wealthy nation, the United States can finance a high rate of consumption by selling off assets for a long time—but not forever. Unless our national saving rate is restored to at least its former level in the 7 percent range, it is very likely that we will be overtaken by a number of our competitor nations within the next few years.

Without increased national saving, it will be impossible to reduce the trade deficit and U.S. dependence on foreign capital without a sharp reduction in the rate of domestic investment, regardless of the investment incentives provided or the trade policies pursued. As a matter of arithmetic, domestic investment can be financed only from domestic saving or from foreign borrowing. Without increases in saving, any increase in investment must result from increased foreign borrowing, which means a larger trade deficit. Conversely, any reduction in the trade deficit caused by a change in exchange rates or trade policies reduces the supply of capital to U.S. firms—thereby raising capital costs dollar for dollar and choking off investment. Only by raising our national saving rate can we reconcile the goals of increasing investment and reducing the trade deficit.

International Consequences of Low National Saving

Low U.S. saving and the resulting large current account deficits have adverse implications not only for the United States but also for the world economy. First, low U.S. national saving and large U.S. borrowing create a worldwide capital shortage. As Figure 8.7 illustrates, the United States absorbed most of the capital exported in the world economy

FIGURE 8.6
Saving and Growth, 1960–1984

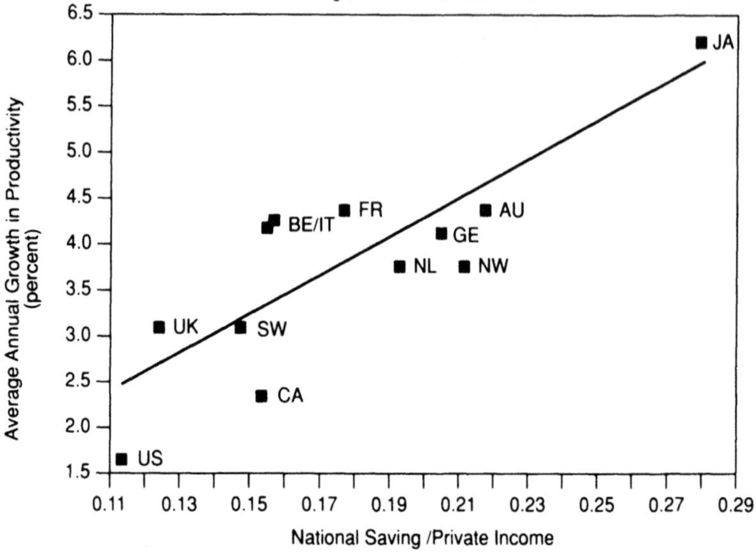

KEY: AU=Austria; BE=Belgium; CA=Canada; FR=France; GE=Germany (West); IT=Italy; JA=Japan; NL=Netherlands; NW=Norway; SW=Sweden; UK=United Kingdom; and US=United States.

Source: Organisation for Economic Co-operation and Development, *National Accounts*.

FIGURE 8.7
1988 World Capital Flows
(billions of U.S. dollars)

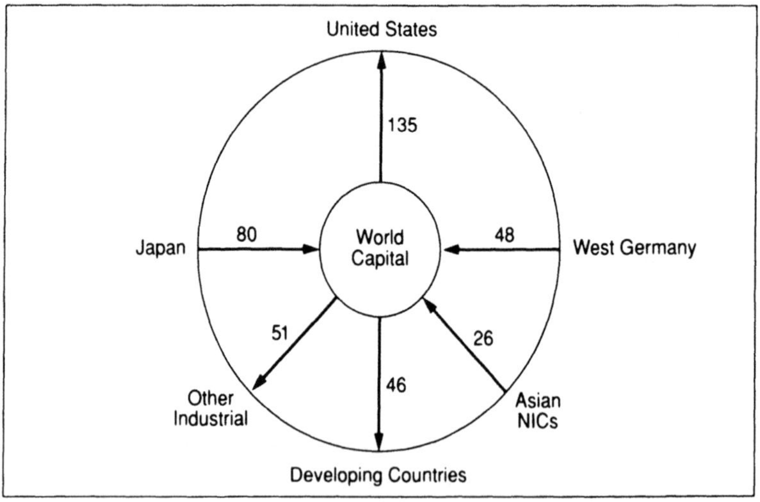

Source: Organisation for Economic Co-operation and Development, *Main Economic Indicators*.

Note: Current account balances do not sum to zero because of statistical discrepancies in the international accounts.

during 1988, thereby crowding out other potential borrowers and increasing world real interest rates. Reduced U.S. national saving has coincided with a sharp increase in world real interest rates. Whereas the real interest rate averaged less than 2 percent in the industrialized economies prior to 1980, it has averaged between 3 and 5 percent in recent years. These high real interest rates increase financial distress. Each 1 point reduction in real interest rates means more than a $5 billion reduction in the debt bills of the major debtor nations. The International Monetary Fund has attributed close to one-fourth of the observed increases in debt-GNP ratios for the seven largest industrial countries to high interest rates. High interest rates also discourage worldwide investment of all kinds.

Second, continuing, large U.S. trade deficits threaten the world's free trading system. Even though I have argued that the magnitude of trade and current account deficits has far more to do with overall levels of national saving and investment than with specific trade practices, this proposition is not widely accepted. As a consequence, large trade deficits call forth increased pressures for protectionist policies in the United States and heighten demands for movements toward a worldwide system of managed trade. These pressures have been contained to some degree so far, but this containment reflects the fact that employment, investment, and output in the U.S. traded goods sector have increased rapidly over the last several years. If and when the next recession comes and manufacturing employment declines rapidly, the pressures for protection will increase greatly. Even if it never comes to pass, fears of U.S. protectionism have adverse consequences for the world economy, encouraging other nations to form trading blocs, to locate plants in ways that would otherwise be economically unsound in an effort to circumvent trade barriers, and to resist U.S. efforts at market opening.

Third, because U.S. trade deficits of the current magnitude are unsustainable, they are likely sources of instability in the world economy. If U.S. trade deficits of the current magnitude continue, the ratio of U.S. foreign debt to GNP will approach one-third by the year 2000 and will be increasing at a rate of nearly $300 billion a year. This is not a sustainable path. If and when foreign investors are no longer willing to loan large amounts of money to the United States on current terms, the result will be a sharp, sudden decline in the value of the dollar. Given the tendency of speculators to follow trends, such a decline may be uncontrollable.

A sudden withdrawal of foreign capital from the United States would pose severe problems for policymakers both here and abroad. U.S. monetary policy would have no attractive choices at a time when interest rates were rising rapidly and a sharply falling dollar was increasing inflationary pressures. Other countries would face a sudden reduction in export demand as the dollar fell. A round of competitive devaluations could reduce worldwide price stability. A "hard landing," although by

TABLE 8.1
U.S. Saving Rate
(percent of GNP)

Year/Period	Components of Saving				
	National	Government	Private	Personal	Corporate
1988	2.7	-2.1	4.8	3.1	1.7
1970s	7.0	-0.9	7.9	5.5	2.4

Source: U.S. Department of Commerce, Bureau of Economic Analysis, *National Income and Product Accounts*

no means a certainty in the near term in the absence of U.S. policy actions, is a continuing threat as long as U.S. policymakers do not act to increase national saving and reduce the U.S. appetite for foreign capital.

WHY IS U.S. NATIONAL SAVING SO LOW?

Whereas federal deficits were the dominant cause of low national saving in the early part of the 1980s, low private saving has been the primary drag on the national saving rate in recent years. As Table 8.1 illustrates, the U.S. national saving rate equaled 2.7 percent of GNP in 1988, compared with an average of 7.0 percent during the 1970s. Of the 4.3 percent decline in the national saving rate, 1.2 percent is the result of an enlarged public-sector deficit, and 3.1 percent is the result of a decline in private saving. More than three-quarters of the decline in private saving is the result of reduced personal saving.

As a number of writers have emphasized, the division of national saving into components is highly arbitrary. For example, in the measurement of saving rates, it may be appropriate to treat only the real component, not the inflationary component, of interest rates as a cost to governments and as income to households. The distinction between personal and corporate saving is especially tenuous. As James Poterba and other analysts have stressed, when a corporation pays a dividend, corporate saving is reduced and personal saving is increased. But the functionally equivalent transaction of repurchasing shares does not affect measured corporate saving. Similar ambiguities arise in connection with corporate pension funding policies. Nonetheless, previous research suggests that regardless of how saving is measured, declining personal saving is an important part of the reason for low U.S. national saving in the 1980s.[3]

A similar conclusion regarding the importance of personal saving is suggested by international comparisons. Table 8.2 contrasts national saving and its components in a number of countries. As has already been demonstrated, U.S. national saving lags badly. The primary reason

TABLE 8.2
International Comparison of Saving Rates
(percent of GDP)

	Components of Saving				
	National	Government	Private	Personal	Corporate
USA	2.7	-2.1	4.8	3.1	1.7
Japan	17.3	3.2	14.1	11.8	2.3
West Germany	8.5	1.0	7.5	5.3	2.2
OECD	7.7	-1.8	9.5	7.8	1.7

Sources: U.S. data are from U.S. Department of Commerce, Bureau of Economic Research, *National Income and Product Accounts.* Other data are derived from information published annually by the United Nations in *National Accounts Statistics: Main Aggregates and Detailed Tables;* reprinted with permission.

Note: U.S. data are for 1988; other data are for 1981–1985.

is low personal saving. It is instructive to consider the reasons for low U.S. personal saving in the 1980s and whether a sharp rise in the saving rate is likely during the 1990s without policy actions. Although these issues have not been resolved definitively, a number of hypotheses have been put forward.

Demographic Factors

The possibility that demographic factors have decreased the personal saving rate during the 1980s and will increase it during the 1990s has received considerable attention. In fact, however, there is little evidence to support the idea that the changing age composition of the population will have a large impact on personal saving. Even though older households do have higher saving rates, the share of total income going to households in different age groups changes only very gradually. For example, from 1968 to 1984, the largest relative change in income shares was a 5.7 percent drop in the share of income going to those aged forty-five to fifty-four. Even if we assume that this age group saves at a 15 percent higher rate than the rest of the population does, this would translate into a reduction in the saving rate of less than 1 percent.

Chris Carroll and I have systematically examined the issue of demographic change and saving by first estimating age-specific saving rates and then using these rates to forecast the effects of the population's changing age composition.[4] Our results, illustrated in Table 8.3, suggest that only a negligible fraction of the decline in personal saving can be attributed to demographic changes. The corollary implication is that the aging of the baby-boom generation is unlikely to appreciably increase personal saving.

TABLE 8.3
Adjustment to Personal Saving Rate for Changing Demographic Composition

Year	Consumer Expenditure Survey	Survey of Consumer Finances
1970	-0.1	0.0
1972	-0.2	0.0
1974	-0.4	0.0
1976	-0.3	-0.1
1978	-0.3	-0.1
1980	-0.4	-0.2
1982	-0.3	-0.4
1984	0.0	-0.4

Source: Author's calculations from data from the Consumer Expenditure Survey and the Survey of Consumer Finances.

Rates of Return

The question of whether increases in after-tax rates of return increase saving continues to be a matter of controversy. Some strong theoretical arguments suggest that consumers should increase saving when real interest rates rise.[5] But the experience of the 1980s was not kind to this point of view. By any measure, real interest rates were far higher than in earlier decades. At least part of the increase could be attributed to fiscal and monetary policies, not increased consumer spending, so theory would have predicted a sharp increase in personal saving. This effect should have been magnified by reduced tax rates and increased saving incentives. Yet personal saving fell, rather than rose. A definitive conclusion is not now possible, but it appears that either rates of return had little empirical effect on saving or other factors had an enormous negative impact on saving during the 1980s.

Debt

A more plausible explanation for low saving in the 1980s emphasizes increased consumer borrowing. By almost any measure, consumer indebtedness increased more rapidly than income during the 1980s. Of greatest importance was increased mortgage borrowing. Whereas downpayments averaged 20 percent of sale price for first-time home buyers in 1980, this figure had fallen to 11.4 percent by 1985. In addition to increased mortgage borrowing at the time of purchase, consumers increased second-mortgage borrowing against their homes. Second-mortgage debt increased from 3.2 percent of all mortgages in 1980 to 10.8

percent in 1987. The combined result of these developments was a sharp increase, from 36 to 45 percent, in the ratio of outstanding mortgage debt to the value of home equity.[6]

International evidence also suggests the importance of consumer debt as a cause of differences in personal saving rates. Vito Tanzi claimed that "the saving rate for countries with generous deductions for consumer interest is almost three times the saving rate for countries with the least generous deductions for consumer interest."[7] The difficulty of consumer borrowing in Japan, where the saving rate is very high, is notorious. Unfortunately, research has not yet succeeded in quantifying the reduction in personal saving that is attributable to increased borrowing.

Precautionary Saving

A great deal of household saving is motivated by retirement or the possibility of death, disability, or large outlays for medical care. There is some evidence that the importance of these motivations for saving has declined in the United States in recent years. For the first time in history, the median income of the elderly is actually greater than the median income of the remainder of the population. The prevalence of life and disability insurance has increased rapidly, as has the share of health outlays that are covered by some form of insurance. Although not amenable to year-by-year, time-series analysis, these factors may have tended to depress U.S. saving over time.

A comparison with Japan is also suggestive in this regard. Social security benefits in Japan are far less generous than they are in the United States. According to Charles Horioka, "41 percent of the elderly surveyed in Japan live with their married sons whereas the corresponding figure for the United States and Europe is only 0.5–3.5 percent." A different source claims that two-thirds of persons older than sixty-five in Japan live with their children.[8] Almost certainly, the need to compensate children for old-age care is an important reason the Japanese saving rate is so high.

Interactions Between Corporate and Household Saving

During the years 1983–1987, more than $400 billion in corporate equity was absorbed by corporate takeovers and share repurchases. These restructurings contributed to rising stock prices, which fueled consumption growth. They may also have contributed more directly to reduced personal saving.

Although repurchases of equity funnel cash to shareholders in much the same way dividends do, these receipts do not show up in disposable income. If consumers consume some part of them, the measured personal saving rate will be depressed. In some recent years, cash funneled to households in restructurings exceeded 4 percent of disposable income. As Figure 8.8 illustrates, takeover receipts alone transferred more than

FIGURE 8.8
Cash Receipts from Takeovers
(percent of disposable income)

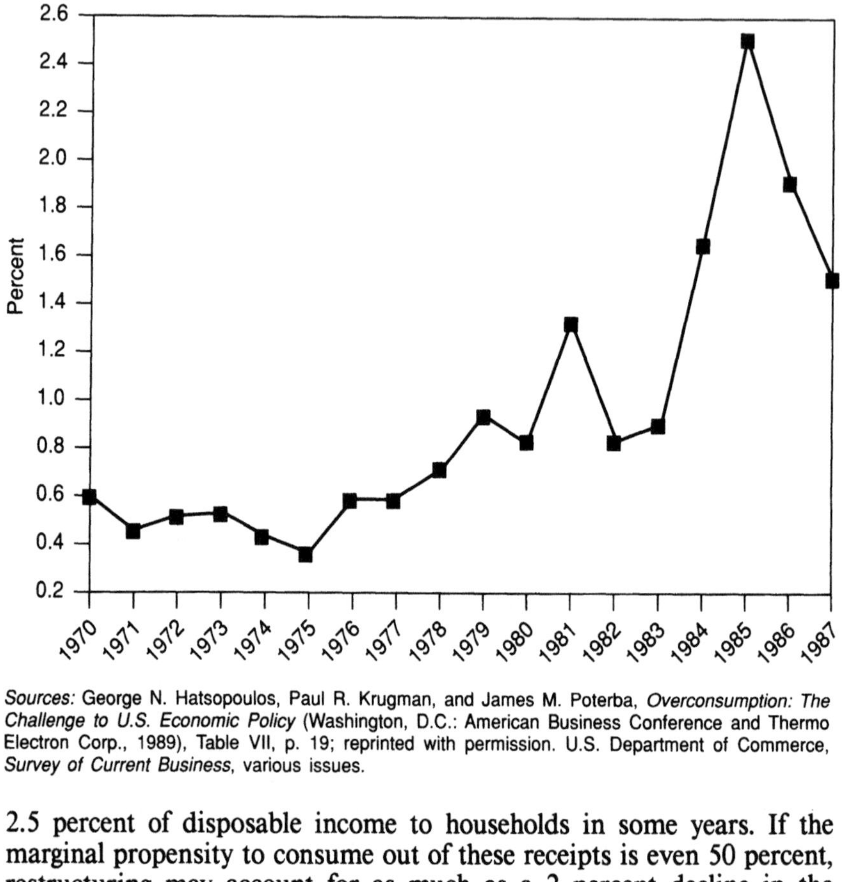

Sources: George N. Hatsopoulos, Paul R. Krugman, and James M. Poterba, *Overconsumption: The Challenge to U.S. Economic Policy* (Washington, D.C.: American Business Conference and Thermo Electron Corp., 1989), Table VII, p. 19; reprinted with permission. U.S. Department of Commerce, *Survey of Current Business*, various issues.

2.5 percent of disposable income to households in some years. If the marginal propensity to consume out of these receipts is even 50 percent, restructuring may account for as much as a 2 percent decline in the measured saving rate.

These effects have probably been enhanced to at least some degree by the increased capital gains realizations caused by lower tax rates. By unlocking assets, capital gains tax reductions have made it easier for consumers to consume out of their wealth and thus have probably operated to increase national saving. Increased tax rates on capital gains are probably one reason for the modest increases in personal saving observed in 1988 and 1989.

HOUSEHOLD SAVING BEHAVIOR

The primary reason U.S. national saving is so low is that most U.S. households save very little. In fact, available statistics suggest that most U.S. households engage in no financial saving. Less than 40 percent of U.S. households reported interest and dividend income of $100 or more in six consecutive years during the early 1980s, and nearly 33 percent never had $100 in gross interest and dividend income. This point may be made in another way. Even at a time when the interest rate on car loans far exceeded the rates people could earn on their money, almost three-quarters of all automobiles and more than one-half of all Cadillacs purchased in the United States were bought on credit.[9]

The failure of most U.S. families to save is understandable when social attitudes toward saving are considered. One recent effort to evaluate public opinions toward saving concluded that "over and over respondents insisted that increased saving would hurt the economy. . . . Many respondents expressed deep ambivalence about the moral value of saving. Most respondents were strongly skeptical of the claim that there is a connection between how much people save and how much is available for investment."[10] Similar public opinion data for Japan are not available, but they would probably suggest a very different conclusion.

In all likelihood, saving declined during the 1980s because institutional changes made it easier for people to act on the basis of prevalent social attitudes. The easier availability of credit, increased cash receipts from corporate restructuring activities, and the reduced need for retirement and rainy-day saving were probably the most important reasons for the recent decline in saving.

CAN PUBLIC POLICY STIMULATE PERSONAL SAVING?

The most effective and reliable way to increase U.S. national saving is to reduce the budget deficit and to move ultimately toward a regime where the United States runs chronic budget surpluses. But the statistics in Table 8.1 make it very clear that even if the United States balanced its budget, U.S. national saving would be woefully inadequate by either historical or international standards. This reality combined with the apparent inability of the political process to produce balanced budgets suggests the importance of policies that stimulate private saving, of which personal saving is the most important component.

Many economists argue that private saving rates are almost immutable and difficult to influence with the tools that government policy has at its disposal. The large drop in the personal and private saving rate in the United States during the 1980s should convince even skeptics that the U.S. personal saving rate is not a constant of nature. More dramatic evidence that public policy can have an important effect comes from a historical comparison of U.S. and Japanese saving rates. As Figure 8.9 illustrates, U.S. saving actually exceeded Japanese saving prior to World War II. Culture does not explain why Japan saves so much, except insofar as Japanese culture is shaped by policies such as the special *maryou* saving incentives adopted in order to ensure rapid recovery after World War II.

FIGURE 8.9
Pre- vs. Postwar Gross Saving Rates
(percent of GNP)

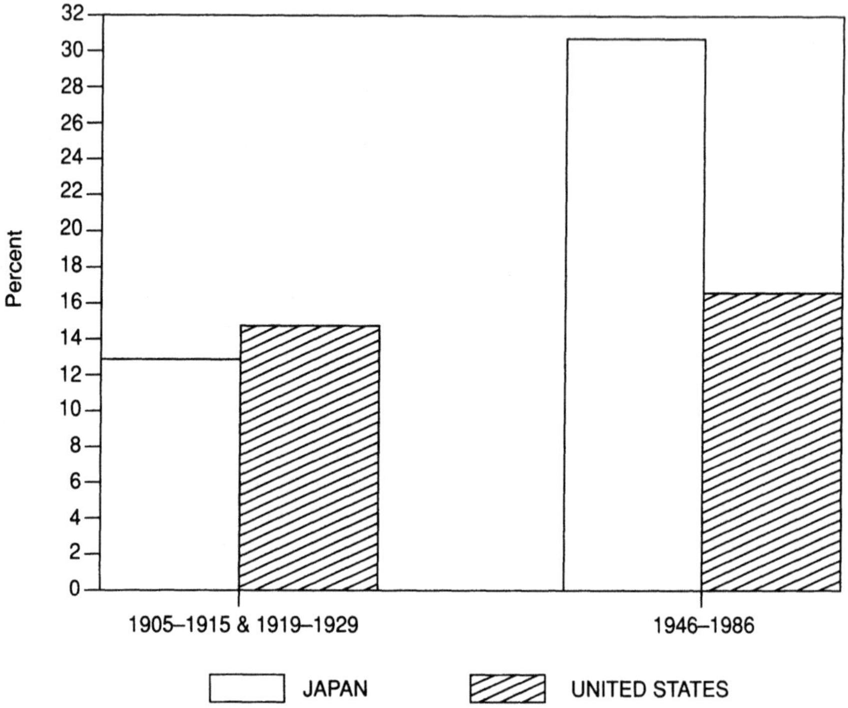

Sources: Japanese data for the period 1905–1929 are from Kazushi Okawa and Henry Rosovsky, *Japanese Economic Growth* (Stanford, Calif.: Stanford University Press, 1973). Japanese data for the period 1946–1960 are from Bank of Japan, *100 Years of Economic Statistics* (Tokyo: Bank of Japan, 1966). Other data for Japan are from Organisation for Economic Co-operation and Development, *National Accounts.* U.S. data for 1905–1929 and for 1946–1969 are from U.S. Department of Commerce, *Historical Statistics,* Series F540-F551 and Series F552-F565, respectively. U.S. data for 1970–1986 are from Organisation for Economic Co-operation and Development, *National Accounts.*

The evidence in the previous section suggests that to be successful, public policies directed at stimulating saving must be directed toward changing public attitudes. In a real sense, saving, like life insurance, is sold—not bought. As with energy conservation, there is ample room for leadership from the "bully pulpit" of the presidency. In addition to rhetoric about the importance of saving, there is scope for additional stimulus to saving in at least three areas: restoration and extension of IRAs, further incentives for employer-provided saving, and limitations on financial engineering.

The Case for Restoring and Expanding IRAs

Although the 1986 Tax Reform Act increased economic efficiency in many ways, the partial revocation of IRAs was unfortunate because the conviction that IRAs are ineffective in stimulating saving is not supported by the available evidence. Even though personal saving rates did decline following the enactment of IRAs, many factors could have been responsible. Without the enactment of IRAs, the U.S. saving rate might well have fallen even further. In fact, IRA contributions accounted for more than one-quarter of all personal saving in 1986.

Simplistic before-and-after comparisons do not shed much light on the incentive effects of IRAs, however. But other evidence does strongly suggest that they have a significant impact on saving. Perhaps the most direct supporting evidence comes from surveys of savers. Respondents in the Federal Reserve's Survey of Consumer Finances were asked whether they made IRA contributions, among other questions about financial affairs. David Wise of Harvard's Kennedy School of Government and Steven Venti of Dartmouth College conducted a series of careful statistical analyses of these data, on the basis of which they concluded that about one-half of the money flowing into IRAs represents new savings, about 30 percent comes from the taxes individuals save by making IRA contributions, and only about 20 percent comes from saving that would have taken place in the absence of IRAs.[11] Similar conclusions were suggested by research carried out by Daniel Feenberg and Jonathan Skinner of the National Bureau of Economic Research.[12]

Other evidence also refutes the claim that most IRA contributions come from a reshuffling of assets. First, the Consumer Expenditure Survey indicated that the median IRA contributor had only $8,000 in fully liquid assets in 1985. For a married couple, this was only two years' IRA contribution. The available data also suggest that most IRA contributors have very little interest and dividend income. It seems unlikely that people with modest asset holdings could finance IRA contributions by reshuffling for very long. Indeed, it is ironic that IRAs were scaled back just when their effectiveness in stimulating new saving should have increased.

Second, nearly two-thirds of IRA contributors do not make the maximum possible contribution, suggesting that they cannot effortlessly move money in order to contribute. Further evidence that many IRA contributions represent incremental saving is provided by the behavior of IRA contributors. In many cases, married couples contribute only the $2,000 allotment permitted to single people rather than the full contribution that they are permitted under law.

Third, the timing of IRA contributions is suggestive. An individual can maximize the tax advantage of an IRA by contributing as early as possible (in January of each tax year). Presumably, taxpayers who were simply shifting assets that were being saved anyway would make their IRA contributions early in the tax year. But taxpayers for whom IRA contributions represent new saving may not have the funds on hand to contribute early in the tax year. Internal Revenue Service statistics reveal that some $15 billion, or 45 percent, of 1984 IRA contributions were actually made in 1985, which suggests that a significant amount of new saving was generated by IRA contributions. It is striking that, holding everything else constant, individuals are more likely to make an IRA contribution if they owe taxes in April than if they expect to receive a refund.

More important than the question of whether IRA saving is financed through borrowing or other saving is the broader effect of IRAs on attitudes toward saving. Given our national saving problem, it is unfortunate that polls reveal that many people regard increasing saving as bad for the economy because it reduces the demand for goods. IRAs and the advertising they generate are a useful counterbalance to this sentiment. The existence of IRAs may cause people to focus more on the need to save for their retirement than they otherwise would. IRAs certainly give banks and other financial institutions a strong incentive to remind people of the need to save for retirement.

Unfortunately, since the partial repeal of IRAs in 1986, this incentive has dwindled. A top executive of one very large New York bank indicated to me that his bank reduced its IRA advertising budget from $23 million to less than $10 million following the 1986 tax act and intended to reduce its budget even further if the law was not changed. This is not atypical. Press reports suggest that many other financial institutions abandoned IRA advertising once the potential market was reduced following the 1986 act. There is evidence that advertising IRAs mattered. Figure 8.10 illustrates that *even among those who remained eligible following the 1986 act, the take-up rate for IRAs declined sharply in 1987.* Moreover, despite their attractiveness for many high-income taxpayers, nondeductible IRAs have not been popular.

International experience confirms the view that saving incentives matter. Most of the nations we compete with have higher saving rates than ours. Most also have more generous saving incentive programs, as Table 8.4 suggests. Especially dramatic evidence of the long-term importance of the hortatory effects of saving incentives comes from Canada, which implemented a retirement savings program like our IRA program in 1972 and significantly liberalized it in 1976. As Figure 8.11 illustrates, the private saving rate in Canada, which had closely tracked that of the United States, took off soon after the 1976 liberalization and has outpaced ours ever since.

The weight of the available evidence suggests that IRAs generated a significant amount of saving that would otherwise not have taken place. If IRAs were reinstated under current law, the government would lose about twenty-five cents for each one dollar of contribution. If more than one-fourth of the money contributed to IRAs represents new saving, IRAs will increase private saving by more than their revenue cost. If this condition is met, the case for reinstating IRAs is clear. Even if it is not, there is still a strong case for saving incentives given that the restoration of IRAs would be likely to come at the expense of other tax breaks rather than at the expense of larger deficits.

FIGURE 8.10
IRA Uptake Rate for Taxpayers
with Income Less than $40,000 Per Year

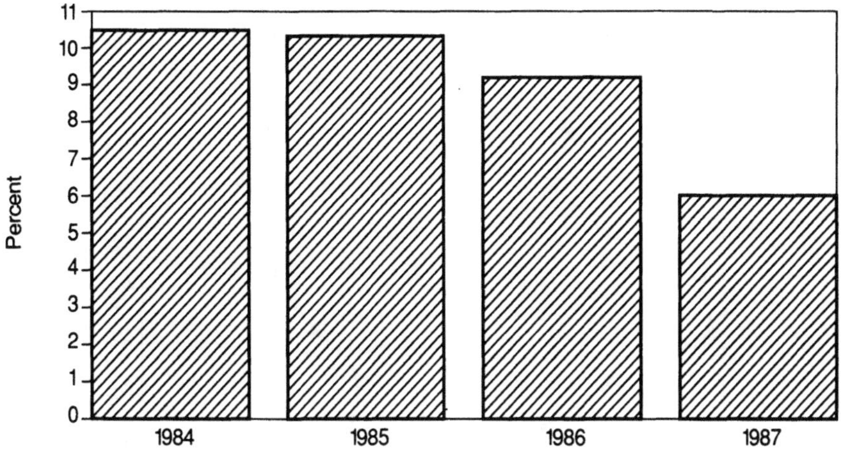

Source: U.S. Internal Revenue Service, *Statistics of Income.*

TABLE 8.4
Saving Incentives: Some International Examples

Belgium:	Income from savings bank deposits is deductible up to a limit (U.S. $800 in 1987).
Canada:	Up to U.S. $750 of investment income is tax free. Savings in registered pension plans (RPPs) and registered retirement savings plans (RRSPs) is tax deductible up to a limit (U.S. $2,640 in 1987). In addition, the income earned accumulates free of tax.
Finland:	All interest from bank deposits and government bonds is tax deductible.
France:	Income from bonds and from shares is deductible up to a limit (U.S. $830 and U.S. $500, respectively, in 1987). Net purchases of shares are deductible up to a limit (U.S. $830 in 1987). There is a flat-rate withholding tax on investments rather than the steeper income tax rates.
West Germany:	Income from capital is exempt from taxation up to a limit (U.S. $440/couple in 1987).
Italy:	Interest from government bonds is tax deductible. Nondividend returns are subject to a flat-rate withholding tax.
Japan:	Prior to 1987, interest on bank deposits, public bonds, mortgaged debentures, stock investment trusts, postal savings, and government bonds was deductible up to very high limits. Interest income or distribution of profits from employee savings accounts is deductible if used for housing or pension purposes (up to U.S. $35,000 in 1987).
Netherlands:	Interest received is deductible up to a limit (U.S. $690 in 1987). Dividends received are tax free up to a limit (U.S. $990 in 1987).
Norway:	Interest and dividend income is tax free up to a limit (U.S. $600/couple in 1987). Investment in special bank plans and in shares is tax deductible up to a limit (U.S. $1,190/couple and U.S. $600/couple, respectively, in 1987).

FIGURE 8.11
Canadian vs. U.S. Private Saving
(percent of GNP)

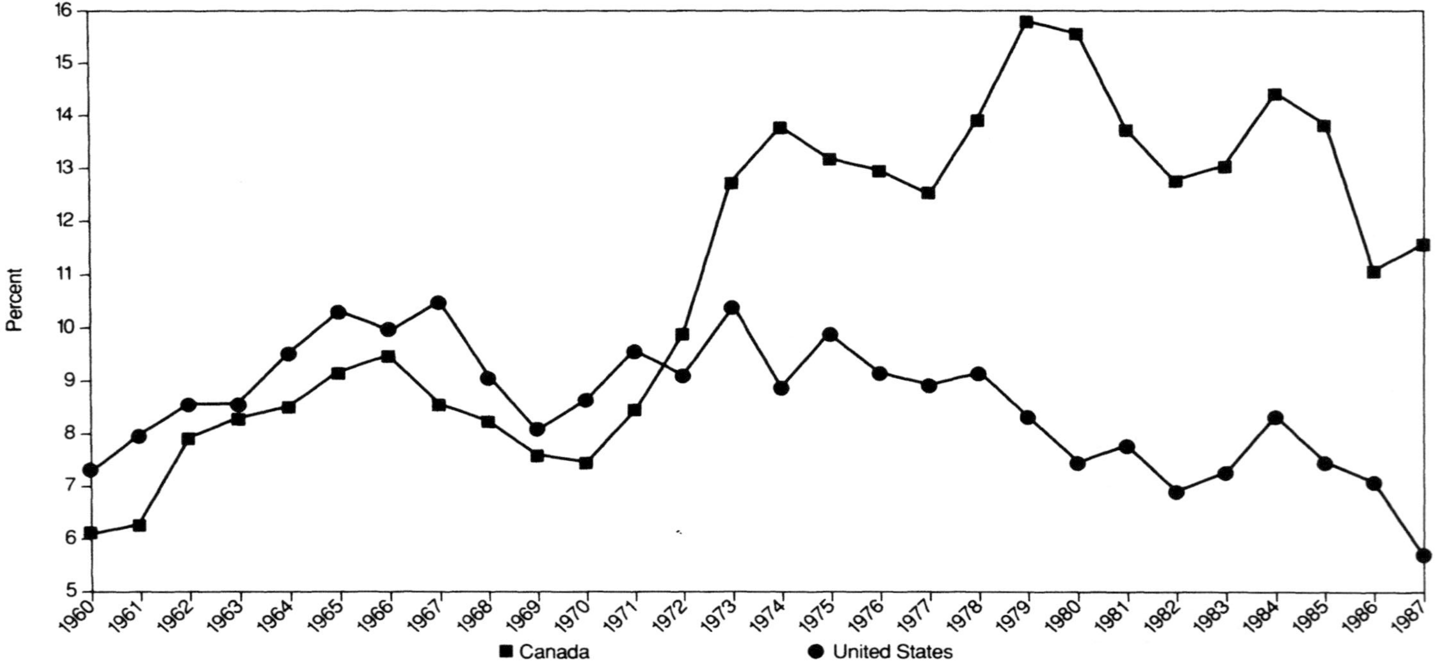

Source: Chris Carroll and Lawrence H. Summers, "Why Have Private Savings Rates in the United States and Canada Diverged?" *Journal of Monetary Economics* 20 (1987), Figure 1A, p. 252; adapted with permission of Elsevier Science Publishers.

Although hard statistical evidence is not available, I believe that IRAs would be more attractive if they could be used to finance new homes and education as well as retirement. The argument that saving for these purposes would not be incremental misses the key point. Most people in the United States do not save at all. Any saving stimulated by IRAs or by the advertising they would generate would be incremental.

Employer-Based Saving

The largest U.S. tax expenditure is the $60 billion devoted to the encouragement of pension saving. Employer contributions to private pensions have accounted for nearly one-half of all personal saving in some recent years. These figures raise the question of whether further steps could be taken to encourage employers to save on behalf of their employees.

Current "top-heavy" and nondiscrimination rules limit employers' ability to provide different benefits to different workers. Typically employers find that generous pension or 401(k) plans are more attractive to high-income than to low-income employees. In order to be able to offer such plans to high-wage employees, employers often have to "bribe" low-wage employees to take advantage of the plans. This has the effect of sharply increasing the rate of return for low-income savers and encourages saving. In many cases, the government gets a great deal of saving bang for its buck, as employers provide matching contributions to encourage some of their employees to save.

Given the importance of "selling" saving, let us consider further ways employers could be induced to encourage their employees, particularly their younger low-income employees, to save. Two possibilities suggest themselves. First, employers could be required to provide employees with 401(k) plans that meet the nondiscrimination rules. Because this mandate would force employers to work hard to convince their low-income employees to save, it would be a cost-effective use of government money. In any event, as with IRAs, it is important to remember that the first-year revenue cost of encouraging saving exceeds the total cost because taxes deferred are eventually collected, with interest.

Second, the uses to which 401(k) money is put could be broadened. As long as Social Security benefits replace a large share of the final salary of low-wage earners, it will be very difficult to convince them to save for retirement. Perhaps it would be easier to encourage saving for other contingencies. This could be accomplished by permitting individuals to borrow for brief periods from the 401(k) for certain established purposes.

Financial Engineering and Capital Gains Taxes

As was previously emphasized, one of the factors propelling consumption upward and saving downward during the 1980s was households' forced realization of capital gains during corporate restructurings. More generally, it is likely that measures that encourage households to convert their wealth from illiquid to liquid forms will tend to encourage consumption. To the extent that reductions in capital gains taxes in 1978 and again in 1981 encouraged wealth holders to turn their assets over more quickly and made corporate restructuring transactions more attractive, these reductions probably operated to increase consumption and reduce personal saving. Even though simple before-and-after comparisons can never be conclusive, it is noteworthy that personal saving dropped off sharply following the 1978 and 1981 tax cuts and increased slightly following the full implementation of the 1986 Tax Reform Act.

This effect is augmented if reduced capital gains taxes also raise asset values. On the other side of the ledger, reduced capital gains taxes raise rates of return, which may encourage some saving, although as we have seen, the evidence of the 1980s does not suggest that this is likely to have a large effect on saving behavior.

Balancing these considerations suggests that *a reduction in capital gains taxes is likely to reduce personal saving* and the supply of capital. This outcome is especially likely in the case of a temporary reduction in capital gains taxes. Because a temporary cut will affect only old assets, it is not likely to stimulate new saving because it has no impact on long-term expected returns. But the strong incentive that a tax holiday gives to cash out past gains is almost certain to encourage consumption and reduce personal saving.

It is true, as proponents of capital gains reform argue, that a capital gains tax cut will increase entrepreneurs', real estate investors', and other beneficiaries' demand for capital. But it will also reduce the supply of capital. Thus, a tax cut will have one of two effects. Either too much demand for capital chasing too little supply will lead to rising interest rates and capital costs that will choke off excess investment demand, or there will be enlarged inflows of capital from abroad and a higher trade deficit.

These possible effects suggest that national saving considerations mitigate against a capital gains tax reduction. If a capital gains cut nonetheless were enacted, its adverse effects on saving could be minimized in three ways. First, relief should be given only when the recipients of capital gains reinvest their earnings. Rollover provisions such as those used with owner-occupied housing would ensure that capital gains cuts did not encourage asset sales to finance consumption. Second, relief should be given prospectively, not on gains already accrued. Rate reductions for old capital raise consumption and do little else. Third, relief should not be given to gains on assets such as land and collectibles that are in fixed supply. Such relief only confers windfalls and encourages consumption.

In a similar vein, any policies that have the effect of slowing money down or making borrowing more difficult are likely to promote saving.

These policies might include securities transactions taxes or penalty taxes on very short-term gains and further restrictions on the deductibility of interest on bonds, which are actually a close substitute for equity. The merits of these policies obviously depend on much more than their overall saving impact.

CONCLUSION

Increasing national saving is the most important economic priority facing the United States. Without increases in national saving, it will be impossible to meet the goals of increasing investment and reducing dependence on foreign capital. Substantial increases in personal saving are necessary if even minimally adequate levels of national saving are to be attained. Overwhelming evidence suggests that public policy can affect saving behavior. Restoring and extending IRAs would be a good place to start. Liberalizing pension and 401(k) rules and reforming the capital gains tax to asset holders to encourage long-term investment would also make contributions to the raising of personal saving.

As long as the public believes that saving is undesirable, it is very unlikely that U.S. saving will increase. New prosaving policies must be coupled with efforts to educate the public about the importance of domestic saving. Presidential leadership is needed both to educate the public on the importance of saving and to enact the policies that will provide the necessary incentives.

NOTES

I am indebted to Jonathan Gruber for research assistance and to Dr. James Poterba for helpful discussions. This analysis draws on earlier work done jointly with Chris Carroll.

1. For a fuller discussion of the relationship between U.S. competitiveness and the national saving rate, see George Hatsopoulos, Paul Krugman, and Lawrence Summers, "U.S. Competitiveness: Beyond the Trade Deficit," *Science*, July 15, 1988, pp. 299–307.
2. Fumio Hayashi, "Is Japan's Saving Rate High?" *Federal Reserve Bank of Minneapolis Quarterly Review* (Spring 1989), p. 9. Business consultant Kenichi Ohmae, "Americans and Japanese Save About the Same," *Wall Street Journal*, June 14, 1988, p. 34, put forth arguments similar to those of Hayashi.
3. See Lawrence Summers and Chris Carroll, "Why Is U.S. National Saving so Low?" *Brookings Papers on Economic Activity* 2 (1987), pp. 607–635.
4. Ibid.
5. See Lawrence H. Summers, "Capital Taxation and Accumulation in a Life Cycle Growth Model," *American Economic Review* (September 1981), pp. 533–544. For some counterarguments, see David A. Starrett, "Effects of Taxes on Saving," in Henry Aaron, Harvey Galper, and Joseph A. Pechman, eds., *Uneasy Compromise: Problems of a Hybrid Income-Consumption Tax* (Washington, D.C.: Brookings Institution, 1988), pp. 237–268.

6. For a thorough discussion of mortgage market developments, see Joyce Manchester and James Poterba, "Second Mortgages and Household Saving," *NBER Working Paper No. 2853* (Cambridge, Mass.: National Bureau of Economic Research, February 1989).

7. Vito Tanzi, "The Tax Treatment of Interest Incomes and Expenses in Industrial Countries: A Discussion of Recent Change," *Proceedings of the NTA, 1987* (Columbus, Ohio: National Tax Association, 1988), p. 134.

8. This paragraph is drawn from Roger S. Smith, "Factors Affecting Saving, Policy Tools, and Tax Reform: A Review," *IMF Working Paper* WP/89/47 (Washington, D.C.: International Monetary Fund, 1989). Charles Horioka is cited on p. 35 of the working paper.

9. For a discussion of heterogeneity in saving behavior, see Chris Carroll and Lawrence Summers, "Consumption Growth Parallels Income Growth: Some New Evidence," *NBER Working Paper No. 3090* (Cambridge, Mass.: National Bureau of Economic Research, September 1989).

10. John Immerwahr, *Saving: Good or Bad? A Pilot Study on Public Attitudes Toward Saving, Investment, and Competitiveness* (New York: Public Agenda Foundation, 1989).

11. Steven Venti and David Wise, "Have IRAs Increased U.S. Saving? Evidence from Consumer Expenditure Surveys," *NBER Working Paper No. 2217* (Cambridge, Mass.: National Bureau of Economic Research, April 1987).

12. Daniel Feenberg and Jonathan Skinner, "Sources of IRA Saving," *NBER Working Paper No. 2845* (Cambridge, Mass.: National Bureau of Economic Research, February 1989).

B. Prospects and Policies for Higher Personal Saving in the 1990s

James W. Christian

INTRODUCTION

In 1973, the personal saving rate in the United States (measured on a national income and product accounts basis) reached a post–World War II high of 9.4 percent and remained more than 9 percent through the recession of 1974–1975. Since that time, however, the personal saving rate has trended downward rather severely, reaching 3.2 percent in 1987.[1] This long, secular decline has given rise to a great deal of concern that the low personal saving rates of the 1980s will, through a variety of channels, lead to lower U.S. standards of living in the 1990s.

My purpose is not to draw out the dire consequences of a low personal saving rate for the economy, capital formation, international competitiveness, or the standard of living. Instead, I take the view that changes in the U.S. tax code that have already been made largely complete the agenda for creating an environment conducive to personal saving. Combined with the impending change in U.S. population demographics, these policy actions create a strong likelihood that personal saving rates will increase in the 1990s. I also note, however, that assuring increases in personal saving requires a new agenda centered on reforms in the pension system that will enhance not only the security of retirement income but personal saving as well.

Major policy actions were taken in the 1980s to create an environment more conducive to higher personal saving rates. The Economic Recovery Tax Act (ERTA) of 1981 raised after-tax rates of return on saving by reducing marginal tax rates for the first time in almost two decades. The Tax Reform Act of 1986 went even further in shifting the balance of tax incentives away from consumption toward saving. Still lower marginal personal income tax rates and the phaseout of tax deductions for consumer interest expenses further increased the after-tax rate of return on saving and raised the after-tax cost of borrowing for consumption.[2] Although the 1986 tax reform legislation was not entirely "prosaving" in that it sharply curtailed the eligibility requirements for individual retirement accounts (IRAs),[3] it is impossible to escape the conclusion that the policy environment is far more favorable to personal saving today than it was a decade ago.

That personal saving rates went into decline at almost the same time the first of these reforms was implemented and reached a post–World War II low in the year immediately following the passage of the second reform measure has tended to discredit the effectiveness of tax measures in promoting personal saving. During this period, however, the baby-boom generation was passing through the "prime buying and borrowing" phase of its life cycle while the baby-bust generation of the 1930s was passing through the "prime saving" phase of its life cycle. Common sense argues that this severe demographic mismatch would produce a decline in the aggregate personal saving rate regardless of the tax regime in place at the time. If the decline in the aggregate personal saving rate during the period 1974–1989 can be attributed largely to "life cycle" demographics, the prospects for significant improvement in the personal saving rate would appear almost certain in the 1990s, when the population demographics will become much more favorable to personal saving.

Taken together with a tax structure that is much more amenable to personal saving, the reversal of adverse demographic trends in the 1990s offers rather bright prospects for higher personal saving rates. Indeed, it appears that the personal saving rate began its trend reversal in 1988, ahead of the turn in the demographics. The increase in the personal saving rate from a forty-year low of 3.2 percent in 1987 to 4.2 percent in 1988 and to 5.4 percent in 1989 may provide the first indication that the Tax Reform Act is working in the desired direction.

The process of setting the personal saving rate back on the road to recovery may not, however, be complete. The decline in the personal saving rate has been accompanied by an equally dramatic increase in the proportion of personal saving flowing into employer-sponsored pension funds. Consequently, personal saving has become much more "contractual" and much less "discretionary," with the personal saving decision in large part passing from the individual to the employer. This analysis suggests that the consequences of this change in saving behavior may offer some scope for further policy action to support other elements now in place that are working toward an improved saving rate in the 1990s.

A PORTRAIT OF PERSONAL SAVING

The portrait of personal saving in the United States during 1974–1989 is not a pretty one. Although personal saving rates have declined generally in most countries around the world, none of those saving rates has fallen as severely as the U.S. personal saving rate.[4]

Figure 8.12 shows a striking parallel between the decline in the personal saving rate and the decline in the ratio of the number of individuals in the prime saving phase of the life cycle (ages forty-five to sixty-four) to the number of individuals in the prime buying and borrowing phase of the life cycle (ages twenty-five to forty-four). Equally promising is the projected turn in the ratio of prime savers to prime buyers/borrowers in the 1990s.[5]

Tax policy actions in the 1980s were therefore being played out on a stage dominated by demographic forces; that is, reductions in marginal tax rates were being implemented at the same time that the life cycle demographics were becoming increasingly unfavorable to personal saving and nominal interest rates were declining as well. Figure 8.13 shows that the decline in the average marginal tax rate roughly tracked the decline in nominal interest rates from their historic highs in 1981. Although the after-tax interest rate fell less than the nominal rate did because of the tax rate reductions, individual perceptions were probably focused more on the fact that nominal rates were declining.

Those in any way involved in marketing IRAs or All Savers Certificates during the early 1980s knew how difficult it was to explain to the general public the pretax equivalent return of these tax-advantaged products, primarily because most individuals were ill-informed about their own marginal tax rates. The major selling feature for the IRA thus became the simpler concept of the tax deductibility of the principal contribution. This same kind of appeal appeared to carry over to individual attitudes toward employer-sponsored pension funds, whose growth during the 1980s restrained the decline in the aggregate personal saving rate. This comparison is shown in Figure 8.14.

As pension fund balances grew and aggregate personal saving drifted downward, conventional measures of personal saving concealed a much

FIGURE 8.12
The Personal Saving Rate and the Saving Demographics

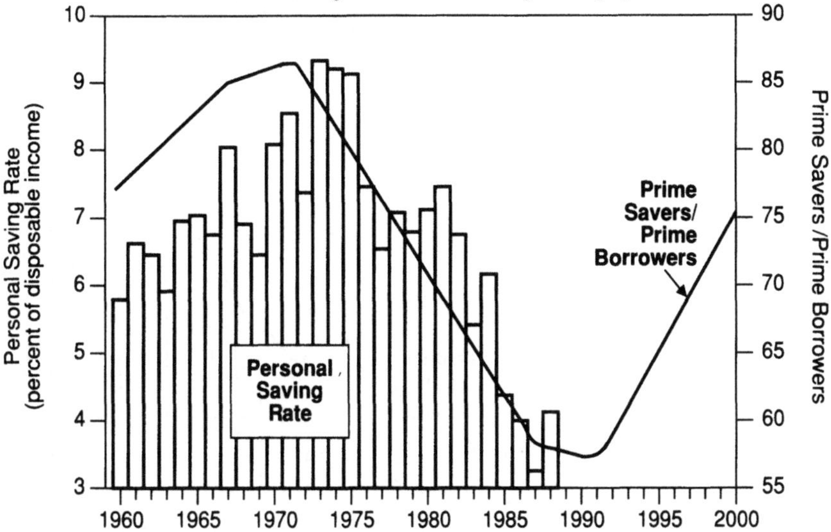

Sources: U.S. Department of Commerce, Bureau of the Census, *P-25 Population Report;* U.S. Department of Commerce, Bureau of Economic Analysis, *National Income and Product Accounts.*

FIGURE 8.13
Average Marginal Tax Rates
and Interest Rates

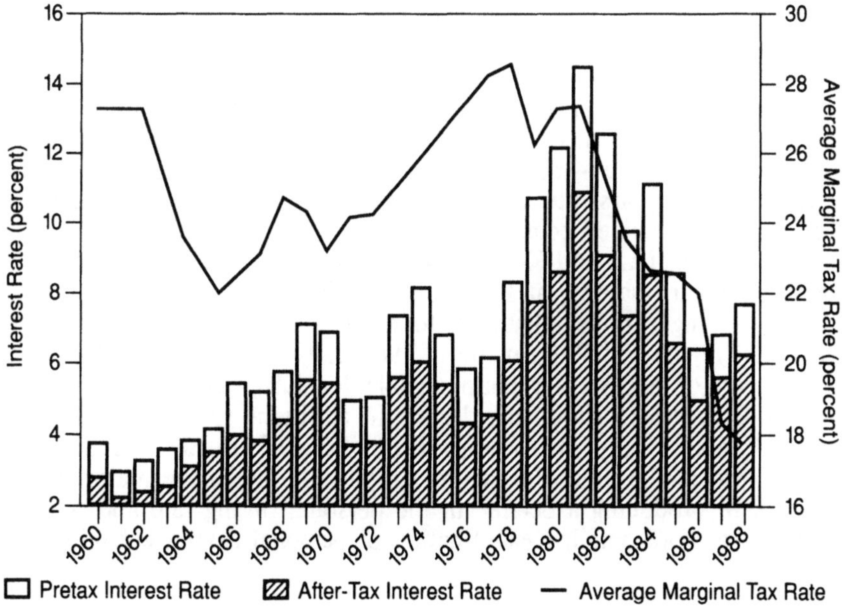

Sources: Board of Governors, Federal Reserve System, *Federal Reserve Bulletin;* Wharton Econometric Forecasting Associates.

FIGURE 8.14
Aggregate Personal Saving and
Pension Contributions and Earnings

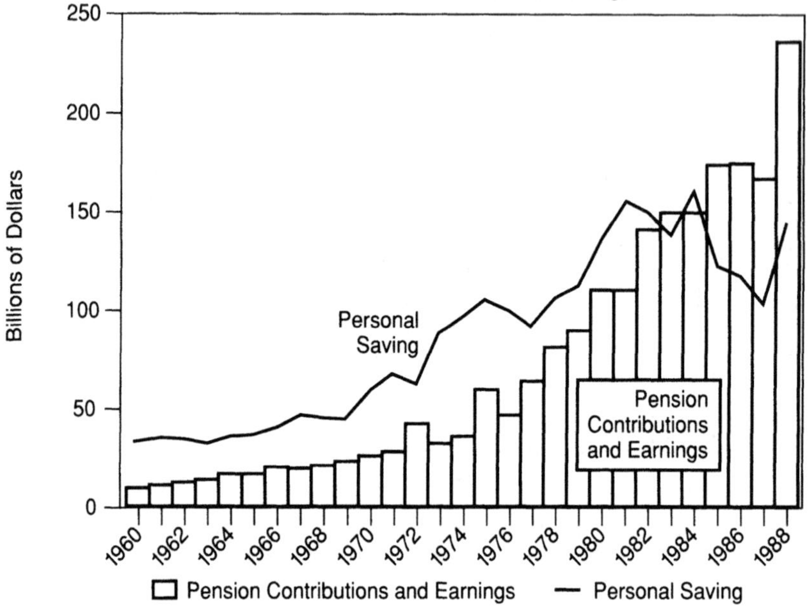

Sources: Board of Governors, Federal Reserve System, *Flow of Funds Accounts;* U.S. Department of Commerce, Bureau of Economic Analysis, *National Income and Product Accounts.*

more serious decline in discretionary personal saving. Personal saving other than annual net pension fund contributions and earnings—discretionary saving—turned *negative* in 1984. This rather serious situation is depicted in Figure 8.15. Several highly socialized countries—Finland, Sweden, and Norway—have also experienced negative personal saving rates in recent years, but the United States does not consider itself to be a highly socialized economy.[6]

Inasmuch as IRA and Keogh contributions and earnings are included in discretionary saving, at least some of the recent decline in discretionary saving can be attributed to the restrictions imposed on IRA eligibility in the Tax Reform Act of 1986, notwithstanding the fact that a majority of taxpayers remain eligible for fully deductible IRA accounts. Figure 8.16 shows the decline in additions to IRA and Keogh account balances after the passage of the Tax Reform Act in 1986. The data shown in the preceding figures graphically depict the major forces at work in producing a decline in the personal saving rate and set the stage for a more detailed examination of personal saving behavior.

DETERMINANTS OF PERSONAL SAVING

The key component of Keynesian consumption and saving theory—that personal consumption and personal saving depend on personal

FIGURE 8.15
Discretionary Personal Saving

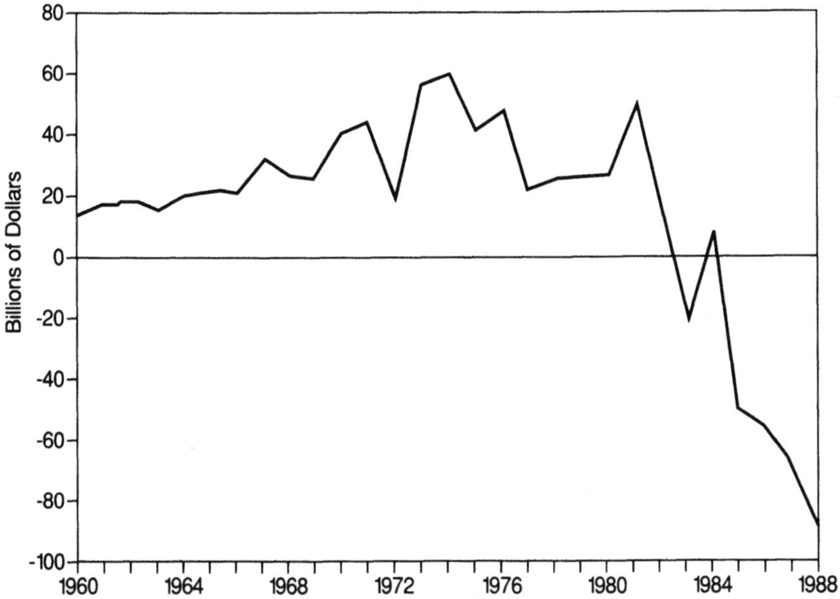

Sources: U.S. Department of Commerce, Bureau of Economic Analysis, *National Income and Product Accounts;* Board of Governors, Federal Reserve System, *Flow of Funds Accounts.*

FIGURE 8.16
Additions to IRA and Keogh Balances

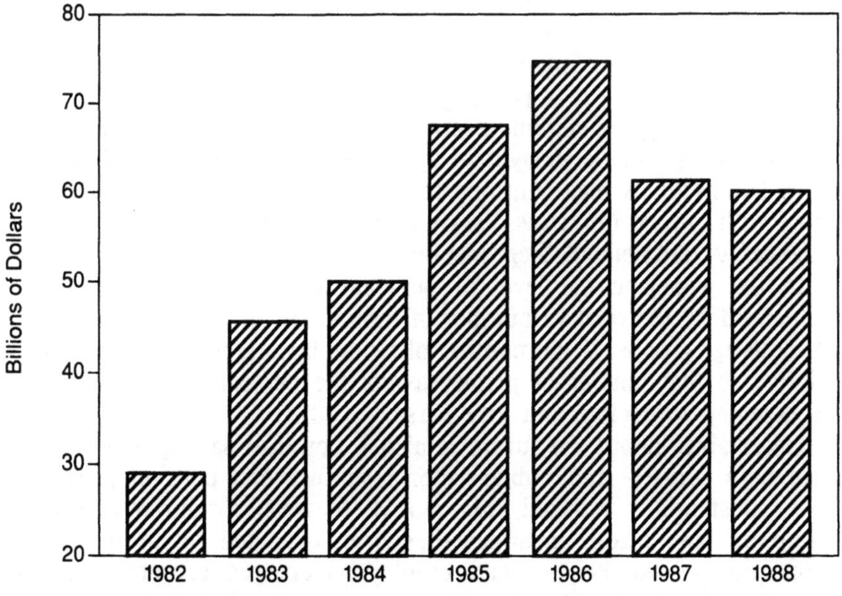

Sources: Employee Benefit Research Institute, *EBRI Issue Brief* (April 1989), Table 5, p. 9; and *Employee Benefit Notes* (January 1990), Table 1, p. 5. Adapted with permission.

disposable income—is widely accepted. There are, of course, variations on the theme, but the sheer common sense of the proposition—a person cannot spend money or save it if he or she does not have it—is compelling. Keynesian theory notwithstanding, common sense suggests that individuals work to earn income in order to buy things. Because people are presumed to prefer consumption today over consumption tomorrow and because saving represents consumption at least temporarily foregone, it follows that they require some inducement to depart from their preferences. Thus, interest rates, dividends, and the prospect of capital gains provide varying inducements to save. In more sophisticated contexts, perhaps the after-tax and/or the inflation-adjusted rate of return is the appropriate variable on which to focus.

The Ando-Modigliani life cycle hypothesis also appeals to common sense and practical experience.[7] The simple version of the life cycle hypothesis is that given personal disposable income, the aggregate level of personal saving will depend significantly on how the population is divided between "prime buyers/borrowers" and "prime savers." Prime buyers/borrowers generally correspond to that segment of the population between the ages of twenty-five and forty-four, roughly that period of the life cycle when families are formed, household capital equipment (homes, furniture, appliances, automobiles) is accumulated, children are educated, and so forth. During this phase of the life cycle, household incomes generally rise, but not as rapidly as the claims placed on them, so households in this age group tend to be net borrowers or dissavers.

In the general course of events, the growth of the claims on income diminishes by the time the household head reaches age forty-five. Moreover, household income is generally somewhat higher, so that a convergence of higher income and lower claims on income provides a wider margin for saving at the same time that household financial attention turns toward impending retirement.

Beyond age sixty-five, when retirement is presumed to occur, saving and dissaving may be thought to approximately balance out. Wealthier retired individuals may continue to save at relatively high rates, while those with limited resources dissave by drawing down their accumulated balances to supplement their income.

In the aggregate the level of personal saving can be seen to be influenced by the relative number of individuals or households in each of these age groups. If the number of prime buyers/borrowers increases relative to the number of prime savers, the personal saving rate can be expected to decline and vice versa.

Uncertainty about the future is also a powerful saving motive, and here both private- and public-sector insurance and pension programs have substantially reduced this motive to save. Employer-sponsored group life and health insurance has been extended to an increasing proportion of workers, as have employer-sponsored retirement plans. Government-sponsored programs such as unemployment insurance, worker's compensation, Medicare, Medicaid, and Social Security also cover a wide segment of the population. To the extent that individuals feel that corporate or governmental provisions have been made for the unforeseen contingencies that might strike them, their motivation to save from current income to meet those contingencies from their own resources is reduced.

Other factors also affect personal saving. In the absence of the broad availability of credit, individuals must "save up" to make large purchases. With credit cards, home equity loans, and liberal standards of creditworthiness so prevalent in the market today, "saving up" has almost become a quaint anachronism of grandfather's day. The spread of various insurance programs and the broad availability of credit remove or weaken motives to save that once were prominent in our economy, leaving the primary motivation that of saving for retirement. All of these factors may combine to explain the secular decline in the personal saving rate in the United States and offer some guidance as to how households may save in the future.

AN ECONOMETRIC ANALYSIS OF PERSONAL SAVING

This econometric analysis of personal saving behavior focuses on the distinctions between aggregate personal saving and discretionary personal saving. Aggregate personal saving includes both discretionary and contractual saving. Most theoretical constructs of personal saving behavior implicitly assume that all saving is discretionary. In fact, individuals have very little discretion over a great deal of personal saving that is undertaken by others on their behalf. How does this saving affect their discretionary saving behavior?

The basic equation serving as the analytical framework for this study explains aggregate personal saving (defined by the national income and product accounts) as a linear function of five independent variables: personal disposable income; the unemployment rate; the number of people in the "prime buying/borrowing" and "prime saving" phases of the life cycle; and the after-tax, one-year Treasury bill rate. The unemployment rate is used here as a proxy for uncertainty or a feeling of economic insecurity that would lead employed individuals to save more. The after-tax interest rate is used to reflect the return on all financial instruments in which personal saving reposes.

Inasmuch as it is reasonable to assume that saving behavior may have changed over time, the functions are estimated over different time period subsets of the years 1960–1989 to determine the stability of the coefficients and their direction of movement. Table 8.5 contains estimates of the regression coefficients of the basic equation, showing the impact of the five independent variables on the personal saving rate. Mean elasticities are given in Table 8.6.

TABLE 8.5
The Basic Personal Saving Function:
Regression Coefficients

Time Period	Disposable Income	Unemployment Rate	Prime Buyers	Prime Savers	After-Tax Interest Rate	R2	DW(1)
1960–1979	.079	6.802	–3.308	2.521	6.190	.960	1.539
1960–1980	.073	6.465	–3.528	2.879	5.259	.968	1.475
1960–1981	.074	7/293	–3.570	2.972	4.868	.976	1.469
1960–1982	.075	5.400	–3.682	3.256	4.423	.976	1.362
1960–1983	.066	6.555	–4.348	3.800	7.201	.965	0.918
1960–1984	.069	5.066	–3.846	3.451	5.975	.967	1.452
1960–1985	.068	6.692	–4.181	3.555	7.975	.964	1.720
1960–1986	.062	6.830	–4.201	3.553	8.183	.964	1.742
1960–1987	.062	6.830	–4.201	3.553	8.183	.964	1.742
1960–1988	.062	6.674	–4.198	3.570	8.077	.966	1.732
1961–1988	.064	6.699	–4.346	3.717	8.050	.963	1.737
1962–1988	.064	6.694	–4.355	3.726	8.051	.960	1.720
1963–1988	.069	6.633	–4.848	4.211	8.120	.958	1.742
1964–1988	.071	6.593	-5.070	4.428	8.159	.952	1.714
1965–1988	.077	6.538	-5.678	5.016	8.248	.948	1.716
1966–1988	.088	6.562	-6.799	6.081	8.402	.942	1.705
1967–1988	.090	6.587	-6.929	6.202	8.410	.933	1.684
1968–1988	.108	7.024	-8.760	7.876	8.607	.927	1.736
1969–1988	.111	7.136	-9.078	8.161	8.628	.912	1.585
Average "t" Values	5.761	4.037	3.624	3.088	5.111		

TABLE 8.6
The Basic Personal Saving Function:
Mean Elasticities

Time Period	Disposable Income	Unemployment Rate	Prime Buyers	Prime Savers	After-Tax Interest Rate
1960–1979	.944	.614	-2.671	1.680	.432
1960–1980	.981	.559	-2.722	1.819	.364
1960–1981	.996	.518	-2.615	1.767	.336
1960–1982	1.016	.435	-2.595	1.844	.301
1960–1983	.909	.525	-3.006	2.089	.484
1960–1984	.976	.391	-2.575	1.816	.393
1960–1985	.913	.509	-2.775	1.834	.519
1960–1986	.938	.512	-2.776	1.804	.522
1960–1987	.982	.507	-2.789	1.792	.518
1960–1988	1.021	.482	-2.755	1.761	.502
1961–1988	1.044	.472	-2.796	1.795	.496
1962–1988	1.046	.458	-2.748	1.761	.494
1963–1988	1.126	.444	-3.001	1.947	.496
1964–1988	1.161	.430	-3.074	1.999	.495
1965–1988	1.262	.418	-3.379	2.213	.496
1966–1988	1.447	.412	-3.972	2.621	.502
1967–1988	1.471	.410	-3.975	2.609	.495
1968–1988	1.782	.434	-4.948	3.240	.502
1969–1988	1.840	.437	-5.036	3.272	.496

The goodness-of-fit statistics for the equation and for individual coefficients are generally acceptable. But the coefficients of disposable income and the demographic variables rise as the analysis concentrates increasingly on the more recent period. These effects are magnified in the mean elasticities. Chow tests across the sample period indicate that saving behavior changed significantly after 1975.[8]

These findings signify that the marginal propensity to save from disposable income has increased over time. This increase's failure to produce higher levels of personal saving can probably be attributed to the increasingly powerful effects of the life cycle demographics. The extreme mismatch of prime buyers/borrowers and prime savers appears to have overwhelmed this effect of higher marginal propensities to save from disposable income and to have produced lower personal saving than disposable income alone would have indicated.

The mean elasticity of the unemployment rate has drifted downward over the period, suggesting that unemployment no longer holds the horror it once did. We have not, for example, had an economic depression comparable to that of the 1930s. Although the recessions of 1974–1975 and 1981–1982 were severe by postwar standards, the years 1960–1989 contain both the longest economic expansion in U.S. history (1961–1969) and the longest peacetime expansion (1983 to the present).

The mean elasticity of the after-tax interest rate is less than unity and displays relative stability in comparison with the other variables. The less-than-unity value for after-tax interest rates does not dismiss the potential importance of tax incentives in promoting personal saving. This value may instead highlight the fact that a growing proportion of personal saving is not only outside individual discretion and therefore insensitive to interest rate movements but is already tax advantaged.

Public policy has offered individuals a tax-deferred means of saving contractually in its treatment of pension funds while leaving most forms of discretionary saving exposed to taxation. Should it be surprising that personal saving has shifted toward the tax-deferred product?

In 1960, households held 6.7 percent of their total financial assets in private and government pension funds. By 1980, this percentage had grown to 14.0 percent, and in 1988, 20.3 percent of total household financial assets were lodged in employer-sponsored pension funds. Moreover, employer contributions to pension funds—excluding earnings on those funds—amounted to 23 percent of aggregate personal saving in 1960, 49 percent in 1987, and 34 percent in 1988. Because these contributions are fully tax sheltered, aggregate personal saving should not be expected to show strong responsiveness to after-tax rates of return.

This consideration leads to a different formulation of the saving function—one that separates saving in the form of employer-sponsored pension funds from aggregate personal saving. Personal disposable income as presented in the national income and product accounts includes employer contributions to pension funds, but inasmuch as savers do not constructively receive this "income," they do not directly decide to save or spend it. Personal disposable income also includes the earnings on pension funds in personal interest and dividend income. Because personal saving in the national income accounts is taken as the difference between personal disposable income and personal outlays, pension fund contributions and earnings on pension fund balances are perforce included in personal saving.[9] (It should be noted, however, that contributions to and earnings attributable to IRA and Keogh accounts are *not* included in pension fund contributions or pension fund earnings.) Personal saving as conventionally measured thus contains both discretionary and contractual elements, and until discretionary personal saving is isolated from aggregate personal saving, after-tax interest rates cannot be expected to show strong effects on personal saving.

There are other aspects of this circumstance that may also have a bearing on personal saving behavior. Participation in an employer-sponsored pension fund serves to relieve anxiety about the future and so weakens a powerful motivation to save from discretionary income. Individuals might therefore be expected to save less from their discretionary income if they are participants in employer-sponsored pension funds.

Discretionary personal saving can be isolated by subtracting employer pension fund contributions and pension fund earnings (net of pension benefits paid out) from both personal saving and personal disposable income. The pension fund effect on discretionary saving can then be analyzed by including the annual net addition to pension funds as an independent determinant of *discretionary* personal saving. These results are presented in Table 8.7. Mean elasticities are given in Table 8.8.

In this formulation of the saving function, the upward drift of the values of the coefficients can again be noted as the period moves away from the 1960s and 1970s and comes to focus increasingly on the 1970s and 1980s. But substantially higher mean elasticities can also be seen for all of the variables, including that of the after-tax interest rate. Indeed, the mean elasticity of discretionary personal saving becomes greater than unity when 1983, the first year in which lower marginal tax rates were fully in effect, is included in the sample.

The life cycle demographics appear relatively stronger, however, and offer the same explanation of the decline in discretionary personal saving as in aggregate personal saving. The demographics still appear to have overwhelmed the income effects and interest rate effects, even though these effects were moving in the direction of producing higher saving. For example, the lower marginal tax rates contained in both ERTA and the Tax Reform Act of 1986 may have elicited the expected response from individuals in the prime saving phase of the life cycle, but because the prime savers were outnumbered by those in the prime buying and borrowing phase of the life cycle, the response of the prime savers was

TABLE 8.7
The Discretionary Personal Saving Function:
Regression Coefficients

Time Period	Disposable Income	Pension Funds	Unemployment Rate	Prime Buyers	Prime Savers	After-Tax Interest Rate	R2	DW(1)
1960–1979	.082	-1.090	6.914	-3.144	2.243	6.036	.769	1.419
1960–1980	.085	-1.115	6.639	-3.308	2.508	5.198	.766	1.357
1960–1981	.084	-1.067	6.304	-3.428	2.748	4.587	.790	1.360
1960–1982	.095	-1.210	5.673	-3.368	2.731	3.972	.779	1.232
1960–1983	.090	-1.284	6.846	-3.936	3.134	6.538	.776	0.942
1960–1984	.098	-1.364	5.905	-3.499	2.740	5.540	.774	1.450
1960–1985	.095	-1.414	7.476	-3.770	2.763	7.342	.856	1.635
1960–1986	.089	-1.354	7.765	-3.881	2.860	8.011	.90	1.581
1960–1987	.089	-1.354	7.765	-3.881	2.860	8.011	.925	0.592
1960–1988	.081	-1.195	6.890	-3.989	3.177	7.718	.945	1.585
1961–1988	.082	-1.196	6.919	-4.151	3.335	7.685	.945	1.588
1962–1988	.082	-1.196	6.917	-4.153	3.338	7.686	.944	1.569
1963–1988	.087	-1.192	6.856	-4.649	3.824	7.754	.945	1.566
1964–1988	.090	-1.189	6.816	-4.872	4.043	7.793	.944	1.559
1965–1988	.097	-1.193	6.760	-5.576	4.716	7.882	.945	1.560
1966–1988	.112	-1.200	6.806	-6.885	5.944	8.036	.946	1.553
1967–1988	.120	-1.213	6.939	-7.510	6.512	8.050	.945	1.546
1968–1988	.149	-1.245	7.568	-9.978	8.726	8.236	.948	1.630
1969–1988	.164	-1.263	8.033	-11.268	9.866	8.283	.947	1.473
Average "t" Values	3.982	4.749	4.256	3.408	2.574	4.822		

TABLE 8.8
The Discretionary Personal Saving Function:
Mean Elasticities

Time Period	Discretionary Income	Pension Funds	Unemployment Rate	Prime Buyers	Prime Savers	After-Tax Interest Rate
1960–1979	2.151	-1.155	1.286	-5.230	3.081	0.868
1960–1980	2.400	-1.325	1.255	-5.584	3.466	0.787
1960–1981	2.441	-1.344	1.173	-5.676	3.692	0.715
1960–1982	2.989	-1.744	1.116	-5.796	3.775	0.660
1960–1983	3.235	-2.202	1.488	-7.389	4.676	1.193
1960–1984	3.840	-2.606	1.327	-6.820	4.198	1.093
1960–1985	4.414	-3.312	1.900	-8.362	4.766	1.597
1960–1986	4.960	-3.884	2.253	-9.921	5.617	1.976
1960–1987	6.145	-4.848	2.643	-11.803	6.607	2.322
1960–1988	7.358	-5.840	2.927	-15.412	9.224	2.822
1961–1988	7.677	-5.999	2.935	-15.066	9.687	2.847
1962–1988	7.922	-6.222	2.938	-16.261	9.786	2.923
1963–1988	8.677	-6.447	2.940	-18.450	11.336	3.035
1964–1988	9.169	-6.675	2.938	-19.529	12.066	3.125
1965–1988	10.419	-7.039	2.980	-22.989	14.361	3.275
1966–1988	12.659	-7.532	3.113	-29.274	18.648	3.491
1967–1988	14.310	-8.103	3.315	-33.093	21.046	3.640
1968–1988	19.645	-9.256	3.939	-47.531	30.279	4.054
1969–1988	23.789	-10.399	4.545	-57.709	36.524	4.398

simply too small to prevent aggregate discretionary saving from falling. This interpretation also offers an explanation for the failure of the universal individual retirement account provided in ERTA to reverse the declining trend in the personal saving rate.

At first blush, these results suggest that with the turn in the life cycle demographics in the 1990s, discretionary personal saving is destined to increase. But this analysis also reveals another aspect of changing saving behavior in the 1970s and 1980s. The regression coefficient of discretionary personal saving with respect to pension fund contributions and earnings is negative and greater than unity, indicating that \$1.00 saved through the pension fund mechanism does not simply displace \$1.00 that would otherwise have been saved at the individual's discretion. Instead, individuals save even less. In the equation for 1969–1988, which reflects the most recent experience, individuals would, ceteris paribus, reduce their discretionary saving by \$1.26 for every \$1.00 added to their pension fund balances.

Although absolute faith should not be placed in econometric findings, this result is quite disconcerting. With life cycle demographics already taken into account in the equation, this finding could indicate that the increases in the personal saving rate suggested by the demographics of the 1990s might fall short of expectations and that we are observing a *behavioral* change prompted, at least in part, by a widespread feeling of current and future economic security.[10]

POLICY ISSUES IMPLIED BY THE ANALYSIS

First, the most readily available policy measure for increasing discretionary saving would appear to be a rollback of the limitations imposed on IRA contributions by the Tax Reform Act of 1986. Although such action raises the issue of the efficiency of the tax incentive, current proposals along these lines may accommodate efficiency concerns.[11]

Second, given the demographics, which will become favorable to personal saving in the 1990s, and given the saving incentives built into the Tax Reform Act of 1986, one realistic policy option is to take no further action. If the economic expansion continues and personal discretionary income continues to grow, the demographics might be relied on to produce a significant increase in personal saving. A "no-action" policy recommendation can be put a bit more forcefully. Individuals require time to adjust their behavior to the kind of tax changes wrought in the 1980s. Although I do not argue that the Tax Reform Act of 1986 is perfect, I do argue for leaving the current tax structure as undisturbed as possible to allow time for saving behavior to respond.

Third, this analysis detects a growing dependency of personal saving on employer pension fund contributions and earnings. Moreover, the analysis suggests that the reliance on pension plans as the primary personal saving vehicle has reduced discretionary saving disproportionately; an additional dollar of pension fund balance appears to have displaced *more than* one dollar's worth of discretionary saving. The finding of a greater-than-unity coefficient for discretionary saving with respect to changes in pension fund balances suggests that pension funds make aggregate personal saving lower than it would otherwise be.

The same conclusion could probably be reached about unemployment insurance and group health and life insurance benefits.[12] But a policy that increased uncertainty and economic insecurity in order to achieve a higher personal saving rate would surely be an unpopular one. The national objectives of maintaining economic security and increasing personal saving need not be in conflict, however. Their compatibility depends to some extent on the distinction between *employer-sponsored defined-benefit plans* and *employer-sponsored defined-contribution plans.*

According to the Department of Labor's most recent employee benefits survey, employers paid the full cost of defined-benefit pension plans for 94 percent of participants. In the case of defined-contribution retirement plans, however, 56 percent of the plans entailed contributions from *both* employers and employees; 86 percent of defined-contribution capital accumulation plans were jointly financed by employees and employers.[13] Thus, in general, defined-benefit plans do not require saving by individual participants whereas a majority of defined-contribution plans do.

Defined-benefit plans accounted for 66.3 percent of the assets of all private employer-sponsored plans in 1985, the latest year for which data are available.[14] Time-series data on pension fund balances by type of plan—defined benefit versus defined contribution—are quite difficult to obtain, however, so an econometric determination cannot be made as to whether defined-benefit plans displace more discretionary saving than defined-contribution plans.

Two factors lead me to the conclusion that defined-contribution plans probably serve the interests of increasing the personal saving rate better than defined-benefit plans do. First, if employees had full understanding of the provisions of their defined-benefit pension plans, they might save much more from their own resources. Vesting periods are typically much longer for defined-benefit plans than for defined-contribution plans, even after a reduction of maximum vesting periods provided in the Tax Reform Act of 1986; if individuals change employers frequently (voluntarily or involuntarily), the likelihood therefore is much lower that they will retain employer contributions with defined-benefit plans than with defined-contribution plans. The well-informed, defined-benefit-plan participant thus should respond to this uncertainty by saving *more* from his or her own resources. The evidence indicates, however, that most defined-benefit-plan participants are *not* well informed about the provisions of their pension plans. Rather than cope with their plans' complexities, participants appear to base their spending and saving decisions on the premise that the plan will provide adequately for their retirement, which results in their saving less from their own resources than they would otherwise.[15]

Second, where defined-contribution plans require that the employee contribute in order to receive an employer contribution, the employee has a powerful incentive to save from his or her own resources because he or she cannot otherwise obtain the employer's contribution. By contrast, employees participating in defined-benefit plans that are fully funded by employer contributions need maintain only their employment with the firm to obtain the *feeling* that they are securing the employer's contribution and providing for their own retirement; they are not obliged to save from their own resources. Workers who change jobs, whose companies fail or are "restructured," or who experience a pension fund reversion typically discover that their perception of retirement security far exceeds the cold-cash reality.

Defined-benefit plans were originally designed to promote employee loyalty to the company in order to secure for the company a stable, experienced work force. But in today's high-tech, takeover-prone corporate environment, defined-benefit plans may no longer serve the interests of either employees or employers. The average employee changes jobs twelve times or more in a working life, far too frequently to realize the full benefits of a defined-benefit plan.[16] Employers may also find that defined-benefit plans inhibit their responses to changing market conditions that require major changes in work force skills.

Current trends indicate that the number and coverage of defined-contribution plans are growing relative to defined-benefit plans. In 1975, 36 percent of all private-sector pension plans were defined-benefit plans, and they covered 87 percent of pension plan participants and held 71 percent of pension fund assets. By 1985, 34 percent of private-sector pension plans were of the defined-benefit type, but they covered only 71 percent of participants and held 66 percent of pension fund assets.[17] Also notable is the rapid increase in 401(k) plans—defined-contribution plans that were first authorized in 1978.[18] In 1983, only 10 percent of the Employee Retirement Income Security Act of 1974 work force had the opportunity to participate in 401(k) plans; by 1988, that proportion had increased to 34 percent.[19]

Defined-contribution plans have the general reputation of being less generous than defined-benefit plans, and this may be so for the employee who devotes a major portion of his or her working life to a single company or to a group of employers enrolled in a single multiemployer pension plan. The reputation for lower benefits accorded to defined-contribution plans may derive, however, from the fact that these plans have traditionally been secondary plans—an additional benefit that employers offer their employees.[20] If a defined-contribution plan is taken as the primary retirement benefit offered by an employer, there is no a priori reason the employer should be less generous.

If it is correct that defined-contribution plans are more likely to encourage personal saving than defined-benefit plans, and if the trend toward defined-contribution plans continues, this provides another reason for expecting higher personal saving rates in the 1990s. Should policy action be taken to accelerate these trends? The answer to this question can be no stronger than "possibly." Not enough is known about the behavioral relationship between personal saving and pensions to offer detailed recommendations. The evidence presented here raises the question but does not provide a definitive answer.

Considerable attention has, however, been paid recently to perceived inequities in the way defined-benefit pension plans work, and Congress has considered several measures to restrict employers' ability to capture the excess balances of overfunded, defined-benefit plans through reversion. Furthermore, in the wake of the shortfalls in the Farm Credit System, the Federal Savings and Loan Insurance Corporation, and the Federal Housing Administration, the continuing insolvency of the Pension Benefit Guaranty Corporation, which insures defined-benefit pension plans, must weigh heavily on the minds of many members of Congress.[21] Yet discussions of pension reform seldom consider the effects of alternative reform measures on personal saving. Such effects belong on the pension reform agenda.

CONCLUSIONS

In identifying the life cycle demographics as the most likely cause of the secular decline in personal saving in the United States during 1974–1989 and in anticipating a reversal of these adverse demographic trends in the early 1990s, I conclude that the prospects for improving personal saving rates are very strong. The major changes in tax policy during the 1980s have already created an environment in which personal saving can flourish in the 1990s if the current tax structure is left largely undisturbed.

The principal concerns that arise from this analysis center on the relationship between discretionary personal saving and pension fund contributions and earnings. Discretionary personal saving appears to decline more than in proportion to increases in pension fund balances. It can be surmised, but not substantiated quantitatively, that this result flows from the preponderance of defined-benefit pension plans in our retirement system, which are fully funded by employer contributions. Most defined-contribution plans, by contrast, are *jointly* funded and require an employee contribution to obtain the contribution of the employer. Individuals participating in defined-contribution plans are therefore saving from their own resources. Although it is not possible to suggest specific pension reform actions that would offer additional assurance of a rising personal saving rate in the 1990s, I do believe that pension reform measures must be evaluated in light of their potential effects on personal saving.

NOTES

1. The lowest personal saving rate during the post–World War II era was 3.1 percent in 1947, immediately following the conversion of U.S. industry from wartime to peacetime production. Inasmuch as personal saving rates during the war years (1942–1945), when consumer goods were unavailable, averaged 23 percent, it is not surprising that the public went on a buying binge soon after the war's conclusion. The 3.2 percent personal saving rate of 1987, however, cannot be excused by any such mitigating factors and therefore should really stand as the postwar record low.

2. These factors have long been held as impediments to higher personal saving in the United States. See, for example, Chris Carroll and Lawrence H. Summers, "Why Have Private Savings Rates in the United States and Canada Diverged?" *Journal of Monetary Economics* (1987), pp. 249–279.

3. The Tax Reform Act of 1986 limited the deductibility of IRA contributions to individuals who are active participants in employer-sponsored pension plans, to couples earning $50,000 or less in adjusted gross income, and to single taxpayers earning $35,000 or less in adjusted gross income. Phased-down deductibility applies to couples earning between $40,000 and $50,000 and to single taxpayers earning between $25,000 and $35,000. It is estimated, however, that 93 percent of single taxpayers, 94 percent of one-earner couples, and 77 percent of two-earner couples remain eligible for fully deductible IRA contributions under the Tax Reform Act. See Employee Benefit Research Institute, *Issue Brief* (Washington, D.C.: Employee Benefit Research Institute, April 1989), p. 9.

4. Every major trading partner of the United States experienced a declining personal saving rate over the 1973–1988 period. Japan's saving rate fell from 20.4 percent in 1973 to 15.1 percent in 1988; Germany's from 13.9 percent to 12.3 percent; France's from 19.1 percent to 11.5 percent; Britain's from 10.7 percent to 5.6 percent; Canada's from 10.7 percent to 9.7 percent; and Australia's from 10.0 percent to 8.4 percent. See Organisation for Economic Co-operation and Development, *OECD Economic Outlook* (June 1989), Table R 12.

5. Note that Figure 8.12 depicts the *ratio* of prime savers to prime buyers/borrowers. The ratio would have a value of 100 if the number of prime savers were equal to the number of prime buyers/borrowers; ratio values less than 100 indicate that prime buyers/borrowers outnumber prime savers.

6. See *OECD Economic Outlook* (June 1989).

7. Albert Ando and Franco Modigliani, "The 'Life Cycle' Hypothesis of Saving: Aggregate Implications and Tests," *American Economic Review* (1963), pp. 55–84.

8. Gregory C. Chow, "Tests of Equality Between Sets of Coefficients in Two Linear Regressions," *Econometrica* (July 1960), pp. 591–605.

9. The national income accounts include separate estimates for employer pension fund contributions but not for pension fund earnings. Accordingly, in this analysis the flow of funds measure of changes in pension fund balances is used. This measure effectively nets out payments from pension funds to retirees.

10. For a similar point of view, see Barry P. Bosworth, "There's No Simple Explanation for the Collapse in Saving," *Challenge* (July-August 1989), pp. 27–32. Also see B. Douglas Bernheim and John B. Shoven, "Pension Funding and Saving," *NBER Working Paper No. 1622* (Cambridge, Mass.: National Bureau of Economic Research, May 1985).

11. In this context, "efficiency" refers to the question of whether the net increase in personal saving is equal to or greater than the tax revenue foregone in the provision of the incentive. If not, the incentive is inefficient in that it takes away more from *national* saving than it adds. Current proposals contemplate allowing a 50 percent deduction of principal contributions for currently ineligible individuals and thereby provide a greater likelihood that the IRA tax incentive will be "efficient." See James W. Christian, *Tax Incentives for Saving: The Idea and the Evidence* (Chicago: U.S. League of Savings Institutions, 1982).

12. For reasons other than the increasing of personal saving, there are some who would restrict these benefits by exposing them to taxation. See Alicia H. Munnell, "It's Time to Tax Employee Benefits," *New England Economic Review* (July-August 1989), pp. 49–63.

13. U.S. Department of Labor, Bureau of Labor Statistics, *Employee Benefits in Medium and Large Firms, 1988*, Bulletin 2336 (Washington, D.C.: U.S. Government Printing Office, August 1989).

14. See Mark J. Warshawsky, "Pension Plans: Funding, Assets, and Regulatory Environment," *Federal Reserve Bulletin* (November 1988), pp. 717–730.

15. A host of news articles in the 1980s reported on the outrage employees and retirees express when employers—quite legally—terminate their defined-benefit pension plans in order to capture the surplus in their overfunded plans. Employees feel that those surpluses are theirs; but, in law, the surplus is the employer's. Defined-benefit plans offer the employer's guarantee of certain benefits on retirement, based primarily on salary and years of service. Unexpected gains that accrue to funds from high interest rates or a booming stock market not only relieve the employer of the obligation to contribute to the fund but may also invite the recapture of the surplus through a process known as "reversion." See, for example, Vicky Cahan, "The Shrinking Nest Egg: Retirement May Never Be the Same," *Business Week*, December 8, 1986, pp. 114–116; and Susan B. Garland, "The Fury over Pension Funds," *Business Week*, July 3, 1989, p. 31.

16. See "The Pension System: Can Its Promises Be Kept?" *Congressional Quarterly Weekly Report,* April 11, 1987, pp. 647–652.

17. U.S. Department of Labor, *Estimates of Participant and Financial Characteristics of Private Pension Plans* (Washington, D.C.: U.S. Government Printing Office, 1983); Warshawsky, "Pension Plans"; and Employee Benefit Research Institute, *Issue Brief* (April 1989).

18. Although 401(k) plans were authorized in 1978, preliminary regulations were not issued until 1981. As a consequence, few employers offered these plans in the five years following authorization. See Congressional Budget Office, *Tax Policy for Pensions and Other Retirement Saving* (Washington, D.C.: Congressional Budget Office, April 1987).

19. Employee Benefit Research Institute, *Issue Brief* (Washington, D.C.: Employee Benefit Research Institute, September, 1989). Also see U.S. General Accounting Office, *401(k) Plans: Incidence, Provisions and Benefits* (Washington, D.C.: U.S. General Accounting Office, March 1988).

20. See Employee Benefit Research Institute, *Issue Brief* (April 1989), p. 6.

21. See, for example, Pension Benefit Guaranty Corporation, *Promises at Risk* (Washington, D.C.: Pension Benefit Guaranty Corp., April 1987); and Congressional Budget Office, *Federal Insurance of Private Pension Benefits* (Washington, D.C.: Congressional Budget Office, October 1987).

ADDITIONAL REFERENCES

American Council of Life Insurance. *Pension Facts: 1988 Update.* Washington, D.C.: American Council of Life Insurance, 1988.

Andrews, Emily S. *The Changing Profile of Pensions in America.* Washington, D.C.: Employee Benefit Research Institute, 1985.

Crenshaw, Albert B. "Shifting the Risk in Pensions." *Washington Post,* June 4, 1989, p. H13.

Erlich, Elizabeth, Vicky Cahan, and Jonathan B. Levine. "Putting the Traditional Pension Out to Pasture." *Business Week,* May 5, 1986, pp. 102–103.

Hendershott, Patric H., ed. *The Level and Composition of Household Saving.* Cambridge, Mass.: Ballinger, 1985.

Institute for Research on the Economics of Taxation. *Save, America.* Washington, D.C.: Institute for Research on the Economics of Taxation, 1989.

Ippolito, Richard A., and Walter W. Kolodrubetz. *The Handbook of Pension Statistics.* Chicago: Commerce Clearing House, 1986.

Kirkpatrick, David. "Will You Be Able to Retire?" *Fortune,* July 31, 1989, pp. 56–66.

Kosterlitz, Julie. "Promises to Keep." *National Journal,* August 29, 1987, pp. 2138–2141.

O'Toole, Patricia. "How Safe Is Your Pension?" *Fortune,* October 27, 1986, pp. 52–56.

Weiss, Stuart. "Fat Pension Funds Can Make Companies Tempting Targets." *Business Week,* November 10, 1986, pp. 106–108.

Discussion

Jacob S. Dreyer

James Christian is fairly optimistic about the prospects for an increase in personal saving in the 1990s, and this benign view is shared by many. I have no quarrel with his prediction, but I am skeptical about the implied extent of the increase in the personal saving rate. If we judge by his forecast of the prime borrowers/prime savers ratio, by the year 2000 the personal saving rate should reach the level of the early 1970s. It may indeed get there, but will it stay there? In my judgment, we should not count on more favorable demographics alone to solve the U.S. saving problem.

Absent from Dr. Christian's estimated saving function is the wealth effect. Nevertheless, study after empirical study has found pervasive negative correlation between changes in personal wealth and the saving rate. This is mirrored in numerous findings of changes in wealth being positively correlated with changes in personal consumption.

From the late 1970s until 1987, during which time the saving rate fell from about 7 percent to 3.2 percent, individuals, especially those in age and income brackets where saving rates were highest, experienced a massive increase in their wealth through an unprecedented, almost simultaneous rise in the value of their equity, debt, and real estate holdings. In 1987, this appreciation of assets was interrupted, and the personal saving rate took off soon thereafter. It is yet to be seen to what extent the rise in the stock market and the much more modest appreciation of debt instruments in 1988–1989 will affect personal saving. The inference must be, however, that unless we are going to experience declining stock prices, rising bond yields and stagnant or falling real estate values, we are not likely to experience the same rapid increases in the personal saving rate that we witnessed in 1988 and 1989.

Another reason for my skepticism about the personal saving rate staying, say, at 8 to 9 percent is the now-famous Boskin, or vintage, effect: The pre-1939ers are more frugal, ceteris paribus, than is the postwar generation. This is reflected in many surveys of saving and spending habits. Contrary to the life cycle hypothesis, the prewar folks, even in their retirement years, *are* prime savers relative to other age cohorts, and the small relative size of the prewar generation notwithstanding, their attrition is bound to have a dampening effect on the overall personal saving rate in the 1990s.

More important, perhaps, is the question of the adequacy of saving even at the 8 percent level. I certainly do not wish to start a discussion on saving adequacy along the lines of the Golden Rule or optimal capital accumulation. But even if a 7 to 8 percent rate of personal saving was deemed sufficient in the late 1960s to early 1970s, it cannot be deemed adequate in the 1990s. The circumstances are simply not the same. Not only will we have to service external debt and maintain a high level of private investment in decaying infrastructure and human capital development; the prospects for the federal sector abandoning its propensity to dissave do not appear to be very promising either.

Although Dr. Christian's analysis and the forecast based on it are uplifting, what the 1990s will bring is by no means a nirvana. The ongoing improvement in the demographic makeup of the population, dramatic as it may be, does not obviate the urgent need to devise ways to induce higher personal saving. The difficulty is, of course, that such inducements, insofar as they are designed as tax concessions, may cost the Treasury money. The long-running debate about IRAs is effectively a dispute about whether the incremental personal saving they induce exceeds or falls short of the *contemporaneous* revenue loss to the federal government. But, as everyone knows, an IRA, as it stands now, is a tax deferment—not a tax deduction. If all IRA contributions were invested in Treasury securities at a yield equal to the Treasury's average interest cost, the rate of accumulation of an IRA account of a given vintage and the rate of discount back to the present of the value of deferred tax collections would be definitionally identical. Therefore, even if every single dollar deposited in an IRA account came out of a taxable account, on a present-value basis, the Treasury would not lose one dime in revenues.

Just because the federal budget accounting is on a cash basis (and because budget projections of the Office of Management and Budget or the Congressional Budget Office do not extend beyond a five-year time horizon) does not mean that the effects of tax deferments on the national saving rate should also be analyzed using the same accounting conventions. One would not think highly of a corporate management team whose criterion for undertaking an investment expenditure is an instantly matching increase in revenues or decrease in costs. But this is exactly the argument advanced in many discussions about the relationship between IRA-induced saving and federal revenue losses.

If the rationality of present-value accounting is combined with the proposition that the compound rate of asset growth in an IRA account invested in a portfolio of stocks, corporate bonds, or longer term certificates of deposit generally exceeds the interest cost of Treasury borrowing, it is clear that even if IRAs failed to generate additional personal saving, the present value of future revenues gained by the Treasury would still exceed the present value of the revenues it foregoes. If, in addition, Venti and Wise, Feenberg and Skinner, Summers and Carroll, Boskin, and many others have their estimates of IRA-induced saving responses even approximately right, every dollar of IRA-induced saving is in fact the icing on the saving cake. Every such dollar increases national saving today *and* tomorrow.

The political reality is such, however, that estimates of revenue losses are static, short term, and measured in current rather than present-value dollars. In other words, for a proposal to be considered politically acceptable, static estimates of near-term tax revenue losses must be minimized. Against this background, the saving inducement proposed by James Christian—a shift from defined-benefit to defined-contribution pension plans—is very appealing. The beauty of his proposal is that such a shift, if it could be implemented, would cost the Treasury nothing and might in fact save the Pension Benefit Guaranty Corporation a lot of money in the long run. Whatever one may think of the change in the pattern of risk bearing resulting from such a shift, it is difficult to assert that an increase in personal saving spurred by his proposal would be negated by an increase in government dissaving.

Proposals for back-loaded IRAs, such as the IRA-Plus proposal championed by Senator William Roth, also deal with the existing political reality in a very ingenious way. The incentive to save today is that the individual will have to pay no taxes tomorrow. But today, or over the five years of the budget planning horizon, the Treasury will experience no loss of revenues as computed by the Office of Management and Budget, the Congressional Budget Office, or the Joint Committee on Taxation. Thus, to the extent that people will respond to this inducement at all, the U.S. saving rate is bound to go up, at least over the politically relevant time horizon. The IRA-Plus scheme is equally ingenious in dealing with another political reality: the so-called tax fairness issue. By requiring people to pay taxes up front, this scheme makes a dollar of delayed tax-free income more costly to taxpayers in higher brackets than it would be to those in lower brackets.

I wish to make two remarks regarding back-loaded IRAs. First, people are frequently myopic in their financial planning. Both Dr. Christian and Dr. Summers cite evidence to this effect. Like the federal government, most individuals mentally keep their books on a cash basis. Reducing a current tax liability is much sweeter than reducing a tax liability twenty or thirty years down the road. Even though earnings on the after-tax contributions accumulate tax free, not just tax deferred, I have my doubts that IRA-Plus would have the same appeal as the pre-1987 IRA. If people were so provident as to bear sacrifices today for the sake of tax-free retirement income to be enjoyed decades from now, we would not have a problem with inadequate personal saving in the first place. In order to convince people to pay taxes on income they cannot currently enjoy, provisions for penalty-free early withdrawals for certain purposes would be desirable, and a substantial and patient educational and marketing effort would also be absolutely necessary.

Second, people may suspect that benefits promised today may be later taken away or otherwise diluted. This point is wholly unrelated to the substantive merit of an IRA-Plus. But the rapid-fire changes in tax laws during the 1980s made many people skeptical of the long-term stability of the tax structure. For the promise of future tax benefits to be credible, iron-clad safeguards—for example, a supermajority requirement to make any changes in the effective tax status of future IRA withdrawals—should be made part and parcel of the bill.

As to the traditional IRAs, so forcefully advocated by Dr. Summers, they can be made even more attractive in several ways. Payroll deductions have been mentioned. Also, those employers who offer retirement plans could be required to credit a portion of their contribution (up to the legal IRA limit) to employees' IRA accounts provided, of course, that employees also contribute. Such an arrangement would not increase the employer's costs. Employees would immediately reap both a matching employer's contribution and a tax deduction—quite a return on the money put into an IRA. This policy would increase, at least marginally, the share of defined-contribution plans in total pension assets. Employees would be immediately vested in the employer's IRA matching contribution. Employees would also have control over how their expanded IRA assets were invested, a collateral advantage of which would be greater dispersion of investment funds across instruments, industries, and companies; less social or political pressure for preferred investments; and, in general, a better-functioning capital market. Most importantly, however, this would be both good pension policy promoting the reliability of retirement income and good tax policy promoting the expansion of personal saving.

Discussion

Ed Jenkins

In the years that I have served on the Ways and Means Committee beginning in 1977, and during the years since 1959 that I have had some connection with Congress either as an employee or as a member, I have not seen as many changes in the tax code as have been effected in the last ten years or so. Although such regular change causes much frustration, I do not believe the passage of the Tax Reform Act of 1986 amounted to the Ten Commandments. I believe that we should reexamine a number of issues raised by the 1986 act to determine whether our policies are working. Capital gains is one of those issues.

I have observed that with a 20-plus percent tax rate versus a higher ordinary income tax rate, people reinvested their gains on Main Street, in a manufacturing plant, a new business, or an activity of great benefit to the community. I also think that as we look at the benefits of lower capital gains tax rates, we must consider the distributional effect of capital gains versus any other type of saving vehicle. I believe that the capital gains tax rate is a factor in the cost of capital and that capital gains rates are important from the standpoint of international trade. Most of the European Community nations either do not tax capital gains of individuals at all or tax them very lightly. Practically all of the Pacific Rim countries, for example, have no capital gains tax. Only Great Britain and Indonesia have capital gains tax rates higher than that of the United States. I think there is some correlation between what our trading partners have done with respect to capital gains taxes and their growth rates versus the U.S. rate of growth and between their saving rate versus the U.S. rate of saving. I believe that the track record reinforces my belief in a capital gains tax rate differential.

My interest in the capital gains differential and my belief in its viability are not new. As a freshman on the Ways and Means Committee in the late 1970s, I joined with Bill Steiger to reduce the capital gains tax rate in the 1978 tax bill. I heard the same argument then as is advanced now—that reducing the capital gains rates would create a terrible drain on federal revenues. Even in 1986, the Ways and Means Committee did not increase capital gains rates. When we reported the tax reform bill, there was no support for increasing the capital gains rates by 50 percent. An increase was not in the package that went to the House floor. Neither did the House propose an increase in the capital gains rates in 1986. After the tax package left the House and went to the Senate, a further reduction, from 35 to 33 percent, was made in ordinary income tax rates. That action, together with some other changes that were made, led to an increase in the capital gains tax rate.

In 1986 my colleagues in the House of Representatives voted to retain a lower capital gains tax rate. Tom Foley supported the lower capital gains tax rate in 1986, as did Dan Rostenkowski, the committee chair. Dick Gephardt also voted for the lower capital gains tax rate in 1986, and so did I. I continue to believe in it.

There can be legitimate debate as to the proper form of a tax subsidy or of a tax benefit to encourage saving. Certainly the capital gains differential is not the panacea of all means to encourage saving, nor is it the primary factor to be considered in lowering the cost of capital. But it is one factor to be considered, and it is beneficial.

The capital gains proposal that passed the House in 1989 results in a net revenue loss of $1.4 billion over the first five years. The people who opposed it said, "But consider how much it will cost us twenty years from now, or ten years from now." They were asking that the capital gains proposal measure up to standards of ten years or fifteen years down the road. But $300 million a year would not qualify even as an asterisk on the budget. This projected loss would have no adverse impact; it would have a positive impact.

Let me explain why this 1989 capital gains proposal, the Jenkins-Archer-Flippo bill, outlined only a two-year rate cut. Although I happen to favor a permanent differential in capital gains rates, I nonetheless live in the real world. In 1989, I had to get nineteen votes in the Ways and Means Committee in order to get the bill to the floor of the House for a vote. In order to get enough votes in the committee, I had to settle for less than what I wanted. I hope that a future bill contains a permanent capital gains differential.

Some have raised the issue that capital gains tax reductions would contribute to excessive timber harvesting. I am not very knowledgeable about the economics, but I do know something about trees. Ten-year-old pine trees are not harvested unless the owner is trying to make toothpicks. Tree farmers have not delayed harvesting mature trees as they became ready for market in anticipation of a capital gains tax cut. Tree farmers do not cut a tree until the time is right. We are in a world marketplace as far as timber is concerned. I have heard some people genuinely concerned that we would have a wholesale massacre of timber in this nation if a capital gains differential passed. That is not going to happen, even if only a two-year provision is passed.

Many of the environmental groups have supported a permanent differential, including one for timber, primarily because it is otherwise very difficult to get private individuals to plant trees and hold them for thirty-five years. Under the present passive loss rules, a tree farmer cannot deduct the expenses of maintaining those trees over their lifetime. To ask tree farmers to hold trees for thirty-five years and then when they cut the trees to pay 40 percent of the income from the sale in state and federal income taxes simply does not make sense to me.

Taxing capital gains at the same rate as ordinary income has restricted the range of the individual investor and thus the base of our capital. Today, along with venture capital, we depend more and more on pension funds as a source of investment. Such dependence has positive and negative effects. Pension plans are probably better able in today's climate to make venture capital and other types of investments than are individual investors.

Nevertheless, I have problems with an investment climate that destroys individual initiative. Individuals need incentive to save and make long-term investments in a variety of capital opportunities. It seems risky to me to depend primarily on one source of investment.

Look at the savings and loan failures. What if savings and loans had been the only vehicle of investment? I have served on the board of a bank, and I have represented a savings and loan. I have no problems with these institutions making lots of investments, except that in fact not many of their board members have day-to-day involvement with the actual investment decisions. Small banks depend primarily on their chief operating officer. When a pension fund has the same operation, real difficulties are possible if there is not sufficient scrutiny over investment decisions. I believe this is the situation today in the pension fund investment field.

I would feel safer letting the individual who accepts a private investment risk make the investment decision, rather than depending entirely on pension plans to make those types of investment decisions. I know that we can spend $150 billion on the savings and loan bailouts over the next twenty years and say, "That was just a result of deregulation, bad investments, the real estate market." Although all of these certainly contributed, they are a drop in the bucket compared to the losses that could occur from bad pension fund investments. I am not certain that the federal government today gives the necessary scrutiny to pension funds.

I am delighted that the research presented here is somewhat bullish on the need to increase our saving rate because I agree that this is one of the real danger points in our country. In conclusion, I believe a capital gains differential has worked in the past to increase saving and investment. That is the reason I favor it.

9

Capital Gains Taxation and the Cost of Capital

A. Capital Gains Tax Differential: Impact on Capital Costs

George N. Hatsopoulos

INTRODUCTION

Two of the most frequently cited reasons for the decline of U.S. international competitiveness are the low rate of investment and the shortsightedness of U.S. industry, both of which can be ascribed to the high cost of capital prevailing in the United States. This country no longer possesses the overwhelming advantages it had at the end of World War II, and we can no longer compete successfully while handicapped by a cost of capital that is substantially higher than that of other nations.

Because lagging competitiveness means lagging standards of living, economic policy debates are increasingly centered around finding politically acceptable ways to reduce the cost of capital. One of the many possible ways to reduce the cost of capital is to maintain a tax rate differential between capital gains and all other types of income. It is my purpose here to examine the past and possible future effects of such a differential with respect to the cost of capital, particularly that component of the cost of capital that most directly influences corporate foresight.

CORPORATE INVESTMENT, PLANNING HORIZONS, AND THE COST OF CAPITAL

One of the many factors affecting the rate of corporate investment in plant and equipment is the cost of capital, especially with respect to long-term rather than short-term investment rates. Over the short term, the investment rate is primarily governed by demand for the product or service and by the rate of capacity utilization. In the long run, however, corporations decide among alternative technologies to produce a given output on the basis of the prevailing cost of capital in relation to the cost of labor. Cost of capital plays a critical role in corporate decisions affecting the development of new ventures and innovative products.

The cost of capital for an investment in a physical asset is usually expressed as the annual pretax cost associated with that asset's use. Equivalently, the cost of capital is the minimum pretax return that the corporation must earn in order to justify the investment. Such a return must cover the depreciation of the asset; the taxes to be paid on the return, less depreciation allowances and tax credits; and the required payments to the investors and lenders supplying the funds used to make the investment. Because the funds used by corporations involve both equity and debt, the determinants of the cost of capital are the tax code parameters, the depreciation rate of the asset, the cost of equity (the rate of return on equity demanded by stockholders), and the cost of debt (the interest rate demanded by lenders).

Manufacturing, the principal U.S. industry involved in international competition, has been investing less in plant and equipment per worker since World War II than have similar industries in any other industrialized nation. It is no coincidence that the United States has also experienced the lowest rate of long-term productivity growth. This point is dramatized when one compares the two industrialized nations occupying the opposite ends of the investment/productivity spectrum: the United States and Japan. Japanese manufacturers invest almost twice as much per worker as do their U.S. counterparts. This might seem surprising until one takes into account the difference in the cost of capital between the two countries. Given the large differential, there is no reason to suggest that Japanese manufacturers have any more fundamental propensity to invest than do U.S. manufacturers.[1]

Apart from low levels of physical investment, perhaps the most common indictment of U.S. management is that it is myopic. Critics charge that this shortsightedness not only leads managers to forego profitable long-term investments in research and development (R&D) but also makes managers more reluctant than their overseas competitors to invest in other long-term ventures such as the development of foreign markets.

There is ample anecdotal evidence to show that both the rate of intangible investment by Japanese industry and its planning horizons are much greater than those of U.S. industry. For this reason I believe that the critics are correct in characterizing U.S. industry as shortsighted. As in the case of tangible assets, however, there is no reason to believe that the behavior of U.S. managers is less rational than that of their Japanese counterparts. The cost of long-term intangible investments is the cost of equity, which in turn is one component of the cost of tangible assets. This has a decisive bearing on U.S. planning horizons because the difference in the cost of equity between the United States and Japan is even greater than the difference in the cost of tangible capital.[2] (For a discussion of the factors affecting the cost of tangible and intangible capital for U.S. firms, see Appendix 9.A.)

THE IMPORTANCE OF INTANGIBLE INVESTMENTS TO U.S. COMPETITIVENESS

The United States has long paid higher manufacturing wages than any other country in the world. Some countries, such as West Germany, have surpassed us recently in the level of wages, and others, such as Japan, are rapidly approaching our level. When we say our nation should strive to remain competitive, we mean that we should do so while maintaining high wages, for competitiveness with low wages is clearly an undesirable solution. Many challengers to the U.S. industrial leadership have the same goal: competitiveness with high wages.

The only way any country with high wages can compete effectively is by specializing in industry segments with output that is in demand and is difficult for others to produce. A prime example of such a strategy is the shift in emphasis of Japanese manufacturing from basic industry segments, such as steel, to high-technology segments, such as semiconductors. The United States has a big advantage in carrying out such a strategy because it continues to be the most inventive and innovative country in the world. The reasons for such an advantage are both economic and cultural. On the cultural side, we place a high value on individualism and entrepreneurship and provide encouragement and support to those who want to build their own businesses. On the economic side, our society has developed institutions, such as venture capital firms, that can provide funds for creative individuals to start their own businesses. Digital Equipment Corporation and Apple Computer are just two of hundreds of internationally competitive enterprises that were started after World War II by individual entrepreneurs who were financed with venture capital. Even our most successful international challengers, such as Japan, are envious of our ability to create innovative new industries.

Another advantage with regard to innovation is the number and variety of U.S. institutions for higher education, which are second to none in the world. Equally important are this country's broad-based activities in basic research. On this latter point it should be noted that although Japan spends more than we do for nondefense R&D in relation to gross national product, it spends a trivial amount for basic research compared to the United States.

This is our plus side. On the negative side, the United States incorporates its innovation and technology into internationally marketed products and services at a rate that is scandalously less than our true potential. In fact, Japan appropriates and commercializes U.S. technology at a much higher rate than we do. Why? The answer is simple: U.S. managers are required by their stockholders to achieve a much higher return on equity than that demanded of their Japanese counterparts.

Embodiment of innovation into markets in general, and foreign markets in particular, requires rates of intangible investment far greater than those of tangible investment. Even though our industry still lags behind other countries in this respect, U.S. manufacturing began shifting from basic industries to high-tech industries in the 1980s. This shift was reflected in the fact that R&D expenditures in manufacturing rose from 40 percent of gross investment in plant and equipment in 1980 to more than 70 percent in 1988.

R&D is only part of the intangible investment our industry must make in order to regain competitiveness. Investing to penetrate foreign markets will be just as costly and just as necessary because there are more opportunities to increase exports than there are opportunities to reduce imports of innovative products and services. Given that the ability of managers to make intangible investments is, as noted earlier, dictated by the required rate of return on equity, U.S. competitiveness strategy must focus on ways to reduce the gap in the cost of equity that exists between this country and our leading competitors.

WHAT DETERMINES THE COST OF EQUITY?

The standard approach to this question is to assume that individuals hold both debt and equity, and arbitrage away any difference in the risk-adjusted, after-tax rate of return they get from these two types of financial instruments. Thus, if i_o is the prevailing interest rate on risk-free debt, the risk-free, after-tax return an investor would demand from an equity investment is $i_o\ (1-\tau_i)$ where τ_i is the debtholder's personal marginal tax rate.

For that condition to be satisfied, the risk-free marginal return ρ_o that a corporation must earn on stockholder equity is given by the general relation:[3]

$$\rho_o = i(1-\tau_i)/[f_d(1-\tau_d)/Q+(1-f_d)(1-\tau_c)] \qquad (1)$$

where f_d is the corporation's payout ratio
τ_d is the personal tax rate on dividends
τ_c is the personal tax rate on capital gains,
and
Q is the ratio of the market value of corporate equity divided by its replacement value (Tobin's Q).

Beyond this point there are two views. The traditional view assumes that Q is unity.[4] Moreover, since τ_d has always equaled τ_i in the United States, (1) becomes:

$$\rho_o = i/[f_d + (1-f_d)(1-\tau_c)/(1-\tau_i)]. \quad (2)$$

The new view contends that the portion of corporate equity represented by retained earnings is less valuable to stockholders than the portion that was paid in because retained earnings are subject to personal taxation when they are eventually paid out.[5] As a result, the value of Q must always be less than unity and must be related to tax rates τ_i and τ_c by the expression:

$$Q = (1-\tau_i)/(1-\tau_c). \quad (3)$$

According to the new view, the risk-free marginal return ρ_o of (1) required for reinvesting retained earnings becomes:

$$\rho_o = i[(1-\tau_i)/(1-\tau_c)]. \quad (4)$$

Actually, Tobin's Q is generally less than unity. I believe, however, that this is so not because of taxation but because corporations reinvest retained earnings at actual rates of return less than those required by the stockholders. The appropriate expression for ρ_o is therefore:

$$\rho = i/[f_d/Q + (1-f_d)(1-\tau_c)/(1-\tau_i)] \quad (5)$$

where Q is a number less than or at most equal to unity.[6]

In any case, all of the expressions (2), (4), and (5) show the importance that the taxation ratio $(1-\tau_i)/(1-\tau_c)$ plays in the relation between ρ_o and i. The smaller this ratio is, the smaller is the cost of equity ρ_o relative to the risk-free bond rate i.

For example, if we assume that τ_d were 0.5, Q were unity, and the marginal traders in stocks were in the top tax bracket of 70 percent and held the stock one year or less,[7] the change in the maximum tax rate on capital gains from 49.1 percent in 1977 to 28 percent in 1979 would reduce the ratio ρ_o/i from 74 percent to 59 percent. If, however, the marginal traders were in the 50 percent bracket and held the stock one year or less, the ratio ρ_o/i would have been 87 percent in 1977 and 77 percent in 1979.

The assumption that taxpayers in any one tax bracket determine the performance of the stock market is, of course, simplistic. Taxpayers in all brackets, as well as tax-free institutions, contribute to the determination of stock prices and consequently to the cost of equity. Nevertheless, the theory indicates, at least qualitatively, the direction in which markets should move in response to changes in the tax code.

EMPIRICAL STUDY OF THE COST OF EQUITY

As discussed in the preceding section, prevailing theories predict that for a given risk-free interest rate, the cost of equity to a corporation depends on the spread between the personal marginal tax rate on interest incomes and the personal marginal tax rate on capital gains. Thus, the lower the capital gains tax rate is in relation to the tax rate on interest, the lower is the required rate of return on equity. In order to find out whether there is any empirical support for the cost-of-capital theories, it would be useful to examine the cost of equity under varying tax regimes.

In this section, I present the results of an empirical study that revises and updates a 1987 study I co-authored with Stephen Brooks.[8] The methodology used is similar to what I first presented in a 1983 study.[9] The methodology is based on the premise that the principal mechanism by which stockholders express and possibly enforce their demand for a company to achieve a certain rate of return on its investments is the auctioning of the company's stock. If the rate of return on the replacement value of the company's net worth is lower than that required by the stockholders, the market value of the company is reduced to less than its replacement value; that is, Tobin's Q is reduced to less than unity. That Q is usually less than unity, both here and abroad, is understandable. A conscientious manager wants his or her company to grow and have that growth reflected in the company's stock price. Accordingly, the manager will make increasingly more investments at increasingly lower returns until the price of the company's stock is adversely affected. As a result, an equilibrium is reached at an investment rate that is somewhat lower than the return demanded by the stockholders.

The equation used in evaluating the cost of equity ρ_e from corporate data is:

$$\rho_e = r_i + y(1-Q) \tag{6}$$

where r_i is the expected rate of return of a firm on its incremental investments, y is the expected cash-payment rate divided by the current market value of corporate shares, and Q is the ratio of the market value of equities to their replacement value. The equation was applied to the nonfinancial corporate sector of the United States.[10]

The expected rate of return r_i was estimated as follows. First, total nominal profit of the corporate sector for each year was calculated by adding dividends to the increase in the replacement value of corporate equity and subtracting new equity issues. This profit included capital consumption adjustments, inventory valuation adjustments, and revaluation of physical assets.

Nominal return on equity was obtained by dividing nominal profit by the replacement value of equity. To estimate the expected rate of return r_i, I smoothed the actual return over time by means of a third-degree, five-point, least-square procedure.[11] Smoothing is appropriate to account for cyclical factors as well as for periodic data adjustments implemented at the Federal Reserve System.[12] Actual and smoothed nominal returns are shown in Figure 9.1. Also shown in this figure is the return with capital consumption and inventory valuation adjustments but before revaluation of physical assets. Both actual and smoothed nominal returns show two humps, one in 1974 and one in 1979, which

FIGURE 9.1
Nominal Returns to Equity

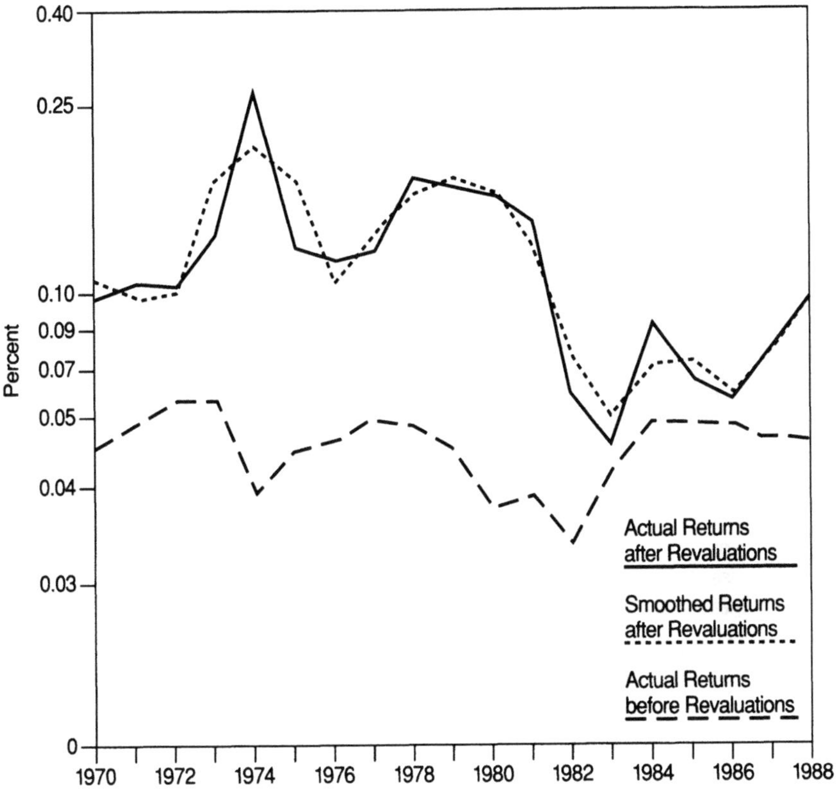

coincide with the surge in inflation resulting from the two oil shocks during the 1970s.

To evaluate y, I proceeded as follows. I first divided dividends paid by the replacement value of equity. Because the resulting series was surprisingly smooth, I set y equal to the dividend-to-equity ratio divided by Tobin's Q. In following this procedure, I disregarded the fact that in recent years corporations have transferred cash to stockholders by repurchasing shares as well as by paying dividends. I did this because the dividend payout ratio has remained relatively constant, and, therefore, stock repurchases can be viewed as a temporary result of a change in the debt-to-equity ratio.

The results obtained for the cost of equity are listed in Table 9.1. The first column of the table lists the smoothed nominal return of Figure 9.1. The second column is the actual dividend-to-equity ratio. The third column shows the resulting nominal cost of equity. The fourth column indicates the interest rate on ten-year Treasury notes. The fifth column lists the nominal cost of equity as a percent of the

TABLE 9.1
The Cost of Equity of the Nonfinancial Corporate Sector

Year	Smoothed Nominal Returns to Equity	Dividends (percent of equity)	Nominal Cost of Equity (percent)	Interest Rate on Ten-Year Treasury Notes (percent)	Nominal Cost of Equity (percent of interest rate)
1970	10.3	3.0	11.5	7.3	156
1971	9.6	2.9	10.6	6.2	172
1972	9.9	2.8	10.7	6.2	172
1973	17.2	2.8	19.8	6.8	289
1974	20.0	2.6	25.6	7.6	339
1975	17.0	2.2	22.5	8.0	282
1976	10.2	2.3	13.9	7.6	183
1977	13.3	2.5	18.0	7.4	243
1978	15.9	2.5	22.2	8.4	264
1979	17.1	2.4	23.9	9.4	253
1980	16.3	2.4	21.7	11.5	189
1981	12.6	2.3	17.3	13.9	124
1982	7.4	2.3	11.5	13.0	88
1983	5.5	2.4	8.8	11.1	80
1984	7.0	2.4	10.2	12.4	82
1985	7.1	2.4	9.9	10.6	93
1986	6.1	2.6	8.0	7.7	104
1987	7.2	2.7	9.0	8.4	108
1988	9.7	2.8	11.8	8.8	134

FIGURE 9.2
Ratio of Cost of Equity to Cost of Debt

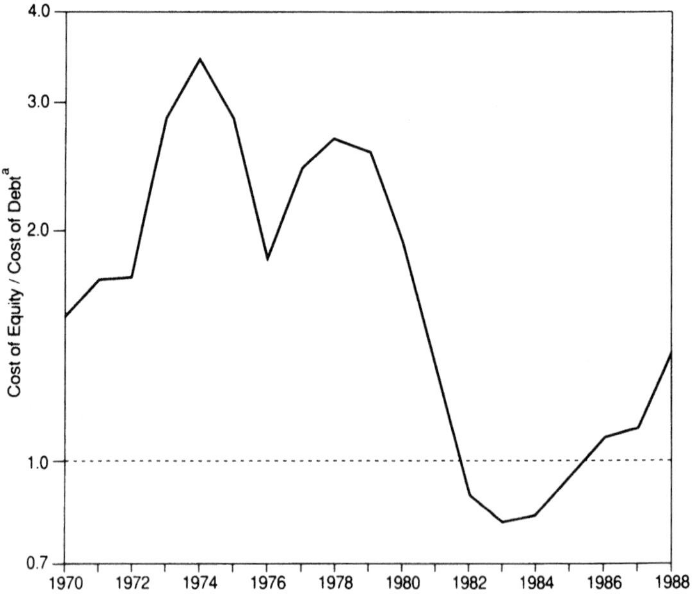

[a] interest rate on ten-year Treasury notes

interest rate on ten-year Treasury notes. The ratio of the cost of equity to the interest rate is also shown in Figure 9.2.

The precipitous decline of the cost of equity–interest rate ratio around 1979 and its rise in 1986 coincided with the increase and the elimination of the capital gains exclusion, respectively. The change around 1979, however, was several times greater than what could possibly be expected from theory. Other factors therefore must have been at work. For example, risk premiums for equities were excessively high in the 1970s, as several authors have observed.[13] But the rise after 1986 is not inconsistent with theory.

Unlike the risk-free cost of equity discussed in the preceding section, the values shown in Table 9.1 include the risk premium demanded by the market. It is therefore very surprising that the cost of equity from 1982 through 1987 was kept to about the rate for risk-free, ten-year U.S. Treasury notes.

To determine the degree to which the foregoing results represent reality, I examined a number of sources of uncertainty. The first relates to the rate of return. The Federal Reserve System estimates the flow of funds to the nonfinancial corporate sector first from the income, or supply, side and then from the investment, or use, side. The two sides differ by an appreciable discrepancy that fluctuates with time. Returns to equity were calculated both ways. When smoothed over time and compared, the standard deviation of one from the other was less than 5 percent (about 0.4 percentage point), and in any one year the difference was less than 10 percent (about 0.7 percentage point).

The second source of uncertainty relates to the expected payout yield. The assumption made in arriving at the results shown in Table 9.1 was that the large repurchases of corporate shares that occurred in the period 1984–1988 were a temporary phenomenon and should not be expected to be significant over the long run. Had stock repurchases been assumed to continue indefinitely at the rate that occurred in 1984–1988, the cost of equity in those years would be higher than shown by an amount that is less than 10 percent, whereas the cost of equity for years prior to 1984 would have remained unaltered.

There are two possible reasons for the cost of equity to be much higher than what was calculated. One is that the value of Tobin's Q is much less than what is shown in the balance sheets of the Federal Reserve. This possibility is plausible because the Federal Reserve considers only tangible assets in evaluating the replacement value of corporate equities. In addition to tangible assets, corporations possess intangible assets such as patents, technology, and market position as indicated by the fact that many corporations are sold at prices above the replacement value of their tangible net worth. An adjustment for intangible assets may change the level of the curve in Figure 9.1 but is unlikely to change its shape. A second possible reason is that the marginal profit rate during the early 1980s was greater than the average profit rate. The relative constancy of the average profit rate, however, casts doubt on this explanation.

It appears, therefore, that there are good reasons to believe that the cost of equity relative to interest rates declined after 1979 and rose after 1986. A decline in risk premiums probably overshadowed any effect the increase in the capital gains differential had on the cost of equity after 1979. But given that there is no apparent reason for risk premiums to increase after 1986, the observed increase in the cost of equity relative to risk-free interest rates is probably mostly due to the elimination of the capital gains differential that year.

The capital gains differential produces values of the cost of equity relative to interest rates that would be unattainable in a tax-free world. This observation raises the question of whether the differential introduces an undesirable disturbance to the market. I believe it does not for the following reasons. It is well known that intangible investments in innovation, technology, or the opening of new markets produce social returns in excess of the returns that accrue to the investor. For example, many of the innovations my own company has made have been copied by others; patent protection is actually quite limited. This argument has also been used repeatedly to justify the R&D tax credit. I prefer the capital gains differential because it applies to a broader base of investments, it is very cost effective when applied prospectively, and it is very important in the maintaining of our leadership in creating new enterprises. In fact, we currently lag so far behind our international competitors that both the tax credit and a capital gains differential are justifiable.

THE EFFECTS OF CORPORATE TAX RATES ON FORESIGHT AND INVESTMENT

The real cost of equity is, by definition, the rate at which future inflation-adjusted, after-tax profits from an equity investment are to be discounted for comparison with the equity outlay. Because the primary objective of a corporation is to serve its stockholders, the cost of equity is the principal determinant of what weight the future is given compared to the present. Moreover, the after-tax cost of equity depends only on what stockholders demand and is independent of corporate taxation. The time horizon of a corporation therefore should depend only on three factors: the taxation of stockholders, competing investment vehicles such as bonds, and the stockholders' perception of risk.

Nevertheless, the traditional measure of the cost of capital, which is used to determine the optimum use of capital in relation to other factors of production such as labor, is evaluated gross of tax simply because the costs of other factors are tax deductible. The expression commonly used for the real cost of capital C* is that derived by Robert Hall and Dale Jorgenson,[14] namely:

$$C^* = (r^* + \delta)(1 - ITC - \tau z)/(i - \tau) - \delta \qquad (7)$$

where r^* is the real, after-tax cost of funds of the corporation
δ is the depreciation rate of the asset
ITC is the investment tax credit
τ is the corporate income-tax rate
and
z is the present value of depreciation allowances.

This cost does depend in general on the corporate tax rate, both explicitly and because the after-tax cost of funds r^* is a composite of the cost of equity and the cost of debt, which is deductible. In most cases, the cost of capital declines with declining tax rates.

For intangible investments with no ITC, the Hall-Jorgenson expression reduces to:

$$C^* = r^* \tag{8}$$

because such investments can be written off for tax purposes.[15] Thus, the pretax cost of capital for such investments becomes the after-tax cost of funds. If a company has no debt, r^* and C^* are the real cost of equity. If a company has debt, r^* is usually lower than the cost of equity because the after-tax cost of debt is usually lower than the cost of equity.

The conclusion that can be drawn from either this analysis or the one given earlier is that the reduction, or even elimination, of corporate income taxes would not improve either the planning horizons of corporations or the incentive for corporations to increase the rate of intangible investments. The only tax measure that can influence both planning horizons and the rate of intangible investments, other than targeted tax credits such as those for R&D, is a tax rate on capital gains that is lower than the tax rate on interest income.

CONCLUSIONS

The establishment of a rate differential between the personal taxation of interest and the taxation of long-term capital gains on corporate equities can play an important role in restoring the international competitiveness of the U.S. economy. A high-wage country such as the United States cannot compete in unrestrained world markets unless the planning horizon of its industry is comparable to that of its competitors. This means that U.S. industry must be able to make long-term investments in product development and the development of foreign markets at a rate comparable to that of its leading foreign competitors.

The economic determinant of both the planning horizon and the rate of investments that produce profits only in the long run is the rate at which future corporate earnings are discounted. Such a rate of discount, which is also called the cost of equity, depends primarily on two factors: the prevailing interest rate and the capital gains differential. Empirical results show the cost of equity of U.S. corporations declining around 1979 in relation to the interest rate of U.S. Treasury notes and rising around 1986. These changes coincided with the increase and subsequent elimination of the capital gains exclusion in those two years, respectively. The change around 1979 was several times greater than what could possibly be expected from theory. Other factors, therefore, must have been at work. The rise in the late 1980s, however, is not inconsistent with theory.

The United States is at a severe disadvantage compared to its major competitors on both of the two factors that determine the cost of equity. First, this country provides no relief from the double taxation of either retained earnings or dividends. All other industrialized nations provide such relief through a capital gains differential. Second, the United States suffers from high real interest rates. Interest rates, which reflect the necessity to balance the supply and demand for funds, are high in the United States because our national saving rate is extremely low.

Appropriate taxation of capital gains would not only lower the cost of equity; it would also help reduce interest rates by encouraging people to save. Efforts to achieve the saving objective can be treacherous, however. Although investment inducements increase saving, the income realized from such investments increases consumption.[16] Ideally, the high returns on saving should be offered for the future, and penalties should be imposed for early realizations. Induced realizations of capital gains produce tax revenues and as a result may give the impression that national saving has increased. This does not actually occur, however, because for national saving to increase, consumption must decrease, and there is no mechanism by which early realizations can induce anyone to consume less.

The short-run problem facing U.S. economic policymakers is the need to increase saving and at the same time maintain a high level of production. An increase in national saving requires that consumption be reduced. To avoid a recession, consumption must be replaced with increased net exports and increased investment. A capital gains tax rate differential stimulates preferentially those investments needed to expand exports without encouraging consumption.

Finally, a capital gains differential would in the long run partly correct the imbalance between the taxation of corporate equities (taxed at both the corporate and personal levels) and the taxation of debt (taxed only at the personal level). This imbalance, which was exacerbated by the several tax changes during the 1980s, has provided such an advantage to debt financing that the rate of debt-financed takeovers and leveraged buyouts has escalated in recent years to a level far beyond what could be justified on economic grounds alone.

APPENDIX 9.A: FACTORS AFFECTING THE COST OF TANGIBLE AND INTANGIBLE CAPITAL

The issue of corporate planning horizons usually refers to a company's willingness to make intangible investments such as R&D. It is true that one electric utility, for example, could be thought to have more foresight than another because it built a power plant that proved to be needed ten years later. In manufacturing, however, most cases of foresight involve intangible investments, and because of this, the parameters governing planning horizons differ from those governing tangible capital formation.

The principal difference between a tangible investment and an intangible investment is the way that each is treated by the accounting profession. Tangible investments are capitalized, and therefore, their annual effect on the income statement of the corporation is equal to the cost of capital multiplied by the value of the investment. An intangible investment is usually expensed in the current year. As a result, the effect of an intangible investment on the income statement is the full value of the investment. Accountants and business leaders are fully cognizant of this defect in accounting principles, but no one has ever suggested a satisfactory solution.

An added difference between tangible and intangible investments is that banks and other lenders, as well as debt-rating agencies, almost completely disregard intangible assets in arriving at their assessment of a company's viability. Yet these same institutions consider other nontangible factors, including the growth rate of the company's served market.

The result of these differences between tangible and intangible investments is that the criteria used by management in making investment decisions and the parameters governing such decisions differ from one type of investment to another. For a tangible investment, the potential pretax return is in effect compared to the pretax cost of capital. In contemplating an intangible investment that will reduce the company's current earnings, however, managers must assure themselves that the future earnings from that investment, discounted at the after-tax cost of equity, will exceed the cost of that investment. As a result, interest rates affect the two types of investments differently. For tangible investments, on the one hand, interest rates play a significant role, especially for general purpose investments such as office buildings that can be easily financed, mostly by debt. For intangible investments, on the other hand, the cost of equity plays the dominant role and interest rates are a factor only to the extent that they influence the cost of equity.

Unlike tangible investments and capital, there is only partial information available about industry's intangible investments and capital, either for this country or for other nations. There are data concerning research and development, but these expenses constitute only one part of corporate intangible investments. This is especially true for Japanese industry, which has spent enormous sums to penetrate markets in other countries.

APPENDIX 9.B: EVALUATION OF THE COST OF EQUITY FROM CORPORATE DATA

Stockholders invest in corporate equities in order to have future monetary returns. Corporations invest the stockholders' equity and make an after-tax profit; part of that profit is paid back to investors, and part is retained and reinvested. The purpose of the reinvestment is to generate progressively larger profits so as to allow progressively higher cash payments to stockholders.

Let ρ_e be the cost of equity of the corporation, that is, the rate of return stockholders demand before paying taxes. Let NI be the net income of a corporation, ER the replacement value of its net worth, and EM its market value. First consider the case in which a corporation pays out to its stockholders all of its income, NI. The market value, EM, of the firm would then have to be NI/ρ_e because there would be no sellers at less than that price and no buyers at more than that price. Consequently, we can empirically determine ρ_e by dividing net income by market value. Moreover, if the return, r_e, on the replacement value, ER, that is NI/ER, equals ρ_e, the market value, EM, will be identical to ER. If, however, r_e is less than ρ_e, EM would be less than ER. That is, the ratio EM/ER (or Tobin's Q) would be less than unity. This point illustrates the general proposition that stockholders will bid down the market value of a corporation below the replacement value when the company returns less than its stockholders demand.

The situation becomes more complicated when the corporation pays out a fraction, f_d, of its income, NI, and reinvests the remaining fraction, $(1-f_d)$. The market value of the firm will depend not only on NI, f_d, and ρ_e but also on how quickly the stockholders expect NI to grow as a result of reinvestments. Moreover, how quickly the net income of the corporation grows depends on the incremental rate of return on incremental investments. In this case, neither the return NI/ER nor the return NI/EM can be used as a proxy for the cost of equity.

In general, the market value of a corporation is the present value of payments P_t to its stockholders discounted at the rate ρ_e. Thus,

$$EM_o = \int_o^\infty P_t \exp(-\rho_e t)dt \, . \tag{A1}$$

This expression can be evaluated if we project a constant payout rate, f_d, and a constant incremental rate of return, r_i, on incremental investments as follows:

The payment rate P_t at time t will be:

$$P_t = f_d NI_t \, . \tag{A2}$$

The income NI_t rate at time t will be:

$$NI_t = NI_o + r_i(ER_t - ER_o) \tag{A3}$$

where ER_t is the equity replacement at time t.
But because ER changes by virtue of retained earnings,

$$d(ER_t)/dt = NI_t - P_t. \tag{A4}$$

Substituting into (A4) from (A3) and NI_t from (A2) we get:

$$dP_t/dt = r_i(1-f_d)P_t \tag{A5}$$

or

$$d(\ln P_t)/dt = r_i(1-f_d), \tag{A6}$$

which when integrated yields:

$$P_t = P_o \exp[r_i(1-f_d)t] \tag{A7}$$

where P_o is the company's current payment rate to stockholders.

By substituting (A7) into (A1), integrating, and rearranging, we get:

$$\rho_e = (P_o/EM_o) + r_i(1-f_d) \tag{A8}$$

or

$$\rho_e = y + r_i(1-f_d) \tag{A9}$$

where y denotes the payment yield ratio P_o/EM_o.

Equation (A9) can also be written in the form

$$\rho_e = r_i + y(1-Q) \tag{A10}$$

where Q is the ratio of the market value EM_o of the corporate equity divided by its replacement value ER_o.

NOTES

I gratefully acknowledge the invaluable assistance of James M. Poterba, professor of economics at the Massachusetts Institute of Technology, for his review of this chapter and for his constructive suggestions. I also thank Stephen H. Brooks, an economist with S. H. Brooks Co., Inc., who provided critical data.

1. George N. Hatsopoulos, Paul R. Krugman, and Lawrence H. Summers, "U.S. Competitiveness: Beyond the Trade Deficit," *Science* 241 (July 15, 1988), pp. 209–307.

2. George N. Hatsopoulos and Stephen H. Brooks, "The Cost of Capital in the United States and Japan" (Paper presented at the International Conference on the Cost of Capital, Kennedy School of Government, Harvard University, Cambridge, Massachusetts, November 20, 1987).

3. The derivation of (1) is as follows: An investor who buys corporate shares at market price, EM, has a claim on after-tax income, NI, of the corporation. If a fraction, f_d, of this income is distributed in the form of dividends, the stockholder would have received $f_d \times NI$ in cash, and the corporation would have retained $(1-f_d) \times NI$. Let the ratio of the market value, EM, divided by the replacement value, ER, be Q, and let Q be constant. As a result of the retention, the corporate shares would appreciate by $(1-f_d) \times NI \times Q$. If τ_d is the personal tax rate on dividends and τ_c that on capital gains, the after-tax return to the stockholder would be:

$f_d \times NI \times (1-\tau_d) + (1-f_d) \times NI \times Q(1-\tau_c)/EM = (NI/EM) \times [f_d(1-\tau_d) + (1-f_d)Q(1-\tau_c)]$

or by substituting $(ER \times Q)$ for EM and equating this return to the return $i_o(1-\tau_i)$ on bonds, we get:

$i_o(1-\tau_i) = (NI/ER) \times [f_d(1-\tau_d)/Q+(1-f_d)(1-\tau_c)]$.

The ratio (NI/ER) is the corporation's return ρ on the replacement value of its equity.

4. James M. Poterba and Lawrence H. Summers, "The Economic Effects of Dividend Taxation," in E. Altman and M. Subrahmanyan, eds., *Recent Advances in Corporate Finance* (Homewood, Ill.: Dow Jones Erwin, 1985), pp. 227–284.

5. Alan J. Auerbach, "Wealth Maximization and the Cost of Capital," *Quarterly Journal of Economics* 93, no. 4 (August 1979), pp. 443–446.

6. If Q is found to be greater than unity, it means that the corporation possesses an intangible asset such as a patent or know-how that was omitted in the evaluation of the replacement value of the corporate equity.

7. Longer holding periods reduce the effective tax rate on capital gains.

8. Hatsopoulos and Brooks, "The Cost of Capital in the United States and Japan."

9. George N. Hatsopoulos, *High Cost of Capital: Handicap of American Industry* (Washington, D.C.: American Business Conference and Thermo Electron Corp., April 26, 1983).

10. The derivation of this equation is summarized in Appendix 9.B. The sources of the data were Federal Reserve System, *Balance Sheets for the U.S. Economy* (Washington, D.C.: Board of Governors of the Federal Reserve System, April 1989); and Federal Reserve System, *Flow of Funds Accounts* (Washington, D.C.: Board of Governors of the Federal Reserve System, June 1989).

11. See Francis B. Hildebrand, *Introduction to Numerical Analysis* (New York: McGraw-Hill, 1956), p. 296.

12. For example, the Federal Reserve Reconciliation Tables recorded large revaluations in 1974, most of which were "catch up."

13. Franco Modigliani and Richard A. Cohn, "Inflation, Rational Valuation, and the Market," *Financial Analysts Journal* (March-April 1979), pp. 24–44.

14. Robert E. Hall and Dale W. Jorgenson, "Tax Policy and Investment Behavior," *American Economic Review* 57, no. 3 (June 1967), pp. 391–414.

15. Intangible investments depreciate, but when the asset is expensed for tax purposes in the absence of ITC, the depreciation rate ρ cancels out.

16. Realized capital gains induce higher consumption than do equivalent returns in the form of unrealized but accruing appreciation of assets. See George N. Hatsopoulos, Paul R. Krugman, and James M. Poterba, *Overconsumption: The Challenge to U.S. Economic Policy* (Washington, D.C.: American Business Conference and Thermo Electron Corp., 1989).

B. Capital Gains Taxation and the Cost of Capital for Mature and Emerging Corporations

Yolanda K. Henderson

The role of capital gains taxes in impeding capital formation is a perennial topic in policy circles. The discussions have taken on greater significance since the Tax Reform Act of 1986 eliminated the 60 percent exclusion for long-term capital gains received by individuals. The revised capital gains treatment was undertaken largely to satisfy concerns about the effect of the tax revision on the distribution of income, but this revision will tend to reduce overall national income somewhat in the long run because of its adverse effects on corporate investment.

This study examines the impact of the individual capital gains tax increase for the corporate sector. This discussion goes beyond the usual aggregated statistics to examine the effect on the cost of capital for corporations at different stages of development. Two central conclusions emerge from the analysis. First, the higher capital gains tax rates accounted for one-half of the overall increase in the cost of corporate capital under the 1986 tax reform. Second, emerging corporations bear an especially pronounced burden of taxation because they rely disproportionately on equity finance.

This study begins with "An Overview of Capital Gains Taxation." It continues with "Characteristics of Emerging and Mature Corporations." Because they have not yet reached the relatively low growth rates associated with maturity, young corporations tend to retain their earnings and seek additional external funding for their investments. The discussion of the relative cost of capital for different firms appears in the next four sections: "Access to Debt," "Issues in Measuring the Cost of Equity Capital," "Institutional Ownership of Equity and Debt," and "Production Processes and the Mix of Capital Assets." Although additional imperfections in capital markets could also contribute to differences in capital costs, this discussion concentrates largely on disparities that can be adjusted through changes in tax policy. Finally, this study's conclusion offers a starting point for renewed policy discussions by briefly indicating the relative benefits and difficulties of reforming capital gains taxes, on the one hand, and the corporate income tax, on the other.

AN OVERVIEW OF CAPITAL GAINS TAXATION

Capital gains taxes paid by shareholders are only one element of the cost of funds for corporations. This section provides a perspective on how capital gains taxes factored into the set of changes introduced in the Tax Reform Act of 1986 and considers how taxes distort incentives for capital allocation and capital formation through differential effects on assets, financial instruments, and sectors. Emerging corporations may differ from mature corporations in their sources of funding, lines of business, and production processes. The effects of capital gains taxation are especially important for the analysis in later sections of the study, which deal more directly with companies at different stages of development.

By eliminating the 60 percent exclusion rate for assets held more than six months, the Tax Reform Act subjected realized long-term capital gains from the holding of corporate stock to the same effective tax rates to which ordinary income is subject. Simultaneously, the act reduced marginal tax rates. With 100 percent of long-term capital gains includable in taxable income, households now face marginal tax rates on capital gains ranging from 15 percent to 33 percent. The rate for the highest income filers is 28 percent.

The net effect of eliminating the capital gains exclusion and lowering statutory tax brackets was to raise the effective tax rates on capital gains. Prior to the passage of the Tax Reform Act, the top rate on ordinary income was 50 percent; the 60 percent exclusion produced a top capital gains rate of 20 percent. The increase for other filers was

TABLE 9.2
Changes in the Cost of Corporate Capital
Under the Tax Reform Act (TRA) of 1986
(percent)

Asset	Prior Law	Tax Reform Act of 1986: All Provisions	Tax Reform Act of 1986: Capital Gains Provisions Only	TRA Percent Difference from Prior Law: All Provisions	TRA Percent Difference from Prior Law: Capital Gains Provisions Only
Machinery and Equipment	4.2	6.9	4.6	66.3	9.4
Nonresidential Structures	7.2	7.9	7.6	10.6	6.9
Public Utility Structures	6.3	7.8	6.7	24.0	6.7
Inventories	7.9	7.6	8.5	–4.2	7.7
Land	8.3	7.9	8.9	–4.0	7.4
Total[a]	6.5	7.5	7.0	14.5	7.8

Source: Author's calculations and data in Don Fullerton, Yolanda K. Henderson, and James Mackie, "Investment Allocation and Growth Under the Tax Reform Act of 1986," *Compendium of Tax Research 1987* (Washington, D.C.: Department of the Treasury, Office of Tax Analysis, 1987), pp. 173–201.

Note: Calculations assume a net-of-tax rate of return equal to 4 percent.

[a]Using each asset's share of the total capital stock in 1984: machinery and equipment, 29.2 percent; nonresidential structures, 15.1 percent; public utility structures, 11.3 percent; inventories, 34.3 percent; and land, 10.1 percent.

more pronounced because their marginal tax brackets were reduced to a lesser extent.

This increase in capital gains taxation was responsible for about one-half of the overall increase in the corporate sector's cost of capital that resulted from the Tax Reform Act. The entries in Table 9.2 indicate the pretax real rates of return that corporations must earn on investments in order to return an inflation-adjusted 4 percent net of all taxes they and their shareholders and creditors pay. These representative calculations use a Hall-Jorgenson approach to estimating costs of a prospective investment, taking into account statutory rates of tax, investment tax credits and depreciation allowances, and separate provisions for interest, dividends, and capital gains. These calculations assume that investments are financed using one-third debt and two-thirds equity, that the debt and equity are held by the observed mix of taxable and nontaxable investors, and that the expected inflation rate is 4 percent. The calculations aggregate costs of specific types of machinery and equipment, structures, land, and inventories according to their observed fractions of the corporate capital stock. Using these assumptions combined with statutory changes, the Tax Reform Act raised the corporate cost of capital by almost 15 percent, from 6.5 percent to 7.5 percent. From the changes in capital gains taxes alone, the cost of capital increased by about 8 percent, to 7.0 percent.[1]

This increase in the cost of capital has tended to discourage capital formation and to misallocate resources away from businesses into lightly taxed investments such as owner-occupied housing. Unlike some of the other changes introduced under the Tax Reform Act, the increased taxation of capital gains has no offsetting advantages in terms of allocative effects within the corporate sector. For example, before the reform, corporations in different industries had differing effective capital costs because of their mix of assets. By rescinding the 10 percent investment tax credit and lowering the top statutory corporate income tax rate from 46 percent to 34 percent, the act tended to equalize the tax treatment of corporations using large proportions of machinery and equipment and those using large proportions of structures and nondepreciable assets. This narrowing of capital costs across corporations may have outweighed the harmful effects of increasing the overall cost of capital. For example, Don Fullerton, James Mackie, and I found that national output would increase slightly in the long run from this combination of tax changes.[2] By contrast, however, the higher taxation of capital gains affected all assets fairly equally, so this policy did not help to improve the allocation of capital across corporations. Considered alone, the increased capital gains taxes will have a negative effect on national output in the long run because they deter capital formation.

The simple Cobb-Douglas rule of thumb maintains that a 1 percent change in the cost of capital would lead to a commensurate change in the opposite direction in corporations' desired capital stock. Under this assumption, the 1986 capital gains tax increase would lead to close to an 8 percent decrease in corporate capital. Simulation with the model used in the Fullerton, Henderson, and Mackie study indicates an eventual drop of about 5.5 percent because corporations are not as sensitive to capital costs as the Cobb-Douglas model assumes. The simulations assume that households' loss of purchasing power from the capital gains tax increase would be restored by other tax cuts. Also, the simulations assume that part of the rise in the cost of capital is offset as lower investment depresses interest rates. The model indicates that national income would eventually fall by about 0.5 percent, which reflects both the contribution of corporate capital to gross national product (GNP) and some reallocation of resources to unincorporated sectors.

The increase in the capital gains rate also exacerbated the tax differential between corporate equity and debt, in opposition to the improved financial incentives caused by the reduction in the corporate income tax rate. Table 9.3 indicates some representative calculations of tax rates on interest and capital gains, assuming once again that the underlying assets are held by the observed mix of taxable and nontaxable investors and using standard assumptions about holding periods for corporate stock. (Alternative assumptions are discussed later in "Institutional Ownership of Equity and Debt.") The computations in Table 9.3 abstract from changes in depreciation allowances and the investment tax credit introduced in the Tax Reform Act.

TABLE 9.3
Federal Taxation of Nominal Corporate Interest and Capital Gains, 1986 and 1988
(percent)

	1986	1988
Interest		
Households[a]	21.5	18.5
Insurance Companies	46.0	34.0
Weighted Average Tax Rate, Including Tax-Exempt Institutions	14.9	12.2
Capital Gains		
Corporate Income Tax Rate	46.0	34.0
Households		
Weighted Average Statutory Individual Income Tax Rate	41.0	26.7
Inclusion Rate	40.0	100.0
Tax Rate on Capital Gains	16.4	26.7
Advantage of Deferral and Step-up of Basis at Death	25.0	25.0
Net Tax Rate	4.1	6.7
Insurance Companies[b]	14.0	17.0
Weighted Average Tax Rate, Including Tax-Exempt Institutions	47.7	37.2
Differential Tax between Capital Gains and Interest	32.8	25.0

Source: Author's calculations using methodology in Mervyn A. King and Don Fullerton, *The Taxation of Income from Capital* (Chicago: University of Chicago Press, 1984).

Note: The computations hold capital cost recovery provisions fixed; they abstract from changes in depreciation allowances and the investment tax credit introduced in the Tax Reform Act of 1986.

[a]Including an adjustment for untaxed imputed interest.

[b]Including an adjustment for deferral.

Interest payments are deductible by corporations but are taxable to households and other entities holding corporate debt. Some interest payments are also received by untaxed institutions. On average, the tax on one dollar of interest fell from about fifteen cents to about twelve cents because of reductions in marginal tax brackets. By contrast, corporate equity is "double taxed," with the provisions depending on whether the income is paid out as a dividend or retained in the corporation. As will be discussed, the measurement of disincentive effects caused by taxation of equity income is controversial, but at least one theory emphasizes the role of capital gains taxation over dividend taxation. Although the tax on equity at the corporate level was reduced from 46 percent to 34 percent, the effective tax on shareholders rose. If we consider both the change in marginal tax rates and the elimination of the capital gains exclusion, the weighted rate for individuals rose from 16 percent to 28 percent. In contrast to most taxes that are paid on income as it accrues, capital gains taxes are postponed until assets are sold. Also, appreciation on assets held until the individual's death escapes the capital gains tax. Various analysts have assumed that these features combine to reduce the effective capital gains tax rate on average to one-quarter of its statutory level.[3] If the reduced corporate rate, the increased capital gains rate for individuals, and taxation of institutional holders are combined, the result is a total effective tax rate on corporate capital gains that dropped from 48 percent in 1986 to 37 percent in 1988. Thus, although the differential tax between debt and equity fell, it remained very significant at 25 percentage points and was accentuated by the increase in the capital gains tax.

The tax differential between debt and equity looks even larger once inflation is considered. Capital gains are not indexed to inflation, so the effective tax is a larger fraction of real gains. The lack of indexation of interest means that the taxable income of corporations is understated in times of inflation, but this is exactly matched by an overstatement of taxable income for their creditors. Corporations are in a higher statutory tax bracket than their creditors on average, and therefore the effective tax cut is greater than the effective tax increase once a correction is made for the impact of inflation on interest.

This analysis of the various real and financial decisions distorted by capital gains taxation sets the stage for an examination of different types of corporations. As the remainder of this study indicates, capital gains taxes are particularly onerous for emerging corporations because of their reliance on equity finance.

CHARACTERISTICS OF EMERGING AND MATURE CORPORATIONS

There is no universally accepted definition of an "emerging" as opposed to a "mature" corporation, nor do data sources typically provide information separately on these two categories of firms. This section provides a conceptual definition and then discusses how this definition relates to available statistics.

Mature corporations tend to be larger than emerging corporations and grow at rates approximately equal to those of their industry group. They issue relatively little new equity to finance their expansion, relying primarily on retained earnings and borrowings. They are likely to pay out dividends to their shareholders and, especially in recent years, may actually repurchase previously issued shares. Those that grow relatively quickly are likely to achieve their growth by merging with other businesses as opposed to expanding from within. Emerging corporations, by contrast, actively seek to increase their market share. They look to external finance to accommodate their expansion plans.

Some statistical data are available by size of company, but size in itself is not a definitive indicator of "maturity." For example, mature manufacturing firms tend to be larger than mature services firms because of greater possibilities for economies of scale in manufacturing. Therefore, comparisons by size must also distinguish by industry. Data by age are harder to come by, but they would also not be a definitive indicator of whether a company is mature. For example, in some cases fairly stable companies take on new growth strategies as a result of changes in ownership or management. The next section uses some statistics on financial ratios from a sample of corporations in the Standard and Poor's Compustat database, contrasting them with corporations that had just made an initial public stock offering. By and large, companies in the latter sample are substantially smaller and younger, and even those that are large and of long standing could be considered "emerging" because their decision to tap into national equity markets signals a planned change in scale or scope. In later sections that consider policies to retain earnings or pay out dividends, direct data are not readily available, so the analysis is based on presumed characteristics of mature and emerging corporations rather than on hard numbers.

ACCESS TO DEBT

Because of tax laws, corporations prefer to finance capital expansion by means of debt rather than equity. The use of debt means that income generated by new investments is subject to only one layer of tax, whereas income from equity is taxable both to the corporation and its shareholders. Therefore, restricted access to debt could raise the relative cost of capital for emerging corporations. A comparison of debt-asset and debt-equity ratios from the Compustat database and a sample of newly public corporations confirms that emerging corporations have relatively limited access to debt markets. The data are presented for disaggregated industries in order to control for nontax obstacles to the use of debt that vary across the economy. For example, corporations with highly cyclical cash flows are especially reluctant to incur an obligation to make regular interest payments.

Ideally, one would want to compare emerging and mature corporations with respect to their financing of new investment projects. But about the best that can be done is an overall comparison of debt accumulated to finance existing assets or debt relative to shareholders' equity. The data for mature corporations come from more than twenty-four hundred corporations in the Standard and Poor's Compustat Industry Aggregate Database. The average book value of assets per company was estimated at $781 million for manufacturing corporations; $1,444 million for transportation, communication, and utilities; $331 million for trade; and $207 million for services.[4] The ratios in each industry are measured as the sum of debt divided by the sum of assets or equity, so they give added weight to larger corporations.

For emerging companies, data are taken from *Going Public: The IPO Reporter*. This publication covers essentially all corporations making initial public offerings (IPOs). Because of the large number of IPOs in 1986, that year was chosen for the comparisons. Total assets, long-term debt, and shareholders' equity were available for 237 of the 416 domestic, nonfinancial corporations making initial public offerings in 1986.[5] Many of these companies were of recent vintage, but some had started as divisions of larger corporations, and others had been privately held for a number of years. The IPO sample is less concentrated in manufacturing than is the Compustat data base. The average size of assets in 1986 was much smaller: $102 million in manufacturing; $148 million for transportation, communication, and utilities; $73 million for trade; and $26 million for services. These mean values far overstate the size of a typical firm. For example, one-half of the manufacturing firms had assets valued at less than $26 million, and one-half of the services firms had assets valued at less than $12 million.[6] Although these companies are very much smaller than those in the Compustat data base, they are still significantly larger than what is usually referred to as "small business."

Debt-to-Asset and Debt-to-Equity Ratios

Table 9.4 indicates debt-to-asset ratios for mature and emerging corporations in 1986. Table 9.5 presents debt-to-equity ratios for the same groupings. Debt consists of interest-bearing liabilities. By accounting identity, assets equal the sum of shareholders' equity, debt, and other liabilities such as accounts payable, tax liabilities, and other accrued expenses. (The contribution of these other liabilities may cause some divergence in the patterns indicated between Table 9.4 and Table 9.5.[7])

The first three columns of numbers in each table compare long-term debt for mature and emerging companies. As indicated in Table 9.4, the ratio of long-term debt to assets for mature companies ranged from 17.4 percent in manufacturing to 34.1 percent in services. The ratios for the emerging companies were generally substantially smaller.[8] In services industries, the emerging companies' average debt ratio was 17.3 percent, about one-half that of the mature companies. In trade, the long-term debt ratios were one-third lower than for the mature companies, and in manufacturing, they were one-tenth lower. Only in transportation, communication, and utilities were the emerging companies comparable to the mature companies in the Compustat sample. The third column presents median values rather than means for the emerging corporations sample. Many emerging companies have very low long-term debt ratios, and the industry averages are brought up by relatively few companies using large amounts of debt (see Figure 9.3).

TABLE 9.4
Debt-to-Asset Ratios for Mature and Emerging Corporations by Industry, 1986[a]
(percent)

	Long-Term Debt			Total Debt			Sample Size	
	Mature	Emerging		Mature	Emerging[b]		Mature	Emerging
		Mean	Median		Mean	Median	(number of companies)	
Total Nonfinancial	23.0	18.5	9.8	28.5	25.9	18.9	2,422	237
Manufacturing	17.4	15.7	8.0	23.7	23.7	17.8	1,245	93
Food and Tobacco	22.4	14.6	7.8	32.1	25.3	18.4	93	6
Chemicals	18.1	10.4	1.3	25.6	18.1	11.9	137	12
Industrial and Computing Equipment	13.2	25.5	3.9	22.2	29.2	13.8	224	8
Electronic Equipment	12.3	7.9	4.6	18.9	14.3	14.2	123	17
Measuring Instruments	11.7	26.6	2.5	18.1	34.2	11.4	99	11
Miscellaneous Manufacturing	21.0	7.6	1.1	31.3	24.6	23.5	41	7
All Other Manufacturing	18.9	17.5	14.0	23.5	25.4	22.3	528	32
High-Technology Industries[c]	n.a.	16.9	3.0	n.a.	22.5	12.4	n.a.	38
Non-High-Technology Industries	n.a.	14.8	10.4	n.a.	24.6	20.9	n.a.	55
Transportation, Communication, Utilities	31.6	31.5	27.4	34.9	35.5	33.0	370	26
Wholesale Trade	24.2	16.0	11.3	31.7	26.3	23.8	153	15
Retail Trade	24.1	17.0	14.2	32.7	27.2	24.3	291	30
Services	34.1	17.3	7.2	40.1	23.4	15.6	249	69
Technology-Oriented Industries[d]	n.a.	16.6	5.6	n.a.	23.0	14.0	n.a.	47
Non-Technology-Oriented Industries	n.a.	18.8	7.7	n.a.	24.3	16.3	n.a.	22

Sources: Data from Compustat Industry Aggregate Database and *Going Public: The IPO Reporter.*

[a]For mature corporations, the ratios are value-weighted means. Bernanke and Campbell have indicated that means and medians are similar in the Compustat sample. For emerging corporations, they are means and medians of ratios for individual companies averaged before and after their initial public stock offers. Individual industries are shown separately if there are at least six observations of companies going public in 1986. See Ben S. Bernanke and John Y. Campbell, "Is There a Corporate Debt Crisis?" *Brookings Papers on Economic Activity* 1 (1988), pp. 83–125.

[b]Short-term debt component estimate based on the observed ratio of short-term debt to liabilities, excluding long-term debt in mature corporations.

[c]SIC codes 283 (drugs), 286 (industrial organic chemicals), 357 (office and computing equipment), 366 (communications equipment), 367 (electronic components), 372 (aircraft), 376 (missiles), and 380 (instruments). Definition from U.S. Congressional Budget Office, *Federal Financial Support for High-Technology Industries* (Washington, D.C.: U.S. Government Printing Office, June 1985).

[d]SIC codes 737 (computers and data processing), 7389-7399 (business services not elsewhere classified), 805-809 (health services), 8731 (commercial physical research), and 8734 (testing laboratories).

TABLE 9.5
Debt-to-Equity Ratios for Mature and Emerging Corporations by Industry, 1986[a]
(percent)

	Long-Term Debt			Total Debt			Sample Size	
		Emerging			Emerging[b]		Mature	Emerging
	Mature	Mean	Median	Mature	Mean	Median	(number of companies)	
Total Nonfinancial	58.6	122.5	22.2	72.8	191.5	56.9	422	210
Manufacturing	42.4	115.3	20.1	57.8	213.1	54.5	245	86
Food and Tobacco	62.3	86.1	17.3	89.3	156.0	131.5	93	5
Chemicals	43.4	64.7	2.3	61.2	96.9	17.5	137	10
Industrial and Computing Equipment	30.1	37.9	9.3	50.6	57.1	37.5	224	8
Electronic Equipment	26.8	39.8	16.7	41.2	66.0	26.9	123	17
Measuring Instruments	25.9	91.6	5.1	40.3	139.3	45.8	99	9
Miscellaneous Manufacturing	48.5	112.6	2.8	72.5	318.0	127.9	41	7
All Other Manufacturing	47.8	213.3	49.6	59.5	384.1	86.5	528	30
High-Technology Industries[c]	n.a.	43.9	6.1	n.a.	66.0	30.1	n.a.	37
Non High-Technology Industries	n.a.	165.1	43.7	n.a.	314.1	84.2	n.a.	53
Transportation, Communication, Utilities	82.6	241.9	80.5	91.3	283.3	125.6	370	21
Wholesale Trade	67.6	348.4	39.2	88.4	453.5	111.8	153	14
Retail Trade	76.5	89.2	43.6	103.7	145.4	83.7	291	26
Services	106.8	42.9	16.3	125.6	72.0	37.5	249	60
Technology-Oriented Industries[d]	n.a.	39.6	13.5	n.a.	69.4	34.0	n.a.	40
Non Technology-Oriented Industries	n.a.	49.3	19.4	n.a.	77.2	46.5	n.a.	20

Source: Data from Compustat Industry Aggregate Database and *Going Public: The IPO Reporter.*

[a]For mature companies, the ratios are value-weighted means. Bernanke and Campbell have indicated that means and medians are similar in the Compustat sample. Ben S. Bernanke and John Y. Campbell, "Is There a Corporate Debt Crisis?" *Brookings Papers on Economic Activity* 1 (1988), pp. 83–125. For emerging corporations, they are means and medians of ratios for individual companies averaged before and after their initial public stock offering. Observations are omitted if equity is negative. Individual industries are shown separately if there are at least six observations of companies going public in 1986. All ratios are book values.

[b]Short-term debt component estimated based on the observed ratio of short-term debt to liabilities, excluding long-term debt in mature corporations.

[c]SIC codes 283 (drugs), 286 (industrial organic chemicals), 357 (office and computing equipment), 366 (communications equipment), 367 (electronic components), 372 (aircraft), 376 (missiles), and 380 (instruments). Definition from U.S. Congressional Budget Office, *Federal Financial Support for High-Technology Industries* (Washington, D.C.: U.S. Government Printing Office, June 1985).

[d]SIC codes 737 (computers and data processing), 7389–7399 (business services), 805–809 (health services), 8731 (commercial physical research), and 8734 (testing laboratories).

FIGURE 9.3
Frequency Distribution of Long-Term
Debt-to-Asset Ratios for Emerging Corporations

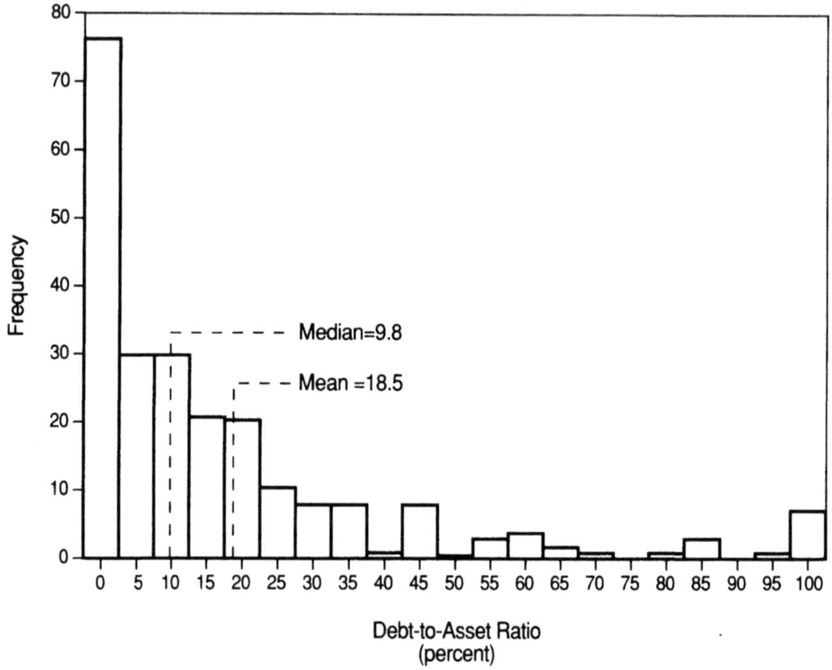

Source: Calculated from data from *Going Public: The IPO Reporter.*

The median values, which mark the division between the bottom and top halves of the sample, are a better indicator for the "typical" emerging company in each industry. (The mature company sample does not appear to have such an asymmetric distribution, according to other research using observations for individual companies. Therefore, means and medians are approximately equal.[9]) Within both manufacturing and services, the overall median ratios for the emerging companies are less than 10 percent, and for each disaggregated manufacturing industry the median ratio is much less than the counterpart in the mature company sample.

In Table 9.5, the long-term debt-to-equity ratios for mature corporations average 42.4 percent in manufacturing and 106.8 percent in services, and they take on intermediate values in the other industry groups. The mean ratios for the emerging companies are typically higher (except for services) but are distorted upward not only by selected companies with high use of debt but also by selected companies with very low values of shareholders' equity as a result of operating losses in early years. The median values of debt-to-equity confirm the findings of low usage of debt: The ratio is 20.1 percent in manufacturing and

16.3 percent in services. Except for transportation, communication, and utilities and for manufacturing industries not shown separately (because of low instances of initial public offerings), the ratios are substantially less than those measured for mature industries.

The accessibility of long-term debt is important for the analysis of the cost of fixed capital, such as plant and machinery. Because these assets have relatively long lives, risk-averse firms are unlikely to finance them with short-term loans that must be renegotiated each year. The relevant choice is between long-term debt and equity. Nevertheless, total debt is relevant for considering aggregate investment, which includes assets such as inventories. Some economists believe that it is also misleading to associate different investments with particular sources of finance. Victor Andrews and Peter Eisemann have argued that the fungible nature of funds means that once companies acquire financing, it may be used for any cash need.[10] In particular, they observed that small businesses make use of a variety of sources to finance the purchase of fixed assets. Whether this informal financing of capital is possible once corporations become larger than those in the Andrews and Eisemann study is open to debate.

For corporations in the Compustat sample, adding in short-term interest-bearing liabilities contributes 6 percentage points to the debt-to-asset ratio on average (Table 9.4). The ratio in manufacturing is 23.7 percent and in services 40.1 percent, for example. Unfortunately, the *IPO Reporter* does not provide short-term debt, so an approximation was used. For each industry, other liabilities were computed by subtracting long-term debt and shareholders' equity from total assets. Then it was assumed that short-term debt constituted the same proportion of this total as it did in the Compustat sample (with the remainder attributable to items such as accounts payable, tax liabilities, and other accrued expenses[11]). The results continued to indicate a lower debt-to-asset ratio than for mature companies, especially when median values were used. In manufacturing, the overall median ratio for the emerging corporations averaged 5 percentage points less than that for mature companies and usually exhibited a bigger difference in the individual industries with a substantial concentration of IPOs. The ratio for emerging corporations was 75 percent as large in trade and only about 40 percent as large in services compared to the Compustat sample. The debt-equity ratios showed less of a difference than the debt-asset ratios but were still very much lower for new companies in services than for established companies.

Among the mature corporations, those in the services sector had the highest debt ratios in 1986. It might be expected that an industrial structure shifting toward services and away from manufacturing would tend to raise the proportion of debt used to finance corporate investment. But the IPO sample indicates the opposite because the emerging services corporations had lower debt-asset and debt-equity ratios than the emerging manufacturing corporations. Apparently the nature of these new services companies is different from that of more mature companies.

Technology-Oriented Companies

Finally, for the emerging corporations, an analysis was performed to determine whether technology-oriented companies differ from other companies in their use of debt. Many analysts believe that these companies are important for international competitiveness because of their own potential for high growth and because of the spillover benefits of their research for other sectors.[12] To the extent that high-tech companies use specialized equipment and invest in additional assets not suitable for collateral, they may have a hard time attracting credit. In services, the results were clear. Companies in technology-oriented industries such as computers and medical and other research laboratories had far less access to debt than did companies in industries with less of an orientation toward technology. In manufacturing, the results held up if median debt-asset ratios or debt-equity ratios were used but not if mean debt-asset ratios were used.

Comments and Caveats

The empirical results in this section indicate that the typical young corporation planning significant expansion finances a lower fraction of its assets using debt than does the large, established corporation. The results tend to carry over to comparisons of debt-equity ratios. Lower availability of debt, all else equal, means that emerging corporations face a higher cost of capital because of their inability to take advantage of tax incentives for this form of finance. These findings conflict with the results of a previous study by Andrews and Eisemann that emphasized the reliance on debt finance by small businesses, but their focus tended to be on very small businesses, and they did not control for industrial mix.[13]

No data set is perfect for analyzing these issues, and the current ones contain some shortcomings that deserve comment. First, the debt-asset ratios of mature firms may be understated because debt is usually amortized faster than assets are depreciated in financial accounts.[14] Because companies in the Compustat data base are older on average, their reported debt-asset ratios may be low relative to those in the IPO data base. For some industries, however, particularly services, the reported discrepancy is so large that it seems unlikely to disappear with alternative accounting procedures.

The measured debt-equity ratios appear to have a weakness that would work in the opposite direction. Shareholders' equity in newly emerging corporations tends to be reduced because of negative or low earnings in the initial period of a company's history. Several years later, the company may be using more equity (and relatively less debt) to finance new investments than is apparent from ratios reflecting its entire history.[15] Because of this relative overstatement of the use of debt by young companies in the IPO data base, it is even more striking that the debt-equity ratios for typical companies in each industry are as low as indicated.

Finally, the data did not permit an analysis of flows of funds but assumed that new capital would be financed in a manner reflecting the cumulation of historical decisions for both sets of companies. Clearly, more research is needed.

ISSUES IN MEASURING THE COST OF EQUITY CAPITAL

The previous section indicated that emerging corporations tend to have a higher cost of capital than mature corporations do because they are less able to finance their investments by debt. This section examines the contribution of tax policy to the cost of equity capital. For most corporations, the capital gains tax is the most important element of the personal tax on income from equity ownership. But the theory of the relative role of dividend and capital gains taxes is a matter of dispute among economists; therefore, it is impossible to say unambiguously whether tax policy favors emerging or mature corporations in this respect. The calculations used for Table 9.2 adopted the so-called new view of dividend taxation, which maintains that emerging corporations are disadvantaged relative to mature corporations. The old view holds that emerging corporations have a lower cost of equity capital than mature corporations do (keeping nontax factors constant) but that their relative advantage shrank under the Tax Reform Act of 1986. Finally, a recent line of research emphasizes the costliness of external finance beyond what can be measured by tax factors alone. This suggests that emerging corporations face especially high costs when they issue new shares to finance their expansion.

Taxes on Shareholders and Equity Costs: An Unresolved Dispute

The old view and the new view are identical with respect to their measurement of capital gains taxes and dividend taxes. Equity that is retained and reinvested generates accrued capital gains that are not taxed until realization. If the shares are held until death, they escape taxation altogether. Because of these deferral and forgiveness features, capital gains are effectively taxed at a lower rate than dividends are, even now that both types of income face identical rates when they are reported on individuals' tax returns. The reasons that firms pay dividends are largely still a mystery, although economists have tried to measure nontax factors, such as the value of the signals that dividends can convey to shareholders.

The old view and new view of dividend taxation differ in the relative weights they assign to the relatively highly taxed dividends compared to capital gains in the overall cost of equity finance (see Table 9.6). The new view of dividends stresses financial decisions at the margin. To retain one more dollar of earnings, the corporation must forego a dividend payment. The opportunity cost of this dollar of retentions is equal to one dollar *less* the dividend tax that would have to be paid. When the returns from the reinvested retained earnings are ultimately paid out to shareholders, they are subject to dividend tax. But because the dividend tax enters into the calculation of the opportunity cost of retaining earnings, the return to shareholders relative to dividends foregone initially is independent of the dividend tax. Therefore, in the calculation of the cost of retained earnings, only capital gains taxes matter. The dividend tax, however, does affect the cost of new share issues. To invest an additional dollar, the corporation issues a dollar of new shares. These earn a rate of return that is ultimately taxed at the dividend tax rate when paid out to shareholders.

For corporations as a whole, new share issues are a minor source of equity capital. Mervyn King and Don Fullerton estimated that 93 percent of equity is raised through retained earnings and only 7 percent from new shares.[16] Therefore, capital gains taxes are the predominant form of taxation of equity income under the new view. This theory implies that emerging corporations are especially disadvantaged by the tax code because their proportion of finance through new share issues is higher than average. In effect, they face the higher dividend tax on a relatively greater proportion of their equity.

The old view of dividends emphasizes observed ratios of retained earnings and dividend payouts. Historically, U.S. corporations in the aggregate have retained about 60 percent of their profits and paid out about 40 percent.[17] The old view takes these weights for the capital gains tax and the dividends tax, respectively. Extension of this theory to emerging and mature corporations implies that emerging corporations have a relatively low cost of equity capital because they usually do not pay dividends. The theory also leads to the conclusion that by increasing capital gains tax rates and decreasing dividend tax rates, the Tax Reform Act of 1986 hurt emerging corporations relative to mature corporations.

Unfortunately, empirical evidence on the role of dividend taxation has been inconclusive. In separate studies, David Bradford and Alan Auerbach found evidence in support of the new view, whereas James Poterba and Lawrence Summers rejected it.[18] So although I employ the new view of dividend taxation in my calculations of the cost of capital, policymakers should realize that the economics profession does not speak with one voice on this issue.

Cash-Flow Constraints

A related line of research suggests that emerging corporations face a substantial cost disadvantage in having to seek external equity finance

TABLE 9.6
Personal Income Taxation of Corporate Equities under Alternative Theories

	Tax Rate on Equity Capital		Effect of 1986 Tax Reform	
	Corporations in General	Emerging vs. Mature Corporations	Corporations in General	Emerging vs. Mature Corporations
New View of Dividend Taxation	Capital gains tax rate × (retained earnings/equity finance) + dividend tax rate × (new share issues/equity finance). Estimated weight observed for capital gains tax = 0.93; for dividend tax = 0.07.	Rate for mature corporations is dominated by capital gains tax because they tend not to issue new shares. As a result, tax policy lowers the cost of equity capital for mature corporations relative to that for emerging corporations.	Taxation of equity capital increased substantially because of the increase in the capital gains tax rate.	Changes tended to raise the cost of capital for mature corporations relative to that for emerging corporations.
Old View of Dividend Taxation	Capital gains tax rate × (retained earnings/profits) + dividend tax rate × (dividends/profits). Estimated weight observed for capital gains tax = 0.6; for dividend tax = 0.4.	Rate for emerging corporations is dominated by capital gains tax because they tend not to pay dividends. As a result, tax policy lowers the cost of equity capital for emerging corporations relative to that for mature corporations.	Taxation of equity capital changed minimally because the increased capital gains tax rate was offset by the decreased dividend tax rate.	Changes tended to raise the cost of capital for emerging corporations relative to that for mature corporations.

beyond the disadvantage suggested purely on the basis of tax measures. The problem arises because potential shareholders do not know how to interpret new share issues. In some cases, the issuance of new shares implies that existing shareholders have information that leads them to expect low future earnings, and they are therefore willing to dilute their ownership of the company. In other cases, issuance simply means that profitable investment opportunities outstrip internal funds. Because prospective shareholders cannot distinguish good opportunities from bad opportunities, they demand a premium to buy shares. This raises the cost of external equity finance. In support of this theory, Steven Fazzari, Glenn Hubbard, and Bruce Petersen found that internal cash flow often serves as a constraint on investment beyond the constraint that would be expected based on tax theories alone.[19] Applying these results to emerging corporations with limited ability to borrow and with investment opportunities in excess of their retained earnings, the study suggested that the high cost of new share issues puts these companies at a competitive disadvantage.

INSTITUTIONAL OWNERSHIP OF EQUITY AND DEBT

The measurement of the cost of capital in "An Overview of Capital Gains Taxation" depended on an assumed mix of taxable and nontaxable entities providing financing to corporations. If funds are provided by institutions that are not taxed, such as pension funds, the corporation's cost of funds should be lower because investors demand a higher rate of return from corporations if they must pay taxes on the capital gains, dividends, and interest they receive. This section discusses what is known about the ownership of equity and debt and concludes that greater institutional ownership of the securities issued by mature corporations gives them a capital cost advantage over emerging corporations.

The calculations in Table 9.2 assumed that debt and equity finance were provided to corporations in line with observed ownership. Households are the most common supplier of equity finance (see Table 9.7); they accounted for 64 percent of corporate equity ownership in 1988. Untaxed institutional investors, especially pensions, accounted for most of the remainder. For corporate debt, households accounted for less than one-half of total ownership, and most of this was "indirect" ownership through shares of mutual funds that purchased corporate bonds and through deposits at banks and savings institutions that made loans to corporations. The role of institutional investors was greater in debt markets than in equity markets.

Evidence from securities markets indicates that untaxed investors are more important for large, established corporations than for smaller corporations whose shares are held largely by households. On the New

TABLE 9.7
Distribution of Ownership of Corporate Equity and Debt, 1988[a]
(percent of total)

	Equity	Debt
Households[b]	64	45
Pension Funds	23	34
Foreigners	5	9
Nonprofit Institutions	4	—[c]
Insurance Companies	3	11

Source: Calculated by the author from Board of Governors, Federal Reserve System, *Flow of Funds Accounts* using the methodology in Mervyn A. King and Don Fullerton, *The Taxation of Income from Capital* (Chicago: University of Chicago Press, 1984).

[a]Excluding finance provided by other nonfinancial corporations.

[b]Including indirect ownership through mutual funds, savings institutions, commercial banks, and other financial intermediaries. Excludes estimate attributable to nonprofit institutions.

[c]Not available separately; included under households.

TABLE 9.8
Sources of Finance for Private, Independent Venture Capital Funds, 1988

Finance Source	Percent of Total
Pension Funds	46
Foreigners	14
Nonprofit Institutions	12
Corporations	11
Insurance Companies	9
Households	8

Source: Data reprinted with permission from Venture Economics, *Venture Capital Yearbook 1989* (Needham, Mass.: Venture Economics, 1989), p. 23.

York Stock Exchange, noninstitutional investors have accounted for only about 10 percent of total volume since 1987. Even before the rise in capital gains tax rates in 1987, they accounted for just 30 percent.[20] By contrast, in the over-the-counter market, where smaller firms' shares are traded, noninstitutional investors account for about 80 percent of total volume.

Institutions are important investors for certain young businesses, however. For example, during the 1980s institutions were major providers of capital through venture capital funds. Pension funds, foreigners (who face no capital gains taxes in the United States), and nonprofit institutions together provided more than 70 percent of funds raised by the venture capital industry in 1988 (see Table 9.8). But it is important not to exaggerate the significance of organized venture capital. In recent years, initial public offerings of companies backed by venture capital were only one-fifth of total IPOs.[21] Wealthy individuals and entrepreneurs remained an important source of funds, as did corporations through their funding of divisions or subsidiaries that later made public offerings.

Established corporations also have a disproportionate access to untaxed institutional investors through the bond market. Younger companies rely heavily on financial intermediaries such as banks rather than on direct credit.[22] In effect, younger companies are borrowing funds from households that have accounts at these institutions and face taxes on interest received.

PRODUCTION PROCESSES AND THE MIX OF CAPITAL ASSETS

The preceding analysis has emphasized the financial distinctions between emerging and mature corporations. The current section examines potential differences in production processes. Before the passage of the Tax Reform Act of 1986, effective tax rates varied widely across assets. Even now, machinery and equipment are taxed at somewhat lower rates than are other assets because of accelerated depreciation. If emerging and mature corporations differ in their asset mix, this would be another factor contributing to differences in the cost of capital.

No study has looked specifically at this issue, but a comparison by Don Fullerton and Andrew Lyon of high-technology industries with economywide averages indicated very little difference in capital costs because of differences in asset composition.[23] Using a methodology very similar to that used to generate Table 9.2, they found that high-technology industries (identified according to research and development intensity) had slightly *lower* capital costs than did all industries in the early 1980s based on their observed use of machinery, equipment, and structures. Measured in terms of an effective tax rate, the difference in any given year was never larger than 3 percentage points, however.

To the extent that these results carry over to a general comparison of emerging and mature corporations, they indicate that differences in production activity are not important contributors to disparate capital costs. Because the Tax Reform Act succeeded in narrowing distinctions in taxation of different capital assets, this conclusion is more likely to hold now than in previous years.

CONCLUSIONS

This study has found that increases in capital gains taxes contributed about one-half of the overall rise in the corporate cost of capital from the Tax Reform Act of 1986. The elimination of the capital gains preference raised these costs about 8 percent for the average corporation, even when the offsetting effects of lower marginal tax brackets are considered and lags between accrual and realization of capital gains and their forgiveness at death are taken into account. That is, to earn a return of 4.0 percent net of all taxes, the typical corporation's threshold pretax return has risen from 6.5 to 7.0 percent as a result of higher capital gains taxes, if we assume that the corporation uses a financing mix of one-third debt and two-thirds equity. This increase has deterred capital formation without improving the allocation of capital resources.

Any increase in the cost of equity funds is likely to impose a disproportionate burden on emerging corporations, thereby discouraging their growth. The typical young corporation finances a lower proportion of its assets by issuing debt and has a lower debt-to-equity ratio than does the typical mature corporation. This comparison is especially sharp in the services sector.

Technology-oriented companies also have particularly low access to debt. Although economists disagree on exactly how capital gains taxes and dividend taxes affect the cost of equity, and therefore on whether equity is more expensive for emerging than for mature corporations, they generally recognize capital gains taxes as a significant element of this cost. Furthermore, recent research indicates that a lack of internally generated funds serves as a constraint on investment beyond what an analysis based solely on tax policy would indicate. The need of young corporations to issue new shares hampers their capital expansion plans.

The cost of funds—both equity and debt—depends on whether investors and creditors are subject to taxation on their income. Mature corporations have relatively greater access to untaxed institutional investors such as pension funds and can therefore afford to undertake investments with pretax returns lower than those undertaken by emerging corporations. Investors in young corporations are more likely to be individuals subject to capital gains taxes.

Finally, these financial distinctions between emerging and mature corporations are more important than distinctions based on production activity. Differences in the reliance on equipment as opposed to structures are not particularly striking between high-technology businesses and others, and any existing differences were mitigated by the Tax Reform Act of 1986.

This study has concentrated on evidence regarding capital costs, leaving to other researchers and policymakers the task of formulating a detailed policy response. Achieving an appropriate balance between goals for income distribution and for capital formation is always problematic. Considerations of fairness deserve a prominent role in policy discussions but have been omitted from this study. Nevertheless, it might be appropriate to conclude with a few general comments on policy lessons regarding capital formation.

Tax reformers interested in lowering the cost of investment in corporations relative to the cost of tax-preferred investments such as owner-occupied housing and consumer durables should attempt to eliminate the "double tax" on corporate equities. This would also serve to equalize capital costs between mature and emerging corporations. Lowering the effective tax rate on capital gains from corporate stock could form part of this response. Policymakers still have to weigh alternative mechanisms for achieving this result, including the reintroduction of an exclusion for capital gains or the adjustment of the basis for computing gains. Considerations of effects on particular investments and investors, as well as of revenues, enter into this decision. Also, policymakers must decide whether considerations of equity or administrative ease imply that favorable treatment should be extended to assets outside the corporate sector as well as to gains on existing investments in addition to new investments. But whichever decision is made, a reduction in capital gains taxes could be enacted rather easily.

A reduced effective tax rate on capital gains still leaves in place significant distinctions between the tax treatment of debt and equity. These differences stem from the existence of a separate tax on corporate income in addition to taxes on shareholders. The original plans for tax reform in the mid-1980s included a proposal for partial tax integration through a corporate deduction for dividend payments. This plan never won the support of the business community because it appeared to discourage the retention and reinvestment of earnings and because other aspects of the reform package were more universally popular.

Researchers and policymakers interested in eliminating penalties on investment in corporate equities may wish to revisit the possibilities for tax integration. A successful blueprint would encompass corporations that raise equity capital through retained earnings as well as new share issues and corporations that pass returns to shareholders through capital gains as well as dividends. Tax integration would be a very ambitious undertaking, but it has the potential to encourage significant capital formation by corporations.

NOTES

The research assistance of Jeffrey B. Liebman is gratefully acknowledged. The view expressed here are those of the author and do not necessarily reflect official positions of the Federal Reserve Bank of Boston or the Federal Reserve System.

1. For further discussion of the methodology used to calculate the changes in the cost of capital that resulted from the Tax Reform Act of 1986, see Yolanda K. Henderson. "Lessons from Federal Reform of Business Taxes," *New England Economic Review* (November-December 1986), pp. 9–25; and Don Fullerton, Yolanda K. Henderson, and James Mackie, "Investment Allocation and Growth Under the Tax Reform Act of 1986," *Compendium of Tax Research 1987* (Washington, D.C.: U.S. Department of the Treasury, Office of Tax Analysis, 1987), pp. 173–201.
2. See Fullerton, Henderson, and Mackie, ibid.

3. See Chapter 6; and references in Mervyn A. King and Don Fullerton, *The Taxation of Income from Capital* (Chicago: University of Chicago Press, 1984). Shorter holding periods would cause the effective rate to be closer to the statutory rate.

4. The data base consists of observations by industry, not by corporation. Average assets were computed by dividing total assets in the industry by the reported number of corporations, and then the level was corrected using direct evidence on 500 large corporations.

5. The data for shareholders' equity refer to common equity only, but corporations that had issued preferred stock usually converted it to common stock prior to making a public offering.

6. The IPO corporations were assigned to industries on the basis of registries issued by the Securities and Exchange Commission and Standard and Poor's, supplemented by telephone conversations with employees of the Securities and Exchange Commission. For further financial information on these corporations, see Yolanda K. Henderson, "The Emergence of the Venture Capital Industry," *New England Economic Review* (July-August 1989), pp. 64–79.

7. If debt were measured as the total of interest-bearing and noninterest bearing liabilities, then the ranking of companies by debt-to-asset ratios and debt-to-equity ratios would be identical. Because this discussion focuses on the tax treatment of interest, it is necessary to distinguish interest-bearing debt from other liabilities. As a result, the ranking of companies by debt intensity depends on which concept—debt to assets or debt to equity—is used. Consider a corporation with shareholders' equity (E) equal to 300, debt (D) equal to 200, and other liabilities (L) equal to 500. Total assets (A) would equal 1,000 (E + D + L). Assume that for a second corporation, E = 300, D = 100, L = 50, and A = 450. The first corporation has the higher debt-equity ratio (2/3, compared to 1/3 for the second corporation). The second corporation has the higher debt-asset ratio (2/9, compared to 1/5—or 2/10—for the first corporation). Because of this ambiguity, both measures of debt usage are indicated in the tables.

8. The IPO ratios in Tables 9.4 and 9.5 take assets and equity averaged before and after the public stock offering. Prior to the offering, the ratios might understate companies' desired levels of equity. But given fixed costs of issuing stock, companies tend to make only periodic offerings, so the postoffering ratios might overstate companies' desired levels of equity.

9. Ben Bernanke and John Campbell have reported a mean (short-term plus long-term) debt-asset ratio of 27.3 percent and a median ratio of 28.9 percent for a sample of more than six hundred Compustat companies in 1986. See Ben S. Bernanke and John Y. Campbell, "Is There a Corporate Debt Crisis?" *Brookings Papers on Economic Activity* 1 (1988), pp. 83–125.

10. Victor L. Andrews and Peter C. Eisemann, "Who Finances Small Business Circa 1980?" Working Paper (Washington, D.C.: Interagency Task Force on Small Business Finance, Studies of Small Business Finance, November 1981).

11. Total other claims were a far larger fraction of liabilities for the IPO companies than for the Compustat companies, so the procedure of allocating a fraction to short-term debt is subject to considerable error. A spot check of the financial statements for several electronics industry companies indicates that the procedure may understate short-term debt on average. A more definitive analysis would require amassing this information for the many remaining corporations.

12. See Ralph Landau and Dale Jorgenson, eds., *Technology and Economic Policy* (Cambridge, Mass.: Ballinger, 1986).

13. See Andrews and Eisemann, "Who Finances Small Business Circa 1980?"

14. Richard W. Kopcke, "The Roles of Debt and Equity in Financing Corporate Investments," *New England Economic Review* (July-August 1989), pp. 25–48.

15. Other related factors ignored in the foregoing analysis are the incomplete deductibility of interest payments when operating income is low, as well as imperfect loss carry forward provisions.

16. King and Fullerton, *The Taxation of Income from Capital.*

17. James M. Poterba, "Tax Policy and Corporate Saving," *Brookings Papers on Economic Activity* 2 (1987), pp. 455–515.

18. David F. Bradford, "The Incidence and Allocation Effections of a Tax on Corporate Distributions," *Journal of Public Economics* 15 (1981), pp. 1–22; Alan J. Auerbach, "Taxes, Firm Financial Policy, and the Cost of Capital: An Empirical Analysis," *Journal of Public Economics* 23 (1984), pp. 27–57; and James M. Poterba and Lawrence H. Summers, "The Economic Effects of Dividend Taxation," in Edward I. Altman and Marti G. Subrahmanyam, eds., *Recent Advances in Corporate Finance* (Homewood, Ill.: Richard D. Irwin, 1985).

19. Steven M. Fazzari, R. Glenn Hubbard, and Bruce C. Petersen, "Financing Constraints and Corporate Investment," *Brookings Papers on Economic Activity* 1 (1988), pp. 141–195.

20. Securities Industry Association, *Investor Activity Report* (New York: Securities Industry Association, 1989), various monthly issues, 1986–1989. The data since 1987 may not be comparable to data prior to 1987 because of revisions by the Securities Industry Association that removed all dividend capture activity and three-fourths of program trading activity from the retail and other category and allocated it to the institutional category starting in 1987.

21. Henderson, "The Emergence of the Venture Capital Industry."

22. Mark Gertler and R. Glenn Hubbard, "Financial Factors in Business Fluctuations," *NBER Working Paper No. 2758* (Cambridge, Mass.: National Bureau of Economic Research, 1988).

23. Don Fullerton and Andrew B. Lyon, "Does the Tax System Favor Investment in High-Tech or Smoke-Stack Industries?" *Economic Inquiry* 24 (1986), pp. 403–416.

ADDITIONAL REFERENCES

Investment Dealers' Digest. *Going Public: The IPO Reporter.* New York: Investment Dealers Digest, various issues.

U.S. Congressional Budget Office. *Federal Financial Support for High-Technology Industries.* Washington, D.C.: U.S. Government Printing Office, June 1985.

Discussion

Bill Archer

I have been a long-time advocate of lowering the cost of capital by reducing the capital gains tax rate. In the first session of the 101st

Congress, we came very close to another breakthrough, which was reminiscent of the 1978 experience with capital gains rate cut legislation that led to passage of the Steiger-Archer amendment. Of course, Bill Steiger clearly played the lead role on the measure overall, but it was in that legislation that I initiated within Congress the concept of indexing the cost basis of capital gains for inflation. The amendment passed both in committee and on the House floor in separate bipartisan votes. Unfortunately, the Senate was not as wise as it became in later years and did not adopt the indexing provision—with the result that indexing was dropped in the conference committee. In 1989, we again came close to passage of that concept.

It has fascinated me over the years that there has been little help from the business community for the indexing of the cost basis of capital. We politicians are often asked why we cannot anticipate problems and make the tough decisions long in advance. But the business community is really no different. I have been told over and over by business executives, "Indexing may help us twenty years out, but I am going to be CEO for only five years, so it does not do anything for me."

Had we put indexing of the cost basis of capital on the books in the 1970s, consider the tremendous benefit that would now exist for capital gains transactions. Today the prospects are more favorable because economists of all persuasions consider indexing a valid reform, even though they may favor other concurrent changes. The capital gains tax is the most direct tax on capital saving that exists within the tax code. If we want capital saving to flourish, we must reduce the rate of tax on capital gains.

It is fascinating to listen to the government estimators. For the first time in 1989, we had a wide divergence between the estimators at the Department of the Treasury and those at the Joint Committee on Taxation. Admittedly, anticipating the behavioral response to a capital gains tax reduction is not easy, and the estimators on both sides are trying to do a conscientious job. But I firmly believe that there is an optimum capital gains tax rate that will maximize revenues, and it is not 28 or 33 percent; it is a figure much less than that. I am told by people whom I respect within the economic community that 70 to 80 percent of economists agree that the optimum capital gains tax rate for maximizing revenue is somewhere between 15 and 22 percent. If that is true, we will get *more* tax revenue, not less, as a result of a permanent rate reduction on capital gains.

As far as revenue is concerned, a lower capital gains tax rate yields a type of revenue that is positive and helpful. This revenue comes from a more dynamic economy that grows faster and produces more normal ordinary income taxes for the Treasury. Regardless of how we debate the question of the revenue that comes in from the capital gains tax, we cannot ignore its positive macroeconomic impact on the entire economy. When we debate the revenue impact of a capital gains tax cut, we act as if there is some guru who knows precisely what the revenue is going to be. Michael Darby dispels that in his remarks in this chapter. My own view, which I believe has been mostly overlooked, is that we need to talk about incentives for *new* risk investment in our society *and* about how to protect the reservoir of capital saving that has been accumulated and invested and that *already exists* in the marketplace.

There are those within the Bush administration who believe that we should not pay much attention to existing capital investments, that our main challenge is to increase incentives for new investments. I do not disagree that we should have an incentive for new investments. We all know that a reduction in the capital gains tax rate will be an incentive for new investments because it reduces the hurdle rate and the cost of capital.

But if, in fact, we are trying to increase incentives for future investment through individual retirement accounts or other mechanisms, we have to be concerned about the nucleus of capital that is already out there. If we do not, we are going to become more dependent on foreign sources of capital as the only means to build new plants, to put new tools in place, to improve our standard of living, and to have better jobs.

If we are willing to accept greater dependence on foreign capital, we do not need to worry. But I do not accept this view. We should do all we can to alter our current posture of greater dependence on foreign ownership. Such dependence creates a lien on our productivity for generations to come in the way of rent, interest, and dividends that must be paid out of the productivity of this country into foreign hands.

It is extremely important that we have flexibility and mobility of capital. If the capital gains rate is too high, we are going to lock in bigger and bigger portions of that reservoir of existing capital investments so that they will not seek their highest and best use.

Perhaps we should examine some of the arguments of those who oppose reducing the tax rate on capital gains. One is alleged "fairness." Is it fair to give a tax rate reduction to the rich? I have heard that question until I am blue in the face. IRS data show that 74 percent of the taxpayers who reported capital gains income in 1988 had other income of less than $50,000 a year. Opponents also lose sight of the fact that people may be presumed "rich" because for one year in their lives they sell a home, a small business, or a farm. The people who show up in the statistics are different every year.

We should encourage people to save, and they should look forward to that time when they will have a capital gain in their lives, even though it will not be every year. We won on the floor of the House in 1989 because the public understands this, just as it did when George McGovern promised voters $1,000 a year from the Treasury if they earned less than $17,000. At that time, more than 70 percent of U.S.

workers earned less than $17,000 a year; McGovern thought he had a winning ploy to get 70 percent of the vote. But surveys taken after the election showed that those who earned $17,000 or less did not think they would *always* be earning at that level; and by George, when they began earning *more than* $17,000, they did not want $1,000 of their tax money going to somebody who was earning *less than* $17,000 a year. That same healthy spirit permeates the U.S. public relative to capital saving investment in their home, small business, farm, or other type of saving.

The second argument used by those who in 1989 opposed a capital gains cut after their populist demagogic rhetoric failed was that a lower capital gains tax rate would lose revenue for the federal Treasury, bust the budget, and create a catastrophic fiscal situation for the country. But empirical data resulting from the Steiger-Archer amendment in 1978 indicates that contrary to the government estimators' predictions, in every succeeding year revenues *increased* instead of declining—until 1987, when Congress raised capital gains tax rates.

The reality is that we *gained* revenue. The estimators were wrong, and there is an optimum lower rate that will increase revenues. I believe that we are going to get a capital gains tax reduction in the near future. It will not be easy, but we have solid bipartisan majorities. A capital gains tax reduction can have only a positive impact on the flexibility and mobility of capital, permitting it to seek the highest and best use.

Discussion

Michael R. Darby

George Hatsopoulos reasons that the cost of equity is the principal determinant of corporate planning horizons and of the rate of intangible investment in R&D and expenditures to develop goods and services for foreign markets. The relatively high cost of equity in the United States has shortened planning horizons, lowered investment incentives, and contributed to the decline in U.S. competitiveness. The key to lengthening planning horizons, strengthening investment, and restoring competitiveness, in his view, is to reinstate a permanent reduction in the capital gains tax rate relative to the rate on other income. I concur that the restoration of the capital gains differential is absolutely essential.

Dr. Hatsopoulos cautions, however, that the effort to raise saving can be treacherous and that a tax differential might cause an increase in interest rates because the differential stimulates investment. I would like to elaborate on this technical, but important, point lest it be misunderstood.

Even though restoring the capital gains differential is vital to the long-run health and competitiveness of our economy, the effect this move would have on the trade deficit is indeed ambiguous. The trade deficit is determined by the gap between desired investment and saving. A lower tax rate on capital gains will increase both desired investment and saving, so the net effect on interest rates and the trade deficit will depend on whether it is investment or saving that is shifted upward by a larger amount. The belief that U.S. competitiveness has dropped developed with the appearance of the trade deficit, but the trade deficit itself was not a product of either a sudden and dramatic decline in the underlying competitiveness of the United States or a sharp increase in the government deficit. It was primarily the reflection of increased investment opportunities in the United States, accompanied by lower domestic saving rates that resulted from rational responses to temporarily lower income and, later, real money balances.

The changes in tax law and regulatory climate that were inaugurated in 1981 and the dramatic decline in the rate of inflation shortly thereafter greatly raised investment demand in the United States. Increased desire by both U.S. and foreign investors to invest here was reflected first by higher real interest rates and an appreciating dollar and then with the usual two-year lag by an increase in both the trade deficit and the gap between investment and national saving.

The dominant role of shifts in investment demand also explains the timing of the dollar depreciation in early 1985. The Tax Reform Act was proposed in early 1985 and enacted in the fall of 1986. At the same time, the business climate was improving abroad, and business taxes there were being lowered. In contrast to shifts in investment relative to saving, changes that improved the competitiveness of particular industries, without affecting desired investment or saving, caused dollar appreciation and eventual adverse effects on other industries.

Would a cut in capital gains tax rates raise government revenues, lower government dissaving, and lift the U.S. saving rate? The analysis at the Department of the Treasury shows that a drop in the capital gains tax rate does raise revenue. It is clear that the revenue-maximizing rate is much lower than the current capital gains rate. In addition, the optimal rate should always be less than the revenue-maximizing rate.

The effect of changes in the deficit on national saving is muted, however, by normal offsetting movements in private saving. This result appeared during the 1982 increase in the deficit as well as the decline in 1987. So the direct effect of a lower capital gains rate is a small, net increase in national saving. And, in addition, there is an indirect effect because saving should rise further due to the higher net returns to saving that result from cutting the antisaving tax distortion. An upward shift in private saving relative to investment is essential in reducing our trade deficit. By lowering real interest rates in the United States, the shift in saving would also stimulate the rate of intangible investment that Dr. Hatsopoulos emphasizes.

Yolanda Henderson documents a large impact of the change in the capital gains provision in the Tax Reform Act of 1986 on the cost of capital. As I mentioned earlier, this is part of the change in environment that led to the decline in the value of the dollar. Dr. Henderson also documents the generally lower debt-to-equity ratios of emerging corporations compared with mature corporations. As a result, she indicates that any increase in the cost of equity is likely to impose a disproportionate burden on emerging corporations, especially technology-oriented companies. The data for emerging companies are taken from a sample of corporations making initial public offerings of equities. These firms apparently financed investment expenditures to a large extent with internal funds and net increases in debt before seeking new equity. This pattern fits the financing sequence of firms suggested by other research. Although a drop in the cost of equity would benefit these emerging firms, a decline in interest rates would do so as well, and the lower interest rates would aid those small firms not yet able to tap equity markets.

As President Bush has made clear, a cut in the capital gains tax rate is a vital component of policy, and a reduction should encourage saving as well as investment. But whether the goal is more intangible investment, some relief for emerging businesses, or a reduction in our trade deficit, there is also a basic need for a rise in national saving relative to investment. For this reason, the administration is also committed to restraining spending on government goods and services as the most effective way to increase national saving and to developing supplementary policies focused on promoting national saving. The reason we should reduce capital gains tax rates is primarily because it would have such a positive effect on national welfare. Nonetheless, the reality is that we are in a world in which policies that adversely affect the budget deficit are restrained or put on hold.

My reading of the evidence is that it used to be true that we just did not know about the revenues that a capital gains rate cut would generate. There was a wide diversity of opinion. But there has been a lot of research that has contributed to a quantum leap in our knowledge. The recent research at Treasury, which looks at individual tax returns over many years using different models by different researchers, all comes to the same conclusion: The current capital gains rate is much greater than the revenue-maximizing rate and greater still than the optimal rate. Had the revenue estimates made by Treasury early in 1989 been based on that research, the implicit elasticity of realizations in those estimates would have been much larger and the revenue estimates much higher.

A restoration of the differential capital gains rate cannot do all that needs to be done. But because the current tax rate is so much greater than the revenue-maximizing rate, indeed well into the prohibitive range, a permanent capital gains tax differential should be enacted in order to lower the budget deficit and increase national saving.

10

Tax Policies for Increasing Business Saving

James M. Poterba

Most of the decline in the U.S. saving rate during the 1980s was due to extraordinary peacetime federal deficits and an unusually low personal saving rate. As a result, proposals to increase saving have focused either on reducing the federal budget deficit or on increasing personal saving. Corporate saving, which has historically accounted for nearly 40 percent of national saving, has received limited attention in recent policy discussions. This is especially surprising because the political difficulty of deficit reduction and the controversial efficacy of personal saving plans have limited the consensus for either of these approaches to increasing national saving.

This chapter examines the importance of corporate saving and how tax policies affect it. The first of the four sections that follow ("The Importance of Corporate Saving") considers the relative importance of personal, corporate, and government saving, showing that corporate saving increased during the 1980s as the two other components of national saving declined. The second section ("Does Corporate Saving Matter?") reviews the long-standing controversy about whether households "pierce the corporate veil," reduce their personal saving to offset changes in corporate saving, and thereby nullify policies that raise corporate saving. The empirical results surveyed in this section suggest that although households consider corporate saving in formulating their saving plans, they do not completely offset it. Policies that raise corporate saving are therefore likely to increase national saving.

Section three ("Policy Options to Increase Corporate Saving") considers several policies that would increase corporate saving, including reductions in corporate income taxes, expanded investment incentives, and changes in dividend and capital gains taxation. The analysis examines the effects of each tax policy on corporate and national saving. It also considers how these policies would affect the cost of capital, an important determinant of the relative competitiveness of U.S. and

TABLE 10.1
The Components of National Saving, 1950–1988
(percent of net national product)

	Personal Saving	Corporate Saving	Government Saving
1950–1959	5.2	3.1	-0.2
1960–1969	5.1	3.8	-0.3
1970–1979	6.2	2.7	-1.1
1980–1988	4.3	2.0	-2.9
1985–1988	3.2	2.2	-3.1

Source: U.S. Department of Commerce, Bureau of Economic Analysis, *National Income and Product Accounts.*

foreign firms. The most attractive options appear to be revenue-neutral increases in corporate investment incentives. Finally, section four ("Conclusion") summarizes the study findings.

THE IMPORTANCE OF CORPORATE SAVING

National saving is the sum of personal, corporate, and government saving. The national income accounts define saving as the fraction of an economic entity's earnings that is set aside for future consumption. For households, this corresponds to the difference between disposable income and consumption; for corporations, saving equals retained earnings, the component of after-tax profits that is not distributed to shareholders.[1]

Table 10.1 shows the contributions of corporate and personal saving to private saving from 1950 to 1988. Corporate saving accounts for approximately one-third of private saving and declined much less than personal saving did during the 1980s. Corporate saving is clearly sensitive to business cycle conditions and declines during recessions, when depressed profits combine with stable dividend payments to lower retained earnings.

Table 10.1 chronicles the decline in the U.S. national saving rate by nearly 5 percent of net national product (NNP) between the 1970s and the 1980s. Reduced personal saving and increased government deficits each accounted for 2 percentage points of this decline. Although corporate saving also declined, by 0.8 percent of NNP, it has been the most stable component of national saving.

The corporate saving measure in Table 10.1 can be refined to better reflect economic profits and thus saving. First, net corporate interest payments should be measured in real terms. Although the national accounts correct depreciation and inventory profits for the effects of inflation, they record nominal rather than real interest payments. Nom-

TABLE 10.2
Nonfinancial Corporate Saving, 1953–1988
(percent of net national product)

	Unadjusted National Accounts	Adjustments		
		Inflation	Inflation and Repurchases	Inflation, Repurchases, and Pensions
1953–1959	2.3	2.6	2.6	3.2
1960–1969	3.1	3.6	3.6	4.4
1970–1979	2.2	3.4	3.3	4.5
1980–1988	2.1	2.6	1.8	3.0

Sources: Author's calculations based on data from U.S. Department of Commerce, Bureau of Economic Analysis, *National Income Accounts;* and Board of Governors, Federal Reserve System, *Flow of Funds.* For detailed data descriptions, see James M. Poterba, "Tax Policy and Corporate Saving," *Brookings Papers on Economic Activity,* 2 (1987), pp. 455–503.

inal interest payments include an inflation premium that compensates borrowers for the inflationary erosion of their real principal. Because corporations are net debtors, they benefit from the inflationary devaluation of debt *and* pay higher nominal interest rates when lenders anticipate such devaluation. Measured corporate profits and corporate saving, the undistributed component of profits, should therefore be augmented by the inflationary gain on corporate liabilities.

Second, the national accounts debit corporate saving when firms pay dividends but not when cash is distributed by repurchasing shares. Nondividend cash payouts grew dramatically during the 1980s. To the extent that these transactions substitute for dividends, excluding them from the column of debits to corporate savings yields a misleading picture of corporate saving patterns over time.[2]

Third, the national accounts treat all pension contributions as deductions from corporate earnings and credit them as personal income. Nearly three-quarters of corporate pension plans, however, are defined-benefit plans, which commit firms to provide specified benefits to retirees regardless of their pension plan's net worth. Contributing to the pension fund therefore does not affect the firm's pension liability because contributions are effectively investments on corporate account. These contributions should therefore augment corporate saving.[3]

Table 10.2 shows the importance of these various corrections, focusing on saving by nonfinancial corporations (NFCs). The first column shows reported (national accounts) NFC saving as a share of NNP. NFC saving fell less than total corporate saving in the period 1980–1988, averaging 2.2 percent of NNP in the 1970s compared to 2.1 percent in 1980–1988. The decline in total corporate saving in Table 10.1 is largely the result of lower retentions by financial firms, such as insurance companies and real estate holding companies, which experienced relatively low profit rates in the 1980s. The second column of

Table 10.2 reports the effect of subtracting only real interest payments from corporate earnings. By this measure even nonfinancial corporate saving declined, from 3.4 percent of NNP during the 1970s (higher than the national accounts measure because rapid inflation led to substantial overstatement of real interest costs) to 2.6 percent in the period 1980–1988.

The third column in Table 10.2 shows the effect of correcting for both inflation and share repurchases. Correcting for share repurchases yields an even sharper decline in corporate saving. In this case NFC saving drops from 3.3 percent to 1.8 percent of NNP from the 1970s to the 1980s. Share repurchases averaged $35.4 billion (1988 dollars) during 1980–1988 but were virtually nonexistent during the 1970s. The final column indicates the impact of correcting for pension contributions as well as inflation and repurchases. This correction increases the level of corporate saving throughout the postwar period, but it does not change the magnitude of the decline during 1980–1988.

DOES CORPORATE SAVING MATTER? THE CORPORATE VEIL CONTROVERSY

There is no clear rationale for encouraging corporate saving as opposed to either personal or government saving. *National* saving, the sum of these three components, is the central determinant of interest rates, the trade balance, and investment levels. Proposals to raise corporate saving must therefore be evaluated in terms of their *net effect on national saving*, rather than their *partial effect on corporate behavior*. It is therefore important to recognize that many plans to encourage corporate retentions affect the government deficit, in some cases reducing or offsetting positive effects on corporate saving. Similarly, links between corporate and personal saving must be evaluated. If households "pierce the corporate veil," taking full account of corporate saving in formulating their own saving plans, policies that encourage corporate saving with no effect on government saving will be undone by equal and opposite changes in personal saving. This section briefly reviews the evidence on whether households behave in this highly rational fashion.

The logic suggesting that households pierce the corporate veil is simple. Households are the ultimate owners of most corporate equity. When a corporation saves by reducing its dividends and using the proceeds to purchase assets, dividends fall but share values rise. If share values increase by the amount of the foregone dividend and there are no taxes, household wealth is unaffected by the firm's dividend payment. If the firm pays dividends, households can use their cash receipts either to consume goods and services or to purchase additional stock. If the firm reduces its dividends and buys assets, households can either sell their shares to finance consumption spending or do nothing and increase their equity position. Household consumption decisions are therefore independent of corporate saving, and changes in corporate saving will be offset dollar for dollar by changes in personal saving.

There are three reasons for skepticism about the extent to which households pierce the corporate veil. First, imperfections in the market for corporate control may permit managers of established, dividend-paying firms to undertake projects with marginal returns that are less than the market's required return. In this case one dollar of retained earnings may increase share values by less than one dollar, thereby reducing shareholder wealth relative to what it would have been if the cash were paid out. Shareholders will not reduce their saving by one dollar if their wealth has increased by less than one dollar, so in this case raising corporate saving would have a positive net effect on private saving at the cost of some investment inefficiency.[4]

Second, households may follow rules of thumb in formulating their consumption plans, consuming at higher rates from dividend income than from accruing capital gains. They may view fluctuations in share values as transitory, may face transactions costs in selling shares or borrowing against them in order to finance consumption, or may be unable to disentangle the increase in share values due to asset purchases from other variations. If such behavior is widespread, the division of corporate income between cash payout and retained earnings may affect consumption.

Third, many policies that affect corporate saving do so by altering the distribution of after-tax incomes across households. Reductions in the relative tax burdens on corporations transfer resources among the owners of corporate equity and away from other households. Households with large asset stocks and those near the top of the income distribution exhibit lower marginal spending propensities than do households with less income or wealth. This may reflect different preferences or the presence of liquidity constraints that prevent lower income households from borrowing to smooth fluctuations in their income. These differences in spending rates mean that changes in corporate saving can affect national saving. Even if households that own stock pierce the corporate veil and adjust their saving to offset a corporation's retained earnings, their higher average saving rate implies that resource transfers to them will raise national saving.

Table 10.3 demonstrates the high concentration of direct ownership of corporate stock. Although only 1 percent of all households reported adjusted gross income for 1984 of more than $100,000, this group reported 6 percent of all labor income and nearly 33 percent of dividend receipts. The skewed distribution of equity ownership is confirmed by direct surveys of asset holdings that show that 85 percent of corporate equity is held by those in the top decile of the wealth distribution, and 43 percent of equity is held by those in the top one-half of 1 percent of the wealth distribution.[5]

TABLE 10.3
Ownership of Corporate Stock, 1984

Adjusted Gross Income Category (dollars)	Percent of Tax Returns	Percent of Dividends	Percent of Wages & Salaries
< 25,000	68.44	23.19	34.18
25- 50,000	24.81	20.77	42.80
50-100,000	5.74	22.89	16.50
100-500,000	0.97	21.94	5.62
>500,000	0.04	11.19	0.90

Source: Author's calculations based on Internal Revenue Service, *Statistics of Income—1984 Individual Income Tax Returns* (Washington, D.C.: U.S. Government Printing Office, 1986).

Numerous econometric studies have tested whether households adjust their saving completely in response to changes in corporate saving. Even though many studies fail to reject the view that households pierce the corporate veil, the results usually suggest less than complete offset. For example, Martin Feldstein found evidence that households raise consumption in response to retained earnings but that the consumption effects of dividends (approximately seventy-six cents per dollar) were larger than the effects of retentions (about fifty cents per dollar).[6] In their recent examination of the postwar U.S. data, Alan Auerbach and Kevin Hassett, even when focusing on tax-induced changes in payout, did not reject the view that households pierce the corporate veil.[7] As with many previous studies, however, their point estimates suggested incomplete saving offset. Kul Bhatia, and later Patric Hendershott and Joe Peek, found evidence *for* a corporate veil.[8] The study by Hendershott and Peek was notable for its conclusion that the negative correlation between corporate and personal saving in earlier studies was primarily the result of opposite-signed inflationary biases in the two saving series. All of these studies are somewhat difficult to interpret because much of the variation in corporate saving results from higher profits or other shocks that may change household as well as corporate saving.

One source of evidence that avoids these problems examines the reaction of corporate and personal saving to tax reforms that affect corporate payout incentives. These tax reforms affect the distribution of corporate earnings between payout and retentions without changing the level of corporate earnings. Results of my previous studies suggest that households offset between 30 and 80 percent of fluctuations in corporate saving.[9] These studies investigate the historical experience of the United States, Canada, and the United Kingdom; the results from all three nations confirm the presence of a "corporate veil." These empirical findings suggest that policies that alter corporate saving will *not* be completely nullified by offsetting changes in personal saving.

POLICY OPTIONS TO INCREASE CORPORATE SAVING

The basic accounting identity linking corporate earnings to corporate saving is a useful starting point in an analysis of the determinants of corporate saving:

$$\text{Corporate Saving} = \text{Earnings} - \text{Taxes} - \text{Interest} - \text{Dividends} - \text{Repurchases}.$$

My analysis treats pretax earnings as beyond the government's control and focuses on how changes in tax policy affect the other components of this identity. I consider two classes of tax policies to encourage corporate saving: policies that lower corporate taxes, implemented by either cutting the statutory rate or expanding investment incentives, and policies designed to change payout rates by either raising the dividend tax or reducing capital gains tax rates. This section evaluates each of these policies with regard to their net effects on national saving and their implications for the cost of capital facing U.S. firms.

Reducing the Corporate Tax Rate

The most direct way to increase corporate saving is to increase the pool of after-tax earnings that managers allocate between dividends and corporate saving by reducing corporate taxes. Corporate saving depends on both the average corporate tax rate, which determines the amount of after-tax earnings available for retention or distribution, and the marginal tax rate, which affects incentives to retain earnings and reinvest.

To illustrate how corporate tax policy affects saving, consider a rate reduction that lowers corporate taxes by $1 billion. Corporate saving will not increase by the entire amount tax reduction because higher after-tax corporate profits will raise dividends or repurchases. Estimates of corporate payout behavior suggest that when profits increase by one dollar, dividend payments increase by about twenty-five cents.[10] Reducing corporate taxes by $1 billion therefore would raise corporate saving by about $750 million. This policy transfers resources to the corporate sector; it is not simply an increase in corporate saving financed by a dividend reduction. The extent to which personal saving will offset this increase in corporate saving therefore depends on the marginal propensities to consume of those who gain and lose from the tax reform rather than simply on the extent to which households that own equity pierce the corporate veil.[11]

A corporate tax reduction would increase personal consumption as households respond both to higher dividends and to increased wealth in corporate shares. If we assume that households spend 50 percent of their dividend receipts and 3 percent of their accruing capital gains, consumption would rise by approximately $150 million for each $1 billion corporate tax reduction, yielding an increase of $850 million in private saving.[12] This ignores, however, the possibility that the personal saving rate will increase in response to higher after-tax returns as the total tax burden on capital income from the corporate sector is reduced.

If corporate taxes were lowered but were not offset by tax changes to achieve revenue neutrality, the policy's net effect would be a *reduction* in national saving. The federal deficit would widen by the full amount of the tax cut, so for the parameters chosen previously, each $1 billion of tax reduction would lower national saving by $150 million. If a corporate tax reduction were paired with other revenue-raising reforms, the net saving effect would depend on whether the marginal saving propensities for those who were burdened by the substitute tax were higher or lower than the saving propensities for those who owned corporate stock. Given the skewed nature of corporate equity holdings, such a revenue-neutral substitution would probably raise national saving.[13]

A revenue-neutral corporate tax reduction is an expensive way to encourage corporate investment because it provides a windfall to the owners of existing corporate assets. This is an inefficient use of tax incentives because tax policy can never lead to the production of more "old capital." Further rate reductions would compound the effects of the 1986 Tax Reform Act, which Lawrence Summers estimated would reduce taxes on existing assets by $68 billion between 1987 and 1991 while raising tax burdens on new capital by $184 billion.[14] Other potential changes in the taxation of corporate capital income would have larger incentive effects for the same revenue cost.

A more attractive option for reducing corporate taxes would be expanded investment incentives, either with more generous depreciation policies or restoration of the investment tax credit. These reforms would raise the after-tax return on reinvested corporate earnings and therefore encourage firms to retain rather than distribute profits. Increased investment incentives would lower average corporate tax rates but avoid transfers to the owners of existing assets.

The principal drawback of such policies is their cost. Restoring the investment tax credit on equipment investment, for example, would cost nearly $40 billion per year and would reduce national saving even if it encouraged corporate saving. Revenue-neutral policies that raise the statutory corporate tax rate and use the proceeds to enhance investment incentives would still increase corporate saving. These policies deserve consideration. Combining an investment tax credit with an increase in the statutory corporate tax rate is an example of such a reform. Such reforms raise the tax burdens on existing assets to finance incentives for new investment, thereby maximizing the incentive effect per dollar of foregone revenue.

The desirability of shifting tax burdens from corporations to other sectors is quite sensitive to views about optimal tax progressivity.

Because these policies affect saving by raising the wealth of high-income and high-wealth households—households with greater-than-average marginal propensities to save—they make the after-tax income and wealth distribution less equal. This is a basic tradeoff in analyzing the saving effects of tax reforms: Because high-income households save a larger fraction of their incomes than their low-income counterparts do, reforms that increase private saving usually lead to a less equal after-tax income distribution.

Changing Payout Incentives

A second strategy for increasing corporate saving involves raising dividend taxes, or reducing the capital gains tax burdens, to reduce the incentives for firms to pay dividends. The links between such tax changes and corporate saving are complex, however. To illustrate the issues, I will first consider a dividend tax increase and then contrast its effects with those from reducing the capital gains tax rate. The tax options for raising dividend tax burdens include increased dividend taxes on shareholders as well as split-rate corporate taxes of the type used in the United States in 1936–1937, which placed higher tax burdens on distributed profits than on retentions.

The traditional analysis of how higher dividend taxes would affect corporate saving would hold that such reforms would raise corporate saving by discouraging firms from paying dividends. According to this reasoning, these reforms would make investments in the corporate sector less attractive relative to noncorporate investments, perhaps discouraging equity issues to finance new firms, but would influence the allocation of returns on existing capital to increase corporate retentions. Substantial empirical literature suggests that the relative tax burden on dividends and retained earnings affects corporate payout rates. My own estimates imply that a 1 percent increase in the average shareholder's after-tax income from dividends, as opposed to capital gains, increases dividend payments by roughly 2 percent.[15]

This analysis assumes that firms distribute profits to equity holders through dividends and that equity holders cannot avoid dividend taxes by relying on debt finance. Because higher dividend taxes raise the total tax burden on equity-financed projects, such taxes encourage firms to find alternatives to cash dividend distributions to equity holders and to substitute debt for equity finance. Financial innovations during the 1980s made these alternatives readily available to many firms. Table 10.4 shows that during 1983–1988, cash distributed through share repurchases grew from a negligible amount to nearly one-half of dividend payments. In conjunction with other transactions such as cash-financed purchases of other firms' equity in corporate takeovers shown in the last column of Table 10.4, repurchases contributed to a *decline* in the outstanding equity of U.S. corporations.

TABLE 10.4
Cash Flow from Corporations to Households, 1970–1988
(constant 1988 dollars)

Year	Cash Dividends	Share Repurchases	Cash Acquisitions
1970	53.5	3.5	—
1971	50.5	1.9	—
1972	52.5	5.5	—
1973	51.6	3.9	—
1974	48.7	4.7	—
1975	50.7	4.3	—
1976	53.4	3.7	—
1977	57.5	6.1	7.8
1978	62.6	5.9	12.1
1979	60.6	6.9	26.1
1980	64.4	7.1	18.5
1981	68.9	5.2	37.8
1982	72.4	9.8	31.8
1983	77.6	9.0	24.8
1984	78.3	90.0	72.3
1985	78.9	45.2	76.6
1986	79.4	44.2	79.4
1987	84.1	56.1	64.3
1988	83.0	52.1	65.2

Sources: Column 1: U.S. Department of Commerce, Bureau of Economic Analysis, *National Income and Product Accounts.* Columns 2 and 3: Yolanda K. Henderson, "Is Leverage a Tax Dodge—or Not?" *New England Economic Review* (March–April 1990), pp. 11–32; reprinted with permission.

The rapid rise in repurchases during the 1980s had many sources. First, firms gradually became aware that the Internal Revenue Service would not tax repurchases as if they were cash dividends. Second, financial innovations that permitted large-scale takeovers increased pressure on managers to distribute "free cash flow." Third, recent tax reforms made debt more attractive than equity and provided an incentive for firms to replace equity with debt in their capital structures.

The tax incentives for debt finance depend on the taxes on investors as well as on corporations. During the 1980s, reductions in the top marginal tax rate on interest income (from 70 percent in 1980, to 50 percent in 1981, to 28 percent in 1986) reduced the tax burden on corporate borrowing and increased the attractiveness of corporate debt for individual investors. In 1980, a top-bracket individual received thirty cents in after-tax interest payments if the corporation earned one dollar and paid this dollar as interest, compared with thirty-one cents if the

FIGURE 10.1
Net Debt and Equity Issues, 1952–1988

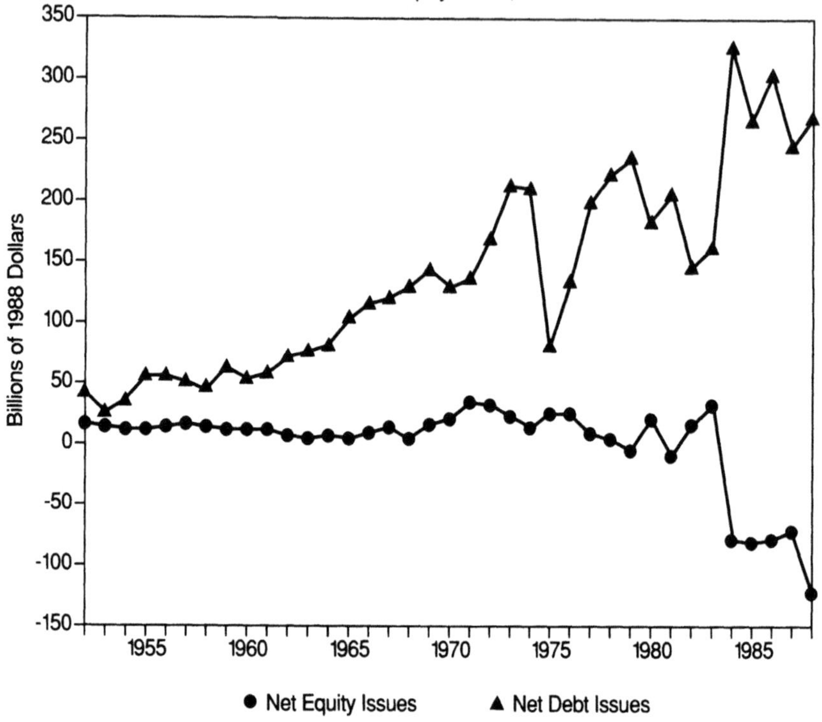

Source: Board of Governors, Federal Reserve System, *Flow of Funds Accounts.*

individual held corporate equity. (This assumes a payout rate of 50 percent and an effective capital gains tax rate of 14 percent because of the benefits of tax deferral on accruing gains.) For 1989, the analogous after-tax incomes were seventy-two cents for debt and fifty-two cents for equity. The after-tax return from holding debt has increased faster than that from holding equity, thus prompting changes in corporate capital structure.

Figure 10.1 shows net borrowing and net equity issues by nonfinancial corporations from 1952 to 1988. Net equity issues were approximately zero, or slightly positive, until the mid-1980s, when they became substantially negative. During the late 1980s, net equity in nonfinancial corporations declined by nearly $400 billion. Not all repurchases were debt financed, however; Auerbach estimated that one-third of the funds used for repurchases represent foregone dividends.[16]

Share repurchases affect national saving through several channels. First, they reduce corporate saving. Second, even though households receive cash payments that would enable them to increase their saving to offset the decline in corporate asset values, there is evidence that households with accrued but unrealized capital gains are less likely to consume than are households with "forced realizations" in debt-for-equity recapitalizations or takeovers. George Hatsopoulos, Paul Krugman, and I estimated that each one dollar of payout in cash takeovers raises consumption by more than fifty cents.[17] Although this probably provides an upper bound on the effects of forced realizations, other evidence such as Lawrence Atkins's study of lump-sum, pension-benefit recipients suggests that large cash receipts trigger consumption.[18] Finally, because debt is taxed less heavily than equity is, debt-for-equity swaps reduce tax revenues and thereby widen the budget deficit. Revenues may rise in the short run as stockholders realize capital gains during the debt-for-equity conversion. Yolanda Henderson demonstrated, however, that the net effect on the present value of revenues is likely to be negative.[19]

The central question for analyzing the effects of dividend taxes on saving is whether the sensitivity of repurchases to dividend tax changes is large enough to offset the potentially positive saving effects of reduced dividend payout. There is no satisfactory empirical evidence on this issue. There are other grounds, however, for avoiding dividend tax increases.

First, higher dividend tax burdens would tie funds to the firms where they are generated, placing greater reliance on internal than external capital markets. If the free cash flow explanation for the recent takeover wave proposed, for example, by Michael Jensen, is accurate, internal capital markets may deliver projects with less-than-market returns.[20] Raising dividend tax burdens would exacerbate these inefficiencies while also discouraging new funds from entering the corporate sector.

Second, higher dividend taxes increase the cost of capital, an important determinant of corporate investment decisions.[21] A higher cost of capital discourages new investment and could adversely affect the rate of U.S. productivity growth. Changes in the cost of capital have the largest effect on investment in very long-horizon projects, such as research and development, which may have important effects on the future growth of living standards.[22] It is noteworthy that most of our major trading partners provide *subsidies* for dividend payout in an attempt to alleviate the double-tax burden rather than levying additional taxes. Canada, France, West Germany, and the United Kingdom all provide shareholder tax credits for corporate taxes; this reduces the cost of capital relative to the double-tax system currently in place in the United States. Increasing dividend tax rates and magnifying the difference between the United States and other nations may therefore be inappropriate.

Finally, dividend taxes exacerbate the artificial tax distinction between debt and equity finance and encourage firms to find ways to label risky payments to investors as interest rather than as dividends. The development of high-yield debt markets during the 1980s facilitated corporate borrowing when the underlying cash flows were much riskier than those in traditional debt-financed projects. High corporate debt levels may impose social costs by raising the risk of bankruptcy or financial distress. Further widening of the tax disparity between debt and equity would encourage additional borrowing.

These arguments suggest that raising dividend tax rates would exacerbate several real and financial distortions and would have uncertain effects on corporate saving. A more attractive method of encouraging retentions is to reduce the capital gains tax. This would lower the tax burden on capital gains relative to dividend income, thereby making investors more willing to reinvest earnings within the firm.

The effects of such a policy on corporate saving would be small, however, for two reasons. First, individual investors are direct owners of only one-half of outstanding corporate stock.[23] Even though individual investors indirectly hold the assets of pension funds and other financial intermediaries, the individual capital gains tax rate does not affect the tax burden on gains accruing through these channels. Second, deferral implies that the *effective* capital gains tax rate rises less than point for point with increases in the statutory capital gains tax rate. For example, when the inflation rate is 4 percent per year and capital gains are taxed at a statutory rate of 28 percent, an asset that appreciates at 10 percent per year and is held for twenty years faces an effective tax rate equivalent to that from taxing *accruing* gains at 15.3 percent. These calculations ignore the reduction in effective capital gains tax rates provided by the current step-up of basis at death. Some estimates suggest that this tax provision halves the effective tax rate.[24]

A reduction in the statutory tax rate to 20 percent would reduce the effective tax rate by less than 4 percentage points. The average after-tax income that shareholders receive per dollar of dividends relative to what they receive in after-tax capital gains when the firm retains a dollar would decline by approximately 2 percent. Based on the estimates of dividend payout response in one of my earlier studies,[25] this would translate to a 4 percent ($3.6 billion) reduction in dividend payments. Even though corporate saving would increase, it would be offset in part by a reduction in personal saving as households recognized the increase in corporate assets. If we assume that household saving responds by one-half the change in corporate saving, such a capital gains reform would increase private saving by approximately $2 billion. There might also be positive effects on personal saving as the after-tax return to some classes of investment increases, but again these effects would probably be small. The net effect of such a tax change on national saving, however, would depend critically on its ultimate (but highly controversial) effect on federal revenues.

Reducing the capital gains tax rate avoids a number of the disadvantages associated with higher dividend taxes as corporate saving incentives. For example, lower capital gains rates reduce the cost of capital and narrow the tax differential between debt and equity finance. The distributional effects of such a reform, however, are similar to those from a corporate tax reduction: Most capital gains accrue to high-wealth households. These distributional effects could be minimized by restricting the capital gains tax reduction to future gains, thereby avoiding windfalls to existing asset holders, and by restricting the rate reduction to corporate stock to limit the magnitude of the redistribution while encouraging corporate saving.

Other Options

The foregoing policies do not exhaust the options for affecting the level of corporate saving. Reforms in the tax deductibility of interest payments, for example, would alter the balance of corporate financing between debt and equity. Policies that discourage borrowing by, for example, disallowing interest deductions for some or all corporate liabilities would reduce interest payout and lead to increased use of equity in corporate capital structures. Such policies might raise corporate saving because the payout rate on equity would typically be lower than that on debt, but they would also raise the cost of capital.[26]

CONCLUSION

Corporate saving is an important component of national saving. Even though corporate saving did not decline as much as personal or government saving did during the 1980s, a national saving campaign should not ignore policies to raise corporate saving. More importantly, tax reformers should recognize the potential impact of tax changes—particularly those affecting the tax burdens on dividends, capital gains, and corporate borrowing—on corporate saving.

Increasing corporate saving was not a consideration in the design of the Tax Reform Act of 1986. The act raised corporate tax burdens, reduced investment incentives while providing windfalls to the owners of existing assets, and raised capital gains tax rates. All of these changes discouraged corporate saving. Strong corporate profits in the years since 1986 and increased corporate borrowing that reduced corporate tax collections have masked the effect of these changes. It is nevertheless important to avoid compounding these effects with future tax reforms.

The most promising way to raise corporate saving in the United States would be to expand investment incentives. This would encourage firms to reduce their payouts to shareholders, both through dividends and share repurchases, and to reinvest the funds in new projects. A key component of such a program, if it is to raise national and not simply corporate saving, is to find alternative revenue sources to offset reduced corporate taxes. Even if increased investment allowances were coupled with a higher corporate tax rate so that the policy was revenue neutral, it would have a positive effect on corporate saving.

NOTES

I thank Benjamin Friedman for his very useful suggestions.

1. Saving can also be measured as the change in an economic entity's net worth. There are two disadvantages of this approach to defining corporate saving, however. First, the values of corporate stock and bonds change for many reasons beyond managers' control and therefore need not reflect *choices* regarding the intertemporal allocation of income. Second, asset fluctuations are not necessarily associated with capital formation. A land price increase may raise net worth with no effect on the capital stock.

2. Repurchases financed from corporate earnings that otherwise would have been distributed as dividends should be subtracted from corporate saving; those financed by issuing new securities such as high-yield debt should not be. Although it is difficult to distinguish the two, Alan Auerbach and Yolanda Henderson have suggested that a substantial fraction of repurchases is financed from internal cash flow. See Alan Auerbach, "Tax Policies and Corporate Borrowing" (Philadelphia: University of Pennsylvania, 1989, mimeograph); and Yolanda K. Henderson, "Is Leverage a Tax Dodge—or Not?" *New England Economic Review* (March-April 1990), pp. 11–32.

3. The correct pension adjustment would credit contributions to defined-benefit plans while debiting changes in accrued liabilities to plan participants. Unfortunately, information needed to make accurate calculations of accruing liabilities is not available. My correction therefore *overstates* the true correction. For the 1980s, however, when much of the variation in pension contributions was the result of unanticipated stock market gains on pension assets, the extreme correction may be nearly correct.

4. The argument that some firms reinvest their earnings at submarket returns should be contrasted with Bruce Greenwald and Joseph Stiglitz's claim that because of credit market constraints, an additional dollar of cash flow may facilitate investments with a market value of *more* than one dollar. See Bruce Greenwald and Joseph Stiglitz, "Financial Structure and the Incidence of the Corporation Income Tax" (Princeton, N.J.: Princeton University, 1987, mimeograph). Steven Fazzari, Glenn Hubbard, and Bruce Petersen presented evidence of firm heterogeneity. Young firms with no payout history may be credit constrained, whereas more mature firms may be better described by the model with imperfect managerial control. See Steven Fazzari, R. Glenn Hubbard, and Bruce Petersen, "Financing Constraints and Corporate Investment," *Brookings Papers on Economic Activity* 1 (1988), pp. 141–196.

5. Tabulations from the 1983 Survey of Consumer Finances are presented in Robert B. Avery and Gregory E. Elliehausen, "Financial Considerations of High-Income Families," *Federal Reserve Bulletin* 72 (March 1986), p. 175.

6. See Martin S. Feldstein, "Tax Incentives, Corporate Saving, and Capital Accumulation in the United States," *Journal of Public Economics* 2 (1973), pp. 159–171.

7. Alan Auerbach and Kevin Hassett, "Corporate Saving and Shareholder Consumption," in B. Douglas Bernheim and John Shoven, eds., *The Economics of Saving* (Chicago: University of Chicago Press, forthcoming).

8. See Kul B. Bhatia, "Corporate Taxation, Retained Earnings, and Capital Formation," *Journal of Public Economics* 11 (1979), pp. 123–134; and Patric H. Hendershott and Joe Peek, "Aggregate U.S. Private Saving: Conceptual

Measures and Empirical Tests," in Robert E. Lipsey and Helen S. Tice, eds., *The Measurement of Saving, Investment, and Wealth* (Chicago: University of Chicago Press, 1989), pp. 185–226.

9. Reported in James M. Poterba, "Tax Policy and Corporate Saving," *Brookings Papers on Economic Activity* 2 (1987), pp. 455–503; and James M. Poterba, "Dividends, Capital Gains, and the Corporate Veil: Evidence from Canada, the U.K., and the U.S.," in Bernheim and Shoven, eds., *The Economics of Saving.*

10. The estimate of a twenty-five-cents dividend increase per one dollar of after-tax cash flow is reported in Poterba, "Tax Policy and Corporate Saving."

11. Lower corporate tax rates would also reduce the incentives for corporate borrowing and therefore induce a shift from debt to equity finance, although the magnitude of this effect is uncertain.

12. This analysis presumes that the tax reduction will reduce future government spending or that households do not save to offset any higher future taxes generated by a current tax reduction.

13. Feldstein imputed each firm's tax payments to its shareholders in order to estimate how shifts from corporate to individual taxation affect the tax burden across income classes. See Martin S. Feldstein, "Imputing Corporate Tax Liabilities to Individual Taxpayers," *National Tax Journal* 41 (1988), pp. 37–60.

14. Lawrence H. Summers, "A Fair Tax Act That's Bad for Business," *Harvard Business Review* (March-April 1987), pp. 53–59.

15. Reported in Poterba, "Tax Policy and Corporate Saving."

16. Auerbach, "Tax Policies and Corporate Borrowing."

17. George N. Hatsopoulos, Paul R. Krugman, and James M. Poterba, *Overconsumption: The Challenge to U.S. Economic Policy* (Washington, D.C.: American Business Conference and Thermo Electron Corp., 1989).

18. G. Lawrence Atkins, *Spend It or Save It? Pension Lump-Sum Distributions and Tax Reform* (Washington, D.C.: Employee Benefit Research Institute, 1986).

19. Henderson, "Is Leverage a Tax Dodge—or Not?"

20. Michael C. Jensen, "The Takeover Controversy: Analysis and Evidence," *Journal of Economic Perspectives* 4 (1988), pp. 6–32.

21. Poterba and Summers sketched the "traditional view" of dividend taxation in which higher tax burdens raise the cost of capital. See James M. Poterba and Lawrence H. Summers, "The Economic Effects of Dividend Taxation," in Edward I. Altman and Marti G. Subrahmanyam, eds., *Recent Advances in Corporate Finance* (Homewood, Ill.: Richard Irwin, 1985), pp. 227–284. A similar criticism applies to proposals to reduce the exchange of debt for equity by raising tax burdens on debt finance. Such proposals would discourage corporate borrowing but also raise the cost of funds to U.S. firms, making them less competitive in the world marketplace.

22. These policies also widen the wedge between the pretax return earned by corporations and the posttax return these firms can deliver to their shareholders, thereby magnifying distortions in intertemporal consumer behavior and potentially discouraging personal saving.

23. This tabulation is based on data from the Federal Reserve Board Flow of Funds, excluding nontraded "closely held shares" that are included in the equity aggregate. This calculation is described in greater detail in Kenneth French and James Poterba, "Who Owns Corporate Stock?" (Boston: Massachusetts Institute of Technology, Department of Economics, 1989, mimeograph).

24. For details on the calculation of effective accrual tax rates, see James M. Poterba, "Venture Capital and Capital Gains Taxation," in Lawrence Summers, ed., *Tax Policy and the Economy* 3 (Cambridge, Mass.: MIT Press, 1989), pp. 47–68. The standard source of estimates on how deferral and basis step-up affect effective tax rates is Martin J. Bailey, "Capital Gains and Income Taxation," in Arnold Harberger and Martin Bailey, eds., *The Taxation of Income from Capital* (Washington, D.C.: Brookings Institution, 1969), pp. 11–49.

25. Poterba, "Tax Policy and Corporate Saving."

26. Some argue that disallowing interest deductions would raise national saving by increasing corporate tax payments and thereby reducing government dissaving. Higher taxes are principally a transfer from corporate to government saving, however.

Discussion

Benjamin M. Friedman

What we need to do to correct the now chronic problem of inadequate saving in the United States is by now abundantly clear. The federal government needs to implement either spending cuts or tax increases, or some combination of the two, sufficient to achieve a sizable reduction of its dissaving. But because our political leadership has been unwilling to address the problem in this way, we are driven to search, ever more extensively, for other ways of addressing it. Therefore, the best way to understand the rationale underlying James Poterba's analysis, like several others in this book, is as part of the search for something that we may be *willing* to do in place of doing what we know we *ought* to do.

The place to begin any discussion of public policy directed toward our national saving is to focus on our national investment performance. After all, the reason we care about national saving in the first place is that under normal circumstances more saving means more investment, which in turn enhances our economy's productivity growth and competitiveness and, ultimately, its ability to deliver a high and rising standard of living to the citizenry.

Unfortunately, the U.S. economy's investment performance in the 1980s was a pretty sorry affair. Despite high hopes in many quarters at the outset of the decade, and certainly in contrast to the splendid rhetoric with which President Reagan first introduced his new approach to economic policy, the share of our national income that we devoted to net new investment in business plant and equipment was lower in the 1980s than in any previous period since World War II. On average in the 1950s, the 1960s, and the 1970s, we devoted three and three-tenths cents of every dollar of our national income to net business fixed investment. That share was already too low, for many of the reasons carefully identified in this book. On average during the 1980s, however, the share of our national income that we devoted to net business investment declined yet further, to just two and one-tenth cents of every dollar.

Those who defend our current economic policies usually prefer to focus on gross rather than net investment. Gross investment did indeed proceed at a higher average rate during the 1980s than during the prior post–World War II experience. But on closer inspection, gross investment also declined as a share of our national income throughout the 1980s. The postwar peak by this yardstick occurred in 1981, when we devoted twelve and one-tenth cents of every dollar of our national income to gross investment in plant and equipment. Since then, it has been all downhill. In 1988 we devoted just ten cents of each dollar of our national income to gross new investment.

With our investment in new plants and new machinery down rather than up, our productivity performance has continued to be disappointing despite a number of factors—an older and more experienced labor force, cheaper energy prices, and reduced regulation, among others—that might otherwise have enhanced our productivity growth. At the same time, our ability to compete in world markets, as well as to defend our own markets at home against foreign producers, has deteriorated in a way that would never have been imagined just a decade ago. Worse yet, with such slow productivity growth, except for a few specific areas of the economy, the real (inflation-adjusted) wage of the average worker in U.S. business has fallen in every year since 1984. In his remarks in Chapter 4, Paul Volcker asks why we feel poor. In an era in which the average worker's real wage is falling, not just relatively but absolutely, the answer is that people are losing ground and they know it.

The principal reason for this decline in U.S. business investment—and this brings us to James Poterba's analysis—is the decline in our national saving. The decline in our saving has been due, in roughly equal proportions, to a sharp drop in private saving as a share of our national income and to a sharp rise in the federal government's dissaving. Saving by corporations (in other words, their retained earnings) has typically accounted for about one-third of all private saving in the United States, with personal saving accounting for the other two-thirds. Corporate saving and personal saving both declined in the 1980s, compared with either the 1960s or the 1970s. Therefore, a logical question to ask and the question that motivates Dr. Poterba's discussion—is whether measures to stimulate corporate saving in particular may be a sensible way to help resuscitate our overall national saving and with it our overall national investment.

As Dr. Poterba makes clear, it is far from obvious that the answer is "yes." One reason, which he carefully explains, is that at least if past experience is any guide, having corporations save more—for example, by paying out less of their profit in dividends—would simply cause households to save less. The extent to which reduced personal saving would offset increased corporate saving is less than one for one, but it is clearly enough to matter and matter importantly.

Another reason stimulating corporate saving may not really solve the problem is that in today's political climate, changes in the tax code are eligible for polite public discussion only if they will result in lower Treasury revenues: in other words, no new taxes. To the extent that any tax change intended to stimulate corporate saving would also further widen the federal government's budget deficit, it would increase national saving only if the induced additional corporate saving were sufficient to offset *both* the consequent decline in personal saving and the increase in government dissaving.

Moreover—and here I differ with a principal implicit thrust of Dr. Poterba's analysis—at this point there is little reason to have great confidence in the ability of changes in the tax code to influence private saving behavior. Surely one of the strongest lessons of the 1980s was that personal saving did not increase in anything like the way that advocates of tax reduction and tax reform had predicted would happen if several changes in the relevant environment took place.

Three specific changes that occurred in the 1980s are especially relevant in this context. First, with federal borrowing requirements so large and, importantly, with an anti-inflationary monetary policy in place, real returns on saving instruments issued and traded in U.S. markets reached record highs in the 1980s, even on a pretax basis. It is an error to think of the 1980s as a decade of low interest rates in the sense that matters for saving behavior. Nominal interest rates fell, to be sure, but interest rates net of price inflation were at record levels throughout the decade, even on a pretax basis.

Second, because of lower tax rates, real interest rates for taxable investors have gone up even more on an after-tax basis. Dr. Poterba reminds us that the top marginal tax rate on interest income earned by individuals has fallen from 70 percent to 28 percent. He also indicates that the net tax rate on corporate income distributed to shareholders has declined from 52 percent to 31 percent (assuming a 50 percent payout rate). At this point in his discussion, the emphasis is on whether or not this change has tilted the debt-equity incentives operating within the corporate sector. But the equally important point is that both the decline from 70 to 28 percent at the direct individual level and the decline from 52 to 31 percent for corporate distributions have been enormous compared to what advocates of tax reduction and tax reform said would be sufficient to stimulate private saving in an important way.

Third, inflation has slowed dramatically—the one genuine economic policy success of the 1980s. Slower inflation also matters for saving behavior, at least in principle, because our tax code is not neutral with respect to inflation. Once again, the impact has been to make after-tax, after-inflation returns even greater to taxable investors.

Yet despite all this, personal saving has *declined*, either sharply or modestly depending on the specific measure of saving one uses. In the wake of this stark failure to stimulate personal saving, it is no longer clear why anyone would now have confidence in our ability to affect any aspect of private saving behavior—personal or corporate—by what would surely amount to only marginal changes in the tax code.

Yet a further reason for being dubious of tax changes as a way of stimulating corporate saving is the question of whether, even if corporate saving did rise, corporations would then use the additional retentions to increase their investment in new plants, new machinery, and new research. As Dr. Poterba explains, whereas dividend payments are normally considered a *reduction* in corporate saving, corporations' purchases of their own or other firms' shares are conventionally treated as a *use* of corporate saving. The question therefore arises whether, especially in the current financial climate, an increase in corporate retentions would merely provide further wherewithal for the enormous wave of mergers, acquisitions, stock repurchases, and leveraged buyouts that has swept over so much of the corporate United States since the mid-1980s.

It is important to put this question in the proper context. The entire amount of net saving by U.S. corporations during 1984–1988—the quantity that is the subject of Dr. Poterba's discussion—was $437 billion (not $437 billion per year, but $437 billion in total over the five years). By comparison, the amount of equity paid down by U.S. corporations during these same five years, measured in excess of the proceeds of new share issues by all corporations issuing new shares, was $443 billion—that is, marginally more than the entirety of net corporate saving. The ongoing debate over why all this is happening and, even more importantly, over whether the corporate reorganizations that this process has entailed are good or bad for our economy is a proper subject for another book. But there is one principle on which everyone should agree: To the extent that part of the motivation for this massive substitution of debt for equity in the capital structures of U.S. corporations is an artificial tax incentive arising purely from the tax code's differential treatment of debt and equity, there is certainly no reason to make that incentive any stronger.

Beyond that—and here there is substantially less agreement—I think there are also good reasons to view the economywide implications of this massive substitution of debt for equity with some concern. On average in the 1950s and 1960s, it took sixteen cents of every dollar of corporate earnings (measured before interest and taxes) to pay corporations' interest bills. On average in the 1970s, it took thirty-three cents of corporate earnings to pay the interest bill. On average in the 1980s, it took fifty-six cents of every dollar of corporate earnings to pay the interest bill. Worse yet, there was no tendency for U.S. corporations' interest coverage ratios to improve as the 1980s progressed, despite steep declines in nominal interest rates and despite seven years of sustained economic expansion, with healthy growth in corporate earnings.

Not surprisingly, both the rate at which U.S. firms went bankrupt and the dollar volume of bankrupted firms' liabilities (compared to gross national product) were at record levels throughout the 1980s. It was only natural that in 1981–1982, when the economy experienced the worst business recession since the 1930s, the bankruptcy rate likewise rose to a record post-1930s high. What has been unprecedented, however, is that the bankruptcy rate did not fall back to prerecession levels when the recession ended. Instead, it continued to rise for four more years into the expansion. Even now, after a welcome but modest decline, the bankruptcy rate is still far above anything in the postwar experience before 1981.

All this has raised fears of some kind of impending disaster, typically presumed to be most likely to occur in the form of a massive, and perhaps cumulative, default experience next time there is a business recession of any significant magnitude. As I have written elsewhere,[1] I regard the possibility of a systemic default on a scale that would threaten the soundness of the U.S. economy as relatively remote. But the reason I do not think the recent rise in corporate indebtedness threatens a financial crisis does lead me to fear that it will ultimately impose a severe cost on our economy in the form of a return to high inflation.

The logic behind this argument is that because policymakers in the Federal Reserve System are completely aware of the implications of high and rising corporate indebtedness, they will be reluctant to pursue a genuinely tight monetary policy whenever doing so presents the risk of a serious business recession. But even a quick glance backward at the experience of inflation and recession during the post–World War II period in the United States immediately suggests that if corporate indebtedness has now locked monetary policy into a no-recession stance for the foreseeable future, that policy will inevitably turn out to be a proinflationary policy.

For all of these reasons, I conclude that tax policy action—or, for that matter, any other action—specifically aimed at stimulating corporate saving is not the right way to address the profound inadequacy of saving and investment that is slowly, subtly, and surely eroding the basis for our national prosperity and also slowly but not so subtly eroding the basis for the role that the United States has played in world affairs within our lifetime. What, then, is the right way to solve this problem? As a political matter, perhaps we would like to think that there must be policy options other than cutting government spending or raising taxes. Unfortunately, there is no real alternative. If we are serious about increasing our national saving and investment, and thereby boosting our productivity growth and our competitiveness, we must go back to the basics.

NOTES

1. See, for example, Benjamin M. Friedman, "Implications of Increasing Corporate Indebtedness for Monetary Policy," Group of Thirty Occasional Paper no. 29 (New York and London: Group of Thirty, 1990).

Discussion

Harry D. Garber

James Poterba provides an excellent point of departure for a discussion of strategies to increase business saving. I would like to expand on his implicit and explicit conclusions, drawing, as appropriate, on my knowledge of public policy and my business experience. As a starting point, I would like to highlight two points that Dr. Poterba makes. The first is the fact that business saving has traditionally accounted for 30 to 40 percent of national saving. By mere virtue of size, therefore, business saving is important to overall national saving.

The second point is that business saving levels are related to both individual saving levels and government saving levels. Dr. Poterba discusses the relationship between business saving and individual saving at some length. The relationship of business saving to government saving stems from the effects any federal actions to improve business saving might have on the federal budget deficit. Incentives to improve business saving will have an adverse effect on government saving unless the revenue loss from these incentives is offset by increased revenue elsewhere or by reduced expenditures. If business taxes are increased to provide the offsetting revenues, there might still be an improvement in net business saving, but this improvement would be marginal at best.

Although Dr. Poterba does not make this point explicitly, I believe it is fair to conclude from his analysis that if business tax incentives do not increase business pretax income, they will have, at best, only a marginal impact on overall national saving. In these circumstances, the most important issue to be addressed in pursuing the goal of increased business saving is how to increase business pretax income through federal policy and actions. This suggests that economic growth itself is the key question. In the remainder of my remarks, I will seek to address two questions in this respect: Are there effective tax incentives that can increase business saving through an increase in business pretax income? What additional (nontax) federal policy initiatives are available to increase business pretax income?

I would like to consider the second question first. It is important to recognize that businesses save to achieve certain goals—not simply for the joy of saving. Traditionally, businesses have saved for the repayment of debt, future investment in plant and equipment to increase capacity and/or efficiency, acquisitions, or increased safety in ever-changing economic conditions. More recently, these four traditional business saving goals have been modified by the sweeping changes in the financial markets. These changes have included, on the one hand, the easier availability of credit through "junk bonds" and the expanded commercial paper market and, on the other hand, the relatively lower market valuations accorded companies that are not viewed by the stock market as using corporate resources (including cash) effectively. The critical test for business saving today is whether or not such saving is the most effective way to meet certain business needs such as increased capacity, increased efficiency, improved market penetration, retention of current market share, development of new markets, or changes in market position. Businesses must have some identified need for additional saving, and that need must be best satisfied through increased business saving. If there is no business need and/or if borrowing funds or selling stock is a less costly or easier option, there will be no incentive for increased business saving. In summary, increased business saving will be driven principally by business needs and financial market conditions—not by federal tax incentives.

In Chapter 3 Federal Reserve vice chairman Manuel Johnson describes the appropriate role of government in the economy. This role is to foster an economic environment that promotes economic growth, saving, and investment. Such an environment would be one in which inflation is controlled and the relative responsibilities of business and government are well understood and stable over time. It is an environment in which requirements on business to shoulder more of society's burdens are made only after careful study and discussion.

Unfortunately, this environment too often does not exist. The business sector is being required to take responsibility for a vast array of societal problems with unknown risks and costs. And "to add insult to injury," these government interventions not only require businesses to act; they also specify *how* business must act and then require them to file voluminous reports with some bureaucratic organization to "prove compliance." Prominent current (or prospective) examples of such legislative burdens include Section 89, the uncontrolled tort liability system, proposals to mandate health care insurance (with its uncontrolled cost structure), and the Americans with Disability legislation.

Business is increasingly being viewed by a revenue-short federal government (and by some state governments) as the vehicle to solve political problems. These actions are rarely, if ever, supported by any credible analysis as to whether the additional burdens on business will have a materially adverse impact on business investment or competitive position, whether there are existing federal programs that have lesser priority and could be reduced or eliminated, or whether the purported problem is sufficiently serious that any action is required at all. This is the present reality, and it is the antithesis of the ideal environment just described.

I want to describe what I believe is a classic case in this respect. It involves a series of actions taken by Congress over a fifteen-year period that has irrevocably undermined what government officials have long regarded as the fundamental building block of the nation's private pension system. The victim in this case is the defined-benefit pension plan.

It is a fascinating case because the actions were for the most part taken by supporters of this type of pension arrangement who had as their purpose the "perfection" of this vehicle. But the actions taken were not well researched, and, with hindsight, it is now clear that these actions were misguided. They have fatally wounded this arrangement—just the opposite result of that intended. (I am aware that pension accumulations are in fact considered personal saving, but this case exemplifies the inadvertent effects that government actions can have on the behavior of business.)

Defined-benefit pension plans generally provide lifetime retirement benefits to employees in amounts that usually recognize salary history, length of service, and so on. The benefits are usually integrated with Social Security old-age benefits and are sometimes indexed for changes in the cost of living. A defined-benefit plan is what everyone thinks of when the term *pension plan* is mentioned.

Defined-benefit plans grew tremendously after World War II. They offered employers considerable flexibility in the timing of contributions, the investment vehicles used, and so on. There was a favorable tax structure in which employers could deduct the contributions made, the investment income on pension funds was not taxed, and employees were not taxed until the income (from employer contributions and investment income) was received.

Funding flexibility inevitably produced cases in which there were, when companies failed, underfunded plans and pension promises that could not be fulfilled. Studebaker was a prominent example. There were also cases of misuse of pension funds and of fraud and carelessness in the investment of such funds. In order "to protect" this institution and to carry out certain other purposes, Congress passed the Employee Retirement Income Security Act (ERISA) in 1974. Some of the provisions of ERISA for defined-benefit plans were the following:

- Minimum annual funding requirements were established with supporting actuarial valuations and reports.
- Boards of directors were made fiduciaries for pension fund investments.
- The Pension Benefit Guaranty Corporation (PBGC) was established to provide a guarantee of the defined-benefit obligations of terminated plans and/or insolvent companies. The PBGC was funded by a tax on all existing defined-benefit plans.

- A cap on the amount of annual income that could be paid under a defined-benefit plan was established. (If I recall correctly, the original cap affected only one corporate executive in the nation.)

These seemed, at the time, like prudent and helpful changes. Let me describe what happened after ERISA, starting with the area of funding. Long before ERISA, company pension fund managers had discovered that common stocks offered the highest return over long periods of time. In many cases the majority of a company's pension funds was invested in common stocks. Although stocks had historically produced higher returns than fixed-income obligations did, actuaries, encumbered by their legal obligations under ERISA, were reluctant to assume that investment portfolios would earn much more than fixed-income-level returns, even for portfolios heavily invested in common stocks. This judgment was "supported" by the stock market performance in the mid- to late 1970s. Because of this judgment, higher contributions were required than would have been the case if higher earnings rates on stocks had been assumed, but the companies continued what they believed to be the right investment decisions—to have a high percentage of funds in common stocks. The inevitable consequence when common stocks produced their historical return rates in the 1980s was an overfunding of many defined-benefit pension plans. When companies tried to recapture the excess funds that ERISA "required them to contribute," there was a political outcry, followed by a series of legislative prohibitions of and/or punitive taxes on such recoveries. Although this issue has not yet been fully resolved, it is hard to believe that we will ever again see an unencumbered return of unneeded pension funds.

The fiduciary obligations imposed by ERISA on company boards of directors and managements have caused most day-to-day management of pension funds to be delegated to independent managers. The competition among these managers has recently raised concerns about a perceived overemphasis on short-term results, the instability in stock markets that is often attributed to this short-term emphasis, and the inadvertent assistance to takeover specialists that results from the normal operations of these managers.

The cap on the amount of annual income that could be received by an individual for a qualified plan is now lower in dollars than it was originally (and much lower in economic value). It is at a level where corporate executives will typically receive more from a combination of defined-contribution plans, nonqualified supplementary plans, and stock options than from the qualified defined-benefit plan, with a consequent loss of interest in and attention to the company's defined-benefit plan.

The PBGC, which was never operated using basic insurance principles, now has several billion dollars more in known liabilities than it has in existing assets, and it must be bailed out by higher charges on existing defined-benefit plans. But even this is not the end. The 1986

Tax Reform Act increased vesting requirements and reduced the degree of possible Social Security integration with consequent increased benefits (and costs) for many defined-benefit plans. And, finally, there is considerable pressure to require portability in defined-benefit pensions as employees change jobs, with further increases in benefits and costs.

To sum up, it can be seen that although the original intent of ERISA was to protect plan participants, the actual burdens imposed by this act, its subsequent modifications, and related legislation removed all of the attractiveness of defined-benefit plans to employers but left them with the basic risk of guaranteeing a result. It should be no surprise that no new defined-benefit plans are being formed, that the emphasis has shifted to defined-contribution arrangements, and that existing defined-benefit plans are being frozen, reduced in scope, or phased out. As this case illustrates all too well, the basic problem with many government actions is that they are not well researched and their likely consequences are not well understood. Because of this poor foresight, they often have unintended consequences that are worse than the original problem. It is this type of well-intentioned but shortsighted activity that must be avoided if we are to achieve the kind of business climate that promotes saving, investment, growth, and, along with all of these, business saving.

My other question—whether there are effective federal tax incentives for business that will increase business growth, saving, and investment—has provoked a great deal of controversy and debate. Many believe that incentives like the investment tax credit or accelerated depreciation methods are effective tools for increasing capital investment by business. Although there is no question that the United States needs a favorable environment for capital investment, the real question is whether direct tax incentives are an effective way to achieve this desired result.

I am skeptical about the effectiveness of such incentives. There is not much evidence that tax incentives such as those just mentioned have produced *sustained* increases in capital investment. And there is considerable evidence that federal tax legislation cannot be targeted effectively. The political process tends to add many unnecessary and undeserving beneficiaries to the list of those receiving tax incentives. A good example is the recent real estate "boom and bust" that was fueled principally by the 1981 tax law. Furthermore, there is also considerable evidence that the possible addition and/or renewal of tax incentives has sustained a cottage industry in Washington, D.C., of tax lawyers, lobbyists, tax accountants, and so on, supporting the enactment, enlargement, and/or retention of tax incentives. (This is the unquestioned growth industry produced by federal tax incentives.)

The ability of the federal government to fashion tax incentives that hit the target and do not have materially adverse side effects is poor. And the instability that results from continued tinkering with these incentives is debilitating to the economy and to business saving. The basic problem is that the corporate income tax is a highly leveraged structure. The base of taxable income is small, the tax rates are high, and it makes an enormous difference to companies how different types of transactions are treated. This highly leveraged structure leads to an environment in which corporate actions may be determined more by the ever-changing vagaries of the tax law than by the basic economics involved. I suspect that abandoning this structure in favor of a low-rate business transfer tax (with border adjustments) might do more for sustained business investment and growth than all of the suggested targeted tax incentives combined.

In summary, I would like to reemphasize four points. First, business saving cannot be looked to as the principal source of improved saving; it will in fact be less important than either individual or government saving. Second, if the United States provides a favorable environment for business investment and growth, business saving will continue to be an important segment of the total national saving. Third, if the United States does not provide this type of environment, business saving and investment will be smaller and individual and government saving will have to take up the slack—or economic growth will suffer. Fourth, tax incentives are probably not the best means of increasing business saving over the long term; conflicting and changing political objectives do not permit such incentives to be targeted initially or to be sustained.

Discussion

Jim Moody

I want to begin this commentary with three assumptions. First, total aggregate saving is more a function of income than it is of any particular tax regime or even of the prevailing interest rate. I am a strong believer in the permanent income hypothesis, and although perturbations in personal household saving are doubtlessly a result of impacts on those households, in the long term they adjust and tend to be a rather constant fraction of income.

Second, the flow of saving between the different uses does depend on the after-tax impacts on those flows. Therefore, the allocation of saving is susceptible to tax policy and other government intervention. The maximum impact on total saving would result from deficit reduction rather than from an increase in corporate or household saving.

Third, households tend to act as though they are pursuing a target saving. If we look at the data on individual retirement accounts (IRAs) and some of the other current data, we will see that people are acting as though they are striving for a target of saving and some precautionary or retirement motivation. That has important policy implications. As we change our policies in Medicare and in Social Security, and as we change other policies rather than simply raise taxes, we change those targets because people presumably want to save some of those government safety nets.

As we consider any tax change, whether in the household or the corporate sector, we must determine the effect on national saving. If every one dollar in tax incentives for either the household or the corporate sector yields one dollar in deficit increase or a one dollar increase in government dissaving, we have to make some heroic assumptions about the marginal propensity to save for those who receive those tax benefits. One dollar of saving in the government sector, however, does not produce one dollar in saving increase in either of the two private sectors. This would be true even with some tax regimes that would tend to lock in dividend increases, but it is less true for flows going to households because we know their marginal propensity to save is certainly far less than one. This sheds light on the capital gains issue as well as the issues raised by Dr. Poterba in this chapter.

With this as background, I will turn to the possible ways of raising the corporate saving rate. Lowering corporate taxes does push more resources into the corporate sector. What happens after that depends on the corporation's dividend policy, for example. Insofar as corporations use additional resources to increase dividends, the saving increases are reduced. Insofar as lowering the corporate tax rate raises deficits, it reduces total aggregate saving. The net impact would be moderate, or even negligible, depending on the empirical relationships.

For each of the four devices that Dr. Poterba outlines, what are the empirical strengths of the flow of forces? I am a strong supply-sider, but I have never believed that the incentives created by supply-side policies were strong enough empirically to overcome other impacts on the deficit and on other factors. Raising dividend taxes tends to skew the debt-equity structure referred to by both Dr. Poterba and Dr. Friedman. If we think that is an adverse effect, we want to avoid it. If we think locking in retained earnings is good, we might wish to have it.

If we pursue policies that tend to lock in retained earnings, we must ask if that is the most efficient use of those dollars. If they are retained as corporate saving, that does not necessarily promote the freer flow of capital and get the biggest bang for the buck. The goal is not just to maximize saving; the goal is also to maximize the efficiency of saving. So locking saving up in one sector may tend to actually lower the total efficiency of saving. We are concerned about increasing our national income, not just producing saving.

Raising taxes on dividends increases the cost of all forms of capital for all sectors. I believe in the Harberger model, whereby the net returns of capital tend to equalize over time between different forms of business organization. Higher dividend taxes can increase the bias against equity and the fragility of the system and raise the amount of risk that exists in the corporate sector.

Reducing the capital gains tax produces a windfall for the household sector. I question whether we are going to get our bang for the buck in saving terms because we are increasing the deficit and because the marginal propensity to save is far less than one.

Target investment incentives such as the investment tax credit and more generous depreciation allowances begin to offer some real leverage on the goals we are seeking to achieve. They have the obvious deficit-increasing effects and therefore increase dissaving in the public sector, but these can be overcome by revenue-neutral devices that leave the net incentive to accumulate and invest capital in the corporate sector stronger than it was without those incentives.

It is important to remember that the U.S. corporate sector does not exist in a vacuum. It competes with international corporations, which in turn are competing for capital and other resources. The international effects have become titanic. We now are borrowing approximately 3 percent of our gross national product from foreign sources, mostly private, and it obviously affects our competitiveness as a nation.

With the deficit as high as it has been and with the total national federal debt as high as it is, it may be that our tolerance for additional levels of debt is nonlinear. A discussion about how one additional dollar of saving in the corporate sector may yield one additional dollar of dissaving in the public sector may ignore the fact that the impacts are nonlinear. The level of interest rates in the United States is tremendously dependent on the level of federal debt. I suspect that this, too, may be a nonlinear relationship. There is feedback through the deficit side of the budget because if we raise interest rates 100 basis points, we suddenly have $28 billion more in spending because of the $2.8 trillion stock of debt. Government dissaving has a multiplier effect on interest rates that may be very symmetrical as we trade one pot of saving for another.

11

The Federal Deficit, National Saving, and Economic Performance

Joel L. Prakken

INTRODUCTION

Nineteen eighty-nine marked the seventh consecutive yearly increase in the real gross national product (GNP) of the United States, making the current recovery one of the longest in our nation's peacetime history. Yet the expansion has proved as remarkable in its imbalances as in its longevity. Contrary to previous experience, the structural federal deficit rose sharply as the economy rebounded, the real rate of interest climbed to highs not sustained since the Great Depression, and large trade deficits transformed the United States from the world's largest lender to the world's largest debtor.

The persistence of these imbalances has spawned concern that the mix of fiscal and monetary policies adopted during the 1980s has created an environment hostile to saving and investment. Figure 11.1 depicts the share of net domestic product devoted to net private domestic investment during the postwar era; years in which the economy is estimated to have reached full employment are marked with a "P" to denote a cyclical peak.[1] The figure makes clear that investment as a share of output, despite rebounding sharply at the onset of the current recovery, is well below the levels witnessed late in other postwar expansions.[2]

Furthermore, that the manner in which investment is financed has shifted dramatically since 1980 is made clear by considering Table 11.1. In 1979, the year in which the economy last reached full employment, virtually all of net private saving went to finance net private domestic investment; government and foreign saving were only minor factors. By contrast, in 1988 almost one-half of net investment in the United States was financed by foreigners, as nearly three-quarters of private national saving was absorbed by the federal deficit.[3]

FIGURE 11.1
Net Investment
(percent of NDP)

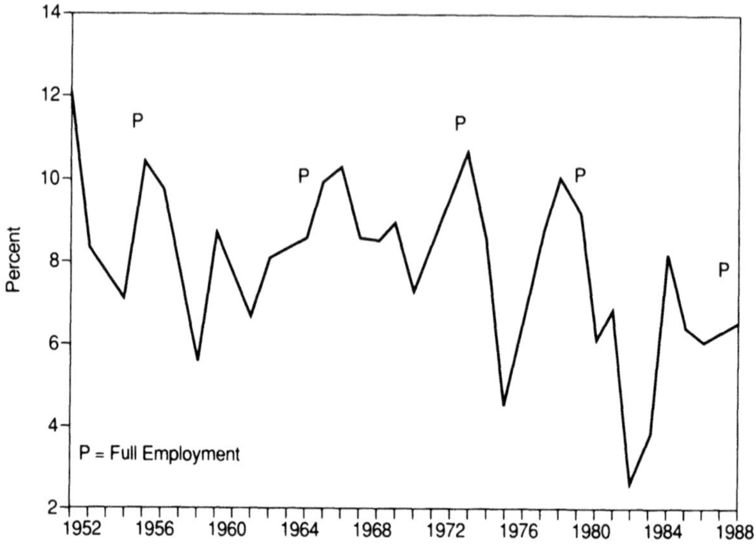

Source: U.S. Department of Commerce, Bureau of Economic Analysis, *National Income and Product Accounts.*

TABLE 11.1
Net Saving and Investment, 1979 and 1988

	Billions of Dollars, Seasonally Adjusted Annual Rates	
	1979	1988
Net Private Domestic Investment	189	237
financed by:		
Net National Saving	190	120
Private	178	216
Government	12	-96
Federal	-16	-146
State and Local	28	50
Foreign Saving	-1	117
	Percent of GNP	
	1979	1988
Net Private Domestic Investment	7.5	4.9
financed by:		
Net National Saving	7.6	2.4
Private	7.1	4.4
Government	0.5	-2.0
Federal	-0.6	-3.0
State and Local	0.7	1.0
Foreign Saving	-0.0	2.4

Source: U.S. Department of Commerce, Bureau of Economic Analysis, *National Income and Product Accounts.*

One popular explanation of these events focuses on the role of the federal budget deficit as a vehicle for converting private saving into public consumption. According to this view, large budget deficits in the 1980s drove up the real rate of interest, *crowding out* domestic investment and thereby discouraging economic growth. Were it not for the dramatic inflow of foreign saving during this period and, to a lesser extent, an increase in saving by state and local governments, the rise in the real interest rate and the decline in net investment associated with the burgeoning federal deficit would have been even more pronounced. Furthermore, the argument goes, unless the so-called twin deficits of the budget and the balance of trade are reduced, U.S. economic growth will languish while foreign claims against the United States, both direct and indirect, will increasingly undermine our nation's standard of living.

Nowadays, in any discussion of saving and investment, there is a natural inclination to focus on the role of the federal deficit. The federal deficit is the component of national saving that changed most dramatically during the 1980s. And whereas policies to enhance private saving typically rely on incentives to *induce* changes in private behavior, policies to alter spending and/or taxes seemingly operate on national saving directly. Yet there is considerable uncertainty about the role that balancing the budget might play in improving national economic performance. If the deficit is eliminated, will total saving advanced rise equivalently, or will there be offsetting reductions in private and foreign saving? If so, how large might those offsets be? What are the potential gains in national income and product to be realized by reducing the deficit? What factors do these gains depend on, and how quickly do they accrue? Does the manner in which we choose to reduce the deficit have an impact on the real interest rate, saving, investment, and economic growth? If so, are these considerations of primary or secondary importance?

The remainder of this analysis is organized as follows. The second section ("Conceptual Issues") presents a discussion of the conceptual issues raised by proposals intended to increase national saving by reducing the federal deficit. The details of a simple but powerful analytical model of saving and economic growth are relegated to Appendix 11.A. Section three ("Simulation Analysis") presents the results generated with the Washington University macroeconomic model of the U.S. economy of five different plans to eliminate the federal deficit by 1995 and then maintain the budget in proximate balance through the year 2008. Section four ("Summary and Conclusions") summarizes the findings and the implications of the results.

CONCEPTUAL ISSUES

A stylized, classical analysis of economic growth (see Appendix 11.A) suggests that in the long run, the economy expands at a rate determined by (1) the rate of growth in the labor force and (2) the rate of (disembodied and labor-augmenting) technological advance.[4] Growth in the labor force is governed primarily by demographic considerations that in the first instance are considered unrelated to macroeconomic policy. Technical advance is the growth in labor's productivity that cannot be explained by variations in the amount of physical capital that workers have at their disposal. By definition, technological advance is exogenous. Consequently, *in the long run the growth of real output is independent of the saving rate and is not influenced by policies to promote national saving and investment.*

The saving rate, however, can play a pivotal role in determining the *level* of output as well as its *near-term* rate of growth. An exogenous increase in the nation's saving rate—that is, an increase in the propensity to save at any given real rate of interest—generally reduces the equilibrium real interest rate. A decline in the real interest rate in turn induces an increase in the equilibrium ratio of capital to output. The resulting *capital-deepening* raises the level of labor's productivity so that for a given labor force there is an increase in the level of potential output. During the transition from the lower to the higher level of potential output, the rate of economic growth temporarily rises above its long-run value, the latter being determined solely by demographics and technical advance.

This analysis is depicted in Figure 11.2, which graphs the logarithm of output against time. Line A represents the long-term path of output under a low national saving rate and a high real rate of interest. Line C represents the long-term path of output under a high national saving rate and a low real interest rate. The lines are of equal slope, reflecting the fact that long-term growth is independent of the national saving rate. Suppose initially that output is growing along A but that fiscal authorities then implement a program of gradual deficit reduction that succeeds in raising the national saving rate. During the transition from a high to a low deficit, the real interest rate declines gradually and the resulting capital-deepening boosts economic growth above the long-term rate. Consequently, output rises along line B as it moves from the lower to the higher long-term path. When the desired reduction in the deficit is achieved, the real interest rate stabilizes at a lower level, economic growth reverts to the long-term rate, and output grows along C. The onetime increase in the level of output associated with the reduction in the deficit is reflected in the vertical distance between the two long-run paths of output. One way to gauge the implications for social welfare of reducing the deficit is simply to measure the increase in the level of output. Another is to calculate the cumulative gain in output, represented in Figure 11.2 by the shaded area. As the level of output is higher perpetually, however, the cumulative gain is most meaningful if measured in terms of its present value.

The foregoing analysis is simplistic in two important respects. First, it assumes that an exogenous increase in government saving necessarily

FIGURE 11.2
Deficit Reduction and Economic Growth

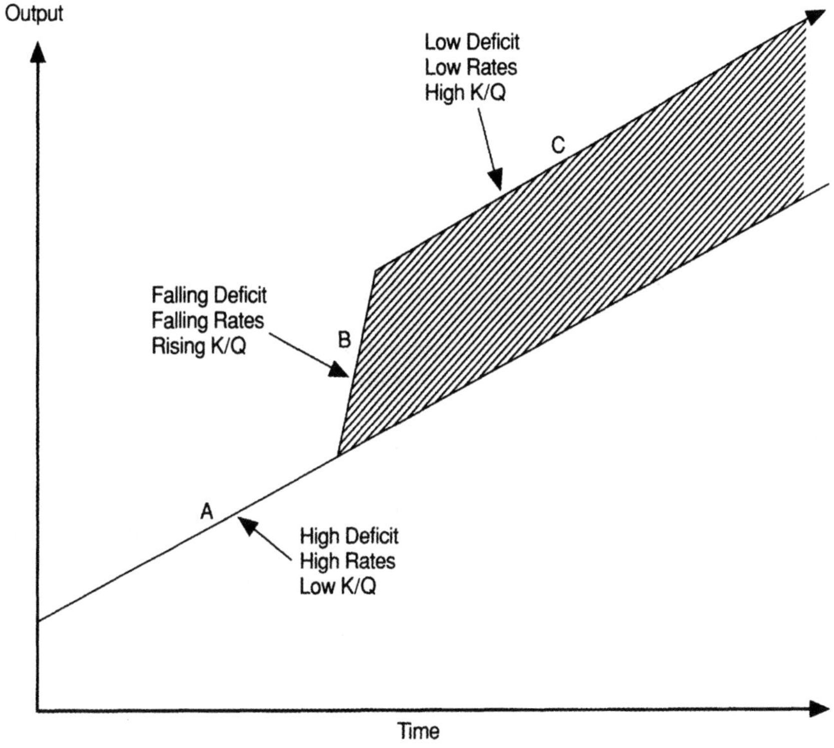

Note: K/Q is the capital-to-output ratio.

leads to an increase in total saving. Second, it makes no allowance for the fact that policies to reduce the deficit may have an impact on potential output other than through the real interest rate. A more comprehensive view of the process is presented in Figure 11.3. Although the figure takes some liberties in portraying interdependencies of saving, investment, and output, it does serve as a useful point of reference for understanding the primary channels through which a reduction in the federal deficit influences the level of output.

Consider a reduction in the deficit accompanied by an easier monetary policy intended to maintain the economy at full employment during the transition from a lower to a higher level of potential output. Other things equal, government saving rises and the real rate of interest falls. But as shown in Figure 11.3, there are two possible offsets to saving. First, domestic private saving may decline if the private saving rate depends positively on the real interest rate. Second, the flow of saving advanced by foreigners may atrophy if as a result of reducing

FIGURE 11.3
Deficit Reduction and Potential Output

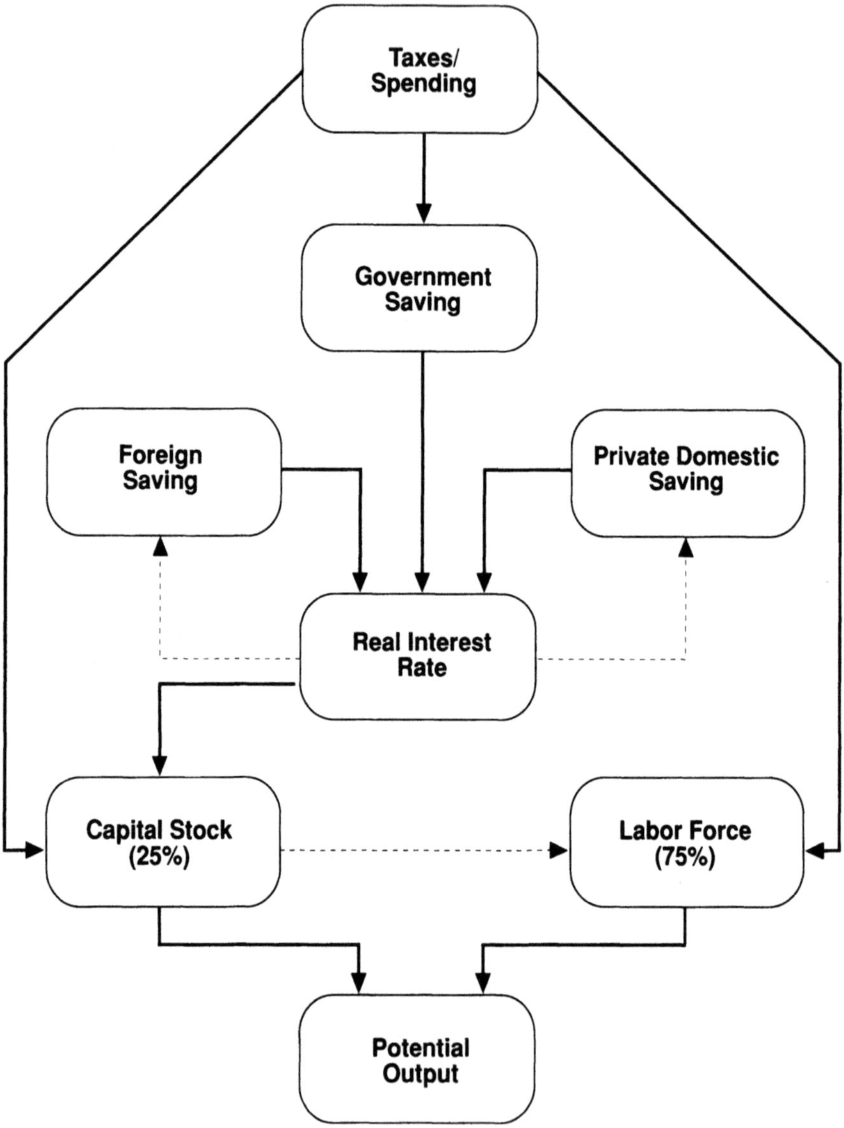

the deficit, the domestic interest rate falls relative to the rate of return earned abroad. Put somewhat differently, restrictive fiscal policy accompanied by easier monetary policy reduces the real rate of interest and stimulates the interest-sensitive sectors of aggregate spending. But to the extent that consumption and exports rather than business fixed investment strengthen as the interest rate falls, the gains in output associated with a reduction in the deficit are limited.

The lion's share of (net) private saving is, of course, personal saving. Thus, the key parameter in this regard is the interest sensitivity of the personal saving rate. Theories of household behavior suggest that personal saving may rise *or* fall as the interest rate declines, depending on whether the reduced incentive to substitute saving for consumption at the margin (the so-called substitution effect) is offset by the desire to reduce consumption as disposable income falls with the rate of interest (the income effect). Empirically, the issue is further confused by how both saving and income are defined and measured. For example, the calculation of the personal saving rate in the national income and product accounts (NIPAs) treats expenditures on consumer durables as consumption and defines personal income to exclude capital gains. Consumer theory suggests that any net increase in the stock of durables be regarded as saving and that income be defined to include capital gains. Be that as it may, at the aggregate level there is some evidence to suggest that the personal saving rate is positively associated with the real interest rate.[5] In that case, any increase in national saving wrought by a reduction in the federal deficit is likely to be offset partially by a reduction in private saving. Obviously, the extent of the offset is crucial in determining the macroeconomic benefits of reducing the deficit.[6]

A reduction in foreign saving would be reflected in a depreciation of the exchange value of the dollar and a concomitant increase in net exports. The magnitude of this offset depends partly on how sensitive foreign investors are to a change in the international differential in interest rates. Even more important is the question of whether, as apparently happened in the 1980s, a marked shift in domestic fiscal policy would in fact result in an international differential in yields. If so, how long might the differential persist?

Policies to reduce the deficit may influence potential output through channels other than the decline in the real interest rate that results from the change in the mix of fiscal and monetary policies. In particular, the size of the labor force and the equilibrium ratio of capital to output may depend directly on taxes and spending. For example, if the deficit is reduced through new taxes on investment, the result will be to increase the cost of capital at any given interest rate, undermine the extent of capital-deepening otherwise associated with reduction of the deficit, and thereby limit any increase in potential output. A tax that does not affect the equilibrium capital-output ratio directly—for example, a consumption-based value-added tax—is therefore likely to provide a less costly way to reduce the deficit than does a tax that directly increases the cost of capital.

The impact that changes in the tax code might have on investment was actively debated prior to the passage of the Tax Reform Act of 1986.[7] But the impact of fiscal policy on potential output via the cost of capital may not be nearly as important as its impact via the labor force, particularly because labor accounts for three-fourths of the value of production. In theory, if leisure is a normal good, the supply of labor declines when nonlabor (transfer) income increases. The labor force may rise or fall as the tax rate on wages rises, depending on whether the reduced incentive to work at the margin (the substitution effect) is offset by the desire to reduce the consumption of leisure as disposable income falls (the income effect). Even though the empirical evidence on the directions and magnitudes of these responses is not wholly compelling, at the aggregate level it does suggest that the labor force declines as transfers rise and as the marginal tax rate on wages increases.[8]

In that case, a proposal to reduce the deficit by raising income taxes might have importantly different implications for the macroeconomy than would a plan that stressed restraint in spending. Although both would promote capital-deepening by fostering a lower interest rate, a proposal to restrain the growth of all outlays (including transfers) would increase the labor force and would have no direct deleterious impact on the cost of capital. In contrast, not only would a plan to increase income taxes reduce the labor force; it would also directly raise the cost of capital.

In summary, two sorts of effects are engendered by policies to increase government saving. First, the *change in the mix of fiscal and monetary policies* leads to a lower interest rate, higher investment, and an increase in potential output whose magnitude is partly determined by the extent to which consumption and exports "crowd in" as the deficit declines. Second, changes in tax and expenditure rates may have important *supply-side effects* on investment and/or the supply of labor at any real rate of interest. The overall impact on output depends on the direction and magnitudes of both types of effects. Generally, a change in the mix of policy toward fiscal restraint and monetary ease leads unambiguously to higher output. Supply-side effects, however, may be contrary, particularly those arising from increased tax rates. Consequently, different approaches to the balancing of the budget may have different implications for social welfare.

There are, of course, important reservations to be stated about the model that underlies this discussion. Perhaps most important is that the analysis treats federal outlays as current consumption, when in fact it may be argued reasonably that at least part of that spending is on public capital that augments future private output. Thus, if the deficit is reduced by cutting public investment in, say, education,[9] research and development, or the infrastructure,[10] a simple growth analysis might overstate the advantages of increased government saving. Nor does the model address the possibility that competing plans to reduce the deficit may have very different implications for the distribution of income and wealth in the United States, for the environment, or for other intangible aspects of the quality of life not adequately (if at all) reflected in the measurement of output. Finally, this analysis treats labor as a homogeneous commodity when in fact the productivity of labor is partly dependent on investment in human capital. If a reduction in the deficit leads to a lower real interest rate and as a result to an increase in private investment in education and job training, the consequent increase in output may exceed that implied by the simple classical model of growth.

SIMULATION ANALYSIS

The Washington University Macroeconomic Model

This section reports the results of simulations generated with the Washington University macroeconomic model of the U.S. economy. The model, built and maintained by Laurence H. Meyer & Associates (LHM&A), is a structural quarterly econometric system of roughly 350 equations and 500 variables.[11] The model has an income-expenditure structure in which near-term movements in real GNP are determined primarily by fluctuations in aggregate demand. But the fully developed *supply side* of the model makes it an ideal vehicle for simulating the long-run effects on the macroeconomy of competing proposals to reduce the deficit. At full employment the equilibrium level of output is determined by a neoclassical growth model completely consistent with the earlier discussion. In particular, potential output is determined by (disembodied, labor-augmenting) exogenous technology, the labor force, and the ratio of capital to output.

The supply of labor is governed primarily by demographics. Nevertheless, LHM&A also estimates that the elasticity of the labor force with respect to per capita real transfers is −0.05 and with respect to the marginal after-tax real wage is 0.15. Thus, leisure is a normal good for which the substitution effect dominates the income effect. The capital-output ratio depends on the rental price of capital (the latter formulated in the standard Jorgensonian fashion to depend on the real rate of interest), the relative price of investment, the depreciation rate of capital goods, and the treatment of capital in the tax code. The elasticity of substitution between capital and labor is unitary.

With the exception of interest payments on the national debt and certain cyclical components of transfer payments, real federal expenditures are exogenous to the model. Therefore, although, strictly speaking, government saving is not exogenous, the federal deficit is directly affected by changes in the exogenous components of outlays and taxes. Personal saving, which constitutes most of net private saving, is determined by a life cycle model in which the average personal saving rate rises with the real interest rate. The elasticity of the personal saving rate (as defined in the NIPAs) with respect to the real interest rate is roughly 0.15.

Saving advanced by foreigners, the opposite of what in the NIPAs is referred to as net foreign investment, is in absolute value the sum of net exports and federal payments to foreigners. (A third component, personal transfers to foreigners, is insignificantly small.) The latter is composed primarily of interest payments to foreigners but also includes direct federal grants. Net exports depend importantly on the real exchange rate, which in turn is determined by the difference between the real interest rate in the United States and that abroad. Any differential that arises is assumed to dissipate over a period of two years. This structure endows the model with the property that a change in fiscal policy—say, for example, a sharp increase in the structural deficit—does not have associated with it a lasting change in either the exchange rate or the trade deficit. (This issue is addressed further in "More on International Considerations.")

Defining the Baseline

To assess the macroeconomic impact of a policy that reduces the deficit, one must first develop a *baseline* scenario that describes the economic environment that would prevail in the absence of that policy. There is a necessary element of arbitrariness in this process, for if the policy actually is implemented, the baseline goes unobserved and thus unknown. In the present case, however, theoretical considerations provide some guidance in defining a baseline because a simple growth model (see Appendix 11.A) suggests that it is variations in the size of the deficit *relative to output* that are associated with changes in potential output. Therefore, the baseline was constructed by first assuming the current tax code to remain in force through the year 2008 and then managing the exogenous components of federal outlays to maintain the deficit at roughly 3 percent of gross national product, the same share as in recent years. Monetary policy was managed to maintain the actual unemployment rate at the estimated natural rate of 5.3 percent, so that growth in actual output is exactly growth in potential output.

The rate of technical advance is assumed to be 1.2 percent annually, the same (we estimate) as during the current recovery. The labor force grows 1.2 percent per year, consistent with projections prepared by the Department of Labor and based on projections of population developed by the Bureau of the Census using middle-series assumptions about fertility. Thus, for an unchanged ratio of capital to output, the growth of potential output in the private business sector is 2.4 percent. Because by usual convention no growth of productivity in the public sector is assumed, growth in potential domestic output is actually close to 2.3 percent.

The baseline simulation is summarized in Table 11.2. From 1988 through 2008, real gross national product grows at an average annual rate of 2.19 percent. The unemployment rate averages 5.3 percent, inflation averages 3.9 percent, and the real rate of interest remains practically unchanged at 5.4 percent. The federal deficit, which averages 3 percent of GNP over the period, rises to $473 billion by 2008; interest payments alone reach $596 billion. The ratio of federal debt to GNP eventually stabilizes at roughly 48 percent.

Over the twenty years, net private domestic investment averages 4.6 percent of GNP; one-half (2.3 percent) of that is financed by net national saving, the other half by saving advanced by foreigners. Private net national saving averages 4.9 percent of GNP but is offset by government dissaving of 2.6 percent. The private saving rate rises over the first fifteen years of the simulation, primarily because demographic considerations raise the personal saving rate (as defined in the NIPAs) by 1.6 percentage points, from 5.2 percent to 6.8 percent, by the year 2000.

In the Washington University macroeconomic model, the real exchange rate depends on the international differential in the real rate of interest. Even though movements in the differential as sharp as those in the 1980s have pronounced effects on the exchange rate, the model implies that the mobility of capital eliminates any differential over a period of two years. Thus, as the domestic real interest rate is constant in the baseline simulation, there also is little movement in the real exchange rate. Consequently, the trade deficit remains a fairly constant share of GNP, with net foreign investment falling to $356 billion by 2008. U.S. indebtedness as a share of GNP reaches almost 30 percent by 2008; it would stabilize at a somewhat higher level several years thereafter.

In the baseline simulation, the imbalances that currently characterize the economy are sustained: The U.S. public continues to support fiscal policies that engender large federal deficits, while foreigners continue to absorb sizable flows of dollar-denominated assets at the prevailing rate of interest. In this regard it is important to emphasize that the baseline is not a forecast of what will be or even of what might reasonably be expected. Instead, it is intended only as a benchmark against which to measure the implications of alternative fiscal initiatives.

Balancing the Budget by Managing Only Outlays

In this first experiment, the budget is balanced by restraining the growth of spending sufficiently to permit the economy to grow its way out of the deficit. In particular, outlays other than Social Security and interest payments are held constant in real terms until the deficit is eliminated—in essence, the flexible freeze proposed during President

TABLE 11.2
The Baseline Simulation: Deficit = 3% of GNP

	1988	1989	1990	1991	1992	1993	1994	1995	1996	1997	1998	1999
Gross Ntl Prod (bil $82). .	4024	4146	4237	4327	4413	4499	4586	4682	4783	4888	4994	5099
Net Pay by For (bil $82). .	28	27	23	20	16	11	7	3	0	-3	-7	-10
Gross Dom Prod (bil $82)	3996	4119	4213	4307	4397	4487	4579	4678	4783	4892	5001	5110
GNP Deflator ('82 = 100).	121.3	126.3	131.5	136.8	142.2	147.7	153.5	159.5	165.7	172.1	178.8	185.7
Unemployment Rate (%)	5.5	5.3	5.3	5.3	5.3	5.3	5.3	5.3	5.3	5.3	5.3	5.3
Real Exchange Rate ('88 = 100)	100.0	106.6	106.4	105.2	103.5	102.4	102.4	102.4	102.4	102.4	102.4	102.3
Money Stock (M1, $ bil). .	776	801	848	898	952	1010	1070	1134	1203	1275	1351	1432
Treasury Bill Yield (%) . .	6.7	7.8	7.7	7.7	7.7	7.6	7.5	7.5	7.4	7.4	7.4	7.3
Corporate Bond Yield (%)	9.7	9.5	9.3	9.4	9.4	9.4	9.3	9.3	9.3	9.3	9.2	9.2
Real Interest Rate (%)	6.2	5.6	5.4	5.5	5.5	5.5	5.4	5.4	5.4	5.4	5.4	5.4
Expected Inflation (%)	3.5	3.9	3.9	3.9	3.9	3.9	3.9	3.9	3.9	3.9	3.9	3.8
— Private Nonfarm Business —												
Gross Product (bil $82). .	3127	3234	3309	3384	3455	3527	3601	3682	3767	3856	3945	4037
Labor Force (mil).	121.7	124.0	125.5	127.0	128.6	130.1	131.7	133.2	134.8	136.5	138.1	139.7
Output/Hour ($82/hr). .	19.9	20.1	20.3	20.5	20.7	20.9	21.1	21.3	21.5	21.8	22.0	22.3
Tech Adv ('88 = 100)	100.0	101.2	102.4	103.6	104.9	106.1	107.4	108.7	110.0	111.3	112.7	114.0
Capital/Output (%).	62.5	62.3	62.0	61.6	61.2	60.8	60.4	60.1	59.9	59.7	59.5	59.3
Fix Wt Defl ('82 = 100). . .	109.8	114.4	119.0	123.7	128.5	133.4	138.6	144.0	149.5	155.3	161.3	167.5
Hourly Comp ($/hr)	15.6	16.4	17.2	18.1	19.0	19.9	20.9	21.9	23.0	24.2	25.4	26.7
—Investment & Saving— (Percent of GNP)												
Gross Pvt Domestic Investment	15.4	15.0	15.1	15.1	15.0	15.1	15.2	15.5	15.7	15.9	15.9	15.9
Depreciation.	10.5	10.5	10.6	10.6	10.7	10.8	10.8	10.9	11.0	11.0	11.1	11.2
Net Pvt Dom Investment	4.9	4.6	4.5	4.4	4.3	4.3	4.4	4.6	4.8	4.9	4.9	4.8
Net National Saving. . . .	2.4	2.5	2.2	2.1	2.0	2.0	2.1	2.3	2.5	2.6	2.5	2.5
Private.	4.4	4.4	4.0	3.9	3.9	4.1	4.5	4.8	5.1	5.2	5.3	5.3
Government	-2.0	-2.0	-1.8	-1.8	-1.9	-2.1	-2.3	-2.5	-2.6	-2.7	-2.8	-2.9
Federal	-3.0	-2.9	-2.7	-2.7	-2.8	-2.9	-3.0	-3.0	-3.0	-3.1	-3.1	-3.1
State & Local	1.0	0.9	0.9	0.9	0.8	0.7	0.6	0.5	0.5	0.4	0.4	0.3
Foreign Saving	2.4	2.1	2.3	2.3	2.3	2.3	2.3	2.3	2.3	2.3	2.3	2.3
— Addenda —												
Federal Deficit (bil $). . . .	-145	-152	-150	-160	-173	-189	-208	-224	-241	-257	-277	-298
Federal Net Int (bil $) . . .	151	171	182	195	208	222	236	252	269	287	307	327
To Foreigners (bil $). . .	29	33	35	38	40	43	46	49	52	55	59	63
Federal Dbt/GNP (%) . . .	42.0	42.2	42.4	42.6	42.8	43.2	43.6	44.1	44.5	44.9	45.3	45.8
Net Exports (bil $).	-73	-62	-79	-85	-87	-92	-94	-100	-107	-114	-123	-130
Net Exports (bil $82). . . .	-74	-56	-63	-67	-66	-61	-57	-56	-57	-59	-61	-62
Net For Invest (bil $)	-117	-109	-130	-138	-145	-153	-159	-169	-181	-193	-206	-219
Foreign Dbt/GNP (%) . . .	10.0	11.5	13.0	14.5	16.0	17.4	18.6	19.8	20.9	21.9	22.9	23.8
Personal Saving Rate (%)	4.2	5.2	4.6	4.5	4.6	4.9	5.5	6.0	6.3	6.5	6.6	6.7

TABLE 11.2 (Cont.)

	2000	2001	2002	2003	2004	2005	2006	2007	2008	Annual Averages 1989-2008 Growth	Level
Gross Ntl Prod (bil $82)..	5208	5321	5440	5565	5691	5818	5945	6074	6209	2.19	5096
Net Pay by For (bil $82)..	-14	-17	-20	-24	-27	-30	-34	-37	-40		-8
Gross Dom Prod (bil $82)	5222	5339	5461	5589	5718	5848	5980	6111	6250	2.26	5104
GNP Deflator ('82 = 100).	192.9	200.4	208.2	216.2	224.6	233.3	242.4	251.8	261.6	3.92	186.6
Unemployment Rate (%)	5.3	5.3	5.3	5.3	5.3	5.3	5.3	5.3	5.3		5.3
Real Exchange Rate ('88 = 100)	102.3	102.4	102.4	102.5	102.6	102.6	102.6	102.5	102.6		103.0
Money Stock (M1, $ bil)..	1518	1609	1706	1808	1917	2032	2154	2283	2420	5.85	1471
Treasury Bill Yield (%) ..	7.3	7.3	7.4	7.4	7.4	7.4	7.5	7.5	7.5		7.5
Corporate Bond Yield (%)	9.2	9.2	9.2	9.2	9.2	9.3	9.3	9.3	9.3		9.3
Real Interest Rate (%)	5.4	5.3	5.4	5.4	5.4	5.5	5.5	5.5	5.5		5.4
Expected Inflation (%)	3.8	3.8	3.8	3.8	3.8	3.8	3.8	3.8	3.8		3.9
— Private Nonfarm Business —											
Gross Product (bil $82)..	4129	4225	4327	4433	4540	4647	4755	4862	4976	2.35	4035
Labor Force (mil).....	141.4	143.1	144.8	146.6	148.3	150.1	151.9	153.7	155.6	1.24	139.2
Output/Hour ($82/hr)..	22.5	22.7	23.0	23.3	23.6	23.8	24.1	24.4	24.6	1.07	22.2
Tech Adv ('88 = 100)	115.4	116.8	118.2	119.6	121.0	122.5	124.0	125.5	127.0	1.20	113.6
Capital/Output (%).	59.1	59.0	58.8	58.7	58.6	58.5	58.4	58.3	58.2	-0.36	59.7
Fix Wt Defl ('82 = 100)...	173.9	180.5	187.4	194.5	201.9	209.6	217.5	225.8	234.3	3.86	168.0
Hourly Comp ($/hr).....	28.0	29.4	30.9	32.4	34.0	35.7	37.5	39.4	41.3	4.99	27.1
—Investment & Saving — (Percent of GNP)											
Gross Pvt Domestic Investment...........	16.0	16.0	16.0	16.0	16.0	16.0	16.0	15.9	15.8		15.7
Depreciation........	11.2	11.3	11.3	11.3	11.4	11.4	11.4	11.4	11.4		11.1
Net Pvt Dom Investment	4.7	4.7	4.7	4.7	4.7	4.6	4.6	4.5	4.4		4.6
Net National Saving....	2.4	2.4	2.4	2.4	2.4	2.4	2.3	2.2	2.2		2.3
Private.............	5.3	5.4	5.4	5.3	5.3	5.3	5.2	5.1	5.0		4.9
Government	-2.9	-3.0	-3.0	-2.9	-2.9	-2.9	-2.9	-2.8	-2.8		-2.6
Federal	-3.2	-3.2	-3.2	-3.1	-3.1	-3.1	-3.0	-3.0	-2.9		-3.0
State & Local	0.3	0.2	0.2	0.2	0.2	0.2	0.2	0.1	0.1		0.4
Foreign Saving	2.3	2.3	2.3	2.3	2.3	2.3	2.3	2.2	2.2		2.3
— Addenda —											
Federal Deficit (bil $)....	-319	-339	-359	-376	-395	-415	-435	-455	-473		-295
Federal Net Int (bil $) ...	350	374	400	428	458	490	523	559	596		342
To Foreigners (bil $)...	68	72	77	83	89	95	101	108	116		66
Federal Dbt/GNP (%) ...	46.3	46.7	47.1	47.4	47.7	47.9	48.1	48.2	48.3		45.5
Net Exports (bil $)......	-136	-144	-152	-161	-169	-178	-185	-191	-197		-129
Net Exports (bil $82)....	-63	-64	-65	-67	-69	-70	-70	-69	-69		-64
Net For Invest (bil $)	-231	-245	-260	-276	-293	-309	-325	-340	-356		-222
Foreign Dbt/GNP (%)...	24.7	25.6	26.3	27.0	27.7	28.3	28.9	29.4	29.8		22.4
Personal Saving Rate (%)	6.8	6.8	6.8	6.7	6.6	6.6	6.5	6.4	6.2		6.0

Bush's 1988 presidential campaign. Given the projected growth in potential output, the deficit is eliminated by 1995, at which time outlays excluding interest have been reduced roughly 10 percent relative to the baseline. Thereafter, spending is managed to keep the budget in proximate balance.

The shift toward fiscal restraint is accompanied by an easier monetary policy that maintains the unemployment rate at the natural rate of 5.3 percent. This differs importantly from the usual approach to monetary accommodation. For example, in testimony before the National Economic Commission, the Congressional Budget Office (CBO) in 1988 presented results in which "accommodative" monetary policy maintained a baseline path of *output* in the face of fiscal restraint. While serving to illustrate that the Federal Reserve could engineer a smooth transition toward a balanced budget, the CBO's choice of methodology obscured the fact that altering the mix of monetary and fiscal policies could change the level of output produced at full employment.[12]

The results of this alternative are presented in Table 11.3. The shift in the mix of policy leads to a pronounced reduction in the real interest rate. By 1995, when the budget moves into balance, the real bond yield has fallen 2 percentage points relative to the baseline presented in Table 11.2; ultimately, it declines by roughly 3 full percentage points. Over the entire twenty years, growth in real gross national product averages 2.37 percent annually, 0.16 percent higher than in the baseline. In 2008, gross product of the private nonfarm business sector is 3.8 percent higher than in the baseline. Of this increase, 3.5 percentage points arise from the increase in labor productivity attributable to the capital-deepening induced by the decline in the real interest rate. In addition, however, the labor force rises by 0.3 percent as both the increase in the real wage associated with capital-deepening and the restriction of real transfers work to induce an increase in the supply of labor.

The results also shed light on the extent to which exogenous changes in government saving are offset by induced changes in either domestic private saving or in saving advanced by foreigners. In the baseline, net private domestic investment averages 4.6 percent of GNP over the next twenty years. One-half (2.3 percent) is financed by national saving, the other half by foreign saving. Net national saving is composed of private saving, which averages 4.9 percent of GNP through 2008, and government (dis)saving, which averages −2.6 percent. The federal deficit averages 3 percent of GNP over the period, while state and local governments run small surpluses that average 0.4 percent of nominal output. In the alternative simulation, the average federal deficit falls to 0.4 percent of GNP. If there were no offsetting changes in the other components of saving, net domestic investment as a share of output would rise from 4.6 percent to 7.2 percent. In fact, it rises to only 5.5 percent. Expressed differently, roughly two-thirds of the increase in federal saving is offset by a reduction in saving from other sources.

TABLE 11.3
Balancing the Budget by Managing Only Outlays

	1988	1989	1990	1991	1992	1993	1994	1995	1996	1997	1998	1999
Gross Ntl Prod (bil $82)	4024	4148	4239	4334	4426	4521	4617	4719	4832	4949	5069	5183
Net Pay by For (bil $82)	28	27	23	20	16	12	9	6	3	1	-1	-3
Gross Dom Prod (bil $82)	3996	4120	4216	4314	4409	4508	4608	4713	4828	4948	5070	5187
GNP Deflator ('82 = 100)	121.3	126.3	131.4	136.6	141.9	147.3	152.9	158.7	164.6	170.8	177.2	183.9
Unemployment Rate (%)	5.5	5.3	5.3	5.3	5.3	5.3	5.3	5.3	5.3	5.3	5.3	5.3
Real Exchange Rate ('88 = 100)	100.0	106.2	105.5	104.3	102.4	101.1	101.0	101.1	101.7	101.8	101.5	101.8
Money Stock (M1, $ bil)	776	805	859	917	981	1051	1126	1206	1278	1367	1452	1549
Treasury Bill Yield (%)	6.7	7.5	7.0	6.8	6.5	6.1	5.7	5.3	5.6	5.1	5.1	4.9
Corporate Bond Yield (%)	9.7	9.3	8.9	8.7	8.3	8.0	7.6	7.3	7.2	6.8	6.8	6.6
Real Interest Rate (%)	6.2	5.4	5.0	4.8	4.5	4.1	3.8	3.4	3.4	3.1	3.1	2.8
Expected Inflation (%)	3.5	3.9	3.9	3.9	3.9	3.9	3.9	3.8	3.8	3.8	3.8	3.7
— Private Nonfarm Business —												
Gross Product (bil $82)	3127	3235	3311	3390	3466	3546	3628	3714	3810	3909	4011	4111
Labor Force (mil)	121.7	124.0	125.6	127.1	128.7	130.3	132.0	133.6	135.2	136.9	138.5	140.2
Output/Hour ($82/hr)	19.9	20.1	20.3	20.5	20.7	20.9	21.2	21.4	21.7	22.0	22.3	22.6
Tech Adv ('88 = 100)	100.0	101.2	102.4	103.6	104.9	106.1	107.4	108.7	110.0	111.3	112.7	114.0
Capital/Output (%)	62.5	62.3	62.0	61.7	61.4	61.1	61.0	61.1	61.2	61.4	61.7	62.0
Fix Wt Defl ('82 = 100)	109.8	114.4	119.0	123.6	128.4	133.3	138.5	143.8	149.2	154.8	160.7	166.7
Hourly Comp ($/hr)	15.6	16.4	17.2	18.1	19.0	19.9	21.0	22.0	23.2	24.3	25.6	26.9
— Investment & Saving — (Percent of GNP)												
Gross Pvt Domestic Investment	15.4	15.1	15.2	15.3	15.4	15.7	16.0	16.5	16.9	17.2	17.5	17.5
Depreciation	10.5	10.5	10.6	10.6	10.7	10.8	10.9	11.1	11.2	11.3	11.4	11.6
Net Pvt Dom Investment	4.9	4.6	4.7	4.7	4.7	4.8	5.1	5.4	5.7	5.9	6.0	6.0
Net National Saving	2.4	2.5	2.3	2.4	2.5	2.7	3.0	3.4	3.8	4.0	4.1	4.0
Private	4.4	4.3	3.6	3.4	3.2	3.1	3.2	3.4	3.7	3.8	4.0	4.0
Government	-2.0	-1.8	-1.3	-1.0	-0.7	-0.4	-0.2	0.1	0.1	0.1	0.1	0.0
Federal	-3.0	-2.8	-2.2	-1.7	-1.3	-0.9	-0.5	-0.1	0.0	0.1	0.2	0.2
State & Local	1.0	0.9	0.8	0.7	0.6	0.5	0.3	0.2	0.1	0.0	-0.1	-0.1
Foreign Saving	2.4	2.1	2.3	2.3	2.2	2.1	2.0	2.0	2.0	2.0	2.0	1.9
— Addenda —												
Federal Deficit (bil $)	-145	-144	-119	-102	-82	-59	-33	-6	3	12	15	15
Federal Net Int (bil $)	151	170	178	184	188	189	189	184	180	176	171	166
To Foreigners (bil $)	29	33	34	35	36	36	36	35	35	34	33	32
Federal Dbt/GNP (%)	42.0	42.2	42.0	41.3	40.4	39.1	37.5	35.6	33.5	31.4	29.4	27.5
Net Exports (bil $)	-73	-62	-79	-83	-86	-89	-90	-94	-102	-110	-123	-128
Net Exports (bil $82)	-74	-56	-61	-63	-61	-55	-49	-46	-48	-53	-58	-59
Net For Invest (bil $)	-117	-109	-129	-134	-138	-142	-144	-148	-156	-165	-178	-183
Foreign Dbt/GNP (%)	10.0	11.5	13.0	14.5	15.8	17.0	18.1	19.0	19.8	20.6	21.3	22.0
Personal Saving Rate (%)	4.2	5.0	4.0	3.5	3.1	3.0	3.2	3.3	3.7	3.7	4.0	4.0

TABLE 11.3 (Cont.)

	2000	2001	2002	2003	2004	2005	2006	2007	2008	Annual Averages 1989–2008 Growth	Level
Gross Ntl Prod (bil $82)..	5308	5439	5575	5715	5857	5997	6137	6278	6429	2.37	5189
Net Pay by For (bil $82)..	-6	-8	-9	-11	-12	-14	-16	-17	-18		0
Gross Dom Prod (bil $82)	5314	5447	5585	5726	5870	6011	6153	6296	6448	2.42	5189
GNP Deflator ('82 = 100).	190.8	197.9	205.3	213.1	221.2	229.6	238.3	247.4	256.6	3.82	184.6
Unemployment Rate (%)	5.3	5.3	5.3	5.3	5.3	5.3	5.3	5.3	5.3		5.3
Real Exchange Rate ('88 = 100)	101.6	101.8	101.8	101.9	102.0	102.1	102.2	102.3	102.3		102.3
Money Stock (M1, $ bil)..	1652	1759	1874	1995	2124	2259	2401	2552	2713	6.46	1596
Treasury Bill Yield (%) ..	4.8	4.7	4.6	4.5	4.5	4.5	4.4	4.4	4.3		5.3
Corporate Bond Yield (%)	6.5	6.3	6.2	6.1	6.1	6.0	5.9	5.9	5.8		7.0
Real Interest Rate (%)	2.7	2.6	2.5	2.4	2.3	2.3	2.2	2.2	2.1		3.2
Expected Inflation (%)	3.7	3.7	3.7	3.7	3.7	3.7	3.7	3.7	3.7		3.8
— Private Nonfarm Business —											
Gross Product (bil $82)..	4217	4330	4446	4565	4687	4805	4922	5040	5167	2.54	4116
Labor Force (mil).....	141.9	143.6	145.4	147.1	148.9	150.7	152.5	154.3	156.1	1.25	139.6
Output/Hour ($82/hr)..	22.9	23.2	23.5	23.9	24.2	24.5	24.8	25.2	25.5	1.25	22.6
Tech Adv ('88 = 100)	115.4	116.8	118.2	119.6	121.0	122.5	124.0	125.5	127.0	1.20	113.6
Capital/Output (%).	62.3	62.6	63.0	63.4	63.7	64.1	64.4	64.8	65.1	0.20	62.5
Fix Wt Defl ('82 = 100)...	172.9	179.3	186.0	192.9	200.1	207.6	215.3	223.3	231.5	3.80	167.1
Hourly Comp ($/hr).....	28.3	29.7	31.3	32.9	34.6	36.4	38.2	40.2	42.2	5.10	27.4
—Investment & Saving— (Percent of GNP)											
Gross Pvt Domestic Investment	17.7	17.9	18.0	18.1	18.2	18.2	18.1	18.0	18.0		17.0
Depreciation........	11.7	11.8	12.0	12.1	12.2	12.3	12.3	12.4	12.4		11.5
Net Pvt Dom Investment	6.0	6.0	6.0	6.0	6.0	5.9	5.8	5.6	5.5		5.5
Net National Saving....	4.1	4.1	4.2	4.2	4.2	4.2	4.1	4.0	3.9		3.6
Private.............	4.1	4.1	4.1	4.1	4.1	4.1	4.1	4.0	3.9		3.8
Government	0.0	0.0	0.0	0.0	0.1	0.0	0.0	0.0	0.0		-0.2
Federal	0.2	0.2	0.2	0.2	0.2	0.1	0.1	0.0	0.0		-0.4
State & Local	-0.1	-0.1	-0.1	-0.1	-0.1	-0.1	-0.1	-0.1	0.0		0.2
Foreign Saving	1.9	1.9	1.9	1.8	1.8	1.8	1.7	1.7	1.6		2.0
— Addenda —											
Federal Deficit (bil $)....	16	17	18	19	19	16	10	4	0		-19
Federal Net Int (bil $) ...	161	157	152	148	144	141	138	135	133		164
To Foreigners (bil $)...	31	30	29	28	28	27	26	26	25		31
Federal Dbt/GNP (%) ...	25.8	24.1	22.5	21.0	19.6	18.3	17.1	16.1	15.1		29.0
Net Exports (bil $)......	-138	-147	-156	-165	-174	-181	-187	-192	-199		-129
Net Exports (bil $82)....	-61	-64	-67	-69	-71	-72	-73	-73	-74		-62
Net For Invest (bil $)	-194	-204	-214	-224	-235	-243	-251	-259	-267		-186
Foreign Dbt/GNP (%) ...	22.6	23.1	23.6	24.0	24.3	24.6	24.9	25.1	25.2		20.5
Personal Saving Rate (%)	4.1	4.1	4.1	4.0	4.0	4.0	3.9	3.8	3.7		3.8

Private saving falls by almost one-quarter, from 4.9 percent of GNP to 3.8 percent, while foreign saving falls by roughly one-eighth, from 2.3 percent to 2 percent.

Private saving relative to GNP mirrors the personal saving rate, which as measured in the NIPAs drops from an average of 6 percent of personal disposable income in the baseline to only 3.8 percent under the flexible freeze. The personal saving rate falls partly because the decline in the real rate of interest reduces the share of personal income attributable to interest income and from which we estimate the propensity to consume is small. But the lower real interest rate also encourages personal consumption expenditures relative to income by lowering the cost of durable goods and by raising the value of household net worth.

Perhaps the most interesting aspect of the simulation is the dynamic path of interest payments and the resulting implication for future fiscal policy. Even with constant interest rates, interest payments in the baseline simulation grow slightly faster than GNP as the ratio of debt to output asymptotically approaches roughly 49 percent. In the alternative, and once the budget is balanced, interest payments are roughly constant in absolute terms and decline between 6 percent and 7 percent annually as a share of GNP. As a result, if the flexible freeze is maintained beyond 1995, the budget moves sharply into surplus. To prevent this occurrence, starting in 1996 growth in the exogenous components of federal spending is raised above the rate of growth in potential output. Therefore, from 1996 through 2008, federal spending, excluding interest and measured as a share of GNP, gradually rises toward its value in the baseline (see Figure 11.4). A similar pattern is prevalent in all ensuing simulations of deficit reduction and underscores an important conclusion. Policies to reduce the deficit now generate a kind of fiscal dividend later that can, in principle, be used to repay part of the national debt, to reduce taxes, or, as here, to fund additional spending. As will become apparent, it is the disposition of this fiscal dividend that most distinguishes the macroeconomic impacts of competing plans to reduce the deficit.

Finally, before the implications of alternative proposals to reduce the deficit are considered further, a methodology for contrasting them must be established. The convention adopted here is to compare the cumulative present discounted value of the gains in potential output (relative to the baseline) realized over the next twenty years. The computation is made using the real interest rate associated with the balanced budget. Thus, for example, through 2008 the present value of the cumulative gain in real GNP associated with the flexible freeze is $1,108 billion, or 28 percent of the 1988 level of output.

Balancing the Budget by Managing Only Income Taxes

In this second experiment, a tax surcharge is imposed on personal and corporate income; the surcharge is gradually raised to eliminate

FIGURE 11.4
Expenditure Rates
(managed outlays relative to base)

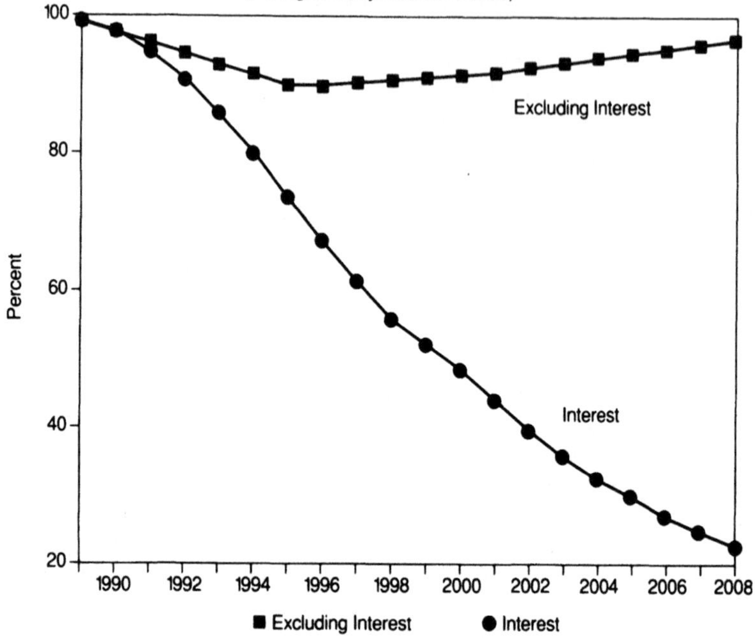

FIGURE 11.5
Tax and Expenditure Rates
(managed taxes relative to base)

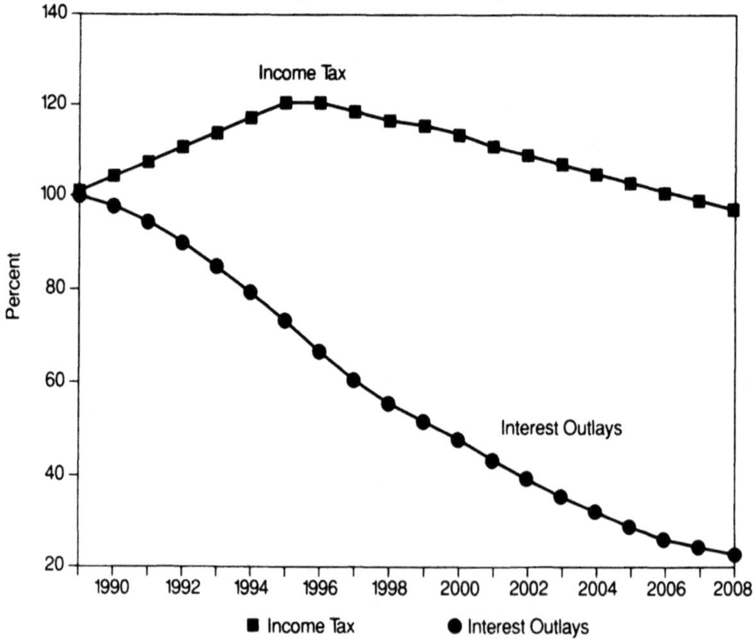

the deficit by 1995, the same year that a balanced budget was achieved under the flexible freeze. The surcharge itself reaches 24 percent of tax rates in the baseline by 1995 but then is gradually reduced to maintain the budget in proximate balance as interest payments shrink relative to the GNP. By 2008, income tax rates have returned to their value in the baseline (see Figure 11.5). The initial shift toward fiscal restraint is accommodated by an easier monetary policy that keeps the unemployment rate at the natural rate of 5.3 percent. The results of the simulation are summarized in Table 11.4. The patterns of the real interest rate, saving, and investment are broadly similar to those considered at length in the preceding discussion of the flexible freeze. By 2008, the level of GNP under the income tax surcharge is 3.1 percent above the baseline, seemingly not much different from the 3.5 percent increase realized under the flexible freeze. Yet this comparison obscures that for most of the twenty years, the level of output under the income tax surcharge is substantially less than under the freeze, and for the first ten years it is even below the level of the baseline. Thus, the present value of the cumulative gain in GNP under the surcharge is just $259 billion, or roughly 6 percent of 1988 GNP, and only one-quarter of the gain accrued through restraint on spending.

This result arises because marginal income tax rates, although not much different by 2008 than in the baseline, are on average some 14 percent higher over the entire twenty years. Higher marginal rates reduce potential output in two ways. First, because the supply of labor is an increasing function of the after-tax real wage rate, the higher personal income tax rate reduces the labor force 0.4 percent below the baseline on average. This is in contrast to the flexible freeze, under which the restriction of real transfers *raises* the labor force by 0.3 percent. Second, the higher corporate income tax rate raises the cost of capital associated with any real rate of interest, thereby mitigating the extent of capital-deepening associated with the balanced budget.

Balancing the Budget by Managing Outlays and Income Taxes

In this third experiment, a flexible freeze is imposed until the deficit is eliminated in 1995. Thereafter, the opportunity provided by the declining share of interest in GNP is used to embark on a gradual reduction in the tax rates on personal and corporate income while maintaining the budget in proximate balance. By 2008, marginal tax rates are reduced 20 percent relative to the baseline (see Figure 11.6). The initial shift toward fiscal restraint is accommodated by an easier monetary policy that keeps the unemployment rate at the natural rate of 5.3 percent. The results are summarized in Table 11.5.

This plan incorporates the best elements of the previous two. Initially, restraint on the growth of spending leads to a substantial reduction in the real interest rate that raises potential output primarily via capital-

TABLE 11.4
Balancing the Budget by Managing Only Income Taxes

	1988	1989	1990	1991	1992	1993	1994	1995	1996	1997	1998	1999
Gross Ntl Prod (bil $82) . .	4024	4144	4225	4309	4388	4465	4544	4632	4737	4854	4975	5095
Net Pay by For (bil $82) . .	28	27	23	19	15	10	7	3	1	-1	-3	-6
Gross Dom Prod (bil $82)	3996	4116	4202	4290	4373	4454	4537	4628	4736	4856	4979	5101
GNP Deflator ('82 = 100) .	121.3	126.3	131.5	136.8	142.1	147.6	153.3	159.2	165.2	171.5	177.9	184.6
Unemployment Rate (%)	5.5	5.3	5.3	5.3	5.3	5.3	5.3	5.3	5.3	5.3	5.3	5.3
Real Exchange Rate ('88 = 100)	100.0	106.5	105.9	104.3	102.4	101.2	101.1	100.9	101.2	101.7	101.7	101.7
Money Stock (M1, $ bil) . .	776	801	851	907	967	1030	1099	1175	1252	1331	1418	1512
Treasury Bill Yield (%) . .	6.7	7.7	7.3	7.1	6.7	6.4	6.0	5.6	5.5	5.4	5.3	5.2
Corporate Bond Yield (%)	9.7	9.4	9.1	8.9	8.6	8.3	8.0	7.6	7.3	7.2	7.0	6.9
Real Interest Rate (%)	6.2	5.5	5.2	5.0	4.8	4.4	4.1	3.7	3.5	3.4	3.2	3.1
Expected Inflation (%)	3.5	3.9	3.9	3.9	3.9	3.9	3.9	3.8	3.8	3.8	3.8	3.8
— Private Nonfarm Business —												
Gross Product (bil $82) . .	3127	3231	3299	3367	3432	3495	3560	3634	3722	3822	3924	4029
Labor Force (mil)	121.7	124.0	125.3	126.6	127.9	129.2	130.5	131.8	133.3	135.0	136.8	138.6
Output/Hour ($82/hr) . .	19.9	20.1	20.3	20.5	20.7	20.9	21.1	21.3	21.6	21.9	22.2	22.4
Tech Adv ('88 = 100)	100.0	101.2	102.4	103.6	104.9	106.1	107.4	108.7	110.0	111.3	112.7	114.0
Capital/Output (%) .	62.5	62.3	62.0	61.6	61.3	61.0	60.8	60.7	60.6	60.7	60.8	61.0
Fix Wt Defl ('82 = 100) . . .	109.8	114.4	119.0	123.6	128.4	133.4	138.5	143.8	149.3	154.9	160.8	166.9
Hourly Comp ($/hr)	15.6	16.4	17.2	18.1	19.0	19.9	20.9	22.0	23.1	24.3	25.5	26.8
— Investment & Saving — (Percent of GNP)												
Gross Pvt Domestic Investment	15.4	15.0	15.1	15.1	15.2	15.3	15.6	16.0	16.4	16.7	16.9	17.1
Depreciation	10.5	10.5	10.6	10.7	10.7	10.9	11.0	11.1	11.1	11.2	11.3	11.4
Net Pvt Dom Investment	4.9	4.6	4.5	4.5	4.4	4.5	4.6	4.9	5.2	5.5	5.6	5.7
Net National Saving	2.4	2.5	2.2	2.2	2.2	2.3	2.6	2.9	3.3	3.6	3.7	3.8
Private	4.4	4.3	3.6	3.2	2.9	2.7	2.7	2.7	2.9	3.2	3.3	3.5
Government	-2.0	-1.9	-1.4	-1.0	-0.7	-0.4	-0.1	0.2	0.4	0.4	0.3	0.3
Federal	-3.0	-2.8	-2.2	-1.8	-1.4	-1.0	-0.6	-0.1	0.1	0.2	0.2	0.1
State & Local	1.0	0.9	0.9	0.8	0.7	0.6	0.5	0.4	0.3	0.2	0.2	0.1
Foreign Saving	2.4	2.1	2.3	2.3	2.2	2.1	2.0	1.9	1.9	1.9	1.9	1.9
— Addenda —												
Federal Deficit (bil $)	-145	-146	-124	-108	-89	-68	-41	-7	9	13	14	12
Federal Net Int (bil $) . . .	151	171	180	187	193	196	196	193	188	184	179	174
To Foreigners (bil $) . . .	29	33	35	36	37	38	38	37	36	35	34	34
Federal Dbt/GNP (%) . . .	42.0	42.2	42.2	41.7	41.0	39.9	38.5	36.7	34.5	32.3	30.2	28.3
Net Exports (bil $)	-73	-62	-78	-82	-83	-84	-83	-85	-91	-101	-112	-121
Net Exports (bil $82)	-74	-56	-61	-62	-59	-51	-43	-39	-40	-45	-50	-53
Net For Invest (bil $)	-117	-109	-128	-134	-137	-140	-140	-143	-149	-159	-171	-180
Foreign Dbt/GNP (%) . . .	10.0	11.5	13.0	14.5	15.9	17.2	18.3	19.2	20.0	20.6	21.3	21.9
Personal Saving Rate (%)	4.2	5.1	4.1	3.5	3.1	3.0	3.0	2.9	3.1	3.3	3.5	3.7

TABLE 11.4 (Cont.)

	2000	2001	2002	2003	2004	2005	2006	2007	2008	Annual Averages 1989-2008 Growth	Level
Gross Ntl Prod (bil $82)	5220	5352	5490	5636	5784	5934	6087	6240	6403	2.35	5126
Net Pay by For (bil $82)	-8	-10	-11	-13	-14	-15	-16	-17	-18		-1
Gross Dom Prod (bil $82)	5229	5362	5502	5649	5799	5950	6103	6258	6422	2.40	5127
GNP Deflator ('82 = 100)	191.6	198.8	206.2	213.9	221.9	230.1	238.7	247.6	256.7	3.82	185.1
Unemployment Rate (%)	5.3	5.3	5.3	5.3	5.3	5.3	5.3	5.3	5.3		5.3
Real Exchange Rate ('88 = 100)	101.8	101.9	101.9	102.0	102.0	102.1	102.1	102.1	102.1		102.3
Money Stock (M1, $ bil)	1612	1720	1834	1957	2088	2229	2378	2538	2708	6.45	1570
Treasury Bill Yield (%)	5.0	4.9	4.8	4.7	4.6	4.5	4.4	4.3	4.2		5.5
Corporate Bond Yield (%)	6.7	6.6	6.5	6.3	6.2	6.1	6.0	5.9	5.8		7.2
Real Interest Rate (%)	3.0	2.8	2.7	2.6	2.5	2.4	2.3	2.2	2.1		3.4
Expected Inflation (%)	3.8	3.7	3.7	3.7	3.7	3.7	3.7	3.6	3.6		3.8
— Private Nonfarm Business —											
Gross Product (bil $82)	4137	4249	4368	4493	4620	4747	4877	5006	5144	2.52	4058
Labor Force (mil)	140.4	142.3	144.2	146.1	148.1	150.1	152.1	154.1	156.1	1.25	138.6
Output/Hour ($82/hr)	22.7	23.0	23.4	23.7	24.0	24.4	24.7	25.0	25.4	1.23	22.5
Tech Adv ('88 = 100)	115.4	116.8	118.2	119.6	121.0	122.5	124.0	125.5	127.0	1.20	113.6
Capital/Output (%)	61.2	61.5	61.7	62.0	62.4	62.7	63.0	63.4	63.8	0.10	61.7
Fix Wt Defl ('82 = 100)	173.1	179.6	186.2	193.1	200.2	207.6	215.1	223.0	231.0	3.79	167.1
Hourly Comp ($/hr)	28.2	29.6	31.1	32.7	34.4	36.1	37.9	39.9	41.9	5.06	27.3
—Investment & Saving— (Percent of GNP)											
Gross Pvt Domestic Investment	17.3	17.5	17.6	17.8	17.9	18.0	18.0	18.0	18.0		16.7
Depreciation	11.5	11.6	11.7	11.8	11.9	12.0	12.1	12.1	12.2		11.4
Net Pvt Dom Investment	5.8	5.8	5.9	6.0	6.0	6.0	6.0	5.9	5.8		5.4
Net National Saving	3.9	3.9	4.0	4.1	4.2	4.2	4.2	4.2	4.2		3.4
Private	3.6	3.8	3.9	4.0	4.1	4.1	4.2	4.1	4.1		3.5
Government	0.2	0.1	0.1	0.1	0.1	0.1	0.1	0.0	0.0		-0.2
Federal	0.1	0.1	0.1	0.1	0.1	0.1	0.1	0.0	0.0		-0.4
State & Local	0.1	0.1	0.0	0.0	0.0	0.0	0.0	0.0	0.0		0.3
Foreign Saving	1.9	1.9	1.9	1.8	1.8	1.8	1.7	1.7	1.6		1.9
— Addenda —											
Federal Deficit (bil $)	10	9	8	10	10	9	7	4	4		-23
Federal Net Int (bil $)	170	165	161	157	153	149	146	142	139		171
To Foreigners (bil $)	33	32	31	30	29	29	28	27	27		33
Federal Dbt/GNP (%)	26.5	24.8	23.2	21.7	20.3	19.0	17.8	16.7	15.7		29.7
Net Exports (bil $)	-130	-139	-149	-159	-169	-178	-186	-191	-198		-124
Net Exports (bil $82)	-56	-59	-62	-65	-68	-70	-71	-71	-72		-58
Net For Invest (bil $)	-190	-200	-211	-222	-233	-243	-252	-260	-268		-183
Foreign Dbt/GNP (%)	22.5	23.0	23.4	23.8	24.2	24.5	24.7	24.9	25.0		20.5
Personal Saving Rate (%)	3.8	4.0	4.0	4.0	4.0	4.0	4.0	3.9	3.8		3.7

FIGURE 11.6
Tax and Expenditure Rates
(managed outlays/taxes relative to base)

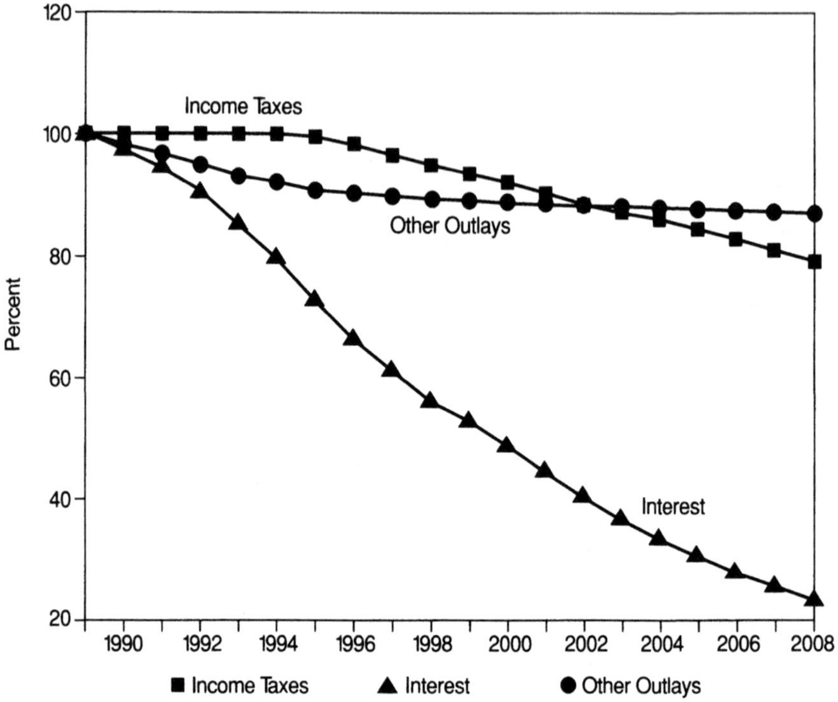

deepening; a reduction in real transfers also induces a small increase in the labor force. The fiscal dividend gained from balancing the budget is then used to reduce marginal tax rates. The effect is to induce both further increases in the labor force and a gradual reduction in the cost of capital associated with any real rate of interest. Both factors augment the increases in potential output already generated by the earlier elimination of the deficit.

Over the full twenty years, the average rate of growth in real GNP is raised by 0.29 percentage point relative to the baseline. By 2008, the level of real gross product in the nonfarm business sector is higher by 6 percent; the labor force is up by 2 percent, and labor productivity rises by 4 percent. The cumulative gain in the present value of real GNP associated with the policy is $1,534 billion, or 38 percent of 1988 GNP. The gain associated with this plan exceeds by 36 percent the gain in output realized under the flexible freeze, and it is more than six times greater than the gain achieved when the budget is balanced with taxes alone.

Balancing the Budget with a Value-Added Tax

In this fourth experiment, the deficit is eliminated through the introduction of a consumption-based value-added tax (VAT) that grad-

TABLE 11.5
Balancing the Budget by Managing Outlays and Income Taxes

	1988	1989	1990	1991	1992	1993	1994	1995	1996	1997	1998	1999
Gross Ntl Prod (bil $82). .	4024	4148	4239	4334	4426	4521	4617	4720	4840	4960	5084	5209
Net Pay by For (bil $82). .	28	27	23	20	16	12	9	6	4	1	0	-3
Gross Dom Prod (bil $82)	3996	4120	4216	4314	4409	4508	4608	4713	4836	4959	5084	5212
GNP Deflator ('82 = 100).	121.3	126.3	131.4	136.6	141.9	147.3	152.9	158.7	164.6	170.8	177.2	183.9
Unemployment Rate (%)	5.5	5.3	5.3	5.3	5.3	5.3	5.3	5.3	5.3	5.3	5.3	5.3
Real Exchange Rate ('88 = 100)	100.0	106.2	105.5	104.3	102.4	101.1	101.0	101.1	101.6	101.9	101.6	101.8
Money Stock (M1, $ bil). .	776	805	859	917	981	1051	1126	1206	1282	1365	1457	1556
Treasury Bill Yield (%) . .	6.7	7.5	7.0	6.8	6.5	6.1	5.7	5.4	5.4	5.2	5.1	4.9
Corporate Bond Yield (%)	9.7	9.3	8.9	8.7	8.3	8.0	7.6	7.3	7.2	6.9	6.8	6.6
Real Interest Rate (%)	6.2	5.4	5.0	4.8	4.5	4.1	3.8	3.4	3.3	3.2	3.0	2.9
Expected Inflation (%)	3.5	3.9	3.9	3.9	3.9	3.9	3.9	3.8	3.8	3.8	3.8	3.7
— Private Nonfarm Business —												
Gross Product (bil $82). .	3127	3235	3311	3390	3466	3546	3628	3715	3818	3920	4025	4135
Labor Force (mil).	121.7	124.0	125.6	127.1	128.7	130.3	132.0	133.6	135.3	137.1	138.9	140.7
Output/Hour ($82/hr). .	19.9	20.1	20.3	20.5	20.7	20.9	21.2	21.4	21.7	22.0	22.3	22.6
Tech Adv ('88 = 100)	100.0	101.2	102.4	103.6	104.9	106.1	107.4	108.7	110.0	111.3	112.7	114.0
Capital/Output (%).	62.5	62.3	62.0	61.7	61.4	61.1	61.0	61.1	61.2	61.4	61.7	62.0
Fix Wt Defl ('82 = 100). . .	109.8	114.4	119.0	123.6	128.4	133.3	138.5	143.8	149.2	154.9	160.7	166.7
Hourly Comp ($/hr)	15.6	16.4	17.2	18.1	19.0	19.9	21.0	22.0	23.2	24.3	25.6	26.9
—Investment & Saving — (Percent of GNP)												
Gross Pvt Domestic Investment	15.4	15.1	15.2	15.3	15.4	15.7	16.0	16.5	16.9	17.2	17.5	17.7
Depreciation.	10.5	10.5	10.6	10.6	10.7	10.8	10.9	11.1	11.1	11.3	11.4	11.5
Net Pvt Dom Investment	4.9	4.6	4.7	4.7	4.7	4.8	5.1	5.4	5.8	6.0	6.1	6.1
Net National Saving. . . .	2.4	2.5	2.3	2.4	2.5	2.7	3.0	3.4	3.8	4.0	4.1	4.1
Private.	4.4	4.3	3.6	3.4	3.2	3.1	3.2	3.4	3.8	4.0	4.2	4.3
Government	-2.0	-1.8	-1.3	-1.0	-0.7	-0.4	-0.2	0.0	0.0	0.0	-0.1	-0.2
Federal	-3.0	-2.8	-2.2	-1.7	-1.3	-0.9	-0.5	-0.1	0.0	0.0	0.0	0.0
State & Local	1.0	0.9	0.8	0.7	0.6	0.5	0.3	0.2	0.1	0.0	-0.1	-0.1
Foreign Saving	2.4	2.1	2.3	2.3	2.2	2.1	2.0	2.0	2.0	2.0	2.0	2.0
— Addenda —												
Federal Deficit (bil $). . . .	-145	-144	-119	-102	-82	-59	-33	-8	-2	-1	-1	-3
Federal Net Int (bil $) . . .	151	170	178	184	188	189	188	184	180	177	173	168
To Foreigners (bil $). . .	29	33	34	35	36	36	36	35	35	34	33	32
Federal Dbt/GNP (%) . . .	42.0	42.2	42.0	41.3	40.4	39.1	37.5	35.6	33.5	31.5	29.7	27.9
Net Exports (bil $).	-73	-62	-79	-83	-86	-89	-90	-94	-103	-113	-124	-133
Net Exports (bil $82). . . .	-74	-56	-61	-63	-61	-55	-49	-46	-49	-54	-59	-62
Net For Invest (bil $)	-117	-109	-129	-134	-138	-142	-144	-148	-157	-167	-179	-189
Foreign Dbt/GNP (%) . . .	10.0	11.5	13.0	14.5	15.8	17.0	18.1	19.0	19.8	20.6	21.3	22.0
Personal Saving Rate (%)	4.2	5.0	4.0	3.5	3.1	3.0	3.2	3.3	3.8	4.0	4.2	4.3

TABLE 11.5 (Cont.)

	2000	2001	2002	2003	2004	2005	2006	2007	2008	Annual Averages 1989–2008 Growth	Level
Gross Ntl Prod (bil $82)	5339	5475	5622	5773	5925	6080	6237	6395	6563	2.48	5225
Net Pay by For (bil $82)	-5	-6	-8	-9	-10	-11	-12	-12	-13		1
Gross Dom Prod (bil $82)	5344	5482	5630	5783	5935	6092	6249	6408	6576	2.52	5224
GNP Deflator ('82 = 100)	190.7	197.7	205.0	212.6	220.4	228.6	237.0	245.8	254.8	3.78	184.2
Unemployment Rate (%)	5.4	5.4	5.3	5.3	5.3	5.3	5.3	5.3	5.3		5.31
Real Exchange Rate ('88 = 100)	101.8	101.9	101.9	101.9	102.0	102.0	102.0	102.0	102.1		102.3
Money Stock (M1, $ bil)	1661	1773	1892	2020	2157	2302	2458	2624	2797	6.62	1614
Treasury Bill Yield (%)	4.8	4.6	4.5	4.4	4.3	4.2	4.1	4.0	3.9		5.2
Corporate Bond Yield (%)	6.5	6.3	6.2	6.0	5.9	5.8	5.7	5.5	5.5		7.0
Real Interest Rate (%)	2.7	2.6	2.5	2.4	2.3	2.1	2.0	1.9	1.9		3.2
Expected Inflation (%)	3.7	3.7	3.7	3.7	3.7	3.6	3.6	3.6	3.6		3.8
— Private Nonfarm Business —											
Gross Product (bil $82)	4246	4363	4490	4619	4749	4881	5014	5147	5289	2.66	4149
Labor Force (mil)	142.6	144.5	146.4	148.3	150.3	152.2	154.2	156.2	158.3	1.32	140.3
Output/Hour ($82/hr)	22.9	23.2	23.6	23.9	24.3	24.6	24.9	25.3	25.6	1.27	22.6
Tech Adv ('88 = 100)	115.4	116.8	118.2	119.6	121.0	122.5	124.0	125.5	127.0	1.20	113.6
Capital/Output (%)	62.3	62.7	63.1	63.5	63.9	64.3	64.8	65.2	65.6	0.24	62.6
Fix Wt Defl ('82 = 100)	172.8	179.2	185.7	192.5	199.5	206.8	214.2	222.0	230.0	3.77	166.8
Hourly Comp ($/hr)	28.3	29.7	31.2	32.8	34.5	36.3	38.1	40.0	42.0	5.08	27.3
— Investment & Saving — (Percent of GNP)											
Gross Pvt Domestic Investment	17.8	18.0	18.2	18.3	18.4	18.5	18.5	18.5	18.5		17.2
Depreciation	11.7	11.8	11.9	12.0	12.1	12.2	12.3	12.4	12.5		11.5
Net Pvt Dom Investment	6.1	6.2	6.2	6.3	6.3	6.3	6.2	6.1	6.0		5.7
Net National Saving	4.2	4.2	4.3	4.4	4.4	4.4	4.4	4.4	4.4		3.7
Private	4.4	4.5	4.6	4.6	4.6	4.7	4.7	4.6	4.6		4.1
Government	-0.2	-0.3	-0.2	-0.2	-0.2	-0.2	-0.2	-0.2	-0.2		-0.4
Federal	-0.1	-0.1	-0.1	0.0	0.0	0.0	-0.1	-0.1	-0.1		-0.5
State & Local	-0.2	-0.2	-0.2	-0.2	-0.2	-0.2	-0.2	-0.2	-0.1		0.1
Foreign Saving	2.0	1.9	1.9	1.9	1.9	1.8	1.8	1.7	1.7		2.0
— Addenda —											
Federal Deficit (bil $)	-5	-7	-5	-4	-5	-6	-7	-10	-11		-31
Federal Net Int (bil $)	164	160	157	153	150	146	143	140	137		166
To Foreigners (bil $)	32	31	30	29	29	28	27	27	26		32
Federal Dbt/GNP (%)	26.3	24.8	23.4	22.0	20.7	19.5	18.4	17.3	16.4		29.5
Net Exports (bil $)	-142	-152	-163	-174	-184	-193	-202	-208	-216		-135
Net Exports (bil $82)	-65	-68	-71	-75	-77	-79	-80	-81	-81		-65
Net For Invest (bil $)	-198	-209	-221	-233	-243	-254	-264	-272	-281		-191
Foreign Dbt/GNP (%)	22.6	23.1	23.6	24.0	24.4	24.7	25.0	25.3	25.4		20.5
Personal Saving Rate (%)	4.4	4.5	4.5	4.4	4.4	4.3	4.2	4.1	4.0		4.0

ually rises to 6 percent by 1995. Thereafter, marginal tax rates on both personal and corporate income are reduced to maintain the budget in proximate balance as the share of interest payments in GNP declines. By 2008, income tax rates fall by roughly 20 percent relative to the baseline. The initial shift toward fiscal restraint is accompanied by an easier monetary policy that keeps the unemployment rate at the natural rate of 5.3 percent. The results are summarized in Table 11.6.

In the Washington University model, a value-added tax raises consumer prices relative to wages, thereby reducing the real wage received by households and, as a consequence, discouraging the supply of labor. Thus, in one regard the introduction of a VAT followed by a reduction in income tax rates is conceptually similar to the previous experiment in which income taxes are raised and then lowered. But unlike an increase in income tax rates, imposition of the VAT does not itself raise the cost of capital. Accordingly, balancing the budget with a VAT is likely to prove more advantageous than relying on income taxes but less advantageous than restraining the growth of outlays.

These suppositions are indeed manifested in the results. By 2008, real GNP is 3.5 percent above the baseline, the same increase as under the flexible freeze. As in the case of the income tax surcharge, however, this comparison conceals that for part of the twenty years the level of output is actually below that of the baseline. Thus, the present value of the cumulative gain in GNP under the surcharge is just $582 billion (14 percent of 1988 GNP), one-half the gain accrued under the flexible freeze and only one-third the gain realized by restraining spending and then lowering taxes.

More on International Considerations

In the previous experiments, the real exchange rate, which in the model depends importantly on the differential between the real rate of interest in the United States and that abroad, remains relatively unchanged over the twenty years of the simulations. The reason for this constancy is that while the domestic real interest rate falls with the changing mix of monetary and fiscal policies in the United States, the foreign real interest rate is assumed to follow the domestic yield down with a lag sufficiently short (two years) that a sustained differential never arises. This seems contrary to the experience of the 1980s, when sharply divergent fiscal policies here and abroad temporarily raised the real interest rate in the United States some 6 percentage points relative to the real yield earned abroad. If as the deficit declined the real interest rate in the United States temporarily did fall relative to that abroad, the real exchange rate would fall temporarily and real exports would rise temporarily, thereby absorbing a portion of national saving that would otherwise be allocated to domestic investment and undermining both the decline in the domestic real interest rate and the increase in

TABLE 11.6
Balancing the Budget with a Value-Added Tax

	1988	1989	1990	1991	1992	1993	1994	1995	1996	1997	1998	1999
Gross Ntl Prod (bil $82)..	4024	4145	4231	4318	4401	4485	4570	4665	4774	4889	5012	5127
Net Pay by For (bil $82)..	28	27	24	21	17	13	10	7	3	0	-4	-8
Gross Dom Prod (bil $82)	3996	4118	4206	4296	4384	4471	4560	4658	4770	4890	5016	5136
GNP Deflator ('82 = 100).	121.3	126.6	132.6	138.8	145.2	151.7	158.6	165.7	172.4	178.8	185.5	192.4
Unemployment Rate (%)	5.5	5.3	5.3	5.3	5.3	5.3	5.3	5.3	5.3	5.4	5.3	5.4
Real Exchange Rate ('88 = 100)	100.0	106.4	105.7	104.5	102.7	101.5	101.5	101.3	101.9	102.3	101.9	102.0
Money Stock (M1, $ bil)..	776	805	863	925	992	1064	1143	1231	1307	1388	1477	1574
Treasury Bill Yield (%) ..	6.7	7.6	7.2	7.0	6.7	6.4	6.0	5.6	5.9	5.6	5.6	5.3
Corporate Bond Yield (%)	9.7	9.3	9.0	8.8	8.5	8.2	7.9	7.6	7.6	7.3	7.3	7.1
Real Interest Rate (%)	6.2	5.4	5.0	4.9	4.7	4.4	4.1	3.8	3.8	3.6	3.5	3.4
Expected Inflation (%)	3.5	3.9	3.9	3.9	3.9	3.9	3.9	3.8	3.8	3.8	3.8	3.7
— Private Nonfarm Business —												
Gross Product (bil $82)..	3127	3233	3303	3373	3442	3511	3582	3662	3755	3854	3960	4063
Labor Force (mil).....	121.7	124.0	125.4	126.8	128.1	129.5	131.0	132.4	134.0	135.7	137.5	139.3
Output/Hour ($82/hr)..	19.9	20.1	20.3	20.5	20.7	20.9	21.1	21.4	21.6	21.9	22.2	22.5
Tech Adv ('88 = 100)	100.0	101.2	102.4	103.6	104.9	106.1	107.4	108.7	110.0	111.3	112.7	114.0
Capital/Output (%).	62.5	62.3	62.0	61.6	61.3	61.1	60.9	60.9	61.0	61.1	61.3	61.5
Fix Wt Defl ('82 = 100)...	109.8	114.4	119.0	123.6	128.4	133.3	138.4	143.7	149.1	154.7	160.5	166.5
Hourly Comp ($/hr).....	15.6	16.4	17.2	18.1	19.0	19.9	20.9	22.0	23.1	24.3	25.5	26.8
— Investment & Saving — (Percent of GNP)												
Gross Pvt Domestic Investment...........	15.4	15.1	15.2	15.3	15.3	15.6	15.9	16.4	16.8	17.1	17.4	17.5
Depreciation.........	10.5	10.5	10.6	10.7	10.8	10.9	11.1	11.2	11.3	11.4	11.5	11.6
Net Pvt Dom Investment	4.9	4.6	4.6	4.6	4.5	4.6	4.8	5.2	5.5	5.7	5.9	5.9
Net National Saving....	2.4	2.5	2.2	2.1	2.1	2.1	2.4	2.7	3.0	3.1	3.2	3.2
Private.............	4.4	4.3	3.5	3.1	2.7	2.6	2.5	2.6	2.9	3.1	3.3	3.4
Government	-2.0	-1.8	-1.3	-0.9	-0.7	-0.4	-0.2	0.1	0.1	0.0	-0.1	-0.2
Federal	-3.0	-2.7	-2.1	-1.7	-1.3	-0.9	-0.5	0.0	0.0	0.0	0.0	-0.1
State & Local	1.0	0.9	0.8	0.8	0.6	0.5	0.3	0.1	0.0	0.0	-0.1	-0.1
Foreign Saving........	2.4	2.1	2.4	2.4	2.4	2.5	2.5	2.5	2.6	2.6	2.7	2.7
— Addenda —												
Federal Deficit (bil $)....	-145	-143	-119	-101	-82	-61	-35	-3	3	2	0	-5
Federal Net Int (bil $) ...	151	170	178	185	190	193	193	190	187	184	181	178
To Foreigners (bil $)...	29	33	34	36	37	37	37	37	36	35	35	34
Federal Dbt/GNP (%) ...	42.0	42.1	41.7	40.8	39.7	38.3	36.6	34.5	32.4	30.4	28.6	27.0
Net Exports (bil $)......	-73	-63	-85	-93	-101	-112	-121	-136	-151	-168	-187	-201
Net Exports (bil $82)....	-74	-56	-60	-61	-58	-52	-45	-43	-46	-53	-60	-63
Net For Invest (bil $)	-117	-111	-134	-145	-156	-168	-179	-194	-210	-227	-248	-262
Foreign Dbt/GNP (%)...	10.0	11.5	13.0	14.5	16.0	17.4	18.8	20.0	21.3	22.6	23.8	25.1
Personal Saving Rate (%)	4.2	5.1	4.0	3.5	3.2	3.1	3.2	3.3	3.7	3.9	4.2	4.3

TABLE 11.6 (Cont.)

										Annual Averages 1989-2008	
	2000	2001	2002	2003	2004	2005	2006	2007	2008	Growth	Level
Gross Ntl Prod (bil $82). .	5257	5389	5521	5665	5816	5965	6115	6268	6429	2.37	5152
Net Pay by For (bil $82). .	-12	-15	-18	-20	-23	-25	-27	-28	-30		-4
Gross Dom Prod (bil $82)	5269	5405	5539	5686	5840	5990	6142	6297	6460	2.43	5157
GNP Deflator ('82 = 100).	199.5	207.0	214.7	222.6	230.9	239.4	248.4	257.6	267.1	4.03	191.8
Unemployment Rate (%)	5.3	5.3	5.3	5.3	5.3	5.3	5.3	5.3	5.3		5.31
Real Exchange Rate ('88 = 100)	101.6	101.9	102.0	101.9	102.0	101.9	101.9	102.0	102.0		102.4
Money Stock (M1, $ bil). .	1683	1792	1909	2038	2176	2322	2478	2644	2821	6.67	1632
Treasury Bill Yield (%) . .	5.1	5.1	4.9	4.8	4.7	4.6	4.5	4.4	4.3		5.6
Corporate Bond Yield (%)	6.9	6.8	6.6	6.5	6.4	6.2	6.1	6.0	5.9		7.3
Real Interest Rate (%)	3.2	3.1	2.9	2.8	2.7	2.6	2.5	2.3	2.2		3.5
Expected Inflation (%)	3.7	3.7	3.7	3.7	3.7	3.7	3.7	3.6	3.6		3.8
— Private Nonfarm Business —											
Gross Product (bil $82). .	4176	4290	4404	4528	4658	4785	4912	5042	5179	2.55	4086
Labor Force (mil).	141.1	143.0	144.9	146.7	148.6	150.6	152.6	154.6	156.6	1.27	139.1
Output/Hour ($82/hr). .	22.8	23.1	23.4	23.8	24.1	24.4	24.8	25.1	25.4	1.23	22.5
Tech Adv ('88 = 100)	115.4	116.8	118.2	119.6	121.0	122.5	124.0	125.5	127.0	1.20	113.6
Capital/Output (%).	61.7	62.0	62.2	62.5	62.9	63.2	63.6	64.0	64.4	0.15	62.1
Fix Wt Defl ('82 = 100). . .	172.6	179.0	185.7	192.5	199.5	206.8	214.4	222.2	230.3	3.77	166.7
Hourly Comp ($/hr)	28.2	29.6	31.1	32.7	34.3	36.1	37.9	39.8	41.9	5.06	27.2
— Investment & Saving — (Percent of GNP)											
Gross Pvt Domestic Investment	17.8	18.0	18.0	18.2	18.4	18.4	18.5	18.5	18.5		17.1
Depreciation.	11.8	11.9	12.0	12.1	12.2	12.3	12.4	12.4	12.5		11.6
Net Pvt Dom Investment	6.0	6.1	6.0	6.1	6.2	6.2	6.1	6.0	6.0		5.5
Net National Saving. . . .	3.3	3.4	3.4	3.5	3.5	3.6	3.6	3.5	3.5		3.0
Private.	3.6	3.7	3.7	3.8	3.8	3.8	3.8	3.8	3.7		3.4
Government	-0.2	-0.3	-0.3	-0.3	-0.3	-0.3	-0.3	-0.2	-0.2		-0.4
Federal	-0.1	-0.1	-0.1	-0.1	0.0	0.0	0.0	0.0	0.0		-0.5
State & Local	-0.2	-0.2	-0.2	-0.2	-0.2	-0.2	-0.2	-0.2	-0.2		0.1
Foreign Saving	2.7	2.7	2.7	2.6	2.6	2.6	2.6	2.5	2.5		2.5
— Addenda —											
Federal Deficit (bil $). . . .	-5	-8	-11	-8	-4	-4	-4	-3	0		-30
Federal Net Int (bil $) . . .	174	171	167	164	161	158	155	151	148		174
To Foreigners (bil $). . .	33	33	32	32	31	30	30	29	28		33
Federal Dbt/GNP (%) . . .	25.4	24.0	22.7	21.4	20.1	18.9	17.8	16.8	15.8		28.8
Net Exports (bil $).	-219	-235	-250	-268	-287	-304	-320	-335	-351		-199
Net Exports (bil $82). . . .	-67	-70	-72	-75	-79	-82	-83	-84	-85		-65
Net For Invest (bil $)	-281	-298	-314	-333	-353	-372	-389	-406	-425		-260
Foreign Dbt/GNP (%) . . .	26.2	27.2	28.2	29.1	29.9	30.7	31.4	32.0	32.5		23.6
Personal Saving Rate (%)	4.4	4.6	4.6	4.5	4.4	4.4	4.3	4.2	4.0		4.0

potential output that would otherwise be associated with a balanced budget.

To assess the potential magnitude of this offset, a fifth and final experiment was constructed. In this experiment (1) the deficit is eliminated in 1995 by restraining the growth of spending; thereafter, marginal income tax rates are gradually reduced to maintain the budget in proximate balance. (2) The initial shift toward fiscal restraint is accommodated by an easier monetary policy that keeps the unemployment rate at the natural rate of 5.3 percent; thus, the mix of monetary and fiscal policies is the same as in the third alternative. (3) Through 1995, the foreign real interest rate is prevented from declining relative to the baseline, with the result that an international differential in favor of the foreign yield temporarily arises. In the three years after 1995, the differential is permitted to dissipate. The results are summarized in Table 11.7.

By 1995, the real exchange rate falls 11 percent relative to the baseline, and real net exports actually move into surplus. The real interest rate falls to only 4.1 percent, however, as compared to 3.4 percent when the international interest rate differential did not arise. As a share of GNP, net private domestic investment is 0.5 percent lower than in alternative three. After 1995, the differences between this and the third alternative begin to dissipate as the international differential in interest rates narrows and the real depreciation of the dollar is reversed. Nevertheless, by 2008 the level of real GNP is 4.7 percent above baseline, compared to 5.7 percent in alternative three; the present value of the cumulative gain in real GNP over the entire twenty years is $1,053 billion (or 26 percent of GNP), one-third less than in the third alternative.

SUMMARY AND CONCLUSIONS

This analysis investigates the impact of eliminating the federal deficit on national saving, investment, and product. It concludes that if implemented, proposals to eliminate the deficit would lower the real interest rate in the United States by as much as 3 percentage points, raise domestic saving and investment, and produce savings in federal interest payments sufficiently large that a balanced budget could be achieved and maintained without permanent reductions in federal spending (other than interest) and without permanent increases in tax rates.

The economic benefits of balancing the budget could be substantial. For example, it is estimated that if through restraint of the growth of spending the deficit were eliminated by 1995 and the budget were then maintained in proximate balance through the year 2008, the level of the nation's real gross national product would at the end of the twenty years stand 3.5 percent higher than if the deficit remained at 3 percent

TABLE 11.7
Balancing the Budget Under Enhanced Offsets in Foreign Saving

	1988	1989	1990	1991	1992	1993	1994	1995	1996	1997	1998	1999
Gross Ntl Prod (bil $82). .	4024	4148	4237	4331	4422	4512	4606	4707	4813	4928	5047	5169
Net Pay by For (bil $82). .	28	27	23	20	16	13	9	7	5	4	3	1
Gross Dom Prod (bil $82)	3996	4120	4213	4311	4406	4499	4596	4699	4807	4924	5044	5167
GNP Deflator ('82 = 100) .	121.3	126.3	131.4	136.6	141.8	147.2	152.7	158.5	164.5	170.8	177.3	184.1
Unemployment Rate (%)	5.5	5.3	5.3	5.4	5.3	5.3	5.3	5.3	5.3	5.3	5.3	5.3
Real Exchange Rate ('88 = 100)	100.0	106.0	103.8	100.9	97.7	95.1	93.4	91.8	91.4	94.3	97.0	99.8
Money Stock (M1, $ bil). .	776	805	857	913	971	1033	1102	1174	1248	1319	1414	1506
Treasury Bill Yield (%) . .	6.7	7.5	7.1	7.0	6.9	6.6	6.3	6.1	6.1	6.1	5.7	5.6
Corporate Bond Yield (%)	9.7	9.3	8.9	8.8	8.6	8.4	8.2	8.0	7.8	7.9	7.5	7.5
Real Interest Rate (%)	6.2	5.4	5.0	4.9	4.8	4.6	4.3	4.1	4.0	4.1	3.7	3.7
Expected Inflation (%)	3.5	3.9	3.9	3.9	3.8	3.9	3.9	3.8	3.8	3.8	3.8	3.8
— Private Nonfarm Business —												
Gross Product (bil $82). .	3127	3235	3309	3387	3463	3538	3618	3703	3792	3888	3988	4093
Labor Force (mil).	121.7	124.0	125.6	127.1	128.7	130.3	131.9	133.5	135.1	136.8	138.6	140.4
Output/Hour ($82/hr). .	19.9	20.1	20.3	20.5	20.7	20.9	21.1	21.4	21.6	21.9	22.1	22.4
Tech Adv ('88 = 100)	100.0	101.2	102.4	103.6	104.9	106.1	107.4	108.7	110.0	111.3	112.7	114.0
Capital/Output (%).	62.5	62.3	62.0	61.6	61.3	61.0	60.8	60.6	60.5	60.5	60.5	60.5
Fix Wt Defl ('82 = 100). . .	109.8	114.4	119.0	123.6	128.4	133.3	138.4	143.7	149.2	154.9	160.7	166.8
Hourly Comp ($/hr)	15.6	16.4	17.2	18.1	19.0	19.9	20.9	22.0	23.1	24.2	25.4	26.7
— Investment & Saving — (Percent of GNP)												
Gross Pvt Domestic Investment	15.4	15.1	15.2	15.3	15.4	15.5	15.8	16.2	16.6	16.8	16.9	17.0
Depreciation.	10.5	10.5	10.6	10.7	10.8	10.9	11.0	11.2	11.3	11.3	11.4	11.4
Net Pvt Dom Investment	4.9	4.6	4.6	4.6	4.6	4.6	4.8	5.1	5.3	5.4	5.5	5.5
Net National Saving. . . .	2.4	2.5	2.3	2.4	2.5	2.7	3.0	3.4	3.8	4.1	4.1	4.1
Private.	4.4	4.3	3.6	3.4	3.3	3.3	3.5	3.7	3.9	4.2	4.3	4.4
Government	-2.0	-1.8	-1.3	-1.0	-0.8	-0.7	-0.5	-0.3	-0.1	-0.2	-0.2	-0.4
Federal	-3.0	-2.8	-2.2	-1.8	-1.4	-1.1	-0.8	-0.4	-0.1	-0.1	-0.1	-0.1
State & Local	1.0	0.9	0.8	0.8	0.6	0.5	0.3	0.2	0.0	-0.1	-0.1	-0.3
Foreign Saving	2.4	2.1	2.3	2.2	2.1	2.0	1.8	1.6	1.5	1.3	1.3	1.4
— Addenda —												
Federal Deficit (bil $). . . .	-145	-144	-121	-106	-90	-75	-56	-31	-9	-10	-7	-6
Federal Net Int (bil $) . . .	151	170	178	185	191	195	197	198	197	196	194	192
To Foreigners (bil $). . .	29	33	34	36	37	38	38	38	38	38	37	37
Federal Dbt/GNP (%) . . .	42.0	42.2	42.0	41.5	40.6	39.6	38.3	36.6	34.7	32.8	30.9	29.2
Net Exports (bil $).	-73	-62	-80	-81	-80	-77	-70	-66	-58	-53	-61	-77
Net Exports (bil $82). . . .	-74	-56	-59	-55	-44	-26	-8	6	21	25	15	-3
Net For Invest (bil $)	-117	-110	-129	-133	-133	-131	-126	-122	-115	-112	-120	-137
Foreign Dbt/GNP (%). . .	10.0	11.5	13.0	14.5	15.8	16.9	17.8	18.4	18.9	19.1	19.3	19.5
Personal Saving Rate (%)	4.2	5.0	4.1	3.6	3.5	3.7	4.0	4.3	4.6	5.0	4.9	5.0

TABLE 11.7 (Cont.)

	2000	2001	2002	2003	2004	2005	2006	2007	2008	Annual Averages 1989–2008 Growth	Level
Gross Ntl Prod (bil $82) . .	5294	5428	5576	5720	5873	6026	6178	6339	6501	2.43	5193
Net Pay by For (bil $82) . .	0	0	-1	-3	-4	-5	-6	-7	-8		5
Gross Dom Prod (bil $82)	5294	5429	5577	5723	5877	6031	6185	6347	6509	2.47	5188
GNP Deflator ('82 = 100) .	191.1	198.3	205.6	213.3	221.3	229.6	238.2	247.1	256.3	3.81	184.6
Unemployment Rate (%)	5.3	5.3	5.3	5.3	5.3	5.3	5.3	5.3	5.3		5.305
Real Exchange Rate ('88 = 100)	100.2	100.2	100.9	101.3	101.5	101.8	101.8	101.8	102.2		99.1
Money Stock (M1, $ bil) . .	1623	1734	1843	1964	2099	2237	2393	2551	2715	6.46	1575
Treasury Bill Yield (%) . .	5.2	5.1	5.1	5.0	4.9	4.8	4.6	4.6	4.5		5.7
Corporate Bond Yield (%)	7.0	6.9	6.8	6.6	6.5	6.4	6.3	6.2	6.1		7.5
Real Interest Rate (%)	3.3	3.2	3.1	2.9	2.8	2.8	2.6	2.5	2.5		3.7
Expected Inflation (%)	3.8	3.7	3.7	3.7	3.7	3.7	3.7	3.7	3.7		3.8
— Private Nonfarm Business —											
Gross Product (bil $82) . .	4198	4312	4439	4562	4693	4823	4952	5088	5224	2.60	4115
Labor Force (mil)	142.3	144.2	146.1	148.0	150.0	152.0	154.0	156.0	158.0	1.31	140.1
Output/Hour ($82/hr) . .	22.7	23.0	23.3	23.7	24.0	24.3	24.7	25.0	25.3	1.21	22.5
Tech Adv ('88 = 100)	115.4	116.8	118.2	119.6	121.0	122.5	124.0	125.5	127.0	1.20	113.6
Capital/Output (%) .	60.6	60.8	61.1	61.4	61.8	62.2	62.6	63.1	63.5	0.08	61.4
Fix Wt Defl ('82 = 100) . . .	173.0	179.4	186.1	193.0	200.1	207.5	215.1	222.9	231.1	3.79	167.0
Hourly Comp ($/hr)	28.1	29.5	31.0	32.6	34.3	36.0	37.9	39.8	41.8	5.05	27.2
— Investment & Saving — (Percent of GNP)											
Gross Pvt Domestic Investment	17.1	17.3	17.6	17.7	17.9	18.0	18.0	18.0	18.0		16.8
Depreciation	11.5	11.6	11.6	11.7	11.8	11.9	12.0	12.0	12.1		11.4
Net Pvt Dom Investment	5.6	5.8	6.0	6.0	6.1	6.1	6.0	6.0	5.9		5.4
Net National Saving	4.1	4.2	4.3	4.4	4.4	4.5	4.4	4.4	4.4		3.7
Private	4.4	4.4	4.5	4.6	4.6	4.7	4.6	4.6	4.6		4.1
Government	-0.3	-0.3	-0.2	-0.2	-0.2	-0.2	-0.2	-0.2	-0.2		-0.5
Federal	0.0	0.0	0.1	0.1	0.1	0.1	0.1	0.0	0.0		-0.5
State & Local	-0.3	-0.3	-0.3	-0.3	-0.3	-0.3	-0.3	-0.2	-0.2		0.1
Foreign Saving	1.5	1.6	1.6	1.6	1.6	1.6	1.6	1.6	1.5		1.7
— Addenda —											
Federal Deficit (bil $)	0	3	8	8	11	10	8	7	3		-30
Federal Net Int (bil $) . . .	187	182	178	174	170	166	162	158	155		181
To Foreigners (bil $) . . .	36	35	34	33	33	32	31	30	30		35
Federal Dbt/GNP (%) . . .	27.5	25.8	24.1	22.6	21.2	19.8	18.5	17.4	16.3		30.1
Net Exports (bil $)	-95	-112	-125	-138	-149	-160	-168	-176	-182		-104
Net Exports (bil $82)	-22	-34	-44	-50	-55	-60	-63	-65	-66		-32
Net For Invest (bil $)	-155	-172	-186	-200	-212	-224	-233	-243	-250		-162
Foreign Dbt/GNP (%) . . .	19.8	20.2	20.5	20.9	21.2	21.5	21.8	22.0	22.2		18.7
Personal Saving Rate (%)	4.6	4.6	4.7	4.7	4.6	4.6	4.5	4.4	4.3		4.4

FIGURE 11.7
Present Value of Cumulative
Output Gain from Deficit Reduction

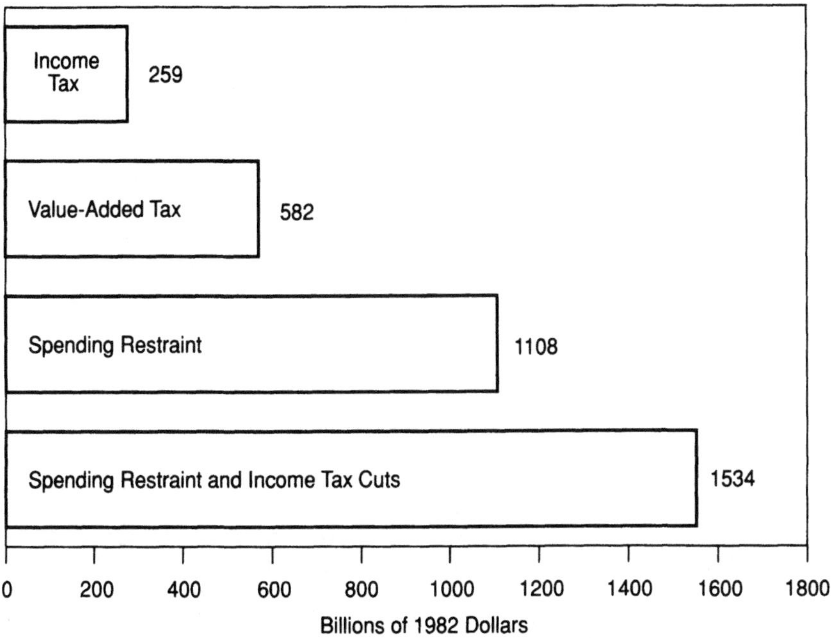

of GNP. In present value, the cumulative gain in output through 2008 would amount to $1,108 billion, or 26 percent of the value of GNP in 1988. It is possible to design plans with even larger cumulative gains.

There are, however, important differences in the gains realized under the five alternative schemes to balance the budget. Although all plans to eliminate the deficit reduce the real interest rate and thereby encourage capital formation, proposals that do so with higher tax rates entail disincentives that partially offset the benefits of lower yields. For example, an increase in the tax rate on corporate income would raise the cost of capital associated with any real rate of interest, thereby discouraging investment. Likewise, an increase in the tax rate on personal income would lower the after-tax wage rate, thereby reducing the supply of labor and undermining the increase in output otherwise resulting from a decline in the real interest rate. Thus, it is estimated that if through an increase in income taxes the deficit were eliminated by 1995 and the budget were then maintained in proximate balance through the year 2008, the present value of the cumulative gains in real GNP over that period would amount to only $259 billion, just one-quarter of the gains achieved through restraint on spending (see Figure 11.7).

While provocative, these findings are qualified by the limitations of the classical growth theory that underlies them. In particular, the analysis is based on two presumptions: that aggregate output is an appropriate measure of economic advantage and that no part of federal spending represents public investment in the future. In fact, it is reasonable to argue that considerations other than GNP—such as increased inequality in the distribution of income, limitations on the general availability of public services, or adverse impacts on the environment—should weigh importantly in the assessment of any scheme to cut the deficit. Similarly, it is important to recognize that some elements of federal spending—such as aid to education, subsidies for research and development, and funds spent to improve the nation's infrastructure—are investment; cuts in these will undermine the advantages of any resulting increase in private investment.

APPENDIX 11.A: A SIMPLE CLASSICAL MODEL OF ECONOMIC GROWTH

A useful point of departure in assessing the qualitative relationships among the federal deficit, the real interest rate, national saving, and economic performance is a simple classical model of economic growth. Even though the simple model lacks the richness of structural detail found in the Washington University macroeconomic model used to generate the results presented in section three, it nonetheless serves the very useful purpose of isolating qualitatively the primary channels by which fiscal policy can affect potential output.

Let output (Q) supplied at time t be governed by Cobb-Douglas production technology in capital (K) and labor. In this simple model, the latter is assumed to be a fixed share of population (N); that is, the labor force participation rate is fixed. Thus, up to a scalar, the production function can be written as:

$$Q = K^{a}(e^{zt}N)^{1-a} \,. \tag{A1}$$

There are constant returns to scale, and labor-augmenting technical advance occurs at the exogenous rate z. In competitive factor markets, a and $1-a$ represent the respective shares of income earned by capital and labor.

The capital stock varies in proportion to output and in inverse proportion to the rental price of investment (q):

$$K = aQ/q \,. \tag{A2}$$

If the tax code is neutral with respect to the treatment of capital, the rental price of investment is simply the sum of the real interest rate (i) and the depreciation rate of capital (d):

$$q = i + d \,. \tag{A3}$$

Combining (A1) through (A3) yields the following expression for the equilibrium level of output (up to a scalar) supplied at time t:

$$Q = e^{zt}N(i + d)^{-a/(1-a)}. \tag{A4}$$

Thus, with existing technology and for a given population, the supply of output increases as the real rate of interest declines because as the interest rate falls, the capital stock rises and the resulting capital-deepening enhances the average productivity of labor.

The time-derivative of (A4) is approximately:

$$\dot{Q} = \dot{z} + \dot{N} - [a/\{(1 - a)(i + d)\}]\Delta i \,. \tag{A5}$$

That is, economic growth (Q) is determined by the rate of labor-augmenting technical advance, the rate of growth in population (N), and *changes* in (as opposed to the *level* of) the real interest rate. In steady state, the real interest rate is constant ($\Delta i = 0$), so that equilibrium growth is simply the sum of the rate of technical advance and the rate of growth in population:

$$\dot{Q} = \dot{z} + \dot{N} \,. \tag{A6}$$

Although this result is well known, it underscores an important conclusion: Unless the magnitude of the budget deficit permanently affects the rate of technical advance and/or the rate of growth in the labor supply, the level of government saving (or dissaving) has no impact on economic growth in the long run.

Output is allocated between personal consumption (C), gross private domestic investment (I), government purchases of goods and services (G), and exports (X) net of imports (M):

$$Q = C + I + G + X - M \,. \tag{A7}$$

Personal consumption is a fixed share of after-tax income:

$$C = (1-s_p)(1-t)Q \,, \tag{A8}$$

where s_p is the personal saving rate and t is the exogenous income tax rate, defined net of government transfer payments.

Gross private investment has two components: net investment (I_n) and depreciation of the existing stock of capital (I_d). Net investment is the change in the capital stock, which in steady state and using equations (A2), (A3), and (A5) can be written as:

$$I_n = \dot{K} = a(\dot{z} + \dot{N})Q/(i + d). \tag{A9}$$

That is, in equilibrium the share of output allocated to net investment is inversely related to the level of the real interest rate. Depreciation is simply the depreciation rate multiplied by the stock of capital, which using equation (A2) can be written as:

$$I_d = dK = aQ/(i + d) \,, \tag{A10}$$

so that depreciation as a share of output is also inversely related to the real rate of interest.

Both exports (X) and imports (M) are expressed as shares (x, m) of domestic output. Here, these shares are treated as fixed:

$$X = xQ, \tag{A11}$$

$$M = mQ. \tag{A12}$$

Finally, government purchases of goods and services are an exogenous share (g) of output that is determined by the fiscal authorities:

$$G = gQ. \tag{A13}$$

Equations (A6) through (A13) can be solved for the equilibrium level of the real interest rate:

$$i = a(\dot{z} + \dot{N} + d)/[S_p(1-t) + S_f + S_g] - d. \qquad \text{(A14)}$$

Here $S_g = t - g$ is the government saving rate (government saving as a share of output). A reduction in the deficit as a share of output corresponds to an increase in S_g.

$S_f = m - x$ is foreign saving supplied to the United States (the negative of net exports) as a share of domestic output. A worsening trade deficit thus implies an increase in foreign saving in the United States.

Next, consider an increase in S_g accomplished by reducing government purchases of goods and services. Equation (A14) implies that as the government saving rate rises, the real rate of interest falls sufficiently to augment private investment by the amount of the additional government saving, provided that there are no offsetting declines in either private saving (S_p) or foreign saving (S_f). From equation (A4), it follows that there is an associated onetime increase in the level of output. Equation (A5) implies that while the interest rate is falling, economic growth rises above the equilibrium rate defined in (A6). And equations (A9) and (A10) reveal that the equilibrium shares of output allocated to net investment and to depreciation both rise.

If, however, either S_p or S_f falls as S_g rises, the decline in the real interest rate is mitigated, the increase in total saving available to support additional investment is reduced, and the magnitude of the onetime increase in output associated with a smaller government deficit is curtailed. The principal reason that such offsets might be of importance is that private saving and foreign saving themselves may be positively related to the real interest rate.

In summary, simple although it is, this model offers four important insights into the relationship between government saving and economic performance. First, an increase in the government saving rate (that is, a decrease in the deficit as a share of output) does, other things equal, reduce the real rate of interest. Second, for a given amount of labor, the reduction in the real interest rate generates a onetime increase in the capital stock and thus in output. During the period of declining interest rates and capital-deepening, economic growth temporarily rises. Third, the magnitude of the onetime increase in output depends importantly on the response of private and foreign saving to the real rate of interest. Fourth, in the long run the rate of economic growth is not affected by fiscal policy, being determined solely by the rate of technical advance and the growth in population.

A thorough econometric analysis of the macroeconomic impact of eliminating the federal deficit is presented in section three of the main body of this analysis. But the proximate magnitude of the effects is gleaned from a simpler, static analysis only slightly more complicated than that just developed. Consider a standard Jorgensonian formulation for the rental price of investment:

$$q = (P_k/P)(1-tz)[r(1-tl) - \dot{p}^e + d]/(1-t). \qquad \text{(A15)}$$

Here P_k is the price of capital goods, P is the price of output, t is the corporate income tax rate, z is the present value of depreciation allowances permitted under the current tax code, r is the nominal pretax rate of return, l is the leverage ratio, p^e is the expected rate of inflation, and d is the depreciation rate of capital. For current values of these variables and parameters, the rental price of investment is 22.2 percent.

Suppose that were the federal deficit eliminated, the real rate of interest would fall from its current level of 6 percent to 3 percent, closer to the postwar norm. This in turn reduces the rental price of investment by 13.5 percent (to

19.2 percent). For a Cobb-Douglas production function, the resulting increase in the equilibrium capital-output ratio is 13.5 percent. If capital's share of income (that is, the parameter a in equation [A1]) is 0.25, the associated rise in output is 3.4 percent. If adjustment to this higher level of output is spread over, say, twenty years, the result is to raise the average rate of growth in real output by 0.17 per year over that period.

These results suggest that a failure to reduce the deficit will not precipitate a calamitous decline in domestic output. Rather, the United States will likely experience a protracted period of marginally slower growth. That the impact is relatively modest is attributable to two separate factors: (1) because the depreciation rate of capital is sizable relative to the real rate of interest, the halving of yields reduces the rental price of investment by considerably less than that percentagewise; (2) relative to labor, capital plays a minor role in the production function.

This simple exposition does not incorporate the direct impacts that tax and expenditure rates may have on either the capital-output ratio or the supply of labor. Instead, it focuses on the increase in output associated with a change in the mix of fiscal and monetary policies. It is, however, a relatively simple matter to introduce supply-side incentives into the model. For example, at current values of the relevant variables and parameters, equation (A15) implies that an increase in the corporate income tax rate would raise the cost of capital at any interest rate. The resulting reduction in the equilibrium ratio of capital to output would limit the rise in potential output that would otherwise be associated with a change in the mix of policy that balanced the budget by raising income taxes. In a similar vein, if tax and expenditure rates had a bearing on the labor force participation rate, the supply of labor at full employment and thus the increase in potential output that otherwise would be associated with a change in the mix of policy that balanced the budget might be importantly influenced by the manner in which the deficit is reduced.

NOTES

I thank Laurence H. Meyer and Chris P. Varvares for their insightful discussions with me during the preparation of this study. Any errors, however, are entirely my responsibility.

1. Net private domestic investment is nominal gross private domestic investment less nominal depreciation, as defined in the national income and product accounts (NIPAs). Much the same picture results if net investment, depreciation, and net product are defined in constant prices.

2. Despite the conceptual superiority of net investment as a measure of capital accumulation, some observers argue that the inadequate measurement of depreciation dictates a reliance on gross investment instead. Measured in gross terms, recent weakness in investment is less apparent than in Figure 11.1. The difference, however, is attributable largely to recent sharp increases in the share of investment allocated to computing equipment, for which the rate of depreciation is relatively high.

The equilibrium share of net domestic product devoted to net investment is not necessarily constant over time. In particular, it is positively correlated with the sum of the underlying rate of exogenous technical advance and the exogenous rate of growth in the labor force. Therefore, one reason that net investment relative to net output is lower now at full employment than, say, during the 1960s, is that the decade of the 1960s was characterized by relatively rapid growth in potential output.

3. Net private saving is defined here as the sum of personal saving, undistributed profits, the inventory valuation adjustment, the capital consumption adjustment, government wage accruals, and a statistical discrepancy, all as measured in the national income and product accounts. Government saving is composed of the federal deficit and the deficits of state and local governments, again on a NIPA basis. Foreign saving, the opposite of net foreign investment, is the sum of federal interest paid to foreigners, federal transfers to foreigners, and personal transfers to foreigners less net exports of goods and services.

4. The decomposition of growth in output into the contributions made by growth in labor and by the rate of technical advance dates back to the seminal article by Robert M. Solow, "Technical Change and the Aggregate Production Function," *Review of Economics and Statistics* 39 (August 1957), pp. 312–320.

5. The most noteworthy studies in this regard are Michael J. Boskin, "Taxation, Saving, and the Rate of Interest," *Journal of Political Economy* 86, no. 2, part 2 (April 1978), pp. S3–S27; Lawrence Summers, "Tax Policy, the Rate of Return, and Saving," *NBER Working Paper No. 995* (Cambridge, Mass.: National Bureau of Economic Research, 1982); and Alan Auerbach and Laurence J. Kotlikoff, *Dynamic Fiscal Policy* (Cambridge: Cambridge University Press, 1987).

6. Some have argued that these offsets are potentially quite large. For example, Lawrence Summers estimated that changes in private saving, foreign saving, and state and local government saving might offset as much as 60 percent of a change in the federal deficit. See Lawrence Summers, "The Legacy of Current Macroeconomic Policies," in George R. Hulten and Isabel V. Sawhill, eds., *The Legacy of Reaganomics* (Washington, D.C.: Urban Institute, 1984), pp. 179–198. Others have found little evidence to support the existence of such large offsets. See, for example, Benjamin M. Friedman, "Implications of the Government Deficit for U.S. Capital Formation," *Federal Reserve Bank of Boston Conference Series*, no. 27 (October 1983), pp. 73–95.

7. See, for example, Joel L. Prakken, "The Macroeconomics of Tax Reform," in Charls E. Walker and Mark A. Bloomfield, eds., *The Consumption Tax: A Better Alternative?* (Cambridge, Mass.: Ballinger, 1987), pp. 117–166.

8. Three studies that support this conclusion are Jerry A. Housman, "Labor Supply," in Henry J. Aaron and Joseph A. Pechman, eds., *How Taxes Affect Economic Behavior* (Washington, D.C.: Brookings Institution, 1981); John Kendrick, "The Implications of Growth Accounting Models," in Hulten and Sawhill, eds., *The Legacy of Reaganomics,* pp. 19–43; and Gary Burtless, "The Supply-Side Legacy of the Reagan Years: Effects on Labor Supply" (Paper presented at the Conference on the Economic Legacy of the Reagan Years: Euphoria or Chaos? Oakland University, Oakland, California, June 30–July 1, 1989).

9. Dale Jorgenson and Barbara Fraumeni carefully document the relationship between economic growth and investment in education in Chapter 3.

10. Most work suggests that the rate of return on investment in the infrastructure is quite low. See, for example, Donald A. Nichols, "Federal Spending Priorities and Long-Term Economic Growth," in Hulten and Sawhill, eds., *The Legacy of Reaganomics,* pp. 151–173.

11. A more detailed description of the Washington University macroeconomic model is found in Laurence H. Meyer & Associates, *The WUMM Model Book* (Saint Louis: Laurence H. Meyer & Associates, 1989).

12. U.S. Congressional Budget Office, "The Economic Effects of Deficit Reduction in Commercial Econometric Models: A Report to the National Economic Commission" (Washington, D.C.: Congressional Budget Office, December 7, 1988).

Discussion

Martin Feldstein

Joel Prakken's very interesting analysis shows the powerful effects of deficit reduction. Those of us who have received scars for trying to reduce the budget deficit know that this indeed describes the promised land that was held out for deficit reduction.

I want to comment on four issues that Dr. Prakken raises. First, the most overlooked important point in general discussions of the effects of deficit reduction is that the *expectation* of deficit reduction has the effect of lowering interest rates, which actually reduces the deficit because of the magnitude of our outstanding government debt. As Dr. Prakken shows in his calculations, this effect is really very large. With a debt of some $2 trillion, a 3-percentage-point reduction in interest rates brings down the deficit by some $60 billion; that then feeds into the next year's deficit and further reduces interest outlay in the future. These mechanisms act as a kind of perpetual motion machine that does indeed produce something for nothing. If people really believe that the deficit is going to come down, the actual reductions in the government's noninterest outlays or increases in taxes needed to balance the budget are not all that great. That indeed was a large part of the strategy that made the Bush administration's flexible-freeze numbers work as well as they did on paper. But the key is expectations; having a plan in place that the administration and Congress are clearly committed to will have the effect on financial markets of lowering interest rates.

The first round of that occurred in 1985 with the budget resolution early in that year and the subsequent Gramm-Rudman legislation. Interest rates did come down very substantially. One of the significant reasons our budget deficit is smaller than was projected in 1985 is that interest rates are much lower than they were in real terms back in 1985.

What does all this mean for the kind of budget policy we should be looking for in the fiscal 1991 budget? The key is, again, a multiyear commitment—a tougher version of the Gramm-Rudman-Hollings approach. But to make it convincing, after the experience of a fair amount of smoke and mirrors, we need something tougher that goes beyond the narrow range of items in the existing eligible categories for Gramm-Rudman sequestration cuts.

In addition to the current range, we must put taxes and entitlements back on the table. If taxes and entitlements are on the table, and if the overall program promises incremental percentage reductions in entitlements and incremental percentage increases in taxes if the targets are not met, we should see a very substantial interest rate reduction, although perhaps not as large as Dr. Prakken suggests. Those interest rate reductions make it unnecessary to trigger the "second-stage automatic deficit reduction." In other words, if Congress takes the kind of relatively small measures that are likely within the existing budget and if interest rates drop, this hidden power of potential further cuts in entitlements and increases in taxes will never have to be triggered. The key is a credible, multiyear program.

A second issue is the international trade effects of deficit reduction. Dr. Prakken's analysis shows that the effects of a reduction in U.S. interest rates on the trade balance are temporary—that after a relatively short period of time, interest rates abroad will also come down and there will be no further reason for a change in capital flows. On the contrary, I think that a fall in our interest rates will not bring down foreign interest rates, except by a change in the capital flow. The reason we expect interest rates to be arbitraged around the world is that when our interest rates come down, there is less incentive to move capital here and there is more capital remaining in Europe and Japan, where interest rates become lower than they would otherwise be. The key point is that a lower U.S. budget deficit and a correspondingly higher national saving rate will (1) result in greater domestic investment and (2) shrink the trade deficit. The impact on *domestic* GNP growth will not be as large if we have less foreign capital, but our *national* GNP growth will not be diminished by this process.

A third issue is how budget deficits should be reduced. I agree with Dr. Prakken's basic proposition, which Senator Warren Rudman seconds, that lower spending would be preferable to increases in taxes. And I agree that accomplishing this through changes in entitlements for the nonpoor should be part of that process. Slowing the growth of transfer of payments to the aged, in particular the nonpoor aged, is the big missing piece in outlay control.

If taxes are going to be part of the process, what kind of taxes should they be? My own preference would be to start with selective excise taxes on products where the effect of a tax increase would have benefits for the nation other than just higher revenue. For example, the evidence shows that an increase in the excise tax on cigarettes would reduce smoking by young people. Higher gasoline excise taxes would have a favorable effect on the environment and, by reducing the speeds at which people choose to drive, on accidents.

What about a value-added tax? Dr. Prakken's simulations indicate a certain virtue of a value-added tax relative to the income tax, as measured by GNP. He is very careful in his introductory remarks to remind us that GNP does not include the value of leisure. Therefore, to the extent that an income tax, in contrast to a value-added tax, changes the amount of work effort, Dr. Prakken may be overstating the gains from a VAT in terms of the standard of living.

Whatever the economic virtues of a value-added tax—and my sense is they are less than is usually claimed—a new value-added tax is not appropriate when what we need is, at most, a small increase in revenue. If Dr. Prakken's simulations are in the right ballpark, we may need only a temporary increase in revenue; taxes as a share of GNP can later be brought down because of the higher growth of GNP. If we put a value-added tax on the books, it is very unlikely that we will take it off the books five or ten years later. It is much more likely that it would get ratcheted up as people discover new, otherwise unfinanced "needs" that the country could pay for in that way.

A fourth issue is private saving. It is certainly true that deficit reduction is a direct way of increasing the national saving rate. But we must not lose sight of the need to raise private saving as well. After all, the reduction in private saving as a share of GNP in the 1980s contributed 3 percent to the fall in our national saving rate while the increase in the budget deficit contributed only 1 percent. We should be looking very hard at ways of encouraging more private saving.

I am grateful to Dr. Prakken for a very stimulating discussion that makes concrete how the impact of deficit reduction is magnified through interest rates and the changes that are actually required in taxes and revenue. If that can be a guiding principle to the fiscal 1991 budget, we can see tougher commitments in the same spirit as the original Gramm-Rudman legislation, and we will really be on the road to dealing with the deficit problem.

Discussion

Warren B. Rudman

I agree with much of what Joel Prakken says. The one thing absent, of course, is the political reality. If I were king, I would probably call for an immediate, truly flexible freeze without a lot of flex in it that would probably adjust for inflation. Six years from now, we would be in a position to prove that supply-side economics works as long as one end of it is frozen. That is not going to happen, so we are facing what is politically possible.

The deficit as a percentage of GNP was 5.9 percent in 1985. In fiscal year 1990 it stands at about 2.3 percent. Total U.S. government spending before Gramm-Rudman-Hollings was growing 10.5 percent annually; since the law was established, the annual growth rate has been about 5.6 percent. In 1988, the increase in government spending was lower than at any time since 1968. So we are making progress, but not enough.

After speaking to many economists, I firmly believe that the best thing for our economy would be to hold down the rate of increase of government spending and leave the tax code pretty much alone. If we could do that, we would eventually grow our way out of the deficit situation. That is essentially what Dr. Prakken suggests, and that would be the preferred way.

But looking at the numbers makes it clear that the political realities of holding down the increase in federal government spending are very, very difficult. Roughly 45 to 50 percent of the fiscal 1990 budget was in entitlement programs—automatic spending programs such as Social Security, Medicare, Medicaid, certain student loans, agricultural subsidies, veterans benefits, and federal and military retirement. Defense was about 25 percent; interest was about 12 percent. Thus, everything else we call government was 15 percent. When we talk about a freeze, we are talking about that 15 percent, which includes items such as education and research and development that we probably do not want to freeze because there might be a deleterious effect on the other end of the economy.

The situation is similar to that of a Fortune 500 chief executive officer (CEO) whose board says, "You are going to cut overhead 10 percent next year." The CEO says, "Ten percent?" The board says, "That's the good news. The bad news is that all you can touch is telephone and stationery."

So where does this deficit saving come from? It has come out of defense. Look at the Reagan budget as it forecast defense for 1990–1995. With the positive events in Eastern Europe, we may be lucky. What Dr. Prakken does not show in his tables and figures is that over the next ten years, our defense expenditures as a percentage of GNP may be less than we predicted. That would be excellent because the strategic part of our spending in defense is, by far, the least expensive part. The most expensive part is labor accounts.

But the real issue is the entitlement programs. About twelve members of the Senate are willing to vote for a meaningful amount of means testing in the entitlement programs. When we talk about freezes we are really talking about the defense budget—which is already coming down; interest—which cannot be frozen; and discretionary spending—which has been held to some fairly restrained amounts.

The first time we put some kind of a means test on the people who benefited from entitlement programs, we had a revolution. This leads me to believe that I was right when I said that people in this country really believe that there is somebody else out there to pay for the benefits that they receive. Deficit spending has taught them this lesson. There is no doubt in my mind that if we could do what many of us would like to do, the impact on saving, on interest rates, and on the balance of payments in our trade area would be incredible.

I believe that it will be a while before we get to a balanced budget. We will not make it by 1993, when Gramm-Rudman calls for a balanced budget. The deficit for 1989 was forecast at $310 billion when we passed the Gramm-Rudman-Hollings legislation in 1985; the deficit for 1989 was actually $152 billion. We miss the targets every year, but that is no reason to lose faith.

12

Social Security Surpluses: How Will They Be Used?

Alicia H. Munnell

One mechanism available to help raise the low U.S. saving rate is the Social Security trust funds. Under current law, old-age, survivors and disability insurance (OASDI) receipts are projected to exceed outlays for the next thirty years, producing assets equal to nearly 30 percent of gross national product (GNP) by the year 2018. Although current law also provides that these accumulated reserves decline as a percentage of GNP between 2018 and 2046, proposals are already emerging in Congress to raise taxes to maintain the reserves once amassed. Hence, by accumulating assets in the Social Security trust funds, the federal government can create government saving and thereby contribute to higher levels of future output.

The following four sections address both the desirability and the feasibility of increasing national saving through the Social Security program. The first step is to separate the implications of prefunding for the Social Security program itself from those for the economy in general. Toward this end, section one ("Financing the Social Security System") explains how the Social Security program, which for three decades was financed more or less on a pay-as-you-go basis, began to accumulate a significant surplus. This section also addresses the implications of alternative ways of financing social security over the next seventy-five years. The conclusion is that the OASDI system can be financed equally well on a pay-as-you-go basis or on a prefunded basis. But although prefunding may not be necessary for the financial health of the Social Security system, it may be the most desirable course for the economy. This issue is raised in the second section ("The Economics of Increasing National Saving Through Social Security"). This section explores how trust fund surpluses can reduce the burden of supporting future generations of retirees. Equally important, it highlights the fact that whether or not saving actually occurs depends on how Congress reacts to the buildup in the Social Security trust funds. If Congress substitutes the increase in reserves for a tax hike or spending cut to finance current consumption—that is, to pay for current outlays in the rest of the budget—no real saving will occur. But if the federal government alters its spending and taxing patterns to produce surpluses in its unified accounts—not just in the Social Security trust funds—the nation will enjoy higher saving and investment. Therefore, if reserves are to be accumulated, it is important to determine how to translate public pension accumulations into national saving.

The United States is not the first country to attempt to prefund its public pension system. Canada, Japan, and Sweden, for example, have each accumulated a large public pension trust fund reserve in an effort to ease the burden of future pension costs. Section three ("Foreign Experience") explores the experiences of these three countries to determine if they suggest any policies or procedures that might help ensure that pension fund surpluses are used to augment national saving and investment. The final section ("Conclusion") presents recommendations for the financing of Social Security over the next few years and for the long term.

FINANCING THE SOCIAL SECURITY SYSTEM

This section makes three points. First, the history of Social Security financing has included periods of both reserve accumulation and pay-as-you-go financing; both approaches have proven workable. Second, the currently scheduled reserve accumulation is the result of efforts in 1977 and 1983 to address short- and long-run financial problems, not a deliberate policy response designed to increase national saving. Therefore, the slate is clean and the options are open. Third, the future costs of the OASDI program are manageable, regardless of whether reserves are accumulated in advance.

A Brief History of Social Security Financing

The Social Security system is projected to accumulate substantial reserves over the next thirty years, peaking as a percent of GNP in the year 2018.[1] Even though outlays will exceed revenues after 2018 in nominal terms, fund assets will continue to grow until the year 2029 as a result of interest income; after 2029 the dollar value of trust fund assets is scheduled to decline as bonds are redeemed to pay current benefits. This buildup of reserves is not without precedent; a look at the first two decades of the program reveals the accumulation of substantial reserves and the repeated enactment of tax schedules that would have eventually produced large trust funds.

Although the system was never intended to be fully funded, the original 1935 legislation did provide for the creation of a substantial trust fund.[2] Accumulated reserves were projected to grow to $47 billion by 1980, and interest on these reserves was slated to finance 40 percent of annual benefit payments. To guarantee the buildup, payroll tax payments started five years before benefits, and several tax hikes were scheduled under the act.

Shortly thereafter, however, Congress amended the legislation, substantially altering the nature of the program and the role of the reserve fund. The critical 1939 amendments expanded the beneficiary population, moved up the date of the first benefit payment, and postponed the scheduled payroll tax increases for three years. Congress designed these changes both to improve benefit protection and to move the system to pay-as-you-go financing in which the reserve fund served as a "contingency fund to insure ready payment of benefits at all stages of the business cycle and under varying conditions."[3]

Despite this 1939 policy change to pay-as-you-go financing, the old-age and survivors trust fund generated annual surpluses until 1956, causing reserves to grow rapidly (see Figure 12.1). The accumulation of reserves is almost inevitable during the early phase of a contributory system; eligibility requirements keep benefit payments low in the early years, while contribution rates are generally set to cover long-term commitments.

Tax schedules enacted by Congress further violated the intent of the 1939 amendments. The typical practice was to set current tax rates at a level that produced revenues roughly equal to outlays for the next couple of years; scheduled rate increases then resulted in the accumulation of large trust fund surpluses in the future. These surpluses generated significant interest earnings to help meet future benefits, assuring long-run balance between income and outlays under the assumption of static wages and prices. The date of the projected accumulations was continually postponed, however, because long-run surpluses emerged when wage and price increases inevitably occurred and were incorporated into new cost and revenue estimates. Faced with the appearance of an overfinanced system, Congress updated the benefit provisions to keep them in line with the growth in wages and prices, postponed rate increases not needed currently, and set up a new tax schedule producing large trust fund surpluses in the future. Thus, even though reserve accumulation was constantly projected, the continual postponement of these accumulations produced pay-as-you-go financing on an ad hoc basis.

After more than fifteen years of ad hoc, pay-as-you-go financing, the approach was adopted as the official financing mechanism in 1971. The 1971 Advisory Council on Social Security explicitly rejected the historical pattern of enacting contribution and benefit schedules that produced a substantial accumulation of trust balances in future years. Instead, the council recommended that contribution rates be set at a level sufficient to cover annual benefit and administrative costs and that the trust fund be maintained as a contingency reserve at a level approximately equal to one year's outlays. Thus, the Social Security

FIGURE 12.1
Annual Surplus or Deficit and Balance in the OASDI Trust Funds for Selected Years
(percent of GNP)

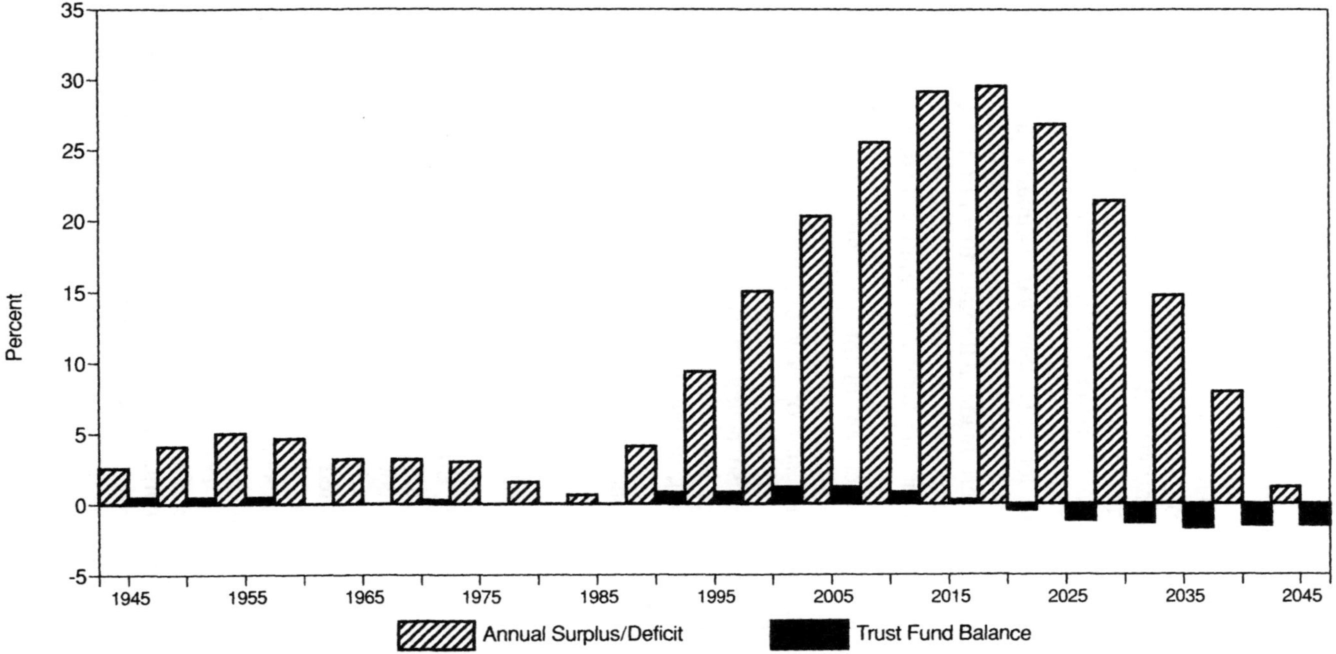

Sources: Social Security Administration, *Social Security Bulletin, Annual Statistical Supplement, 1987,* Tables 23 and 25, pp. 98–100; and Social Security Administration, *1989 Annual Report of the Board of Trustees of the Federal Old-Age and Survivors Insurance and Disability Insurance Trust Funds*, Tables F1, F3, and F4, pp. 128–134.

Note: Figures for 1945–1985 represent the average of the annual surplus or deficit and balance in the OASDI trust funds over the preceding five years. Figures for 1990–2045 are annual figures projected under alternative assumption II-B of the 1988 OASDI Trustees Report.

system has been financed under a number of schemes, and a variety of alternatives are feasible for the future.

Origins of the Trust Fund Buildup

Ironically, reforms initiated in 1972 to revise the historical funding patterns and ensure pay-as-you-go financing set off the chain of events that has led to the projected buildup. In order to implement the new financing recommendations, in 1972 Congress introduced automatic indexing for both taxable wages and benefits and enacted a revised contribution schedule. To cover the increasing costs of the program that will arise when the baby-boom generation starts to retire, Congress scheduled a rate hike for 2011 that was estimated to be sufficient to finance all benefits over the rest of the seventy-five-year period for which the estimates were made. Although this rate increase would have produced some accumulation of reserves if allowed to take effect in 2011, the intent was, as the year 2011 approached, to spread out the tax increases to match the rising costs, not build up a large trust fund.

Shortly after the enactment of the 1972 amendments, the long-range estimates were substantially revised, showing a significant increase in costs, primarily as a result of new assumptions about inflation, productivity, fertility, and disability rates. A few years later it became clear that the system was also facing short-run financial problems because economic performance had been weaker than expected. In order to strengthen the financing of the program, Congress passed legislation in 1977 that extensively revised both the revenue and benefit provisions.

Most of the additional revenue in the 1977 legislation came from an increase in the planned 2011 rate hike and a change to make it effective in 1990. This meant that the rate hike originally scheduled to coincide with rising benefit costs as the baby boomers retired would take effect while costs were declining as a percent of payrolls. The combination of increased revenues and lower costs was projected to produce surpluses in the program through the year 2010. The 1978 annual report of the trustees projected trust fund assets equal to 2.5 times annual outlays by the year 2005.[4] Because the 1977 legislation established actuarial balance for only fifty years, the trust fund reserves were then scheduled to be depleted in the early 2020s.

Revenues and costs did not turn out as expected, and further remedial legislation was needed. The 1983 amendments were designed both to relieve a short-term financing crisis and to remove the long-term deficit left by the 1977 amendments. In the process, the legislation greatly increased the size and extended the duration of the reserve buildup. This was accomplished primarily by increasing revenues somewhat through the taxation of benefits and by reducing costs significantly through the extension of the retirement age. As a result of the 1983 legislation, the intermediate cost estimates indicate that fund assets will equal 4.3 times annual outlays in 2005, rather than 2.5 times as projected under the 1977 legislation. Assets will ultimately rise to a peak of 5.5 times annual outlays in 2018. The nominal value of fund assets will continue to increase until 2029 but will eventually be drawn down as bonds are redeemed to cover annual deficits in the years between 2029 and 2046.

The main point is that the projected buildup was a by-product of, first, moving a scheduled tax rate from the year 2011 to 1990 in the 1977 legislation and, second, decreasing long-run costs significantly in the 1983 legislation. No one involved in the process ever considered the advantages or disadvantages of trying to increase our national saving rate through the Social Security program. If someone had, Congress would not have come up with the plan of building up reserves and then drawing them back down to cover a permanent increase in costs per worker because of the decline in the birth rate.

In short, the history of these surpluses indicates that the slate is clean and that policymakers can choose any future course of action deemed desirable. They can use Social Security surpluses to increase national saving, use Social Security reserves to fund other government spending, or return the system to a pay-as-you-go basis.

Outlook for Social Security Financing

Each year the Social Security trustees prepare a report on the outlook for the system's financing over the next seventy-five years. This report includes four sets of projections based on alternative demographic and economic assumptions. Demographic factors are important because they determine the number of people who will be receiving benefits as compared to the number of workers who will be paying taxes. The lower the birth rate, the fewer are the number of workers per retiree and the higher are the projected costs per active worker. Similarly, the longer the life expectancy, the higher is the per-worker cost. Economic considerations are important because in an automatically adjusted system such as ours, costs depend crucially on the difference between the rate of increase in prices and the rate of increase in wages. This is true because tax revenues increase with the growth of wages and benefits rise with the increase in prices.

The central estimates prepared by the trustees assume that the fertility rate will remain at its present, low level of 1.9 children per woman of childbearing age, that life expectancy at age sixty-five will ultimately be eighteen years for men and twenty-two years for women, and that the difference between the growth of wages and prices will be 1.3 percentage points. These very reasonable assumptions produce the projected costs and asset accumulation shown in Figures 12.2 and 12.3. Costs significantly less than tax receipts (predominantly payroll taxes but also income from taxation of benefits) over the period 1990–2015 will result in the rapid accumulation of reserves, as illustrated by Figure 12.2. If current law remains unchanged, these reserves will be drawn

FIGURE 12.2
OASDI Income and Cost Rates for Selected Years
(percentage of taxable payroll)

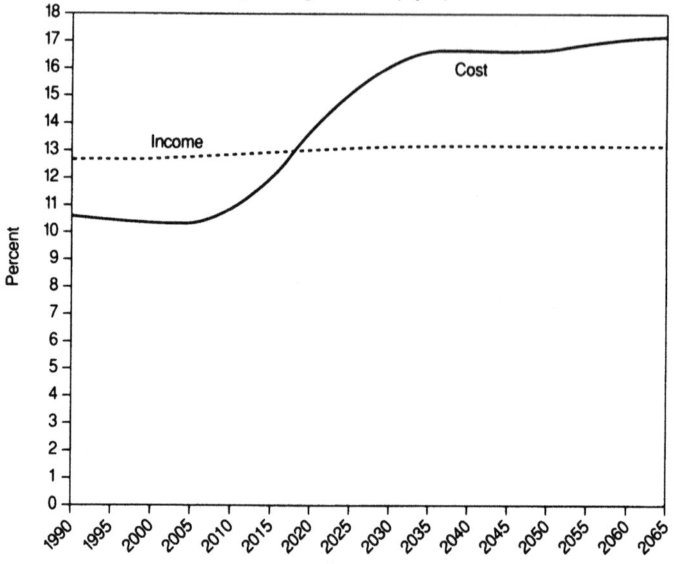

Source: Social Security Administration, *1989 Annual Report of the Board of Trustees of the Federal Old-Age and Survivors Insurance Trust Funds* (Washington, D.C.: Social Security Administration, 1989), Table 26, p. 69.

FIGURE 12.3
OASDI Trust Fund Accumulation for Selected Years
(percentage of annual outgo)

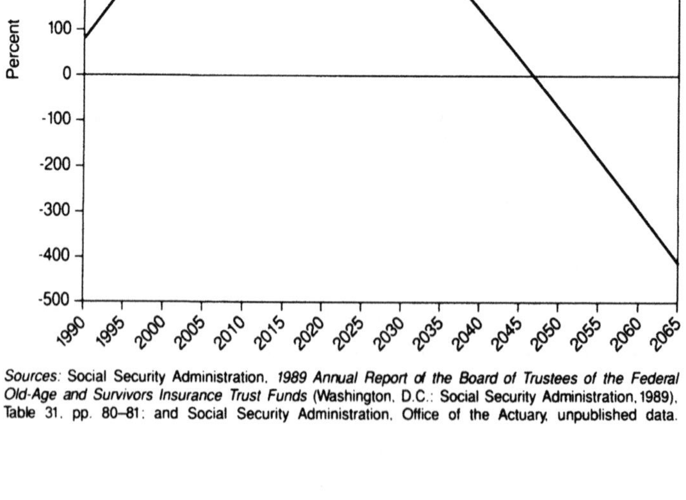

Sources: Social Security Administration, *1989 Annual Report of the Board of Trustees of the Federal Old-Age and Survivors Insurance Trust Funds* (Washington, D.C.: Social Security Administration, 1989), Table 31, pp. 80–81; and Social Security Administration, Office of the Actuary, unpublished data.

down to cover the excess of costs over revenues in the period 2018 through 2046. Thereafter, a tax rate increase will be required to finance the system on a current-cost basis; according to these intermediate projections, the combined employee-employer payroll tax will have to rise from its present level of 12.4 percent to roughly 17.0 percent in 2046.

If reserves are not accumulated, payroll tax rates could be significantly lower than the present 12.4 percent for the next twenty-five years but would have to rise thereafter. A rate hike to about 16 percent in 2018 and another increase to 17 percent in 2046 would probably be required to finance the program on a more or less pay-as-you-go basis. In other words, rates would be lower through 2017, higher between 2018 and 2046, and the same after 2046 as they would have been under the scheduled funding scheme. (It should be noted that the required tax rate increases are of roughly the same magnitude as those experienced by workers over the 1968–1990 period and are therefore completely manageable.)

Prefunding as scheduled under current law allows the system to maintain a constant tax rate until about 2050. This will be true regardless of whether the buildup in the trust funds actually produces increased national saving or the reserves are used to finance other government programs. In either case, benefits for the average worker will remain roughly 41 percent of preretirement earnings, and the combined employer-employee OASDI tax rate (under the intermediate assumptions) will stay at 12.4 percent over the entire projection period. On a superficial level, how the trust fund reserves are used will have no effect on the Social Security program. What difference, then, does it make whether or not the buildup of reserves actually produces increased national saving?

THE ECONOMICS OF INCREASING NATIONAL SAVING THROUGH SOCIAL SECURITY

In the broadest terms, increased saving matters not because it will affect the *proportion* of the budget pie required for Social Security but because greater saving will expand the *size* of the pie available for everyone. If the trust fund assets are used to increase national saving and investment, future workers will have more money with which to pay retirement benefits for the baby boomers and for subsequent generations of retirees, and future levels of retirement benefits will be higher. The specific pattern of sacrifice and gain over time, however, depends on the precise nature of the experiment. This section briefly discusses the plan incorporated in current law under which trust fund reserves are accumulated and then drawn down, describes an alternative approach whereby periodic tax increases ensure that accumulated trust funds are maintained, and explores the possibility that the buildup of trust fund reserves may not produce any new saving.

Impact of Building Up and Drawing Down Reserves

This discussion assumes that the buildup of Social Security reserves actually does result in a net positive accumulation of funds at the federal level. That is, the accumulation of reserves in the Social Security trust funds represents net saving by the government and, unless it is offset completely by a reduction in private saving, implies that a higher proportion of current output will be devoted to capital formation.[5]

If the current level of national saving is too low and if monetary and other nonfiscal policies ensure full employment, surpluses at the federal level will lead to a higher rate of long-term growth in the supply of capital and greater future levels of output and income. Until 2018, Social Security surpluses will come from two sources: an excess of tax income over outgo and interest received on accumulated assets. Even though outlays will begin to exceed tax revenue after 2018, the Social Security system will continue to add to national saving because of interest payments through 2029. After 2029, the trustees of the Social Security trust funds will have to redeem their holdings of government bonds to pay benefits. During this second period, the process will work in reverse. The redemption of the government bonds and the transfer of these funds to the public will represent dissaving by the federal government. This means that a lower portion of current output will be devoted to capital formation, unless offset by an increase in private saving.

The exercise is primarily one of shifting the pattern of consumption from the early half of the period to the later. That is, people living during the period of accumulation will have lower per capita consumption than they would otherwise have. During the period of drawdown consumption will receive a boost from two sources. First, the increased saving and capital accumulation from the buildup of the trust funds will start to pay off in the form of higher levels of national output and consumption. Second, the drop in saving brought on by the drawing down of the trust fund assets could create a consumption boom similar to the one we have just experienced.

The rationale for such a shift in consumption patterns, of course, is that the people contributing during the period of accumulation are part of the baby-boom generation. This very large cohort would place a significant burden on the following generation if all of its retirement benefits as well as its health care benefits were financed on a pay-as-you-go basis. Because of the magnitude of this potential burden, the argument goes, this generation should pay for some of its retirement in advance by accumulating reserves in the Social Security trust funds.

The other side of the argument is that because of its large size, the baby-boom generation has had a difficult time. These people attended overcrowded schools, experienced difficulties finding jobs, and found slow advancement once on the job. The mere size of this group has contributed to the virtual freezing of real wages for a decade and has made it difficult to find affordable housing. Whether or not this generation should be the one to contribute to its own retirement in addition to financing benefits for current retirees is an issue that should be part of the funding debate.

Another factor that should be considered is the wisdom of drawing down the trust fund reserves once they are accumulated. The discussion surrounding this part of the proposal seems to imply that the United States is facing a temporary blip in the cost of Social Security as the baby-boom generation passes through—a pig being swallowed by a python. In other words, the implication is that the number of beneficiaries per hundred workers will go from its current level of thirty up to fifty-five and then back down. This is not the case. This country is facing a permanent increase in the ratio of beneficiaries to workers because the fertility rate, which has been reduced by nearly one-half since 1960, is expected to remain around its present level. The number of beneficiaries per hundred workers will rise from the present level to fifty-five and remain there, and the pay-as-you-go costs of the Social Security program will increase proportionately. Hence, if the decision is made to prefund some Social Security benefits, it makes more sense to build up the fund and keep it as a permanent source of partial funding rather than draw it down. This would require a tax increase around the year 2018. This issue should also enter the funding controversy.

Impact of Accumulating and Maintaining Reserves

A recent Brookings Institution study examined the economic implications of building up a trust fund and maintaining it.[6] According to the study, the creation of a permanent fund is the natural outcome of the assumption that payroll tax rates will be increased whenever long-term deficits emerge in the Social Security program over the next seventy-five years. The emergence of long-term deficits is inevitable because each successive annual seventy-five-year projection will contain one fewer early year with a large surplus and one additional later year with a large deficit. Eliminating these periodic deficits requires several separate increases cumulating at 2.4 percentage points between 1990 and 2060. With this system of adjusted tax rates in place, the authors employed a model of the economy to estimate the effect on the capital stock, output, wages, and benefits of using the Social Security surpluses to increase national saving.

The results are very interesting: Saving through the Social Security system does relieve the burden of supporting the added numbers of retirees in the future, but the difference between the worlds with and without the trust fund buildup is not dramatic. If the productivity growth underlying the Social Security trustees' intermediate projections materializes, the net wage in 2020 after the Social Security tax is paid will be 199 percent of today's level without the additional saving, 211 percent with it.[7] At lower levels of productivity growth, the incremental contribution of the additional saving becomes more important. If productivity growth should fall as low as 0.4 percent per year, the net wage would be only 127 percent of today's level without the saving and 138 percent with it.

On the benefit side, the Brookings study revealed a similar pattern. Under the intermediate productivity assumptions, real benefits in 2020 would be 129 percent of today's level without the Social Security saving and 135 percent with it. With very low productivity, the difference would be 100 percent versus 107 percent. Because of the repeated Social Security tax increases, a substantial reserve fund continues to exist at the end of the forecast period. But the differences between net after-tax wages and benefits with and without the saving in 2060 are very similar to those in 2020.

The Brookings results indicate that building up and maintaining a trust fund may well be desirable public policy because prefunding can eliminate all the added pension costs generated by the increasing proportion of beneficiaries in the total population. But the results highlight the fact that the difference in welfare between the saving and no-saving scenarios is relatively small, particularly compared to the impact of other factors such as the rate of productivity growth.

Translating Reserve Accumulation into National Saving

The necessity of prefunding may be open to debate, but a result that almost all commentators agree should be avoided is one in which the reserves amassed in the Social Security trust funds are spent on current consumption. Since the origins of the Social Security program in the 1930s, opponents of funding have argued that Congress will use the assets in the trust funds to pay for current consumption. This potential problem is typically, albeit imprecisely, characterized as using surpluses in the Social Security trust funds to cover deficits in the rest of the budget. The real concern, however, is not one of deficits but rather one of behavioral response. That is, critics worry that the surpluses in the Social Security trust funds will encourage Congress either to spend more money or to raise less in taxes than it otherwise would. Thus, the issue is one of fiscal discipline. By removing pressure to scrutinize the merits of alternative spending proposals, the Social Security reserves could allow Congress either to liberalize Social Security benefits or to finance marginal projects in the non–Social Security portion of the budget, thereby producing higher spending than would otherwise occur. Alternatively, by appearing to be available to cover general government outlays, the Social Security surpluses could reduce incentives to raise taxes.

One would think that the likelihood of producing this type of behavioral response would vary inversely with the availability of trust fund revenues for general budget purposes. One factor in this regard is probably whether the Social Security programs are included in some type of unified budget or are accounted for separately. When trust fund activity is integrated with other federal functions and the total is reported as a single figure, as has been true in the United States since 1969,[8] Congress and the public are encouraged to think that the trust fund reserves are available to cover general government outlays. This tendency is reinforced if Social Security is included in deficit reduction targets, as has been true under the Gramm-Rudman-Hollings legislation.

Another closely related factor is the ease with which the Treasury can borrow from the trust funds. This depends on the extent to which the administration and the finances of the Social Security trust funds and the rest of the government are intertwined. In the United States, the secretary of the Treasury is also the managing trustee of the trust funds, and the finances of the Social Security trust funds and the rest of the budget are closely intermingled. In the same vein, the extent to which the trust funds are a captive market of the Treasury may also affect the extent to which Social Security surpluses produce additional investment. If trust fund surpluses are used to cover current consumption, they will have contributed nothing to overall saving and capital accumulation and taxpayers will be no richer than they would have otherwise been. The burden of supporting beneficiaries in the second half of the period will be the same as if the system had all along been financed on a pay-as-you-go basis. The only effect of accumulating Social Security surpluses will have been to alter the composition of federal revenues over time. General government expenditures during the first half of the period would be financed by the relatively regressive payroll tax rather than by the more progressive income tax, and future benefit payments would be financed by general revenues. Reserve accumulation under these circumstances would create no economic benefit and would produce very undesirable distributional consequences.

FOREIGN EXPERIENCE

This section examines the experiences of other countries that have attempted to prefund their public pensions. These experiences may aid us in assessing the feasibility of embarking on a similar program in the United States.

Evaluating whether trust fund reserve accumulations have increased national saving entails answering two questions. The first is, Did the existence of the surpluses in the public pension plans generate greater government expenditures or lower tax revenues in the rest of the budget? If the overall government budget deficit remained unchanged, the public pension buildup probably caused the government to spend more money or to raise less revenue than it would otherwise have done. In this case, additional saving probably did not occur.

This may not always be the case, however. An exception would be those instances in which the government increased expenditures but through investment in physical or human capital rather than through consumption. Thus, the second question is, What was the nature of the additional government expenditure? The building of roads, bridges, and other types of physical infrastructure is just as much an investment as is the construction of any factory in the private sector. Equally important is investment in human beings because future output will depend on a healthy and educated work force. Thus, in evaluating the experience of other countries, we must assess the composition of government spending as well as determine whether the trust fund accumulations encouraged either greater expenditures or reduced tax revenues.

Sweden, Japan, and Canada have all attempted to increase national saving by accumulating large trust fund reserves in an effort to ease the burden of future pension costs. These countries have accumulated substantial amounts of money in their public pension plans; pension reserves currently amount to 30 percent of gross domestic product (GDP) in Sweden, 18 percent of GDP in Japan, and 8 percent of GDP in Canada. The individual countries, however, have had varying degrees of success in translating their pension fund accumulation into national saving. The following sections summarize the results of a more extensive study that attempted to assess the extent to which the reserves were used to increase national saving as opposed to cover current expenses in the rest of the budgets.[9] The study was based on government accounts data prepared by the Organisation for Economic Co-operation and Development. These data were particularly valuable because they attempted to standardize for differences in accounting and included separate figures for government deficits (revenues less outlays) and for government saving (revenues less outlays plus net capital investment).[10]

Sweden

Sweden has two public pension programs: the basic social security pension and the national pension, Allman Tillaggspension (ATP). The basic social security program, established in 1913, pays old-age benefits to all people aged sixty-five and older regardless of their labor force status; the ATP, established in 1958 after the workers' trade-union movement pushed for reforms, pays earnings-related pensions to those with substantial labor force attachment and their dependents.

The decision to prefund the new ATP supplementary earnings-related pension reflected concerns that increasing benefits would lead to decreased private saving and that ATP benefits would absorb a growing share of resources as the ratio of beneficiaries to workers increased. Thus, the rationale for setting up the National Pension Insurance Fund (Allmanna Pension foden, or AP fund) in 1959 was twofold: to counteract the expected drop in private saving resulting from the establishment of the new pension plan and to increase the long-run level of Swedish national saving. In order to build up the AP fund, payment of full benefits was delayed until 1979.

TABLE 12.1
Swedish Government Saving and Deficit or Surplus, 1960–1986
(percent of GDP)

	General		Central and Social Security		Central		Social Security		Local	
Year	Saving	Deficit or Surplus	Saving	Deficit or Surplus	Saving	Deficit or Surplus	Saving	Deficit or Surplus	Saving	Deficit or Surplus
1960	5.25	2.01	3.39	2.01	2.62	1.24	.77	.77	1.86	0
1961	6.72	3.47	5.37	4.03	4.34	3.01	1.03	1.02	1.36	-.56
1962	7.63	4.04	5.78	4.41	3.97	2.61	1.81	1.80	1.86	-.37
1963	7.27	2.93	5.42	3.76	3.07	1.42	2.35	2.35	1.84	-.83
1964	7.68	2.92	5.87	4.09	3.21	1.43	2.66	2.66	1.81	-1.17
1965	9.22	4.53	7.34	5.49	4.43	2.59	2.91	2.90	1.89	-.96
1966	9.11	4.20	6.49	4.73	3.27	1.51	3.23	3.22	2.62	-.53
1967	9.07	3.68	5.77	3.95	2.18	.36	3.59	3.59	3.30	-.27
1968	9.64	3.97	6.26	4.52	2.08	.34	4.18	4.18	3.38	-.55
1969	9.86	4.63	6.80	5.14	2.52	.86	4.28	4.28	3.07	-.50
1970	9.77	4.42	7.96	6.05	3.83	1.91	4.14	4.14	1.80	-1.63
1971	10.08	5.20	8.88	7.02	4.40	2.54	4.48	4.48	1.20	-1.82
1972	9.14	4.42	6.77	4.66	2.10	-.02	4.68	4.67	2.37	-.24
1973	7.87	4.08	6.03	4.21	1.61	-.21	4.42	4.42	1.84	-.13
1974	5.43	1.96	4.09	2.41	-.13	-1.81	4.22	4.22	1.34	-.45
1975	5.79	2.75	5.39	3.93	1.49	.03	3.90	3.90	.40	-1.18
1976	7.57	4.54	7.28	5.64	3.12	1.49	4.16	4.15	.29	-1.10
1977	5.38	1.68	4.53	2.53	.46	-1.54	4.08	4.07	.85	-.85
1978	3.46	-.47	.95	-1.37	-2.84	-5.16	3.80	3.79	2.50	.90
1979	1.43	-2.95	-.58	-3.43	-3.99	-6.84	3.41	3.40	2.01	.49
1980	-.22	-3.74	-1.84	-3.78	-5.05	-7.00	3.22	3.21	1.62	.04
1981	-1.27	-4.91	-2.89	-4.90	-6.14	-8.14	3.24	3.24	1.62	0
1982	-2.51	-6.35	-4.07	-6.50	-7.05	-9.47	2.97	2.97	1.57	.15
1983	-1.39	-4.98	-2.81	-5.07	-5.51	-7.77	2.70	2.70	1.42	.09
1984	-.07	-2.60	-1.23	-2.63	-4.08	-5.48	2.85	2.85	1.16	.03
1985	-1.28	-3.76	-1.91	-3.29	-4.42	-5.80	2.51	2.51	.63	-.47
1986	1.53	-.72	1.21	-.14	-1.33	-2.68	2.54	2.54	.32	-.58

Sources: 1974–1986: OECD, Department of Economics and Statistics, *National Accounts: 1974-1986*, vol. 2, 1988, Detailed Tables, Swedish tables 1, 6.1, 6.3, 6.4; 1970–1973: OECD, unpublished data; 1960–1969: OECD, *National Accounts of OECD Countries: 1960–1977*, vol. 2, 1979, Detailed Tables, Swedish tables 1, 10, 11, 12.

From the inception of the Swedish plan in 1959 until the mid-1970s, large annual surpluses in the social security programs—frequently exceeding 4 percent of GDP—were augmented by somewhat smaller surpluses in the central accounts to produce significant saving at the federal level (see Table 12.1). In the second half of the 1970s, the non-social security portion of the budget ran annual deficits, but this development appears to have been the result of a weak economy rather than a response to the buildup of pension reserves. Productivity growth slowed in Sweden after 1973, as it did in other developed countries during the widespread recession of 1974–1975. In an effort to stave off unemployment, the Swedish government continued a high level of public spending that far exceeded the growth in tax revenues and led to large deficits in the central accounts, which dwarfed the surpluses in the social security trust funds.

A return to balance in the non–social security portion of the budget has been an important goal of Swedish economic policy since 1982, and significant progress has been made. Once achieved, however, balance in the central accounts will be combined with declining surpluses in the social security account as the proportion of public pension disbursement covered by interest income increases. The federal government will therefore not be a major source of national saving in the future.

Although the experiment may be over, the Swedish effort to increase national saving by accumulating assets in the AP fund appears to have been quite successful. This success may be attributable in large part to the separateness of the ATP system. The ATP is treated separately from other budget activities in both the process and government documents. Budget documents and deficit targets exclude the ATP system, and in practically all Swedish statistical publications government spending is defined as that of the central government excluding social security. Furthermore, ATP premiums are set without reference to the central accounts. On the investment side, although the government imposes some restrictions on the options open to the AP fund's governing boards, these boards retain a significant amount of control over their investment choices. They can invest directly in the public sector, and in the private sector they can purchase corporate bonds and promissory notes of intermediary credit institutions.

Japan

The Japanese experience, although very different, has probably been successful in its own way. Japan has two partially funded public pension programs. The National Pension (NP) covers all residents of working age (twenty to fifty-nine) and provides a universal basic benefit at age sixty-five regardless of employment status. The Employees' Pension Insurance (EPI) pays an additional, wage-related pension for most retired private-sector employees.

From the beginning the Japanese government intended both the NP and EPI systems to be substantially funded. The motives to increase national saving or equalize burdens across generations were not as explicit as in Sweden, however. When the Employees' Pension Program was established in 1941, it was charged with raising funds for the war effort as well as providing security for workers in their old age. This interest in accumulating immediate funds may explain why the payment of full benefits was delayed until forty years after the program was initiated.

The decision in 1959 to build up assets in the NP fund was more probably attributable to its founders' recognition that the ratio of elderly to working-age population was going to increase sharply. Because of concern over the prospect of dramatically rising costs, payment of the contributory portion of the pension did not start until 1971, twelve years after the plan was established.

Although the precise reasons for the initial funding decisions are difficult to determine, Japanese officials and commentators now tend to view the lack of full funding of the public pensions as a failing. In fact, the Japanese are frequently reluctant to provide international organizations with data on reserves in the NP and EPI funds; they believe these moneys provide a misleading picture of the health of the government because the public pension programs face unfunded liabilities for future benefits that dwarf the magnitude of the assets on hand. In other words, the Japanese appear to view full funding as the norm and deviations from this standard as undesirable.

At first glance Japan's large, unified account deficits seem to indicate that despite reserves equal to 18 percent of GDP, the public pension system has not contributed to national saving (see Table 12.2). Nevertheless, if the increased government spending takes the form of investment that would otherwise not have taken place, the expenditure of the social security buildup can also add to national saving and investment. In fact, the Japanese government maintains a capital budget through which the public pension reserves are directed.

A brief explanation of the Japanese investment procedures may be useful. The Japanese budget consists of four parts: the general budget, thirty-eight special accounts, eleven government-affiliated agencies, and the Fiscal Investment Loan Program (FILP), which is characterized as the Japanese capital budget. The EPI and NP programs each maintain special accounts and deposit any surpluses after payment of benefits with the Trust Fund Bureau, which also maintains a special account (see Figure 12.4). The assets of the Trust Fund Bureau, along with those of the Industrial Investment Special Account and the Postal Life Insurance Fund, and bonds and borrowings guaranteed by the central government are then made available to the Fiscal Investment Loan Program. The FILP provides funds for housing, hospitals, power plants, and other public endeavors by purchasing bonds from a variety of special accounts, government-affiliated agencies, local governments, and public corporations. The primary mandate governing the capital budget agenda is that its funds be used on a sound and profitable basis to meet public needs. In this manner, the Japanese government directs a large portion of the EPI's and the NP's reserves toward productive investment. In other words, the Japanese government does indeed spend the surpluses, but it spends them on public-sector investments. This spending pattern explains the significant difference in Table 12.2 between "deficit or surplus" and "saving" for the central and social security accounts combined.

Even though it appears that the Japanese government invests the reserves productively, the net impact of these surpluses on national

TABLE 12.2
Japanese Government Saving and Deficit or Surplus, 1960–1986[a]
(percent of GDP)

	General		Central and Social Security		Central		Social Security[b]		Local	
Year	Saving	Deficit or Surplus	Saving	Deficit or Surplus	Saving	Deficit or Surplus	Saving	Deficit or Surplus	Saving	Deficit or Surplus
1960	5.73	1.75	n.a.	n.a.	n.a.	n.a.	n.a.	n.a.	n.a.	n.a.
1961	6.62	2.44	n.a.	n.a.	n.a.	n.a.	n.a.	n.a.	n.a.	n.a.
1962	6.43	1.41	n.a.	n.a.	n.a.	n.a.	n.a.	n.a.	n.a.	n.a.
1963	5.94	1.03	n.a.	n.a.	n.a.	n.a.	n.a.	n.a.	n.a.	n.a.
1964	5.72	.81	n.a.	n.a.	n.a.	n.a.	n.a.	n.a.	n.a.	n.a.
1965	5.25	.45	n.a.	n.a.	n.a.	n.a.	n.a.	n.a.	n.a.	n.a.
1966	4.85	-.32	n.a.	n.a.	n.a.	n.a.	n.a.	n.a.	n.a.	n.a.
1967	5.51	.76	n.a.	n.a.	n.a.	n.a.	n.a.	n.a.	n.a.	n.a.
1968	5.64	.83	n.a.	n.a.	n.a.	n.a.	n.a.	n.a.	n.a.	n.a.
1969	5.96	1.19	n.a.	n.a.	n.a.	n.a.	n.a.	n.a.	n.a.	n.a.
1970	7.06	1.81	4.62	2.24	2.30	-.03	2.32	2.27	2.44	-.43
1971	6.62	.51	4.34	1.59	1.71	-.99	2.63	2.58	2.28	-1.08
1972	6.82	.18	4.55	1.36	1.99	-1.14	2.55	2.50	2.27	-1.18
1973	8.14	2.07	5.72	3.09	2.98	.41	2.74	2.68	2.42	-1.02
1974	6.33	-.04	4.12	1.25	1.33	-1.47	2.79	2.72	2.21	-1.29
1975	2.25	-3.81	1.39	-1.61	-1.18	-4.11	2.57	2.50	.87	-2.20
1976	2.15	-3.67	.95	-2.05	-1.51	-4.43	2.46	2.38	1.20	-1.62
1977	2.18	-4.25	.85	-2.40	-1.95	-5.12	2.80	2.72	1.33	-1.86
1978	2.93	-4.28	1.15	-2.52	-1.36	-4.94	2.50	2.42	1.78	-1.76
1979	2.68	-4.52	.57	-3.15	-2.13	-5.76	2.70	2.62	2.12	-1.38
1980	3.01	-4.13	.83	-2.82	-1.95	-5.52	2.78	2.70	2.18	-1.31
1981	3.02	-3.76	.86	-2.50	-2.04	-5.31	2.90	2.81	2.16	-1.26
1982	2.94	-3.46	.60	-2.51	-2.21	-5.24	2.82	2.73	2.34	-.95
1983	2.86	-2.99	.60	-2.22	-2.22	-4.94	2.82	2.73	2.26	-.77
1984	3.47	-1.87	1.26	-1.26	-1.70	-4.12	2.97	2.85	2.21	-.61
1985	4.42	-.79	1.88	-.51	-1.46	-3.74	3.34	3.23	2.55	-.28
1986	4.58	-.54	2.09	-.12	-1.01	-3.11	3.10	2.98	2.49	-.41

Sources: 1974–1986: OECD, Department of Economics and Statistics, *National Accounts: 1974-1986.* vol. 2, 1988, Detailed Tables, Japanese tables 1, 6.1, 6.3, 6.4; 1960–1973: OECD, unpublished data.

Note: N.a. = not available.

[a]Government data for 1970–1986 are on a fiscal-year basis, while GDP remains on a calendar-year basis.

[b]Includes health insurance provided by local governments.

FIGURE 12.4
Relationship of Japan's EPI and NP Systems
to the Fiscal Investment Loan Program

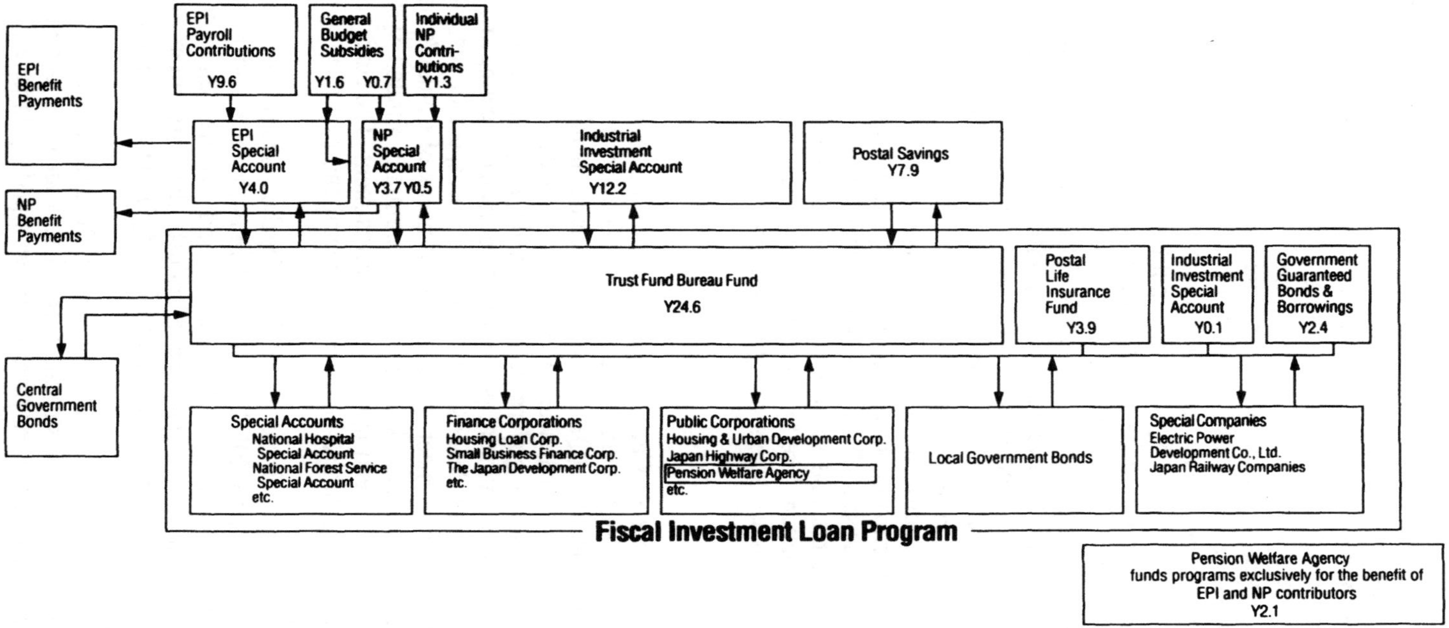

Sources: Ministry of Finance, Budget Bureau, *The Budget in Brief* (Tokyo: Ministry of Finance, 1987); Yukio Noguchi, "National Budget," in *Kodansha Encyclopedia of Japan* (New York: Kodansha International, 1983), vol. 1, pp. 204–206; and Douglas Ostrom, *Japan's Fiscal Policy*, Japan Economic Institute Report no. 18A, 1988.

Note: Yen amounts (Y) are in trillions and refer to the FY 1987 Initial Budget.

saving could be eroded if they caused larger deficits in the general budget. The history and structure of Japanese fiscal policy indicate that this is probably not the case. First, the deficits that emerged in the central accounts after 1974 can be most easily explained by the shock of the oil crisis that hit Japan along with the rest of the world. Tax revenues were dramatically reduced and did not rebound to their pre-oil-crisis levels until 1978. Second, Japanese fiscal policy has always been framed in terms of the general budget, with almost no attention to the special accounts, the budgets of the affiliated agencies, or the budget of the FILP. Specifically, public statements and documents calling for a return to balanced budgets in the wake of the deficits of the 1970s focused only on central account revenues and outlays and never mentioned the surpluses in the EPI and NP special accounts.

As in the case of Sweden, the way Japanese fiscal policy targets are framed makes it impossible for the government to count the increase in public pension fund reserves as part of the effort to balance the budget. It is therefore unlikely that the reserves have led to larger deficits in the central accounts. Unlike the government of Sweden, the Japanese government has maintained control over the accumulated reserves and directed them into government-sponsored companies and other investments that serve public purposes. Despite the difference in its approach, Japan, like Sweden, appears to have invested in a manner that ensures higher levels of future income.

Canada

The experience of Canada is significantly less encouraging. Canada's two public pension plans—the Canada Pension Plan (CPP) and the Quebec Pension Plan (QPP)—were developed in the 1960s in response to the growing inadequacies of the existing federal universal pension system. The federal government originally proposed a pay-as-you-go system, but the provincial governments objected. Feeling the effects of almost a decade of deficits and facing the prospect of massive investments in schools to meet the educational needs of Canada's baby-boom generation, the provinces favored a substantially funded system, with annual surpluses reverting to them for investment. The current financing represents a compromise between the federal and provincial government positions.

Rather than participate in the CPP, Quebec elected to create its own public pension, the QPP. Because contributory rates and benefits have always been the same for both plans and because their buildups of assets in relation to outgo are identical, they are often referred to together. The investment practices of the QPP have been very different, however.

Table 12.3 shows that although the CPP and the QPP have consistently produced annual surpluses equal to roughly 1 percent of GDP, since 1974 these surpluses have been swamped by large annual deficits

TABLE 12.3
Canadian Government Saving and Deficit or Surplus, 1960–1986
(percent of GDP)

	General		Central and Social Security		Central		Social Security[a]		Local[b]		Provincial		Municipal[b]	
Year	Saving	Deficit or Surplus	Saving	Deficit or Surplus	Saving	Deficit or Surplus	Saving	Deficit or Surplus	Saving	Deficit or Surplus	Saving	Deficit or Surplus	Saving	Deficit or Surplus
1960	.60	-1.71	-.49	-.58	-.49	-.58	c	c	1.09	-1.13	.47	-.54	.62	-.58
1961	.47	-2.06	-.70	-1.01	-.70	-1.01	c	c	1.17	-1.05	.11	-.69	1.05	-.35
1962	1.12	-1.60	-.94	-1.15	-.94	-1.15	c	c	2.07	-.45	.74	-.13	1.32	-.32
1963	1.32	-1.32	-.42	-.60	-.42	-.60	c	c	1.74	-.71	.61	-.21	1.13	-.50
1964	2.51	.19	.80	.67	.80	.67	c	c	1.72	-.47	.77	-.16	.95	-.32
1965	3.06	.36	1.28	.95	1.28	.95	c	c	1.78	-.59	.90	0	.88	-.59
1966	3.52	.66	1.81	1.47	.70	.36	1.11	1.11	1.71	-.80	.65	-.27	1.06	-.53
1967	3.05	.22	1.55	1.17	.26	-.12	1.29	1.29	1.50	-.95	.47	-.49	1.03	-.47
1968	3.20	.67	1.69	1.33	.35	-.01	1.34	1.34	1.51	-.65	.65	-.07	.86	-.58
1969	4.53	2.32	2.90	2.59	1.55	1.24	1.35	1.35	1.63	-.27	1.06	.39	.57	-.65
1970	2.91	.80	1.93	1.63	.58	.28	1.35	1.35	.98	-.82	.30	-.29	.67	-.53
1971	2.46	.03	1.52	1.18	.20	-.14	1.32	1.32	.94	-1.15	.42	-.50	.52	-.64
1972	2.32	-.04	1.24	.78	-.03	-.49	1.27	1.27	1.08	-.83	.25	-.67	.83	-.16
1973	3.05	.89	2.01	1.51	.85	.34	1.16	1.16	1.04	-.62	.70	-.09	.34	-.53
1974	4.22	1.89	2.54	2.01	1.37	.84	1.17	1.17	1.68	-.12	1.32	.47	.36	-.60
1975	-.07	-2.52	-.52	-1.07	-1.70	-2.25	1.18	1.18	.44	-1.45	-.07	-1.00	.51	-.45
1976	.22	-1.81	-.07	-.59	-1.18	-1.70	1.11	1.11	.29	-1.22	-.08	-.74	.37	-.48
1977	-.58	-2.53	-1.86	-2.36	-2.89	-3.40	1.04	1.04	1.28	-.16	.37	-.27	.92	.10
1978	-1.40	-3.19	-3.03	-3.51	-4.06	-4.53	1.02	1.02	1.63	.32	1.05	.42	.58	-.10
1979	-.52	-2.02	-2.17	-2.44	-3.15	-3.42	.98	.98	1.64	.42	.61	0	1.03	.42
1980	-1.26	-2.80	-2.18	-2.49	-3.15	-3.47	.98	.98	.92	-.31	.40	-.18	.52	-.13
1981	-.03	-1.48	-.89	-1.15	-1.81	-2.07	.92	.92	.86	-.33	.27	-.30	.59	-.02
1982	-3.86	-5.96	-3.68	-4.44	-4.69	-5.45	1.02	1.02	-.18	-1.53	-.84	-1.53	.66	0
1983	-4.82	-6.97	-4.41	-5.42	-5.21	-6.21	.79	.79	-.41	-1.55	-.96	-1.56	.56	.01
1984	-4.73	-6.70	-5.07	-6.15	-5.81	-6.88	.73	.73	.34	-.55	-.12	-.56	.46	0
1985	-5.13	-7.06	-5.24	-6.05	-5.91	-6.72	.67	.67	.11	-1.01	-.47	-1.07	.58	.06
1986	-3.80	-5.51	-3.64	-4.29	-4.26	-4.91	.62	.62	-.16	-1.22	-.68	-1.27	.52	.05

Sources: 1974–1986: OECD, Department of Economics and Statistics, *National Accounts: 1974–1986*, vol. 2, 1988, Detailed Tables, Canadian tables 1, 6.1, 6.2, 6.3, 6.4; 1960–1973; OECD, unpublished data.

[a]Canada and Quebec Pension Plans only. [b]Includes hospitals. [c]The Canada and Quebec Pension Plans were not instituted until 1966.

in the central accounts, which has produced substantial overall deficits at the federal level. As discussed earlier, deficits in the non-social-security portion of the budget do not indicate, in and of themselves, that the effort to increase national saving and investment has failed. The issue is whether the existence of the pension fund surpluses caused general government expenditures to be higher or taxes to be lower than they would have otherwise been. To a large extent, this depends on how social security is treated in the budget.

CPP financing is entirely off budget; the reserves are not included in budget totals, and deficit targets are established only for the non-social-security portion of the budget. Moreover, the fund is in no way a captive market for Treasury securities; the vast majority of reserves is loaned to the provinces, and only a small residual may be used by the federal government. But because the provinces have such easy access to the accumulated pension reserves, we must consider the behavioral response not only of the members of Parliament but also of the provincial governments.

The provinces might increase their expenditures in response to the CPP commitment for several reasons. The average (and marginal) interest rates that the provinces have to pay on this debt are below market level. The provinces may also be able to lower their own open market rates by reducing the supply of provincial bonds sold to the general public. If the provincial deficits are large, the implicit reduction in interest costs may be substantial. Lower interest costs may thus induce more current consumption of government goods and services.

Most commentators simply assume that the availability of ready credit has encouraged more spending by the provincial governments. The only effort to document increased expenditures was a 1981 study prepared for the Economic Council of Canada,[11] which found that the borrowings induced the Atlantic provinces to reduce their own-source revenues and to increase expenditures. Although difficult to say with certainty, it appears that the CPP loans did induce greater provincial spending.

The issue remains, however, as to whether this increased spending produced additional consumption or greater investment. The data in Table 12.3 tend to indicate that provincial spending on investment did not increase in response to the ability of the provinces to borrow from the CPP. Provincial saving was 0.61 percent of GDP from 1960 to 1966 and did not increase noticeably after the provinces were permitted to borrow. In fact, provincial saving remained at its pre-1966 rate through 1974, after which it became negative. This pattern is also evident in the figures for provincial expenditures on gross capital formation, which have declined steadily since the inception of the plan from a high of 14 percent of total provincial expenditures in 1964 to less than 4 percent in 1986.[12] Thus, it appears that the provincial governments have allocated a large share of the CPP surpluses to current consumption.

The story of the QPP is quite different from that of the CPP. The assets of the QPP, along with those of other Quebec public employee pensions, are invested through the Caisse des Depots in regional business and crown corporations with an eye toward the highest possible return. The fund can also purchase private corporate equities, although it may not own more than 40 percent of the voting stock in any one firm. The investment patterns of the QPP contrast sharply with those of the CPP; by placing its funds directly into regional businesses, the QPP augments private-sector investment.

In summary, except in the case of Quebec, the Canadian government appears to have failed to prefund its public pension system in a meaningful way. On balance, the buildup in the trust funds seems to have stimulated increased consumption at the provincial level and to have reduced the incentive to raise provincial taxes. The buildup of reserves in the trust funds therefore probably has not increased investment or economic growth, and the pie may well be no larger than it would have been in the absence of prefunding.

Lessons from Foreign Experience

Although this brief international excursion seems to have revealed two successes and only one failure, the results are not all that encouraging for the United States because of several dissimilarities. The successes have occurred in countries with stable and disciplined political environments where the same party has been in power almost continuously since the experiment began. In addition, the government plays a more active role in Sweden and Japan than it does in the United States. The country most like us—Canada—was not able, with the exception of the province of Quebec, to translate pension fund reserve accumulation into increased national saving.

Nevertheless, the task is not impossible, and international survey suggests some institutional changes that might increase the chances of success. The key concern in the United States is that Congress will increase its spending or reduce its tax-raising efforts in response to the existence of large reserves in the Social Security trust funds. The likelihood of the members of Congress responding to the Social Security surpluses in this manner surely depends on their ability to count the surpluses toward overall deficit reduction. All three countries studied keep their social security accounts very separate from the rest of the budget, and this appears to have discouraged their legislatures from incorporating social security surpluses in their general budget decisions or their deficit reduction efforts. As long as the United States retains a unified budget, Congress will be tempted to keep one eye on the surpluses when voting on tax and expenditure proposals. Ensuring that Social Security does indeed go off budget when the Gramm-Rudman-Hollings legislation expires is therefore an important first step.

The separateness of the Social Security program as an institution seems to be another important dimension. The U.S. program is really only a Department of the Treasury account, with the secretary of the Treasury as managing trustee. This setup would probably not be desirable in an environment where the Social Security trust funds were being used to increase national saving. If that were desired, the secretary of the Treasury should not have easy access to Social Security funds, as occurred in 1985 in the case of a debt ceiling crisis, nor should the secretary consider the trust funds available as a captive market for federal debt.

The solution for the United States may rest in resurrecting a proposal to make the Social Security Administration an independent agency. This change, which has long been advocated to ensure the program's integrity and administrative effectiveness,[13] may become essential in an era of reserve accumulation. If such a change were adopted, control over revenues and investment decisions should reside with a board that is totally separate from the Treasury. Institutional changes of this type may help, but there is no doubt that the task of using the Social Security trust funds to increase national saving is a difficult one.

CONCLUSIONS

Circumstances have created a situation in which by accumulating assets in the Social Security trust funds, the United States has a convenient mechanism for augmenting its low level of national saving. This is probably the most desirable course of action. Saving in advance would make it easier to support the additional burden that will be created by the retirement of the baby-boom and subsequent generations.

The issues concerning the desirability and feasibility of accumulating OASDI reserves are complicated, however. Fortunately, we do not have to determine today the course of fiscal policy for the next sixty years. Regardless of what we decide to do for the long run, the most prudent short-run agenda is clear: The trust fund accumulation should continue.

Two factors lie behind this recommendation. First, the present reserves equal only 57 percent of annual outlays, an amount that is insufficient to weather the kind of back-to-back recessions experienced during the 1970s. Calculations indicate that contingency reserves should be at least 150 percent of outlays. The most recent projections by the Social Security Administration indicate that this level of contingency funding will not be reached until 1993.

The second argument for continuing the prefunding policy, at least for the next few years, is that the federal government needs all the revenue it can get. If payroll taxes were reduced immediately to the pay-as-you-go level for OASDI, other expenditures would have to fall, or other revenue sources or debt in the hands of the public would have to rise by an additional $64 billion in 1990. Prospectively, the problem is even greater because returning to pay-as-you-go financing for Social Security would require program cuts or revenue increases of an additional $94 billion to meet the Gramm-Rudman targets in 1993. Such a change would put unreasonable pressure on other government programs.

Only after OASDI has an adequate contingency reserve and some deficit reduction has been successfully achieved should we consider our long-run agenda. At that time the optimal choice would be to balance the non-Social Security portion of the budget and run surpluses in the Social Security trust funds.

What many fear may happen, however, is that reserves amassed in the Social Security trust funds will be used to finance current consumption—that is, to pay for current outlays in the non-Social Security portion of the budget. Although the Social Security program would look exactly the same under this scenario, no saving would occur and paying for baby-boom and subsequent retirement benefits would be just as burdensome as it would have been without the reserve accumulation. This scenario would also have the undesirable distributional consequence of financing current general government activities with the more regressive payroll tax.

A better alternative to this type of "pseudofunding" is to return to explicit pay-as-you-go financing. This would eliminate the impression that we are planning in advance for the retirement of the baby-boom generation when in fact we are not increasing saving at all; such a shift would also remove the undesirable distributional effects of financing current government outlays with the payroll tax. Pay-as-you-go financing is a perfectly workable option. If OASDI reserves are not accumulated between now and the year 2018, OASDI taxes will have to be raised sooner rather than later to finance annual deficits on a current-cost basis. It is important to note, however, that the payroll tax rate increase required would be roughly 2 percent each for the employer and the employee. These are not small amounts, but they are manageable.

NOTES

The views expressed are solely those of the author and do not necessarily reflect those of the Federal Reserve Bank of Boston or the Federal Reserve System.

1. The precise date at which the accumulation ceases and the drawing down of assets begins can be defined in three ways. In nominal terms, even though outlays exceed tax income after 2018, fund assets continue to grow until 2029 as a result of interest income, and the drawing down of trust fund assets occurs only between 2029 and 2046. If income and outlays are expressed in constant dollars, then interest enables the fund to continue growing for only three years after outlays exceed tax income, and the real value of fund assets declines after 2021. Expressed as a percentage of GNP, trust fund assets begin to decline as soon as annual outlays exceed tax revenues. Because this latter measure offers

the most relevant indicator of the impact of trust fund behavior on the economy, it is used in the following analysis. The exact dates at which fund assets reach their peak come from unpublished data obtained from the Social Security Administration, Office of the Actuary.

2. The following discussion draws heavily on Alicia H. Munnell and Lynn E. Blais, "Do We Want Large Social Security Surpluses?" *New England Economic Review* (September-October 1984), pp. 5–21.

3. U.S. Congress, Senate, *Advisory Council on Social Security Final Report, December 10, 1938*, S. Doc. 4, 76th Cong., 1st sess., 1939, p. 25.

4. Board of Trustees, Federal Old-Age and Surviors Insurance and Disability Insurance Trust Funds, *1978 Annual Report* (Washington, D.C.: U.S. Government Printing Office, 1978).

5. It is possible to suggest two reasons increased government saving might lead to some reduction in private saving. First, higher government saving in an economy maintained at full employment will lead to a reduction in real interest rates. Lower real rates of interest will encourage private households to consume more and save less. Although economists agree on the direction of the response of saving to such a change in interest rates, they have not reached a consensus as to the magnitude of this response. An average of the extreme estimates, however, would indicate that a 10 percent decline in interest rates (say, from 6.0 to 5.4 percent) would reduce the private saving rate by only about 2 percent (say, from 10.0 to 9.8 percent). Thus, any reduction of private saving in response to a decline in the interest rate as a result of an accumulation of trust fund assets should be relatively small. See Michael J. Boskin, "Taxation, Saving, and the Rate of Interest," *Journal of Political Economy* 86 (April 1978), pp. S3–S27; and Philip E. Howrey and Saul H. Hymans, "The Measurement and Determination of Loanable Funds Saving," *Brookings Papers on Economic Activity* 3 (1978), pp. 655–685.

Another mechanism by which private saving might respond inversely to changes in government saving is a model in which individuals take into account the effect of current surpluses on the welfare of their children. Robert Barro has suggested that parents, realizing their offspring will have a higher standard of living, might reduce their own saving and bequests in order to offset the effect of government actions. Although Barro's model raises interesting theoretical questions, it seems unlikely that individuals actually adopt the long-run perspective implied by the theory, and thus the magnitude of any Barro-type effect would probably also be small. See Robert J. Barro, "Are Government Bonds Net Wealth?" *Journal of Political Economy* 82 (November-December 1974), pp. 1095–1117.

6. Henry J. Aaron, Barry P. Bosworth, and Gary Burtless, *Can Americans Afford to Grow Old? Paying for Social Security* (Washington, D.C.: Brookings Institution, 1989).

7. Ibid., Table 5-4.

8. Until fiscal 1969, the financial activity of Social Security and other trust funds was reported separately from the administrative budget; after fiscal 1969, trust fund activity was integrated with other functions and the total reported as the unified budget. The Gramm-Rudman-Hollings legislation enacted in 1985 moved Social Security "off budget" but retained it for the purpose of calculating whether Congress has met the deficit targets. When Gramm-Rudman-Hollings expires in 1993, Social Security will be "off budget" for all purposes.

9. Alicia H. Munnell and C. Nicole Ernsberger, "Public Pension Surpluses and National Saving: Foreign Experience, *New England Economic Review* (March-April 1989), pp. 16–38.

10. The OECD uses the system of national accounts (SNA) developed by the United Nations to calculate government surpluses or deficits and government saving. According to the SNA, a government's surplus or deficit equals the amount that it has to lend or needs to borrow after financing its total expenditures. In other words, the surplus or deficit equals total revenue minus total outlays.

Total revenue falls into two classifications: current and capital. Current revenue includes tax receipts (other than those from estate or inheritance taxes), property income, proceeds from nonindustrial and incidental sales, cash operating surpluses of departmental enterprises, fees and charges, fines, forfeits, private donations, and financial grants from other governments. Capital revenue equals proceeds from sales of capital items plus capital transfers from other sectors and governments. Capital transfers also include death duties, such as inheritance taxes, as well as donations of durable goods made by the private sector or by other governments.

Like revenues, expenditures are categorized as current or capital. The SNA defines current outlays as purchases of services and nondurable goods, financial transfers to individuals, financial grants to other governments, and all military expenditures. Capital outlays include expenditures for acquisitions of land, intangible assets, government stocks, or nonmilitary durable goods with a life expectancy of more than one year. Transfers of capital assets to other governments and sectors are also considered capital outlays.

Government saving, according to the SNA, equals the surplus or deficit plus net capital investment (capital outlays minus capital income minus depreciation). Depreciation is defined as a government's consumption of fixed capital or the reduction in value of its reproducible fixed assets resulting from normal wear and tear and foreseen obsolescence. The SNA calculation includes wear and tear of government buildings but does not depreciate other forms of government construction, such as roads. Reductions in value that result from unforeseen catastrophes and depletion of natural resources are also not included in depreciation.

Because the U.S. Bureau of the Census does not distinguish between current and capital receipts and outlays of governments, U.S. economists typically consider a government's saving equal to its surplus or deficit. This analysis, however, is more concerned with the productivity of government spending than with the level and consequently uses the SNA definition of saving. See U.N. Department of Economic and Social Affairs, *A System of National Accounts,* Series F, no. 2 (New York: Winterthur Swiss Insurance Co., 1968); and International Monetary Fund, *A Manual on Government Finance Statistics* (Washington, D.C.: International Monetary Fund, 1986).

11. Keith Patterson, *The Effect of Provincial Borrowings from Universal Pension Plans on Provincial and Municipal Government Finance,* Discussion Paper No. 192 (Ottawa: Economic Council of Canada, 1981).

12. Canadian Ministry of Finance, *Quarterly Economic Review: Annual Reference Tables* (Ottawa: Ministry of Supply and Services, June 1987), Table 52.

13. U.S. Congressional Panel on Social Security Organization, *A Plan to Establish an Independent Agency for Social Security* (Washington, D.C.: U.S. Government Printing Office, 1984).

ADDITIONAL REFERENCES

Board of Trustees, Federal Old-Age and Survivors Insurance and Disability Insurance Trust Funds. *1989 Annual Report of the Board of Trustees of the Federal Old-Age and Survivors Insurance and Disability Insurance Trust Funds.* Washington, D.C.: U.S. Government Printing Office, 1989.

Organisation for Economic Co-operation and Development, Department of Economics and Statistics. *National Accounts of OECD Countries: 1960–1977,* Vol. 2. Paris: OECD, 1988.

——. *National Accounts: 1974–86,* Vol. 2. Paris: OECD, 1988.

Discussion

Henry J. Aaron

I agree with Alicia Munnell that the accumulation of reserves in the Social Security system provides an economic opportunity. Because capitalizing on that opportunity poses formidable political difficulties, I propose in the following discussion specific rules that Congress could adopt that would significantly increase the likelihood that additions to Social Security reserves actually do add to national saving.

The economic implications of reserve accumulation are fairly clear and are increasingly widely understood. What is gradually being realized is that Social Security financing matters from an economic standpoint only to the extent that it affects national saving and, through saving, the rate at which the United States increases its wealth and thus its capacity to meet the added costs of future retirees.

Once one adopts that perspective, the additions to the Social Security reserves are just one component of national saving and more particularly of government saving. The question then is not, Is the accumulation of reserves necessary for the financing of Social Security? As Dr. Munnell has shown, this is a nonquestion. Social Security benefits can be paid for by a schedule of taxes that leads to the accumulation of reserves or by one that does not. In either case, roughly the same quantity of resources will have to be transferred to retirees, the disabled, and survivors.

That quantity is increasing, but by much less than many people seem to think. In the last fifty years, the cost of Social Security pension benefits rose from nothing to 5 percent of gross national product. Over the next fifty years, the cost will rise from 5 percent to 7 percent, an added 2 percent of national output. While significant, this increase is hardly backbreaking.

The proper economic question in thinking about Social Security financing becomes, Is the United States saving enough to underwrite the growth necessary to meet all future obligations to the dependent population? And, if not, can the accumulation of reserves in the Social Security system make a contribution?

On the desirability of increased saving, Dr. Munnell is mildly supportive and focuses on what we should do if we wish to boost national saving. She points out that a policy of using additions to reserves to finance deficits elsewhere in government is a species of fiscal fraud and argues, in my view correctly, that almost any other course of action is superior to this policy. The best target for fiscal policy is balance on operations of government other than Social Security (or more ambitiously, on operations of government other than those that entail long-term commitments to provide benefits of all kinds for future retirees, disabled, and survivors). But if that goal proves unattainable, she argues, again correctly in my view, that a return to pay-as-you-go financing would be preferable to the continued use of payroll taxes—an instrument whose principal merit is that it is closely related to the base used for calculating pension benefits—to pay for interest on the debt, national defense, and other government activities. Even though the economic case for achieving balance (or some other reasonable target) on government operations other than Social Security is increasingly understood and accepted, the political problem of how to reach it remains elusive. It is to this problem that I will address the remainder of my comments.

Based on the experience of three other countries, Dr. Munnell concludes that additions to Social Security reserves can add to national saving. She infers from these experiences that the chances that reserves will be left alone are heightened if the pension agency is independent of general government. Administrative independence is important, but I think that two other conditions are also important in the U.S. context.

The indices used to measure the status of the general government's budget must exclude the operations of the social insurance system. The purpose of the additions to reserves in the social insurance system is to promote saving, add to capital formation, and ease the task of future workers in meeting the costs of Social Security. It is imaginable, if unlikely, that the public might be brought to understand that Congress should aim for an overall budget surplus about the size of the annual additions to Social Security reserves and that this surplus should change each year in line with the balance of the Social Security accounts.

Surely public understanding of fiscal requirements would be improved if Congress declared that it is aiming for balance (or some other target) for "the budget," meaning current operations of government, and that the Social Security trust fund should be set up as a completely separate account. The target on the current operating budget might be balance, or it might be a small deficit if, as some have urged, government investment in physical and human capital were greatly expanded. But whatever the target, the purpose of accumulating Social Security reserves would be defeated if changes in Social Security reserve accumulation simply continued to obscure deficits elsewhere.

If Social Security is regarded as a pension system that happens to be managed publicly, it should be treated as an independent financial entity. Doing so would require removing Social Security taxes from government revenues and Social Security expenditures from government outlays and adding the interest payments on government debt held in Social Security reserves to government outlays.

When Prudential Life Insurance or Teachers' Insurance and Annuity Association (TIAA) buys government bonds to add to reserves against future pension liabilities, the interest income each receives is treated as real income to the pension fund, and the payment of that interest is a real cost to the federal government. I can think of no justification for treating the interest payments on debt held by the Social Security Administration against future pension liabilities differently from interest payments on federal debt held by TIAA against future pension liabilities. Recognizing that interest payments on the national debt should receive the same budgetary treatment whether they are paid to pension funds under private management or to pension funds under public management leads to three observations.

First, Dr. Munnell is right to say that the Social Security system will continue adding to national saving until 2029, the first year when outlays will exceed taxes plus interest income on Social Security reserves. Just as TIAA would continue to add to national saving if a surplus of revenues over outlays arose only from interest earnings, so should the Social Security system.

Second, members of Congress and others who say that Social Security reserves will not be available when needed to cover retirement benefits because they are being borrowed by the federal government and spent now are simply confused. The trustees of TIAA know full well that their portfolio of government securities is their most secure asset and that it will assuredly be available when needed to support pensions for retired professors. The trustees may have well-founded doubts about the effects of government economic policy on national saving and thus on the political environment in which promises now being made will come due. But this concern has absolutely nothing to do with current policy on the financing of Social Security or of the investment of reserves. It has everything to do with the stubborn refusal of the president and Congress to change a fiscal policy that continues to cut the heart out of national saving.

Third, Senator Phil Gramm is right in suggesting that the next target for deficit reduction should be based on the deficit excluding Social Security taxes and outlays. But he is wrong to claim that the government budget should not be charged for interest on the Social Security trust fund. Ignoring the interest cost on previous borrowing makes about as much sense as saying that the government should not count as an expenditure interest payments on federal debt paid to private pension funds. This is to say that it makes no sense at all. I can think of no reason for treating interest paid on debt held by a publicly managed pension system any differently from interest payments on federal debt held by private pension systems.

I hasten to add that this last point should not be read as an endorsement of a revised set of annual deficit reduction targets. Previous deficit reduction targets have failed utterly to produce detectable deficit reduction. They have been Olympian successes in spawning a long and growing list of dishonest budgetary practices that have been scorned with bipartisan impartiality by past directors of the Congressional Budget Office and economists of both parties.

In short, the first two steps in effectively using additions to Social Security reserves to boost national saving are to promote some measure of formal administrative autonomy to the Social Security system, as Dr. Munnell suggests, and to adopt a method of presenting budget information to the public that promotes understanding of the separate fiscal requirements of general government and of long-term pension programs. These two steps, although necessary, are not sufficient to create the political conditions for ensuring that additions to Social Security reserves will increase saving. Indeed, in a democracy, no formal conditions can take the place of an informed public and political leadership. But additional steps, together with the first two, would go a very long way toward promoting disciplined management of the social insurance funds themselves.

The history of the Social Security system provides comfort that such discipline can be sustained. Unlike many other countries, the United States has long required annual projections of the costs, revenues, and balance of the Social Security system stretching into the distant future. The Social Security actuaries have long reported to Congress on whether the system is within close actuarial balance—that is, that outlays measured over seventy-five years are between 95 percent and 105 percent of revenues. Even though Congress has not always promptly corrected long-term imbalances, it has done so invariably. Furthermore, the announcement of deficits has promoted public debate that encouraged action to correct such deficits.

Many observers are worried that the accumulation of large Social Security reserves will irresistibly tempt elected officials to use those reserves to expand benefits, especially if reserves are managed through an independent agency. Paradoxically, these large reserves and the attendant concern about the temptation to boost benefits arise at the same time that Social Security has slipped from long-term actuarial balance into deficit. In 1989, the Social Security actuaries revised a number of economic assumptions and made some other technical changes in their long-run projections. As a result, the seventy-five-year projection published in 1989 indicated that revenues were a bit less than 95 percent of long-run costs. The additions to reserves under current law, large although they may be, are insufficient to cover the cost of later deficits—hence, the absence of actuarial balance measured over seventy-five years.

To minimize the risk that additions to Social Security reserves will be used to raise benefits, I suggest the following three steps. First, the trustees of an independent Social Security Administration should be legally required to continue reporting annually to Congress and the public on the long-run actuarial balance of the Social Security system. The technical details of this projection are now under study, and amendments to current practice may be justified. But the projections, prepared according to specified rules, should continue.

Second, the agency should be prohibited from recommending any increase in benefits if the Social Security system is in long-run actuarial deficit. Third, Congress should adopt the procedural rule that if the system is in long-run deficit, any proposal to increase benefits will be subject to a point of order and require a qualified majority—two-thirds in the House of Representatives and three-fifths in the Senate—to pass unless it satisfies two conditions. One condition is that any proposal to raise benefits will have to be accompanied by a payroll tax increase at a flat percentage amount spread over the seventy-five-year planning horizon of Social Security that is *at least* sufficient to prevent any increase in a long-run Social Security deficit. Another condition is that if the cost of the benefit increase is front loaded, the accompanying tax increase will have to be sufficient to prevent the new benefit from reducing projected reserve accumulation over the next five years.

This set of procedures would go a long way toward assuring that the projected accumulation of reserves under current law would not be reversed by congressional temptation to raise benefits now and pay for them later. Any benefit increase would have to be accompanied by a tax increase of sufficient size to prevent any worsening of the short-run or long-run balance.

Such a rule would not require Congress to correct the long-run deficits that are certain to arise for the reasons cited by Dr. Munnell. Although action to correct long-run deficits as soon as they appear would be desirable, I can think of no procedural device likely to be acceptable to Congress that would force action to achieve this objective. In any event, although it would be desirable if Congress continually adjusted the long-run financing of Social Security to maintain actuarial balance, the more important and pressing concern is that Congress will be seduced by large additions to reserves into unduly liberalizing benefits in the near future. The procedures I have outlined here would significantly increase the likelihood that currently projected reserves will actually be accumulated.

Discussion

Stephen J. Entin

Dr. Munnell has been an eloquent defender of the Social Security system for many years, and she does not deviate from that position in her contribution to this chapter. Indeed, it is not entirely clear whether she is concerned primarily with promoting economic growth or promoting the continued growth of Social Security. Before I comment on the question of the trust fund surpluses, I would like to discuss Dr. Munnell's rather sanguine view of the system and its impact on the economy.

Dr. Munnell suggests that the system is in relatively good shape. Although current surpluses are temporary, and followed by enormous deficits, she says nothing about trimming the growth of future benefits. Instead, the whole burden of adjustment is to come from payroll tax increases totaling about 4.5 percent of payroll. She describes these as "manageable" because we have survived similar tax increases in the past. That is a little like the old joke about the man who has fallen off the 102nd floor of the Empire State Building. As he passes the 51st floor, he remarks to himself that if the second half of the drop is as smooth as the first, it will have been a lovely trip.

A 4.5-percentage-point increase in the payroll tax rate is only half the story. With deficits looming in Medicare's Hospital Insurance (HI) program, the necessary increase is nearer 9 percentage points. This would reduce the after-tax wage by about 15 percent and cut employment by about 5 percent, which translates into 7 to 10 million jobs lost in the second quarter of the next century. In fact, it is not true, as Henry Aaron states, that Social Security affects the economy only by its impact on the federal budget and national saving. There is also a direct, adverse excise effect of higher tax rates on the cost of labor and on employment.

In view of the enormous growth in real Social Security benefits per retiree that is projected over the seventy-five-year planning period, one must question the need to leave the current benefit formula untouched. The future benefit growth is displayed in Table F6 of the 1989 Social Security trustees report. A portion of Table F6 is reproduced here in Table 12.4.

An upper income worker retiring today receives about $11,000, or $16,500 with spouse. By 2065, a similar retiree will be getting almost $32,000, or $48,000 with spouse, in today's dollars, after inflation. These benefits are neither necessary nor desirable. They arise from a benefit formula that keeps giving each new cohort of retirees, generation after generation, the same percent of preretirement income, no matter how high real income rises over time. It makes better sense to let replacement rates fall as the ratio of workers to retirees declines over time, rather than struggle to maintain constant replacement rates as the demographics move against the system.

It would also make no sense to pay the benefits only to tax them back. The current method of taxing benefits forces the elderly to report as taxable income $.50 in Social Security benefits for each $1.00 by which total income exceeds certain thresholds. This means that an extra $1.00 of wages or interest and dividend income is recorded for tax

TABLE 12.4
Estimated Real Benefit Amounts Payable to Retired Workers upon Retirement[a]

Calendar Year	Constant 1989 Dollars			Percent of Earnings		
	Low[b]	Average	Maximum[c]	Low[b]	Average	Maximum[c]
1989	$5,016	$8,022	$10,795	57.5	41.4	24.0
1990	5,031	8,286	11,210	56.9	42.2	24.4
1995	5,212	8,609	11,959	55.8	41.5	24.6
2000	5,547	9,162	13,208	55.8	41.5	25.4
2005	5,852	9,685	14,448	55.3	41.2	26.1
2010	6,228	10,305	15,829	55.3	41.2	26.8
2015	6,631	10,969	17,173	55.3	41.2	27.3
2020	7,053	11,669	18,350	55.3	41.2	27.4
2025	7,455	12,355	19,398	54.9	41.0	27.2
2030	7,933	13,147	20,648	55.0	41.0	27.3
2035	8,441	13,989	21,963	55.0	41.0	27.3
2040	8,982	14,886	23,374	55.0	41.0	27.3
2045	9,559	15,841	24,874	55.0	41.0	27.3
2050	10,171	16,855	26,469	55.0	41.0	27.3
2055	10,823	17,936	28,164	55.0	41.0	27.3
2060	11,517	19,086	29,966	55.0	41.0	27.3
2065	12,255	20,309	31,883	55.0	41.0	27.3

Source: Board of Trustees of the Federal Old-Age and Survivors Insurance and Disability Insurance Trust Funds, *1989 Annual Report* (Washington, D.C.: U.S. Government Printing Office, 1989), Table F6, p. 138.

[a]The data assume retirement at the normal retirement age at which full benefits are payable—currently age 65. This age will rise to 66 in stages (two months per year) for those reaching age 62 between 2000 and 2005, and to 67 in stages for those reaching age 62 between 2022 and 2027. Pre-retirement earnings levels are based on Alternative II-B assumptions.

[b]Earnings equal to 45 percent of average.

[c]Earnings equal to the SSA contribution and benefit base (maximum covered earnings).

purposes as $1.50, effectively increasing marginal tax rates on millions of the elderly by one-half (for example, from 28 percent to 42 percent). This penalizes private saving for retirement. It even cripples the utility of front-ended individual retirement accounts (IRAs) by putting people into higher tax brackets after retirement than before retirement, which makes it undesirable to move taxable income from working years to retirement years. This is another excise, or microeconomic, effect of Social Security financing not captured by national income accounting reshuffling.

THE NATURE OF THE SOCIAL SECURITY SURPLUSES

The OASDI *cash* surpluses from 1989 through 2017 are actually quite modest—about $3 trillion, or about 0.8 percent of GNP. They end in about 2018, followed by deficits. By 2031, when the trust funds peak at about $12 trillion, the whole amount consists of interest transfers from the Treasury. None of this is real money, of course. It is merely budget authority, permitting the system to order the Treasury to pay benefits out of general revenues or new borrowing from the credit markets without bothering Congress for an appropriation. This is all the trust funds represent—spending authority. All these figures are much reduced when one adds in HI, or Medicare Part A, which will be moving off budget shortly to join OASDI. One wonders how this added bit of cosmetics will affect the debate.

As Dr. Munnell points out, the magnitude of the OASDI surplus is accidental. Congress could pass legislation to double or halve the size of the trust fund tomorrow, and it would have no current impact whatsoever on the credit market. The trust fund balance is an accounting artifact devoid of economic consequence until it is used as permission to spend real money. Then, and not until then, will the system's trust fund affect the economy, and it will do so through its tax or credit market impact in the year the spending occurs.

Thus, the sanguine view of the system's condition comes only from looking at OASDI in isolation. With $12 trillion in legal spending authority, the system will be in great shape, at least from a budget politics standpoint. Meanwhile, the Treasury's tax and borrowing divisions will be reeling as they scramble in the future to raise revenue or borrow in the credit markets to obtain the cash to pay benefits.

SEGREGATING THE SURPLUSES

Dr. Munnell shares the view that it would be desirable to create a rest-of-the-budget balance, with taxes high enough to cover the trillions of dollars of interest transferred from the Treasury's general fund to OASDI, so that the total trust fund buildup becomes a total on-and-off-budget surplus. Such suggestions are based on the questionable argument that deficit reduction per se is good for national saving and helps promote investment, thereby expanding economic capacity and generating additional future real output for future retirees to consume.

Toward that end, she favors moving Social Security not only off budget but way off budget and out of the Gramm-Rudman-Hollings deficit reduction targets. As Michael Boskin states in Chapter 2, the real impact of the federal budget on the credit markets includes the effect of Social Security; to pretend otherwise is not helpful. It is the total budget that should be balanced. There is no need to go further.

Dr. Munnell's rationale for segregating OASDI is to keep Congress from regarding it as a source of funds. I doubt that Congress can be fooled in this way. One cannot keep a bear out of the honey tree by putting a "do not disturb sign" on the lowest branch. I suspect this suggestion is also designed to shelter the system from taking its share of spending cuts in near-term deficit reduction. This could backfire later when the system begins running deficits of its own.

DEFICITS, NATIONAL SAVING, AND INVESTMENT

As for the deficit argument, a smaller government deficit, or a larger surplus, would not necessarily result in more investment. As Joel Prakken (Chapter 11) and others have noted, it is *investment* that is the real goal, not *saving* per se. It should not be assumed that added investment would be the natural outcome of any and all measures undertaken to run federal budget surpluses.

The desired level of the physical capital stock (plant, equipment, and structures) is determined by the after-tax return on physical capital, which in turn is set by technology, the amount of labor and other factors of production available for the capital to work with, and the tax structure. The deficit per se does not affect these variables; thus, deficit reduction does not lead directly to an increase in the capital stock in the absence of an improved tax treatment of capital investment. The deficit also has limited impact on interest rates.[1]

The ability to add to the capital stock is measured by national saving, which in real terms is the GNP not consumed by the private sector or government. Government purchases of goods and services, however financed, detract from national saving and investment insofar as government spending is for consumption and is not itself investment. A cut in government consumption spending may improve national saving and investment, but a tax increase leaving government spending unchanged—or worse, increased—will not necessarily raise national saving and investment.

The credit market and its financial flows reflect these real activities and are not a separate influence. To count the flow of funds in addition to real national saving is double counting. Unfortunately, those who focus on the credit markets and try to predict interest rates by the size of the deficit are often guilty of partial analysis. They argue for a tax increase to reduce government borrowing from a flow of funds that they assume to be constant; they also assume this will increase real national saving, lower interest rates, and raise investment.

This argument in favor of large federal surpluses founders on an invalid hidden assumption: that private saving is unaffected by a tax increase. In reality, tax increases come predominantly out of saving, not consumption. A study by Michael Darby, Robert Gillingham, and John Greenlees of the U.S. Treasury's Office of Economic Policy found that at least in the first several years, a rise in taxes and government saving is largely offset (by about 80 percent) by a decline in private saving and only reduces consumption slightly (by about 20 percent of the tax increase).[2] By contrast, a cut in government spending primarily reduces national consumption (by about 80 percent of the cut) and raises the national saving rate. These authors concluded that spending cuts are approximately four times more effective than tax increases in promoting national saving. Other researchers may find a tax increase split between saving and consumption of only three to one or even two to one, but the saving impact is large. This brings the financial flows analysis into line with the foregoing real activities analysis.

Dr. Munnell does acknowledge in a footnote the possibility that private saving may react to offset a tax increase. She admits only two reasons. One is a possible drop in interest rates, which I am skeptical would actually occur. The other is the Ricardian equivalence view, as propounded by Robert Barro. Barro has suggested that taxpayers with perfect foresight save any tax cut because they see that the resulting deficit, compounded at interest, will force a future tax increase equal to the original tax cut plus interest; they are so solicitous of their children that they leave this saving, plus interest, as a bequest if the tax increase has failed to arrive by the time they die. Dr. Munnell dismisses both the Barro explanation and the phenomenon he has tried to explain.

The ancient Greeks observed that the sun rises in the east and sets in the west. They thought this was because Apollo hauled it across the sky in his chariot. They were wrong about Apollo, but they were right about the sun rising in the east. There are many non-Barro, common-sense reasons a tax increase primarily reduces private saving. But perhaps the simplest approach is the best.

There are three types of private saving: personal saving, retained earnings of corporations, and capital consumption allowances. A corporate tax rate increase reduces on a dollar-for-dollar basis retained earnings and private saving. A worsening of depreciation schedules (as in the Tax Reform Act of 1986) cuts capital consumption allowances. By eliminating the investment tax credit, the Tax Reform Act cut retained earnings, as did many of the so-called loophole closings. Tax reform devastated two of the three elements of private saving dollar for dollar with the tax increases. Not only do these types of tax increase reduce the funds from which to save; they raise the cost of capital and lower the desire to invest. Thus, these tax increases have two effects, either of which could almost guarantee a drop in national saving and investment.

On the individual side, a tax increase on individuals with families to feed and mortgages to pay comes mainly out of saving and may even force some families to borrow. Income tax increases and IRA cutbacks also reduce the incentive to save. An income or payroll tax increase on labor reduces investment as well because there is less and more costly labor for the capital to work with, which again lowers the rate of return on capital. Consumption taxes reduce saving via the income effect; although they do not create added disincentives to save, like the income tax, they do not improve the incentive to save either and are not a realistic way out of the saving problem.

The effect of a tax increase on the deficit and government dissaving is not likely to be as expected either. As the tax increase weakens the economy, some of the revenue gains anticipated by static analysis fail to materialize. Also, Congress is sure to spend a portion of the anticipated revenue increase. For both reasons, there is no way the deficit will fall by the projected amount of the tax increase. Indeed, the only way a tax increase can raise national saving is if the government has a lower propensity to spend out of added income than the private sector does. Just saying this brings a chuckle. If that were true, why is government a debtor of some note and the private sector a net lender?

Most people take it for granted, without much analysis, that a cut in the deficit will raise national saving, at least somewhat. If we are not in a perfectly Ricardian world, that is true. But the evidence is pretty clear that it does make a difference *how* we cut the deficit. A cut in government's absorption of real factor inputs makes it cheaper and easier to produce more consumption or investment goods. But if spending remains uncut, even a cut in taxes will only shift resources into investment if it lowers the cost of investment relative to consumption. This is virtually impossible to achieve with a tax increase, particularly one that raises the cost of capital.

Even a consumption tax increase fails to achieve this objective. Some have recommended adding a particular type of consumption tax, a value-added tax (VAT), to the tax code to reduce the deficit. A consumption tax or a VAT, as an add-on tax, does not favor saving and investment over current consumption, as it taxes both current and future consumption at the same rate, giving no incentive to postpone consumption to the future. Such a tax does not lower the cost of capital. It can be helpful only as a *substitute* for other taxes as part of a major reduction in the taxes on capital, a highly unlikely trade from a political standpoint.

SHOULD WE RUN TOTAL BUDGET SURPLUSES?

This brings me to the specific question of whether it would be a good idea for national saving and investment to balance the rest of the budget and run large total budget surpluses in the Social Security accounts. I think not for four reasons. First, this is an inefficient way to raise national saving. Spending cuts are superior, and Social Security should do its share.

Second, even if we could arrive at a total budget surplus through spending cuts alone, and even if this raised national saving, a surplus is not an efficient way to increase investment, which is the real goal. Running budget surpluses and buying back the national debt do not accomplish that task by themselves. In fact, it would be better to define saving as the purchase of sources of future income (investment in a productive asset). This generally excludes government debt. (In his remarks in this chapter, Henry Aaron comments that if insurance companies count federal debt as an asset, one cannot say that federal debt held by the Social Security trust funds is not a real investment, too. The point is, federal debt is *economically* unproductive, regardless of who holds it, including insurance companies. There is a difference between economics and accounting.)

Third, if we were in the happy situation of confronting large surpluses anywhere in the federal budget, the appropriate course of action would be to use the surpluses to further reduce taxes on capital and labor. This could include accelerating depreciation until it is of equal value to first-year write-off or restoring the investment tax credit to achieve similar results; expanding IRAs and cutting the double taxes on dividends and capital gains to reduce the tax bias against saving at the personal level; and reducing income and payroll tax rates. Any of these steps would reduce the cost of capital directly and favor saving and investment over consumption. They would be preferable to simply reducing the national debt. The estimates presented by Joel Prakken in Chapter 11 of how this would work in practice are a good illustration of the benefits to be had from spending restraint and tax rate reduction.

Fourth, I agree with Dr. Munnell that a pay-as-you-go system for Social Security is feasible and superior to the running of large trust fund surpluses that do not promote real investment, employment, and growth. I differ with her in that I see no way in which large surpluses could be made to increase total national saving and promote investment, and I would eliminate such surpluses if they materialized in a total budget sense with payroll or other tax cuts. A pay-as-you-go system is also far superior to an industrial policy whereby the government tries to steer funds to favored industries. By all means, let us do our own saving and direct it as we see fit. We do not need federal bureaucrats to direct it on our behalf.

THE MOVE TO PUT SOCIAL SECURITY FURTHER OFF BUDGET

I believe that the economic argument for taking Social Security out of the total budget is simply wrong. Not only will it not work to improve the economy, it is feeding the political movement to put Social Security outside the Gramm-Rudman-Hollings deficit reduction targets. As there is no economic merit in doing so, I view the effort as a political one. It stems from four motives. First, there are those who have honestly been taken in by the misguided surpluses-are-good-for-investment rationale debunked in the preceding discussion.

Second, there is the political desire to assure the elderly that current retirement benefits will not be cut. This is only a gesture. The current Congress cannot bind any future Congress, and the Social Security system can be reached no matter how far off budget it goes if Congress has the will. The fact is that the system is in long-run deficit, especially including HI, and must be revisited eventually.

Third, there is the hidden agenda to force a tax increase near term, which must surely be the outcome if we try to balance the rest of the federal budget by 1995 or 1998. The rest of the budget must indeed cease to rely on the payroll tax when OASDI and HI begin running combined deficits, but that weaning of the budget away from those moneys can be done through spending restraint over twenty years. There is no need to rush the job in a way that will merely lead to greater government spending over time.

Fourth, by isolating the system now, its supporters hope to prevent longer term cuts in Social Security and force another tax increase in the future. After the system has been ignored for twenty years, until its own crisis is upon it, it will be time to engineer another payroll tax increase. Indeed, if Congress waits twenty years before focusing on the system's long-term imbalances, a tax increase will be the only answer. Millions of baby boomers will then be too close to retirement to permit a cutback in the benefit increases that are scheduled under current formulas. It is the nature of benefit changes that they must be phased in very slowly, beginning years ahead of the time they are needed. Now is the time to begin building a consensus that a tripling of real benefits is not going to happen. This will be easier if Social Security is not hidden away off off budget outside the Gramm-Rudman-Hollings spotlight.

NOTES

1. For a discussion of the limited relationship between deficits and the level of interest rates, see U.S. Treasury, Office of Economic Policy, *The Effect of Deficits on Prices of Financial Assets: Theory and Evidence* (Washington, D.C.: U.S. Treasury, Office of Economic Policy, March 1984).

2. Michael R. Darby, Robert Gillingham, and John S. Greenlees, *The Impact of Government Deficits on Personal and National Saving Rates*, Research Paper No. 8702 (Washington, D.C.: U.S. Treasury, Office of Economic Policy, April 1989).

Discussion

Sander M. Levin

Our experience with the economy these last years indicates that there is a lot of necessary uncertainty in anyone's prognostications. But it is nevertheless important to speak with some bluntness, albeit with an edge of uncertainty. That is what I would like to do.

The more I see of Washington, D.C., and of government, the more I am convinced that we need to ask ourselves, "Does everyone really believe there is a problem?" My own feeling is that despite the rhetoric not everyone believes that our present course, the deficit, and our saving rate are all tied together. There is a lot of lip service given to the danger of the deficit but little action. A good reason is that there are some very different assumptions and different feelings about the danger of our present situation.

I am somewhat amused by the talk about Congress and the references to Congress by Dr. Munnell—whose contribution to this chapter is first rate. The majority party in Washington is the one that holds the White House and sets the most basic tone. The possessor of the White House, whether a Democrat or a Republican, holds the power. That is one basis for my humility. I know where most of the power resides.

There are some differences of opinion about whether we are in a fix. I think the underlying assumption of the Bush administration is that we are not and that the status quo is basically acceptable and sustainable. I think Steve Entin expresses this general view in his remarks in this chapter. There is another view: that the present situation is not acceptable and is not sustainable. I acknowledge that those of us who have been saying that for a number of years have not been right, although perhaps the stock market crash in October 1987 indicated we were not altogether wrong.

A *Wall Street Journal* article summed up the situation. The article said that "public concern over the budget deficit seems to be waning. The deficit is shrinking as a percentage of the nation's total output and financial markets no longer see it as a cause of economic instability. Budget deficits are passé subjects on Wall Street. They won't let you into a party in Manhattan if you talk about the budget deficit."[1] I am not sure the test is whether one is allowed into a party in Manhattan, but I think it states rather colloquially where we presently are.

My own view is that our present circumstance ties into our high real interest rates and into our trade deficit, which I believe is destined to stay at least where it is, if it does not worsen. I think our present operational deficit obscures unmet needs in this country that range from the need to build up our physical infrastructure—not only bridges and roads but our basic industry as well—to the need to fight a real war on drugs. Our attack on these problems is not only obscured; it is misshaped by our budget deficit. We say we have only $7 billion, most of it not new money, to fight a war on drugs; we say that there is not $200 million to help the Philippines; we say we do not need a substantial package to assist Poland and Hungary. Although the argument against more spending for these items is put in economic terms sometimes, I think it is also driven by our budget deficit.

I think the strategy of the administration is basically to slide through 1992, and the capital gains proposal very much fits into this strategy. Raise $5 billion, or maybe even $10 billion in year one, another $5 to $10 billion in year two. Continue to fudge the figures in year one and year two. When these moneys are put together with a $10 billion leeway within Gramm-Rudman-Hollings, the administration is within $20 to $30 billion of meeting the deficit reduction targets, and it can slip through until November of 1992. This is a viable strategy if the basic assumptions are correct and if the present scenario is as rosy as it appears.

I lean toward not letting the Social Security surplus obscure, or distort, our operational deficit. There will be efforts to take Social Security off budget, partly as a matter of budget honesty or, as many of us would put it, budget reality, but also because we are concerned about our rate of saving. And economists differ about whether this is really an issue. The rate of saving in this country has not changed dramatically from decade to decade. But I think it does represent a pressing problem.

There are several problems with the suggestion that we increase the rate of saving through the Social Security fund. First, distributionally, this is not a very equitable way to generate saving. Studies have shown rather dramatically that there was a distributional change in real income in the United States in the 1970s. And I worry about generating increased saving through the present, high payroll tax.

Second, we must ask ourselves about the generating of this large surplus and how it will be handled by the administration and Congress. Congress is no more sensitive to the demands of seniors than the administration is. When it came to the issue of catastrophic health insurance, the administration skated around the issue and then pulled the rug out from under the secretary of health and human services, Louis Sullivan, at the last minute. Congress did not act with any more courage. But I think we must ask ourselves whether we really want to generate saving through the payroll tax,' with its problems of equity and with questions about whether it will add to the pressure to increase benefits.

We need to challenge each other's basic assumptions if we are going to make any progress in finding a resolution. I have become convinced through this five-year battle, and it has been endless, that we are drifting because we are not laying our basic attitudes and assumptions on the table. In conclusion, I do think there is a saving crunch, if not a crisis, in the United States. It is part of an overall failure of this country to look at where we are going in the long term and to consider the impact of an operational budget that has now added up to a national debt.

NOTES

1. Alan Murray and John E. Yang, "Lingering Animosity from Capital-Gains Fight Threatens Bipartisan Efforts on Cutting Deficit," *Wall Street Journal*, October 5, 1989, p. A30.

13

Consumption Taxes Versus Income Taxes for Deficit Reduction and Tax Restructuring

John B. Shoven

INTRODUCTION

The low level of national saving is the greatest single long-run problem facing the U.S. economy. On the basis of the national accounts definitions of income, consumption, and saving (upon which I tend to rely, although I am aware of their shortcomings), U.S. saving averaged roughly 3.5 percent of gross national product (GNP) in the last half of the 1980s, down from the 7 to 8 percent of GNP level that prevailed between 1950 and 1980.

One direct consequence of inadequate national saving relative to investment is our need to import foreign financial capital. Another consequence is that a saving rate of 3.5 percent of GNP translates to a saving-wealth ratio of only about 1 percent. This means that in the long run, real wealth will grow at a rate of only about 1 percent per year, and real wealth per capita will not grow much, if at all. It is hard to believe that the United States can compete with the rest of the developed world in terms of economic growth with such anemic saving behavior.

My own initial goal would be to return to a U.S. saving rate of roughly 8 percent of GNP. Although this is a rather arbitrary target, it is both ambitious and barely adequate. To reach that goal in five years would require that consumption growth be held down relative to GNP growth by 1 percent per year. I believe that can be accomplished only with increased incentives for private saving and with decreased federal government dissaving in terms of the deficit. We will need simultaneously to restructure taxes, increase taxes, and reduce government spending. There are encouraging signs that at least some of the following necessary elements may be seriously considered: the liberalization of individual retirement accounts (IRAs), reduced taxation of nominal capital gains, a possible restructuring of the corporate tax, and reduced defense expenditures in the wake of the thawing cold war.

In the second section ("The Tax Reform Act of 1986"), I offer an assessment of the 1986 Tax Reform Act. A natural question is, Why consider major tax restructuring so soon after the massive 1986 tax overhaul? Despite my sympathy with the "leave-it-alone" position, I think the tax system could and should be nudged in a new direction, namely, toward consumption taxation and away from income taxation.

The third section ("The Case for a Consumption Tax") makes the case for consumption taxation. Although we cannot be certain that consumption taxation would indeed encourage saving and also raise economic welfare, some statistical evidence lends significant credence to the argument that a move toward this taxation mode would have these desirable effects.

The fourth section ("Cost of Capital for the United States and Japan") reviews some work that Doug Bernheim and I did estimating the cost of capital for the United States and Japan.[1] Our methodology is briefly described, the results are presented for the two countries in 1980 and 1988, and some discussion is offered on how tax restructuring would affect the cost of capital. Both corporate tax integration and a switch to a consumption tax are considered.

The final section ("Conclusion and Policy Recommendations") offers some policy conclusions about tax restructuring and considers both the desirable form of incremental revenue sources and the possibility of shifting the entire basis for our existing tax system. My general conclusion is that some fairly fundamental changes in the structure of the U.S. tax system are needed.

THE TAX REFORM ACT OF 1986

The political process that produced the 1986 Tax Reform Act in the United States began in 1984 with the goals of producing a tax system that promoted neutrality and economic efficiency, fairness, economic growth, and simplicity. Although the resulting bill has been hailed by some as landmark legislation and the realization of the impossible dream, not everyone shares this view. I would give the 1986 tax bill decidedly mixed grades on these early design criteria: a B− on efficiency and neutrality; an F on economic growth; a B on fairness; and a gentleman's C on simplicity. I think we could have done better. With a report card like this, it is worth looking at what happened and what went wrong. For the purposes of this analysis, the failing grade on economic growth is of greatest concern.

The complete failure of the Tax Reform Act of 1986 to promote economic growth stems from the fact that it did nothing to address this country's totally inadequate level of national saving. In fact, it made the problem worse. It certainly did not encourage private saving—

just the opposite—and it did nothing to reduce federal government dissaving.

In terms of private saving incentives, the tax reform act greatly reduced the advantage of IRAs, 401(k) accounts, and other supplementary retirement accounts for middle- and high-income taxpayers. This seems counterproductive in that the best evidence available indicates that roughly one-half of IRA saving was incremental private saving.[2] The full taxation of capital gains that resulted from the 1986 tax reform also amounts to an extra tax burden on equity saving and can be expected to weaken saving somewhat. The removal of saving incentives at the household level was not offset at the corporate level. In fact, the net tax advantage of debt for corporations (over equity) may encourage firms to reduce retained earnings and to finance investments with debentures or junk bonds, which would have the likely net effect of reducing corporate saving. The boom in corporate restructurings, partially caused by the bias in the tax system toward debt, has probably depressed saving via another mechanism. In most restructurings in the 1980s, the existing shareholders were paid cash for their shares. The marginal propensity to consume out of this money has been estimated to be 0.5, which means that only one-half of that wealth is retained while half is spent on immediate consumption.[3]

IRAs, capital gains, and the tax advantage of debt are only details. The larger missed opportunity in terms of encouraging saving was the failure to move to a consumption-based tax rather than an income tax. (The consumption tax alternatives are discussed at some length later.) The other massive mistake was not to address the government's negative contribution to national saving. The federal deficit is a huge contributor to the weakness in national saving and to our need for foreign capital. The initial design guideline of revenue neutrality, at a time when the government roughly had a $200 billion deficit, is hard to justify. The deficit today is still around $160 billion if the Social Security trust fund account is separated from other government revenues and expenditures and permitted to build up the surplus to deal with the retirement of the baby-boom generation. Not only did the 1986 reform fail to address the need to reduce the deficit; the official projections of the Department of the Treasury found the reform to be revenue losing after the first five years. It can be characterized as revenue neutral only because it uses some front-loaded revenue devices, several of which—such as the onetime Treasury windfall in 1986 that resulted from the massive amount of capital gains realized before the end of the exclusion—have already run out of steam. There is a near consensus among economists that a tax increase is necessary to bring the deficit under control and to permit the economy an adequate level of saving. The only arguments involve the timing and nature of the tax increase and the political problems in enacting one.

The failure to stimulate growth and saving either by continuing to rely on such programs as individual retirement accounts or by moving toward consumption taxation was only one of the big flaws in the tax reform. I do not fully agree with the goal of establishing a broad-based, low-rate income tax system (in contrast to a consumption tax), but even if one accepts that target, the 1986 tax reform fell very far short of correctly implementing an income tax. First, it failed to index the definition of income for inflation—an enormous problem, particularly for capital gains, because nominal capital gains are not even a reasonable approximation of real capital gains. Martin Feldstein and Joel Slemrod found that individuals paid tax on $4.6 billion of nominal capital gains on corporate stocks in 1973,[4] which translated to a total $1 billion real loss on these transactions. Even the sign of the magnitude was wrong in the aggregate, as it doubtlessly was for many individual cases. This huge divergence between real and nominal realized capital gains was not only a 1973 problem; it occurs year after year in an inflationary economy such as ours. Taxation of nominal capital gains is more of a random wealth transactions tax than an income tax. The old 60 percent exclusion was clearly a very crude instrument for converting nominal to real gains, but it probably was better than nothing. We must recognize that inflation is a fact of life in the United States. In most years, nominal returns are at least twice real returns on safe assets, meaning that full taxation of realized gains, even with the deferral advantage, usually implies an overtaxation of real gains.

If one must stay within the framework of an income tax, one cannot do much better than the solutions for dealing with inflation and the definition of income that were proposed in 1984 in Treasury I.[5] For capital gains, the correct indexation requires restating the cost basis in terms of today's dollars, which was precisely what Treasury I proposed. Such a solution would not have to be complex.

Once one accepts the view that nominal capital gains are not even an approximation of real gains and that cost bases should be indexed, the definition of income must be indexed throughout the code. For instance, taxing only real gains and allowing full nominal interest deductibility open enormous opportunities for arbitrage. Treasury I recognized this and proposed a useful, although imperfect, formula for separating real and nominal interest expenses that would have permitted only the deduction of real interest costs. Symmetrically, Treasury I would have taxed only real interest receipts.

The correct calculation of real capital gains and real interest income and expenses is an important aspect of "fairness," although one that does not receive much attention. An income tax system cannot be deemed fair when it fails even to calculate real income correctly. It is clear that the gain that indexation achieves on fairness comes at an inescapable cost in terms of adding complexity. The truth is that taxing real economic income is necessarily very complex, which is one of the chief arguments in favor of a consumption tax.

If real incomes are taxed while a separate corporate income tax is left in place, the definition of corporate income must also reflect the effects of inflation. Unfortunately, the 1986 Tax Reform Act did not achieve any such definition. The items that must be adjusted to measure corporate income correctly include depreciation allowances, interest costs, and cost of goods sold (or inventory accounting). The failure to adjust depreciation deductions was made even more costly in that depreciation lifetimes were extended for many assets.

The second major flaw in the 1986 Tax Reform Act in terms of enacting a broad-based income tax was its complete failure to address the double taxation of corporate equity earnings. In fact, although it is traditional to talk about the double taxation of corporate equity earnings, it is more accurate to term the current treatment *triple taxation* because corporate equity is purchased with after-tax money (and, therefore, one level of tax is "prepaid"). In addition, the earnings on the investment face two levels of tax—one at the corporate level and the other at the personal level. The 1986 reform actually increased our revenue reliance on the separate corporate income tax by transferring roughly $24 billion per year (for the first five years) in tax burden from households to corporations. This permitted the misleading claims of the proponents of tax reform that 80 percent or more of households would pay less tax with a revenue-neutral reform. Such claims ignore the personal burden of the corporate income tax; the first basic principle of tax incidence theory is that all taxes are ultimately borne by households. Nonetheless, roundabout taxes (such as the corporate tax) are politically appealing because their incidence is well hidden from the general public.

The corporate income tax is not just an indirect means of taxing wealthy households. It distorts the allocation of assets in the economy in that it applies only to the return on corporate assets (and not to such important categories of physical assets as housing and most farms). Even for corporate assets, the income tax applies only to investments that are equity financed because interest payments to debt holders are deductible from the corporate income tax base. That debt payments avoid the corporation income tax is a major factor in the merger and acquisition wave in this country as well as the numerous leveraged buyouts, share repurchases, and corporate restructurings. The tax code strongly favors highly leveraged companies.

A third flaw in the 1986 tax reform was that it continued to allow a major form of capital income—the imputed rent on owner-occupied housing—to escape taxation. With housing amounting to from 20 to 25 percent of the entire capital stock of the United States, it is impossible to implement the much-heralded policy of a "level playing field" if the return to corporate equity capital is taxed twice (at both the corporate and personal levels) while the imputed rent on owner-occupied housing is not taxed at all.

The 1986 corporate tax changes—including the deceleration of depreciation deductions, the elimination of the investment tax credit, and

TABLE 13.1
Corporate Tax Reform, New and Old Capital
(billions of dollars)

	1987	1988	1989	1990	1991	1987–1991
Taxes on Old Capital	0.8	-8.6	-17.1	-20.1	-23.3	-68.3
Taxes on New Investment	24.3	32.5	39.6	43.5	48.5	188.4
Total	25.1	23.9	22.5	23.4	25.2	120.1

Source: Lawrence H. Summers, "Reforming Tax Reform for Growth and Competitiveness" (Cambridge, Mass.: Harvard University, 1987, mimeograph).

Note: Taxes on new capital include capital cost, minimum tax, and some accounting provisions of the 1986 Tax Reform Act. The other changes are treated as applying to old capital.

the lowering of the marginal corporate tax rate from 46 to 34 percent—have the somewhat perverse effect of increasing the taxation of new investments and decreasing the taxation on old capital. Table 13.1 shows that over the first five years of the 1986 law, the taxation of existing capital is reduced by $68.3 billion, while the taxation of new investment is increased by $188.4 billion. This same conclusion was reached in the cost of capital studies by Patric Hendershott; Don Fullerton, Yolanda Henderson, and James Mackie; and Doug Bernheim and me.[6] Each of these three studies found that the 1986 law increased the cost of capital facing firms on new investment. (The fourth section of this analysis presents new evidence on the cost of capital and calculates the impact of moving to corporate tax integration or to a consumption tax.)

To defend briefly the other grade that I have given the 1986 Tax Reform Act in terms of simplicity, the tax law was made more simple for relatively low-income households whose tax was already straightforward. But the law was made more complex for many investors as a result of the new distinction between passive and active income. Finally, there was the missed opportunity for the added simplicity offered by consumption taxation.

THE CASE FOR A CONSUMPTION TAX

I will not review all of the literature that has been written on the advantages or effects of the U.S. switching to a consumption tax. The American Council for Capital Formation Center for Policy Research held a conference on this subject in 1986 and subsequently published a compilation of the papers delivered at the conference;[7] a recent survey of the literature is particularly thorough.[8] Instead, I give my views regarding the relative importance of the various arguments and then briefly analyze how certain we can be about the effects if a consumption tax were adopted.

The relative desirability of consumption and income taxes cannot be determined on a purely theoretical basis. It is clear that a consumption tax would eliminate an intertemporal distortion of the income tax stemming from the double taxation of saving. It has long been recognized, however, that while consumption taxation reduces intertemporal distortions, it also contributes to the distortion of labor-leisure choices. A priori, there is no particular reason to believe that either effect is quantitatively more important than the other.

It is therefore necessary to evaluate consumption taxes on the basis of models that are somewhat "realistic." This observation has led to the emergence of a large number of articles that study various reform proposals in the context of reasonably complex models. These articles share an important feature: The impact of consumption taxation is determined computationally rather than analytically. In general, this literature suggests that our current policy of taxing income is rather costly. In his study, Lawrence Summers found that a complete shift to consumption taxation might raise steady-state output by as much as 18 percent and consumption by 16 percent.[9] Alan Auerbach and Laurence Kotlikoff suggested that the steady-state capital-to-output ratio would more than double.[10] In our study of a progressive consumption tax, Don Fullerton, John Whalley, and I found that it would result in gains to the economy of roughly 1 percent of the present value of future national income.[11]

Some of the efficiency gains offered by a consumption tax do not derive from intertemporal efficiency considerations but from the fact that interasset efficiency is enhanced by taxing housing and nonhousing assets symmetrically. A recent article by Jane Gravelle found that a consumption tax offers only very small improvements in the present value of economic welfare when compared to a pure income tax.[12] Nevertheless, the consideration that the imputed rent on owner-occupied housing is practically untaxable on an income tax basis still means that a consumption tax offers considerable benefits from the standpoint of economic efficiency.

None of these studies emphasized the simplicity advantage of a consumption tax, although that theme has been foremost in David Bradford's arguments and was featured in a recent article by Charles McLure.[13] I agree with the spirit of their analysis—that it is much easier to implement a consumption tax on a conceptually clean basis than to implement the principles of a pure income tax. The three greatest advantages of a consumption tax are intertemporal efficiency, neutrality with respect to housing and other assets, and simplification. This raises the question, How certain can we be that a consumption tax would improve efficiency and also increase private saving?

One problem in assessing the findings of economists with respect to the desirability of a consumption tax is that these findings come from extremely complex numerical general equilibrium models. Usually such models are developed, parameter values are assigned, and the model's predictions are computed. From an outsider's viewpoint, however, the whole process involves a point estimate emanating from a black box. Uncertainty about the model structure and disagreements about the appropriate values of key parameters are common. In addition, these computations are usually based on a large number of parameters, many of which are known with very little precision. It is certainly possible that the cumulative impact of uncertainty concerning these parameters may dwarf the quantitative effects predicted by these models.

In a recent article with John Karl Scholz and B. Douglas Bernheim, I began to address at least some of these issues.[14] We attempted to translate uncertainty about parameter values such as key elasticities into standard errors for the outcome of a general equilibrium model. We did this for an evaluation of the adoption of a consumption tax. Thus, although we did not resolve the uncertainty of model structure, we did deal directly with the uncertainty regarding key elasticity parameters. Our study was largely methodological, and its application to the adoption of a consumption tax was based on the pre-1980 U.S. tax system. In that sense, the analysis was dated, although I doubt that this affected the qualitative results. Our findings revealed that one can be quite confident that a consumption tax would improve the present value of economic welfare. The positive point estimate of the welfare gain exceeded its standard error by a factor of between 1.5 and 3.0. The short- and medium-run effects on saving (over the first fifteen years) were very certain, but there was less certainty thereafter. The effects of a consumption tax adoption on labor supply were more ambiguous, although probably positive in the short and medium run. This research suggests that as policy predictions go, we can be quite confident that a consumption tax could improve aggregate welfare. When I add in the simplification possibilities that have not been accounted for, I advocate a consumption tax without hesitation.

COST OF CAPITAL FOR THE UNITED STATES AND JAPAN

The issue regarding the structure of taxation and its effects on saving and investment is often captured by the concept of the cost of capital. The alleged high cost of capital in the United States is commonly blamed as the cause of a variety of economic maladies afflicting the country: the slowdown in economic growth, the disappointing rate of productivity improvement, and the lack of competitiveness of U.S. firms. I agree that the cost of capital is partly responsible for these things, but I am surprised that there is so little agreement as to even the definition of the cost of capital. There are precious few numerical studies, and I believe there are serious shortcomings in those that are available.

Looking at the literature on cost of capital, one finds three common definitions of the concept: the real interest rate on short, safe securities; the weighted average cost of capital; and measures that combine the interest rate and somewhat detailed taxation factors.[15] All of these measures are seriously flawed; measures that combine interest, risk, and tax factors are required. A fairly well-developed body of theory incorporates risk into cost-of-capital measures.[16] Similarly, detailed tax considerations have been taken into account by several authors.[17] But few analyses have combined the two considerations (risk and taxes), and there has been relatively little empirical application of the theoretical approaches that have been suggested. An exception was a study by George Hatsopoulos and Steven Brooks, which included both risk and tax factors,[18] although its theoretical structure is somewhat different from my 1989 study with Bernheim.[19]

In that study Bernheim and I developed a cost-of-capital model and measure that included the three important factors: the interest rate (or time discounting), the risk premia (or risk discounting), and a moderately detailed description of the personal and corporate income tax systems. Because the model development was somewhat lengthy and involved somewhat complicated mathematical expressions, I will only sketch it out here. After its presentation, we tried to assign numerical values to the model's parameters in order to assess the cost of capital in the United States and Japan, both before and after their recent tax reforms. I report here on those findings and add some analysis of the effects of adopting a consumption tax or corporate tax integration on the cost of capital.

Before I proceed to the model description, let me state explicitly our definition of the cost of capital. We define it in the standard way, as the expected pretax rate of return that new investments must offer in order to satisfy the requirements of the financiers (or financial markets) and the tax authorities. One of the big differences in our current work relative to most earlier work, including our own, is how we capture the returns required in capital markets. Most earlier work is based on the real interest rate offered on safe, short-term government bonds, bills, or notes. To us, at least now, this basis seems completely inadequate. It is well known that the expected return on risky investments must be higher than that on safe investments. Empirically, over the very long term, premia for risky investments are extremely large. One indication of just how large can be assessed by noting that the average real pretax return for the Standard and Poor's (S&P) 500 stocks (dividends plus capital gains) since 1926 is 8.9 percent, while the average real return on Treasury bills is 0.4 percent. This difference in average returns of more than 8 percent compounded annually presumably reflects considerable risk aversion on the part of financiers and a considerable cost for those who contemplate undertaking a risky real physical investment. This gap exists even though interest income has been taxed at the personal level more heavily than has equity return.

FIGURE 13.1
Relationships Between Risk and Return

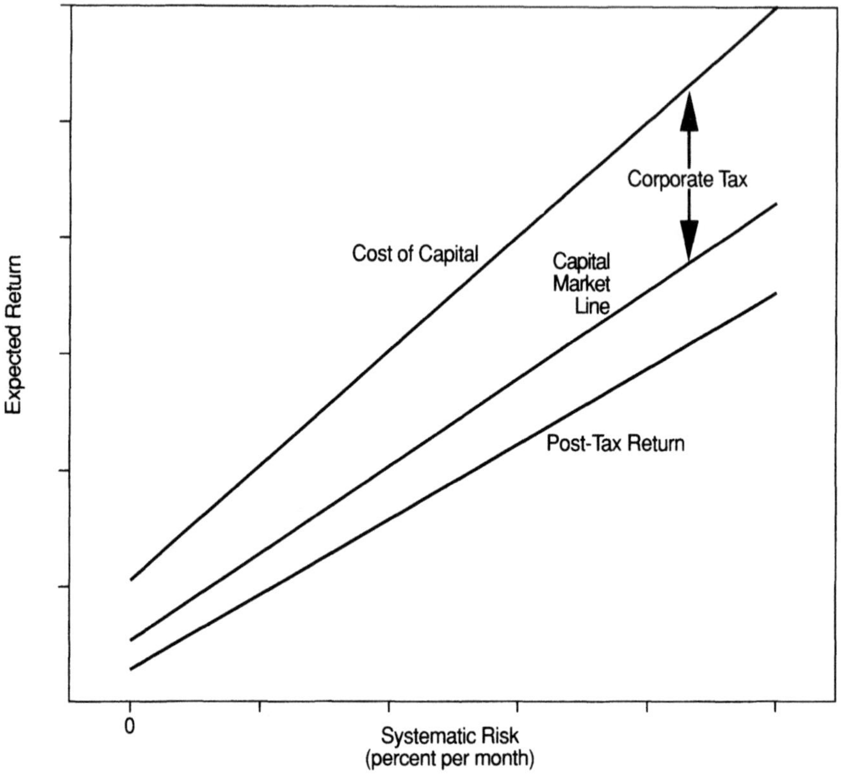

The historical evidence of financial markets is sufficient to make it clear that risk premia are extremely important elements in the cost of capital for risky real investments. The strategy that Bernheim and I follow is to identify three schedules of expected rates of return for investments of different degrees of riskiness. One is the "capital market line," which reflects the expected return as a function of the standard deviation of systematic (undiversifiable) risk in financial markets. The capital market line shows the expected return on assets of different riskiness after corporate- or business-level taxation. From it one can compute (using the details of the tax law and certain equilibrium conditions) the other two schedules: the cost of capital and the post-personal tax return to investors. The three lines are shown in Figure 13.1.

The first step in our approach is to determine the position of the post-corporate-tax capital market line. This turns out to be quite difficult in its own right. Then we assume that all assets must offer equal "certainty equivalent" rates of return. We use the slope of the capital market line to determine the risk premia, which permits us to compute certainty equivalent yields for risky investments. The basic arbitrage condition is that all assets must be competitive with Treasury bills on an after-tax certainty equivalence basis.

In our analysis, new physical investments are subject to two separate kinds of risk: first, the uncertainty as to the contemporaneous marginal product of capital and, second, the uncertainty about the actual depreciation that will be realized on the asset over the next accounting period. In equations, the output of a firm in any period is given by $f(k)(1 + \varepsilon_\delta)$, where k is the capital stock and ε_δ is a zero-mean random variable. In any particular period, actual depreciation is $k(\delta - \varepsilon_\delta)$, where δ is the expected exponential rate of depreciation and ε_δ is another independent zero-mean random variable. This bifurcation of risk into two components has been suggested elsewhere in the literature[20] and is particularly appropriate here because the corporation's income tax applies to shifts in earnings due to income (ε_δ) fluctuations but not to unanticipated depreciation (e_δ).

Without taxes, the cost of capital would be equal to the real interest rate adjusted for the risk premia associated with these two types of risk. The cost of capital would not be a single number but rather a schedule or line as shown previously in Figure 13.1. The precise cost of capital figures for any particular project could be looked up on this schedule once the riskiness of the project had been determined. In a world without taxes, this cost of capital would be exactly the same regardless of whether the incremental investment was financed by debt or by equity. This brings us to one of the first lessons of the Bernheim-Shoven analysis: The risk included in the cost of capital computation is associated with the physical investment, not with the financial instruments used to raise the funds. Some companies (General Motors, for example) could finance a risky project with safe debt. In order to decide whether such a project adds to the value of the firm, the manager should compare the project's expected return to the cost of capital associated with the riskiness of the *investment itself*, not the riskiness of the *bonds*.

Taxes influence the cost of capital in a variety of ways. The corporate tax rate, the pattern of depreciation, the personal tax on interest and dividends, the taxation of realized capital gains, and the lack of inflation indexation of the income definition are some of the important considerations. The taxation of an investment also depends on a firm's behavior with respect to dividend policy and the financial instruments used.

Bernheim and I calculate the cost of capital for equity-financed and debt-financed projects. Unlike the situation in a world without taxes, there is a difference in the cost of capital of a given project depending on whether it is debt or equity financed. This is due to the different taxation of the returns. (Interest payments are deductible from the corporation's income tax base but fully taxable at the household level;

equity return is taxable at the corporate level and also at the personal level, although with special treatment for capital gains.)

Even before presenting some estimates, I can relate one of our findings straight from the theoretical model. Our cost of capital formulae (like those of others) have a multiplicative term of $(1 - A)/(1 - \tau)$, where A is the present value of the tax savings due to depreciation deductions and credits (per dollar of investment) and τ is the corporate tax rate. In fact, that multiplicative term is the only term involving the corporate-level tax, and it affects both the intercept and the slope of the cost of capital line. This means that if A were equal to τ, as with immediate expensing, the corporate tax would not be a distortionary influence on the cost of capital. It also means that the extent to which the corporate tax is distortionary depends crucially on the nominal interest rate. With a zero nominal interest rate, depreciation deductions, even if spread out over thirty years, are equivalent to expensing and the corporate tax therefore is nondistortionary. With a 10 percent interest rate, however, deductions occurring more than, say, fifteen years in the future are worth twenty cents on the dollar or less. This means that A, the present value of the taxes saved with the depreciation deductions, is substantially less than the corporate tax rate, and $(1 - A)/(1 - \tau)$ is significantly greater than unity, thus raising the cost of capital. This crucial importance of the nominal interest rate may be what reconciles the conflicting views as to whether the corporate income tax is more or less distortionary in Japan than in the United States. The corporate tax rate is unambiguously higher in Japan. Depreciation schedules are roughly similar. But the Japanese corporate tax system may be less distortionary because of the lower nominal interest rates and, therefore, the more adequate present value of depreciation deductions; that is, in Japan, A is much closer to τ.

Without elaborating on the remainder of the theory, I discuss implementation. The first problem is determining the capital market line. What is the expected return on the market portfolio, and what is its risk? What is the expected return on an absolutely safe investment? If these two points can be determined, they define the capital market line. If one makes a set of assumptions that basically rule out the importance of higher moments of the distribution of returns, all assets must compete with linear combinations of the safe asset and the market portfolio. This means that all assets must offer terms on the line defined by those two points.

The expected returns on a market portfolio (such as the S&P 500) cannot be determined with complete satisfaction. If the monthly real total (dividends plus real capital gains) rates of return on the market were independently drawn from an identical distribution, the average of a large number of realizations would give an accurate measure of the expected future returns. Similarly, the standard deviation of realizations would give an accurate guide to the standard deviation of the constant underlying real rate of return distribution. The real returns in the U.S. and Japanese equity markets do not seem to conform to the independent draws from an identical distribution model, however. The long-term average realization is still very sensitive to the precise period covered. An extreme example is that the ten-year average of real monthly returns (120 draws) for the S&P 500 equities looking backward from September 1984 was 0.704 percent per month, whereas the 120-month backward-looking average calculated from January 1984 was 0.301 percent per month. The two averages have 112 common entries; yet the 8 substitutions cause the average realization to more than double. Even though this example is one of the sharpest changes observed over recent years, it is not unique. The monthly real return series for the S&P 500 appears to reflect "regime changes" or shifts in the underlying distribution. Similarly, the return series based on the Tokyo Stock Exchange securities seem not to conform to independent draws from an identical distribution.

An example of the lack of stability in the return distribution of Japanese securities is that the annual total inflation-adjusted rate of return realized by the Tokyo Stock Exchange Index I companies was 61.02 percent per year for 1971 and 1972, −1.83 percent per year for the period 1973–1982, and 24.84 percent per year from 1983 through 1988. The return series of both countries exhibit a high coefficient of variation, so a small set of observations cannot hope to indicate the expected outcome. Nevertheless, extending the averaging over very long periods of time (such as twenty years or more) increases the likelihood that the distant observations were drawn from a different regime. Unless the movements in the distribution itself can be described, there is no easy way out of this dilemma. Despite these significant problems, finance economists and practitioners find it useful to construct and evaluate capital market lines based on past realizations over five or ten years. I have examined the consequences of following this practice but am wary of its appropriateness given the apparent lack of stability of the underlying distributions. A more thorough presentation of the cost of capital using this method of measuring expectations is found in Bernheim and Shoven.[21]

An alternative measure of the expected return on equity shares can be taken from the price-earnings ratio (P-E), or more precisely from the earnings themselves. The pattern of price-earnings ratios in the United States and Japan from 1970 to 1988 is shown in Figure 13.2. Basically, the P-E of the Japanese stock market, which started the period at one-half the level of the U.S. market, more than doubled between 1970 and 1973, remained relatively flat between 1973 and 1982, and then more than doubled again between 1982 and 1988. Clearly, most of the recent appreciation of the Japanese market was due to the rise in the P-E ratio rather than to an increase in earnings themselves. The P-E ratio of the U.S. market sagged in the mid-1970s

FIGURE 13.2
Price-Earnings Ratios for the United States and Japan

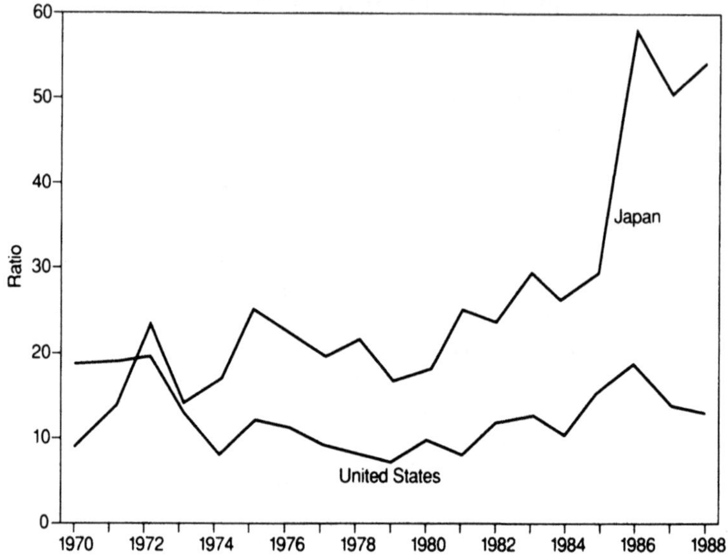

Source: Kenneth R. French and James M. Poterba, "Are Japanese Stock Prices Too High?" Paper presented at the Center for Research in Security Prices Seminar on the Analysis of Security Prices, Chicago, Illinois, May 4, 1989.

FIGURE 13.3
Adjusted Price-Earnings Ratios
for the United States and Japan

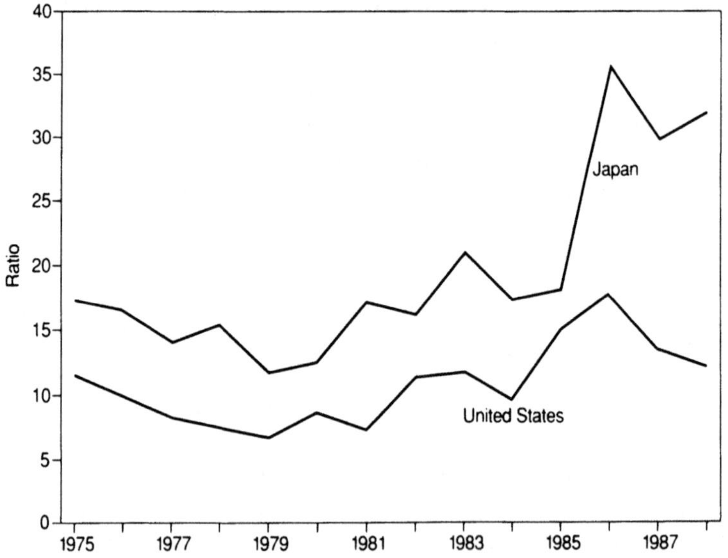

Source: Kenneth R. French and James M. Poterba, "Are Japanese Stock Prices Too High?" Paper presented at the Center for Research in Security Prices Seminar on the Analysis of Security Prices, Chicago, Illinois, May 4, 1989.

to early 1980s. The U.S. P-E ratio does not show the dramatic ratcheting up displayed by the P-E ratio of the Japanese market.

International comparisons of price-earnings ratios are dangerous due to several factors including differential accounting practices and tax rules. A recent article by Kenneth French and James Poterba attempted to correct the P-E ratios of the United States and Japan for accounting differences and for double counting due to intercorporate ownership.[22] The adjusted P-E results (based on estimates of Japanese earnings using U.S. accounting practices) are shown in Figure 13.3 for the 1975–1988 period. Accounting differences explain some of the difference in the P-E ratios between the two countries, but even after the adjustments, the P-E ratio in Japan in 1988 was 2.74 times the P-E value in the United States.

The reciprocal of the P-E ratio, or the earnings-price ratio (E-P), is an alternative candidate for the expected return of holding stock. If we ignore the potentially serious accounting problems, a firm's earnings reflect equity profits after corporate taxes and after depreciation allowances sufficient to maintain the physical capital of the firm. If these earnings were fully paid out to shareholders, the firm's capital stock and thus its "earnings power" would remain intact. As long as the ratio of the stock market valuation of the firm to the value of the underlying capital stock remains constant (and in the long run one would assume that this ratio has to be unity), the real rate of return of the shareholder would be given by the earnings-price ratio. Using the E-P ratio as the expected rate of return involves several assumptions. The two most important of these are that the current earnings rate on real physical capital gives the expected future earnings rate on physical capital and that the expected real change in the market price of a constant capital stock is zero.

For some individual firms, the E-P ratio understates expected future returns because of anticipated growth in earnings. One should note, however, that growth in earnings because of retentions is already reflected in today's E-P ratio. The only growth in earnings that would cause the expected rate of return to exceed the E-P ratio would be an anticipated increase in earnings from a constant capital stock. Although some firms may be in such a position (biotechnology companies, for example), others find themselves in declining industries. It is my feeling that anticipated growth in real earnings per unit of capital is not likely to be significant at the aggregate level (for the market as a whole), even though it may be an important consideration for individual securities.

In this analysis, I report the results obtained if the adjusted earnings-price ratio is used as a proxy for the expected return on the market. It should be noted that proceeding with this proxy has important consequences. First, some serious accounting problems may remain. Second, there is a dramatic divergence between the expectations obtained with this approach and those that would be obtained using a realizations-based measure (particularly for Japan). Third, the earnings and price figures refer not only to reproducible capital such as plant and equipment but to goodwill, research and development, and land. Despite these many warnings, I believe the adjusted earnings-price ratio is the best available proxy for the expected after-corporate-tax returns that must be offered equity financiers.

Fortunately, establishing the expected return on a safe investment is a little easier to determine because short-term, nominal interest rates are readily observable. But converting these nominal rates to real rates involves unobserved inflation expectations. For simplicity, Bernheim and I have taken inflation expectations to be the average monthly rate of inflation over the previous six months, and we subtracted this from the monthly rate on T-bills to get our measure of the expected real safe interest rate. Even though we were aware that T-bills are not perfectly safe in real terms, we followed the usual practice of ignoring this inflation-induced risk.

The market lines, determined by using the adjusted E-P proxy for expectations, are shown in Table 13.2 and Figure 13.4 for the United States and in Table 13.3 and Figure 13.5 for Japan. As these figures reveal, the capital market line is lower in Japan in each of the years displayed, and the slope of the line is much smaller (the price of risk or the degree of risk aversion displayed in markets is lower).

Translating these results on the capital market line to those on the cost of capital requires the application of our modeling of the tax system and the conditions of asset equilibrium. The reader interested in the full model is referred to our 1989 study. Nevertheless, the key parameters and the assumed parameter values for the United States and Japan are shown in Table 13.4. In all cases, the corporate and personal tax rates are meant to reflect subnational levels of taxation as well as national taxation. The α and α_ε parameters reflect the tremendous amount of dividend smoothing that takes place in both countries.

Bernheim and I examined two types of physical investments: an automobile and a plant. We assumed that cars actually depreciate exponentially at a rate of 1/7 per year in both countries, whereas plants lose productivity at a common exponential rate of 1/31.5. Table 13.4 shows the shortest available depreciation lifetimes for these assets. We assumed that firms use the most accelerated form of depreciation permitted by the tax authorities. In the United States, of course, the 1986 tax reform involved a deceleration of depreciation deductions. Previously, firms could use 150 percent, declining-balance methods for plants, but now plant depreciation must be straight line over thirty-one and one-half years. The depreciation deductions on autos were also decelerated, primarily because the minimum lifetime was increased from three years to five years. The investment tax credit on equipment investments (including autos), which is included in A in Table 13.4, was also eliminated in 1986.

TABLE 13.2
Expected Short-Term Rates of Return and the Earnings-Price Ratios for the United States
(percent per month)

Year	December Expected Short-term Return	Monthly Earnings-Price Ratio
1980	0.59097	0.95785
1981	0.29259	1.09649
1982	0.56591	0.75075
1983	0.44561	0.70028
1984	0.42511	0.88652
1985	0.32707	0.58685
1986	0.29428	0.47619
1987	0.20870	0.64599
1988	0.32512	0.71225

Source: B. Douglas Bernheim and John B. Shoven, "Comparison of the Cost of Capital in the U.S. and Japan: The Roles of Risk and Taxes," *CEPR Working Paper No. 179* (Stanford, Calif.: Center for Economic Policy Research, 1989); reprinted with permission.

FIGURE 13.4
U.S. Capital Market Lines
(using earnings-price proxy)

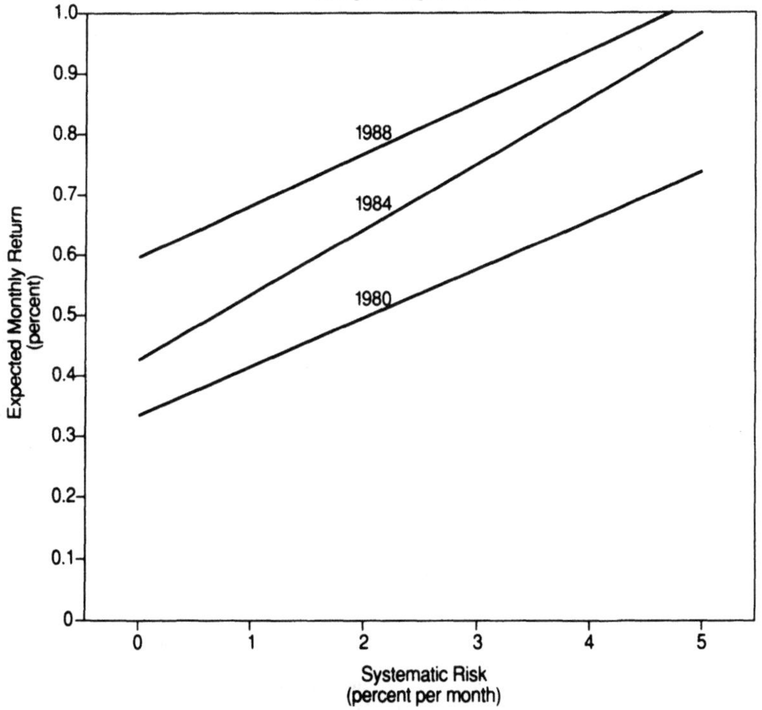

Source: B. Douglas Bernheim and John B. Shoven, "Comparison of the Cost of Capital in the U.S. and Japan: The Roles of Risk and Taxes," *CEPR Working Paper No. 179* (Stanford, Calif.: Center for Economic Policy Research, 1989); reprinted with permission.

TABLE 13.3
Expected Short-Term Rates of Return and the Earnings-Price Ratios for Japan (percent per month)

Year	December Expected Short-term Return	Monthly Earnings-Price Ratio
1980	0.58653	0.66138
1981	0.41560	0.48733
1982	0.43624	0.51125
1983	0.44567	0.39494
1984	0.30574	0.47619
1985	0.56956	0.45788
1986	0.46694	0.23343
1987	0.33611	0.27964
1988	0.24211	0.25961

Source: B. Douglas Bernheim and John B. Shoven, "Comparison of the Cost of Capital in the U.S. and Japan: The Roles of Risk and Taxes," *CEPR Working Paper No. 179* (Stanford, Calif.: Center for Economic Policy Research, 1989); reprinted with permission.

FIGURE 13.5
Japanese Capital Market Lines (using earnings-price proxy)

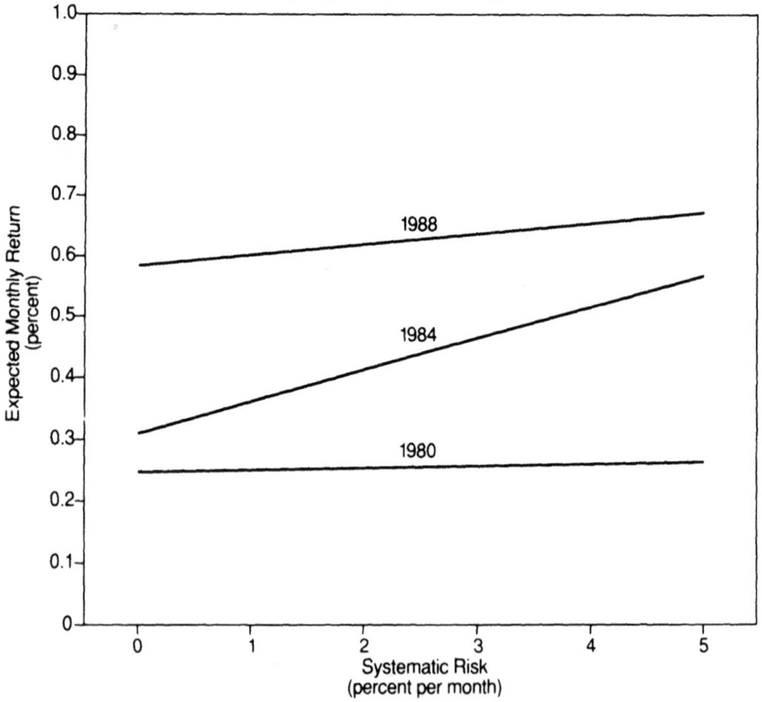

Source: B. Douglas Bernheim and John B. Shoven, "Comparison of the Cost of Capital in the U.S. and Japan: The Roles of Risk and Taxes," *CEPR Working Paper No. 179* (Stanford, Calif.: Center for Economic Policy Research, 1989); reprinted with permission.

TABLE 13.4
Parameter Values Used in the Calculation of the Cost of Capital

	United States		Japan	
	1980	1988	1980	1988
Corporate Tax Rate—τ	.495	.380	.526	.499
Average Marginal Personal Tax Rate on Interest and Dividends—m	.475	.300	.124	.200
Effective Average Marginal Personal Tax Rate on Retained Earnings—z	.25	.21	.06	.08
Effective Average Marginal Tax Rate on Purely Nominal Capital Gains—z_n	.14	.13	.0	.02
Fraction of Long-term Earnings Paid as Dividends—α	.5	.5	.33	.33
Fraction of Transitory Earnings Paid as Dividends—α_ϵ	.02	.02	.02	.02
Fraction of Total Risk Attributable to Capital Risk—η	.9	.9	.9	.9
Short-term Nominal Interest Rate—i	.1566	.0809	.09756	.04092
Expected Rate of Inflation—π	.0858	.0418	.027204	.011904
Exponential Rate of Depreciation for Autos and Plants—δ	1/7, 1/31.5	1/7, 1/31.5	1/7, 1/31.5	1/7, 1/31.5
Tax Depreciation Lifetimes for Autos and Plants—L	3/25	5/31.5	4/26	4/26
Present Value of the Tax Value of Depreciation Deduction and Tax Credits for Autos and Plants—A	.5342 .1659	.3325 .1418	.465 .250	.473 .344
Expected Real Rate of Return on Market Portfolio from Past Realizations—r_1^e	.0964	.1142	.13495	.1549
Expected Real Rate of Return on Market Portfolio from Adjusted Earnings-Price Ratio—r_2^e	.1149	.0855	.0794	.0312

Sources: The corporate and personal tax rates for the United States for 1980 are taken from M.A. King and D. Fullerton, *The Taxation of Income from Capital* (Chicago: National Bureau of Economic Research-University of Chicago Press, 1984); © 1984 by the National Bureau of Economic Research, Institut für Wirtschaftsforschung, and Industriens Utredningsinstitut. All rights reserved. The 1980 tax rates for Japan come from J.B. Shoven and T. Tachibanaki, "The Taxation of Income from Capital in Japan," in John B. Shoven, ed., *Government Policy Towards Industry in the United States and Japan* (Cambridge: Cambridge University Press, 1988); reprinted with permission. The 1988 Japanese figures come from J.B. Shoven, "The Japanese Tax Reform and the Effective Rate of Tax on Japanese Corporate Investments," *NBER Working Paper No. 2791* (Cambridge, Mass.: National Bureau of Economic Research, 1989); reprinted with permission.

The results of plugging these parameter values into the Bernheim-Shoven cost of capital model cannot be summarized easily with simple numbers, only with schedules or lines. Figures 13.6A through 13.6D and 13.7A through 13.7D show the cost of debt- and equity-financed investments in the United States and Japan. In each figure, the higher of the two essentially parallel lines is the cost of equity-financed projects, whereas the lower line is the cost of debt-financed projects. The less steep line is the capital market line. That the cost-of-capital line is

FIGURE 13.6A
Cost of Capital in the United States
for Equity- and Debt-Financed Autos,
1980

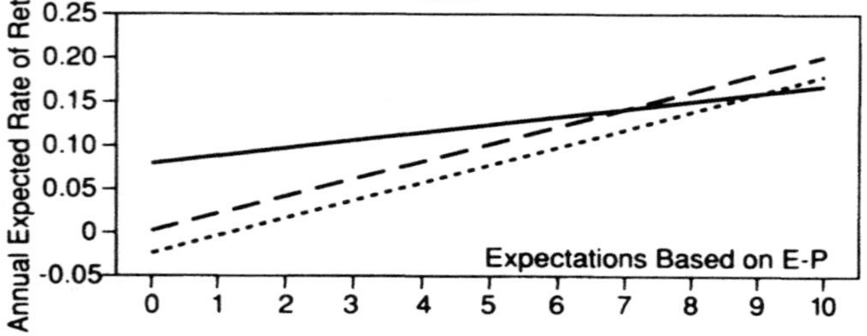

FIGURE 13.6B
Cost of Capital in the United States
for Equity- and Debt-Financed Plants,
1980

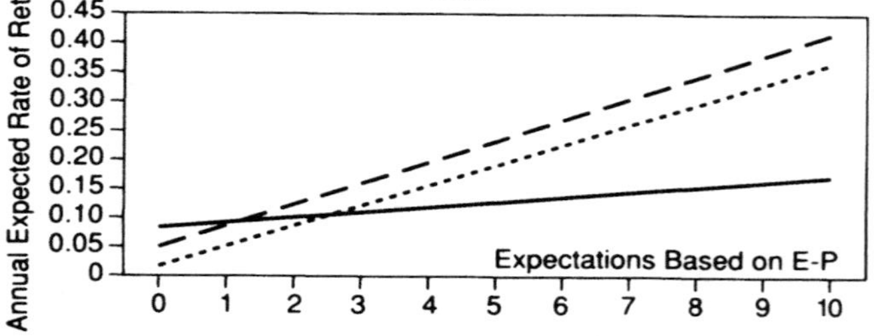

FIGURE 13.6C
Cost of Capital in the United States
for Equity- and Debt-Financed Autos,
1988

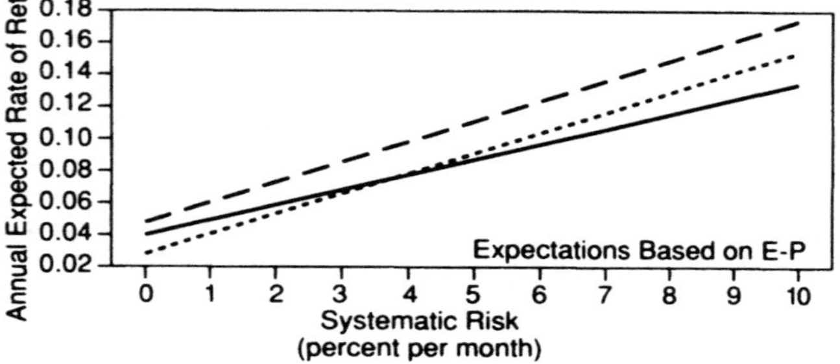

FIGURE 13.6D
Cost of Capital in the United States
for Equity- and Debt-Financed Plants,
1988

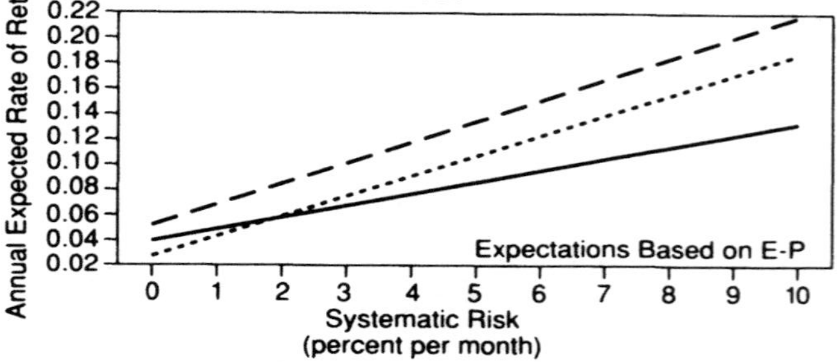

——— Capital Market Line — — — Cost of Equity Capital -------- Cost of Debt Capital

Source: B. Douglas Bernheim and John B. Shoven, "Comparison of the Cost of Capital in the U.S. and Japan: The Roles of Risk and Taxes," *CEPR Working Paper No.179* (Stanford, Calif.: Center for Economic Policy Research, 1989); reprinted with permission.

FIGURE 13.7A
Cost of Capital in Japan for
Equity- and Debt-Financed Autos,
1980

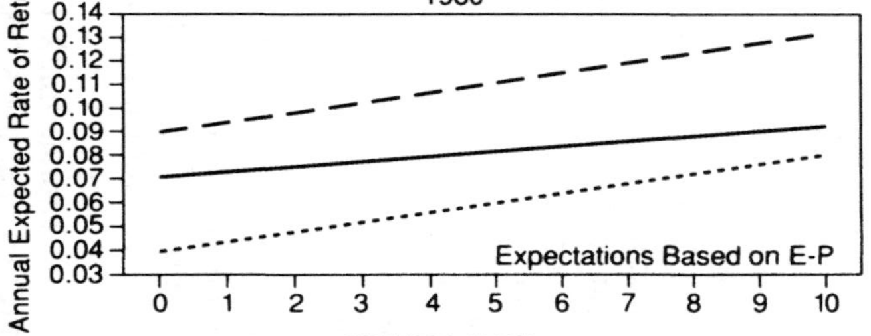

FIGURE 13.7B
Cost of Capital in Japan for
Equity- and Debt-Financed Plants,
1980

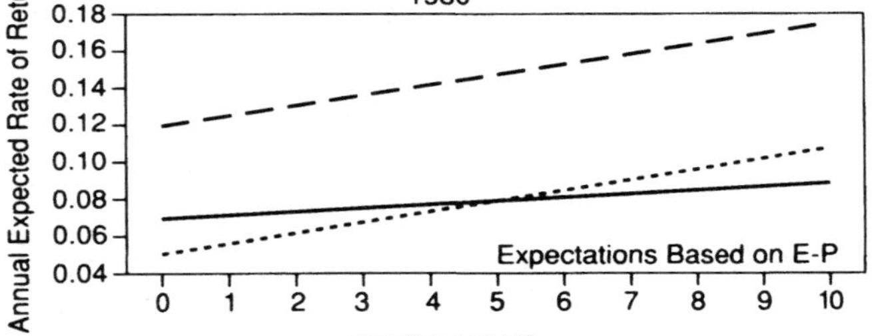

FIGURE 13.7C
Cost of Capital in Japan for
Equity- and Debt-Financed Autos,
1988

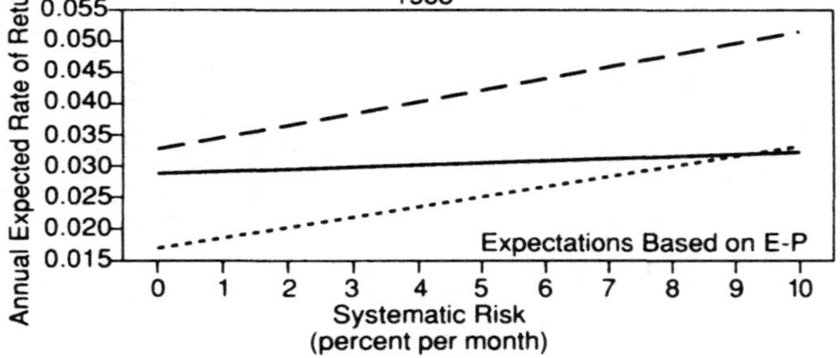

FIGURE 13.7D
Cost of Capital in Japan for
Equity- and Debt-Financed Plants,
1988

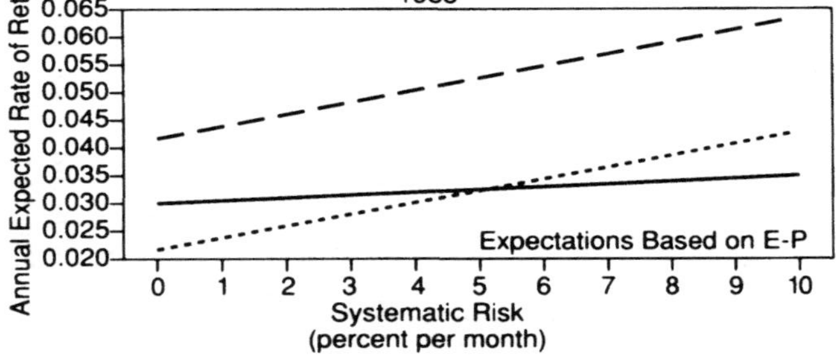

——— Capital Market Line — — — Cost of Equity Capital - - - - - - - - Cost of Debt Capital

Source: B. Douglas Bernheim and John B. Shoven, "Comparison of the Cost of Capital in the U.S. and Japan: The Roles of Risk and Taxes," *CEPR Working Paper No. 179* (Stanford, Calif.: Center for Economic Policy Research, 1989); reprinted with permission.

always dramatically steeper than the capital market line in the United States indicates that the U.S. tax system discriminates against risky investments. That is, the difference between the cost of capital and the market's expected return (the government's wedge) is much higher for more risky investments.

In the United States in 1980, the cost of capital for both debt- and equity-financed autos was less than the return to financiers represented by the capital market line. This was the result of rapid, three-year depreciation; the investment tax credit; relatively light capital gains tax treatment on some of equity's return; and interest deductibility from the corporate income tax.

The comparison of the cost of capital in the United States and in Japan is shown most clearly in Figures 13.8A through 13.8D, which illustrate that the United States has a much higher price of risk for both years and for both assets. In 1980, however, the cost of capital was comparable in the two countries, particularly for equity-financed investments in automobiles. In 1988, the U.S. cost of capital was unambiguously higher (with this approach), and the price of risk also was much greater.

Despite the fact that our approach requires that cost of capital information be transmitted as a schedule rather than a number, there seems to be a substantial demand for single-number summaries of the results. Because of that, I present Table 13.5, which shows the annual cost of capital for autos and plants whose riskiness is a standardized 4.5 percent per month. This amount of risk is comparable to the long-run risk of a diversified portfolio of stocks in either country. The numbers again show Japan to have had a dramatically lower cost of capital than the United States in 1988. For example, the cost of capital for an equity-financed plant was approximately 12.6 percent in the United States but only 5.1 percent in Japan. The contrast was equally sharp for autos and for debt-financed investments. In 1980, the U.S. cost of capital was more comparable to that in Japan, particularly for autos and equipment. The combination of accelerated depreciation and the investment tax credit kept the U.S. cost competitive. The cost-of-equity-capital numbers in Table 13.5, ranging from 8.9 to 20.7 percent for the United States and from 4.1 to 14.5 percent for Japan, agree much more closely to the statements of businesspeople regarding hurdle rates than do the 3.0 to 6.0 percent figures generated by approaches that fail to factor in risk premia.

How would the adoption of a consumption tax affect the cost of capital? A true consumption tax would eliminate the entire wedge between the firm and the investor. The cost-of-capital line, the capital market line, and the investor's expected after-tax return line would all be coincident. The question that cannot be answered here is how such a tax reform would affect the position of the capital market line. To the extent that the line is determined by international investors, it might

FIGURE 13.8A
Cost of Capital for Equity-Financed Autos in the United States and Japan, 1980

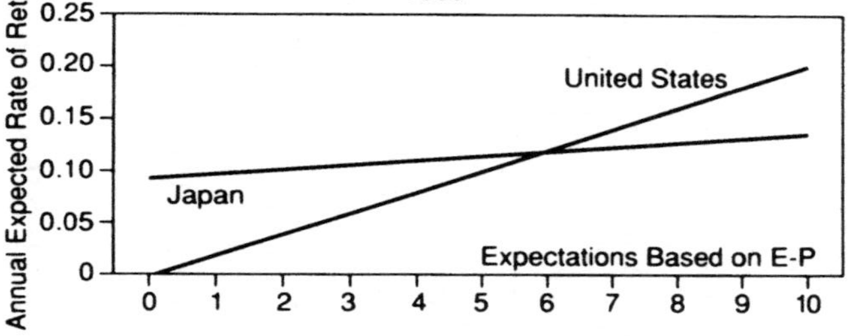

FIGURE 13.8B
Cost of Capital for Equity-Financed Plants in the United States and Japan, 1980

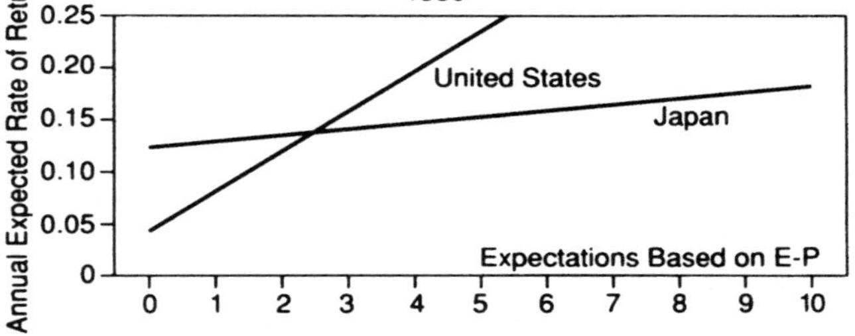

FIGURE 13.8C
Cost of Capital for Equity-Financed Autos in the United States and Japan, 1988

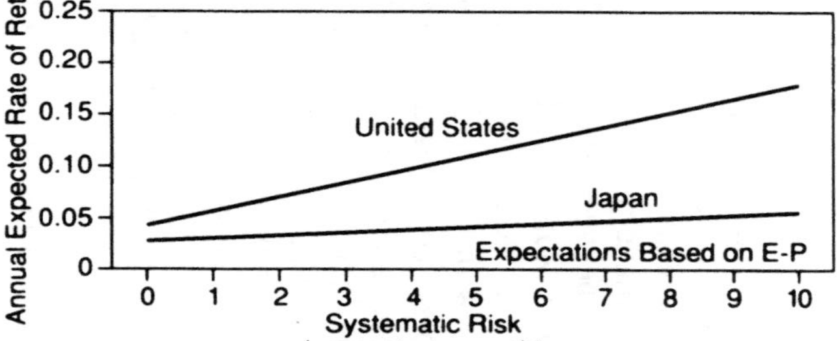

FIGURE 13.8D
Cost of Capital for Equity-Financed Plants in the United States and Japan, 1988

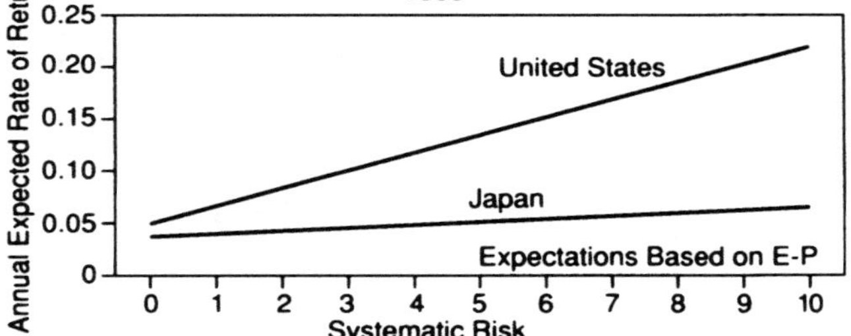

Source: B. Douglas Bernheim and John B. Shoven, "Comparison of the Cost of Capital in the U.S. and Japan: The Roles of Risk and Taxes," *CEPR Working Paper No.179* (Stanford, Calif.: Center for Economic Policy Research, 1989); reprinted with permission.

TABLE 13.5
Cost-of-Capital Estimates for Autos and Plants
with Standardized Riskiness
(standard deviation = 4.5% per month)

	United States		Japan	
	Autos	Plant	Autos	Plant
Equity-Financed				
1980	8.87%	20.73%	10.86%	14.53%
1988	10.37%	12.58%	4.08%	5.12%
Debt-Financed				
1980	6.95%	16.74%	5.82%	7.39%
1988	8.29%	9.73%	2.46%	3.08%

Source: B. Douglas Bernheim and John B. Shoven, "Comparison of the Cost of Capital in the U.S. and Japan: The Roles of Risk and Taxes," *CEPR Working Paper No. 179* (Stanford, Calif.: Center for Economic Policy Research, 1989); reprinted with permission.

Note: Calculations use earnings-price basis.

not change much. The cost of capital for plants would be reduced dramatically in the United States, and the tax penalty faced by risky investments would be eliminated. I draw these conclusions by examining Figures 13.6A–D and assuming that the cost-of-capital lines are rotated to coincide with the capital market line.

The assumption that the capital market line would not move with the institution of a consumption tax is a guess based on the fact that the elimination of the personal and corporate tax wedges would tend to have opposite effects. The elimination of the corporate tax wedge between the cost-of-capital line and the capital market line by itself would tend to raise the capital market line. The tax removal would tend to increase the demand for funds to finance the additional investments made possible by the tax change. The removal of the personal tax wedge between the capital market line and the investor's after-tax return line would tend to lower the capital market line. With the personal tax wedge removed, people will presumably save more. This conforms with the evidence of the previous section.

Corporate-tax integration would also lower the cost of capital in the United States by eliminating the wedge between the cost of capital and the capital market line. But such integration would unambiguously raise the capital market line because it would increase the demand for funds on the original terms without increasing their supply. It is clear that even though corporate-tax integration would offer part of the beneficial effect of the adoption of a consumption tax on the cost of capital, it would not offer the full benefits.

CONCLUSION AND POLICY RECOMMENDATIONS

I have revealed fairly well the policy recommendations suggested by this analysis. First, the tax system affects the cost of capital far more than had been previously recognized because most of the earlier studies did not consider risk. By incorporating risk, one can see that the tax system particularly penalizes risky investments.

If a sweeping tax reform were contemplated, I would favor a consumption tax along the lines of Bradford or of McLure's simplified alternative tax.[23] These reforms would institute a single-level, progressive tax on consumption. The lowering of the cost of capital, particularly for risky investments, would be dramatic. An alternative form of a consumption tax would be a value-added tax (VAT).

The corporate side of a consumption tax could be adopted by moving to a cash-flow tax, which would allow expensing and eliminate interest deductibility. Cash flow returned to either equity or debt holders would be subject to a corporate level tax. From an efficiency perspective, this would be equivalent to corporate-tax integration. The remaining corporate tax would apply only to economic profits. Even though the adoption of either corporate-tax integration or a cash-flow tax would be an improvement, neither has the full advantages of a comprehensive consumption tax.

Politically, it may be more realistic to worry about the structure of new revenue sources rather than to concentrate on the design of the existing tax system. Because the distortions associated with tax increases grow more than proportionately with revenue, the design of marginal revenue sources can be more important than the design of the basic tax system. Thus, it is extremely important that incremental revenue be generated by consumption taxes of one design or another. Certainly, excise taxes can raise more revenue if the increments needed are relatively small. If, however, we need additional tax proceeds of 1 or 2 percent of GNP, a VAT may be the appropriate vehicle. In any case, returning to high income tax rates is not the desirable source for more revenue.

National saving should be an overriding concern in the design of U.S. tax policies. A consumption tax, with its desirable effect of lowering the cost of capital, is clearly the tax design suited for a prosaving government policy.

NOTES

I thank my co-authors on related work, B. Douglas Bernheim and John Karl Scholz. Helpful comments were made by Ralph Landau and James Poterba. The underlying research was supported by the American Council for Capital Formation Center for Policy Research, the Dean Witter Foundation, and the Center for Economic Policy Research, Stanford University.

1. B. D. Bernheim and J. B. Shoven, "Comparison of the Cost of Capital in the U.S. and Japan: The Roles of Risk and Taxes," *Center for Economic Policy Research Working Paper No. 179* (Stanford, Calif.: Stanford University, 1989).

2. S. F. Venti and D. A. Wise, "The Determinants of IRA Contributions and the Effect of Limit Changes," in Z. Bodie, J. B. Shoven, and D. A. Wise,

eds., *Pensions in the U.S. Economy* (Chicago: University of Chicago Press, 1988), pp. 9–52.

3. J. M. Poterba, "Dividends, Capital Gains, and the Corporate Veil: Evidence from Britain, Canada, and the United States" (Paper presented at the National Bureau for Economic Research Conference on Saving, Maui, Hawaii, January 6–7, 1989).

4. M. S. Feldstein and J. Slemrod, "How Inflation Distorts the Taxation of Capital Gains," *Harvard Business Review* (September-October 1978), pp. 20–22.

5. U.S. Department of the Treasury, *Tax Reform for Fairness, Simplicity, and Economic Growth: The Treasury Department Report to the President* (Washington, D.C.: U.S. Department of the Treasury, 1984).

6. See P. H. Hendershott, "The Tax Reform Act of 1986 and Economic Growth," *NBER Working Paper No. 2553* (Cambridge, Mass.: National Bureau of Economic Research, 1988); D. Fullerton, Y. K. Henderson, and J. Mackie, "Investment Allocation and Growth Under the Tax Reform Act of 1986," in *Compendium of Tax Research 1987* (Washington, D.C.: U.S. Department of the Treasury, Office of Tax Analysis, 1988); and B. D. Bernheim and J. B. Shoven, "Taxation and the Cost of Capital: An International Comparison," in C. E. Walker and M. A. Bloomfield, eds., *The Consumption Tax: A Better Alternative?* (Cambridge, Mass.: Ballinger, 1987), pp. 61–86.

7. Walker and Bloomfield, eds., ibid.

8. S. Vogt, "Taxing Consumption as a Fiscal Policy Alternative: A Review of the Debate," *Center for the Study of American Business Working Paper No. 120* (St. Louis: Washington University, July 1988).

9. L. H. Summers, "Capital Taxation and Accumulation in a Life Cycle Growth Model," *American Economic Review* 71 (September 1981), pp. 533–544.

10. A. J. Auerbach and L. Kotlikoff, "National Savings, Economic Welfare, and the Structure of Taxation," in M. Feldstein, ed., *Behavorial Simulation Methods in Tax Policy Analysis* (Chicago: University of Chicago Press, 1983), pp. 459–498.

11. D. Fullerton, J. B. Shoven, and J. Whalley, "Replacing the U.S. Income Tax with a Progressive Consumption Tax," *Journal of Public Economics* 20 (February 1983), pp. 3–23.

12. J. G. Gravelle, "Income, Consumption, and Wage Taxation in a Life Cycle Model: Separating Efficiency from Redistribution" (Washington, D.C.: Congressional Research Service, June 1989, mimeograph).

13. See D. F. Bradford, *Untangling the Income Tax* (Cambridge, Mass.: Harvard University Press, April 1986); and C. E. McLure, Jr., "The 1986 Act: Tax Reform's Finest Hour or Death Throes of the Income Tax?" *National Tax Journal* 41, no. 3 (September 1988), pp. 303–315.

14. B. D. Bernheim, J. K. Scholz, and J. B. Shoven, "Consumption Taxation in a General Equilibrium Model: How Reliable Are Simulation Results?" (Paper presented at the National Bureau of Economic Research Conference on Saving, Maui, Hawaii, January 6–7, 1989).

15. See those based on the Hall-Jorgenson 1967 article—for example, M. A. King and D. Fullerton, *The Taxation of Income from Capital* (Chicago: National Bureau of Economic Research–University of Chicago Press, 1984).

16. See, for example, J. Mossin, *Theory of Financial Markets* (Englewood Cliffs, N.J.: Prentice-Hall, 1973).

17. See, for example, King and Fullerton, *The Taxation of Income from Capital*; and Bernheim and Shoven, "Taxation and the Cost of Capital."
18. G. N. Hatsopoulos and S. H. Brooks, "The Cost of Capital in the United States and Japan" (Paper presented at the International Conference on the Cost of Capital, Kennedy School of Government, Harvard University, Cambridge, Massachusetts, November 19–21, 1987).
19. Bernheim and Shoven, "Comparison of the Cost of Capital in the U.S. and Japan."
20. J. I. Bulow and L. H. Summers, "The Taxation of Risky Assets," *Journal of Political Economy* 92, no. 1 (February 1984), pp. 20–29.
21. Bernheim and Shoven, "Comparison of the Cost of Capital in the U.S. and Japan."
22. K. R. French and J. M. Poterba, "Are Japanese Stock Prices Too High?" (Paper presented at the Center for Research in Security Prices Seminar on the Analysis of Security Prices, Chicago, Illinois, May 4, 1989).
23. See Bradford, *Untangling the Income Tax*; and McLure, "The 1986 Act."

ADDITIONAL REFERENCES

Fullerton, D., R. Gillette, and J. Mackie. "Investment Incentives Under the Tax Reform Act of 1986." In *Compendium of Tax Research 1987.* Washington, D.C.: U.S. Department of the Treasury, Office of Tax Analysis, 1988.

Poterba, J. M., and L. H. Summers. "Mean Reversion in Stock Prices." *Journal of Financial Economics* 22 (1988), pp. 27–59.

Shoven, J. B. "The Japanese Tax Reform and the Effective Rate of Tax on Japanese Corporate Investments." *NBER Working Paper No. 2791.* Cambridge, Mass.: National Bureau of Economic Research, 1989.

Shoven, J. B., and T. Tachibanaki. "The Taxation of Income from Capital in Japan." In *Government Policy Towards Industry in the United States and Japan.* Edited by J. B. Shoven. Cambridge: Cambridge University Press, 1988.

Summers, L. H. "Reforming Tax Reform for Growth and Competitiveness." Cambridge, Mass.: Harvard University, 1987, mimeograph.

______. "Should Tax Reform Level the Playing Field?" Paper presented at the Eightieth Annual Conference of the National Tax Association–Tax Institute of America, Pittsburgh, Pennsylvania, November 8–11, 1987.

Discussion

Benjamin L. Cardin

I agree with much of John Shoven's analysis, and I support a consumption tax. But I would like to put his analysis in context because it is important that we take a look at where we are in Washington today.

The Reagan legacy is the Bush challenge. In the Reagan legacy there are three deficits: the budget deficit, the trade deficit, and the social deficit. We all know these figures, including the budget deficit, which in fiscal 1989 was $152 billion. One figure is the most disturbing: in 1989, the interest payments by the federal government, which amount to 14.7 percent of our outlays; 17.1 percent of revenues go for interest on the public debt. As a percent of on-budget revenues, which exclude Social Security revenues, interest payments rise to 23.2 percent. Our trade deficit is moving in the right direction, but it is still $118 billion. Once the largest creditor nation, our country has become the largest debtor nation. In terms of the social deficit, take a look at the gaps that we have in health care. Many of the elderly have no protection against long-term health care needs. Thirty-seven million workers do not have health insurance. One out of five children lives in poverty. Look at housing. Three hundred thousand to 3 million people are homeless. One out of seven children is at risk of dropping out of school. The social deficit of this country is related to the budget deficit. The budget deficit is clearly our number one problem; we lack the resources to deal with our trade and social problems.

The budget deficit has contributed to very low saving ratios. I agree with Dr. Shoven's observations that the deficit has compounded our low saving ratios and hampered capital formation in our country. Two-thirds of net private saving equals the annual federal deficit. So what do we do about it? Our primary goal must be to reduce the federal budget deficit, and that must be the controlling factor as we look at our policy. The only way to reduce the deficit is to combine new revenues with spending cuts. The problem is that the U.S. public thinks we will use new revenues to increase spending rather than to reduce the deficit. I have introduced legislation that addresses that issue by requiring that every new dollar of revenues be matched by a dollar of spending cuts, so for every $1.00 of increased revenues, the deficit is reduced by $2.00. To put that together properly, the best tax to look at is a consumption-related tax, which rewards saving, penalizes spending somewhat, and can help lower our cost of capital.

The bottom line is that capital costs too much in the United States and that our investment ratios are too small. Saving ratios must be increased. A 1 percent VAT can raise $18 billion, which is considerable revenue. Twenty-two of the twenty-three OECD countries have consumption-related taxes. Adopting a consumption tax could help our country achieve a level playing field in the international trade community.

Some of my colleagues argue that a consumption tax is a regressive tax—that it will tax the poor more than the wealthy. That is perhaps true. But we can work into the proposals tax credits that can address the regressivity of the consumption tax and help low-income people. We have enough revenue to be able to do that, and many states that have consumption taxes have worked in low-income credits, including Hawaii, Idaho, Kansas, New Mexico, South Dakota, Vermont, and

Wyoming. A broad-based consumption tax can be fairer in many respects than an income tax because there is no problem of people avoiding tax, as there is with the income tax, even with the changes that were made in 1986.

We should have some stability in our income tax law. We should not be changing it every few years—which is one reason I do not want to look at the income tax for the revenues that we will need if we are going to make a serious effort to reduce the deficit. Perhaps we should also be considering some reform to deal with Dr. Shoven's concerns about incomplete indexing and the triple tax on corporate investment. His point is well taken: We are overtaxing the investments in corporations.

We might need to address some of the aspects of the income tax law from the point of view of fairness but not, I hope, from the point of view of raising additional revenue. That would be violating a commitment made by Congress when it enacted the 1986 tax reform. Looking at a consumption tax from a political point of view, the Democrats have basically been opposed to it because it is a regressive tax; the Republicans have basically been opposed to it because it is a money machine.

As we consider approaches to reducing the federal deficit, we need to be aware of several issues. First, the public does not believe that the government will actually use new taxes for deficit reduction. The public will support new taxes if they are used for deficit reduction. New taxes must therefore be coupled with spending cuts. Congress cannot move toward a tax unless it is prepared to go forward with real budget cuts along with new revenues. Second, Congress must be prepared to define the deficit properly. Although the economic definition of our deficit may be appropriate, from a political perspective what can be done on Capitol Hill to get around the Gramm-Rudman deficit-reduction law is outrageous. The Gramm-Rudman law does not work; it is a fraud in that it does not capture the spending. An expenditure can be advance-funded to September 30, rather than October 1, because the sequestration trigger mechanism in the current fiscal year is over. Surpluses in certain accounts such as the Social Security trust fund can be counted to make the deficit look smaller. Yet some special accounts that spend money, such as the savings and loan bailout, are not counted toward the Gramm-Rudman target. These types of gimmicks must be removed from the law if Congress is going to win the public confidence that is necessary to pass a tax proposal. A tax proposal must be coupled with spending cuts and a true definition of our deficit. Finally, capital gains or additional incentives for saving can be changed, but long-term planning must be provided along with such changes.

With presidential leadership and bipartisan cooperation in Congress, a solution will be found.

Discussion

Charles E. McLure, Jr.

John Shoven's analysis consists of three essential parts: a critique of the Tax Reform Act of 1986, new estimates of the cost of capital in the United States and Japan, and the case for a consumption tax. I will comment on each of these.

THE 1986 ACT

Dr. Shoven finds great fault with the 1986 act; I share many of his criticisms, but not all. Moreover, I want to reemphasize a point that he suggests: If the Reagan administration and Congress had had the political will to adopt more of the reforms proposed in 1984 in Treasury I,[1] the 1986 act would have been far better. Even so, I give the 1986 act somewhat higher marks than Dr. Shoven does.

Faults in the 1986 Act

Dr. Shoven lists the following failures of the 1986 act: (1) it should have raised more revenue; (2) it should have been more conducive to saving by treating saving for retirement more favorably, not taxing nominal capital gains as ordinary income, not favoring debt finance more than equity finance, and shifting to a tax based on consumption; (3) it fell short of the taxation of real economic income by not including inflation adjustment of capital gains, of interest income and expense, of depreciation allowances, and of costs of goods sold from inventories; (4) it provided no integration of corporate and personal taxes; (5) it retained the tax advantage of owner-occupied housing; and (6) it has proved extremely complicated for some taxpayers.

In Defense of Treasury I

I agree in principle with all of Dr. Shoven's criticisms, except the strength of his endorsement of a shift to a consumption-based tax. It is worth noting (as Dr. Shoven has) that only three of these criticisms—the failure to raise taxes, the sanctity of the home-mortgage deduction, and the choice of the income tax over the consumption tax—can be levied against Treasury I. The Treasury staff knew and emphasized the advantages of favorable treatment of pension saving; of the indexing of the measurement of income, including capital gains; and of reduction of the relative advantages of debt finance via both indexing and integration of the corporate and personal income taxes.

Two of the defects Dr. Shoven identifies were the subject of explicit instructions from President Reagan: no tax increase and the sanctity of the home-mortgage deduction. Although this does not make them good policy, it does help explain bad policy. The third, the choice to retain the income-tax model, deserves further comment.

Income Versus Consumption Taxation

The choice of the income-tax model in Treasury I is best explained by three words: dead on arrival (DOA). This is exactly what a consumption-tax proposal would have been. Richard Nixon was able to go to China, but Jimmy Carter could not have. Carter could have proposed a consumption-based tax, but Ronald Reagan could not have.

Some may think that proposing a consumption tax that was DOA would have been a better outcome than the 1986 tax act, but I do not agree. The 1986 act achieved several objectives to which Dr. Shoven does not give enough attention. First, it eliminated tax on 6 million low-income persons who would otherwise have paid taxes. This step probably would have been taken eventually. But when? It was overlooked when the 1981 act cut taxes for the rest of us.

Second, the 1986 act essentially killed most tax shelters. I believe that it is hard to overstate the importance of this accomplishment. A system of government finance based on voluntary payment of the income tax cannot long survive the erosion of confidence engendered by the specter of wealthy individuals using tax shelters to avoid paying taxes. This is hardly ever taken into account by those who extol the virtues of the excessive tax benefits for investment created by the 1981 act—precisely the benefits that made tax shelters possible.

Third, investment is far less conditioned by tax considerations than it was before the 1986 tax reform. Even though many calculations indicate that the efficiency gains are not tremendous, these calculations may not adequately capture the full benefits of a more nearly level playing field. Of course, the field can hardly be level as long as owner-occupied housing continues to enjoy overwhelming tax benefits and thus to attract investment funds that could better be invested elsewhere. Reexamination of the tax treatment of owner-occupied housing should be high on the agenda of tax reform. Because it is difficult to tax imputed income, it would be appropriate to limit mortgage deductions. A consumption-based tax has the important advantage of making the taxation of nonhousing investment more nearly equal to the taxation of housing by leveling downward.

CALCULATIONS OF THE COST OF CAPITAL

The Shoven-Bernheim calculations of the cost of capital clearly have made an important contribution by adding explicit considerations of risk to the standard methodology. It is especially noteworthy that the Shoven-Bernheim calculations indicate a cost of capital much higher than those calculations that do not consider risk and much closer to the rates business uses. I suggest one important extension of the analysis.

Dr. Shoven presents a three-way comparison of the cost of capital in the United States and in Japan, assuming for the United States current law, a consumption tax, and integration of the income taxes. A natural extension would be to calculate the U.S. cost of capital for a system that provided inflation adjustment in the measurement of income. Inflation adjustment would reduce the cost of capital by increasing depreciation allowances and reducing taxes on capital gains. Given the international mobility of capital, indexation of interest deductions would increase the cost of debt finance; thus, it would also reduce the tax advantages of debt relative to equity. Inflation adjustment would clearly not reduce the cost of capital as much as movement to a consumption tax. But given its superiority to the present system, an inflation-adjusted system (with or without integration) should at least be allowed to enter the race against the consumption tax.

ADVANTAGES OF THE CONSUMPTION TAX

In regard to the advantages of the consumption tax, I can add little to what Dr. Shoven and others have said. There are all the usual caveats about distributional effects, international considerations, and transitional problems—caveats that help to explain further why the consumption tax was not proposed in Treasury I. Rather than repeating these, I want to concentrate on two advantages of consumption-based taxes and a major problem with introducing one form of such a tax.[2]

Dr. Shoven notes that the failure to provide inflation adjustment in the measurement of income from business and capital was one of the chief defects of the 1986 act. It also helps to explain why the cost of capital is so much higher in the United States than in Japan, where the inflation rate has historically been lower. And yet there is no doubt that a comprehensive system of inflation adjustment would add greatly to the complexity of the income tax. One of the primary advantages of consumption-based direct taxation is that no inflation adjustment is needed. This is most easily seen in the case of depreciable assets and capital gains. With expensing, inflation has no chance to erode the value of depreciation allowances. In the case of capital gains, the basis of assets is always zero (or else, in another system, such gains are not even taxed). In the version of the consumption tax that allows no deduction for interest expense and does not tax interest income, there is no issue of inflation adjustment for interest.

One reason the 1986 act is so complicated is that an effort was made to deal with many aspects of the time value of money. (In essence, taxpayers gain from postponing the recognition of income or accelerating deductions, such as those for depreciation.) Thus, we now have tighter rules for installment sales, rules requiring the capitalization of many more expenses, and the inclusion of many more expenses that formerly were simply deducted currently in the value of inventories;

these join such paragons of simplicity as the tightened rules for original issue discount. For an income tax to function properly in a complex economy with sophisticated tax planning, such rules are necessary in order to prevent inequities, opportunities for tax shelters, and the distortion of economic decisionmaking. But no such rules are needed in a system based on consumption, where cash flow is king; either money is received or it is not. This is the second major simplicity advantage of basing direct taxation on consumption rather than on income. More attention should be devoted to these well-known simplicity advantages of consumption-based taxes. There are other ways, at least in principle, to increase national saving; the public deficit could, in principle, be reduced. There is no other way to simplify the income tax than to simplify it.

I want to end with a warning about transition effects. A recent article in the *American Economic Review* should give those who advocate the "tax prepayment approach" to the implementation of a consumption-based tax reason to pause.[3] The author's point was really very simple: If the new tax is phased in by raising its rate while reducing the rate of the income tax, there will be an incentive to postpone investment. This is true because expensing of investment occurs at a lower tax rate than the one at which the resulting income is taxed. As a result, such a substitution may not increase welfare, as is commonly assumed, even if labor supply is not reduced by the necessity of levying higher taxes on labor income. More generally, it may be dangerous to introduce such a tax if the tax rate cannot be held constant over time. The "qualified accounts," or individual cash-flow variant, of a consumption tax does not suffer from this liability. Unfortunately, it is more complicated than the tax prepayment approach.[4]

NOTES

1. U.S. Department of Treasury, *Tax Reform for Fairness, Simplicity, and Economic Growth: The Treasury Department Report to the President* (Washington, D.C.: U.S. Department of the Treasury, 1984).

2. The discussion that follows draws heavily on several studies. See George R. Zodrow and Charles E. McLure, Jr., "Implementing Direct Consumption Taxes in Developing Countries," *World Bank Discussion Paper*, Series WPS131 (Washington, D.C.: World Bank, December 1988); Charles E. McLure, Jr., "The 1986 Act: Tax Reform's Finest Hour or Death Throes of the Income Tax?" *National Tax Journal* 41, no. 3 (September 1988), pp. 303–315; and Charles E. McLure, Jr., "Lessons for LDCs of U.S. Income Tax Reform," in Malcolm Gillis, ed., *Tax Reform in Developing Countries* (Durham, N.C.: Duke University Press, 1989), pp. 347–390.

3. See Peter Howitt and Hans-Werner Sinn, "Gradual Reforms of Capital Income Taxation," *American Economic Review* 79, no. 1 (March 1989), pp. 106–124.

4. See Zodrow and McLure, "Implementing Direct Consumption Taxes in Developing Countries."

About the Editors and Contributors

ABOUT THE EDITORS

Mark A. Bloomfield, Esq., is president of the American Council for Capital Formation and its economic education and research affiliate, the ACCF Center for Policy Research. Mr. Bloomfield testifies frequently before congressional committees on capital formation issues, in particular before the House Ways and Means and Senate Finance Committees. A speaker and author on economics, tax policy, and politics, he is frequently quoted in the *New York Times*, the *Wall Street Journal*, and the *Washington Post* and has appeared on PBS's "The MacNeil-Lehrer NewsHour" and "Adam Smith's Moneyworld," NBC's "Strictly Business," ABC's "Nightline," and C-SPAN. Mr. Bloomfield is a co-editor of or contributor to five other books on tax and economic policy.

Dr. Margo Thorning is chief economist of the American Council for Capital Formation and director of research of the organization's affiliated ACCF Center for Policy Research. Dr. Thorning writes and lectures on tax policy and economics and is frequently quoted in the national and local press. She has testified before congressional committees, including the House Ways and Means Committee. Dr. Thorning previously held positions as staff assistant to the deputy administrator of applied analysis at the U.S. Department of Energy, supervisory economist at the U.S. Department of Commerce, and economist at the Federal Trade Commission.

Dr. Charls E. Walker is chairman of the American Council for Capital Formation and its affiliate, the ACCF Center for Policy Research. Dr. Walker also is chairman of Charls E. Walker Associates, Inc., a Washington, D.C.–based consulting firm. He served as deputy secretary of the Treasury from 1968 to 1972 and as assistant and principal adviser to the secretary of the Treasury from 1959 to 1961. He holds the Alexander Hamilton Award, the highest honor granted by the U.S. Department of the Treasury. Dr. Walker is co-editor of *New Directions in Federal Tax Policy for the 1980s* (1983) and *The Consumption Tax: A Better Alternative?* (1987).

ABOUT THE CONTRIBUTORS

Dr. Henry J. Aaron is a senior fellow at The Brookings Institution, where he is involved in research on taxation, health care, Social Security, and other issues. Dr. Aaron is also a professor of economics at the University of Maryland and a senior associate with the Policy Economics Group of KPMG Peat

Marwick. From 1977 to 1978, he served as assistant secretary for planning and evaluation at the Department of Health, Education, and Welfare. The author of numerous books and articles and an associate editor of the *Journal of Economic Perspectives*, Dr. Aaron most recently wrote *Can America Afford to Grow Old?* (coauthored with Barry Bosworth and Gary Burtless, 1988). He is a member of the research advisory council of the Joint Center for Political Studies, Inc., vice president of the National Academy of Social Insurance, and a member of the National Academy of Sciences Institute of Medicine.

Hon. Bill Archer (R-Tex.), who has represented the seventh district of Texas in the U.S. House of Representatives for almost two decades, is ranking Republican on the Ways and Means Committee and a member of the Joint Committee on Taxation. Representative Archer has become known for his flexibility and effective leadership and was named "most respected" Texas representative by *Texas Business Magazine.* He has also received the Tax Foundation's Distinguished Public Service Award, the National Federation of Independent Business's Guardian of Small Business Award, the National Taxpayers Union's Taxpayers' Best Friend Award, and the National Associated Business Watchdog of the Treasury Award. Representative Archer served in the Texas House of Representatives for four years before his election to the U.S. Congress in 1970.

Dr. C. Fred Bergsten is director of the Washington, D.C.–based Institute for International Economics. Dr. Bergsten previously served in government as assistant secretary of the Treasury for international affairs (1977–1981), functioning as under secretary for monetary affairs during 1980 and 1981, and as assistant for international economic affairs to Dr. Henry Kissinger on the senior staff of the National Security Council (1969–1971). The author of eighteen books and numerous articles on international economic issues, Dr. Bergsten most recently wrote *America in the World Economy: A Strategy for the 1990s* (1988). He was cited by *Time* in 1974 as one of "America's 200 Young Leaders," by the *National Journal* as one of the "One Hundred Fifty Who Make a Difference" to U.S. national policy, and by *U.S. News & World Report* as part of "The New American Establishment: Who Runs America."

Hon. Michael J. Boskin is chairman of the President's Council of Economic Advisers. Dr. Boskin is on leave from Stanford University, where he is Burnet C. and Mildred Finley Wohlford Professor of Economics. He is also on leave as a research associate of the National Bureau of Economic Research. Dr. Boskin is the recipient of numerous professional awards and citations, including the first National Tax Association Outstanding Dissertation Award in 1971 and Stanford University's Distinguished Teaching Award in 1988. He is the author of more than eighty books and articles on U.S. saving behavior, government spending, tax theory and policy, capital formation, and other topics.

Dr. David F. Bradford is professor of economics and public affairs at Princeton University, where he has taught since 1966. Dr. Bradford is also the associate dean of the Woodrow Wilson School of Public and International Affairs and directs the John M. Olin Program for the Study of Economic Organization and Public Policy. Since 1977, he has been a research associate of the National Bureau of Economic Research and director of the NBER's Tax Program. Dr. Bradford served as deputy assistant secretary of the Treasury for tax policy from 1975 to 1976. His recent work has focused on the effects of income taxes on private investment, saving, and financial decisions. Dr. Bradford's book *Untangling the Income Tax* (1986) provides a comprehensive review of income taxes and their alternatives, including consumption taxes.

Hon. Nicholas F. Brady became the sixty-eighth secretary of the Treasury on September 15, 1988. Secretary Brady served in the U.S. Senate from April 20, 1982, through December 27, 1982. In 1984, President Reagan appointed him chairman of the President's Commission on Executive, Legislative, and Judicial Salaries. He has also served on the President's Commission on Strategic Forces and the National Bipartisan Commission on Central America and as chairman of the Presidential Task Force on Market Mechanisms. Secretary Brady's career in the banking industry spans thirty-four years. He joined Dillon, Read & Co., Inc., in New York in 1954, rising to chairman of the board. Secretary Brady has been a director of the NCR Corporation, the MITRE Corporation, and the H. J. Heinz Company, among others, and is currently a member of the Council on Foreign Relations, Inc.

Hon. Benjamin L. Cardin (D-Md.) has represented Maryland's third congressional district in the U.S. House of Representatives since 1987. He serves on the Ways and Means Committee and as assistant majority whip. Before his election to Congress, Representative Cardin had a twenty-year career in the Maryland House of Delegates, to which he was elected in 1966 at the age of twenty-three. He served as chairman of the Ways and Means Committee from 1974 until 1979, when he became the youngest speaker in the history of the Maryland House. Representative Cardin was vice chairman of the Democratic State Legislative Leaders Caucus from 1983 to 1986 and a member of the Governor's Commission on Excellence in Higher Education in 1985.

Dr. James W. Christian is senior vice president, chief economist, and director of the economics department of the United States League of Savings Institutions. An internationally recognized expert on housing finance systems in developing countries, Dr. Christian is the author of numerous journal articles and monographs. Before joining the U.S. League in 1980, he held positions as senior vice president and chief economist for the National Savings and Loan League, director of the international division of the Federal Home Loan Bank Board, and professor of economics at Iowa State University.

Clive Crook is the economics editor of *The Economist* of London. He previously worked as an official in Her Majesty's Treasury and as *The Economist*'s Washington correspondent.

Hon. Michael R. Darby is under secretary of commerce for economic affairs. Before this appointment, Mr. Darby was assistant secretary of the Treasury for economic policy and received the department's highest honor, the Alexander Hamilton Award, in recognition of his leadership and service. He has been a professor of economics at the University of California at Los Angeles, an assistant professor of economics at Ohio State University, a research associate of the National Bureau of Economic Research, and a vice president and director of Paragon Industries. Mr. Darby served as editor of the *Journal of International Money and Finance* from 1981 to 1986 and has been a member of the editorial board since 1986. He has written extensively on money and banking, macroeconomics, and international finance.

Dr. Jacob S. Dreyer is vice president and chief economist at the Investment Company Institute. Dr. Dreyer is also adjunct professor of economics at Virginia Polytechnical Institute and State University. From 1976 to 1988, he held various federal government positions, including director of the Offices of Monetary Research and Quantitative Studies at the Department of the Treasury (1978–1981), deputy assistant secretary of the Treasury for international economic analysis (1981–1982), deputy to the under secretary of the Treasury for monetary affairs (1982–1983), and deputy assistant secretary of the Treasury for economic policy coordination (1983–1984). When he left the government in 1988 to join the Investment Company Institute, Dr. Dreyer was deputy assistant director and acting assistant director in the Fiscal Analysis Division of the Congressional Budget Office.

Stephen J. Entin is a resident scholar at the Institute for Research on the Economics of Taxation. As deputy assistant secretary of the Treasury for economic policy during the Reagan administration, Mr. Entin participated in the preparation of economic forecasts for the president's budgets and the development of the 1981 tax cuts, including the "tax indexing" provision. Mr. Entin also represented the U.S. Department of the Treasury in the preparation of the annual reports of the board of trustees of the Social Security system and conducted research on the long-run outlook for the system. Prior to his Treasury appointment, he was a staff economist with the congressional Joint Economic Committee.

Dr. Martin Feldstein is George F. Baker Professor of Economics at Harvard University. Dr. Feldstein is also president of the Cambridge, Massachusetts–based National Bureau of Economic Research. From 1982 to 1984, he was chairman of the Council of Economic Advisers and President Reagan's chief economic adviser. Dr. Feldstein's research and teaching have focused on the problems of the national economy and the economics of the public sector. In 1977, he was the recipient of the John Bates Clark Medal of the American Economic Association, a prize awarded every two years to an economist younger than forty who is judged to have made the greatest contribution to economic science. Dr. Feldstein, who holds honorary doctorate degrees from the University of Rochester, Marquette University, and Bentley College, is the author of more than two hundred articles on a wide range of economic issues.

Dr. Barbara M. Fraumeni is associate professor of economics at Northeastern University and a research fellow of the Program on Technology and Economic Policy at the Kennedy School of Government, Harvard University. She received her B.A. in economics from Wellesley College in 1972 and her Ph.D. from Boston College in 1980. She taught at Wellesley and Tufts University before joining the Department of Economics at Northeastern in 1982. Her fields of research include human and nonhuman capital, productivity, and economic growth. She is the coauthor of *Productivity and U.S. Economic Growth* (1987) with Dale W. Jorgenson and Frank M. Gollop.

Dr. Benjamin M. Friedman is William Joseph Maier Professor of Political Economy at Harvard University. Dr. Friedman's latest work has focused on the role of the financial markets in shaping how monetary and fiscal policies affect overall economic activity. His most recent book, *Day of Reckoning: The Consequences of American Economic Policy Under Reagan and After* (1988), received the George S. Eccles Prize awarded annually by Columbia University for excellence in writing about economics. He is currently an associate editor of the *Journal of Monetary Economics.* Before joining the Harvard faculty in 1972, Dr. Friedman was with Morgan Stanley & Co. He has also held positions with the Board of Governors of the Federal Reserve System, the Federal Reserve Bank of New York, and the Federal Reserve Bank of Boston.

Harry D. Garber is vice chairman of the board of The Equitable Life Assurance Society of the United States. Mr. Garber joined Equitable after graduation from Yale University in 1950 and has been with the firm almost forty years, except for a two-year leave of absence from 1952 to 1954 to serve in the U.S. Navy. In his current position, to which he was elected in 1984, Mr. Garber is actively involved with federal legislation and tax policy as well as with corporate strategic policy. He is a member of the boards of directors of The Equitable Variable Life Insurance Company; Genesco, Inc.; the American Academy of Actuaries; and the American Council for Capital Formation. Mr. Garber also is chairman of the board of the American Women's Economic Development Corporation and vice chairman of the board of Howard University.

Hon. Lee H. Hamilton (D-Ind.), who has represented Indiana's ninth district in the U.S. House of Representatives since 1965, is chairman of the Joint Economic Committee, ranking member of the Committee on Foreign Affairs, and a member of the Committee on Science, Space, and Technology. Representative Hamilton has built "a reservoir of respect few members can match, thanks to his intellectual power and his unquestioned personal integrity," according to *Politics in America, 1990.* He has received numerous awards for public service, including the Central Intelligence Agency Medallion (1988), the Defense Intelligence Agency Medallion (1987), the DePauw University McNaughton Medal for Public Service (1987), and the Indiana Trial Lawyers Association Freedom Award (1987).

Dr. George N. Hatsopoulos is the founder, chairman of the board, and president of Thermo Electron Corporation. Dr. Hatsopoulos was a member of the faculty of the Massachusetts Institute of Technology from 1956 to 1962 and is currently senior lecturer. He testifies frequently at congressional hearings on national energy policy and capital formation and serves on national committees on energy conservation, environmental protection, and international exchange. Dr. Hatsopoulos is a member of the board of directors of the American Council for Capital Formation Center for Policy Research, chairman of the Federal Reserve Bank of Boston, a member of the governing council of the National Academy of Engineering, a vice chairman of the American Business Conference, and a member of the executive committee of the board of directors of the National Bureau of Economic Research.

Dr. Patric H. Hendershott is professor of finance and John W. Galbreath Chairholder in Real Estate at the Ohio State University. Dr. Hendershott is also a research associate at the National Bureau of Economic Research. Before joining Ohio State in 1981, he taught finance and economics at Stanford University, New York University, the University of Florida, Purdue University, Northwestern University, and Georgetown University. He has also worked as a research economist at the Federal Reserve Board. Dr. Hendershott, who is the editor of the *Journal of the American Real Estate Board and Urban Economics Association* and an associate editor of the *Journal of Money, Credit and Banking* and the *Journal of Financial Services*, has published more than one hundred articles in business, real estate, and economic journals.

Dr. Yolanda K. Henderson is an economist with the Federal Reserve Bank of Boston. Dr. Henderson is also a research affiliate at the National Bureau of Economic Research. She has taught economics at Amherst College and Boston University, served as a visiting scholar at the American Enterprise Institute, and worked as a research economist at the Congressional Budget Office and Data Resources, Inc. Dr. Henderson, who is the author of numerous articles on tax policy and investment issues, is also a referee for several prestigious business and economic journals.

Hon. Ed Jenkins (D-Ga.), a member of the U.S. House of Representatives from Jasper, Georgia, is a member of the Ways and Means Committee and serves on the Trade Subcommittee. Representative Jenkins is a designated official adviser to U.S. delegations to all international conferences, meetings, and negotiation sessions relating to trade agreements. He also serves on the House Budget Committee. In his twelve years in the U.S. House of Representatives, Representative Jenkins, who is a co-author of the Jenkins-Archer capital gains tax cut initiative, has earned a reputation as an able negotiator, working behind the scenes to effect compromises on major pieces of legislation. His vigilance on behalf of small business owners has earned him the National Federation of Independent Business's Guardian of Small Business Award every year he has been in Congress.

Hon. Manuel H. Johnson is vice chairman of the Board of Governors of the Federal Reserve System. His full term as a member of the board will end January 31, 2000; his four-year term as vice chairman will end August 21, 1990. Dr. Johnson served as assistant secretary of the Treasury (1982–1986) and deputy assistant secretary (1981–1982). While at the Treasury, he was instrumental in designing the Economic Recovery Tax Act of 1981 and the Tax Reform Act of 1986 and received the Alexander Hamilton Award, the department's highest honor. Dr. Johnson is the author and co-author of four books on political economy and public policy and has published more than fifty articles in academic journals and other publications. He sits on the board of trustees of both the Center for Study of Public Choice Foundation and the George Mason University Foundation.

Hon. Roberts T. Jones is assistant secretary of labor for the Employment and Training Administration. Mr. Jones has held this position since his appointment by President Reagan and subsequent Senate confirmation in August 1988; he was appointed to the position by President Bush in March 1989. Mr. Jones oversees the administration of the Job Training Partnership Act, Unemployment Insurance Program, U.S. Employment Service, Job Corps, Trade Adjustment Assistance, and the Bureau of Apprenticeship and Training. Since joining the Department of Labor in 1971, Mr. Jones has served in a variety of executive positions; he was deputy assistant secretary of labor from 1985 to 1988. Mr. Jones was awarded the highest recognition for civilian government service by President Reagan in 1986 as well as the 1987 Phil Arnow Award, the Department of Labor's highest award.

Dr. Dale W. Jorgenson is Frederic Eaton Abbe Professor of Economics at Harvard University, where he has been a professor of economics since 1969. He is also director of the Program on Technology and Economic Policy at the Kennedy School of Government. Dr. Jorgenson has been a professor of economics at the University of California at Berkeley, a visiting professor of economics at Stanford University and the Hebrew University of Jerusalem, a visiting professor of statistics at Oxford University, and Ford Foundation Research Professor of Economics at the University of Chicago. A recipient of the John Bates Clark Medal of the American Economic Association (1971), he is the author or co-author of more than one hundred seventy-five articles and books on economics. Dr. Jorgenson's most recent book is *Productivity and U.S. Economic Growth* (1987), co-authored with Frank M. Gollop and Barbara M. Fraumeni.

Mervyn A. King is a professor of economics at the London School of Economics, where he has taught since 1984. Professor King previously taught at the Massachusetts Institute of Technology, as a visiting professor of economics; at the University of Birmingham, as Esmée Fairbairn Professor of Investment; at Harvard University, as a visiting professor of economics; and at Cambridge University, as a lecturer in the Faculty of Economics. He is the author of four books on public policy and taxation and more than fifty journal and book articles. Professor King is currently associate editor of the *Journal of Public Economics*. He is also a director of the Bank of England, a fellow of the Econometric Society, a research associate at the National Bureau of Economic Research, and an associate member of the Japanese Ministry of Finance's Institute of Fiscal and Monetary Policy.

Hon. Sander M. Levin (D-Mich.) has represented Michigan's seventeenth district in the U.S. House of Representatives since 1983. Representative Levin serves on the Ways and Means Committee and is also a member of the Select Committee on Children, Youth, and Families. *Politics in America, 1990* said of Representative Levin: "After just three House terms, he has won considerable respect as a thoughtful and judicious legislator determined to find right answers even if they are not simple answers." Prior to his election to Congress, Representative Levin served for six years in the Michigan State Senate and as an administrator in the Agency for International Development under President Carter.

Dr. Charles E. McLure, Jr. is a senior fellow at the Hoover Institution at Stanford University. As deputy assistant secretary of the Treasury for tax analysis from 1983 to 1985, Dr. McLure had primary responsibility for developing the Treasury report to President Reagan that became the basis for the president's tax reform proposals to Congress. Dr. McLure has also served as a senior economist on the staff of the President's Council of Economic Advisers, as vice president of the National Bureau of Economic Research, and as Cline Professor of Economics and Finance at Rice University. A specialist in the economics of taxation, Dr. McLure has written extensively on federal tax reform, the value-added tax, and taxation in developing countries. He is a member of the board of directors of the American Council for Capital Formation Center for Policy Research.

Dr. Jacob Mincer is Buttenwieser Professor of Economics and Human Relations at Columbia University, a chair he has held since 1979. He is also on the research staff of the National Bureau of Economic Research. Dr. Mincer has taught at the University of Chicago, the Stockholm School of Economics, the Hebrew University of Jerusalem, and the City College of New York. He is currently on the editorial board of the *Economics of Education Review* and of the *Journal of Labor Economics*. The author of numerous journal and book articles, monographs, papers, and books, Dr. Mincer has focused on the labor force and human capital issues. His most recent works include "Wage Structures and Labor Turnover in the U.S. and in Japan," in *The Journal of the Japanese and International Economy* (June 1988) and "Human Capital and the Labor Market," in *The Educational Researcher* (May 1989).

Hon. Jim Moody (D-Wisc.), a member of the Ways and Means Committee, has represented Wisconsin's fifth district in the U.S. House of Representatives since 1983. Representative Moody is a congressional delegate to the U.S.-Soviet arms reduction talks in Geneva, chairs the bipartisan Congressional Coalition on Population and Development, and is vice chair of the Congressional Budget Task Force. He served in the Wisconsin State Assembly and Senate from 1977 to 1982 and earlier taught graduate and undergraduate economics at the University of Wisconsin. Representative Moody, who holds a Ph.D. in economics from the University of California at Berkeley, has worked as an economist for the U.S. Department of Transportation and the World Bank, as a loan officer with the Agency for International Development, and as a Peace Corps official in Pakistan and Bangladesh.

Dr. Alicia H. Munnell is senior vice president and director of research at the Federal Reserve Bank of Boston. Her prior experience includes teaching positions at Boston University, Harvard University, and Wellesley College and a position as research assistant to Dr. Joseph Pechman at The Brookings Institution. Currently, Dr. Munnell is a member of the Commission to Review the Massachusetts Anti-Takeover Laws, the American Association of Retired Persons national steering committee for New Roles in Society, and the advisory council for Economics and Politics of Fiscal Policy, American Enterprise Institute. The author and co-author of six books, numerous chapters in books, and dozens of journal and newspaper articles, Dr. Munnell is frequently called on to testify on Social Security policy and private pension plans at congressional hearings.

Dr. James M. Poterba is a professor of economics at the Massachusetts Institute of Technology, where he has taught since 1982. Dr. Poterba is also a research associate at the National Bureau of Economic Research and a fellow of the Econometric Society. His current research focuses on the economic effects of taxing corporate capital income as well as on statistical modeling of stock price movements. Dr. Poterba, who has published widely in professional journals and serves on a number of editorial boards, is a co-author of two recent studies, *Manufacturing in America's Future* (1988) and *Overconsumption: The Challenge to U.S. Economic Policy* (1989), that examine national saving in the United States.

Dr. Joel L. Prakken is vice president and co-founder of Laurence H. Meyer & Associates, a St. Louis–based private consulting firm specializing in econometric modeling, forecasting, and policy analysis. He also serves as an associate adjunct professor of economics at the Washington University School of Business in St. Louis. He previously held positions as senior economist at IBM Corporation, economist with the Federal Reserve Bank of New York, and adjunct professor of finance at New York University's Graduate School of Business. Dr. Prakken has authored studies on the economic implications of tax reform and deficit reduction for the Council of Economic Advisers, the Center for the Study of American Business, and the American Council for Capital Formation. He also has testified on tax reform before the House Ways and Means Committee and the Senate Finance Committee.

Hon. Warren B. Rudman (R-N.H.), the junior senator from New Hampshire, was first elected to the Senate in 1980. Senator Rudman is a member of the Committees on Appropriations, Budget, and Governmental Affairs and is vice chairman of the Ethics Committee. Called "one of the Senate's more sensible men" by syndicated columnist David Broder, Senator Rudman is an architect of the Gramm-Rudman-Hollings deficit reduction law. An outdoorsman, he has been active in environmental issues such as toxic waste cleanup and advancement of acid rain control legislation. Senator Rudman's work on defense-related issues led to his appointment as a member of the prestigious North Atlantic Assembly's Subcommittee on Defense Cooperation. He is a member of the senior advisory committee on the John F. Kennedy School of Government at Harvard University. Senator Rudman served as attorney general of New Hampshire from 1970 to 1976.

Hon. Paul S. Sarbanes (D-Md.) is serving his third term in the U.S. Senate, where he is Maryland's senior senator. Senator Sarbanes, who has been called "one of the Senate's leading intellects," is vice chairman of the Joint Economic Committee and a member of the Foreign Relations Committee and the Banking, Housing, and Urban Affairs Committee. He also is vice chairman of the Democratic Policy Committee and chairman of the Maryland congressional delegation. Prior to his election to the Senate, Senator Sarbanes served three terms in the U.S. House of Representatives and four years in the Maryland House of Delegates. Earlier, he was administrative assistant to Walter W. Heller, chairman of President Kennedy's Council of Economic Advisers; executive director of the Charter Revision Commission of Baltimore City; and an associate in two Baltimore law firms.

Dr. Charles L. Schultze is director of The Brookings Institution's Economic Studies Program. Dr. Schultze was chairman of President Carter's Council of Economic Advisers, an associate professor at Indiana University and professor at the University of Maryland, director of the U.S. Bureau of the Budget under President Johnson, distinguished visiting professor of research at Stanford University's Graduate School of Business, and Lee Kuan Yew Distinguished Visitor at the National University of Singapore. A prolific writer, Dr. Schultze most recently co-edited *American Living Standards: Threats and Challenges* (1988). He is currently a fellow of the National Association of Business Economics and a member of the international advisory board of AB Volvo.

Dr. John B. Shoven is professor of economics at Stanford University and director of Stanford University's Center for Economic Policy Research. He is also West Coast director of the National Bureau of Economic Research. Dr. Shoven's research concentrates on personal and corporate taxation, saving behavior, and pensions and the economics of the elderly. Three books now in press will add to the six books and more than seventy professional articles that Dr. Shoven has published: *The Economics of Saving* (University of Chicago Press), *Taxes and Corporate Restructuring* (Brookings), and *Applying General Equilibrium* (Cambridge University Press). Dr. Shoven heads the Provost's Task Force on Faculty and Staff Retirement at Stanford and is a member of Sigma Xi, a fellow of the Econometric Society, and a member of the board of directors of the American Council for Capital Formation Center for Policy Research.

Dr. Lawrence H. Summers is Nathaniel Ropes Professor of Political Economy at Harvard University. Dr. Summers was domestic policy economist for the President's Council of Economic Advisers from 1982 to 1983 and a principal economic adviser to the 1988 presidential campaign of Michael Dukakis. In 1987, Dr. Summers was the first social scientist to receive the National Science Foundation's Alan T. Waterman Award. He was also recently recognized by *The Economist* as one of the world's leading young economists. His books, *Tax Policy and the Economy* and *Understanding Unemployment*, are forthcoming from MIT Press. Dr. Summers is the editor of the *Quarterly Journal of Economics*, a research associate of the National Bureau of Economic Research, and a member of the Congressional Budget Office's Panel of Economic Advisers.

Hon. Paul A. Volcker is chairman of James D. Wolfensohn, Inc. and Frederick H. Schultz Professor of International Economic Policy at Princeton University. Mr. Volcker was chairman of the Board of Governors of the Federal Reserve System from August 1979 to August 1987; initially appointed by President Carter, Mr. Volcker was reappointed in 1983 by President Reagan. Mr. Volcker's government service spans almost thirty years and includes high offices under five presidents and two tours of duty as an official of the U.S. Treasury. He also spent more than four years as president of the Federal

Reserve Bank of New York. Since his return to private life in 1987, Mr. Volcker has served as honorary chairman of the privately sponsored Commission on the Public Service, which studies issues relating to the availability of high-caliber people for government service. He is a director or trustee of several organizations, including service as a member of the board of the American Council for Capital Formation.

Index

For Product Safety Concerns and Information please contact our EU representative GPSR@taylorandfrancis.com Taylor & Francis Verlag GmbH, Kaufingerstraße 24, 80331 München, Germany

Batch number: 10732529

Printed by Printforce, the Netherlands